# Adobe® Acrobat® X PDF Bible

## Ted Padova

WILEY

John Wiley & Sons, Inc.

**Adobe® Acrobat® X PDF Bible**

Published by
Wiley Publishing, Inc.
10475 Crosspoint Boulevard
Indianapolis, IN 46256
www.wiley.com

Published by Wiley Publishing, Inc., Indianapolis, Indiana

Published simultaneously in Canada

ISBN: 978-0-470-61291-0

Manufactured in the United States of America

10 9 8 7 6 5 4 3 2 1

For general information on our other products and services or to obtain technical support, please contact our Customer Care Department within the U.S. at (877) 762-2974, outside the U.S. at (317) 572-3993 or fax (317) 572-4002.

Library of Congress Control Number: 2010943054

*For Arnie.*

# About the Author

**Ted Padova** is the former chief executive officer and managing partner of The Image Source Digital Imaging and Photo Finishing Centers of Ventura and Thousand Oaks, California. He has been involved in digital imaging since founding a service bureau in 1990. He retired from his company in 2005 and now spends his time writing and speaking on Acrobat and PDF.

For more than 17 years, Ted has taught university and higher education classes in graphic design applications and digital prepress at the University of California, Santa Barbara, and the University of California at Los Angeles. He has been, and continues to be, a conference speaker nationally and internationally at PDF conferences.

Currently he lives in the Philippines where he consults with Southeast Asian countries on eGovernment and electronic forms processing.

Ted has written more than 40 computer books and is one of the world's leading authors on Adobe Acrobat. He has written books on Adobe Acrobat, Adobe Photoshop, Adobe Photoshop Elements, Adobe Reader, Microsoft PowerPoint, and Adobe Illustrator. Recent books published by John Wiley and Sons include *PDF Forms Using Adobe Acrobat and LiveCycle Designer Bible*, *Adobe Acrobat PDF Bible* (versions 4, 5, 6, 7, 8, and 9), *Adobe Creative Suite Bible* (versions CS, CS2, CS3, CS4, and CS5), *Color Correction for Digital Photographers Only*, *Color Correction for Digital Photographers For Dummies*, *PowerPoint 2007 Just the Steps For Dummies*, *Creating Adobe Acrobat Forms*, *Teach Yourself Visually Acrobat 5*, and *Adobe Acrobat 6.0 Complete Course*. He also co-authored *Adobe Illustrator Master Class — Illustrator Illuminated* and wrote *Adobe Reader Revealed* for Peachpit/Adobe Press.

# Credits

**Acquisitions Editor**
Aaron Black

**Project Editor**
Jade L. Williams

**Technical Editor**
David Williamson

**Copy Editor**
Marylouise Wiack

**Editorial Director**
Robyn Siesky

**Editorial Manager**
Rosemarie Graham

**Business Manager**
Amy Knies

**Senior Marketing Manager**
Sandy Smith

**Vice President and Executive Group Publisher**
Richard Swadley

**Vice President and Executive Publisher**
Barry Pruett

**Project Coordinator**
Katherine Crocker

**Graphics and Production Specialists**
Carl Byers
Timothy C. Detrick
Andrea Hornberger

**Quality Control Technicians**
John Greenough
Lindsay Littrell
Lauren Mandelbaum

**Proofreading**
Christine Sabooni

**Indexing**
Infodex Indexing Services, Inc.

# Contents at a Glance

# Contents

# Contents

# Contents

# Contents

## Part II: Converting Documents to PDF     159

## Chapter 7: Converting Files to PDF. . . . . . . . . . . . . . . . . . . . . . . . 161

# Contents

# Contents

# Contents

# Contents

# Contents

# Contents

# Contents

## Part VI: Using Acrobat PDF Forms          743

## Chapter 30: Understanding Acrobat Form Tools . . . . . . . . . . . . . . . . . . 745

# Contents

# Contents

# Preface

**A**dobe Acrobat X PDF Bible is written for a cross-platform audience. Users of Microsoft Windows 2000 with Service Pack 2, Windows XP Professional or Home Edition, Windows Vista Professional and Home Edition, Windows 7, Tablet PC Edition, and Apple Macintosh computers running OS X v10.2.8, 10.3, 10.5 and later will find references to these operating systems.

## About This Book

Most of the chapters in this book include screenshots from Acrobat running under Windows. The user interface is closely matched between Windows and the Macintosh; therefore, Macintosh users will find the same options in dialog boxes and menu commands as are found in the Windows screenshots. Where significant differences do occur, you'll find additional screenshots taken on a Macintosh to distinguish the differences.

## How to read this book

I have to admit that this publication is not a page-turner that leaves you grasping for more time to finish a chapter before retiring at night. After all, it's a computer book and inasmuch as my editors at Wiley always strive to get me to add a little *drama* to the text, few people will pick up this *Bible* and read it from cover to cover. You should think of this book more as a reference where you can jump to an area and read over the contents to help simplify your work sessions in Acrobat Standard (available only on Windows in versions 8 through X), and Acrobat Professional version X (available on both Windows and Macintosh). Note that Acrobat Pro Extended for Windows is no longer available in Acrobat X. Adobe Presenter on Windows is also unavailable in Acrobat X. Therefore, I deleted a chapter on creating presentations for this edition.

Because Acrobat is such a behemoth program and can do so many things for almost any kind of work activity, most people won't use every feature the program provides. You may be interested in converting files to PDF and setting up reviews, or you may devote more attention to the area of prepress and printing, or perhaps it's accessibility or PDF forms that are part of your work. In these cases, you may ignore some chapters and just want to jump to the area that interests you most.

Regardless of how much experience you have with Acrobat, you should be able to gain a lot of insight and skill at using the new version of Acrobat by focusing on certain chapters. However, don't completely ignore chapters that cover features you think you won't use. You can find many related concepts falling under headings that are not exclusively related to the general topic for each chapter. For example, you may not be interested in creating accessible PDFs for screen readers. However, the Accessibility chapter also includes coverage of document structures and tagging, which will be important if you need to export the content of a PDF to an authoring application.

Because many chapters may include features that relate to the work you want to perform, it's a good idea to concentrate on the features of greatest interest to you and skim over those chapters that appear to be less beneficial to you.

To begin, I recommend you look closely at Chapter 1 where I cover the new changes in the Acrobat user interface (UI). If there is one single greatest change in Acrobat, it's the new, radically changed UI. You may love it or hate it, but before passing judgment, be certain to spend some time becoming familiar with how you access tools and commands in Acrobat X.

Regardless of how much skill you have using Acrobat, you need to understand PDF navigation — especially navigating the new PDF Portfolio documents that I cover in Chapter 11. Look closely at the Help documents and the Help features in Acrobat X that I cover in Chapter 3. Pay particular attention to Chapters 1, 3, 4, 11, 17, 19, and 20. If you've read the *Adobe Acrobat 9 PDF Bible*, these chapters contain a lot of new material in this revision of the book. (The text has also been revised in many other chapters of the book.)

Throughout the book are sections called "Steps." If you find the contents of a given series of steps interesting, follow the steps to see whether you can replicate what is covered in that section. In this book, I've made an effort to expand steps greatly to provide you some tutorial assistance in understanding many concepts.

## Icons

The use of icons throughout the book offers you a quick idea of what content is being addressed. You can jump to this text to get extra information, be warned of a potential problem, or amplify the concept being addressed in the text. In this book you'll find icons for the following:

### Caution

This icon alerts you to a potential problem in using Acrobat, any tools or menus, or any supporting application from which you want to export a document to PDF. Pay close attention to these caution messages to avoid potential problems. ∎

## Cross-Reference

This icon indicates a cross-reference to another area in the book where you can find more information on a topic. It is almost impossible to learn about Acrobat in a linear fashion because it has so many interrelated features, and so covering all aspects of a single feature in a contiguous section of the book just doesn't work. Therefore I have spread out the discussion of some common commands, tools, actions, and tasks over different chapters. In these cases, you'll find a Cross-Reference icon that directs you to another part of the book that covers related information. ■

## New Feature

This icon appears throughout the book where a new feature has been added to Acrobat. Pay special attention to these icons to learn more about what has been added to Acrobat X, Adobe Reader X, and Adobe LiveCycle Designer 8.2. ■

## Note

This icon signifies information may add more clarity to a text passage or help you deal with a feature more effectively. ■

## PDF Workflow

This icon indicates that the text describes tasks or features that apply to workgroups and workflows. This will be important to you if you work in government, education, or a large business, where you are likely to be in a workgroup with common tasks. ■

## Prepress

A lot of support is offered in Acrobat X for the prepress and printing market. If you're a design professional, or you work in a service bureau or print shop, look for this icon throughout the book to find information related to prepress and printing. ■

## Tip

Tips are handy shortcuts. They help you to more quickly produce results, or work through a series of steps to complete a task. Some tips provide you with information that may not be documented in the Help files that accompany Acrobat. ■

# The book's contents

This book is about Adobe Acrobat Standard (on Windows), and Adobe Acrobat Pro (on Windows and the Macintosh). All the content in the book applies to Acrobat Standard, unless I indicate that a specific section applies only to Acrobat Pro. Acrobat Pro features are clearly marked throughout the book so that you know when Acrobat Standard doesn't support a particular feature.

# Preface

Just about everything that you can do with Adobe Acrobat is contained in the chapters ahead. This book touches on Adobe LiveCycle Designer, and contains chapters dedicated to Acrobat PDF forms, collaboration, PDF creation, Acrobat JavaScript, and many other aspects of Acrobat. Although some of these features can take a book of this size to cover in their entirety, this book provides you with a general overview of *all* that Acrobat can do.

If you're interested in Adobe LiveCycle Designer, this book is NOT for you. Because LiveCycle Designer is a completely different application that runs only on Windows, I do not cover it in this book. If you want to learn more about Adobe LiveCycle Designer, see *PDF Forms Using Acrobat and LiveCycle Designer Bible* (Wiley Publishing).

I've made an effort to address the needs of many different types of users. This book covers how to work with the features found in Acrobat Pro, Acrobat Standard, Adobe Reader, and companion products. Individual industries such as digital prepress, engineering, enterprise workflows, and multimedia and Web publishing are covered. Regardless of what you do, you should be able to find out how Acrobat applies to your particular kind of work. Whether you are an accounting clerk, a real estate salesperson, a digital prepress technician, an engineer, a Web designer, or a hobbyist who likes to archive information from Web sites, Acrobat can help make your work easier.

To simplify your journey through the new release of Acrobat, the book is divided into six parts. A total of 32 chapters address Acrobat features and some individual purposes for using the software. The six parts include the following:

**Part I: Introducing Adobe Acrobat.** To start off, I discuss the Portable Document Format and the many new features and refinements of Acrobat X. I cover tools, menus, and panels to help you understand the major changes in the user interface. This section covers the distinctions between different viewer types, navigating through PDFs, and using the Find tool and the Search panel to search PDF files.

**Part II: Converting Documents to PDF.** There are many different ways to create a PDF document, and I cover all these methods thoroughly in this section of the book. I begin by discussing the creation of simple PDF files, and continue through to much more sophisticated PDF file creation. One chapter is devoted entirely to Microsoft Office applications. In addition, I discuss the many application software developers who are supporting PDFs through direct exports from their programs. I discuss the Adobe Creative Suite, and how you can integrate PDF with the Creative Suite applications. The advantages and disadvantages of using all these methods are also discussed.

**Part III: Editing PDFs.** This section covers editing, modifying, and enhancing PDF files for many different purposes. I also cover how to modify and flow content between Acrobat and authoring programs. New features for creating PDF Portfolios and improvements in redacting PDFs are added in this section. I also discuss scanning in Acrobat and converting scans to text with Optical Character Recognition (OCR). Document repurposing is covered in this section for users who want to modify files for different output media. I cover the new Actions Wizard and all the changes Acrobat X offers you when creating batch sequences. This section also includes a chapter on all the enabling features that are available in Acrobat Standard and the Acrobat Professional products.

**Part IV: Using PDF Interactivity.** This section covers interactivity with PDF documents for workgroups by using the Review and Comment tools, shared reviews, and interactive elements such as multimedia, links, and buttons. A chapter devoted to making PDF documents accessible for people using screen readers is also included in this section.

**Part V: Publishing PDF Files.** This section covers some of the more common distribution methods that are available for PDF files today. I begin with security and authentication as your first step in document distribution and then move on to PDF workflows. I discuss creating PDFs for different kinds of distribution, such as eBooks, and offer complete coverage of all the printing and prepress features. Hosting your PDFs on the Web and sending them via e-mail are also covered in this section along with many new changes to Acrobat.com.

**Part VI: Using Acrobat PDF Forms.** This section covers PDF forms and handling form data. All features for creating forms using the Form Edit mode, which are also available to Acrobat Standard users, are covered in this section. Distributing forms through Acrobat.com, collecting form data, and auto field detection are included in this section. I have also included an introduction to JavaScript and writing simple JavaScript routines.

# Staying Connected

It seems like new products and new upgrades are distributed about every five minutes. If you purchase a software product, you can often find an updated revision soon after. Manufacturers rely increasingly on Internet distribution and less on postal delivery. You should plan to make routine visits to the Adobe Web site and the Web sites of third-party product manufacturers. Any software vendor that has a Web site will offer a product revision for download, or offer you details on acquiring the update.

## Internet connection

With newer releases of computer software, an Internet connection is now essential. Programs, including Acrobat, regularly prompt you to check for updates over the Internet. To optimize the performance of your Acrobat software, you should run it on a computer that has an Internet connection.

## Registration

Regardless of whether you purchase Acrobat Professional Extended, Acrobat Professional, or Acrobat Standard, or download the free Adobe Reader software, Adobe Systems has made it possible to register the product. You can register on the World Wide Web or mail a registration form to Adobe. You will find many advantages in being a registered user. First, update information will be sent to you, so you'll know when a product revision occurs. Second, Adobe distributes information that can help you benefit the most from using Acrobat. Who knows — someday you may be asked to provide samples of your work that might get you a hit from the Adobe Web site. By all means, complete the registration — it will be to your benefit.

## Web sites to contact

Obviously, the first Web site to frequent is the Adobe Web site. When Acrobat and the Acrobat plug-ins are revised, downloads for updates become available. You can also find tips, information, and solutions to problems. Visit the Adobe Web site at `www.adobe.com`. Also, make use of the Help⇨Adobe Expert Support menu command in all Acrobat viewers. This command opens a Web page where you can obtain technical support for a nominal fee. To acquire plug-ins for Acrobat, visit the Adobe Store, where you can find a comprehensive list of plug-ins and demonstration software that works with Acrobat. Visit the Adobe Store at `www.adobe.com/store`.

A wealth of information is available on the Adobe Acrobat User Community Web site at `www.acrobatusers.com`. Here you can find tips, techniques, blogs hosted by some of the world's leading Acrobat professionals, and support for starting and maintaining a local Acrobat User Group. You can also e-mail leading professionals who can help you solve problems. You should regularly check this Web site for up-to-date information and assistance.

Acrobat tips are available on many Web sites — all you need to do is search the Internet for Acrobat information. An excellent source of information, as well as a comprehensive collection of third-party plug-ins, is Planet PDF. You can visit them at `www.planetpdf.com`.

More Acrobat plug-ins can be found on the PluginsWorld Web site. Visit `http://acrobat.pluginsworld.com/` for a great selection of Acrobat plug-ins and demonstration software.

Another source of information, articles, and tips about Acrobat and PDF can be found at `www.pdfzone.com`. Visit the PDFzone Web site for up-to-date articles and interviews with industry leaders.

If you are interested in learning more about Acrobat, you can attend regional conferences sponsored by Mogo Media. If you want to meet with some of the world's experts and discuss PDF issues, look for a conference in your area. You can find information at `www.mogo-media.com/`.

If you want to learn JavaScript, you can find a wealth of information on Thom Parker's Acrobat Users blog site. Log on to `http://acrobatusers.com/blogs/thomp` to see Thom's JavaScript Corner, which contains a number of blog posts on using Acrobat JavaScript. Thom also hosts the `www.pdfscripting.com` Web site where you'll find hours of video tutorials, easy copy-and-paste JavaScripts, a generous library of PDF example forms, automation tools, and a comprehensive source of information on using Acrobat JavaScript. When I have trouble debugging my code, Thom is always the one person who helps me correct my errors.

A new conference has appeared in Minneapolis-St. Paul. To find out more about the Acrobat Central Conference, log on to `www.pdfcentralconference.com`.

The Open Publish conference in Sydney, Australia, is an annual conference for design and creative professionals. This organization hosts many PDF-related seminars and workshops annually. Find out more at `www.openpublish.com.au`.

Whatever you may desire is usually found on some Web site. New sites are continually being developed, so look often.

# Contacting Me

If, after reviewing this book, you feel some important information was overlooked or you have any questions concerning Acrobat, you can contact me and let me know your views, opinions, hoorahs, or complaints, or provide information that might be included in the next revision. (If it's good enough, you might even get a credit line in the acknowledgments!) By all means, send me an e-mail at `ted@west.net`.

Chances are that if you have a problem or question about Acrobat, you're not alone and many others might be interested in your question and a response to the question. You can send your questions directly to my blog on Acrobat Users at `www.acrobatusers.com/blogs/ted padova`. You can also visit the Acrobat User Forums at `www.acrobatusers.com/forum`. In addition to my blog, some very talented friends who know much more than I do also host blogs on Acrobat Users. Visit `www.acrobatusers.com/blogs` to see a complete list of their blogs.

If you happen to have some problems with Acrobat, keep in mind that I didn't design the program. Inquiries for technical support should be directed to the software developers of any products you use. This is one more good reason to complete your registration form.

There you have it— a short description of what follows. Don't wait. Keep reading to learn how Acrobat can help you gain more productivity with its amazing new features.

# Acknowledgments

I would like to acknowledge some of the people who have contributed in one way or another to make this edition possible. Barry Pruett, Executive Publisher at Wiley, continually supports all my writing efforts for the company. A special thank-you goes to my Acquisitions Editor, Aaron Black, and Project Editor, Jade Williams, who nicely coordinated the project and kept things moving in a timely manner. Thanks also to Copy Editor, Marylouise Wiack, and Editorial Director, Robyn Siesky, as well as the rest of the Wiley crew who participated in the project.

A great deal of thanks goes to my Technical Editor, Dave Williamson, who superbly analyzed every phrase and word to ensure technical accuracy.

I feel very fortunate in having so much support from the many people at Adobe Systems who were continually available for comments, suggestions, and favors over a seven-month period while Acrobat X was in development. The energy and enthusiasm of the engineering and marketing teams throughout the development period made it evident that this is a group of people with passion and excitement for their work. A hearty thank-you is extended to Rick Brown, Senior Acrobat Product Manager (and Chief Acrobatist), for his support. I so appreciate all the assistance Rick provides me, as well as the contact I have with him throughout the lifecycle of a product version. If there's glue that keeps the development team together through the rigorous schedule to make the deadlines, it's Rick Brown.

Other Adobe employees who were very helpful include David Stromfeld, Product Manager; Randy Swineford, for a number of assists in helping me become familiar with new features; Joel Geraci for his advice and help with Adobe Flex and Adobe Flash; Chris French for help with many of the multimedia features; Ashu Mittal for constant assistance with many installation and debugging issues; and many other Adobe employees in the engineering and marketing divisions who graciously offered feedback and advice during the development of the Acrobat X family of products.

I'd also like to thank Kurt Foss, editor of the Acrobat User Community; Stephanie Baartz-Bowman and Lori Kassuba of Adobe Systems; and my colleagues on Acrobat Users — Thom Parker, Duff Johnson, Dimitri Munkirs, Douglas Hanna, and Patty-Bing-You — for their support in keeping up-to-date information available on the Acrobat User Community Web site and for their willingness to give me help when I needed it. In my local Davao City Philippines Acrobat User Group, I'd like to thank Chris Cubos, Blogie Robillo, and MiGs for all their generous assistance in helping organize Acrobat users in our area.

My most heartfelt thanks goes to the many readers of my previous works who have contacted me through the years with questions, kudos, and helpful remarks that have helped me refine this work. My labors as an author, writing alone behind a computer each day, are really very dull during the project period. What makes it all worthwhile is hearing from people about real-world applications for Acrobat and interacting with all of you — that's the real treasure and the reward for me spending every waking moment putting this thing together over a three- to four-month period.

# Introduction

This book is the seventh edition of the *Adobe Acrobat PDF Bible*. As a result of feedback from many users, this edition reflects my efforts to include coverage of some topics that were missed in the previous version and to add additional material where users asked for more detail. As such, I've made an effort to cover as much of the new version as is possible in this single, comprehensive book.

## What Is Adobe Acrobat?

Acrobat has evolved over time, and long-time users of Adobe Acrobat are familiar with the distinctions between the Adobe Reader software and Adobe Acrobat (either Standard or Professional). However, many users of Adobe Reader are still confused about what it can and cannot do. For example, many folks think that the viewing of Portable Document Format (PDF) documents is all you can do with Adobe Reader. Now in version X, Adobe Reader can do much more in terms of editing PDF documents. A good example is the new ability to add comments to a PDF document without needing to add special permissions to that document.

I explain in Chapter 2 that Adobe Reader is only one small component of Acrobat. Other programs included in the suite of Acrobat software provide you with tools for creating, editing, viewing, navigating, and searching PDF information. Regardless of your familiarity with previous versions of Acrobat, you should carefully review Chapter 2. In Chapter 4, you'll find details on all the new features that have been added to Adobe Reader, as well as how you can add some Reader Extensions to PDF documents that offer you much more functionality than was available in previous versions of Adobe Reader.

Acrobat has evolved through many different changes, both to the features it offers you and to many of the names associated with the various components. In earlier versions of Acrobat, names such as Acrobat Professional, Acrobat Exchange, and then simply Acrobat were used to refer to the authoring application. Version X of Adobe Acrobat continues with the same product names as were found in Acrobat 9 with one exception: Acrobat Pro Extended has been eliminated from the Acrobat product line.

## Nomenclature

The official name for the new release of the high-end Acrobat product is Adobe® Acrobat® X Pro. You'll notice the registered marks that appear in the name. For the sake of ease and clarity, as you read through the book and see any reference to Acrobat, Adobe Acrobat, or

Acrobat Pro (also called Acrobat Professional), keep in mind that the reference is to Adobe Acrobat Pro. For the other authoring application, the official name is Adobe® Acrobat® Standard. When referring to this product, I may use terms such as Acrobat Standard or simply Standard. Where it makes sense, I'll say it like it is supposed to be used; otherwise, I'll use an abbreviated name.

Adobe Reader is the free downloadable Acrobat software. Again, for the purposes of communication and ease, I may refer to Adobe Reader simply as Reader. Remember, however, that the official name should prevail when you communicate with Adobe Systems about these products.

For Windows users, Acrobat X Pro also ships with Adobe® LiveCycle® Designer, which is used for authoring dynamic XML-based forms. I may refer to this product as LiveCycle Designer, Designer, or LCD. Although Designer is referenced in this book, I do not cover using that program.

Why is naming important? Adobe Systems has spent much time, labor, and money on developing branding for their products. With the different changes to product names and the different components of the software, some people using the products don't completely understand the differences or from where each product came. An Adobe Reader installer can be distributed legitimately on CD-ROM, and some end users may not know that it is a product that is available for upgrading at the Adobe Web site. Therefore, using the formal name can help users understand a little bit more about the software.

And there's another very good reason for helping Adobe Systems with the recognition and marketing of its products. If the product doesn't do well in the marketplace, you might one day see it disappear. You won't want that to happen because when you start working with the new release, you'll easily see many great new features and much more sophistication added to the programs. Adobe Systems has done well in bringing the entire Acrobat family of products to maturity and I'm certain you'll find many new uses for Acrobat.

Above all, keep in mind that *Adobe* is not a product. Adobe, or Adobe Systems, is a company. Referring to Adobe when you mean Acrobat or Adobe Reader is improper and promotes confusion. When referring to the products, be certain to include Acrobat, Standard, or Reader.

## Adobe Systems and the Acrobat mission

Adobe Systems began as a company serving the graphic design and imaging markets. With the release of PostScript, its first product, Adobe devoted a lot of development time to imaging programs, font libraries, and tools to help service graphic design professionals. When you speak to graphic designers and advertising people, they connect Adobe Systems with products such as Adobe Photoshop, Adobe Illustrator, Adobe InDesign, Adobe Premiere, and so on. With some of these flagship programs having long histories and large established user bases, some people may think that a product such as Adobe Acrobat takes a back seat to the high-end graphics and multimedia programs.

Adobe sees Acrobat as an integral part of its future and is investing a lot of energy into Acrobat's growth. With more than 750,000,000 installed users of the Adobe Reader software, Acrobat and the PDF file format are among the most popular software products available today.

Acrobat has become a standard in many different industries. In the publishing market, many large newspaper chains, publishing houses, and book and magazine publishers have standardized on the PDF format for printing and prepress. The prepress industry has long adopted PDF as a standard for commercial and quick-print houses. Almost every software manufacturer includes last-minute notes, user manuals, and supporting information in PDF format on installer disks. The U.S. federal, state, and municipal governments and U.S. government contractors have standardized on PDF for everything from forms, applications, notices, and official documents to intra-office document exchanges. Also, PDF has become an international standard adopted by the International Organization for Standardization (ISO).

With the introduction of the Acrobat 6 product line, Adobe Systems expanded existing markets and targeted new markets. The features in Acrobat 6 and 7 Professional appealed to all kinds of engineering professionals. With the support for layers and direct exports from programs such as Microsoft Visio and Autodesk AutoCAD, engineers, planners, and architects welcomed the new additions to Acrobat. In Acrobat 8, users of Acrobat Professional could convert AutoCAD DWG drawings to PDF, complete with layers and comments, without having AutoCAD installed on a computer. Enterprises, in which document flows include different workgroups for almost any industry, welcomed additions to the comment and review tools in Acrobat Professional 8. Additional enabling usage rights for users of Adobe Reader were introduced in Acrobat 8. The already standardized prepress market applauded new features for printing to high-end imaging devices without the use of third-party plug-ins. In Acrobat 9, Adobe added many new features and simplified the creation of PDF forms. Now in Acrobat X, the big emphasis with the new UI design is simplicity for novice users. By eliminating redundant tools and menus, reducing the number of menus to only five, adding a new Tools panel, and customizing a new Favorites toolbar, Adobe is hoping that the new design will attract more users.

## PDF workflows

A workflow can mean different things to different people. One of the nice aspects of working with Acrobat is the development of a workflow environment. Quite simply, workflow solutions are intended to increase productivity in a more automated and efficient fashion. Editing page-by-page and running manual tasks to change or modify documents could hardly be called workflow solutions. Workflows enable office or production workers to automate common tasks for maximum efficiency. Batch processing documents, running them through automated steps, and routing files through computer-assisted delivery systems are some workflow solutions.

Acrobat provides workflow solutions in almost every industry, and new features added to Acrobat X bring some sophistication to an already great product. But the real advance in workflow activity is the introduction of Acrobat.com. Now, instead of having documents flow across wide area networks, people can collaborate in real-time online events without configuring servers. The introduction of Acrobat.com will not only save companies the huge expense of employee travel, but will also increase productivity in workflows through dynamic interaction.

# New Features in Adobe Acrobat Professional

Several changes and refinements have been made in Acrobat X. As I mentioned earlier, the biggest change is a complete overhaul of the user interface, where panels have replaced tools and menu actions. The Comments panel has been removed from the Navigation pane and added as a separate panel on the right side of the Acrobat window. A sharing panel enables you to engage in shared reviews and to access Acrobat.com. Batch sequences have been replaced with a new Actions Wizard and task buttons have almost disappeared from the Toolbar Well.

Much attention has been devoted to security, such as when users of Adobe Reader view PDF files. In addition to other changes, some refinement has been added to redaction and to scanning and OCR conversion, and PDF Portfolios also have a new design.

What haven't changed in Acrobat are the Field Properties windows, Form Edit mode, and a number of other features. Overall, once you master the new changes in the user interface, you won't find a tremendous number of new cool features in Acrobat X.

# Part I

# Introducing Adobe Acrobat

This section begins with an overview of the Acrobat user interface and familiarizes you with tools, menus, and panels. In Chapter 2, you find a detailed description for the Acrobat viewers and how they are distinguished from each other. Chapter 3 follows with opening and managing PDF documents in Acrobat viewers, followed by Chapter 4 where I cover all the features you find in the Adobe Reader software. In Chapter 5, you'll find everything you need to know about viewing and navigating PDF files in Acrobat viewers. This section ends with searching PDF files using the impressive search features you find in all Acrobat viewers.

# Getting to Know Adobe Acrobat

To start off this large book on Adobe Acrobat, let's first take a look at what Acrobat is and what PDF is, and let's try to get a grasp on some of the many options you have for working with PDF files in Acrobat.

## Getting to Know the Viewing Modes

The first time you launch Acrobat X, you immediately notice a big change in the user interface (UI). Of all the changes in this new version over Acrobat 9, the most obvious is the complete rearrangement of tools, panels, and choices for menu options as shown in Figure 1.1. You notice immediately that Acrobat X has newer menus, three buttons in the top-right corner that are to display the Tools, Comment, and Share panels, a single Create task button, and the absence of toolbars. For a more complete description of the various user interface components, see the section "Working in the Acrobat Environment" later in this chapter.

Why this change, you ask? Quite simply, Adobe wants to improve the viewing experience for both the PDF authors and those who read PDF documents. Before I delve into the many features and tasks you can perform in Acrobat, let's take a look at the new UI and the two different modes available for viewing and working on PDF files.

## STEPS: Viewing PDF Files

1. **Launch Acrobat X.** This step presumes you have installed Acrobat from the DVD-ROM or downloaded the program from the Adobe online store. On Windows a short-cut is added to the Desktop that you can pin to the status bar. On the Mac you have an alias that you can add to the Dock to make launching the program easier. Click the shortcut or alias to launch Acrobat.

2. **Open a PDF file.** You should have a PDF document on your hard drive. If not, you can easily download PDF files from the Internet. Look around and you can easily find a file to experiment with. Locate a PDF file and choose File ➪ Open. In the Open dialog box, select a file and click Open. The file opens in the Normal viewer mode.

3. **Examine the user interface.** Notice that the menus at the top of the Acrobat work-space are reduced to five menu choices and the toolbar is sparsely populated with tools, as shown in Figure 1.1.

---

**FIGURE 1.1**

The default view of the Acrobat X workspace when you open a PDF file

4. **Click the Read Mode button in the toolbar.** The button appears as two diagonal arrowheads in the top-right corner of the toolbar, as shown in Figure 1.1. When you click this button, you enter into the new Acrobat X Read Mode, as shown in Figure 1.2.

5. **Examine the toolbar in Read Mode.** Notice the pop-up toolbar that appears when you open a PDF in Read Mode. From left to right, the tools available in this toolbar include:

   - **Save.** Click the floppy disk icon to open the Save dialog box for saving any updates in the file.

   - **Print.** Click the printer icon to open the Print dialog box.

   - **Previous Page.** Click the up-pointing arrow to take you back to the previous page.

   - **Next Page.** Click the down-pointing arrow to take you to the next page.

   - **Go to Page.** Page numbers are displayed in the toolbar. Click on the page number and the Go to Page dialog box opens. Type a number in the Go to Page dialog box and click OK to jump to the target page.

## FIGURE 1.2

The Acrobat X Read Mode view displaying the Read Mode toolbar

Read Mode toolbar

- **Zoom tools.** The minus (-) button is used to zoom out of the document view. The plus (+) button is used to zoom in on the document.
- **Exit Read Mode.** Click this button to return to the default view shown in Figure 1.1.

6. **Click (X) to Exit Read Mode and return to the Normal view.**

Before you go too far in Acrobat, you should become familiar with these two modes. Read Mode is designed for maximizing the viewer experience by reducing the clutter of menus, panels, and tools. You will find yourself toggling the views frequently during all your Acrobat sessions between Read Mode and Normal viewer mode.

When you enter Read Mode, the toolbar appears momentarily and then disappears. To bring the toolbar back into view, move your mouse around the area where the toolbar appears. You exit Read Mode by clicking Exit Read Mode in the toolbar or pressing the Esc key on your keyboard.

# Discovering Adobe Acrobat

Assuming you know little about Adobe Acrobat, I start with a brief description of what Acrobat is and what it is not. As I explain to people who ask about the product, I usually define it as the most misunderstood application available today. Most of us are familiar with the Adobe Reader software, which is a product from Adobe Systems Incorporated that you can download free from the Adobe Web site (www.adobe.com/acrobat/readermain.html). You can also acquire the Adobe Reader from all the installation CD-ROMs for other Adobe software. You can even acquire Adobe Reader from other sources, as long as the Adobe licensing requirements are distributed with the installer program. The Adobe Reader, however, is *not* Adobe Acrobat. Adobe Reader is a component of a much larger product family that has evolved through several iterations over more than a decade.

You're probably a little more sophisticated and realize there is a major difference between these applications, and you may wonder why I even spend any time discussing the difference between Acrobat and Adobe Reader. Unfortunately, many people still believe that Adobe Acrobat is the free Adobe Reader program.

To add a little more confusion, Adobe continues to market several products in the Acrobat family. While Adobe Reader remains a free download from Adobe Systems, there are two additional commercial viewers — Acrobat Standard (on Windows only) and Acrobat Pro (on Windows and the Mac). The former Acrobat Pro Extended on Windows that was available with Acrobat 9 is no longer available in Acrobat X. As I talk about Adobe Acrobat in this chapter and throughout the book, I am referring to Acrobat Pro for both Windows and the Mac and Acrobat Standard for Windows users only. Where the programs differ in features, I point them out.

## Note

There are distinctions between Acrobat Standard (Windows) and Acrobat Pro in terms of tools, commands, and features. Most editing tasks can be handled in both viewers; however, Acrobat Pro does provide more editing features than Acrobat Standard. Throughout this book I delineate the differences and point out when a feature is unique to a given viewer. ■

Adobe Acrobat (Standard and Pro) in version X is the upgrade from Adobe Acrobat 9 (Standard, Professional, and/or Acrobat Pro Extended), and both viewers are the subject of the remaining chapters of this book. Acrobat is the authoring application that provides you tools and commands for a host of features outlined in the following chapters. If you have not yet purchased a copy of Acrobat, either the Standard version (Windows only) or Pro version (Windows and the Mac), you might want to look over Chapter 2 and read some of the comparisons between the viewers. If fewer tools and features suit your purpose, you might find the Standard version satisfactory — but remember, Acrobat Standard is available only on Windows in versions 8 and above. Although some of the features differ between the viewers, they both provide many features for editing, enhancing, printing, and working with PDF documents.

## Note

For the purposes of clarity, henceforth I'll refer to Acrobat when features are common to all viewers. I'll make specific mention of one of the Acrobat products when a particular feature is unique to a given viewer. For a quick comparison of the viewers and related features, be sure to look over Chapter 2. ■

Acrobat is an authoring application, but it has one little feature that distinguishes it from almost any other authoring program. Rather than starting from scratch and creating a new document in Acrobat, your workflow usually involves converting a document, created in just about any program, to a Portable Document Format (PDF) file. Once converted to PDF you use Acrobat to edit and refine the document, add bells and whistles and interactivity, or prepare it for professional printing. In addition to the Acrobat program, Acrobat Pro ships with companion programs such as Adobe Acrobat Distiller, Adobe Acrobat Catalog, and Adobe LiveCycle Designer (Windows only). Acrobat Standard ships only with Acrobat Distiller. These companion products are used to convert PostScript files to PDF, create search indexes, and author XML-based forms.

## Cross-Reference

For information related to Acrobat Distiller, see the Acrobat Help document. For more information on Acrobat Catalog, see Chapter 6. For more information related to LiveCycle Designer, see Creating PDF Forms Using Acrobat and LiveCycle Designer Bible (Wiley Publishing, Padova and Okamoto). ■

Acrobat solutions are greatly extended with other supporting programs from Adobe Systems and many different third-party vendors. If Acrobat can't do the job, chances are you can find a plug-in or companion program to handle all you want to do with a PDF file.

## Cross-Reference

For information related to Acrobat plug-ins and companion products, see Chapter 2. ■

# Understanding PDF

PDF, short for *Portable Document Format*, was developed by Adobe Systems as a unique format to be viewed through Acrobat viewers. As the name implies, it is portable, which means the file you create on one computer can be viewed with an Acrobat viewer on other computers, handheld devices, and on other platforms. For example, you can create a page layout on a Mac computer and convert it to a PDF file. After the conversion, this PDF document can be viewed on a Linux or Windows machine.

Multiplatform compliance (to enable the exchange of files across different computers, for example) is one of the great values of PDF documents.

So what's special about PDF and its multiplatform compliance? It's not so much an issue of viewing a page on one computer created from another computer that is impressive about PDF. After all, such popular programs as Microsoft Excel, Microsoft Word, Adobe Photoshop, Adobe InDesign, Adobe FrameMaker, and Adobe Illustrator all have counterparts for multiplatform usage. You can create a layout on one computer system and view the file on another system with the same software installed. For example, if you have Adobe InDesign installed on a Mac computer and you create an InDesign document, that same file can be viewed on a PC with InDesign running under Windows.

In a perfect world, you may think the capability to view documents across platforms is not so special. Document viewing, however, is secondary to document integrity. The preservation of the contents of a page is what makes the PDF so extraordinary. To illustrate, suppose you have an InDesign document created in Windows using fonts generic to Windows applications. After it's converted to PDF, the document, complete with graphics and fonts intact, can be displayed and printed on other computer platforms. And the other computer platforms don't need the fonts, graphics, or the original authoring application to print the file with complete integrity.

This level of document integrity can come in handy in business environments, where software purchases often reach quantum costs. PDF documents eliminate the need to install all applications used within a particular company on all the computers in that company. For example, art department employees can use a layout application to create display ads and then convert them to PDF so that other departments can use the free Adobe Reader software to view and print those ads for approval.

The benefits of PDF viewing were initially recognized by workgroups in local office environments for electronic paper exchanges. Today users have much more opportunity for global exchange of documents in many different ways. As you look at Acrobat and discover some of the features available for document comment and markup, comparing documents, support for layered files (which adds much more functionality to Adobe Reader), and preparing PDFs for screen readers, you'll see how Acrobat and the PDF have evolved with new technologies.

## Cross-Reference

The term "screen reader" is used extensively throughout this book. When you see a reference to "screen reader," I'm referring to either a hardware device or special software (JAWS, Kurzweil, and so on) used to convert visual information to audio format. For more information on screen readers and making documents accessible to the readers, see Chapter 23. ■

# Repurposing documents

The computer revolution has left extraordinary volumes of data that were originally designed to be printed on paper on computer systems. Going all the way back to UNIVAC, the number crunching was handled by the computer and the expression was the printed piece. Today, forms of expression have evolved to many different media. No longer do people want to confine themselves to printed material. Now, in addition to publishing information on paper, we use CD-ROMs, the Internet, file exchanges, and meeting sessions via the Internet between computers. Sometimes we use motion video, television, and satellite broadcasts. As high-speed access evolves, we'll see much larger bandwidths, so real-time communication will eventually become commonplace.

Technology will advance, bringing many improvements to bandwidth, performance, and speed. To enable the public to access the mountains of digital data held on computer systems in a true information superhighway world, files need to be converted to a common format. A common file format would also enable new documents to be more easily *repurposed*, to exploit the many forms of communication that we use today and expect to use tomorrow.

Acrobat Pro has many tools for helping users repurpose documents. Tools for repairing problem files, downsizing file sizes, porting files to a range of different devices, and eliminating unnecessary data are part of the many features found in Acrobat Pro. In addition, the PDF/A format introduced in Acrobat 8 is designed specifically for archiving documents. A standards committee has developed this format so documents viewed on computer systems 100 years from now will be compatible with future operating systems.

# Using PDF and Adobe PostScript

The de facto standard for nearly all printing in the graphics industry has been Adobe PostScript. While PostScript is still the dominant printing language, this will slowly change because Adobe has announced in 2006 support for PDF as the new print standard.

PostScript is still around in many print houses, but the use of PostScript is diminishing. Acrobat has shipped a companion product to convert PostScript to PDF called Acrobat Distiller. Distiller is still shipped with Acrobat X, but today we are finding much less use of the Distiller program. This book does not cover Acrobat Distiller. To learn more about Distiller, consult the Acrobat Help Guide.

## Cross-Reference

To learn more about accessing help information, see Chapter 3. ■

## Examining a PDF version

Acrobat is now in version X. The version number indicates the number of releases of the product. PDF is a file format, and with it you'll also find a version number — that is, up until version 9 of Acrobat. The PDF version in versions prior to X related to the specifications of the file format; for the end user it's usually not so important to understand all the specifications as much as it is to know what it does for you or what you can expect from it. If you create PDF documents for users of older Acrobat viewers and use the newer PDF format, your users may not be able to view your PDF files. Conversely, creating PDF files with the older version might prohibit you from using some newer features in the recent release.

PDF versions are typically referred to as Acrobat Compatibility. A PDF version 1.7 file, for example, is an Acrobat 8–compatible file. To understand how the PDF version relates to the Acrobat version, simply add the digits of the PDF version together. For example, PDF version 1.4 is Acrobat 5 compatible (1 + 4 = 5). PDF version 1.5 is Acrobat 6 compatible, and so on.

Since version 9, however, PDF has lost its version number — the reason being, Adobe no longer owns the PDF specification. PDF has become an adopted standard by the International Organization for Standardization (ISO). Since the ISO committee sets the standard, it's taken out of the hands of Adobe and no longer carries a version number.

Each release of Acrobat provides support for additional features in PDF documents. It's not as important to know all the features enabled by one version as it is to know which Acrobat compatibility you need to use. For example, to optimize a PDF file for printing, you may need to use PDF version 1.3 or Acrobat 4 compatibility. Or, if you want to embed movie files in a PDF, then you need to use an Acrobat 6–compatible file. Or, you may want to add password security to a PDF that requires a newer Acrobat viewer to open a file using a password.

Whereas you previously may have thought of PDF version files, you now need to think in terms of Acrobat version compatibility. The PDF specification is handled by ISO, but the Acrobat compatibility is handled by Adobe Systems. ISO 32000 is the ISO specification for the current PDF version.

# Understanding PDF Standards

PDF has been adopted as a standard file format in many industries, including engineering, legal, manufacturing, and prepress and printing. Even the United States Federal Government has embraced PDF as a standard file format.

So what are *standards*? Without regulation and approved standards, the computer industry would be chaotic. Fortunately, the International Organization for Standardization (ISO) develops and approves standards for the technical industry. This international committee, an entity apart from Adobe Systems, has approved and developed substandards of the PDF format.

The PDF standards available now include the following:

- **PDF/X.** This standard is a subset of the PDF format used in the printing industry. PDFs meeting PDF/X compliance are typically reliable and, theoretically, can be accurately printed on almost any kind of PostScript device.

- **PDF/E.** This standard is a subset of the PDF format designed for engineers to ensure that industrial designs and drawings comply with a PDF standard.

- **PDF/A.** This standard is a subset of the PDF format used for archiving documents. The standards committee wants to ensure that the files you create today and save as PDFs can be viewed by computers many years in the future. To do so, the PDFs you create for archival purposes can be saved as PDF/A documents.

- **PDF/UA.** Although, as of this writing, this subset of the PDF format is in an early draft stage, you may be hearing more about it in the near future — about one to two years from this writing. The goal of this proposed new standard is to provide universal access (UA) to all users including those persons working with assistive devices (see Chapter 25 for more on PDFs and assistive devices). The proposed new format is in the hands of the AIIMS Standards Board Committee that also proposed the PDF/X and PDF/A standards and submitted them to the ISO. People interested in participating on the committee can find more information at `www.aiim.org/standards.asp?ID=27861`.

# Working in the Acrobat Environment

Acrobat provides you with features such as menu commands, toolbars, and palettes to accomplish work for whatever goal you hope to achieve with PDF documents. When you launch the program you see many of these features in the Acrobat window. Just so you know what is being referred to when I discuss accessing a feature in Acrobat, take a look at Figure 1.3 to understand the names used to describe the various areas of the new Acrobat workplace.

A. **Title bar.** By default, the name of the file you open appears in the title bar. The title appearing in the title bar can change according to an option for displaying the Document Title in the Initial View properties.

## Cross-Reference
For information related to Initial View and displaying Document Titles, see Chapter 5. ∎

B. **Menu bar.** The menu bar (Viewer mode) contains all the top-level menu commands. In Acrobat X, the number of menus has been reduced to five. Many commands found in menus in earlier Acrobat viewers have been moved to panels.

## FIGURE 1.3

The Acrobat Pro workplace contains menus, tools, and panels.

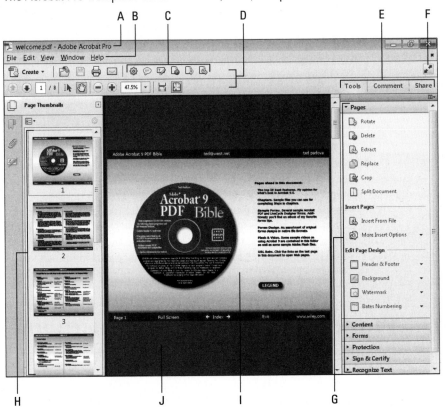

## Cross-Reference

**For information related to link actions and the Execute a menu item command action type, see Chapter 21. For more information on actions with form fields, see Part VI. For making preference choices for viewing PDFs, see "Discovering tools and task buttons" later in this chapter. ∎**

- **C. Favorites toolbar.** Tools are contained in panels along the right side of the Acrobat window. You can customize the Favorites toolbar by adding panel tools to the toolbar.

- **D. Toolbar Well.** Individual tools are nested below the menu bar in the Toolbar Well.

- **E. Panel buttons.** Click one of the panel buttons to open panels in the Panel Bin. Three individual panel groups are available: The Tools panel displays 11 different tool panels. The Comment panel contains all the Annotations and Drawing Markup tools. The Share panel is used for logging on to Acrobat.com, sharing files, and engaging in shared reviews.

F. **Read Mode toggle.** Click this button to enter Read Mode.

G. **Panels.** Click the title of a panel to expand or collapse it. In Acrobat X, many menu commands have been moved to panels.

H. **Navigation pane.** The Navigation pane can be expanded or collapsed. The view in Figure 1.1 is an expanded view showing the Pages panel. Click an icon or press the F4 key on your keyboard to expand and collapse the Navigation pane.

I. **Document.** When you open a PDF file, it appears in the Document pane.

J. **Document pane.** The Document pane is the container for PDF files you see in Acrobat. When no file is open, the Document pane is empty. When you open a PDF document, the document appears in the Document pane.

## Cross-Reference

For more detail on specific menu commands, tools, and palettes, see the related chapters to discover the different options available to you. All of the items discussed here are explained in more depth in subsequent chapters. ∎

## Exploring menus

As with any program operating on a computer system that supports a Windows type of environment, you will notice menu commands at the top level of the Acrobat window. Users of previous versions of Acrobat will notice that there are fewer menus in Acrobat X. Specifically, the Document, Comments, Forms, Tools, and Advanced menus have been eliminated in Acrobat X.

If you are an Acrobat user, don't worry. All the commands from the previous versions of Acrobat still exist. They have just been relocated to panels. If, for example, you want to access the Page Templates command, it has been moved from the Advanced ⇨ Document Processing submenu to the Document Processing panel in the Panel Bin.

- **File menu.** The File menu is where you open and close documents, create PDF files, import and export certain data, access print commands, and find some other nifty new additions in Acrobat such as Acrobat PDF Portfolios and collaboration features. The Mac and Windows operating systems display recent files in different menus. On the Mac in OS X, you'll find recently viewed documents by choosing File ⇨ Open Recent File. This command opens a submenu where you can access recent documents. On Windows, a list of the recently viewed documents is located at the bottom of the File menu.

- **Edit menu.** The traditional Cut, Copy, and Paste commands are located in the Edit menu along with other familiar commands from Acrobat 9. There are no changes to the Edit menu from Acrobat 9.

- **View menu.** The View menu contains all the commands you'll use for viewing PDF documents. The View menu also contains the Cursor Coordinates command. This command displays a tiny window showing the coordinates of the cursor as you move it around the Document pane. The display units are controlled by opening the Preferences (Ctrl/⌘+K) and changing the Units preferences.

- **Document menu.** The Document menu appeared in previous versions of Acrobat. It has been eliminated in Acrobat X and the menu commands have been moved to several panels.

- **Comments menu.** The Comments menu appeared in previous versions of Acrobat. It has been eliminated in Acrobat X and the menu commands have been moved to the Comment panel.

- **Forms menu.** The Forms menu appeared in previous versions of Acrobat. It has been eliminated in Acrobat X and the menu commands have been moved to the Forms panel.

## Cross-Reference

For information on working with Acrobat PDF forms, see Chapters 30 and 31. ■

- **Tools menu.** The Tools menu appeared in previous versions of Acrobat. It has been eliminated in Acrobat X and the menu commands have been moved to several panels.

- **Advanced menu.** The Advanced menu appeared in previous versions of Acrobat. It has been eliminated in Acrobat X and the menu commands have been moved to several panels.

- **Window menu.** The Window menu provides menu commands to assist you in viewing documents. No changes appear in the Window menu in Acrobat X compared to earlier viewers.

- **Help menu.** The traditional help files added to your Acrobat folder at installation are found in the Help menu. Various online help support is also located in this menu.

## Cross-Reference

For information related to Help documents and Help menus, see Chapter 3. ■

- **Submenus.** A number of submenus appear in menus contained in the top-level menu bar and from many different tools contained in panels. Note that on individual panel commands, you see a down-pointing arrow. Clicking the arrow opens a menu; some menus contain submenus. A submenu is denoted in Acrobat by a right-pointing arrow on the right side of a given menu command, as shown in Figure 1.4 (left). Select a command with one of these arrows adjacent to the command name, and a submenu opens. In a few cases, you can find nested submenus where another right-pointing arrow may be visible in the submenu. In panels, down-pointing arrows signify a drop-down menu, as shown in Figure 1.4 (right). If you want to access the second submenu, move the cursor to the menu option containing a right-pointing or down-pointing arrow. To make a selection from a submenu command, move the cursor to the desired menu command. When the menu command highlights, click the mouse button to execute the command.

**FIGURE 1.4**

To access a submenu, move the cursor to the command containing a right-pointing or down-pointing arrow and slide the cursor over to the submenu options. Click the desired command in the submenu to execute the command.

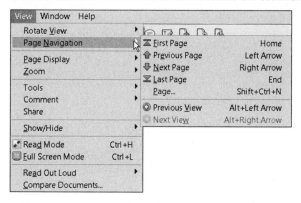

- **Context menus.** Wherever you are in the Acrobat window — the Toolbar Well, panels, Document pane, or the various editing modes — you can gain quick access to menu items related to your task by opening a context menu. Context menus pop up in an area where you either click the right button on the mouse or use an appropriate key modifier. In Windows, right-click the mouse button to open a context menu. On a Mac, when not using a two-button mouse, press the Control key and click the mouse button. Context menu options relate to the particular tool you have selected from a toolbar. Selecting different tools provides you with different menu commands. In Figure 1.5 I opened a context menu with the Hand tool selected.

**FIGURE 1.5**

With the Hand tool selected, right-clicking (Windows) or Control+clicking (Mac) the mouse button opens a context menu. From the menu, scroll the list and select the desired menu command.

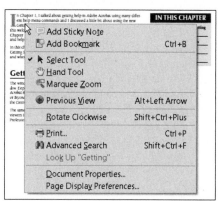

If you change tools in a toolbar and open a context menu, the menu options change to reflect choices with that particular tool. Likewise, a context menu opened on a panel offers menu options respective to the panel. In Figure 1.6 you see a context menu opened while the Edit Document Text tool (known as the TouchUp Text tool in earlier versions of Acrobat) is selected. In Figure 1.7 you see a context menu opened in the Navigation pane.

**FIGURE 1.6**

Changing tools and opening a context menu displays different menu options.

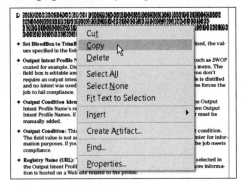

**FIGURE 1.7**

Opening a context menu in the Navigation pane displays a list of available panels that you can access.

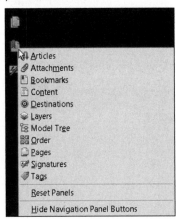

## Tip

Opening a context menu on one of the icons in the Navigation pane opens a menu where you can add or remove panels from the pane. Additionally, you can hide the Navigation panel icons by opening a context menu in the Navigation pane and selecting Hide Navigation Pane Buttons. To bring back the Navigation Pane Buttons, press F4 on your keyboard or select View ⇨ Navigation Panels ⇨ Show Navigation Pane. ■

Context menus are a great benefit during your Acrobat sessions, and using them helps you work much faster. Throughout this book I often make references to the different choices you have in selecting a tool or command. In most incidences, you find mention of context menus. Be certain you know how to open a context menu in Acrobat on your computer. For the remainder of this book, I'll mention opening context menus without walking through the steps for how to open the menu.

- **Keyboard shortcuts.** Pressing one or more keys on your keyboard can also open menus and invoke different commands. When you become familiar with keyboard shortcuts that perform the same function as when using a menu or context menu, you'll find yourself favoring this method for making different menu selections or grabbing a tool from a toolbar. Fortunately, you can learn as you work when it comes to memorizing keyboard shortcuts. As I'm certain you know, several shortcut combinations are noted in menu commands. You can learn these shortcuts when you frequently use a particular command. However, the keyboard shortcuts you see in the menu commands are just a fraction of what is available in Acrobat for quick access to commands and tools. For a complete list of all keyboard shortcuts, look over the Acrobat Help document you open by selecting Help ⇨ Adobe Acrobat X (Standard or Pro) Help or pressing the F1 key.

## Note

Pressing a single key to access a tool requires you to have your Preferences set to accept single keystroke shortcuts. Open the Preferences (Ctrl/Command+L) and click General in the left pane and check the box for Use single-key accelerators to access tools in the right pane. ■

# Discovering tools and task buttons

Tools and toolbars have been dramatically changed in Acrobat X compared to earlier versions of Acrobat. No longer do you find toolbars in Acrobat X. Most of the tools have been moved to panels where they appear more like menu commands than tools. Acrobat allows some customization through the addition of tools to the Favorites menu — essentially the Toolbar Well.

## Exploring the Toolbar Well

The Toolbar Well hosts a task button, default Acrobat tools, and tools that you can add to the Favorites list. More specifically, these items include:

- **Task button.** Acrobat 9 and earlier had several task buttons. In Acrobat X you find a single task button denoted as the Create task button. Notice that the task button includes a drop-down menu. When you click the down-pointing arrow, the menu commands are revealed, as shown in Figure 1.8. You use these commands for converting documents to PDF.

**FIGURE 1.8**

The Create task button drop-down menu

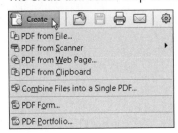

- **Default tools.** By default, there are a number of tools you can use for managing files and changing different document views. These tools, shown in Figure 1.9, are fixed in the Toolbar Well, and you cannot remove or reposition them.

**FIGURE 1.9**

Default tools that are fixed in the Toolbar Well

- **Customized Favorites toolbar.** All the panel commands in Acrobat behave in a similar way to a tool. As such, you can add and remove the items that appear in the panels to and from the Favorites toolbar. In Figure 1.10, tools from the Pages panel appear in the Favorites toolbar.

**FIGURE 1.10**

Tools added to the Favorites toolbar

## Customizing the Favorites toolbar

Panels contain tools and drop down-menus. Menus are indicated by a down-pointing arrow that appears adjacent to a name in the panel. Items without a down-pointing arrow are tools.

You can add each tool and menu in the panels to the Favorites toolbar at the top of the Toolbar Well. When you add a menu item, it is represented as a tool icon with a down-pointing arrow that you can use to access the menu commands.

You add tools and menus to the Favorites toolbar in one of two ways:

- **Context menu command.** Right-click a tool in a panel and choose Add to Favorites Toolbar.

- **Customize Favorites Toolbar command.** Click the plus (+) icon in the Favorites toolbar or open a context menu on the Favorites toolbar and choose Customize Favorites Toolbar. Either action opens the Customize Favorites Toolbar window shown in Figure 1.11.

**FIGURE 1.11**

The Customize Favorites Toolbar window enables you to add, arrange, and delete tools from the Favorites toolbar.

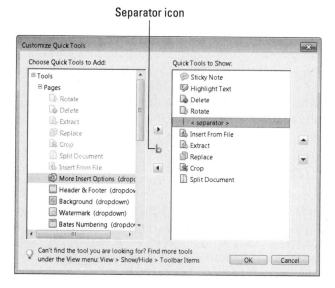

Separator icon

In Figure 1.11, you see a list of the panels contained within the Tools panel on the left side of the window. Click the plus (+) icon to expand a panel. On the right side of the window you see a list of tools that are currently added to the Favorites toolbar.

To add a tool to the Favorites toolbar, click a name in the list on the left side of the window and click the right-pointing arrow. To remove a tool from the Favorites toolbar, click a name in the list on the right side of the window and click the left-pointing arrow.

You can move tools to rearrange them in the Favorites toolbar. To move a tool to a different location, click the tool name in the list on the right side of the panel and click either the up- or down-pointing arrow. If you want to segment groups of tools, add a separator bar by clicking the icon with the vertical line, as shown in Figure 1.11. A separator is added to the bottom of the list on the right. Click <separator> and click the up-pointing arrow to move the separator line to a different location.

Acrobat limits the number of tools you can add to the Favorites toolbar. When the toolbar is fully populated with tools, you cannot add more tools. Instead, you must delete some tools if you want to add more tools.

After you add and arrange tools, click OK in the Customize Favorites Toolbar window, and the tools appear to the right of the plus (+) icon in the Favorites toolbar.

## Tip

You can add a complete panel's tools to the Favorites toolbar by clicking the panel name and then clicking the right-pointing arrow. All tools in the panel are added to the Favorites toolbar. ∎

# Using Panels

In Acrobat X, all the tools formerly found in toolbars have been moved to panels appearing on the right side of the Acrobat window. On the left side of the Acrobat window you find the traditional navigation panels nested in the Navigation pane. The only change to the Navigation pane is that the Comments panel has been moved from the Navigation pane to a separate panel on the right side of the Acrobat window.

## Using the Navigation panels

Acrobat displays a series of panels docked in a well when you first launch the program. The Navigation pane hosts several panels along the left side of the Acrobat window. By default, the Navigation pane is collapsed; however, you can save PDF documents in such a manner where a panel expands when a file is opened in any Acrobat viewer. These settings are document-specific and can be toggled on or off for individual PDF documents.

## Cross-Reference

For more information about setting opening views for panel displays, see Chapter 5. ∎

### Touring the Pages panel

Acrobat users have been familiar with the thumbnail view of each page since the early days of Acrobat. A mini view of each page in the active PDF document is displayed in the Pages pane, as shown in Figure 1.12. The Pages pane offers you menu options for arranging, deleting, inserting, and editing pages in a number of ways. You can zoom in to the thumbnail views as large as or even larger than a page viewed in the Document pane.

**FIGURE 1.12**

Thumbnails are found in the Pages panel in all Acrobat viewers. The thumbnail view of document pages can be sized larger and smaller using context menu commands.

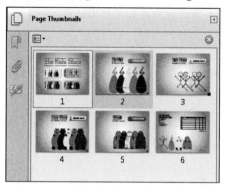

## Cross-Reference

**For a complete description of working with pages (thumbnails), see Chapter 15.** ■

### Looking at the Bookmarks panel

The second default panel in the Navigation pane is the Bookmark panel. You can save PDF documents in a manner where the bookmarks are visible when the file opens in Acrobat. Bookmarks are visible in an open Navigation pane, as shown in Figure 1.13. You can open and close the Navigation pane by pressing F4. You can also grab the vertical separator bar at the right edge of the Navigation pane and move it left and right to size the pane.

**FIGURE 1.13**

Bookmarks can be displayed in the Navigation pane when a file opens.

Bookmarks are navigation buttons that can launch a page, a view, or one of many different Action types similar to link and button actions. Anyone familiar with Acrobat already knows much about bookmarks and how to navigate pages by clicking individual bookmarks in the panel.

## Cross-Reference

To learn how to create and manage bookmarks and add actions, see Chapter 21. ■

### Using the Signatures panel

Digital signatures help you manage signed documents. The Signatures panel enables you to perform tasks such as displaying signatures in the Signature pane, verifying signatures, clearing them, deleting them, and so on. All these editing tasks with signatures are still available in Acrobat Professional and Acrobat Standard as is signature validation, which is also available in all Acrobat viewers.

## Cross-Reference

For a complete description of creating and managing digital signatures, see Chapter 24. ■

### Using the Attachments panel

The Attachments panel (see Figure 1.14) in all Acrobat viewers is used to display, manage, and extract file attachments. You can attach files in Acrobat and extract file attachments using all Acrobat viewers including Adobe Reader.

---

**FIGURE 1.14**

---

The Attachments panel provides options for managing file attachments. Attachments can be extracted from within Adobe Reader.

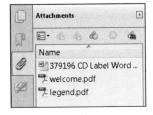

## Cross-Reference

For a complete description of adding file attachments to PDF documents, see Chapter 11. ■

### Viewing hidden panels

As with toolbars, you can choose to view additional panels through menu commands. You can choose to display a number of other panels in the Acrobat window and dock them in the Navigation pane. To open a hidden panel, choose View ➪ Show/Hide/Navigation Panes. From the submenu, you'll find all the panels available.

Another way to access the Navigation panels is through a context menu. Right-click (Windows) or Control+click (Mac) on the Navigation pane and a menu shows all the

Navigation panels. Choose a panel to open, and it opens docked in the navigation pane. Opening a context menu also offers a menu command for Show/Hide Navigation Pane as shown in Figure 1.15.

Navigation panels opened from a context menu appear docked in the Navigation pane.

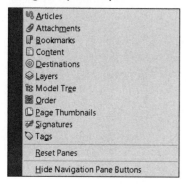

The list includes the default panels. If you select a default panel, the Navigation pane opens and the panel is selected. When you select a hidden panel — in other words, a panel other than those docked in the Navigation pane when you first launch Acrobat — the panel opens in the Acrobat window as a floating panel with one or more panels contained in the window. Drag a panel to the Navigation pane and it docks and then becomes visible in a context menu opened from the Navigation pane.

- **Articles.** The first of the hidden panels listed in the Navigation Panels submenu is Articles. Choose View ➪ Navigation Panels ➪ Articles to open a floating panel. Articles enable you to create article threads to help users follow passages of text in a logical reading order. You won't find any new features added to the Article tool since Acrobat 5.

## Cross-Reference
For information on creating article threads and managing them, see Chapter 21. ∎

- **Content.** A panel designed for managing the structural content of PDF documents is found in the Content panel. When you choose View ➪ Navigation Panels ➪ Content, the Content panel opens in a floating panel as shown in Figure 1.16. Content features help you reflow tagged PDF files and manipulate the structure of tagged documents.

**FIGURE 1.16**

The Content panel opens in a floating panel where the structural content of the open file is reported.

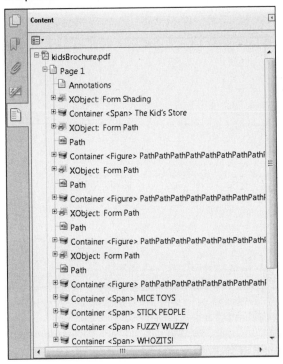

## Cross-Reference

For information on working with the Content panel and tagged PDF documents, see Chapter 23. ■

- **Destinations.** Destinations work similarly to bookmarks, in that specific views are captured and listed in the panel. Clicking a destination opens the associated page in the Document pane, whereas clicking a bookmark opens the associated view (page and zoom).

## Cross-Reference

For information on creating destinations and managing them, see Chapter 21. ■

- **Layers.** If you create documents containing Adobe PDF layers, the Layers panel permits you to toggle layer views and work with layer properties. In Figure 1.17, the Layers panel is open, showing visible and hidden layers.

**FIGURE 1.17**

The Layers panel enables you to manage layer visibility.

- **Model Tree.** The Model Tree panel lets you examine information related to 3-D drawings. You can review assets, hide and show drawing parts, toggle views, review comments, and more on 3-D drawings. In Figure 1.18 you can see the model tree shown for a 3-D image.

**FIGURE 1.18**

The Model Tree panel is designed to work with 3-D drawings.

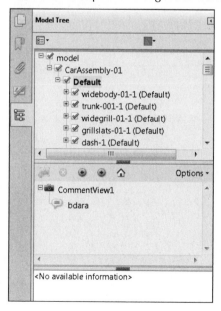

- **Order.** You use the Order panel to manage reading order of documents. This panel also relates to document accessibility, like the options available in the Tags panel. The Order panel enables you to add tags to a document, clear tags, and reorder a page's contents to change a reading order that might be read aloud by a screen reader.

## Cross-Reference

**For information on working with the Order panel, understanding screen readers, and document accessibility, see Chapter 23. ■**

- **Tags.** Tagged PDF files provide more editing capability with PDF documents, and the files can be made accessible to adaptive devices such as screen readers. For adding, editing, and annotating tags in PDF documents, use the Tags panel. Together with the Content panel options, you have much control over document accessibility.

## Cross-Reference

**To understand accessibility and the advantages of creating tagged PDF documents, see Chapter 23. ■**

### Working with panel menus

Each of the panels contains its own pull-down menu. When a panel is open in the Navigation pane or in a floating window, select the Options down-pointing arrow to open a pull-down menu, as shown in Figure 1.19. Menu commands found in panels may or may not be available from the top-level menu bar. Additionally, some panels, like the Attachments panel, offer you several pull-down menus.

**FIGURE 1.19**

Panel Options menus provide menu commands specific to each panel function.

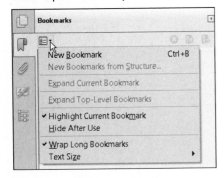

### Using context menus

Context menus can display different options for panel choices depending on where you open a context menu. If you move the cursor to an empty area when all text and objects in a panel are deselected and open a context menu, the menu options may be different than when you select text or an object in a panel. However, this is not always the case, because a few panels provide you with the same options regardless of whether something is selected or not. In Figure 1.20 a context menu is opened within the Bookmarks panel. In this case you need to open the menu on a bookmark name. If you attempt to open a context menu in an empty area in the pane, no menu opens.

---

**FIGURE 1.20**

A context menu opened on a bookmark

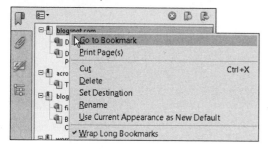

## Getting familiar with the Tools panels

If you are already an Acrobat user, then all the items related to Navigation panels are familiar to you. The only new thing in the Navigation pane is the absence of the Comments panel. What follows is completely new in Acrobat X, where a host of panels contain commands that were previously available from the top-level menus.

At first glance you may think that Adobe has eliminated some functionality in Acrobat when you look through the top-level menus. Notice that the Document, Comment, Forms, and Advanced menus have been eliminated from Acrobat X. Don't worry, however: what you may be familiar with in earlier versions of Acrobat as menu commands have now been nested in the Tools panel.

The Tools panel contains items reorganized in several different groups. Adobe has made an effort to nest similar tools and commands in panels related to certain tasks. When you click the Tools button in the Toolbar Well, 11 different panels open, as shown in Figure 1.21. The Tools panels include:

- **Pages.** Not to be confused with the Pages panel in the Navigation pane, the Pages panel here contains commands related to page editing such as rotating, inserting, extracting, removing, cropping, and splitting pages.

## Cross-Reference

For more on using the Pages panel and editing pages, see Chapter 15. ■

**FIGURE 1.21**

Click the Tools button to open the Tools panel bin.

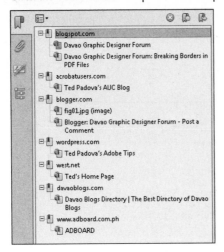

- **Content.** The Content panel contains tools for editing page content, such as adding headers and footers, editing text, replacing images, and adding buttons and multimedia.

## Cross-Reference

For more on using the Content panel, see Chapters 21 and 22. ■

- **Protection.** The Protection panel contains tools for adding security and all the redaction tools.

## Cross-Reference

For more on using the Protection panel for redaction and security, see Chapters 13 and 24. ■

- **Sign and Certify.** This panel is used for adding electronic signatures and certifying documents.

## Cross-Reference

For more on using the Sign and Certify panel for digital signatures and certifying documents, see Chapter 24. ■

- **Forms.** Commands formerly found in the Forms menu in earlier versions of Acrobat are now placed in the Forms panel. To open Form Edit mode, click Edit in the Forms panel.

## Cross-Reference

For more on using form tools and working in Form Edit mode, see Chapters 30 and 31. ■

- **Document Processing.** The former Advanced ⇨ Document Processing menu commands in earlier Acrobat viewers are now placed in this panel. You can also find Acrobat Scan, Web Capture, and the Articles tool here. For more on using the Document Processing commands, look over Parts I and II.

- **Print Production.** All the tools found in the Print Production toolbar in earlier versions of Acrobat are contained in this menu.

## Cross-Reference

For more on using the Print Production panel, see Chapter 29. ■

- **JavaScript.** This panel contains all the commands related to developing JavaScripts.

## Cross-Reference

For more on using the JavaScript panel, see Chapter 32. ■

- **Make Accessible.** The Make Accessible panel contains commands for making documents accessible and checking accessibility.

## Cross-Reference

For more on accessibility, see Chapter 23. ■

- **Analyze.** This panel contains the Measuring tools and geospatial information. For more information on how to use these tools, see the Acrobat Help menu.

- **Actions Wizard.** What was referred to in earlier versions of Acrobat as Batch Sequencing is now referred to in Acrobat X as Actions. This panel is used to create Actions sequences.

## Cross-Reference

For more on using the Actions Wizard, see Chapter 17. ■

# Understanding Preferences

Preferences enable you to customize your work sessions in Acrobat. You can access a Preferences dialog box from within any Acrobat viewer and from within a Web browser when viewing PDFs as inline views. A huge number of preferences exist that all relate to specific tool groups or task categories, and it would not make as much sense to cover them here in the opening chapter as it would within chapters related to using tools and methods influenced by preference choices.

Preferences are contained in the dialog box shown in Figure 1.22. You make a topic selection in the list on the left side of the dialog box and the related preferences are shown to the right side of the dialog box. You make choices for preferences by selecting check boxes or making menu selections from drop-down lists. When you complete making your preference choices, click OK at the bottom of the dialog box.

Almost all the preferences you change in the Preferences dialog box are dynamic, which means you don't need to quit Acrobat and relaunch the program for a preference choice to take effect. Preferences remain in effect until you change them again. If you quit Acrobat and relaunch the program, the preferences you last made are honored by Acrobat. However, if for some reason the program crashes and you don't shut it down properly, any new preference changes will not be recognized when the program is launched again.

**FIGURE 1.22**

Press Ctrl/⌘+K to open the Preferences dialog box. Click a category on the left and the choices are reflected to the right of the Categories list.

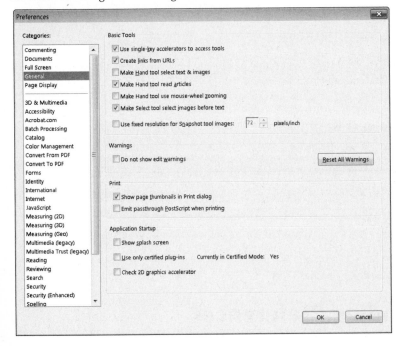

If you find some operation in Acrobat not working as you think it should, first take a look at the Preferences dialog box. In many cases you'll find a check box or menu command not enabled to permit you to perform a task. As you become familiar with specific tool groups and menu commands, make a habit of routinely visiting the Preferences dialog box so you understand all the toggles and switches that affect tool and viewing behavior.

# Summary

This chapter offers you a general introduction to working in Acrobat Standard and Acrobat Pro and helps you understand the environment, the user interface, and some of the many new features that have been added to the commercial Acrobat products. At the very least, you should know how to go about finding help when you first start working in the program. Some of the more important points discussed in this chapter include the following:

- Adobe Acrobat is a multifaceted program designed to provide solutions for many different business professionals. Several types of Acrobat viewers exist, with a range of features to suit different user needs. Adobe Reader is the free PDF viewer available from Adobe Systems. The commercial viewers are Acrobat Standard (Windows only) and Acrobat Pro.

- PDF, short for Portable Document Format, was developed by Adobe Systems and was designed to exchange documents between computers and across computer platforms while maintaining file integrity.

- The PDF language format has changed version numbers along with the Acrobat viewers. Beginning in Acrobat 9, the PDF specification is no longer owned by Adobe. The International Organization for Standards now regulates the PDF specification.

- Tasks are performed through the use of menus, tools, and panels that can be accessed through mouse selections and keyboard shortcuts.

- The extensive list of tools appears in an abbreviated form when you open Acrobat and view the default collapsed Tools panel. You can add individual tools to the Favorites toolbar via the Customize Favorites Toolbar window.

- Panels contain tools formerly assigned to individual toolbars in earlier Acrobat viewers. Panels contain individual tools and drop-down lists.

- You can customize the Acrobat workplace to suit your work style through the use of different preference choices. When preferences, panels, and tools are changed from their default views, the new views are saved when you quit your Acrobat session. They remain unchanged until you change them again or reset them to defaults.

- Preferences are settings that apply globally to Acrobat and influence the behavior of tools and menu commands.

# Using Acrobat Viewers

In Chapter 1 you got a feel for some of the tools and menu commands provided in Acrobat Standard and Acrobat Pro. If you're a PDF author and you use Acrobat Standard or Pro, knowing the capabilities of one viewer versus another is important for job efficiency and productivity, as well as usefulness to the end user. You may want to add multimedia to a PDF document. Therefore, you need to know what authoring tool is needed to import video and sound. You may be sending out a document for review and want to solicit comments. Therefore, you need to know what viewer a user needs to send comments back to you.

At times you may find that none of the Acrobat products can help you do some editing tasks needed in your workflow. Fortunately, you have options for acquiring Acrobat plug-ins developed by third-party manufacturers that add much more functionality to the Acrobat tools and menu commands.

Many of the chapters ahead give you an idea of the distinctions between Acrobat Standard and Acrobat Pro and the tools accessible from one viewer versus the other. This chapter introduces you to the Acrobat viewers, points out some differences among them, and shows you how to use Acrobat plug-ins when you need more features than the viewers provide.

# Exploring Viewer Distinctions

Adobe Reader, Acrobat Standard (Windows only in version 8 through X), and Acrobat Pro are designed to serve different users with different purposes. It should be obvious to you that Adobe Reader, as a free download from Adobe's Web site, is much more limited in features and performance than the products you purchase. For a general overview, take a look at the following descriptions of the Acrobat products.

## Using Adobe Reader

Adobe Reader is available for download from Adobe's Web site free of charge. The Adobe Reader software is distributed for the purpose of viewing, printing, and searching of PDF files created by users of Acrobat Standard and Acrobat Pro. Additionally, Adobe Reader is used for filling in forms on PDFs created with Acrobat Standard and Acrobat Pro. The major features of Adobe Reader include:

- **Viewing and printing.** These features are common across all Acrobat viewers. You can view, navigate, and print PDF documents with Adobe Reader.

- **Forms completion and submission.** Adobe Reader enables you to complete forms but not save the form field data unless the forms carry special usage rights for Adobe Reader users. Forms are submitted through the use of buttons created on forms for emailing or submitting data to Web servers.

## Cross-Reference

For more information on enabling PDFs with usage rights, see Chapter 18. ■

- **Comment and Review.** PDFs can be enabled with usage rights for commenting and review in Acrobat Pro. Once enabled, Reader users can participate in a review workflow and save PDFs locally with comments and markups. New in Adobe Reader X are limited commenting features that can be used without enabling a PDF file.

- **Adobe LiveCycle Reader Extensions ES.** If an organization uses the Adobe LiveCycle Reader Extensions ES product available from Adobe Systems to enhance PDF files, Adobe Reader users can digitally sign documents and save form data.

  A distinction exists between enabling PDFs with usage rights from within Acrobat Standard and Acrobat Pro and using the Adobe LiveCycle Reader Extensions ES. Licensing restrictions do apply when enabling documents, and you should be aware of these restrictions. See Chapter 18 for all you need to know about enabling PDFs and licensing restrictions.

In addition to the preceding, Adobe Reader provides support for eBook services and searching PDF documents, as well as extended support for working with accessible documents.

## Cross-Reference

For more information on using tools in Adobe Reader, see Chapter 4. ■

# Deciding between Acrobat Standard and Acrobat Pro products

Acrobat Standard is available only on Windows in versions 8 through X of Acrobat. The Mac version was discontinued when Acrobat 8 was released. Adobe Systems is a company that tries hard to respond to user needs, but there are limitations. If a product does not support the development costs, then it is likely to be discontinued. This is the case with Acrobat Standard on the Mac. Many users of Acrobat on the Mac acquire Acrobat Pro in a bundled purchase with the Adobe Creative Suite. Independent sales of Acrobat Standard were minimal on the Mac during the Acrobat 7 life cycle. Therefore, Adobe could not justify the development costs for continuing the product. On Windows, sales of Acrobat Standard were much greater, and therefore you see Acrobat Standard still available.

In Acrobat version 9, Acrobat Pro Extended was available. In Acrobat X you find only Acrobat Pro on both the Mac and Windows.

Acrobat Standard is the lightweight of the authoring programs. However, Acrobat Standard still offers many tools for PDF creation and authoring. Without going into every tool that differs between Acrobat Standard and Acrobat Pro, the major differences include the following limitations:

- **Form field authoring.** The Forms toolbar was added to Acrobat Standard 9.0. This was a major upgrade for Acrobat Standard users. You can create PDF forms with field objects, add JavaScripts, distribute forms, and collect form data. Acrobat Standard also supports enabling forms for Adobe Reader users.

## Cross-Reference
For information on writing JavaScripts, see Chapter 32. ∎

- **Professional printing.** Acrobat Standard does not provide options for soft proofing color, preflighting jobs, or commercial printing using such features as color separations, frequency control, transparency flattening, and so on. All these print controls are contained only in Acrobat Pro.

## Cross-Reference
For information on preflighting, soft proofing color, and commercial printing, see Chapter 29. ∎

- **Adding Adobe Reader usage rights.** You can add usage rights that enable Adobe Reader users to extract file attachments from PDF documents, and in Acrobat X Standard, add usage rights for Reader users to save form field data and add digital signatures.

- **Redaction.** The tools for redacting documents are not available to Acrobat Standard users.

- **Batch processing.** Acrobat Standard does not support batch processing and running batch commands.

- **Creating index files.** Acrobat Catalog is not part of Acrobat Standard. You can create index files only with the Acrobat Pro products through a menu command that launches Acrobat Catalog.

- **Creating PDFs.** Acrobat Standard offers support for an impressive range of file types that can be converted to PDF. However, Acrobat Standard doesn't support creating PDFs from certain file types such as AutoCAD, Microsoft Visio, and Microsoft Project. Acrobat Standard does use Acrobat Distiller, but the Acrobat Standard Distiller does not support PDF/X, PDF/E, and PDF/A compliance. Additionally, Acrobat Standard does not support Adobe Presenter features.

## Cross-Reference

For information on adding usage rights for Adobe Reader users, see Chapter 18. For information on using the Redaction tools and redacting documents, see Chapter 13. For information on creating batch sequences, see Chapter 17. For information on creating index files, see Chapter 6. For information on using Acrobat Distiller, see the Acrobat Help file. ■

- **Engineering tools.** Acrobat Standard does not support some features used by engineers and technical illustrators, such as merging and flattening layers.

The preceding items are some of the major differences between Acrobat Standard and the Acrobat Pro viewers. You will discover subtle differences as you work with the programs. For example, Acrobat Standard doesn't support comparing documents, migrating comments, Bates numbering, show and snap to grids, converting .dwg and .indd files, and does not contain the PDF Optimizer for repurposing files, and so on.

If your mission is to recommend the product for purchase or make the decision for your own use, be aware of the three primary distinctions between the products: Acrobat Standard does not support professional printing, engineering tools, or adding Adobe Reader usage rights for review and comment and forms data saving and digital signatures. If your work is in one of these areas, you need to purchase Acrobat Pro.

# Using Plug-ins

All Acrobat viewers support a plug-in architecture. Plug-ins are installed during your Acrobat installation and loaded when you launch Acrobat. Many of the features you find when exercising commands and using tools are made possible by the use of plug-ins. To view the current plug-ins loaded with the viewer you use, choose Help ➪ About Adobe Plug-ins. The About Adobe Plug-Ins dialog box opens as shown in Figure 2.1.

The list in the left side of the dialog box lists the names of the installed plug-ins. Click a name to see a description for the plug-in, including whether the plug-in is certified, the version number, creation date, text description, and dependencies. To examine different plug-ins, select them in the left pane and view the description on the right side of the dialog box.

## FIGURE 2.1

The About Adobe Plug-Ins dialog box lists all the plug-ins accessible to your viewer.

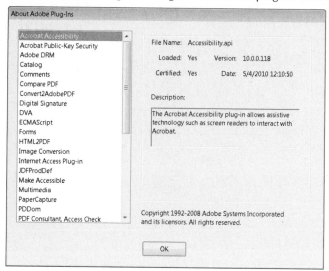

Acrobat plug-ins are created by Adobe Systems and third-party developers. All plug-ins from Adobe Systems are *certified* plug-ins. No third-party plug-ins are certified. Some features in Acrobat require that only certified plug-ins be loaded before the feature is enabled. Working with eBooks is one example where only certified plug-ins can be used.

## Note

**Any time a document has Adobe DRM (Digital Rights Management) protection, such as eBooks and/or documents protected with the Adobe LiveCycle Rights Management ES Server, the viewer is launched in certified plug-in mode. This mode loads only Adobe plug-ins and disables all third-party plug-ins. ∎**

In order to instruct your Acrobat viewer to open with only certified plug-ins, open the Preferences dialog box by choosing Edit ➪ Preferences. Click General in the left pane and select the Use only certified plug-ins check box, as shown in Figure 2.2. When you quit your Acrobat viewer and relaunch the program, only certified plug-ins will load.

Plug-ins developed by third-party developers can also be loaded. The list of available resources for adding to Acrobat functionality in the form of add-ons and plug-ins is almost limitless. As you review all the chapters in this book and find that something you want to accomplish in your workflow is not covered, look for a plug-in developed by a third-party developer. Chances are that you can find a product well suited to do the job.

**FIGURE 2.2**

Select Use only certified plug-ins to allow only certified plug-ins to load upon opening.

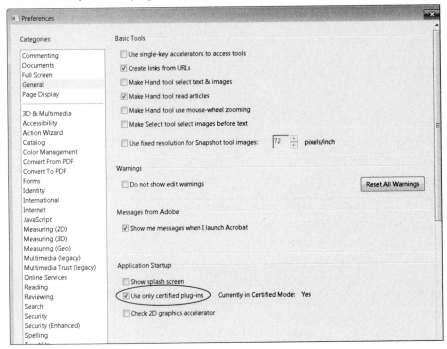

Plug-ins for Acrobat are far too numerous to mention in this book. For a single source where you can view a list of plug-ins, download demonstration copies, and make purchases, visit Acrobat Plug-ins World (http://acrobat.pluginsworld.com), the Planet PDF store at www.pdfstore.com, the Adobe Store at www.adobe.com and click on the Store link, or The PowerXChange at www.thepowerxchange.com. On several Web sites you'll find product descriptions and workflow solutions for almost any third-party product designed to work with Acrobat. When you visit one of the Web sites and review the products, be certain the product you purchase is upgraded to work with Acrobat X and the viewer you use. All products are listed with links to the manufacturer's Web sites, so you can find information on product descriptions, version numbers, and compatibility issues.

## Installing plug-ins

Most plug-ins you acquire from third-party developers are accompanied by an installer program. Installing plug-ins is easy. Open the folder for a plug-in you download from a Web site and double-click the installer icon. The installer routine finds the plug-ins folder inside your Acrobat folder and the plug-in is loaded when you launch Acrobat.

If a plug-in is not accompanied by an installer program, you need to manually add the plug-in to your Acrobat plug-ins folder. On Windows, open the Program Files\Adobe\Acrobat X\ Acrobat\plug_ins folder. Copy the plug-in you want to install to this folder.

On the Mac, open your Applications folder. Open the Adobe Acrobat X Pro folder from within the Applications folder. Press and hold the Control key and click the program icon (Adobe Acrobat X Pro) to open a context menu, as shown in Figure 2.3. From the menu items, click Show Package Contents.

**FIGURE 2.3**

Open the Package Contents on the Mac to gain access to the Plug-ins folder.

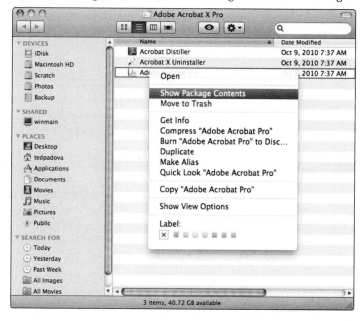

When you open the Package Contents, the Contents folder appears in a single window. Double-click the folder to open it. Several folders appear within the Contents folder, one of which is named Plug-ins. Open this folder and copy your plug-in to it.

## Uninstalling plug-ins

If your plug-in is not accompanied by an uninstaller program, you need to either disable the plug-in or physically remove it from the Acrobat plug-ins folder. A temporary solution is to disable third-party plug-ins by opening the Preferences dialog box, clicking on Startup, and selecting the check box for Use only certified plug-ins, as shown earlier in Figure 2.2.

To permanently remove a plug-in, open the plug-ins folder as described in the previous section, "Installing plug-ins," and drag the plug-in out of the Acrobat plug-ins folder.

## Caution

Some plug-ins are installed in their own folder. To remove a plug-in, drag the folder where the plug-in is installed out of the Acrobat plug-ins folder. Be certain not to remove the Acrobat plug-ins folder from within the Acrobat folder. Doing so disables all tools and menu commands using plug-ins. ■

## Resolving plug-in conflicts

At times you may find a plug-in conflict among several third-party products or a plug-in that may have a bug. If your Acrobat functionality is impaired and you can't launch the program, hold down the Shift key while double-clicking the program icon to launch your viewer. All plug-ins are disabled when you use the modifier key. Open the Preferences dialog box again and select the Use only certified plug-ins check box. Quit and relaunch the program, and the offending plug-in is eliminated during startup.

If a plug-in is creating a problem, you may need to use a process of elimination to figure out which one it is by opening your plug-ins folder and removing all plug-ins. Then add several plug-ins at a time back to the plug-ins folder and launch your viewer. Keep adding plug-ins back into the plug-ins folder until you discover the plug-in that produces the error.

## Working with plug-ins

There are many different plug-ins that provide additional features when working with Adobe Acrobat and Adobe Reader than can be covered in this book. To pick one out among the many is a hard choice. For your own workflow, visit the Planet PDF Store, Adobe Store, Acrobat Plug-ins World, the PowerXChange, or the Acrobat User Community and explore various plug-ins available for download. Try to find a plug-in that offers at least a demo trial period and download it.

Almost all plug-ins come with a ReadMe file or user manual. Before installing a plug-in, be certain to review the installation recommendations by the developer. Install the plug-in and give it a try.

## Summary

In this chapter, you explored the following:

- The three Acrobat viewers include Adobe Reader, Acrobat Standard, and Acrobat Pro. These applications can create Adobe PDFs (with the exception of Adobe Reader).
- Adobe Reader is a free download from Adobe's Web site. All other products require purchase.

- Acrobat Standard offers fewer features than Acrobat Pro and is available in versions 8 through X on Windows only. The primary limitations with Acrobat Standard are no commercial printing and engineering tools. These features are only available in Acrobat Pro.

- Acrobat plug-ins are additions to Acrobat that offer features and tools for adding more functionality to Acrobat viewers. Plug-ins are installed with Acrobat from sources developed by Adobe Systems.

- Plug-ins are available from third-party software manufacturers. A complete list of plug-ins and demonstration products is available at the Planet PDF Store, the Adobe Store, Acrobat Plug-ins World, and The PowerXChange.

# Using Help and Resources

In Chapter 1, I talked about getting help in Adobe Acrobat using some different help menu commands. There's much more to getting help in Acrobat than I covered in Chapter 1. Therefore, a separate chapter detailing the specifics of various help options seems appropriate.

In addition to help documents, there are a number of resources installed in folders that you might want to become familiar with. Many resource files can be edited to customize your PDF creation and editing.

In this chapter, I talk about some of the help documents, Web links, and resources you have with Adobe Acrobat when you start up the program and when you begin to work on some different editing tasks.

## Accessing Help

You can see the number of different commands and tools available in Acrobat is extraordinary — and you haven't yet looked at all the sub-menu options or different preference options accessed from the top-level menu bar. With all these features available to you, your initial Acrobat sessions can sometimes be overwhelming. Fortunately, the great engineers and program designers at Adobe Systems thought about you, and they decided to provide some help.

Help with learning more about Acrobat comes in several forms, and you can choose from several help methods to find the one that works well in your workflow. This section covers different options for getting help in an Acrobat session.

## Using Acrobat help

Acrobat doesn't ship with a user guide. When you open the box, the material of value is the CD-ROM and your serial number. When it comes to documentation, you first need to install Acrobat, and then use the Help menu to find information that will help you learn menu commands, features, and methods for working with the program.

Your first stop in the Help menu is the Adobe Acrobat (Standard or Pro) Help. Choose this command or press the F1 key on your keyboard, and you open the Acrobat X Help Guide shown in Figure 3.1.

FIGURE 3.1

Choose Help ⇨ Complete Adobe Acrobat (Standard or Pro) Help.

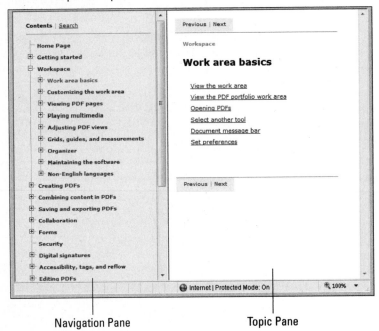

Navigation Pane                    Topic Pane

The Help Guide opens in your default Web browser. From within the Help Guide you have several options for finding help relative to the task at hand.

### Using the Contents tab

By default, the Adobe Help Viewer document opens with the Contents tab exposed as shown in Figure 3.1. In the Navigation pane you'll find a table of contents for the document, shown in a very similar manner to the way bookmarks are listed in a PDF document. Click one of the bookmark topics listed in the Contents tab to see the respective bookmarked page in the Topics pane.

### Using the Search tab

You can use the Search tab to find any word(s) in the help document. Click the Search button and the Navigation pane changes to display a field box where you type your search criteria as shown in Figure 3.2. Type one or more words in the field box and click Search. The results then appear in the Search tab. All text appearing in blue is linked to the page that opens in the Topic pane.

Click Search and type the search criteria in the text box.

### Navigating topics

When you browse topics in the Topics pane, two buttons appear at the top of the pane. Click the Previous or Next button shown in Figure 3.3 to move back or forward in the help document.

Click Previous or Next to scroll back and forth through the help document.

### Printing topics

You can choose File ⇨ Print in your Web browser to print a page; however, a much better alternative is to convert a page to a PDF document. From there, you can keep an electronic file stored on your hard drive or print the PDF document at a later time.

To convert a page to a PDF document in Microsoft Internet Explorer, select all the content on a page in the Topics pane you want to convert to PDF and open a context menu. From the menu commands choose Convert to Adobe PDF as shown in Figure 3.4. The selected area in the Topics pane is then converted to a PDF file.

Select the content you want to archive and choose Convert to Adobe PDF from a context menu.

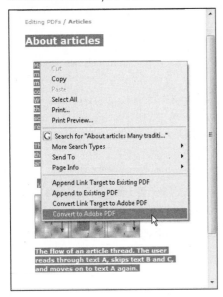

## Note

If using a Web browser other than Microsoft Internet Explorer, you have to convert the entire page to PDF. On the Mac, choose File⇨Print, and print to PDF. You have no options for converting a selection to PDF on the Mac with any Web browser. ∎

### Setting zoom views

The lower-right corner of the Topics pane displays your current zoom view. If you want to zoom in or out of the help document, click the Down Arrow to open a pop-up menu (refer to Figure 3.4). You can choose from preset zoom levels or choose Custom to add a custom zoom. You can also use the keyboard shortcuts Ctrl/⌘++ and Ctrl/⌘+- to zoom in and out of the help document.

# Using Adobe LiveCycle Designer help

Adobe LiveCycle Designer is a separate executable program available to Acrobat Pro users on Windows only. Designer is used for creating dynamic XML forms. Designer also has a help document to assist you in learning the program. To access the Help file, select Help⇨Adobe LiveCycle Designer Help or press the F1 key. The help document shown in Figure 3.5 opens.

**FIGURE 3.5**

Press the F1 key in Adobe LiveCycle Designer ES to open the help document.

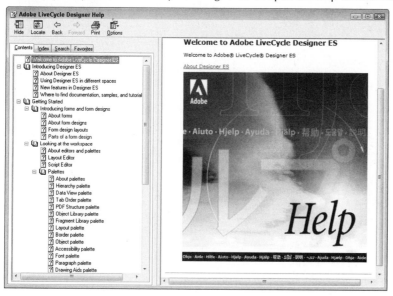

## Using the Contents tab

Like the Adobe Acrobat help document, you find a Contents tab in the Navigation pane. The contents are also listed in a hierarchical tree. Click the plus buttons to expand the contents. Subsequently, click on any item listed in the Contents list and the topics pane opens the respective link.

## Exploring the Index

The Designer help document contains an alpha index. Click the Index tab and the list is exposed. You can scroll the list to find indexed items linked to pages in the Topics pane.

## Using the Search tab

Designer provides you with a more impressive search feature than you find with the Acrobat help guide. Click the Search tab and type the search criteria in the text box at the top of the

Search pane. Click the Display button and your searched word(s) is listed on the page with the first occurrence of the search criteria. Each found word is highlighted by default as you see in Figure 3.6. To find additional pages with search results, click the arrow icons at the top of the Topics pane.

### FIGURE 3.6

All occurrences of searched words are highlighted.

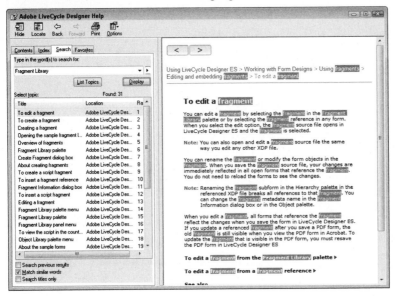

## Storing searches in the Favorites pane

The Favorites pane enables you to store searched items or any particular passage you find in the Topics pane. Click the Favorites tab after performing a search or finding a passage you want to add to a Favorites list. At the bottom of the Favorites pane, you find an Add button. Click Add and the item is listed in the topics list window.

## Using Button tools

At the top of the Contents pane, you find some navigation tools. The tools include:

- **Hide.** Click Hide and the Contents pane hides from view, offering you more room to view the topics pane. When you click Hide, the button changes to Show. Click Show and you reopen the Contents pane.

- **Locate.** Click Locate and the selected item in the Contents pane opens the respective item in the topics pane.

- **Back/Forward.** Click the arrows to move back and forward in the document.

- **Print.** Click the Print button and a dialog box opens, prompting you to choose printing a topic or printing the selected heading and all related topics.

- **Options.** The pull-down menu provides several menu commands similar to the tool options, and additionally offers you a choice for turning the highlighting off. You can eliminate the highlights when searching for items using the Search pane.

## Tip
In addition to the tools, you can also open a context menu in the Contents pane and choose to expand all topics by selecting the Open All menu item, or collapse all items by selecting the Close All menu item. ∎

## Accessing online help for Adobe Acrobat

In addition to the help file that covers working in Acrobat, some additional help and information is available online. Choose Help ➪ Online Support and the submenu displays three online help resources. The resources include:

- **Knowledge Base.** Choose Help ➪ Online Support ➪ Knowledge Base and the Acrobat Support Center Web page opens in your default Web browser. On this site you'll find help documents, error and troubleshooting messages, and general information related to performance problems.

- **Adobe Support Programs.** Choose Help ➪ Online Support ➪ Adobe Support Programs and the Support plans Web page opens. On this site you'll find information related to subscribing to support programs where you can call Adobe Technical Support for help diagnosing problems. A PDF document is available for download that details the specifics related to various support plans provided by Adobe.

- **Accessibility Resource Center.** Choose Help ➪ Online Support ➪ Accessibility to open the Accessibility Resource Center Web site. Here you'll find information related to creating accessible documents.

On the various Web sites you'll also find menus that guide you to other support assistance. You can open the Support menus and find links to customer service, books, training and certification, updates, and more.

## Getting online help for Adobe LiveCycle Designer

Under the Designer Help menu you'll find a link to another Web site dealing with LiveCycle Designer issues. Choose Help ➪ Adobe LiveCycle Development Center and the LiveCycle Development Center Web site opens. Here you'll find some valuable examples for creating dynamic XML forms in LiveCycle Designer.

The online tutorials and PDF documents available for download are valuable resources for anyone wanting to learn more about creating forms in LiveCycle Designer.

## Contacting the Acrobat User Community

Adobe Systems sponsors a user group forum and supports the development of user groups internationally. Some of the world's leading experts on Acrobat participate through providing tips, articles, and hosting blog sessions. You can find some of the most up-to-date information at www.acrobatusers.com. Open the Adobe Acrobat User Community Web page and the opening page appears as shown in Figure 3.7. Here you'll find an easy-to-use Web site filled with many tips and solutions.

If you're interested in learning more about Acrobat, you may find a user group close to your home. If not, you can become one of the many people who start a local user group. You'll find great support from Adobe if you want to start a group. To learn more about the location of user groups and how to go about starting one, search the Adobe Acrobat User Community Web site.

### FIGURE 3.7

Log on to www.acrobatusers.com to find up-to-date information on Acrobat and PDF.

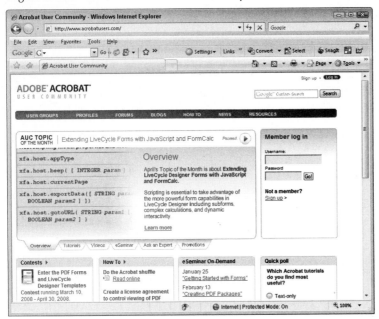

## Using Resources

When you install Acrobat there are a number of files stored in various folders that are used for templates and different resources that assist you in your PDF creation and document editing. Some of these files can be modified and customized to suit your personal PDF creation needs.

# Modifying the coversheet

Users of Acrobat 8 will remember the coversheet that appeared in PDF Packages. The `coversheet.pdf` file was installed with your Acrobat installation. You could modify this file to create a custom coversheet with data relevant to you or your company.

Since PDF Portfolios can only be viewed with the coversheet templates used in Acrobat 9 or X, Adobe created a coversheet that only opens when viewing PDF Portfolios in versions of Acrobat and Adobe Reader earlier than version 9.

The coversheet is a PDF document that resides in the folder:

- `Acrobat X.0/Acrobat/DocSettings/CombineFiles/ENU/coversheet.pdf` (Windows)
- `Applications/Acrobat X Pro/Adobe Acrobat Pro/Contents/Mac OS/DocSettings/CombineFiles/ENU/coversheet.pdf` (Mac)

Note that the ENU folder is for English language installations of Acrobat. Also, note that Mac users need to open the Acrobat X Pro folder and open a context menu on the Acrobat X Pro application file. From the context menu commands choose Show Package Contents to display the Contents folder.

You can replace the file contained in the ENU folder with your own design. Just be certain to name the file `coversheet.pdf`.

## Cross-Reference

For more information about creating custom coversheets for PDF Portfolios, see Chapter 12. ∎

# Modifying Doc Templates

Doc Templates are used with Security Envelopes. When you choose Create Security Envelope from the Secure Task button pull-down menu, a wizard opens where you can choose from three templates installed with your Acrobat installation.

The Security Envelope templates have several form fields that you can modify in Acrobat, or you can create new templates and add them to the folder Acrobat searches the DocTemplates folder for when creating a security envelope. The DocTemplates folder is located at:

- `Acrobat X.0/Acrobat/DocTemplates/ENU/` (Windows)
- `Acrobat X Pro/Contents/Resources/en.lproj/DocTemplates`

Note that you need to open the Adobe Acrobat Pro application folder on the Mac and open a context menu on the program icon. From the menu options choose Show Package Contents to gain access to the Contents folder.

Inside the DocTemplates folder, you'll find the three files installed during your Acrobat installation. You can copy any file to this folder and the template will be shown in the wizard when you create a Security Envelope.

Be certain to add a Document Title in the Document Properties dialog box. The wizard uses the Document Title for a description of the document in the wizard when creating the Security Envelope.

## Cross-Reference

For more information on creating Security Envelopes, see Chapter 24. For more information on adding Document Titles to PDF files, see Chapter 6. ■

## Adding folder level JavaScripts

Whereas Adobe didn't intend to have you interact with the coversheet document or DocTemplates folders, the JavaScripts folder is one that you are encouraged to use when folder level scripts are needed. This is most evident on the Mac because you don't need to drill down through the application supporting folders to find the JavaScripts folder.

- On Windows, open the Acrobat folder and you'll find the JavaScripts folder.
- On the Mac, open your user logon folder and follow the path `Library/Acrobat User Data/10.0_x86/JavaScripts`.

You can add folder level JavaScripts to this folder that are executed at the time Acrobat is launched.

## Cross-Reference

For some examples for using folder level JavaScripts, look over Chapter 32. ■

## Adding custom stamps

Some more resources available to you include the many different stamps images you can add to the Stamp tool in all Acrobat viewers. By default only a few of the files are loaded as stamp libraries.

- On Windows you'll find the libraries at `Acrobat/plug_ins/Annotations/Stamps/ENU`.
- On the Mac you'll find stamps at `Contents/Plug-ins/Comments.acroplugin/Stamps/ENU`.

Before you arrive at the ENU folder inside the Stamps folder you'll find a file called `Words.pdf`. This file has eight different images you can use as Stamp icons. When you open the ENU folder you'll find `Faces.pdf` and `Pointers.pdf`, each containing 11 icons each. Any one of these files can be added as new stamps using the Manage Custom Stamps Wizard in all Acrobat viewers.

## Cross-Reference

For information related to creating and managing custom Stamps, see Chapter 19. ∎

# Using QuickBooks templates (Windows only)

Another folder you find in the Acrobat folder on Windows is the QuickBooksTemplates folder. Open this folder and open the ENU folder and you find seven preinstalled templates for use with QuickBooks. In Figure 3.8, one of the seven templates is shown. You can create new templates and copy the templates to the QuickBooks/ENU folder.

**FIGURE 3.8**

All the template files you use with QuickBooks are forms created in Adobe LiveCycle Designer.

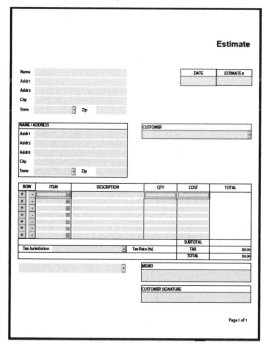

# Using LiveCycle Designer resource files

Inside the Designer 8.2 folder which resides inside the Acrobat folder you find the EN folder. Open this folder and you find two folders with some resource files. The Templates folder contains a number of templates you can use to start a form in LiveCycle Designer. If you create some custom forms and want to use them as templates, copy your template files to this folder.

The Samples folder inside the EN folder is where you'll find some excellent examples of forms created with LiveCycle Designer. If you're new to Designer, be sure to look over the many samples you find here.

# Summary

In this chapter, the following items were covered:

- All Acrobat viewers have a help document you access via a menu command in the Help menu.
- Many online help resources are found via URL links from the Help menu commands.
- A number of resource files can be added to folders inside the Acrobat and LiveCycle Designer folders to customize templates.

# Getting Familiar with Adobe Reader

A s a PDF author you need to be aware of the capabilities and the limitations of the Adobe Reader software. In some situations you can distribute PDF documents to users of the free Adobe Reader software for active participation in your workflow without all your clients and colleagues needing to purchase the full version of Acrobat Standard or Acrobat Pro. In other situations where the Adobe Reader software does not contain tools or commands to properly edit a file for a given workflow, you may need to recommend to others which commercial viewer they need to purchase. Regardless of where you are with PDF creation and editing, at one time or another you'll be called upon to explain some of the differences between Adobe Reader and the other viewers.

Adobe Reader has evolved, and each new upgrade offers users much more functionality than previous versions. Features that users have long requested such as the ability to save form data and add digital signatures were added in Adobe Reader 8. Two more features requested by many users involved having a method for converting application documents to PDF and a no-nonsense easy method for sharing files. Adobe Reader 9, combined with the new online Acrobat.com service, addressed these user requests. In Acrobat X you will find new security features added to help guard against viruses and malware.

# Setting Some Critical Preferences

Like the Acrobat viewers, Adobe Reader has an enormous number of different preference options designed to add more functionality to the program and to help you tailor your workspace and tools to suit personal workflows.

Preferences settings are detailed throughout this book in chapters that specifically relate to tools and commands. A few preference options you want to start with in Reader include some settings to help you prepare for some of the features described in other chapters.

## Establishing an Acrobat.com account

Open Preferences by pressing Ctrl/⌘+K. In the left pane, click Acrobat.com. Preference options you have for adding account information for Acrobat.com are shown in Figure 4.1.

Acrobat.com is a separate service provided free from Adobe. For a number of different tasks you perform in Acrobat including shared reviews, form distribution and collection, and sharing files online, you'll want to take advantage of this service.

### FIGURE 4.1

Press Ctrl/⌘+K to open the Preferences dialog box and click Acrobat.com in the left pane.

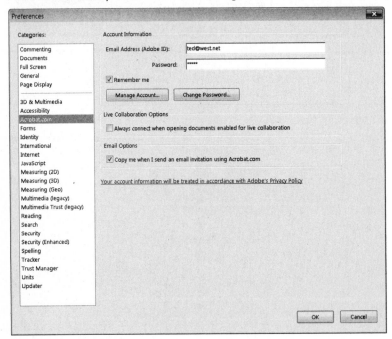

To use Acrobat.com, you need to sign up with an Adobe ID and password. Once you've set up an account, add your email address (from your Adobe ID account) and your password if you want to log on automatically each time you use the service. If you want to connect to Acrobat.com automatically when collaborating on documents set up for collaboration on Acrobat.com, check the Live Collaboration check box. Another check box is an option for copying email messages to your mail client each time you send an invitation for other users to engage in a comment and review session. Check this box if you want to copy messages to your email account.

## Cross-Reference
For information on setting up an account and signing on to Acrobat.com, see Chapter 26. For information on collaboration in shared reviews, see Chapter 20. ■

## Setting general preferences

Open the Preferences dialog box (Ctrl/⌘+K) and click General in the left pane. Check Use single-key accelerators to access tools at the top of the right pane. When this check box is checked, you can access tools by pressing a key on your keyboard. For example, when another tool is selected, you can access the Hand tool by pressing the H key.

## Creating identity preferences

You'll also want to edit identity preferences. When you engage in comment reviews and add comments in review sessions, you're prompted to edit your identity preferences. To prepare your work environment, take time now to add your identity information. Press Ctrl/⌘+K to open the Preferences dialog box and click Identity in the left pane. In the right pane, fill in the text boxes with your personal identity information as shown in Figure 4.2.

**FIGURE 4.2**

Click Identity in the left pane and fill in the text boxes in the right pane to set up your identity preferences.

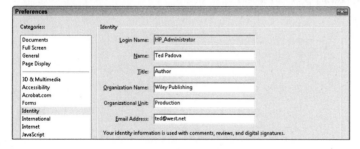

There are many more preferences you can adjust, but these few changes will get the Adobe Reader going for a good many viewing and editing sessions. After you make your edits in the Preferences dialog box, you're ready to go. Reader writes the preferences immediately so there's no need to quit the program and reopen to use the new preference choices.

# Exploring Adobe Reader Tools and Menus

What distinguishes Adobe Reader and other viewers are, in part, the panels and menu commands. Knowing what the user can do with the Reader tools and what tools are not available in Reader is helpful if you intend to distribute documents to Reader users.

The panels and tools (shown in Figure 4.3) in Adobe Reader have counterparts in Acrobat Standard (Windows) and Acrobat Pro. The Reader panels are the same in the other viewers; however, some of the Adobe Reader tools within panels offer more limited features than the same tools used in the other viewers.

## FIGURE 4.3

The Tools panels expanded in Adobe Reader

## Viewing the Reader Tools panel

Adobe Reader has an abbreviated set of panels compared to Acrobat Standard and Pro. When a PDF has been enabled, you find four panels with some tools that are similar to those you find in the other viewers. However, what you can do with tools in Reader is much more limited than what you can do with tools in Acrobat.

## Looking at the Extended Features panel

Unless a file has been enabled with Reader usage rights, the items listed in this panel appear grayed out. For enabled files, you find tools nested in a single panel with categories listed as Content, Sign, Analyze, and Forms. The categories offer:

- **Content.** In the Content area you find tools for editing text and attaching files.

- **Sign.** All the tools in the Sign area are used for applying digital signatures.

- **Analyze**. The Analyze area has three tools. The Object Data tool is available when you open PDFs with object data such as AutoCAD or MS Visio files. The Measuring tool is also available when viewing files such as AutoCAD documents. The third tool is the Geospatial Location tool. This tool is available when PDFs contain geospatial data. The tools in the Analyze panel are specialized for viewing certain kinds of PDF files. For more information on using the Analyze tools, see the Adobe Reader Help document (Help ⇨ Adobe Reader X Help).

- **Forms.** Tools are used for importing and exporting form data.

## Locating the Comments panel

In earlier versions of Acrobat and Reader, the Comments panel was accessed from the Navigation pane and opened in a horizontal view. In Acrobat X, the Comments panel is on the right side of the Acrobat window and opens in a vertical view. To open the Comments panel, click Comments in the Toolbar Well. If special permissions have been added to a PDF file for commenting, the panel opens as shown in Figure 4.4.

---

**FIGURE 4.4**

---

The Comments panel as it appears in Reader when a PDF has been enabled for commenting

All the Annotations and Drawing Markup tools as well as many Comments List commands are available to Reader users when files are enabled with Reader usage rights. For more information on using all of these tools, see Chapter 19. For more information on enabling PDFs for commenting, see Chapter 18.

## New Feature

**Prior to Acrobat X, you needed to enable PDFs with Reader usage rights so that Reader users could add an annotation to a PDF file. In Acrobat X, Reader users can add Sticky Notes and highlight text with comment notes on all files, regardless of whether the usage rights are enabled. In the Toolbar Well, the Add Sticky Note and Highlight text tools appear as defaults when you launch Reader. For more information on using these tools, see Chapter 19. ■**

## Accessing the Share panel

Click Share in the Toolbar Well and the Share Panel opens as shown in Figure 4.5. In this panel, you can access commands for sharing files on Acrobat.com, attaching files to an email message, accessing your Acrobat.com workspace, and sending native document files to Acrobat.com for conversion to PDF. For more information on using the Share options, see Chapter 20.

**FIGURE 4.5**

Click Share in the Toolbar Well to open the Share panel.

## Identifying menu commands

The first thing you notice about Adobe Reader and Acrobat X is that there are fewer menus in the top-level menu bar. Reader and Acrobat X now have only five menus, as following:

- **File menu.** Under the File menu you find options for creating PDFs online; sharing files on Acrobat.com; typical Save, Save As, and Print commands; attaching files to email; and a command for accessing Document Properties. Note that the Save command is only available when files have been enabled with Reader usage rights.

- **Edit menu.** Under the Edit menu, you find options common to many programs, such as Undo/Redo, Cut, Copy, and Paste. This menu also contains the Search and Find commands for searching text in PDF files. See Chapter 6 for more on searching with Reader and Acrobat.

- **View menu.** Under the View menu, you find many different options for viewing documents, tools, and panels. You can access the navigation panels, show or hide the menu bar and toolbars, change modes between Read Mode and Normal Viewer Mode, change zoom levels, rotate pages, and enter Full Screen Mode. For more information on the various viewing options, see Chapter 5.

- **Window menu.** No changes appear in the Window menu compared to earlier Acrobat viewers. You can add new windows, change the display of multiple documents open in Reader (such as tiling and cascading views), and you also see a list of files currently open in the viewer. For more information on the viewing options available in the Window menu, see Chapter 5.

- **Help menu.** Under the Help menu, you find resources for when you need help using Reader and Acrobat. If you don't find what you're looking for in this book, consult the Help Guide. (Choose Help ⇨ Adobe Reader X Help to open the Help Guide.) You can also find links in this menu for online help on the Adobe Web site, accessing Digital Editions, repairing the Reader installation, and checking for program updates. For more information on Digital Editions, see Chapter 27.

## Using navigation panels

Navigation panels that are open by default are docked in the Navigation pane. Depending on the content of a PDF file, you may see different panels open when viewing different documents. For example, if a document containing a digital signature opens in Reader, the Signatures panel is docked in the Navigation pane. If a document contains Adobe PDF layers, the Layers panel is docked in the Navigation pane.

You can open panels in any document by choosing a menu command. To view all the Navigation panels, select View ⇨ Show/Hide ⇨ Navigation Panes. A submenu contains all the Navigation panels you can access in Reader, as shown in Figure 4.6. When you open a panel, it opens as a floating window. Click the panel tab and drag it to the Navigation pane, where you can dock it together with the default panels.

## Cross-Reference

For more information on using navigation panels, see Chapter 1. ∎

**FIGURE 4.6**

Select View ⇨ Navigation Panels to see the navigation panels that are available in Reader. When documents with special usage rights are open, you can access the Document Extensions and Signatures panels.

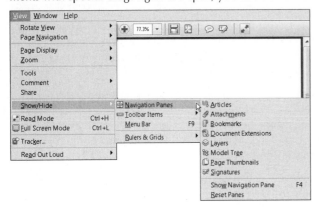

## Working with signatures

Open the Document menu and you find the Sign, Security, and Security Settings commands. If you want Adobe Reader users to digitally sign a document, they must create a digital signature. These commands are used to create signatures, manage signatures, and sign documents.

## Cross-Reference

For more information on digital signatures, see Chapter 24. ∎

# Trying Out PDF Creation at Acrobat.com

Adobe Reader users can create PDFs online and explore a wide range of sharing options. All of what you can do with Acrobat.com and your documents is covered in Chapter 26. In terms of Adobe Reader users, there are a few distinctions you have related to the available services. For starters, Adobe Reader users cannot enable a PDF for commenting and cannot initiate a comment and review session. Therefore, Reader users cannot submit files for review in the same regard as the Acrobat users can.

Reader users, however, can share files on Acrobat.com, and other users of the Acrobat software can add comments. Reader users can also initiate and participate in online meetings for up to three people without purchasing an Acrobat Connect account. Furthermore, Reader users can submit native authoring application documents for PDF creation without any service fees — only five files free as a lifetime service, then offered on a subscription fee basis.

# Creating PDF Files Using Acrobat.com

If your clients or colleagues don't have Acrobat Standard or Acrobat Pro and they need to create an occasional PDF file, they can download the free Adobe Reader 9 and above software and choose File ⇨ Create Adobe PDF Using Acrobat.com. A user needs to have an account to sign on, or they can click Create an Adobe ID to Sign Up for the service. You select a file for conversion in the Select File(s) dialog box that opens when you choose the menu command and click Open. The file is uploaded and converted to PDF.

Create PDF supports many different file formats. The native document formats are as follows:

- **Microsoft Office.** All Microsoft Office files for Mac and Windows.

- **Other Microsoft formats.** Microsoft Publisher is supported.

- **Adobe formats.** Those programs not supporting direct export to PDF, such as earlier versions of PageMaker without the PDF plug-in, are supported. All Creative Suite programs now support export to PDF, and using a service to create PDF files is not necessary.

- **Adobe Flash files.** Adobe Flash .flv and .swf file formats can be converted.

- **AutoDesk AutoCAD.** AutoCAD is supported.

- **CAD File formats.** A huge range of different CAD formats can be converted.

- **Corel WordPerfect Office formats.** Corel WordPerfect files can be converted to PDF.

- **Adobe PostScript formats.** Any program you use that's capable of printing can be printed to disk as a PostScript file. You can submit the PostScript file for conversion to PDF.

- **Text formats.** All ASCII (American Code for Information Interchange) and Rich Text Format (RTF) files can be converted to PDF.

- **Image formats.** Most of the common image formats such as Windows bitmap (.bmp), GIF (.gif), JPEG (.jpg/.jpeg), PCX (.pcx), PICT (Mac) (.pct/.pict), PNG (.png), RLE (.rle), and TIFF (.tif) can be converted to PDF.

## Cross-Reference

For information on converting native application documents to PDF, see Chapters 7 through 9. For information on printing PostScript files and converting PostScript files to PDF, see Chapter 10. ∎

Only a limited number of files can be converted before you have to subscribe to a paid service when using Acrobat.com to convert files to PDF. Users can download free PDF converters from the Internet, such as PDF995, and have a conversion tool ready whenever they want to convert a document to PDF. It's much more efficient and there's no cost involved for unlimited conversions.

# Introducing Protected Mode

Sandboxing is a computer security term. A sandbox is a security mechanism used for separating running programs. If you have Adobe Reader running and an Adobe Flash file playing, this means that you have two separate running programs. Sandboxing helps isolate the runtime operations of the programs and prevents malicious or untested code from executing.

PDFs are huge targets for malicious and malware code executions. Adobe has been constantly adding updates to each version of Acrobat and Adobe Reader to combat newer viruses and malware that can harm your system and extract personal information. With the introduction of sandboxing (available only in Adobe Reader), a tightly controlled set of resources is maintained for running programs.

You can activate sandboxing in the Preferences dialog box. Sandboxing is turned on by default, and you should leave it on when downloading PDFs from the Internet. To turn off sandboxing, open the Preferences dialog box (Ctrl/⌘+K) and click General in the left pane. In the right pane, you find the Enable sandboxing at startup check box, as shown in Figure 4.7. Uncheck the box to disable the sandboxing feature. If sandboxing is disabled, you need to check the box and relaunch Reader.

## FIGURE 4.7

You can enable sandboxing in the General tab of the Preferences dialog box.

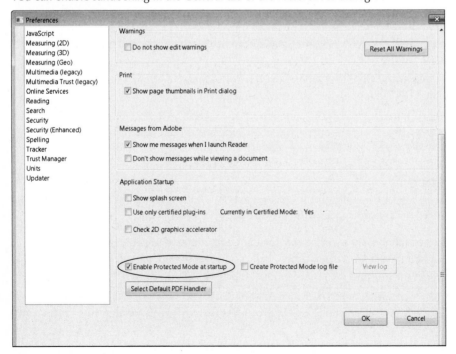

# Adding More Functionality to Adobe Reader

You may look over Adobe Reader X and wish for more features or wonder why Adobe Systems didn't add more to the newest release. If the thought occurs to you, keep in mind that Adobe Systems offers the Reader software free of charge. Adobe Reader is certainly one of the most feature-rich applications that can be acquired without purchase.

If you want more from Adobe Reader, you do have other purchase options available to you from Adobe Systems. From PDF creation to saving form data for enterprise solutions, Adobe does make these features available to you in the form of online services and server-side applications.

For users of earlier versions of Acrobat, Reader Extensions enable users of Adobe Reader versions below 7.0 to perform comment and markup, save forms, and digital signatures functions. Adobe LiveCycle Reader Extensions ES is an enterprise solution intended for large companies that have the technology and resources to offer cost-effective solutions for many users, or those who want to automate processes like adding these enabling rights to PDFs.

The addition of enabling documents for Reader users in Acrobat Standard, Pro, or Pro Extended in version 9 and above to save form data, and Pro/Pro Extended (version 9 and above) to add digital signatures, carries limitations in the End User License Agreement. For enterprise solutions where the needs exceed the licensing limitations, Adobe LiveCycle Reader Extensions ES offers unlimited use of PDF files enabled with usage rights.

For information about Adobe LiveCycle Reader Extensions ES, log on to Adobe's Web site at www.adobe.com/products/readerextensions/. You'll find more information about the server-side software and how to acquire it for your company.

# Summary

In this chapter, you learned a little bit about Adobe Reader.

- Acrobat.com is a separate service offered by Adobe Systems and has nothing to do with Acrobat. However, Acrobat viewers have many menu commands that can access the service for creating PDF files, sharing documents, and engaging in online meetings.

- Acrobat.com services are offered free to everyone in the world.

- Adobe Reader usage rights are enabled in Acrobat Standard (Windows) and Acrobat Pro. When a PDF has been enabled with commenting, form data saving, and digital signatures usage rights, Reader users can comment and mark up a document, participate in an email–based review, save comment updates, save data on PDF forms, and add digital signatures.

- Help and product performance options are available from menu commands in the Help menu.

- Adobe Systems provides an online service for converting files saved in a number of different formats to PDF. You can easily access Acrobat.com where files can be submitted for conversion to PDF via menu commands in Reader.

- Sandboxing is a new security feature added to Adobe Reader X.

- Adobe LiveCycle Reader Extensions ES is a J2EE-based server-side solution intended for automating the addition of user rights as well as meeting the needs for large-scale enablement requirements. With the Reader Extensions Server you can enable PDFs for using Web services, spawning templates, decoding 2-D barcodes, saving form data, and digitally signing PDFs from within Adobe Reader.

# Viewing and Navigating PDF Files

Acrobat viewers provide you with many different kinds of tools to view pages and move around PDF documents. As a visitor to PDFs created by other PDF authors, you can use many tools within the program to browse pages and find information quickly. As a PDF author you can create viewing options and links to views you know will help the end user explore your files. In this chapter, I cover all viewing tools, pages, documents, and the different kinds of viewing options you have available in Acrobat viewers. I leave the authoring items and how-to methods to other chapters. For now, just realize this chapter is an abbreviated form of looking at a huge list of possibilities for viewing and navigation. The amplified explanations follow in several other chapters.

Some of the most dramatic changes in Acrobat X over previous releases are related to viewing PDFs and accessing tools. In this regard, Adobe has made radical changes in the program. Regardless of whether you are an experienced user or a novice, this chapter covers some fundamental ways you work with all Acrobat viewers.

## Using Read Mode

When Adobe engineers went to work on Acrobat X, they made many inquiries to the user community to discover the most common uses for Acrobat and the tools that users most frequently accessed. The engineers discovered that most people use Acrobat and Adobe Reader for viewing PDF files, and that the most frequently used tool is the Rotate tool for rotating pages.

As a result of the responses from the user community, Adobe has implemented a new viewing experience with Read Mode. Read Mode is available when viewing PDF files in an Acrobat viewer or when viewing PDFs inside Web browser windows. To enter Read Mode, do the following:

### STEPS: Reading PDF Files

1. **Open a PDF document.** In an Acrobat viewer, do one of the following: click the Open button on the startup screen, click the Open tool (represented by a folder icon) in the toolbar, press Ctrl/⌘+O, or choose File ⇨ Open. When the Open dialog box appears, select a file and click Open.

2. **Click the View File in Read Mode icon.** This icon appears in the top-right corner of the toolbar and is represented by two opposing diagonal arrows, as shown in Figure 5.1.

**FIGURE 5.1**

Click the View File in Read Mode icon in the toolbar to open a PDF in Read Mode.

3. **Exit Read Mode.** Click the Exit Read Mode icon in the Read Mode toolbar to return to the normal viewer mode.

When you enter Read Mode (shown in Figure 5.2), the Read Mode toolbar appears at the bottom of the document window. In addition, all the toolbars and menus are hidden from view. This mode offers users optimal viewing for the page content of PDF files.

The Read Mode toolbar appears momentarily, and then disappears. To bring the toolbar back, move the mouse and it reappears. The toolbar offers you some viewing choices (reading left to right in Figure 5.2) that include:

- **Save.** Click the floppy disk icon on the far left of the toolbar to save the document.
- **Print.** Click the printer icon to open the Print dialog box.
- **Previous Page.** Click the up-pointing arrow to navigate to the previous page.
- **Next Page.** Click the down-pointing arrow to navigate to the next page.
- **Go to Page.** Click the page icon/numbers to open the Go To Page dialog box. You can type a page number in the dialog box and click OK, and the respective page opens.
- **Decrease Magnification.** Click the minus (-) icon to zoom out of the document page.

- **Increase Magnification.** Click the plus (+) icon to zoom in on the document page.
- **Exit Read Mode.** Click the Exit Read Mode icon to return to normal viewer mode.

**FIGURE 5.2**

The Read Mode view

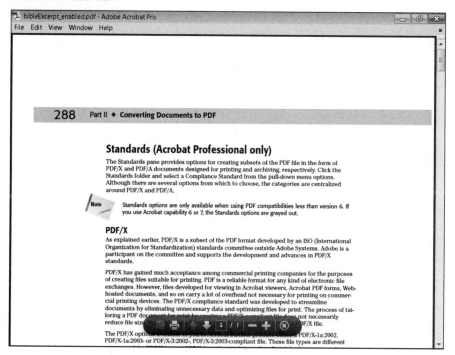

# Customizing the Quick Tools Toolbar

Another radical change from earlier versions of Acrobat is the way you can handle tools and toolbars in the new release. In earlier versions of Acrobat, users loaded tools in toolbars that could float (appear on top of the document pane) or dock them in the Toolbar Well. Acrobat X doesn't actually have toolbars (although Adobe refers to collections of tools as toolbars). Instead of the Toolbar Well, the row of tools appearing below the menu bar is now referred to as the Quick Tools toolbar. Instead of adding tools to individual toolbars, you can now add tools to the Quick Tools toolbar as individual items.

## Finding tools

By default, tools in Acrobat X appear listed in panels. Individual groups are subpanels contained within the panels. For example, when you click a subpanel name in the Tools panel, the subpanel for that tool expands. To open the Tools panel, click Tools on the navigation bar and the panel opens. Click a subpanel name and the subpanel expands. In Figure 5.3, I clicked the Tools button and then clicked Pages to expand the Pages subpanel.

**FIGURE 5.3**

Click Tools to open the Tools panel, and then click a subpanel name to expand the subpanel.

By default, a subpanel opens while closing any subpanel that is currently open. In other words, only a single subpanel in the Tools panel can be open at a time. You can change the default settings for the subpanels by clicking the Show or hide panels icon (located in the top-right corner of the Tools panel), which opens a drop-down menu. The menu lists all available subpanels. Those subpanels with check marks adjacent to their name appear in the Tools panel. The unchecked subpanels are hidden in the Tools panel. Click a subpanel name to add a check mark, and the subpanel is shown in the Tools panel.

To open more than one subpanel at a time, click the first menu item in the Show or hide panels drop-down menu, where you see the command Allow Multiple Panels Open. When you select this command, each time you click a subpanel shown in the Tools panel, the subpanel expands and displays all the tools contained in the respective subpanel.

## Adding tools to the Quick Tools toolbar

After expanding a subpanel, open a context menu on a tool name within the subpanel; the menu item appears as Add to Quick Tools. Click the menu command and the tool is added to the Quick Tools toolbar. You can continue adding tools to the Quick Tools toolbar to fill the first row. When the first row is filled with tools, additional tools are added to a drop-down menu. In Figure 5.4, I added tools to the Quick Tools toolbar. After populating the Quick Tools toolbar, additional tools were added to a drop-down menu.

### FIGURE 5.4

Tools added to the Quick Tools toolbar and additional tools appearing in a drop-down menu

To remove a tool from the Quick Tools toolbar, open a context menu on the tool you want to remove and click Remove from Quick Tools.

## Note

When you add a tool to the Quick Tools toolbar, you can access the tool by clicking it in the Quick Tools toolbar or by clicking the tool in the subpanel from which it originated. In other words, adding a tool to the Quick Tools toolbar does not prevent you from using the same tool in a subpanel. ■

# Navigating PDF Documents

Earlier Acrobat viewers had a Navigation toolbar with several tools that you could use to move around PDF files and to change the view appearance, such as zoom levels and page layouts. They also had several menu commands that duplicated the results of using the tools in the Navigation toolbar.

In Acrobat X, you'll find a lot of redundancy removed from the program compared to earlier versions. Acrobat X does not have a Navigation toolbar, and many of the navigation tasks are now handled in menus.

## Using context menus

Acrobat viewers make use of context menu commands for page navigation. To use a context menu for moving forward and back in PDF pages and documents, select the Hand tool and click the right mouse button (Windows and two-button Macs) or Control+click (Mac) to open the context menu as shown in Figure 5.5.

Context menus opened on a document page using the Hand tool offer navigation commands to move forward and backward one page at a time.

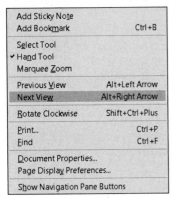

You find the Previous View command in a context menu after you have moved from the default page to another page in the document. The Next View command appears only after you have selected Previous View. These two menu commands permit you to move through pages in a PDF file.

## Using navigation menu commands

The View menu contains all the page navigation commands contained in the Navigation toolbar that was available in earlier versions of Acrobat. In Acrobat X, you mostly change the view in the View menu and with keyboard shortcuts.

When you choose View ➪ Page Navigation, the page navigation commands appear in a submenu, as shown in Figure 5.6.

Those viewing commands allow you to view tools and change page views, and offer alternatives to viewing such as entering Read Mode, Full Screen Mode, Read Out Loud, and scrolling pages automatically. Following is a list of what you can find in the View menu.

**FIGURE 5.6**

The View menu contains many different commands for viewing pages, toolbars, and display modes.

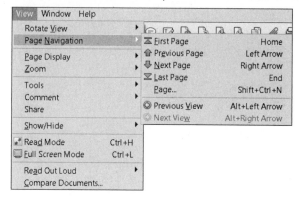

## Navigating pages

The navigation commands are intuitive. You find navigation to the First Page, Previous Page, Next Page, and Last Page. When you click Page, the Go To Page dialog box opens, where you type a page number, click OK, and Acrobat jumps to the page you chose.

## Using the Zoom menu

A submenu provides menu options for zooming to different views. The view options are shown in Figure 5.7. Notice that keyboard shortcuts are shown adjacent to the menu names. The view options include:

- **Zoom To.** Click Zoom To and a dialog box opens where you can type a zoom level. Click OK and the page jumps to the specified zoom.

- **Marquee Zoom.** With Acrobat X, you can access the Marquee Zoom tool from this menu. Select the tool and draw a marquee for the area on a document page where you want to zoom in. Press the Ctrl/Option key and click with the tool to zoom out.

- **Page Layout.** Items listed as Actual Size, Zoom to Page Level (formerly Fit Page in earlier versions of Acrobat), Fit Width, Fit Height, and Fit Visible change the page view to the respective choice from this menu.

- **Pan & Zoom.** With Acrobat X, you can access the Pan and Zoom tool from this menu. Choose the menu item and the Pan and Zoom window opens, displaying a thumbnail of the entire page. When you zoom with this tool, the page zooms according to adjustments you make in the Pan and Zoom window. (For more information on Pan and Zoom, see the "Zooming In and Out" section later in this chapter.)

- **Loupe Tool.** With Acrobat X, you can access the Loupe tool from this menu. This tool is somewhat different from the Pan and Zoom tool. You select the Loupe tool in the View ⇨ Zoom submenu and click on a page where you want to see a zoomed view.

The Loupe tool window displays a zoomed view of the target area while the page in the background remains at the fixed zoom level. (For more information on using the Loupe tool, see the "Zooming In and Out" section later in this chapter.)

- **Reflow.** Document reflow enables users to view PDF documents on adaptive devices for the visually impaired and it is used when copying PDF files to handheld devices and tablets. When you reflow text on-screen or when using other devices, the text in the PDF wraps according to the zoom level of the page or the device viewing area. Therefore, when you zoom in on a paragraph of text and the text moves off the viewing area of your screen, you can use the Reflow command to make the text automatically scroll to your window size.

Reflow only works with tagged PDF documents in Acrobat viewers earlier than version 7. Acrobat 7 through X viewers can reflow any PDF document whether it is a tagged file or not. When you copy PDF documents to iPhones, iPods, iPads, and other mobile devices and handhelds, PDF Reader software wraps text to fit the width of the screen for both untagged and tagged documents.

**FIGURE 5.7**

Zoom submenu commands

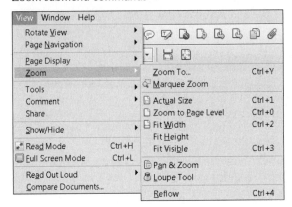

## Cross-Reference

For information about tagging PDF documents, see Chapter 23. ∎

### Changing the Page Display

The Page Display view can be any one of four different layout types. Choices for page layout are contained in the View ➪ Page Display submenu. Depending on the way a PDF file has been saved and depending on what preference choices are made for the Initial View, a PDF layout may appear different on different computers according to each individual user's preference settings. Regardless of how you set your preferences, you can change the Page Display view at any time. The submenu commands for View ➪ Page Display include:

## Cross-Reference

For more information on setting Initial View preferences, see "Setting Initial View Attributes" later in this chapter. ■

- **Single Page.** This layout places an entire page in view when the zoom level is set to Fit Page. When you press the Page Down key or the down-arrow key to scroll pages, the next page snaps into view.

- **Enable Scrolling (formerly known as Continuous in earlier Acrobat versions).** This page layout view shows pages in a linear fashion, where you might see the bottom of one page and the top of another page in the Document pane as you scroll down. The difference between this view and Single Page view is that the pages don't snap to a full page when viewed as Enable Scrolling view.

- **Two Page View.** This view shows two pages — like looking at an open book. When the zoom level is set to Page Level or lower, only two pages are in view in the Document pane.

- **Two Page Scrolling.** This page layout view displays a combination of the preceding two options. When the view is zoomed out, it displays as many pages in the Document pane as can be accommodated by the zoom level.

- **Show Gaps Between Pages.** When you select View ➪ Page Display ➪ Show Gaps Between Pages, the page views for Single Page, Two-Up, and Two-Up Continuous are displayed as you see on the left side of Figure 5.8. Remove the check mark by the menu command and the display shown on the right appears.

**FIGURE 5.8**

Show Gaps Between Pages is turned on in the left side and off in the right side of the figure.

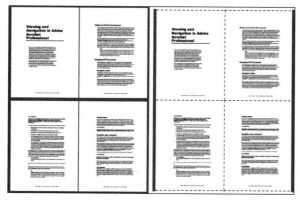

- **Show Cover Page During Two-Up.** When you view a document in a Two-Up page layout, pages 1 and 2 are first shown in the Document pane. Click the Next Page tool and the Document pane shows you pages 3 and 4. If you want to show pages 2 and 3 together, select View ➪ Page Display ➪ Show Cover Page During Two-Up. If a document has more than two pages, the Two Columns and Two Pages views display the first page alone on the right side of the Document pane to ensure proper display of two-page spreads.

- **Automatically Scroll.** This command scrolls pages in the open file at a user-defined speed in all Acrobat viewers. When you select the command, Acrobat automatically switches the Single Page layout view to Enable Scrolling view and Two Page view to Two Page Scrolling view. The pages in the document scroll up, permitting you to read the text without using any keys or the mouse. Attribute changes for automatic scrolling include the following:

  - **Changing scrolling speed.** To change the scrolling speed, press a number key from 0 (slowest) to 9 (fastest) on your keyboard or press the up or down arrow key to speed up or slow down scrolling in increments.

  - **Reverse scrolling direction.** Press the hyphen or minus key.

  - **To jump to the next or previous page and continue scrolling,** press the right or left arrow key, respectively.

  - **Stopping.** To stop using the automatic scrolling feature, press the Esc key.

### Rotating the view

If your PDF opens in Acrobat with a rotated view, you can rotate pages clockwise or counter-clockwise from two submenu commands. The same rotations are also available in the Pages subpanel. Rotate View commands and tools rotate all pages in your PDF document and come in handy if the PDF pages are rotated on the initial view or if you want to view PDFs on eBook readers, tablets, or laptop computers. However, changes made with the Rotate View menu commands are temporary, and any saves you make do not record the rotated views. To permanently save rotated views, use the Rotate tool in the Pages subpanel, and then save the file.

### Using Full Screen Mode

Full Screen Mode displays your documents without toolbars, the menu bar, or the navigation panel. Full Screen Mode enables you to view PDF files without menus, toolbars, and panels.

## Showing and hiding items

A number of panes and panels can be dismissed and hidden from view. To bring back the items, you use menu commands.

### Using navigation panes

Choose View ➪ Show/Hide ➪ Navigation Panes, and a submenu displays all the panes that can be opened in the Navigation pane.

## Cross-Reference

For a description of all the navigation panes, see Chapter 1. ■

### Choosing toolbar items

Although the menu command refers to toolbars, in Acrobat X the items are individual tools. The submenu contains a list of tools, many of which are not found in other commands or panels; these include the Edit tools such as Take Snapshot, Paste, Check Spelling, Advanced Search, and more.

Another command in the Toolbar Items submenu is Quick Tools. Choose this command and the Quick Tools window opens where you can easily manage tools, show and hide them in the Quick Tools toolbar, and add separator marks in the Quick Tools toolbar for managing tools in groups. The Properties Bar is also included in the same submenu. You open the Properties Bar when working with forms and annotations.

## Cross-Reference

For more information on using the Quick Tools window, see Chapter 1. For more information on using the Properties Bar, see Chapters 19 and 31. ■

### Exploring the Menu Bar

Select View ➪ Menu Bar or press F9 (Windows), and the menu bar is temporarily hidden. To bring back the menu bar, press F9 (Windows).

If you're a Mac user working on OS X Leopard or Snow Leopard, the F9 function key used by Acrobat for hiding menu bars is occupied by the OS X default system shortcuts for Spaces and Exposé. If you want to use the Acrobat Function key shortcuts, you need to open the Mac OS X Preferences and reassign the default keys.

### Using rulers and grids

If you need to examine drawings, a grid may help in your analysis. In Acrobat Professional, you can choose to view your file displaying a grid. Grids can be useful when you're authoring PDF files, particularly documents for engineers, architects, and PDF forms. For viewing purposes they can be useful where relationships to objects require some careful examination. To show a grid, choose View ➪ Show/Hide ➪ Rulers & Grid ➪ Grid. By default, the grid displays in the Document pane with blue lines at fixed major and minor gridlines, as shown in Figure 5.9.

If you want to change the distances for the major gridlines and the number of divisions for the minor gridlines, open the Preferences dialog box and select Units & Guides in the left pane. The preference settings enable you to change the units of measure and attributes for the grid layout, as shown in Figure 5.10.

**FIGURE 5.9**

Choose View ⇨ Grid or press Ctrl/⌘+U to access the grid. You can change the grid lines for major and minor divisions in the Preferences dialog box.

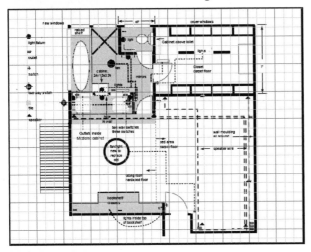

**FIGURE 5.10**

Preference choices for Units & Guides offer you options for changing the units of measure and the grid layout.

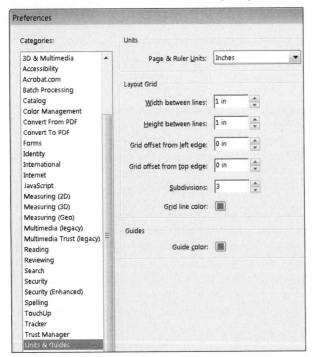

The Units & Guides preference settings are also used for changing attributes for the grid layout and rulers. The attribute choices include the following:

- **Page & Ruler Units.** Five choices are available from the pull-down menu. You can choose Points, Picas, Millimeters, Centimeters, or Inches. Whatever you choose here is reflected in the rulers when you display the rulers (View ⇨ Rulers or press Ctrl/ ⌘+R). Choices here also affect the units of measure found in the Info palette discussed in Chapter 1.

- **Width between lines.** The horizontal distance between the major gridlines is determined in the field box for this setting. You can click on the arrows, enter a number between 0.028 and 138.888 in the field (when inches are selected for the unit of measurement), or press the Up or Down Arrow keys to change the values.

## Note

The limit of 138.888 relates to inches. If you change the units of measure, the limits are roughly the same as the 138.888-inch limit. In points, the range measures between 2 and 10,000. ■

- **Height between lines.** You can change the major gridlines appearing vertically with this field. Use the same methods of changing the values here as for the lines for the Width option.

- **Grid offset from left edge.** Each grid has x and y coordinates indicating where the grid begins on a page. You set the x-axis in this field.

- **Grid offset from top edge.** Use this field to set the starting point of the y-axis.

- **Subdivisions.** The number of gridlines appearing between the major gridlines is determined in this field. The acceptable values range between 0 and 10,000 (when units are set to points).

- **Grid line color.** By default, the color for the gridlines is blue. You can change the grid color by clicking the color swatch. When you click the blue swatch for Grid line color, a pop-up color palette opens, as shown in Figure 5.11. Select a color from the preset color choices in the palette or click Other Color. If you click Other Color, the system color palette opens, in which you can make custom color choices. The Windows and Mac system color palettes vary slightly, as shown in Figure 5.12.

### FIGURE 5.11

Click the color swatch for the Grid line color to choose from a selection of preset colors, or select Other Color to open the system color palette.

**FIGURE 5.12**

When you select Other Color, the Windows system color palette opens (left) or the Mac system color palette opens (right).

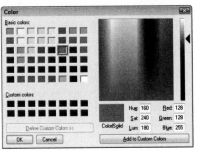

- **Guide color.** Guides are created from ruler wells, and you can manually position them in the Document pane. If you have ruler guides and a grid, you'll want to change one color to easily distinguish the guides from the grid. Both default to the same blue. To change the guide color, click the Guide Color swatch and follow the same steps as described for Grid line color.

## Using Snap to Grid

When you choose View ➪ Show/Hide ➪ Rulers & Grid ➪ Snap to Grid, objects you draw snap to the major and minor gridlines. This feature can be particularly helpful with form designs and engineering drawings.

## Viewing rulers

Acrobat supports viewing rulers, and you can turn them on via the View menu or using the keyboard shortcut Ctrl/⌘+R. When you choose View ➪ Show/Hide ➪ Rulers & Grid ➪ Rulers or use the keyboard shortcut, rulers appear on the top and left side of the Document pane. Inside the top and left ruler is an inexhaustible supply of guidelines. To add a guideline on the document page, place the cursor within the top or left ruler, press the mouse button, and drag away from the ruler in the Document pane. Continue adding as many guidelines as you want by returning to the ruler wells and dragging out more guidelines.

## Tip

You can also add guidelines by double-clicking a ruler. If you want guides positioned at 1-inch increments, as an example, move the mouse cursor to a ruler and double-click the mouse button on each 1-inch increment. Guidelines appear on the page in the Document pane with each double-click of the mouse button. If you attempt to double-click the ruler outside the page area, Acrobat sounds a warning beep and a guideline won't appear outside the document page. If you do want a guideline outside the page area, add a guideline within the page bounding box and drag the guide outside the page area. ■

If you want to move a guideline after it has been placed in the Document pane, select the Hand tool and place the cursor directly over the guideline to be moved. The cursor changes from a hand to a selection arrow. Press the mouse button and drag the line to the desired position.

## Tip

If you have multiple guidelines to draw on a page at equal distances, use the Units & Guides preferences and set the major guides to the distance you want between the guides. Set the subdivision guidelines to zero. For example, if you want guidelines 2 inches apart, set the major Height and Width guides to 2 inches and enter 0 (zero) in the subdivisions. Click OK and you save some time dragging guidelines from ruler wells. ■

To delete a guideline, click the line and press the Delete key on your keyboard. You can also click and drag a guideline off the document page and back to the ruler well to delete it. If you want to delete all guides on a page, open a context menu (see Figure 5.13) on a ruler and select Clear Guides on Page. If you select Clear All Guides, all guides drawn throughout your document are deleted.

**FIGURE 5.13**

To clear guides on a page or throughout all pages, open a context menu on a ruler and select Clear All Guides.

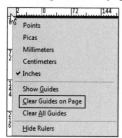

The context menu for rulers also enables you to hide the rulers; you can also use the shortcut keys Ctrl/⌘+R or revisit the View menu. Hidden rulers don't affect the view of the guides that remain visible. Notice that the context menu also contains choices for units of measure, which makes changing units here much handier than returning to the preference settings mentioned earlier. The context menu also offers the option to show and hide guides.

## Using guides

When you draw guidelines the View ➪ Guides menu command is turned on. You can toggle the view of guidelines on and off by selecting View ➪ Guides.

## Choosing line weights

Formerly labeled Wireframe in Acrobat 7, this item appears in both the View menu and the Page Display toolbar. When you zoom in and out of a drawing, the line weights zoom according to the zoom level. For example, a 1-point line zoomed in 400 percent produces a line weight view at 4 points. Zooming out reduces the line weight sizes to where lines can appear almost invisible. When you click the Line Weights tool or select View ⇨ Line Weights, all lines appear at a 1-point size regardless of the zoom level.

## Cross-Reference

**For information related to page layout views, see the section "Setting Initial View Attributes," later in this chapter. ■**

# Reading Out Loud

Read Out Loud is a nice feature in Acrobat that reads text aloud using your operating system's text-to-speech engine. The options for using Read Out Loud are found in the View ⇨ Read Out Loud submenu.

# Using Read Out Loud

This command is a marvelous accessibility tool in all Acrobat viewers. You can have Acrobat PDF documents read aloud to you without having to purchase additional equipment/software such as screen readers. If you want to turn your back on the computer while doing some other activity, you can have Acrobat read aloud any open document. For entertainment purposes, you can gather the family around the computer and have an eBook read to you.

## Cross-Reference

**For information on screen readers, see the sidebar "About Screen Readers" later in this chapter. ■**

When you choose View ⇨ Read Out Loud, a submenu opens with four menu commands. The menu commands all have keyboard shortcuts associated with them, but before you can use the commands you must first select Activate Read Out Loud in the submenu. The menu commands then become active as you see in Figure 5.14. For pausing and stopping the reading, you may want to remember these keyboard shortcuts. The commands include:

- **Activate/Deactivate Read Out Loud** (Shift+Ctrl/⌘+Y). Select Activate Read Out Loud when you start a Read Out Loud session. The menu name then changes to Deactivate Read Out Loud. Make this choice to stop reading out loud.

- **Read This Page Only** (Shift+Ctrl/⌘+V). The current active page in the Document pane is read aloud. Reading stops at the end of the target page.

- **Read To End of Document** (Shift+Ctrl/⌘+B). The reading starts on the active page and continues to the end of the document. If you want to start at the beginning of your file, click the First Page tool before selecting this menu command.

- **Pause/Resume** (Shift+Ctrl/⌘+C). After the reading begins, you see the Pause command active in the submenu. Select Pause or press the keyboard shortcut keys and

Resume appears in the menu. Use the same menu command or shortcut to toggle Pause and Resume.

- **Stop** (Shift+Ctrl/⌘+E). To stop the reading aloud, select the command or use the keyboard shortcut.

---

**FIGURE 5.14**

The Read Out Loud submenu commands provide options for audio output.

| | |
|---|---|
| De<u>a</u>ctivate Read Out Loud | Shift+Ctrl+Y |
| Read This <u>P</u>age Only | Shift+Ctrl+V |
| Read To <u>E</u>nd of Document | Shift+Ctrl+B |
| Pa<u>u</u>se | Shift+Ctrl+C |
| <u>S</u>top | Shift+Ctrl+E |

You change attribute settings for reading aloud in the Preferences dialog box, which you open by choosing Edit ➪ Preferences in Windows, Acrobat ➪ Preferences in Mac OS X, or use the keyboard shortcut (Ctrl/⌘+K). In the left pane shown in Figure 5.15, Reading is selected. The Reading preferences are displayed in the right pane (see Figure 5.15). Preference settings include the following:

- **Reading Order.** Three choices are available from the Reading Order pull-down menu. When in doubt, use the default setting to Infer reading order from document (recommended).

  - **Infer reading order from document (recommended).** With this choice Acrobat makes some guesses about the order for what items are read on the page. If you have multiple columns and the layout is not clearly set up as a page with no layout attributes, the reading order may need some finessing. Acrobat will do its best to deliver the reading in an order compliant to the page layout.

  - **Left-to-right, top-to-bottom reading order.** Reading order delivers the reading, ignoring any columns or heads that may be divided across a page. This choice might be best used for a book designed as text only in a single column.

  - **Use reading order in raw print stream.** Delivers words in the document in the order recorded in the print stream.

- **Override the reading order in tagged documents.** Tagged PDF documents contain structural information, and they are designed to be accessible with reading devices so the proper reading order conforms to the way one would visually read a file. Tagged PDF documents have a designated reading order based on the tree structure. If the PDF document is a tagged PDF with a reading structure defined and you want to ignore the order, deselect the check box. You might make this choice if the tagged PDF does not accurately support the proper reading order and the delivery is more problematic than reading an untagged file.

- **Page vs. Document.** Choices include Only read the current visible pages, Read the entire document, or For large documents, only read the currently visible pages. The difference between the first and last command is when the last item is selected (For large documents, only read the currently visible pages), the field box below the pull-down menu becomes active where you can specify the number of pages to be read.

- **Confirm before tagging documents.** If a document is tagged before reading aloud, a confirmation dialog box opens confirming the file is a tagged document. When the option is checked you can confirm the options that will be used before Acrobat prepares an untagged document for reading. Tagging can be a time-consuming procedure, especially for larger documents. This preference corresponds to the Confirm Before Tagging Documents option in the Accessibility Setup Assistant.

- **Volume.** You adjust volume settings in the Volume pull-down menu. Choose from 1 to 10 to lower or raise the volume.

- **Use default voice.** By default, the Use default voice check box is enabled. If you want to change the voice, deselect the check box and open the pull-down menu adjacent to Voice. The voice availability depends on voices installed with your operating system. Your text-to-speech default voice installed with your operating system is used. By default you may only have a single voice available. If you want additional voices, consult your operating system manual. If no additional voices are installed, you won't be able to change the voice. If you have multiple voices installed, select a voice from the pull-down menu.

- **Use default speech attributes.** The speech attributes are settings for the pitch and the speed the voice reads your file. If you want to change the pitch and/or reading rate, deselect the check box. Pitch can be changed to a value between 1 and 10. To completely understand what's going on with the pitch settings, experiment a little and listen to the various pitch changes with the voice you select from the Voice pull-down menu. Words Per Minute enables you to slow down or speed up the reading. The default is 190 wpm. If you want to make a change, type a new value in the field box.

- **Read form fields.** This setting is designed for use with Acrobat PDF forms. Check the box to have form field default values read aloud. If default text is added to a field, the text is read aloud. If the default text (or any text added to a text field) is replaced, the content of the form fields are read aloud.

## Cross-Reference

For more information about setting form field default values, see Chapters 30 and 31. ■

## Note

Certain PDF readers used with handheld devices don't have the menu commands that are available in Adobe Reader. However, some features, such as Read Out Loud, are available on devices such as the Apple iPad from resources in the operating system (OS). You can read PDF documents using any PDF reader on the Apple iPhone OS 3 and iOS 4. ■

**FIGURE 5.15**

To open Reading preferences, choose the Preferences command or press Ctrl/⌘+K. Click the Reading item in the list at the left side of the Preferences dialog box.

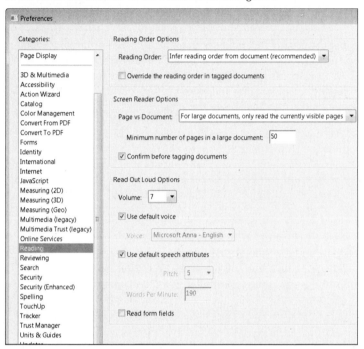

# About Screen Readers

The term *screen reader* as used in this book refers to specialized software and/or hardware devices that enable the reading aloud of computer files. Software such as JAWS and Kurzwiel and a host of other specialized software programs are sold to people with vision and motion challenges for the purpose of voice synthesizing and audio output. Many of these devices deliver audio output from proprietary formatted files or a select group of software applications. Some screen readers read raster image files saved in formats such as TIFF by performing an optical character recognition (OCR) on-the-fly and reading aloud text as it is interpreted from the image files. This method makes scanning pages of books and papers and having the scanned images interpreted by the readers easy.

Because Acrobat has implemented many tools and features for working with accessible files for the vision and motion challenged, screen reader developers have been supporting PDF format for some time. When a PDF is delivered to a reader and you select Read the entire document, the entire PDF file is sent to the reader before the first page is read. If you have long documents, you can choose to send a certain number of pages to the screen reader to break up the file into smaller chunks. When you select For long documents, read only the currently visible pages and the default of 10 pages is selected, ten pages are sent to the screen reader and the reading commences. After the pages are read, another ten pages are sent to the screen reader and read aloud, and so on.

## Cross-Reference

For more information on screen readers, tagged PDF files, and accessibility, see Chapter 23. ∎

# Zooming In and Out

Zooming in and out of document pages is a fact of life with many different programs. Even when you type text in a word processor, you often need to zoom in on text that is set in a style suited for printing, but looks horrible at a 100 percent view on your computer monitor. The same holds true for spreadsheets, all imaging and layout programs, and any kind of program where page sizes grow beyond a standard letter-size page.

Because Acrobat accommodates a page size of up to 200 × 200 inches, PDF documents sporting large page sizes need some industrial-strength zoom tools. Acrobat Professional contains a few more tools than other Acrobat viewers; however, all viewers enable you to zoom in and out of document pages using many tools consistent across all the viewers. The Zoom In and Zoom Out tools used in all viewers permit views from .33 percent to 6,400 percent of a document page.

In all viewers, you can also zoom by clicking the Zoom In or Zoom Out buttons in the Quick Tools toolbar (represented by a + and – symbol) or editing the zoom percentage field in the toolbar — just type a new value in the field box and press the Enter/Return key to zoom. When you click the down-pointing arrow, the preset pull-down menu opens.

The View menu also has a Zoom menu with several options in a submenu for zooming in and out of a document. The View ➪ Zoom ➪ Zoom To command is the first menu item. Select it and the Zoom To dialog box opens, where you can select fixed zoom levels from a pull-down menu or type in a value from 0.5 to 6,400 percent. However, this menu command is redundant because you can also use the Zoom toolbar in the same manner.

## Tip

At first glance you may think that the menu command is useless and unnecessary. However, when viewing PDF documents where the menu bar is hidden or viewing files in Full Screen Mode, you can use the keyboard shortcut Ctrl/⌘+M to open the Zoom To dialog box. You can then change zoom levels without making the menu bar visible or exiting Full Screen Mode. ∎

## Locating the Marquee Zoom tool

When you first launch Acrobat X and look for the Marquee Zoom tool, you may find it difficult to locate. Whereas the Marquee Zoom tool was a default tool that appeared in the Toolbar Well in earlier versions of Acrobat, it isn't visible as a default tool in the Quick Tools menu. To access the tool, choose View ➪ Zoom ➪ Marquee Zoom. Alternately, you can open a context menu with the Hand tool selected and choose Marquee Zoom from the menu.

When you click the Marquee Zoom tool, there are several ways you can use the tool with modifier keys, including:

- **Click and drag.** Drag the tool to create a marquee to zoom in to an area.
- **Alt/Option+click and drag.** Press the Alt/Option key to marquee an area and you zoom the page out.
- **Click.** Click the Marquee Zoom tool and the zoom jumps a fixed percentage.
- **Alt/Option+click.** Press the Alt/Option key and click and you zoom out at fixed percentages.

## Using the Zoom In tool

The Zoom In tool is restricted to its fixed position in the Zoom toolbar. Click the Zoom In (+ icon) tool in the Quick Tools toolbar and you zoom in to the same fixed preset zooms as when using the Marquee Zoom tool.

## Using the Zoom Out tool

The Zoom Out tool works in exactly the same way as the Zoom In tool, only it zooms out rather than in. It also has the same options associated with it as are associated with the Marquee Zoom tool when you press Alt/Option.

## Accessing the Dynamic Zoom tool

When you first use the Dynamic Zoom tool, you may feel like you're watching a George Lucas sci-fi movie. It's downright mesmerizing. This tool is available in all Acrobat viewers and is much handier than drawing marquees with the Marquee Zoom tool.

When you first experience an Acrobat X session, you may think that Adobe no longer includes the Dynamic Zoom tool in this version. This is because it is not accessible from the View⇨Zoom submenu, it doesn't appear in a context menu, and it isn't available in a panel.

To access the Dynamic Zoom tool, first select the Marquee Zoom tool as described earlier in the section "Locating the Marquee Zoom tool." Press the Shift key and the Marquee Zoom tool changes to the Dynamic Zoom tool. Then drag the tool up or down on a page to rapidly zoom in or out.

## Using the Loupe tool

If you use other Adobe programs, such as Adobe Photoshop, Adobe Illustrator, or Adobe InDesign, you know about the Navigator palette. The Loupe tool, available in all Acrobat viewers, works similarly to the Navigator palette found in other Adobe programs but with a little twist. Instead of viewing a complete page in the Loupe Tool window, you see just the zoom level of your selection while the page zoom remains static. This tool can be a great benefit by saving you time to refresh your monitor when you change screen views.

To use the Loupe tool, choose View ⇨ Zoom ⇨ Loupe Tool. Move the cursor to an area on a page you want to zoom to and click the mouse button. The Loupe tool window opens and displays the zoomed area you selected, as shown in Figure 5.16.

Click an area in the Document pane with the Loupe tool, and the target area is viewed at a zoom level in the Loupe window.

You can increase or decrease the magnification of the zoom area by adjusting the slider bar in the Loupe window or clicking the minus or plus symbols in the window. Clicking these symbols offers you smaller incremental changes than when using the Zoom In and Zoom Out tools. If you want the Loupe tool to show a larger portion, you can resize the Loupe Tool dialog box by grabbing a corner of the box and dragging.

When you click in the Document pane with the Loupe tool, a rectangle appears around the area zoomed into the Loupe window (see Figure 5.16). You can place the cursor inside this rectangle and move it around the Document pane to view different areas at the same zoom level. As you zoom in, the rectangle reduces in size. At some point it would be impractical to select the rectangle on the page. If you can't find it, zoom out a little in the Loupe tool window until you see the rectangle on the page. Click and drag it to a new position and you can adjust your zoom.

Notice also in Figure 5.16 the four handles (squares) on the corners of the rectangle marking the Loupe tool zoom area. You can drag the handles in or out to zoom in or out, respectively.

If you have oversized documents that take a long time to refresh, using the Loupe tool helps speed up your PDF viewing. You can keep the document page in the Document pane at a reduced view while using the Loupe tool to examine areas in detail, which won't necessitate screen refreshes.

## Tip

The Loupe window displays the zoom level on an open document and remains fixed to that document until you target a new area. When you have multiple documents open, you can zoom in on one document and switch views in the Document pane to another document; the zoom display in the Loupe tool window remains fixed to the original document view. What you wind up with appears as if it's a picture-in-picture view such as you might see on a television set. ■

## Exploring the Pan & Zoom Window

Whereas the Loupe tool displays the zoom view in its own window and the page in the Document pane remains static, the Pan & Zoom Window works in the opposite manner. The zoom level changes on the page in the Document pane while the original page view remains static in the Pan & Zoom Window. The zoom area is highlighted with a red rectangle in the Pan & Zoom Window. You can change the default red color of the zoom rectangle by opening the Line Color pull-down menu in the window and choosing from preset colors or choosing a custom color.

## Note

If you don't see a red square in the Pan & Zoom Window in the lower-right corner, you need to size the window larger to reveal the pull-down menu. ■

To use the Pan & Zoom Window, choose View ⇨ Zoom ⇨ Pan & Zoom. The window displays a full page with the red rectangle showing the zoom area. If you open the Pan & Zoom Window when your PDF page is in Fit Page view, the page and the red rectangle are the same size.

To zoom a view in the Pan & Zoom Window, select one of the four handles on a corner of the rectangle and resize the rectangle by dragging in or out to zoom in or out, respectively. The page thumbnail view in the Pan & Zoom Window remains the same size while the rectangle is sized, as shown in Figure 5.16.

Also contained in the Pan & Zoom Window are navigation buttons. You can establish a zoom view and then scroll pages in your document with the page tools in the window. As you do so, the page views in the Document pane hold the same zoom level you set in the Pan & Zoom Window.

## Understanding Zoom tool behaviors

A few specific differences exist between the Loupe tool and the Pan & Zoom tool that you should know. The Loupe tool targets an area on an open document and the zoom is fixed to that document while it remains open or until you target a new area. Regardless of the number of files you open, the Loupe tool window displaying your target view stays intact even if another document is brought to the front of the Document pane. If you close a file where the Loupe tool was set to view a zoom, the Loupe tool window clears and displays no view.

The Pan & Zoom tool always shows a target view of the active document brought forward in the Document pane. If you have multiple documents open, open the Pan & Zoom tool, then close a file, the page in view in the next file appears in the Pan & Zoom Window. If you close all files, the Pan & Zoom Window clears.

If you close a file during an Acrobat session, both the Loupe tool and the Pan & Zoom tool return you to the same views. The Pan & Zoom tool displays the opening page at the same zoom level as was last established in the window. The Loupe tool displays the same view last created with the tool. For example, if you zoom to 200 percent on page 25 of a file, close the file, and then reopen it, the Loupe tool window displays page 25 at 200 percent while the Document pane displays the opening page.

You can use both tools together to display different views in different documents. If the page in view in the Loupe window is not the current active document brought forward in the Document pane, you can still manage zooming on the hidden page. Use the slider between the minus/plus symbols to change zoom levels.

# Setting Initial View Attributes

Initial View is the page view you see when you first open a PDF document. You can set several different attributes for an opening view and you can save your settings with the document. These views are document specific so they only relate to a document where you save the settings. When no settings have been saved with a file, the file is saved with a default view.

### Cross-Reference

To understand more about default views, see "Understanding Initial View preferences" later in this chapter. ■

Coincidentally, even though previous versions of Acrobat provided you with options to save an initial view, most PDF authors rarely use them. You can find thousands of PDF files on the Internet and most of them have no settings enabled for an opening view other than the program defaults. I hope that by the time you finish this section, you can see some advantages for saving a particular initial view for the PDF documents you create and edit.

To set the attributes for the opening view, choose File ⇨ Properties or use the keyboard shortcut Ctrl/⌘+D. The Document Properties dialog box opens, displaying a row of tabs at the top. Click the Initial View tab as shown in Figure 5.17.

**FIGURE 5.17**

To set the attributes for the opening view, choose File ⇨ Properties and click the Initial View tab when the Document Properties dialog box opens.

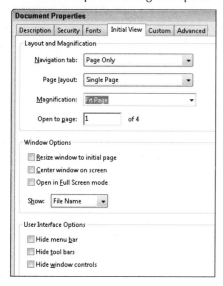

## Note

Initial View settings are not available nor can they be changed in Adobe Reader even when usage rights have been added to the PDF. When Initial Views are saved from Acrobat Standard, Pro, or Pro Extended, PDFs open with the saved views in all Acrobat viewers. ■

Acrobat provides you with many different choices for controlling the initial view of a PDF opened in any Acrobat viewer. Settings you make on the Initial View tab can be saved with your document. When you establish settings other than defaults, the settings saved with the file override the user's default preference settings. The options on this tab are as follows:

- **Layout and Magnification.** The default opening page is the first page of a PDF document. You can change the opening page to another page and you can control the page layout views and magnification by selecting choices from the Layout and Magnification section. The choices include:

## Note

One reason you might want to open a PDF document on a page other than the first page is when you have a cover page or a title page that doesn't include content of interest to the reader. In such cases, you might want to open the PDF document on page 2 where a contents page or the first page of a section or chapter appears. ∎

- **Navigation tab.** Five choices are available from the Navigation tab pull-down menu. Select Page Only to open the page with the Navigation panel collapsed. Use the Bookmarks Panel and Page option to open the Bookmarks panel when the file opens. Use the Pages Panel and Page option to open the Pages panel where the thumbnails of pages are viewed. Use Attachments Panel and Page to open the Attachments panel when the file opens, and use Layers Panel and Page to open the Layers panel when the file opens.

- **Page Layout.** The default for Page Layout is noted in the pull-down menu as Default. When you save a PDF file with the Default selection, the PDF opens according to the default value a user has set for page viewing on the user's computer. To override the user's default, you can set a page layout in the opening view from one of six choices. Your options include:

  **Single Page.** This option opens a single page view that appears the same as when you click the Single Page layout tool.

  **Single Page Continuous.** The same as the Continuous page layout view in earlier versions of Acrobat. This view appears the same as when you click the Single Page Continuous tool.

  **Two-Up (Facing).** The Two-Up (Facing) view shows the first two pages in a file beside each other in a two-page layout. When you scroll, subsequent pages snap to a page view. This view is the same as clicking the Two-Up tool.

  **Two-Up Continuous (Facing).** The view appears very similar to Two-Up (Facing) but when you scroll pages, partial pages can be viewed in the Document pane. For example, the bottom of the previous page and the top of the next page may appear. In other words, this view doesn't snap pages to fit in the Document pane.

  **Two-Up (Cover Page).** The initial view shows one page as in the Single Page view. When you scroll pages, however, the subsequent pages are displayed in a Two-Up (facing pages) view.

  **Two-Up Continuous (Cover Page).** The initial page opens on the right side of the Document pane in a Single Page view. When you scroll pages, the scrolling is similar to the Two-Up Continuous view where facing pages are shown.

- **Magnification.** Choose from preset magnification views in the pull-down menu. If you want the PDF document to open in a fit-in-window view, select Fit Page. Choose from other magnification options or edit the text box for a custom-zoom level. If Default is selected, the document opens according to user preference magnification settings.

- **Open to page.** You can change the opening page to another page by entering a number in the Page number text box. This setting might be used if you want a user to see a contents page on page 2 in a document instead of a title page that appears on page 1.

- **Window Options.** The default window for Acrobat is a full screen where the viewing area is maximized to occupy your monitor surface area. You can change the window view to size down the window to the initial page size, center a smaller window on-screen, and open a file in Full Screen Mode. If you enable all three check boxes, the Full Screen Mode prevails.

- **Show.** From the pull-down menu choose either File Name or Document Title. If you select File Name, the title bar at the top of the Acrobat window shows the filename. If Document Title is used, the information you supply in the Document Properties dialog box for Document Title is shown in the title bar.

## Cross-Reference

Document titles are very important when you're archiving volumes of PDFs and creating search indexes. For information on creating document titles and how they are used, see Chapter 6. ∎

- **User Interface Options.** The Interface Options in the Initial View Document Properties dialog box have to do with user interface items in Acrobat viewers, such as menu bars, toolbars, and scroll bars. You can elect to hide these items when the PDF document opens in any Acrobat viewer. In Acrobat 9, you can hide only two of the three options for the User Interface Controls shown in Figure 5.17. You can choose to hide the menu bar and the window controls as shown in Figure 5.18, the menu bar and the toolbars, or any one of the single items. Acrobat 9 doesn't permit you to hide all three options

  The window controls you see in Figure 5.19 include the scroll bars, the status bar, and the Navigation panel. If you hide the toolbars and menu bar but elect to leave the window controls visible, users can access tools for page navigation.

## Caution

If you elect to eliminate the toolbars and menu bar from view and later want to go back and edit your file, you need to use shortcut keys to get the menu bars and toolbars back. Be certain to remember the F9 key — F9 shows and hides the menu bar and the F8 key shows/hides toolbars. ∎

## Tip

If you open a PDF document with Window Controls hidden, you can open the Navigation pane by opening a context menu on the far-left side of the Document pane and choosing Show Navigation Panel Buttons. ■

When toolbars and the menu bar are hidden, navigating pages requires keyboard shortcuts or navigational buttons on the pages.

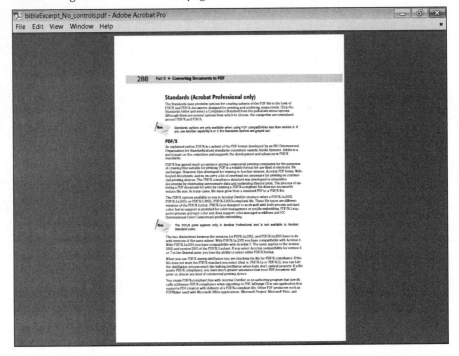

**FIGURE 5.19**

If window controls are visible, users can access tools for page navigation.

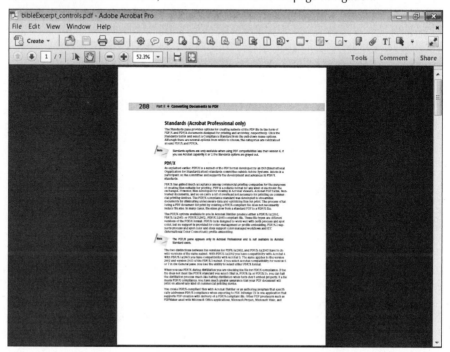

## Setting custom zoom levels

The Initial View options for the page zoom are at fixed magnification levels. If you want a PDF document to open at a zoom level of 69 percent, for example, you don't have the choice for this custom zoom option in the Initial View settings. To set a custom zoom level, you need to use a JavaScript. To add a JavaScript to open a PDF document at a custom zoom level, do the following:

### Steps: Setting Custom Zoom Magnification with JavaScript

1. **Open a document and click Document JavaScripts in the JavaScript subpanel.** The JavaScript Functions dialog box opens. (Note: If the JavaScript subpanel is not shown in the Tools panel, open the Show or Hide panel drop-down menu and check JavaScript.)

2. **Type a name for the script in the Script Name text box.** In my example, I'll name my script *zoom*.

3. **Click Add to open the JavaScript Editor.**

4. **Delete the default text in the JavaScript Editor window and type the following code:**

```
this.zoom=69;
```

5. **Click OK in the JavaScript Editor to return to the JavaScript Functions dialog box as shown in Figure 5.20.**

6. **Close the JavaScript Functions dialog box.**

7. **Save the file.**

FIGURE 5.20

The JavaScript Functions dialog box showing a script to force a zoom magnification of 69 percent.

The preceding code forces the PDF document to open at 69 percent. If you want to use another magnification, just change 69 to another numeric value in the script.

## Cross-Reference

For more information on writing JavaScripts, see Chapter 32. ∎

# Understanding Initial View preferences

If you don't assign Initial View attributes in the Document Properties dialog box and save the file to update it, initial views are determined from individual user preferences. Because each user can set preferences differently, the same PDF may appear with a different page layout mode and a different zoom level on different computers. Depending on the design of your documents and how you want them viewed by end users, potential inconsistency in document views might make viewing difficult for those who view your files.

Users set initial view preferences in the Preferences dialog box. Open the Preferences dialog box by pressing Ctrl/⌘+K, and then click Page Display in the left pane. At the top of the right pane, a pull-down menu appears for Page Layout and another menu appears for Zoom. You can select different page layout and default zoom views from the menus. In Figure 5.21, the Default page layout view is set to Single Page and the Default zoom is set to Fit Page. When you click OK to accept these changes, all PDF documents that have initial views set to Default will open on your computer with the views derived from your preference choices. Other users may choose different options from the pull-down menus, thereby displaying PDF documents with default views according to the choices they make in the Page Display preferences.

Be aware that the initial views you set in a PDF file from the Document Properties override the user preferences in the Page Display preferences pane. Therefore, you can control the initial views for all the PDFs you create. Doing so means your documents are viewed consistently across all computers regardless of the differences between individual user preference choices.

**FIGURE 5.21**

Changing the Default page layout to Single Page and the Default zoom to Fit Page opens all PDFs saved with default initial views with your new preference settings.

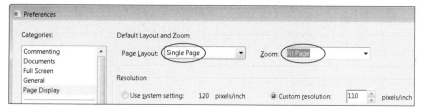

# Saving the Initial View

When you decide what view attributes you want assigned to your document, you can choose one of two save options. The first option updates the file. Click the Save tool in the Acrobat File toolbar or choose File ➪ Save. Any edits you make in the Initial View properties activate the Save command. The Save command is inactive and grayed out by default until you make any changes to your file or reset any kind of preferences that can be saved with the document. The other option is to use Save As. When you select File ➪ Save As, you completely rewrite the file when you click the Save button in the Save As dialog box.

## Cross-Reference

You have different choices for saving files using either Save or Save As. For a more complete understanding of saving and updating PDFs, see Chapter 11. ■

# Viewing Files with the Window Menu

If you open a PDF file and then open a second PDF, the second file hides the first document. If several PDFs are opened, the last opened document hides all the others. Fortunately, the Acrobat viewers have made it easy for you to choose a given document from a nest of open files.

When you load an Acrobat viewer with several open files, you can use tools to help you manage them. If you need to visually compare documents, several different viewing options are available.

The Window menu contains options for helping you manage document views, in particular, multiple documents. The options you find in the Window menu won't be found with tools or in the status bar, so you'll find yourself visiting this menu frequently if you work with multiple open files in Acrobat or if you need to create more than one view in the same document.

## Minimizing and zooming views

By default, when you open PDF files, the Acrobat window appears minimized. In other words, the application window doesn't zoom to the full screen size. This behavior can be a blessing for those with large monitors who want to work in Acrobat and another application alongside the Acrobat window, or a curse for those who want to take advantage of a full-screen size when working in Acrobat alone.

If you leave the preferences at the default, you can zoom the Acrobat application window by clicking the features button on the application window. Click the Maximize button represented by an X in the top-right corner (Windows) and the window zooms to a maximized view. On the Mac, click the plus icon in the top-left corner of the application window, and the application window zooms to a maximized view.

## Opening a new window

New Window was a new feature in Acrobat 7 Professional. When you open a document and select New Window, a duplicate view of your existing document is opened in the Document pane. You can change views and pages in one window while viewing different page views in another window. This feature is handy for viewing a table of contents in one window while viewing content on other pages in the same file.

When you select New Window, Acrobat adds an extension to the filename in the title bar. If you have a document open in Acrobat with a filename like Employee Application and then select New Window, the title bar displays Employee Application:1 on one view and Employee Application:2 on the second view.

New Window can be particularly helpful when viewing PDF Portfolios. You can create a PDF Portfolio and view two or more files within the package in new windows and tiled views.

## Cross-Reference

For more information on PDF Portfolios and viewing options you have with these files, see Chapter 11. For more on tiling views, see "Tiling windows" later in this chapter. ■

## Cascading windows

If you have several files open and choose Window ➪ Cascade, the open files appear in a cascading view with the title bars visible much like you might view cascading Web pages. You can see the name of each file and easily select from any one shown in the Document pane. Click a title bar to bring a document forward.

After bringing a file forward, if you want to see the title bars in a cascading view again, choose Window ➪ Cascade again. The document currently selected in the foreground will appear first when you use this command.

The Window menu also lists the open files by filename at the bottom of the window. When you have multiple files open, the files are numbered according to the order in which they were opened, with the filename appearing in the list, as shown in Figure 5.22. Select any filename from the list in the Window menu to bring the file forward in the Document pane.

**FIGURE 5.22**

Acrobat lists all open files in the Window menu. To bring a document forward in the Document pane, choose the name of the file you want to view from the Window menu.

## Tiling windows

You can also choose to have your documents tiled horizontally or vertically via the Tile submenu in the Window menu. When you choose Window ➪ Tile ➪ Horizontally or Vertically, the PDF files appear in individual windows arranged to fit within the Acrobat window in either a horizontal or vertical view. If you have more than three documents open at one time, the displays for Tile Horizontally and Tile Vertically appear identical. With any number of documents displayed in tiled views, the Navigation panel is accessible for each document. Also, when you choose Window ⇨ New Window and open a second view of the same document, and then tile the views, each window appears in the tiled documents. In Figure 5.23, two documents appear in a vertical tiled view.

Tiling views neatly displays all open documents adjacent to each other within the Acrobat window.

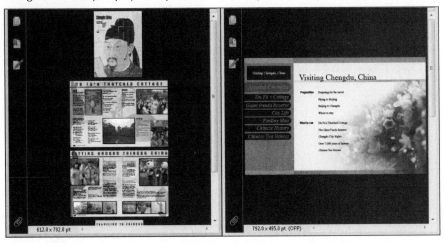

Tiling documents can be helpful when you need to edit documents and exchange pages between two or more PDF files or when you need to compare changes among documents.

## Splitting a window

Choose Window ⇨ Split and the Document pane splits into two horizontal views of the active document, similar to the way you might see a split view in a word processing or spreadsheet program. The two views are independent of each other and offer you much flexibility. You can view the same page in two different zoom views or you can view two different pages at the same zoom level or different zoom views. You can view one pane in a Single page layout and the other pane in one of the other page layout options. You can also combine the Split and Tile option to view two or more documents, each with split views tiled horizontally or vertically. You can adjust the window division by moving the horizontal bar up or down, thereby showing a larger view in one pane and a smaller view in the other pane.

## Using the Spreadsheet Split view

Spreadsheet Split is the same concept as using a Split view except you now have four panes. Just choose Window ⇨ Spreadsheet Split. Click inside the pane whose view you want to change and then zoom in and out and navigate pages as needed. Move the divider bars horizontally and vertically to size the panes to accommodate your viewing needs. Position the cursor at the intersection of the separator bars and you can move the bars vertically and horizontally together. To remove the Spreadsheet Split view, return to the Window menu and select Spreadsheet Split again. The Document pane returns to the default view.

## Tip
**You can exit the Spreadsheet view by double-clicking the intersection of the crossbars. If you want a split view vertically or horizontally, double-click the vertical (or horizontal) crossbar. ∎**

## Viewing in Full Screen Mode

Another viewing option found in the Window menu is the Full Screen Mode. Full Screen Mode displays your PDF document like a slide show and temporarily hides the menus, toolbars, and window controls. You can set up the Full Screen Mode for automatic page scrolling and then walk away from the computer — you'll have a self-running kiosk. You can give a presentation and automatically scroll pages or set preferences for pausing between slides.

# Viewing Links

For the purpose of discussion, links in Acrobat are *hot spots* where you click somewhere in the Acrobat window and some action takes place. With regard to viewing PDF documents, clicking the mouse button on a link takes you to another view, opens a document or Web page, or executes some sort of action. Links can be any one of a number of items, including elements on a PDF page such as buttons, articles, fields, and so on, or they can be part of the user interface such as thumbnails and links you create from options in palettes. In this chapter, I stick to link behavior in Acrobat as it relates to page viewing and locating links.

## Cross-Reference
**For information on creating links and buttons that execute a variety of different actions, see Chapter 21. ∎**

## Viewing the Navigation pane

The Navigation pane contains the default panels discussed in Chapter 1. Most of these panels are connected to certain capabilities for linking to views and other kinds of actions that can be invoked with the click of a mouse button. In some cases, a single click takes you to another view and in other cases a double-click takes you to another view. The panels that contain some form of linking to views include:

## Cross-Reference
**To learn more about the navigation panels, see Chapters 1 and 3. ∎**

- **Pages.** To view thumbnails of each page, click the Pages panel in the Navigation pane. The page thumbnails are links to the respective pages. A single mouse click on a page thumbnail displays the respective page in the Document pane.

## Cross-Reference

For information on working with the Pages panel, see Chapter 21. ■

- **Bookmarks.** All Bookmarks in a PDF file are displayed in a list beside the Bookmarks panel. With a single click of the mouse button, a Bookmark may take you to another page or view, or invoke an action.

## Cross-Reference

For information on creating Bookmarks and setting link actions to them, see Chapter 21. ■

- **Signatures.** The Signatures panel contains a list of all digital signatures in a PDF document. You can open the Signatures panel and navigate to pages where signatures have been added to the file.

## Cross-Reference

For information on creating digital signatures, see Chapter 24. ■

- **Attachments.** The Attachments panel contains a list of all file attachments. Double-clicking an attachment, however, does not navigate to the page where the attachment is placed. Use the Attachments panel to search for the page where the attachment appears because double-clicking an attachment opens the attached file.

## Cross-Reference

For information on working with file attachments, see Chapter 11. ■

- **Comments.** The Comments panel contains any annotations added to the open file. You can navigate to any page where a comment has been added by double-clicking on a comment in the Comments panel.

## Cross-Reference

For information on working with comments, see Chapter 19. ■

# Accessing Additional Navigation panes

You can access the additional panels from the View ➪ Show/Hide ➪ Navigation Panes submenu described in Chapter 1 contain links to the content you create from various panel options. The panels not yet discussed that appear in the Navigation Panels submenu are as follows:

- **Accessibility Report.** When you choose Advanced Editing ➪ Accessibility ➪ Full Check you are prompted to save an Accessibility Report file. Once the file is saved, the report appears in the Navigation pane in the Accessibility Report panel. Here you can analyze the document for compliance with document accessibility.

## Cross-Reference

For information on accessibility, see Chapter 23. ■

- **Articles.** Article threads are like link buttons. You can create article threads in a PDF file and the threads are listed in the Articles panel. Use the panel to open an article thread and click the mouse button inside the article to follow the thread.

## Cross-Reference

For information on creating articles, see Chapter 21. ■

- **Content.** Document content can be displayed in the Content panel. When you open the panel and select individual items, you can highlight the respective content item on the document page. In essence, the Content panel is linked to the content appearing on the PDF pages according to the natural reading order of the PDF file.

## Cross-Reference

For information on using the Content panel, see Chapter 23. ■

- **Destinations.** Destinations are similar to Bookmarks and are linked to a specific location in an open PDF document or to secondary PDF documents. When you click a destination, the view associated with the destination opens in the Document pane.

## Cross-Reference

For information on destinations, see Chapter 21. ■

- **Examine Document.** When you choose Document ➪ Examine Document, the Examine Document panel opens in the Navigation pane. You have a number of options to analyze a document including examining metadata, file attachments, bookmarks, and form fields.

## Cross-Reference

For information on examining documents, see Chapter 13. ■

- **Fields.** In Acrobat 9 and above, you won't find the Fields panel located in the Navigation Panels submenu. The Fields panel has been moved to another interface where form field editing is performed. To see the Fields panel, you need to click Create or Edit in the Forms panel to open Form Edit mode. By default, the Fields panel opens below the Tasks panel when you switch to Form Edit mode. The Fields panel lists all form fields created in the open document. Click a field name in the panel and the field becomes highlighted in the Form Editing window.

## Cross-Reference

For information on creating form fields, see Chapters 30 and 31. ■

## Note

Having the document page size appear by default without having to move the cursor in the lower-left corner of the Acrobat window is a matter of personal choice. I find it helpful having the page size reported when I'm opening PDF documents. As a matter of consistency in viewing the screen shots in this book, I have this preference option turned on for all the figures in the remaining chapters of this book. ■

- **Layers.** The Layers panel shows all Adobe PDF layers contained in a document by layer names. If the panel is empty, no layers are contained in the file. You use the Layers panel to show and hide layers, set layer properties, and manage layers.

- **Model Tree.** Model Tree is used with 3-D graphics within a PDF. You can examine content, change views, shading, and many different aspects of 3-D models. The Model Tree is also opened when you use the Object Data tool.

- **Order.** When you open the Order panel, the reading order of your pages is displayed in the panel and on the document pages. You can easily change the reading order by moving the references in the Order panel around much like you would reorganize Bookmarks.

## Cross-Reference

For information on using the Order panel, see Chapter 23. ■

- **Security Settings.** The Security Settings panel opens in the Navigation pane when a file has security applied to the document. Click Permission Details in the Security Settings panel and the Document Properties Security tab opens displaying the permissions assigned to the document.

- **Standards.** When you create PDF files meeting standards such as PDF/A, PDF/X, PDF/E, and so on. the Standards panel opens in the Navigation pane. Among other things, you can verify compliance to a given standard and click a link to the Preflight tool where you can analyze a document for meeting conditions for a given standard.

## Cross-Reference

For information on using PDF standards and the Preflight tool, see Chapter 29. ■

- **Tags.** Tags list all the structural content in a PDF document. You can highlight an element from within the Tags panel to locate a tagged element. Whereas the Contents panel identifies all the page content in any PDF file, the Tags panel only shows the structure and elements of tagged PDF files. Together with the Order panel, Tags are used with accessible documents.

## Cross-Reference

For information on using the Tags panel and making documents accessible, see Chapter 23. ■

# Using hypertext links

In an Acrobat viewer, hypertext references enable you to move around the PDF or many PDFs, much like surfing the Net. You've probably become so accustomed to clicking buttons on your desktop computer that link navigation is commonplace and needs little instruction. While invoking the action is nothing more than a click with the mouse, what it can do in Acrobat is simply remarkable. To help you gain an understanding of how Acrobat has employed hyperlinks, the following sections describe all the link actions as they can be created in Acrobat and executed in any viewer.

Hypertext references, or *buttons,* are easily identified in a PDF document. As you move the mouse cursor around the document window, a Hand icon with the forefinger pointing appears when you position the cursor over a button or a link. You click, and presto! — the link action is executed!

Link actions can be assigned to any one of several items in Acrobat. You can set a link action to links, fields, Bookmarks, and Page Actions.

All the Link Action types are available with Acrobat Standard and Acrobat Pro. Versions of Acrobat Standard prior to Acrobat 9 did not support creating form fields. The action types available in Acrobat include:

- **Execute a menu command.** This action links to commands found in the Acrobat menus. Unfortunately, many of the Execute a menu command options were removed in Acrobat 8. If you used some Execute menu items that are no longer available in Acrobat 8 and above, you now have to turn to JavaScript programming and completely rework your files.

- **Go to a 3D/Multimedia view.** For PDF documents supporting 3-D views, you can set an action to a specific 3-D view.

- **Go to a page view.** The Go to a page view action opens another view on the existing page, a view to another page in the same document, a view to a named destination, or a view in another document.

- **Import form data.** This action imports data exported from other forms into the active document where form field names match those from where the data were exported.

- **Multimedia Operation (Acrobat 9 and Later).** Use this action when playing media files that support compatibility with Acrobat 9 and later.

- **Open a file.** The Open a file link opens any kind of document. PDFs open in Acrobat. Other file types require having the authoring program installed on your computer. For example, if the link is to a Microsoft Word document, you need Word installed on your computer to open the link.

- **Open a web link.** Opens a URL in your default Web browser.

- **Play a sound.** Plays a sound imported into the active PDF.

- **Play Media (Acrobat 5 Compatible).** Plays a movie file saved in formats compatible with Acrobat 5 and lower viewers. Note: Acrobat 5 compatible media cannot be embedded in a PDF document.

- **Play Media (Acrobat 6 and Later Compatible).** Plays movie files saved in newer formats compatible with Acrobat 6 through Acrobat 9, and movie clips can be embedded in PDFs using this compatibility. This choice uses legacy methodology and requires the user to have a media player installed on their computer.

- **Read an article.** This action navigates to the specified article in the open PDF document or another PDF document.

- **Reset a form.** All the fields or user-specified fields on a form are cleared of data.

- **Run a JavaScript.** Executes JavaScripts written in Acrobat.

- **Set layer visibility.** This action can be set to either hide or show a layer.

- **Show/hide a field.** With form fields, fields are hidden or made visible on a page.

- **Submit a form.** This action is used for submitting data in user-prescribed formats to a specified URL.

The preceding list is a brief description of action types that can be associated with tools that support link actions.

## Cross-Reference

For more detail on how to create link actions and a host of attributes you can assign to them, see Part IV, "PDF Interactivity" and Part VI, "Acrobat PDF Forms." ∎

# Opening PDF Files

As with most computer programs you already use on either Windows or the Mac, you know that files are generally opened via the File ⇨ Open command. In many programs, the keyboard shortcut used to open files is Ctrl/⌘+O. Acrobat uses the same menu and keyboard shortcuts to access the Open dialog box where you browse your hard drive, open folders, and ultimately select a file to open. When you double-click a filename or click the Open button when a file is selected, the file opens in Acrobat.

All Acrobat viewers also offer you a tool to open files. Click the Open tool in the Quick Tools toolbar and the Open dialog box appears just as if you had used the Open menu command or keyboard shortcut. Any one of these methods opens a PDF document or a document of one of many different file types that can be converted to PDF on-the-fly while you work in Acrobat.

## Cross-Reference

For information related to opening files that are converted to PDF with the Open command, see Chapter 7. ∎

When you launch Acrobat and view and/or edit PDF documents, Acrobat keeps track of the most recently opened files. By default, Acrobat keeps track of the last five files you opened. In the Startup preferences you can change the value to as many as ten recently viewed files. The files are accessible at the bottom of the File menu (Windows) or the File ⇨ Open Recent File submenu on the Mac. In Figure 5.24, you can see five filenames at the bottom of the File menu from Acrobat running under Windows.

### FIGURE 5.24

The most recently viewed files appear in the File menu (Windows) or File ⇨ Open Recent File submenu (Mac).

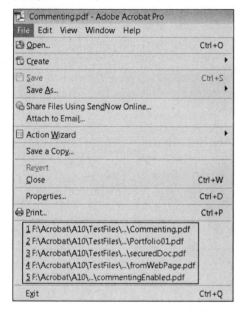

## Summary

This chapter offers you a brief overview of how to go about moving around PDF documents, using viewing tools, panels, and pages, as well as opening and managing files. As you can see, the list is long and there's quite a bit to understand in regard to viewing, navigating, opening, and managing files. Some of the more important points include the following:

- Page navigation tools are available in a toolbar not visible by default. You can place the toolbar in view and dock it to the left, right, top, or below the Document pane for easy access to navigation tools.

- The Read Mode feature optimizes your views for page content. You can easily scroll pages back and forth with simple mouse clicks.

- PDFs can be read aloud and pages can be autoscrolled without the need for any special equipment.

- PDF pages can be viewed in several different layout modes, with grids, guides, and rulers.

- Acrobat contains six tools used for zooming views. The Marquee Zoom tool is a new tool in Acrobat permitting you to zoom in and out by drawing marquee selections. In addition to the Marquee Zoom, Zoom In, Zoom Out, Dynamic Zoom, the Loupe tool, and the Pan & Zoom are available in all Acrobat viewers.

- Initial Views of PDF documents can be displayed with pages and palettes, at different zoom levels, with or without menus, tools, and window controls. These settings are document specific and can be saved with different options for different documents. The settings are established in the Initial View document properties dialog box.

- Links are built into many different Acrobat tools and they can be assigned to items created in Acrobat. Different action types can be assigned to many tools and object elements.

- Acrobat 8 and 9 do not support most of the Execute a menu item commands found in all earlier versions of Acrobat.

- Links can be made to Web pages and URLs.

- PDF files are opened through menu commands or by using the Open tool. The most recently opened files are listed in the File menu (Windows) or the File ⇨ Open Recent File submenu (Mac).

# Searching PDF Files

Acrobat X continues with the search options you had available with Acrobat 9. You'll notice the Find tool and the Search pane are both present in this release.

You can find information contained in PDF documents with the Find tool for open documents. The Search window is available when a document is open in the Document pane or when no document is open. The Search window enables you to search PDFs scattered around your hard drive without the assistance of a search index. However, creating index files with Acrobat Catalog and searching the resultant index files is available to you for more feature-rich and faster searches. In this chapter, I cover all the tools and features available in Acrobat viewers for searching through PDF files and creating and searching index files.

All four Acrobat viewers (Adobe Reader, Adobe Acrobat Standard, Adobe Acrobat Pro, and Adobe Acrobat Pro Extended) support the exact same features for searching PDF content.

## Using the Find Toolbar

In order to use the Find toolbar, you must have a document open in the Document pane. If you have more than one document open, you can search only the active document appearing in the foreground.

Finding words in an open document can be handled in the Find toolbar. The toolbar opens when you press Ctrl/⌘+F or choose Edit ➪ Find.

Type a word in the field box in the Find toolbar and press the Enter/Return key. Acrobat searches the current active document and highlights the first occurrence of the found word. When a word is found, the Previous and Next buttons in the toolbar become active.

Click the Next button in the toolbar, and Acrobat searches for the next occurrence and stops on the page where the word is highlighted again. Clicking Previous takes you to the last found word in the open document (if you click the button after the first search). When you click Next, and then click the Previous button, the search takes you to the previous found word. For example, if you search for a word in a 100-page document and the word appears on pages 5, 6, and 99, the first time you execute the Find, you stop at page 5. Clicking the Previous button takes you to page 99. However, if you click Next while on page 5, the next found word appears on page 6. Clicking Previous on page 6 takes you back to page 5.

The Find toolbar also includes a pull-down menu, as shown in Figure 6.1, containing several menu commands to assist you in narrowing your search.

**FIGURE 6.1**

Open the pull-down menu in the Find toolbar for more search options.

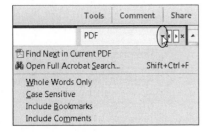

Click the down-pointing arrow to see the following menu commands:

- **Find Next in Current PDF.** The menu command finds the next occurrence of the found word just as it does when clicking the Find Next tool.

- **Open Full Acrobat Search.** Opens the Search window. This command performs the same function as clicking the Search tool or pressing the Ctrl/⌘+Shift+F keys.

- **Whole words only.** Returns words that match whole words only. For example, if you search for a word like *cat*, this command avoids returning words such as *catalog*, *catastrophe*, *category*, and so on.

- **Case-Sensitive.** Finds words that match the letter case of the word typed in the Find toolbar.

- **Include Bookmarks.** Finds words in bookmark descriptions.

- **Include Comments.** Finds words in comment notes.

You can choose one or any combination of the first four options to perform your search. For example, you can select Whole words only, Case-Sensitive, Include Bookmarks, and Include Comments, and Acrobat returns the first occurrence of only whole words matching the letter case in the search criteria whether it be in a bookmark, comment note, or on a document page.

Using the Find toolbar also makes active two other menu commands. After invoking a find, the Next Result and Previous Result commands are accessed by clicking the left and right arrows in the Find toolbar. You can also use the keyboard shortcuts (Ctrl/⌘+G for Next Result and Ctrl/⌘+Shift+G for Previous Result).

# Using the Search Window

You perform searches by accessing a menu command or by using shortcut keys. To open the Search panel from a menu command, choose Edit ⇨ Search, or open a context menu with the Hand tool and select Advanced Search. To use the keyboard shortcut, press Ctrl/⌘+Shift+F and likewise the Search window opens as shown in Figure 6.2. Both the menu commands and the keyboard shortcut allow you to search for a word in an open document, in a collection of PDF files stored on your hard drive, or any type of external media. When you invoke a search, the Search window opens as a floating window. The window can be sized by dragging the lower-right corner out or in to size the width and height.

**FIGURE 6.2**

When you use the Search menu command or the Ctrl/⌘+Shift+F keyboard shortcut, the Search window opens as a floating window.

# Using Exploring basic search options

When the Search window is in view, you type a word or words to be searched for in the field box that appears at the top of the window. You are limited to the actual word(s) you want to find when you perform a simple search. You cannot use Boolean (AND, OR, and NOT) operators or any kind of search expressions if performing a simple search.

## Note

**The area where you type words and phrases to be searched is in the field box following the text "What word or phrase would you like to search for?" in the Search window. Rather than describe this field box by name, the term "first field box" or "search field box" is used throughout this chapter. When you see such a reference, realize it refers to the area where you type words and phrases to be searched. ■**

If you type more than one word in the search field box, the results are reported for the exact phrase. For example, if you search for "Adobe Acrobat Pro," all the occurrences of "Adobe Acrobat Pro" are reported in the results list. Individual occurrences of Adobe, Acrobat, and Pro are not reported. In other words, you don't need to place phrases within any quotes or special characters to find the results.

In the Search PDF window, you choose where you want to search and the options to narrow the search from the list following the first field box. The following sections describe several choices that are available.

### Deciding where to search

The question presented to you is "Where would you like to search?" Two radio buttons appear where you choose whether to search the current open file or search locally on your hard drive, a network server, or a media storage device attached to your computer such as removable media or CD-ROMs. If you select the second radio button for "All PDF Documents in," you can narrow the search to a directory, drive, or media device by opening the pull-down menu and choosing from the hierarchy of drives and folders appearing in the menu options.

Acrobat also permits you to search through bookmarks and comments as the Find toolbar does. Check boxes appear below the pull-down menu for these items. If bookmarks and comments are to be part of your search, check the respective item(s). After you choose the options you want, click the Search button.

The results appear in the Search window, as shown in Figure 6.3. The total number of found instances for your search is noted at the top of the window, and hot links appear in the scrollable list for the words found in the documents according to the search options you selected. Click any text and the respective document page opens in the Document pane with the first occurrence of the searched word highlighted.

**FIGURE 6.3**

The total number of occurrences in a single PDF or all occurrences in all documents searched is noted at the top of the window and search results are reported in a scrollable list. Click any text in the Results list window to open a page where Search found words matching your criteria.

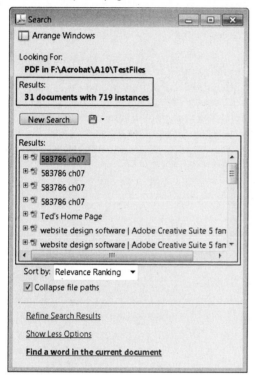

## Navigating search results

Search results are reported in the Search window. Click an item in the list and the respective page opens. You can also find the next and previous results using keyboard shortcuts as follows:

- **Next Document** (Alt/Option+Shift+Right Arrow): Click Next Document to bypass all found instances in the currently viewed file and open the next file listed in the Search results list.

- **Previous Document** (Alt/Option+Shift+Left Arrow): This command offers the opposite response as Next Document — it moves backward through previously viewed documents.

### Stopping a search

When you start a new search, a button appears in the Search window so you can stop the search. Click Stop and the results found prior to stopping are listed in the scrollable list. If you click Stop, you need to search again starting at the beginning of the search to continue. Click the New Search button and the search starts over from the beginning of the file.

### Displaying results

The results list is neatly organized for you in the Search window. If you search the open document, the search results report found words beginning at the front of the document and list occurrences as they are found on following pages. If you search multiple documents, the occurrences are listed in groups according to the individual documents where the words are found. The hierarchy is similar to that of bookmarks. A plus symbol in Windows or a right-pointing arrow in the Mac is shown for each document where results have been found. Click the icon, and the list expands the same way bookmarks and comments expand. The icon changes to a minus symbol in Windows or a down-pointing arrow in the Mac when a list is expanded. Click the icon again to collapse the list.

## Note

You can use Search or the Find toolbar to find words in the open document. Search offers more search criteria options and shows a list of results. As a general rule, using Search is much more efficient than using the Find toolbar. ■

## Cross-Reference

For information on displaying bookmarks, see Chapters 15 and 21. For information on displaying comments, see Chapter 19. ■

### Searching files and folders

If you search through a large collection of PDF files, Search works away loading up the results window. Clicking a link to open a page where results have been found won't interrupt your search. You can browse files while results continue to be reported. To search a hard disk, a media storage device, a network drive, or a folder in any of these locations, open the pull-down menu below All PDF Documents in and select a folder location. The moment you select a folder, the All PDF Documents in radio button is activated.

The pull-down menu lists the drives and servers active on your system. If you want to search a particular folder, select the item denoted as Browse for Location (Windows or Mac) at the bottom of the pull-down menu. The Browse For Folder (Windows) or Browse for Location (Mac) dialog box opens as shown in Figure 6.4. Navigate your hard drive as you would when searching for files to open. When you find the folder to be searched, click the folder name and click OK.

## Tip

When you click a file in the Results window, the Search window becomes hidden by default. If you want to show the Search window after clicking a file in the Results window, click the Arrange Windows button at the top of the Search panel. ∎

After you click OK in the Browse For Folder/Choose a Folder dialog box, the Search window returns. The search does not begin until you click the Search button. Before clicking Search, you can examine the name listed as the target folder. The selected folder is displayed in the Search window by folder name. If all looks as you expect, click Search.

**FIGURE 6.4**

Select the folder to be searched in the Browse For Folder (Windows) or Browse for Location (Mac) dialog box. Select the folder name and click OK (Windows) or Choose (Mac) to return to the Search window.

# Searching PDFs on the Internet

In Acrobat 6, we had Search the Internet using Google in the Search window and as a separate tool. In Acrobat 7, we had Search the Internet using Yahoo! in the Search window and as a separate tool. In Acrobat 8 we had nothing, and nothing in regard to searching the Internet using these search engines appeared in Acrobat 9. The ability to search files on the Internet from a click in the Search window was removed in all Acrobat 8 viewers.

At first glance, you may get a bit annoyed that you lost this feature in Acrobat and Reader. I can't give you a precise reason for the feature disappearing in Acrobat, but my hunch is that the problem lies more with the Web browser developers than it does with Adobe. It may be that Adobe just can't keep up with changes made by other developers when revisions are made to the browsers. Doing so may be cost prohibitive, and the functionality can easily be lost during an Acrobat version life cycle when developers upgrade their products.

For whatever reason we lost the ability to click a link in the Search window to search for PDFs on the Internet, you can still perform this kind of search. Using a search engine such as

Google, just type your search word or phrase in the Search text box in the Google search engine, add a space, and then type **filetype:PDF.** For example if you want to search for Acrobat 8 and have only PDFs reported in your search results, type **"Acrobat" filetype:PDF**. The Google search results report only PDF documents containing your search phrase.

Not all search engines support the extension for searching for PDFs. If you use Yahoo! or Ask. com, for example, you can't use the extension. However, Yahoo! provides you with Advanced Search options. In Yahoo! click the Options pull-down menu and choose Advanced Search. The next page that opens provides you with options for choosing a file type such as PDF.

In some cases, advanced search options in search engines can help you narrow a search to report PDFs with the found results. Check your favorite search engine for advanced options to see if searching PDFs is supported.

## Using additional criteria to define your search

In Acrobat viewers prior to Acrobat X, we had Basic Search Options and Advanced Search Options. In Acrobat X, Basic Search Options are not available. By default, using Acrobat Search displays additional criteria you can use to refine your search as shown in Figure 6.5.

Depending on whether you search an open PDF document or a collection of PDFs stored on drives and external devices, the Advanced Search Options change, offering you different options.

**FIGURE 6.5**

Acrobat Search by default offers options for searching additional criteria.

## Searching an open PDF file

When you select the Current PDF Document from the Look In pull-down menu, the search options shown in Figure 6.5 are available to you. These options are as follows:

- **Whole words only.** When checked, the search results return whole words. If you search for *forgiven*, the search ignores words like *for* and *give* that make up part of the whole word. If the check box is disabled, various stems and parts of a whole word are included with the search results.

- **Case-Sensitive.** Letter case is ignored if the check box is disabled. If enabled, then the search results return only words matching the precise letter case of the searched word.

- **Proximity.** Proximity is a powerful tool when performing searches. If you want to search for two independent words that may appear together in a given context — for example, *Acrobat* and *PostScript* — the Proximity option finds the two words when they appear within a range specified in the Search preferences. The default is 900 words. You can change the proximity range by opening the Preferences dialog box (Ctrl/⌘+K), clicking Search in the left pane, and editing the Range of words for Proximity searches text box.

- **Stemming.** If you want to search for all words stemming from a given word, enable this option. Words such as *header* and *heading* stem from the word *head* in the English language. If you type *head* in the first field box and select the Stemming option, all PDFs containing the search criteria from the word *head* are listed.

- **Include Bookmarks.** When Bookmarks are checked, the search results report the found instances in the bookmarks and the document pages.

- **Include Comments.** Text in comment notes and text on document pages are returned when this option is checked.

- **Include Attachments.** All document file attachments are searchable including file types other than PDF. Select the Include Attachments check box and found results are reported in the Results list for all occurrences of the searched word. Clicking a search result opens the attached file in the Document pane.

If you open a PDF Portfolio, the Search window changes to accommodate searching all files in the package. Select from the Look In pull-down menu and choose In the entire PDF Portfolio and Search will search all files in the package.

You can search PDF Portfolios using either the Basic search options or the Advanced search options. When searching package contents using Basic search options select the radio button for In the entire PDF Portfolio, as shown in Figure 6.6. When using the Advanced options, select In the entire PDF Portfolio from the Look In pull-down menu. Note that both these items are accessible only when you open a PDF Portfolio.

# Cross-Reference

For more information on working with PDF Portfolios, see Chapter 11. ■

**FIGURE 6.6**

Select In the entire PDF Portfolio to search all files in the package.

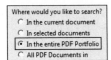

When all the search criteria have been established, click the Search button. The results are reported in the Search window like the searches performed with the Basic Search Options.

### Changing option to search multiple PDFs

When you change the search parameters to search through a collection of PDF documents, the Search Options change, offering you more options to help narrow down your search, as shown in Figure 6.7.

**FIGURE 6.7**

Advanced Search Options offer you additional criteria when searching through multiple PDF documents.

These options are as follows:

- **Return results containing.** Four return result options are available from this pull-down menu:

  - **Match Exact word or phrase.** If you search for something like *Human Resource Forms*, only these three words together in a PDF document are returned as results. The results report the precise order of the words.

  - **Match Any of the words.** Using the same example, words such as *Human, Resource, Forms, Human Resource, Resource Forms, Human Forms,* and *Human Resource Forms* would be reported in the results. Any one of the words or any combination of words in a phrase is reported.

  - **Match All of the words.** In this case, all the words need to be contained in the document, but not necessarily in the order described previously. You might see returns such as Forms Human Resource returned from the search.

  - **Boolean query.** You can search PDF collections using Boolean expressions (AND, OR, NOT) without the assistance of a search index created with Acrobat Catalog. Note that Boolean queries are not available when you search an open document. You need to use the Advanced Search Options to search through a drive, external media, or a folder.

## Cross-Reference

For more detail on using Boolean queries, see the "Using Boolean queries" section later in this chapter. For more information on Acrobat Catalog, see the section "Creating Search Indexes (Acrobat Pro Only)" later in this chapter. ■

- **Use these additional criteria.** Up to three check boxes offer you one or a combination of several different options to help you refine your search. The number of check boxes you have available depends on the vertical size of the Search window. If you reduce the size, you may see only a single check box, as shown in Figure 6.8.

  From the first pull-down menu you select the primary category. The second pull-down menu to the right of each primary category helps refine that particular category. The options for each of the three check box pull-down menus are the same. You might, for example, choose Date Created from the first check box option and define the date from the options contained in the adjacent pull-down menu. You then might add another criterion and ask for the Keywords option. Adjacent to Keywords, you might specify that the file does not contain certain words. In the field box, you type any descriptions for the menu choices you make.

## Note

All the preceding items require that you supply at least one character in "What word or phrase would you like to search for?" The options that follow enable you to search for specific content related to the option of choice, and you do not need to supply a word in the first field box in order to execute a search. When you move around adjusting criteria, the Search button appears active or grayed out. If it is grayed out, you can't perform a search on the options you chose. In some cases, the missing option is a word or phrase that needs to be added to the first field box. ■

From the criteria selection pull-down menu, the choices available to you are as follows:

- **Date Created.** If you look for PDF documents that you know were created before or after a certain date, use the Date Created menu option. You have four choices for options associated with this category available in the second pull-down menu adjacent to the first menu choice. These options are: Is exactly, Is before, Is after, and Is not. These four options are self-explanatory. When you make the choices from the two pull-down menus, your next step is to type the date criteria in the field box appearing below the pull-down menus. If, for example, you select Date Created and Is not, you then add the date you want to exclude from the search. As an additional aid to you, Acrobat offers a calendar when you select the pull-down menu from the field box, as shown in Figure 6.8 (Windows only). Make a date selection from the calendar and move to the option you want to change or click the Search button. If you click the month, a pop-up menu showing all months in a year opens. (Note that the calendar is not available on the Mac.)

### FIGURE 6.8

After setting the date criteria from the pull-down menus, open the pull-down menu from the field box to open a calendar to help you find the date parameters to be searched. Click the month name and a pop-up menu opens showing all months in a year.

- **Date Modified.** The modified date searches for the date the PDF file was last modified. If you create a file on January 1, 2004 and then save some edits on July 1, 2004, the modified date is July 1, 2004. The manner in which you specify a date is the same as searching for the creation date.

- **Author.** The information is derived from the Document Properties in the Description tab. Any data typed in the Author field is searched. This choice and the remaining options offer two menu options in the second pull-down menu. You can select from Contains or Does not contain. In essence, your search includes or excludes the data you supply in the field box immediately following the pull-down menu choices.

## Cross-Reference

**For information related to document descriptions, see the "Understanding Document Descriptions" section later in this chapter. ∎**

- **Title.** Same as the Author search except the Title field is used in the document description.

- **Subject.** Same as the Author search except the Subject field is used in the document description.

- **Filename.** The name you provide for the PDF document is searched.

- **Keywords.** Same as the Author search except the Keywords field is used in the document description.

- **Bookmarks.** When you select this option, Acrobat searches for the words in both the PDF document and in bookmarks. The results list includes the found words in both bookmarks and pages.

- **Comments.** Same as Bookmarks, but the comment notes are searched. The results report the found words appearing in comment notes.

- **JPEG Images.** Narrows the search for files meeting the search text criteria and where JPEG images are contained within the PDF.

- **XMP Metadata.** Searches for words or phrases contained in the document metadata.

- **Object Data.** Certain images contain metadata created from an original authoring application, such as MS Visio, Microsoft Project, and AutoDesk AutoCAD. Select an object with the Object Data tool and click. The metadata information displayed in the Object Data dialog box is searchable as well as the data contained in the Object Data dialog box. If you know certain attributes for images contained in a file, you can narrow your search by searching the object metadata.

## Cross-Reference

For more information on XMP and object metadata, see "Searching metadata" later in this chapter. ■

Below the Use These Additional Criteria pull-down menu options are additional options. These options are the same as those used for the advanced searches on open PDF documents. Jump several pages back in this book to review the descriptions for the items listed at the bottom of the Search window.

### Searching dates

To help you target the precise date with the field box and the calendar, Acrobat offers you several options. To change the year, you can edit the field box and type the year for the date to be searched. In the field box, you can change dates by clicking the day, month, and year, and then use the up or down arrow keys to scroll dates. The dates revolve like an odometer. Select a day, and then click the month to highlight the value and press the arrow keys again until you find the correct month. Move to the year and follow the same steps to select the correct year. You can also select any one of the three values and type new values you want to search for when the text is selected. The text you type replaces all selected text. Acrobat accepts only a legitimate value, so if you type a value not permitted for a date search — for example, entering 33 in the day field — Acrobat will not accept it.

To change dates with the calendar, click the down arrow in the pull-down menu adjacent to the date in the field box to open the calendar. For a month change, left-click on the month name in the title bar of the calendar. For example, if July appears listed in the title bar, click July. Be careful not to left-click the mouse below the title bar because doing so selects a day and closes the calendar. When you left-click on the month name in the title bar, a pop-up menu displays the months of the year. Move the cursor to the desired month and left-click again.

## Note

**You can also change months by scrolling the calendar backward or forward. Click the left arrow in the title bar to scroll backward or the right arrow to scroll forward. As you reach a year beginning or end, the next month in date order is opened. For example, scrolling backward from January 1996 opens December 1995.** ■

When you click to select the desired month, Acrobat leaves the calendar view open so you can still make the year and day selections. To change the year in the calendar, left-click on the year in the title bar. The year becomes visible as editable text. You can edit the field or click the up or down arrows.

After you select the month and year, left-click on the desired day from the calendar displayed below the title bar. Acrobat supplies the new date in the field box, as shown in Figure 6.9, and closes the calendar.

### FIGURE 6.9

Change the date for the calendar and the new date is shown while the current date is reported at the bottom of the calendar.

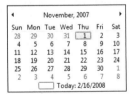

### *Searching metadata*

The ability to search a document's metadata is a powerful tool in Acrobat. In order to use the tool, you need to know just a little bit about what *metadata* is.

Adobe Acrobat 5.0 and later contain metadata in XML (eXtensible Markup Language) format. In Acrobat 7 through X, object metadata are accessible. The metadata of a file or an image is information related to the document structure, origination, content, interchange, and processing. Metadata might include, for example, the document author's name, the creation date, modified date, the PDF producer, copyright information on images, color space on images, and more. When you click Search, the search results report all files where the searched words are contained in a document's metadata.

XMP (eXtensible Metadata Platform) is an XML framework that provides all Adobe programs a common language for communicating standards related to document creation and processing throughout publishing workflows. XMP is a format, and document metadata viewed in XML source code can be exported to XMP format. Once in XMP, it can be exchanged between documents.

To take a look at the XML source code of the XMP metadata for a document, choose File ⇨ Properties and click the Description tab. In the Description tab click on Additional Metadata to open the dialog box shown in Figure 6.10. Click Advanced and expand the listed items by clicking the symbol adjacent to each listed item.

**FIGURE 6.10**

To see document metadata, click the Additional Metadata button in the Description Properties dialog box.

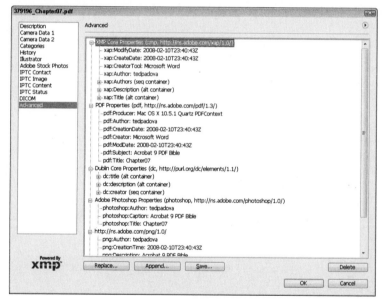

At the bottom of the dialog box are buttons used for replacing, appending, saving, and deleting data. Click Save to export the XMP data that can be shared in workflows across many different file types. For the purposes of searching information, any of the text you see in the source code in the Advanced list can be searched.

## Searching layers

The search criteria discussed on the preceding pages works for documents containing layers. When you invoke a search in documents containing layers, Search automatically searches through all layers for the criteria you specify in the Search window. The results list contains items on any hidden layers as well as all visible layers. When you click a result associated with a hidden layer, Acrobat prompts you in a dialog box, as shown in Figure 6.11, asking whether you want to make the layer visible.

**FIGURE 6.11**

If searched words are found on hidden layers, Acrobat asks whether you want to make the hidden layer visible.

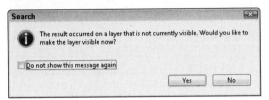

If you click Yes in the dialog box, the layer is made visible and the search stops at the found word. If you select No, the layer remains hidden and you are taken to the next search result.

### Using Boolean queries

The Return results containing pull-down menu in the Search PDF window contains a Boolean query menu option for searching with Boolean expressions. Boolean expressions include AND, OR, and NOT. Acrobat recognizes these Boolean operators when you invoke a search. You can use all the previously listed criteria when you want to use the Boolean expressions option.

To search with Boolean expressions you need to search an index file. Boolean operators are not recognized when searching the current open document or when browsing folders.

## Cross-Reference

For more on searching indexes, see the section "Creating Search Indexes (Acrobat Pro Only)" later in this chapter. ■

- **AND operator.** Use AND between two words to find documents that contain both terms, in any order. For example, type Paris AND France to identify documents that contain both Paris and France. Searches with AND and no other Boolean operators produce the same results as selecting the All Of The Words option.

## Note

When using Boolean operators, the text is not case-sensitive. Uppercase letters for the Boolean expressions are used here to denote a Boolean operator as opposed to text. You can use lowercase letters and the results are reported the same, as long as the Boolean query pull-down menu item is selected. ■

- **OR operator.** Use to search for all instances of either term. For example, type email OR email to find all documents with occurrences of either spelling. Searches with OR and no other Boolean operators produce the same results as selecting the Any Of The Words option.

- **^ (exclusive OR).** Use to search for all instances that have either term but not both. For example, type **cat ^ dog** to find all documents with occurrences of either cat or dog but not both cat and dog.

- **().** Use parentheses to specify the order of evaluation of terms. For example, type **white AND (whale OR Ahab)** to find all documents that contain either white and whale or white and Ahab. The query processor performs an OR query on whale and Ahab and then performs an AND query on those results with white.

- **NOT operator.** Use before a search term to exclude any documents that contain that term. For example, type **NOT Kentucky** to find all documents that don't contain the word Kentucky. Or, type **Paris NOT Kentucky** to find all documents that contain the word Paris but not the word Kentucky.

- **Multiple words.** Words appearing together such as "Acrobat PDF" can be included in quotes. You would supply "Acrobat PDF" in the field box (include the quotes) and all instances where these two words appear together are reported in the search results. If the words are not contained within quotes, the words *Acrobat*, *PDF*, and *Acrobat PDF* would all be returned in the search results. This behavior is similar to how you perform searches in Web browsers.

- **Searching and, or, not.** If you want to search for a term where these three words are part of the term, you can by distinguishing between words you search for and using operators. To search for something like *Ben and Jerry's* as a term, you would type **"Ben and Jerry's"** within quote marks. If you want to search for two terms and a Boolean operator you might use **"Ben and Jerry's" AND "Ice Cream" NOT yogurt**. The results report back to you the documents where the words *Ben and Jerry's* and *ice cream* are contained in the files and the words *Ben and Jerry's yogurt* are not reported in the search results.

## Tip

To learn more about searching with Boolean operators, search the Internet using Boolean searches as your search criteria in any search engine. ■

### Exploring Search preferences

To open preference settings for Search, choose Edit ➪ Preferences (Windows) or Acrobat Preferences (Mac). In the left pane, select Search. The preference options available to you are shown in Figure 6.12.

**FIGURE 6.12**

Choose Edit ➪ Preferences to open the Preferences dialog box. Click Search in the list at the left to display preference settings for using Search.

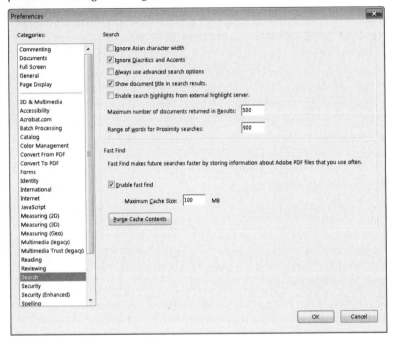

The preference choices listed on the right side of the dialog box are as follows:

- **Ignore Asian character width.** This setting ignores Asian character width and finds both half-width and full-width instances of Asian language characters.

- **Ignore Diacritics and Accents.** A diacritic is an accent mark like you might use on a word such as *resumé* or the cedilla on a word such as *façade* to indicate a special phonetic value. These and other accents are ignored during a search unless you check the box; so for example, if you have it checked Acrobat will find both *resume* and *resumé*. If it is unchecked, Search looks for *resumé* only.

- **Always use advanced search options.** Sets the Advanced Search Options as the default. When the check box is enabled you don't need to keep clicking the Use Advanced Search Options button in the Search window. Enable this setting if you find yourself always using the Advanced Search Options.

- **Maximum number of documents returned in Results.** The acceptable range is between 1 and 10,000. Enter a value and the results are limited to this number.

- **Range of words for proximity searches.** When using Boolean operators, you might want to search for two words within a defined range of words. You can enter a value between 1 and 10,000. Both words need to be within the range when you use a Boolean expression such as AND.

- **Enable fast find.** Searches are logged by Acrobat in a memory cache. If you perform a search and later in another session perform a search on the same information, Acrobat returns to the cache for the information, thus speeding up the search. You can edit the cache size by editing the field box for the number of megabytes on your hard drive you want to allocate to the cache. Be certain you have ample hard drive space when enabling the cache and raising the cache size.

- **Purge Cache Contents.** The cache occupies as much memory as is available on your hard drive. If you want to clear the cache, click the button to erase all the contents.

After changing any settings in the Preferences dialog box, click OK. The changes you make are dynamically reflected in Acrobat and take effect the next time you perform a search.

# Understanding Document Descriptions

Document descriptions are user-supplied data fields used to help you identify PDF files according to title, subject, author, and keywords. At the time you create a PDF document, you may have options for supplying a document description. In other cases, you may add descriptions in Acrobat either individually or with Acrobat's batch processing features.

## Cross-Reference
To learn how to create batch sequences, see Chapter 17. ■

After you add descriptions and save your files, the data added to these fields is searchable via advanced searches and index file searches. Developing an organized workflow with specific guidelines for users to follow regarding document descriptions significantly helps all your colleagues search PDFs much more efficiently.

To add a document description, choose File ⇨ Properties. When the Document Properties dialog box opens, click the Description tab, as shown in Figure 6.13.

The four fields for document descriptions are as follows:

- **Title.** The Title field in this example contains a description of a form. Other forms in a company using a similar schema might use titles such as W-2 Form, Travel Expense, Employee Leave, and so on in the Title field.

- **Author.** In the example, the Author field contains the department authoring the form. Notice that an employee name is not used for the Author field. Rather than use employee names, use departments instead. Using departments is a much better choice because a company typically turns over employees more often than it renames departments.

- **Subject.** In the example, the Subject field contains Form. The Subject here might be used to distinguish a Form from a Policy, Procedure, Memo, Directive, and so on.

- **Keywords.** The first entry in the Keywords field is the form number used by the company to identify the form. Other words in the Keywords field are descriptors related to the form contents. If you want to add an employee author name, add it to the Keywords field.

**FIGURE 6.13**

You add document descriptions to the Description tab in the Document Properties dialog box.

## Tip

Notice the Location item in the Document Properties. The text reports the location on your hard drive where the file is located. This text is a link. Click the text and your file is opened on the Desktop (Finder on Mac) showing you the folder location. ∎

The reason the field information is important for any organization using a PDF workflow is that document description information can be used when someone searches a collection of

PDF files. Each field is searchable by the summary title and the words contained in the fields. Therefore, a user can search for all PDF files where the Title field contains the word *Purchase* and the Subject field contains the word *Form*. The search results display all PDF documents where the Title and Subject fields have these words contained in the document description.

As a comparison, imagine searching for the words *Purchase Order*. The search would return all PDFs where these words appear in either the document summary or the text in the PDF files. *Purchase Order* might be used in memos, policies, procedures, and forms. The user might have to search through many PDFs in order to find the Purchase Order form, thus spending much more time trying to locate the right document.

## Searching document descriptions

To search for document descriptions, you need to use either the advanced search or an index file search. Press Ctrl/⌘+Shift+F to open the Search window in an Acrobat viewer and click Use Advanced Search Options. Select a folder to search from the Look In pull-down menu.

### Cross-Reference

For searching index files, see the section "Searching an index" later in this chapter. ■

Under Use these additional criteria, select one of the description items from the first pull-down menu (Title, Author, Subject, or Keywords). Select either Contains or Does not contain from the pull-down menu adjacent to the first menu. Type the words to be searched in the field box below the pull-down menus. Continue adding additional description fields as desired. In Figure 6.14, two description fields are marked for the search.

---

**FIGURE 6.14**

---

Two description fields are identified. When you click the Search button, Acrobat searches the document descriptions for matches.

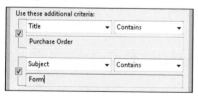

Note that no criteria need to be supplied in the first field box for specific words to be searched in the document. If you click Search in the Search window with the descriptions shown in Figure 6.14, all PDF files in the designated folder with the words *Purchase Order* in the Title field and *Forms* in the Subject field are returned in the results list for files matching the criteria.

## Using document descriptions and Boolean queries

You can add Boolean queries when searching document descriptions. You might know some content in PDF files as well as information contained in the document descriptions. In this case you address the additional criteria items in the same manner and add the Boolean query as discussed earlier in this chapter. In Figure 6.15, document descriptions are added to a Boolean query.

**FIGURE 6.15**

You can add Boolean queries to searches with additional criteria selections such as document descriptions.

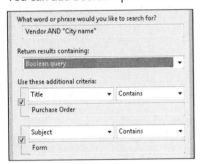

When you click the Search button, the number of results returned in the Search window is significantly reduced compared to searching for individual words — especially when common words are contained in many PDF documents. What the document descriptions offer you is a method for targeting the exact file you're looking for as fast as possible. If you have 100 PDF documents in the search results list, looking through the list and finding the file you want will take some time. Compare that to two or three files listed. Obviously, the document descriptions offer significant time savings as you search PDFs from among very large collections.

# Comparing Full-Text and Index Searches

This section represents a pivotal point in this chapter. What has been covered so far is information about finding content in PDF documents with a very elaborate *find* feature in Acrobat. The name used in Acrobat to refer to what has been discussed so far is "Search." Users of earlier versions of Acrobat may take this to mean using Acrobat Search as it was used in Acrobat viewers earlier than version 6.0. What has been covered thus far, however, is a Search of data files that was greatly improved in Acrobat version 6 and became more powerful in returning results in Acrobat version 8. To understand the difference between the preceding pages and what follows requires a little explanation.

In addition to full-text searches for documents, you can also create a separate index file and search one or more indexes at a time. Index files provide some benefit in that they are quite faster than full-text searches, can be automatically assigned to PDF documents in the Advanced tab in the Document Properties, and can be automatically loaded from a CD-ROM, and multiple indexes can be searched, so files can be scattered on your hard drive in different folders.

# Using Search Index Procedures

I explain the details for working with search indexes in the remaining pages in this chapter. To provide you with an overall summary for how index file creation and management is dealt with in Acrobat, I give you a short summary of the procedures here.

Using index files to perform searches begins with using a current index file or creating a new one. Users who have been working with index files need to make sure that all their previous indexes are updated for compatibility with Acrobat X viewers.

Index files are created and updated with Acrobat Catalog with Acrobat Pro only. Catalog is available in the Document Processing panel. Open the panel and click Full Text Index with Catalog. You open Catalog and make a decision for creating a new index or opening an existing index file for rebuilding or editing in the Catalog window.

After an index file is created or updated, you load the index file into the Search window. Multiple index files can be loaded and searched. When you search index files, the results are reported in the Search window like all the searches discussed earlier in this chapter.

Earlier releases of Acrobat offered you options for various menu selections related to managing indexes and loading new index files. Earlier releases of Acrobat also offered you dialog boxes where results were reported and information about an index file could be obtained. In Acrobat 6.0 and above viewers, you handle all your index file management in the Search window. Menu commands are limited to viewing search results as described earlier in this chapter.

If you edit PDF documents, delete them, or add new documents to folders that have been indexed, you need to rebuild index files periodically. You can purge old data and re-index files in Acrobat Catalog. Index files can be copied to different hard drive locations, across servers, and to external media. When copying files, you need to copy all files and folders associated with the index file. Failure to copy all the files renders the index inoperable.

# Creating Search Indexes (Acrobat Pro Only)

In order to search an index file, you must have one present on your computer, network server, some media storage device, or embedded in a PDF. When you install an Acrobat viewer, a help index file is included during your installation. You can use this file to search for words contained in any of the help documents. If you want to search your own files, you need to create an index. To create an index file, you use Acrobat Catalog.

## Note

**Acrobat Catalog is available only in Acrobat Pro and Acrobat Pro Extended. Search indexes can be used by all Acrobat viewers including Adobe Reader. ■**

To launch Acrobat Catalog from within Acrobat Pro, open the Document Processing panel and click Full Text Index with Catalog. Catalog is robust and provides many options for creating and modifying indexes. After a search index is created, any user can access the search index in all Acrobat viewers to find words using the Search window. However, before you begin to work with Acrobat Catalog, you need to take some preliminary steps to be certain all your files are properly prepared and ready to be indexed.

## Preparing PDFs for indexing

Preparation involves creating PDFs with all the necessary information to facilitate searches. All searchable document description information needs to be supplied in the PDF documents at the time of PDF creation or by modifying PDFs in Acrobat before you begin working with Catalog. For workgroups and multiple user access to search indexes, this information needs to be clear and consistent. Other factors, such as naming conventions, location of files, and optimizing performance should all be thought out and planned prior to creating an index file.

## Note

**Adding document descriptions is not a requirement for creating search indexes. You can index files without any information in the document description fields. Adding document descriptions merely adds more relevant information to your PDF documents and aids users in finding search results faster. ■**

### Creating document descriptions

Document description information should be supplied in all PDF files to be searched. As discussed earlier in this chapter, all document description data are searchable. Spending time creating document descriptions and defining the field types for consistent organization will facilitate searches performed by multiple users.

The first of the planning steps is to develop a flowchart or outline of company information and the documents to be categorized. This organization may or may not be implemented where you intend to develop a PDF workflow. If your information flow is already in place, you may need to make some modifications to coordinate nomenclature and document identity with the document summary items in Acrobat.

Document descriptions contained in the Title, Subject, Author, and Keywords fields should be consistent and intuitive. They should also follow a hierarchy consistent with the company's organizational structure and workflow. The document summary items should be mapped out and defined. When preparing files for indexing, consider the following:

- **Title.** Title information might be thought of as the root of an outline — the parent statement, if you will. Descriptive titles should be used to help users narrow searches within specific categories. The Title field can also be used to display the title name at the top of the Acrobat window when you select viewing titles in the Initial View properties.

## Cross-Reference

For information on how to set document title attributes in the Initial View dialog box, see Chapter 5. ∎

- **Author.** Avoid using proper names for the Author field. Personnel change in companies and roles among employees change. Identify the author of PDF documents according to departments, work groups, facilities, and so on.

- **Subject.** If the Title field is the parent item in an outline format, the Subject would be a child item nested directly below the title. Subjects might be considered subsets of titles. When creating document summaries, be consistent. Don't use subject and title or subject and keyword information back and forth with different documents. If an item, such as employee grievances, is listed as a Subject in some PDFs and then listed as a Title in other documents, the end users will become confused with the order and searches will become unnecessarily complicated.

- **Keywords.** If you have a forms identification system in place, be certain to use form numbers and identity as part of the Keywords field. You might start the Keywords field with a form number and then add additional keywords to help narrow searches. Be consistent and always start the Keywords field with forms or document numbers. If you need to have PDF author names, add them here in the Keywords fields. If employees change roles or leave the company, the Author fields still provide the information relative to a department.

To illustrate some examples, take a look at Table 6.1.

## Tip

Legacy PDF files used in an organization may have been created without a document description, or you may reorganize PDFs and want to change document summaries. To quickly (or efficiently) update these documents, you can create a batch sequence to change multiple PDF files and then run the sequence. Place your PDFs in a folder where the document summaries are to be edited. In the Edit Sequence dialog box, select the items to change and edit each document summary item. Run the sequence to update an entire folder of PDFs. ∎

## Cross-Reference

For more information on creating batch sequences, see Chapter 17. ∎

**TABLE 6.1**

## Document Summary Examples

| Title | Author | Subject | Keywords |
|-------|--------|---------|----------|
| Descriptive Titles Titles may be considered specific to workgroup tasks. | Department Names Don't use employee names in organizations; employees change, departments usually remain. | Subsection of Title Subjects may be thought of as child outline items nested below the parent Title items — a subset of the Titles. | Document numbers and random identifiers You can supply Forms ID numbers, internal filing numbers, and so on in the Keyword fields. If employee names are a *must* for your company, add employee names in the Keywords field box. List any related words to help find the topic. |
| Employee Policies | Human Resources | Vacation Leave | D-101, HR32A, H. Jones, policy, employee regulations |
| FDA Compliance | Quality Assurance | Software Validation | SOP-114, QA-182, J. Wilson, regulations, citations, eye implant device |
| Curriculum | English Department | American Literature | Plan 2010, Martha Evans, senior English, Emerson High, 11th grade |
| Receivables | Accounting | Collection Policy | F-8102, M-5433, Finance, collections, payments |
| eCommerce | Marketing | Products | M-1051, e-117A, golf clubs, sports, leisure |

# Managing Multiple PDF Documents

Books, reports, and manuals can be broken up into separate files and structured in a way that it still appears to the end user as a single document. Assuming a user reads through a file in a linear fashion, you can create links to open and close pages without user intervention. Create navigational buttons to move forward and back through document pages. On the last page of each chapter, use the navigation button to open the next chapter. Also on the last page of each chapter, create a Page action that closes the current document when the page is closed. (See Chapter 22 for creating links and Page actions.) If the end user disables "Open cross-document links in same window" in the Documents category in the Preferences dialog box, the open file still closes after the last page is closed. All the chapters can be linked from a table of contents where any chapter can be opened. If you give your design some thought, browsing the contents of books will appear to the end user no different than reading a book in the analog world.

## Understanding file structure

The content, filenames, and location of PDFs to be cataloged contribute to file structure items. All the issues related to file structure must be thought out and appropriately designed for the audience that you intend to support. The important considerations are as follows:

- **File naming conventions.** Names provided for the PDF files are critical for distributing documents among users. If filenames get truncated, then either Acrobat Search or the end user will have difficulty finding a document when performing a search. This is of special concern to Mac users who want to distribute documents across platforms. The best precaution is to always use standard DOS file-naming conventions. The standard eight-character maximum filename, with no more than three-character file extensions (`filename.ext`), will always work regardless of platform.

- **Folder names.** Folder names should follow the same conventions as filenames. Mac users who want to keep filenames longer than standard DOS names must limit folder names to eight characters and no more than a three-character file extension for cross-platform compliance.

- **File and folder name identity.** In previous versions of Acrobat and Acrobat Catalog you had to avoid using ASCII characters from 133 to 159 for any filename or folder name. Acrobat Catalog in earlier versions did not support some extended characters in this range, and you could experience problems when using files across platforms. (Figure 6.16 lists the characters we used to have to avoid.) In Acrobat 8 through X, with more support for non-English languages and full Unicode characters, you don't need to be worried about file and folder identity that use special characters.

- **Folder organization.** Folders to be cataloged should have a logical hierarchy. Copy all files to be cataloged to a single folder or a single folder with nested folders in the same path. When nesting folders, be certain to keep the number of nested folders to a minimum. Deeply nested folders slow down searches, and path names longer than 256 characters create problems.

---

**FIGURE 6.16**

Extended characters from ASCII 133 to ASCII 159 used to be a problem when using Acrobat Catalog. In Acrobat 8 through X you'll find support for creating index files and searching files and folders containing these characters.

| 133 | à | 139 | ï | 144 | É | 149 | ò | 154 | Ü |
| 134 | å | 140 | î | 145 | æ | 150 | û | 156 | £ |
| 135 | ç | 141 | ì | 146 | Æ | 151 | ù | 157 | ¥ |
| 136 | ê | 142 | Ä | 147 | ô | 152 | ¨ | 158 | ¯ |
| 137 | ë | 143 | Å | 148 | ö | 153 | Ö | 159 | ƒ |
| 138 | è | | | | | | | | |

- **Folder locations.** Windows users must keep the location of folders on a local hard drive or a network server volume. Although Mac users can catalog information across computer workstations, creating separate indexes for files contained on separate drives would be advisable. Any files moved to different locations make searches inoperable.

- **PDF structure.** File and folder naming should be handled before creating links and attaching files. If filenames are changed after the PDF structure has been developed, many links become inoperable. Be certain to complete all editing in the PDF documents before cataloging files.

### Optimizing performance

Searches can be performed very fast if you take a little time in creating the proper structure and organization. If you don't avoid some pitfalls with the way that you organize files, then searches perform much slower. A few considerations to be made include the following:

- **Optimize PDF files.** Optimization should be performed on all PDF files as one of the last steps in your workflow. Use the Save As optimizes for Fast Web View found in the General category in the Preferences dialog box and run the PDF Optimizer located in the Advanced menu (Acrobat Pro and Acrobat Pro Extended only). Optimization is especially important for searches to be performed from CD-ROM files.

## Cross-Reference

**For information on PDF Optimizer, see Chapter 17.** ■

- **Break up long PDF files.** Books, reports, essays, and other documents that contain many pages should be broken up into multiple PDF files. If you have books to be cataloged, break up the books into separate chapters. Acrobat Search runs much faster when finding information from several small files. It slows down when searching through long documents.

## Tip

**If you have a single document such as a book you want to distribute on CD-ROM, you can embed an index file in the PDF. (See "Working with Embedded Index Files" later in this chapter.)** ■

### Creating search help

You can have multiple indexes for various uses and different workgroups. Personnel may use one index for department matters, another for company-wide information, and perhaps another for a research library. In a search, all relevant keywords will appear from indexes loaded in the Index Selection dialog box. When using multiple indexes, employees may forget the structure of document summaries and what index is needed for a given search.

You can create README files and index help files to store key information about what search words can be used to find document summaries. You can create a single PDF file, text files, or multiple files that serve as help. Figure 6.17 shows an example of a PDF help file that might be used to find documents related to a company's personnel policies, procedures, and forms.

## FIGURE 6.17

A PDF help file can assist users in knowing what keywords they need to use for the Title, Subject, Author, and Keywords fields.

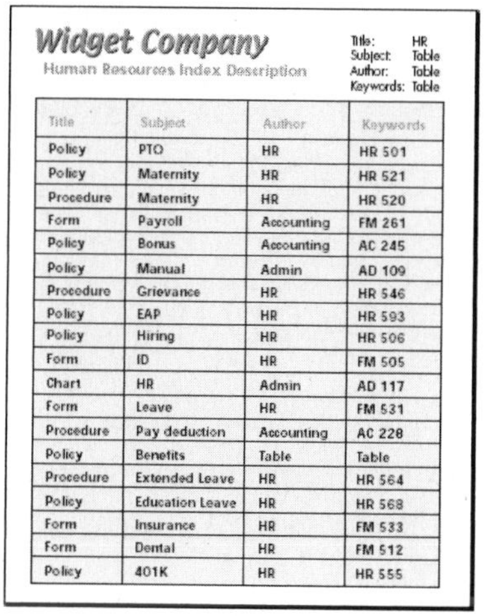

**Widget Company**
Human Resources Index Description

| Title: | HR |
| Subject: | Table |
| Author: | Table |
| Keywords: | Table |

| Title | Subject | Author | Keywords |
|---|---|---|---|
| Policy | PTO | HR | HR 501 |
| Policy | Maternity | HR | HR 521 |
| Procedure | Maternity | HR | HR 520 |
| Form | Payroll | Accounting | FM 261 |
| Policy | Bonus | Accounting | AC 245 |
| Policy | Manual | Admin | AD 109 |
| Procedure | Grievance | HR | HR 546 |
| Policy | EAP | HR | HR 593 |
| Policy | Hiring | HR | HR 506 |
| Form | ID | HR | FM 505 |
| Chart | HR | Admin | AD 117 |
| Form | Leave | HR | FM 531 |
| Procedure | Pay deduction | Accounting | AC 228 |
| Policy | Benefits | Table | Table |
| Procedure | Extended Leave | HR | HR 564 |
| Policy | Education Leave | HR | HR 568 |
| Form | Insurance | HR | FM 533 |
| Form | Dental | HR | FM 512 |
| Policy | 401K | HR | HR 555 |

In the top-right corner of Figure 6.17, the document summary for the help file is listed. The Title fields for this company are broken into categories for policies, procedures, forms, and charts. The Subject fields break down the title categories into specific personnel items, and the Author fields contain the department that authored the documents. Form numbers appear for all Keywords fields.

## Tip

When creating help files that guide a user for searching document information, use a common identifier in the Subject, Author, and Keywords fields reserved for finding only help files. In Figure 6.17, the identifier is "Table." Whenever a user searches for the word table in the Author field, the only returns in the Search Results dialog box will be help files. When using the Title and Author field together, a user can find a specific help file for a given department. In the previous example, the Title is HR and the Author is Table. When these words are searched for the document information, the help file for the HR department is returned in the Search Results. If you reserve keywords for the document Summary fields, any employee can easily find information by remembering only a few keywords. ■

## Creating a new index file

After your files are optimized and saved in final form, it's time to create the search index. Open the Document Processing panel and click Full Text Index with Catalog to open the Catalog dialog box, as shown in Figure 6.18. In the dialog box, you make choices for creating a new index file or opening an existing index file. Click the New Index button to create a new index file.

**FIGURE 6.18**

Click the New Index button in the Catalog dialog box to create an index file.

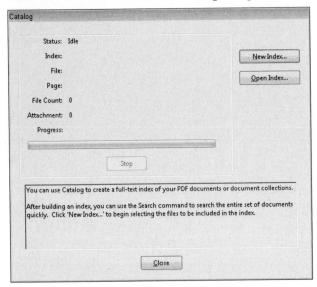

The New Index Definition dialog box shown in Figure 6.19 opens, in which you set specific attributes for your index and determine what folder(s) are to be indexed.

### Creating an index title

The title that you place in this field is a title for the index, but not necessarily the name of the file you ultimately save. The name you enter here does not need to conform to any naming conventions because in most cases it won't be the saved filename. When you open an index file, you search your hard drive, server, or external media for a filename that ends with a .pdx extension. When you visit the Search window and choose Look In ⇨ Select Index, the Index Selection dialog box opens, as shown in Figure 6.20. What appears in the Index Selection dialog box is a list of indexes appearing according to the Index Title names. These names are derived from what you type in the Index Title field in Acrobat Catalog.

## Note

When you get ready to build a file, Acrobat prompts you for the index filename. By default the text you type in the Index Title field is listed in the File name field in the Save Index File dialog box. This dialog box opens when you click the Build button in the Catalog dialog box (see the section "Building the index" later in this chapter). In most cases where you supply a name as a description in the Index Title, you'll want to change the filename to a name consistent with standard DOS conventions (that is, eight-character maximum with a three-character maximum extension). Make this change when you are prompted to save the file. ■

**FIGURE 6.19**

You set attributes for your new index file in the New Index Definition dialog box.

**FIGURE 6.20**

Choosing Select Index from the Look In pull-down menu in the Search window opens the Index selection dialog box. All loaded indexes are listed according to the index title supplied in Acrobat Catalog at the time the index was created.

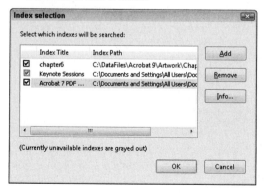

## Caution

If you see an index name grayed out, the index is not available to your Acrobat viewer. You may have moved the index file to another location on your hard drive, deleted the file, or tried to search an index on a CD-ROM that is not mounted. In order to bring back the index and make it available to your viewer, you need to delete the grayed out index name by clicking the Remove button and then add the file or rebuild and Add the file in the Index selection dialog box. ■

### Adding an index description

You can supply as many as 256 characters in the Index Description field. Descriptive names and keywords should be provided so that the end user knows what each index contains. Index descriptions should be thought of as adding more information to the items mentioned earlier in this chapter regarding document descriptions. Index descriptions can help users find the index file that addresses their needs.

When an index is loaded, the index title appears in the Select Indexes dialog box. To get more information about an index file, click the Info button shown in Figure 6.20. The Index information dialog box opens as shown in Figure 6.21. The Index information dialog box shows you the title from the Index Title field and the description added in Acrobat Catalog in the Index Description field.

---

**FIGURE 6.21**

The Index Description is contained in the Index information dialog box. Users can click on the Info button in the Index selection dialog box to see the description added in the Index Description field box in Acrobat Catalog.

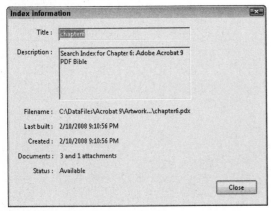

### Including directories

If you add nothing to the Include these directories field, Catalog won't build an index because it won't know where to look for the PDF files to be included in the index. Adding the directory path(s) is essential before you begin to build the index. Notice the first Add button on the right side of the dialog box in Figure 6.19. After you click Add, a navigation dialog box opens, enabling you to identify the directory where the PDFs to be indexed are located. You can add many directories to the Include these directories list. These directories can be in different locations on your hard drive. When a given directory is selected, all subfolders will also be indexed for all directory locations unless you choose to exclude certain folders. When the directories have been identified, the directory path and folder name will appear in the Include these directories field.

### Excluding subdirectories

If you have files in a subdirectory within the directory you are indexing and want to exclude the subdirectory, you can do so in the Exclude these subdirectories field. The folder names and directory paths of excluded directories appear in the Exclude these subdirectories field, as shown in Figure 6.19.

### Removing a directory

If you decide to remove a directory from either the Include these directories or Exclude these subdirectories lists, select an item in the list and click the Remove button. You can add or delete directories in either list prior to building an index or when modifying an index.

## Saving index definitions

Two buttons appear at the top-right corner of the Catalog dialog box for saving a definition. If you begin to develop an index file and supply the index title and a description and want to come back to Catalog later, you can save what you type in the Index Definition dialog box using the Save As button. The Save button does not appear active until you have saved a file with the Save As option or you're working on a file that has been built. Saving the file only saves the definition for the index. It does not create an index file. The Save As option enables you to prepare files for indexing and interrupt your session if you need to return later. For example, suppose you add an index title and you write an index description. If you need to quit Acrobat at this point, click Save As and save the definition to disk. You can then return later and resume creating the index by adding the directories to be cataloged and building the index.

After you have saved a file, you can update the file with the Save button. After a definition is saved, when you return to Acrobat Catalog, you can click the Open button in the Catalog dialog box and resume editing the definition file. When all the options for your search index have been determined, you click the Build button to actually create the index file.

Using Save As or Save is not required to create an index file. If you set all your attributes for the index and click the Build button, Acrobat Catalog prompts you in the Save Index File dialog box to supply a name for the index and save the definition. Essentially, Catalog is invoking the Save As command for you.

If at any time you click the Cancel button in the lower-right corner of the Index Definition dialog box, all edits are lost for the current session. If you add definition items without saving you'll need to start over when you open the Index Definition dialog box again. If you start to work on a saved file and click Cancel without saving new edits, your file reverts to the last saved version.

## Setting options

To the right of the Index Description field is a button labeled Options. Click this button and the Options dialog box appears, allowing you to choose from a number of different attributes for your index file, as shown in Figure 6.22. Some of these options are similar to the Preference settings for Acrobat Catalog you made in the Preferences dialog box. Any edits you make here supersede Preference settings.

## Cross-Reference

For information on setting Catalog preferences, see "Setting Catalog preferences" later in this chapter. ■

**FIGURE 6.22**

Clicking the Options button adjacent to the Index Description field opens the Options dialog box. Here you can assign further attributes to the index file.

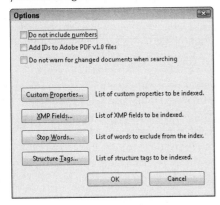

### Excluding numbers

The first item in the Options dialog box is a check box for excluding numbers. By selecting the Do not include numbers option, you can reduce the file size, especially if data containing many numbers are part of the PDF file(s) to be indexed. Keep in mind, however, that if numbers are excluded, Search won't find numeric values.

### Adding IDs to Adobe v1.0 files

Because Acrobat is now in version X, finding old PDF 1.0 files that need to be updated with IDs may rarely happen. If you do have legacy files saved as PDF 1.0 format, it would be best to batch process the older PDFs by saving them out of Acrobat X. As software changes, many previous formats may not be supported with recent updates. For better performance, update older documents to newer file formats.

## Cross-Reference

**For more information on batch processing, see Chapter 17. ■**

If you have legacy files that haven't been updated and you want to include them in your search index, check the box. If you're not certain whether the PDFs were created with Acrobat 1.0 compatibility, check it anyway just to be safe.

### Cancelling the warning dialog box for changed documents

If you create an index file, and then return to the index in Acrobat Catalog and perform some maintenance functions, save the index, and start searching the index, Acrobat notifies you in a dialog box that changes have been made and asks whether you want to proceed. To side-step the opening of the warning dialog box, check the Do not warn for changed documents when searching option.

### Adding custom properties

The Custom Properties button opens the Custom Properties dialog box, as shown in Figure 6.23. Custom Properties are used when customizing Acrobat with the Acrobat Software Development Kit (SDK). This item is intended for programmers who want to add special features to Acrobat. To add a Custom Property to be indexed, you should have knowledge in programming and the PDF format.

You add Custom Properties to the field box and select the type of property to be indexed from the pull-down menu. You type the property values in the field box, identify the type, and click the Add button. The property is then listed in the window below the Custom Property field box.

---

**FIGURE 6.23**

You can add custom data fields to Acrobat with the Acrobat Software Development Kit.

The types available from the pull-down menu are as follows:

- **String.** This is any text string. If numbers are included with this option they are treated as text.
- **Integer.** The integer field can accept values between 0 and 65,535.
- **Date.** This is a date value.

Support for programmers writing extensions and plug-ins and working with the SDK is provided by Adobe Systems. Developers who want to use the support program need to become a member of the Adobe Solutions Network (ASN) Developer Program. For more information about ASN and SDK, log on to the Adobe Web site at `http://adobe.com/go/acrobat_developer`.

### Adding XMP fields

Click XMP Fields and another dialog box opens in which you add to a list of XMP fields. The dialog box is virtually identical to the Stop Words dialog box shown in Figure 6.24. Type a name in the field box and click the Add button. All new XMP fields are added to the list window.

### Inserting stop words

To optimize an index file to produce faster search results, you can add stop words. You may have words such as *the, a, an, of,* and so on that would typically not be used in a search. You can choose to exclude such words by typing the word in the Word field box and clicking the Add button in the Stop Words dialog box. Click Stop Words in the Options dialog box to open the Stop Words dialog box shown in Figure 6.24. To eliminate a word after it has been added, select the word and click the Remove button. Keep in mind that every time you *add* a word, you are actually adding it to a list of words to be excluded.

---

**FIGURE 6.24**

You can eliminate words from an index file by adding words in the Stop Words dialog box. Adding a word to the list excludes it from the index file.

## Tip

You can create an elaborate list of stop words and may want to apply the list to several index files, but Acrobat (as of this writing) does not include an ability to import or swap a list of words to be excluded from an index file. For a workaround, you can open any existing Index Definition field and change all attributes except the stop words. Add a new index title, a new index description, and select a new directory for indexing. Save the definition to a new filename and click the Build button. A new index is built using the stop words created in another index. In workgroups you can save an index definition file without adding directories and use it as a template so all index files have consistent settings for the stop words. ■

### Adding and removing structure tags

If you have a tagged PDF you can search document tags when the tags are included in the search index. Click Structure Tags in the Options dialog box to open the Tags dialog box shown in Figure 6.25. Tagged PDFs with a tagged root and elements can have any item in the tagged logical tree marked for searching. To observe the tags in a PDF file, open the Tags palette and expand the tree. All the tags nest like a Bookmark list. When you want to mark tags for searching, type the tag name in the Tags dialog box and click the Add button. You remove tags from the list window by selecting a tag and clicking the Remove button.

## Cross-Reference

For more information on tagged PDF documents and using the Tags palette, see Chapter 25. ■

**FIGURE 6.25**

You can mark tags for searches in index files by adding tag names in the Tags dialog box.

# Building the index

After you've set all the attributes for the index definition, the index file is ready to be created. Clicking the Build button in the New Index Definition dialog box creates indexes. When you click this button, Acrobat Catalog opens the Save Index File dialog box where you supply a filename and target a destination on your hard drive. The default file extension is .pdx. Do not modify the file extension name. Acrobat recognizes these files when loading search indexes.

The location where you instruct Catalog to save your index file can be any location on your hard drive regardless of where the files being indexed reside. You can choose to save the index file inside or outside the folder that Catalog created during the indexing. Therefore, you have an index file and a folder containing index resources. The relationship between the index file and resource folder locations is critical to the usability of the index. If you move the index file to a different location without moving the supporting folder, the index is rendered unusable. To avoid problems, try to create a folder either when you are in the Save Index File dialog box or before you open Catalog and save your index file to your new folder. Make the name descriptive and keep the index file together in this folder. When you want to move the index to another directory, another computer, or to an external media cartridge or CD-ROM, copy the folder containing the index and supporting files.

Click the Save button in the Save Index File dialog box, and Catalog closes the Index Definition dialog box, returns you to the Catalog dialog box, and begins to process all the files in the target folder(s). Depending on how many files are indexed, the time to complete the build may be considerable. Don't interrupt the processing if you want to complete the index generation. When Catalog finishes, the progress bar stops and the last line of text in the Catalog dialog box reads "Index build successful." If for some reason the build is not successful, you can scroll the window in the Catalog dialog box and view errors reported in the list.

# Understanding the Structure of Index Files

Users who have created index files in all earlier versions of Acrobat are no doubt familiar with the end product of creating a search index. As you may recall, the index file with a .pdx extension and nine subfolders containing all associated files were produced by Acrobat Catalog for every new index. The relationship between the index file and subfolders in terms of directory paths needed to be preserved in order for the index to work properly. When you copied an index file to another directory or source, you needed to copy all the files together and keep the same relative path between the files.

When you produce an index file in Acrobat Pro, you won't find the same nine folders created during the index build with Acrobat version 5 and earlier. Acrobat Catalog 6.0 through X creates a single folder where files with an .idx extension reside. The relative directory path is still a factor in relocating files, but in Acrobat 6.0 through X, you need only copy an index file and a single folder to relocate your index and keep it functional.

The PDX file you load as your search index file is a small file that creates the information in the IDX and .info files. The IDX files contain the actual index entries the end user accesses during a search. When you build an index, rebuild an index, or purge data from an index, the maintenance operation may or may not affect the PDX file and/or IDX files depending on which option you choose. For specific information related to how these files are affected during index creation and maintenance, see the following pages for building, rebuilding, and purging index files.

## Stopping builds

If you want to interrupt a build, you can click the Stop button while a build is in progress. When building an index, Catalog opens a file where all the words and markers to the PDF pages are written. When you click the Stop button, Catalog saves the open file to disk and closes it with the indexed items up to the point you stopped the build. Therefore, the index is usable after stopping a build and you can search for words in the partial index. When you want to resume, you can open the file in Catalog and click the Rebuild button.

## Building existing indexes

When files are deleted from indexed folders and new files are added to the indexed folders, you'll want to maintain the index file and update it to reflect any changes. You can open an index file and click Build for a quick update. New files are scanned and added to the index, but the deleted files are marked for deletion without actually deleting the data. To delete invalid data, you need to use the Purge button. Purging can take a considerable amount of time even on small index files. Therefore, your routine maintenance might be to consistently build a file, and only periodically purge data.

## Creating legacy index files

When you open an index file created with an Acrobat Catalog version earlier than 6.0, a dialog box opens, informing you the index is not compatible with the current version of Acrobat. In the dialog box, you have three options: Create copy, Overwrite old index, and Cancel. Click the Create copy button to make a copy of the index file. A new index file is created leaving the original index file undisturbed. You can click the Overwrite old index button and the file rewrites, replacing the old index. If you choose this option your new index file won't be compatible with Acrobat viewers earlier than version 6.0. Clicking Cancel in this dialog box returns you to the Index Selection dialog box, leaving the index file undisturbed.

If you create a search index using Acrobat Catalog version X, the index file is backward-compatible to Acrobat 6. All Acrobat viewers can use index files suited to the appropriate version.

If you know some users won't be working with the new Acrobat viewers, then be certain to make copies of your index files. Until all users have upgraded to a viewer 6.0 or higher, you may need to organize your indexes according to viewer versions.

## Building index files from secure documents

In Acrobat versions lower than 6.0 you could not create index files from secure PDFs encrypted with either Acrobat Standard Security or Acrobat Self-Sign Security. Version 6.0 of Acrobat afforded complete access to secure files with Acrobat Catalog if the right permissions were applied. When applying Password Security in Acrobat 6 through Acrobat X, you need to enable text access for screen reader devices in order to index a secure file. Creating an index does not compromise your security and doesn't affect all other permissions you set forth when the files are saved.

If you have legacy files that have been secured, you can index them like other files saved in earlier PDF format compatibilities. These files, and any other files you create with Acrobat Pro or Acrobat Pro Extended, can be used only by Acrobat viewers 6.0 and later.

## Cross-Reference

**For more information on encryption and security, see Chapter 24.** ■

## Rebuilding an index

Rebuilding index files completely re-creates a new index. You can open an Acrobat X compatible index file and click Rebuild. The file rewrites the file you opened much like you would use a Save As menu command to rewrite a PDF document. If a substantial number of PDF documents have been deleted and new files added to the indexed folders, rebuilding the index could take less time than purging data.

## Purging data

As indexes are maintained and rebuilt, you will need to perform periodic maintenance and purge old data. A purge does not delete the index file, nor does it completely rewrite the file; it simply recovers the space used in the index for outdated information. Purging is particularly useful when you remove PDF files from a folder and the search items are no longer needed. If you have built a file several times, each build marks words for deletion. A purge eliminates the marked data and reduces the file size. With a significant number of words marked for deletion, a purge will improve the speed when using Search. This operation might be scheduled routinely in environments where many changes occur within the indexed folders.

## Tip

**When changing options for eliminating words and numbers from indexes or adding tags and custom properties in the Options dialog box, first open the index.pdx file in Catalog and purge the data. Set your new criteria in the Options dialog box and rebuild the index. Any items deleted will now be added to the index, or any items you want to eliminate will subsequently be eliminated from the index.** ■

## Setting Catalog preferences

Catalog preference settings are contained in the Preferences dialog box. Choose Edit ⇨ Preferences and click the Catalog item in the left pane as shown in Figure 6.26. Notice that the Index Defaults items use the same settings as found in the Options dialog box from the New Index Selection dialog box. The top three options under Indexing in Catalog preferences are obtained only here in these preference settings.

**FIGURE 6.26**

Open the Preferences dialog box and click Catalog in the left pane to see the options settings for Acrobat Catalog.

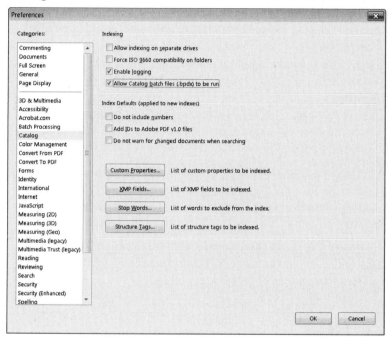

## Indexing Catalog preferences

The four options found in the Indexing section of the Catalog preferences are as follows:

- **Allow indexing on separate drives.** When creating index files where you want to include folders on network servers and/or computers on your network, select this item in the Catalog preferences. The indexing option includes indexing files only on local networks. Unfortunately, you can't index files on Web servers and use indexes from within Web browsers.

- **Force ISO 9660 compatibility on folders.** This setting is a flag that tells Catalog to look for any folders that are not compliant with standard DOS conventions (eight-character maximum with three-character maximum extensions) for folder/directory names. If Catalog encounters a folder name that is not acceptable, the processing stops and an error is reported in the Catalog dialog box. Folder names and directory paths are listed for all incompatible names. You can review the list and manually rename folders. After changing folder names, try to create the index again.

- **Enable logging.** A log file is created during an index build that describes the processing for each file indexed. The file is ASCII text and can be opened in any text editor or word processor. Any errors occurring during the build are noted in the log file. All documents and directory paths are also contained in the log file. If you don't want to have a log file created at the time of indexing, clear the check box to disable the logging. When you disable logging, you are prevented from analyzing problems when you close the Catalog dialog box.

- **Allow Catalog batch files (.bpdx) to be run.** Permits batch processing of index files.

### Choosing index defaults

The options listed in the Index Defaults area of the Catalog preferences are identical to the options you have available in the New Index Description Options dialog box described earlier in this chapter. These default/options settings exist in two locations for different reasons.

When you set the options in the Preferences dialog box, the options are used for all index files you create. When you elect to use the options from the New Index Selection Options dialog box, the settings are specific to the index file you create. When you create a new index file, the options return to defaults.

If you set a preference in the Catalog preferences and disable the option in the New Index Selection Options dialog box, the latter supersedes the former. That is to say, the New Index Selection Options dialog box settings always prevail.

# Using Index Files

As I stated earlier, one reason you create index files is for speed. When you search hundreds or thousands of pages, the amount of time to return found instances for searched words in index files is a matter of seconds compared to searching folders in the Search window.

## Loading index files

To search using an index file, you need to first load the index in the Search window. From the Look In pull-down menu, choose the Select Index menu option, as shown in Figure 6.27.

The Index Selection dialog box opens after you make the menu selection. Click the Add button and the Open Index File dialog box opens. In this dialog box navigate your hard drive to find the folder where your index file is located. Click the index filename and click the Open button.

After selecting the index to load, you are returned to the Index Selection dialog box. A list of all loaded indexes appears in the dialog box. To the left of each filename is a check box. When a check mark is in view, the index file is active and can be searched. Those check boxes that are disabled have the index file loaded, but the file remains inactive. Search will not return results from the inactive index files. If an index file is grayed out as shown in Figure 6.20, the file path has been disrupted and Acrobat can't find the index file or the support files associated with the index. If you see a filename grayed out, select the file in the list and click the Remove button. Click the Add button and relocate the index. If the support files are not found, an error is reported in a dialog box indicating the index file could not be opened.

If you can't open a file, you need to return to the Catalog dialog box and click the Open button. Find the index file that you want to make active and rebuild the index. After rebuilding, you need to return to the Index selection dialog box and reload the index.

**FIGURE 6.27**

Your first step in using indexes is to load the index file(s) by choosing the Select Index menu option from the Look In menu in the Search window.

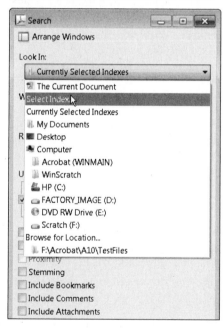

## Note

If you attempt to load an index file from a CD-ROM and the CD is not inserted into your CD-ROM drive, the index filename is grayed out in the Index Selection dialog box. After inserting the CD-ROM containing the index, the index filename becomes active. If you know index files are loaded from CDs, don't delete them from the Index Selection dialog box. Doing so requires you to reload the index file each time you insert a CD. ∎

## Attaching an index file to a document

You can associate an index file with a particular document. Open the Document Properties dialog box (Ctrl/⌘+D) and click the Advanced tab. Adjacent to the Search Index item is a Browse button. Click Browse and the Open dialog box appears. Navigate your hard drive to locate the index file created from a folder containing your document, select it, and click Open. When you save your file and reopen it, you can select Currently Selected Indexes in the Look In pull-down menu and your associated index file is automatically loaded for you.

## Disabling indexes

If an index is to be eliminated from searches, you can deactivate the index by disabling its check box. In a later Acrobat session, you can go back and enable indexes listed in the Index Selection dialog box. You should always use this method rather than deleting an index if you intend to use it again in a later Acrobat session. However, at times you may want to delete an index file. If the index will no longer be used, or you relocate your index to another drive or server, you may want to completely remove the old index. If this is the case, select the index file to be deleted and click the Remove button. Indexes may be enabled or disabled before you select Remove. In either case, the index file is removed without warning.

If you inadvertently delete an index, you can always reload the index by clicking the Add button. Placing index files in a directory where you can easily access them is a good idea. To avoid confusion, try to keep indexes in a common directory or a directory together with the indexed PDF files. Acrobat doesn't care where the index file is located on your hard drive or server — it just needs to know where the file is located and the file needs to keep the relative path with the support files. If you move the index file to a different directory, be certain to reestablish the connection in the Index Selection dialog box.

## Finding index information

When a number of index files are installed on a computer or server, the names for the files may not be descriptive enough to determine which index you want to search. If more detailed information is desired, the information provided by the Index Information dialog box may help identify the index needed for a given search.

### PDF Workflow

Index information may be particularly helpful in office environments where several people in different departments create PDFs and indexes are all placed on a common server. What may be intuitive to the author of an index file in terms of index name may not be as intuitive to other users. Index information offers the capability for adding more descriptive information that can be understood by many users. ∎

Fortunately, you can explore more descriptive information about an index file by clicking the Info button in the Index Selection dialog box. When you click the Info button, the Index information dialog box opens, displaying information about the index file, as shown earlier in Figure 6.21. Some of the information displayed requires user entry at the time the index is built. Acrobat Catalog automatically creates other information in the dialog box when the index is built. The Index information dialog box provides a description of the following:

- **Title.** The user supplies title information at the time the index is created. Titles usually consist of several words describing the index contents. Titles can be searched, as detailed earlier in this chapter, so the title keywords should reflect the index content.

- **Description.** Description can be a few words or several sentences containing information about the index. (In Figure 6.21, the description was supplied in Acrobat Catalog when the index was created.)

- **Filename.** The directory path for the index file's location on a drive or server is displayed with the last item appearing as the index filename.

- **Last built.** If the index file is updated, the date of the last build is supplied here. If no updates have occurred, the date will be the same as the created date.

- **Created.** This date reflects the time and date the index file was originally created and is therefore a fixed date.

- **Documents.** Indexes are created from one or more PDF documents. The total number of PDF files from which the index file was created appears here.

- **Status.** If the index file has been identified and added to the list in the Index Selection dialog box, it will be Available. Unavailable indexes appear grayed out in the list and are described as Unavailable.

## Searching an index

After your index file(s) is prepared and loaded in the Index selection dialog box, it is ready for use. You search index files in the Advanced Search window just as you search multiple files as explained earlier in this chapter. From the Look In pull-down menu, select Currently Selected Indexes.

All the options discussed earlier for advanced searches are available to you. Select from the Return results containing pull-down menu, enter your search criteria, and select the options you want. Click the Search button and you'll find the search results reported much faster than using other search methods.

Index files can be created from PDF collections contained on external media where the index file can remain on your computer without the need for copying the PDF documents to your hard drive. When you insert a media disk such as a CD-ROM, your search index is ready to use to search the media.

Practice searching your new index file using different options and search criteria. To compare the difference between using a search index file and using the advanced search options, you can choose the Browse for Location menu item and search the CD-ROM for the same criteria. Go back and forth to see the differences between searching folders and searching an index file.

# Searching external devices

A computer network server, another computer on your network, a CD-ROM, DVD-ROM, external hard drive, and a removable media cartridge are considered external to your local computer hard drive(s). Any of these devices can be indexed and the index file can be located on any of the devices you index. If you want to save an index file on a device different from where the PDF collection is stored, you need to be certain to open the Preferences dialog box for the Catalog preferences and enable the check box for Allow indexing on separate drives. This preference setting enables you to index across media devices.

## Note
When you want to write index files to read only media such as CD-ROMs and DVDs, you need to create the index file from PDFs stored on your hard drive. After the index file is created, copy the index file, the supporting files, and the PDFs in exactly the same folder structure to your media and burn the disc. ■

When you want to search an index, you can activate the index in the Index selection dialog box and invoke a search whether your external media is mounted and accessible or not. The search index returns results from the index .pdx file and the .idx files without looking at the PDFs that were indexed. You can examine the results of the search in the Search window and find the files where the search criteria match the PDF documents in the index collection.

If you want to open the link to the PDF document where a result is reported, you need to have the media mounted and accessible. If a network server or other computer contains the related files, the server/computer must be shared with appropriate permissions and visible on your desktop. If you use external media storage devices, the media must be mounted and visible on your desktop in order to view the PDFs linked to the search results. If you attempt to view a document when the device is not mounted, Acrobat opens an error dialog box.

If you see an error dialog box, click OK in the dialog box and insert your media, connect an external hard drive, or access a computer or network server. You don't need to quit Acrobat to make your device accessible. Wait until the media is mounted and then click a search result. Acrobat opens the linked page and you're ready to continue your search.

A search index file created on one computer can be moved or copied to another computer. To copy an index file to another computer, be certain you copy the index file (.pdx) and all supporting files in the folder created by Catalog. Be certain you maintain the same relative directory path for the index file and the supporting files. If an index file appears in a root folder and the supporting files appear in a nested folder, copy the root folder to other media. If you place the index file in the same folder as the supporting files, copy the single folder containing all files to your media.

You can load the index file and external media on another computer and perform the same searches as were performed where the index file was created. When distributing CD-ROMs and DVDs you can copy these index files to your media and all users can access the index files. If you access an index file on a network server and the PDF collection is stored on an external device such as a CD-ROM, you cannot open files from another computer unless the

CD-ROM is mounted. You may see your network server, but the associated devices with the server need to be individually mounted in order to open PDF files remotely.

# Working with Embedded Index Files

Index files can be scattered all over your hard drive, and, at times, it can be a chore to load them in the Index selection dialog box. In addition, when sharing PDFs where indexes have been created requires you to either attach an index file to a PDF or send along your index to recipients of your PDFs. Again, the steps involved can be aggravating if you have to spend time finding the index files on your hard drive.

Acrobat 8 simplified the steps for loading index files and sharing them. In Acrobat 8 through X, you can embed an index file in PDFs. Embedding an index file is limited to a single PDF document or a PDF Portfolio and not a collection of PDFs. You won't gain any better performance embedding indexes in one-page PDFs or files containing few pages.

When you embed an index file you bypass all the steps for creating an index using Acrobat Catalog. Indexes are automatically created and embedded by Acrobat Pro and Acrobat Pro Extended through a simple button click in a dialog box.

To understand more about creating an index file and embedding it in a PDF document, follow these steps.

### STEPS: Creating and embedding index files

1. **Open a PDF document in Acrobat Pro.** Try to find a PDF having 500 or more pages or a PDF Portfolio. Longer documents make index embedding more practical when using this feature. In this example I use a file containing 803 pages.

2. **Open the Manage Embedded Index dialog box.** Open the Document Processing panel and click Manage Embedded Index. The Manage Embedded Index dialog box opens, as shown in Figure 6.28.

**FIGURE 6.28**

Click Manage Embedded Index in the Document Processing panel to open the Manage Embedded Index dialog box.

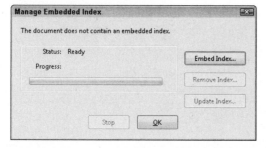

3. **Embed the Index.** Click the Embed Index button in the Manage Embedded Index dialog box.

4. **Click OK.** Click OK after Acrobat completes the index creation and your new index file is now embedded in your PDF. (See Figure 6.29.)

Click OK and your index is embedded in the PDF.

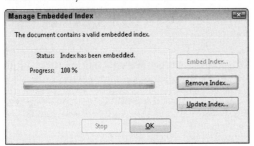

5. **Compare a search using the embedded index.** Open the original PDF without an index embedded in the document and press Ctrl/⌘+Shift+F to open the Search window. Select The Current PDF in the Look In pull-down menu and search for a word in the document. Notice the amount of time it takes to search all pages in the file.

   Bring the file with the embedded index forward in the Document pane or open the file if you closed it. Perform a search using the Current Document option in the Look In pull-down menu. Add the same search criteria in the Search window and search the document. You should see a noticeable difference in the speed for the returned results.

# Summary

Many options discussed for searching PDFs in this chapter included:

- Acrobat X viewers include a Find toolbar used for searching the current active document.

- Searching PDF files occurs in the Search window. When a search is requested, the Search window opens as a floating window.

- The Search window enables basic and advanced searches.

- Basic searches are used to search open PDF files but provide more options than the Find command.

- Advanced searches enable searching multiple PDFs locally, on external media, and across networks with the use of a search index file.

- Acrobat viewers 6.0 and greater support searching content of bookmarks and comments through advanced searches and index file searches. Acrobat 7.0 through X supports searching file attachments.

- Searches for PDFs on the Internet are no longer built into Acrobat. If you want to search for PDFs on the Internet, you need to use a Web search engine that supports searching for PDFs.

- Searches can be made with a variety of options, including Boolean queries, without the use of an index file.

- Search index files are created in Acrobat Catalog in Acrobat Pro or Acrobat Pro Extended only. Searching index files returns results for large collections of PDFs much faster than basic and advanced searches.

- Document descriptions can be searched with advanced searches and via index file searches.

- Index files can be built, rebuilt, and purged with Acrobat Catalog. Old index files created with PDF formats earlier than version 6.0 need to be rebuilt with Acrobat Catalog. Acrobat Catalog X index files are backward-compatible with Acrobat 6.0.

- Tags, XMP data, and object data can be searched with advanced searches and from index searches.

- Index files can be copied to other computers, network servers, and external media storage units. When copying search indexes, you need to duplicate all supporting files and the relative directory path(s) on the destination units.

- Index files can be embedded on a PDF-by-PDF basis in Acrobat 8 through X. A single menu command creates and embeds an index in a PDF opened in the Document pane.

# Part II

# Converting Documents to PDF

This section deals with converting documents from authoring programs to PDF files that can be opened, viewed, and edited in Acrobat Standard (Windows) and Acrobat Professional (Windows and Macintosh). In Chapter 7, you find all the options available for converting files to PDF from within Acrobat. Chapter 8 is dedicated to using the PDFMaker, which is installed with your Acrobat installation, for converting Microsoft Office files. In Chapter 9, I talk about using many Adobe programs that support direct export to PDF. In Chapter 10, I talk about exporting content from PDF files.

# Converting Files to PDF

Unlike almost every other computer program, Acrobat was never designed to support creating new files and editing pages to add content. Where Acrobat begins is with file conversion to the PDF format. Users start with a document authored in another program and the resulting document is converted to PDF using either tools from within Acrobat or tools or commands within programs that support PDF conversion from native documents.

With Acrobat Standard and Acrobat Pro the number of methods you can employ for converting documents to PDF is enormous. Any program file can be converted to PDF through a number of different methods offered by Acrobat, operating systems, and many different authoring applications. The method you use to convert a document to PDF and the purpose for which the PDF is intended require you to become familiar with a number of different options at your disposal for PDF file creation. This chapter begins a new part of the book entirely devoted to PDF creation. In this chapter you learn basic PDF conversion methods available in Acrobat Pro and Acrobat Standard. The following chapters in this part cover more advanced PDF creation methods.

## IN THIS CHAPTER

**Understanding the PDF creation process**

**Changing application documents to PDF**

**Converting PDFs from files**

**Changing scans to PDF**

**Converting Web pages to PDF**

# Understanding How PDFs Are Created

Acrobat offers several choices for converting documents to PDF. You can immediately see options for PDF conversion by opening the File ⇨ Create menu. In the submenu you find choices for:

- **From File.** Use this command to convert a number of different file formats to PDF. For example, convert an MS Word document, an RTF file, an image-formatted file, and many other formats by choosing File ⇨ Create ⇨ From File. The Open dialog box appears where you locate a file, select it, and click the Open button to convert it to PDF.

- **From Scanner.** Choose this option in the submenu and you can scan a document on a flatbed scanner and convert it to PDF with a single button click.

- **From Web Page.** Choose this option to convert a Web page to PDF.

- **From Clipboard.** Any data you copy to the system Clipboard can be converted to PDF by selecting this command.

- **Assemble PDF Portfolio.** Choose File ⇨ Create ⇨ Assemble PDF Portfolio and you find options for adding many different native file formats to a PDF Portfolio. When you add files to a PDF Portfolio, you have choices for converting the documents to PDF or retaining the original file formats.

- **Merge Files into a Single PDF.** Use this option when you want to convert multiple files from a variety of formats into a single PDF document.

- **Batch Create Multiple Files.** This new menu command opens the Actions Wizard where you can create an action. For more on creating actions, see Chapter 17.

# Converting Native Documents to PDF

Many authoring programs offer you methods for converting to PDF, such as exporting or saving to PDF directly, or using a utility installed with Acrobat that supports certain authoring programs. However, when these methods are not available you can use the Print command in your authoring program to produce a PDF document. Virtually any document created in an authoring program that allows printing can be converted to PDF through the use of the Adobe PDF printer (Windows and Mac OS X 10.2 and above).

You access the Adobe PDF printer in the application Print dialog box. Rather than print a file to a printer, you print your file to disk. During this process, the file is temporarily saved as a PostScript file and the PostScript file is distilled in Acrobat Distiller. The Adobe PDF Settings assigned to Distiller control the attributes of the resulting PDF file. The process is relatively the same on both Windows and Mac platforms, but initial printer selection and dialog box selections vary a little.

# Converting with the Adobe PDF printer (Windows)

When you install Acrobat, the Adobe PDF printer is installed in your Printers folder. As a printer driver, the file is accessible from any program capable of printing, including your computer accessories and utilities. Like any other printer you install on Windows 2000 with Service Pack 4, Windows XP Professional, Windows XP Home Edition, Windows Vista, Windows 7, or Tablet PC with Service Pack 2, you can set the Adobe PDF printer as the default printer. Once you have set the default printer, you don't need to make a printer selection each time you want to create a PDF document.

## Note

You may also have the Acrobat Distiller printer installed in your Printer's folder. The features associated with the Adobe PDF printer and the Acrobat Distiller printer are identical. ■

To convert any application document to PDF, choose File ⇨ Print or access the Print dialog box with the menu command in your authoring program. Some dedicated vertical market programs, such as accounting and other office programs, may have print commands located in menus other than the File menu. When you arrive at the Print dialog box, the various printer drivers installed on your computer are shown. Select the Adobe PDF printer in the Print dialog box, as shown in Figure 7.1.

From any authoring program, select the Print command, select the Adobe PDF printer, and click Print to convert the open document to a PDF file.

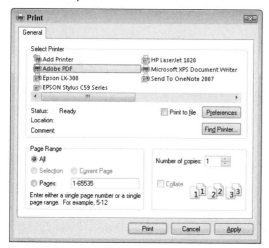

Before printing to the Adobe PDF printer, check your output options by clicking the Preferences button. In Windows 2000 and earlier, you will see Properties appear in the Print dialog box. If you see Properties, click the Properties button. The Adobe PDF Printing Properties dialog box opens, as shown in Figure 7.2. In this dialog box you choose options for the resulting PDF document. Click the Adobe PDF Settings tab to choose the PDF options.

**FIGURE 7.2**

Set your PDF options in the Adobe PDF Printing Preferences dialog box in the Adobe PDF Settings pane.

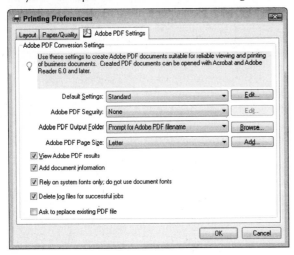

Choices you can make about the PDF file and handling the PDF conversion are contained in the Adobe PDF Settings window. Items you'll want to control include the following:

- **Default Settings.** This item relates to the discussion in the previous section concerning the Acrobat Distiller Adobe PDF Settings. The choices you have from the pull-down menu are nine preset choices (Acrobat Pro) or four choices (Acrobat Standard) provided with your Acrobat installation and any custom settings, if you've created them. It's important to make the proper choice for the options you want. When you print to the Adobe PDF printer, Acrobat Distiller is used in the background and applies the settings you specify in this dialog box.

## Cross-Reference

For a better understanding of Adobe PDF Settings, see the Acrobat Help document. ∎

- **Adobe PDF Security.** If you want to password-protect your document, you can apply security settings at the time the PDF is created. Choose the security options from the choices in the pull-down menu. The default choice for None results in PDF documents created without any password protection.

## Cross-Reference

To learn how to apply password protection to PDF documents, see Chapter 24. ∎

- **Adobe PDF Output Folder.** Choose to save PDF files to a fixed folder and directory path or be prompted for a filename and directory path for the saved file.

- **Adobe PDF Page Size.** A pull-down menu offers an extensive list of page sizes derived from the printer driver and not the PPD (PostScript Printer Description file) for your printer. If you don't have a custom size that matches your document page, click the Add button adjacent to the Adobe PDF Page Size pull-down menu. The Add Custom Paper Size dialog box opens, where you make choices for the custom page size and add the new page option in the pull-down menu, as shown in Figure 7.3.

  Acrobat accepts sizes up to 200 × 200 inches (5,080 × 5,080 millimeters/14,400 × 14,400 points). Enter your new custom page size in the units of measure desired and click the Add/Modify button. Your new page size is added to the Adobe PDF Page Size pull-down menu and selected for you after you click the Add/Modify button. If you want to delete a page after it has been created, click Add in the Printing Preferences dialog box and select the page you want to delete from the Add Custom Paper Size dialog box. Click the Delete button and the page is deleted from both pull-down menus. Clicking Cancel (or pressing the Esc key) in the dialog box returns you to the Adobe PDF Document Properties dialog box without affecting any changes.

---

**FIGURE 7.3**

---

The Add Custom Paper Size dialog box enables you to create a page size up to 200 × 200 inches.

## Cross-Reference

Setting custom pages for the Adobe PDF Printer makes the custom page sizes accessible for this printer driver only. If using other methods for PDF creation such as using the PDFMaker tools in Office programs, you'll want to create custom page sizes in another preferences dialog box. ∎

- **View Adobe PDF results.** When the check box is enabled, the resulting PDF document opens in the Acrobat Document pane. If Acrobat is not open, the program launches after the PDF is created.

- **Add document information.** This item is a little misleading. You are not prompted in a dialog box to add document information. However, when using applications that support certain kinds of document information such as document title and author, the information from the native document is added to the Document Properties Description fields. The document properties in your native document are not translated precisely, though. You may have a Word file with custom properties set up in the Word Document Properties dialog box like a Title, Subject, Author, Keywords, and so on. When the Word file is converted to PDF, you'll find your Title information in Acrobat to be the name of the saved Word file and the Author is your computer log-on name. Regardless of the custom properties you add to the Document Properties text boxes in Word, the results in Acrobat default to descriptions you can't control. If you remove the check box for this setting, all the Document Properties Descriptions in the PDF file are blank.

## Cross-Reference
For more information on document descriptions, see Chapter 6. ■

- **Rely on system fonts only; do not use document fonts.** What this check box does is control whether fonts are put into the PostScript stream that are sent to the Adobe PDF printer. Since 99.9% of the time those fonts are resident on your system, there is no value in having them also embedded in the PostScript stream; it just makes the process of printing to Adobe PDF slower. By default, the check box is ON — it's faster. Leave this setting at the default.

- **Delete log files for successful jobs.** During PDF creation, the processing information is written to a log file in the form of ASCII text. You can open the log file in any text editor and review the steps used to produce the PDF. Each time a PDF is successfully created, the log file is deleted. In the event you want to review the PDF creation process logged in the text file, disable the check box and open the log file in a text editor.

- **Ask to replace existing PDF file.** If you elect to not have Acrobat prompt you for a filename, the PDF file is created using the authoring document filename. If you make changes in the document and want to create a new PDF document, the second creation overwrites the first file if the check box is disabled. If you're creating different versions of PDF files and want to have them all saved to disk, be certain to enable the check box.

After you review all the options in the Adobe PDF Printing Preferences dialog box, click OK. You are returned to the Print dialog box and are ready to create the PDF document. Click Print in the dialog box and the PDF is produced with the options you chose in the Adobe PDF Settings dialog box. If the check box was enabled for View Adobe PDF results, the PDF opens in Acrobat.

Because this method of PDF creation uses a printer driver, you can create a PDF document from virtually any application program. The only requirement is that the program is capable of printing. If you use programs such as Microsoft Office, other Adobe programs, certain CAD drawing programs, high-end imaging programs, or a host of other applications, you may have other methods for creating PDF documents depending on the level of PDF support for the program. It is important to understand when to use the Adobe PDF printer and other methods available to you from different applications. Before you integrate using the Adobe PDF printer into your workflow, be certain to review the next two chapters because they discuss other options for creating PDF documents.

## Cross-Reference

For more information on creating PDFs from Microsoft programs, see Chapter 8. For more information on exporting to PDF from Adobe programs, see Chapter 9. ■

## Converting with the Adobe PDF printer (Mac OS X)

Mac OS X and Adobe PDF are married at the operating system level, and you can find several ways to convert your authoring files to the PDF format. The Acrobat-supported method uses the same type of printer driver you find on Windows. From any authoring program, select the Print command (most commonly accessed by choosing File ⇨ Print). When the Print dialog box opens, select Adobe PDF from the Printer pull-down menu. From the default selection for Copies and Pages, open the pull-down menu and select PDF Options, as shown in Figure 7.4.

PDF Options settings are available after you select the PDF Options pull-down menu command.

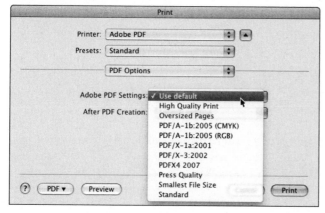

The dialog box changes so that you can access Adobe PDF Settings from a pull-down menu. The default selection is Use Default. If you leave this option active, the most recent settings selected in the Distiller application are used to produce the PDF file. The remaining options are the same as those discussed for Windows users. When you add new custom settings, they appear in the Adobe PDF Settings pull-down menus from the Print dialog boxes on Windows and Mac operating systems.

Another setting for viewing the PDF file appears in the pull-down menu: After PDF Creation. You can choose to view your PDF in the default Acrobat viewer or leave the default at Launch

Nothing, which allows you to go about your work and view the PDFs later. After you choose the settings, click the Print button to convert the file to PDF using the Adobe PDF Settings you selected from the menu choices.

If you open the PDF pull-down menu at the bottom of the dialog box and select Save as PDF (see Figure 7.5), you create a PDF using the PDF engine built into Mac OS X. Checking this option also creates a PDF file, but the PDF creation is not an Adobe-based PDF creation method. This menu choice appears in a generic installation of Mac OS X (Jaguar through Snow Leopard), and creating a PDF this way is supported by the operating system without the use of Acrobat Distiller. When you use Save As PDF, the PDF is created using the native Mac OS X PDF creation tools, which provide adequate PDF creation of non-prepress documents. The PDF documents created using this method will work fine for office uses; however, they will be significantly larger than those created by Adobe Acrobat.

---

**FIGURE 7.5**

Selecting the PDF pull-down menu and choosing Save as PDF creates a PDF file using the Apple OS X PDF creation tools.

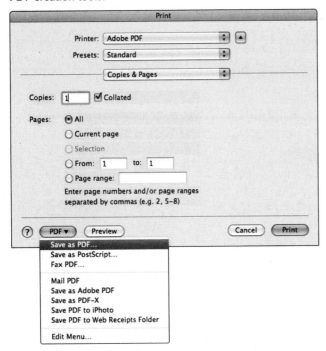

## Cross-Reference

For more information on PostScript and creating PostScript files, see the Acrobat Help file. ■

Save As PDF was designed by Apple to provide users with a PDF version of a document to send to people across the Internet for screen viewing and desktop printing. As a matter of practice, using the Adobe PDF printer is your best choice for creating PDFs suited for purposes other than screen displays.

# Viewing PDFs on the Mac

Mac OS X also supports an Apple-developed PDF viewer called Preview. By default, double-clicking a PDF file opens the PDF in the Preview application. If you want to change the default viewer from Preview to Acrobat, select a PDF document and press ⌘+I to open the Document Info dialog box, as shown in the following figure.

From the Open with menu, select Adobe Acrobat Pro (or the viewer you want to establish as the default PDF viewer). Click the Change All button and all your PDF documents will open by default in Acrobat.

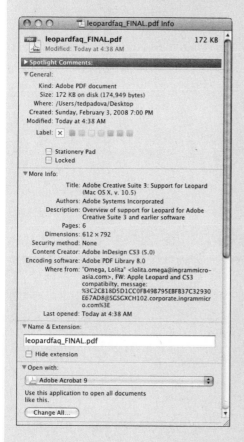

*continued*

*continued*

If you're using Mac OS X Leopard, you have another method for viewing PDF documents with the QuickLook feature. Click a PDF document on the desktop or within a folder and press the Spacebar. The PDF document pops up on the desktop with the first page in view. You can scroll all pages in a PDF file using QuickLook by dragging the slider on the right side of the window up or down.

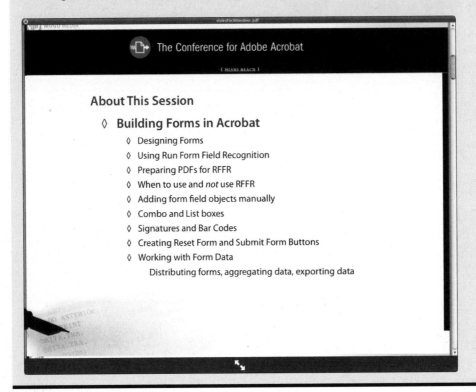

## Caution

**A number of different clone printer drivers and clone PDF creators are distributed from developers and enthusiasts. Using a clone product can often produce unreliable PDF documents. If you purchased Adobe Acrobat, be sure to use the tools Adobe has provided you for PDF creation. Adobe and many Adobe partners that have licensed Adobe technology offer you the best results for reliable PDF creation.** ■

## Using the Adobe PDF Printer driver

On Windows you use the Adobe PDF Printer for authoring applications that don't support exports to PDF. Programs such as the Microsoft Office applications, Autodesk AutoCAD, Lotus Notes, and so on offer you better options for converting directly to PDF via tools installed with your Acrobat installation. Simple text editor documents, vertical market application programs such as accounting programs, shareware programs, and other types of application documents not normally used for professional design purposes are likely candidates for using the Adobe PDF Printer driver. If a program such as a Microsoft Office application supports direct exports to PDF, you're always best served by using the export tools Adobe provides for you when you install Acrobat.

Mac users will find a much more liberal use for the Adobe PDF Printer. Inasmuch as there are some export options for programs like Microsoft Office programs, they generally don't work as well as using the Print dialog box and printing to a PDF document. Additionally, programs like Safari, Firefox, and Apple Mail don't have the same support for PDF creation as you find on Windows with Microsoft Internet Explorer and Microsoft Outlook. Unless you're using the Adobe Creative Suite applications, almost all other application documents on the Mac are best converted to PDF using the Print dialog box.

# Creating PDFs from Files

Adobe Acrobat offers you a number of options for converting application documents to PDF. For PDF creation supported by Acrobat, you don't need to leave the program to produce PDF files from a number of different file formats.

The Create task button pull-down menu offers a few different options for PDF creation, as shown in Figure 7.6 (left). If you choose File ⇨ Create you find many more options for converting documents to PDF as shown in Figure 7.6 (right).

You use Create ⇨ PDF From File to convert any file format supported by Acrobat to a PDF document. You can also use File ⇨ Open to convert to PDF. If using the Open dialog box, be certain to choose All Files (*.*) from the Files of Type pull-down menu (Windows) or Show pull-down menu (Mac).

---

**FIGURE 7.6**

The Create task button (left) offers a few options for PDF file creation. Choose File ⇨ Create (right) and you find many more options for PDF file creation from within Acrobat.

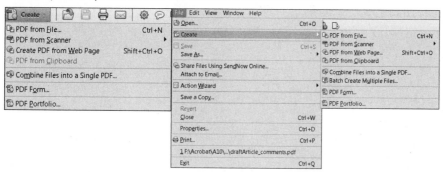

## Tip
You can also convert any file compatible with the Create ⇨ PDF From File menu command by dragging a document on top of the Acrobat window. ∎

# Comparing supported file formats

To convert files to PDF from within Acrobat, you first need to understand all the supported formats. You can try to convert any file format to PDF with the Create PDF tool. If the file format is supported, the document is converted to PDF and opens in Acrobat. If the format is not supported, a dialog box opens informing you that the format is not supported. It won't hurt to try, but knowing ahead of time what formats are supported is better.

Many file formats that are acceptable to Acrobat can also have conversion settings defined by you. Options for the conversion settings are the same as you have available with the Adobe PDF printer, as discussed earlier in this chapter, and they're accessible in the Preferences dialog box. Before you begin converting files to PDF with the Create task button or menu command, be certain to choose Edit ⇨ Preferences (Windows) or Acrobat ⇨ Preferences (Mac) or use (Ctrl/⌘+K) and click the Convert To PDF item in the left pane. On the right side of the Preferences dialog box, you'll see a list of supported file formats, as shown in Figure 7.7 for Windows and Figure 7.8 for the Mac. As you can see at a quick glance, the Mac doesn't support as many file format conversions as Windows.

---

**FIGURE 7.7**

When using the Create ⇨ PDF From File command, you assign PDF Settings to different file formats in the Convert To PDF preferences. The Preferences dialog box lists all supported file formats in the Convert To PDF preferences.

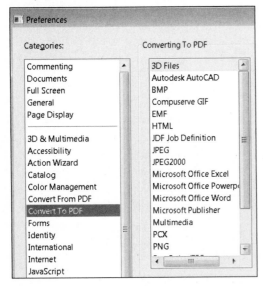

## FIGURE 7.8

Fewer file formats are supported on the Mac.

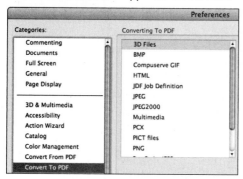

The file formats that are supported by Acrobat Pro include the following:

- **3-D.** A variety of native 3-D formats are supported for conversion to PDF. This feature was supported only in Acrobat Pro Extended in version 9. Acrobat X supports 3-D file conversions on both Mac and Windows.

- **Autodesk AutoCAD (Windows only).** Autodesk's AutoCAD files can be opened in Acrobat directly. Layered files are preserved and opened with data on different layers when layer data are created in the AutoCAD file. AutoCAD is also supported with the PDFMaker utility, which installs Acrobat tools and menu options in the authoring application at the time you install Acrobat.

- **BMP.** Bitmap is a file format that can be saved from many image-editing programs. Bitmap is also commonly referred to as a color mode in Photoshop. As a color mode, the file can be saved in other file formats. For example, a 1-bit bitmap image can be saved as a TIFF-formatted file. In regard to Acrobat, the bitmap file format that is capable of rendering images in 1-bit, 4-bit, 8-bit, and 24-bit color depths can be opened as PDF. Furthermore, a bitmap color mode saved as any of the compatible formats listed here can also be opened as a PDF.

- **CompuServe GIF.** CompuServe's Graphic Interchange Format (GIF) was developed years ago to port image files to and from mainframes and microcomputers. It remains a popular format for Web graphics, and the later version of GIF89a supports interlacing. If using Photoshop, you can either save in the CompuServe GIF87 format or use Photoshop's Save for Web command and choose the GIF89a format. Regardless of what format is used, Acrobat can import either as a PDF.

- **EMF.** Metafile graphics.

- **HTML.** Hypertext Markup Language files are documents written in HTML for Web pages. You can open any HTML file, and the file and file links convert to PDF. Clicking an HTML link in a converted file in Acrobat appends the linked file to the open document.

- **JDF Job Definition.** You find JDF files in prepress workflows. The resultant PDF produces a standardized XML-based job ticket with information about the file for commercial printing uses, such as page size, crop and bleed areas, trapping, colorspace, and so on.

- **JPEG.** Joint Photographic Experts Group (JPEG) images are also used for Web graphics and file exchanges on the Internet. JPEG compression is a lossy compression scheme that can degrade images rapidly when they are compressed at high levels. These files are already compressed. Adding further compression with the PDF conversion options won't compress files smaller than the original compression. Inasmuch as the Settings button is active in the Open dialog box, you can't actually get more compression out of the file when converting to PDF.

- **JPEG2000.** JPEG2000 is a newer compression scheme that also offers a lossless option for compressing images. You can use JPEG2000 with lossless compression for the most discriminating quality required in high-end printing.

- **Microsoft Office/Excel/PowerPoint/Word/Publisher (Windows only).** Microsoft Office files are from the office programs of Excel, PowerPoint, Project, Visio, Word, and Publisher. Each of the Office programs is listed separately because you can edit different settings that apply to each respective program. On the Mac, Office applications are not supported for conversion within Acrobat.

## Cross-Reference
For information related to settings adjustments with Microsoft Office programs, see Chapter 8. ■

- **Multimedia.** Multimedia such as video formats and Adobe Flash can be converted to PDF.

- **PCX.** PCX files are native to the PC and were commonly used as an extension for PC Paintbrush. Adobe Photoshop can export in PCX format, but today it is rarely used for any kind of image representation. The advantage you have in opening PCX files in Acrobat is when converting legacy files saved in this format. Rather than your having to do a two-step operation of opening a PCX file in an image editor and saving in a more common format for file conversions, Acrobat can import the files directly.

- **PICT (Mac only).** The native Apple Mac equivalent to PCX (preceding bullet) is PICT (Picture). Photoshop supports PICT file exchanges in both opening and saving. However, Acrobat supports the format for conversion to PDF only via the From File or From Multiple Files commands.

- **PNG.** Portable Network Graphics (PNG — pronounced *ping*) is a format enabling you to save 24-bit color images without compression. The format was designed for Web use and is becoming more popular among Web designers. Older Web browsers need a special plug-in in order to view the images, which have slowed its wide acceptance. Interestingly enough, PNG images are saved from image editors without compression, yet Acrobat can apply image compression when converting to PDF. You can use all the compression options in the Adobe PDF Settings dialog box with PNG images to reduce file sizes.

- **PostScript/EPS.** PostScript and EPS files were formerly converted only with Acrobat Distiller. In Acrobat 8 you can open the files in Acrobat using the Create PDF tool and Distiller works in the background, handling the conversion to PDF.

- **Text.** Text listed in the Convert to PDF preferences relates to plain text files. Unformatted text from word processors, text editors, and any file saved in a text-only format can be opened in Acrobat.

- **TIFF.** Tagged Image File Format (TIFF) is by far the most popular format among the print people regardless of platform. TIFF files originate from image editors and scans. When scanning text you can save it as a TIFF, import the file in Acrobat, and then convert the image file to rich text with Acrobat's Text Recognition feature.

## Cross-Reference

For more information on Scan to PDF and Text Recognition, see Chapter 16. ■

- **XPS.** XPS (XML Paper Specification) is a paginated representation of an electronic paper in an XML-based format. XPS documents can be converted to PDF from within Acrobat. The Settings adjustments let you choose from any of the Adobe PDF Settings, except the Standards formats such as PDF/A and PDF/X.

## Cross-Reference

For more on PDF Standards formats, see Chapter 29. ■

## Applying settings

Many of the file formats supported by Acrobat can have PDF Options or other settings applied during conversion. These settings are available to all formats except CompuServe GIF, HTML, JDF Job Definition, JPEG2000, and Text. Depending on the file type to be created, you can edit the settings and apply some different options. You edit settings by selecting a file type from those listed in the Preferences dialog box shown in Figure 7.7 and clicking the Edit Settings button. If the settings cannot be adjusted, the Edit Settings button is grayed out.

Settings options for the different file formats include the following:

- **Autodesk AutoCAD.** AutoCAD files can be converted with bookmarks and links, with layers, embedded data, and support for the new Engineering (PDF/E-1) standard as shown in Figure 7.9. The Adobe PDF Settings and Security options are also available with AutoCAD .dxf conversions. Click the Edit Settings button after selecting a file type to open the Adobe PDF Settings dialog box shown in Figure 7.9.

  In the Adobe PDF Settings for Autodesk AutoCAD documents dialog box, you find a Configuration Preferences button. Click the button and the Adobe PDFMaker dialog box opens, where you can choose folders for AutoCAD resource directories. Choosing folders containing resource information instructs Acrobat to search the selected folders for embedding data when files are converted to PDF.

**FIGURE 7.9**

The Adobe PDF Settings for Autodesk AutoCAD documents dialog box offers an elaborate set of options for converting AutoCAD files.

- **BMP/JPEG/PCX/PNG/PICT (Mac only)/TIFF.** These file formats all use identical settings. Whereas many other file formats use the Acrobat Distiller application in the background and have Adobe PDF Settings applied during file conversion, these image file formats don't use Distiller, and no Adobe PDF Settings are applied during file conversion. Different conversion settings can be applied from the same options lists to each of the file types individually. Therefore, a BMP file, for example, can be converted with one level of image compression and a TIFF file can be converted with another level of compression.

  All of these file formats are image formats, and the types of settings you apply to them relate to image options, such as file compression and color management. The same set of options available from pull-down menus exists for all the different color modes listed in the Adobe PDF Settings dialog box shown in Figure 7.10.

## Note

Inasmuch as the Adobe PDF Settings dialog box appears the same for all image formats, some options may be grayed out depending on the type of file to be converted. For example, TIFF images can have compression applied during PDF conversion, whereas JPEG images cannot. Therefore, the compression options for JPEG images are grayed out. ■

FIGURE 7.10

Adobe PDF Settings for image files are available for file compression and color management.

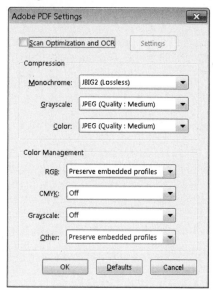

The top of the Adobe PDF Settings dialog box offers you options for scanning and OCR conversion. If your source document is to be scanned, check the box and choose settings for your scanner.

## Cross-Reference

**For more information on scanning and OCR conversion, see Chapter 16.** ■

The next group is for file compression. Choose from options in the drop-down menus for compression levels.

The lower section of the Adobe PDF Settings dialog box handles color management. You have choices for applying settings to the three common color modes: RGB, CMYK, and Grayscale. The Other option at the bottom of the dialog box handles special color considerations such as spot colors you might find in duotones, tritones, and quadtones.

## Cross-Reference

**For more information on color management and understanding different color modes, see Chapter 29.** ■

The color management policies you can apply to each color mode are identical, and they all include options from one of three choices:

- **Preserve embedded profiles.** If you work with images that have been assigned a color profile, choosing this option preserves the profile embedded in the document. Theoretically, no color changes occur when porting the files across platforms and devices.

- **Off.** If a color profile is embedded in an image, the profile is discarded.

- **Ask when opening.** If you select this option, Acrobat prompts you in a dialog box to use the embedded profile or discard it. You can make individual selections as you open files.

## Cross-Reference

For more detail on color management and working with color profiles, see Chapter 29. ■

- **Microsoft Office/PostScript/EPS.** The Microsoft Office and PostScript/EPS options include choices for Adobe PDF Settings and Adobe PDF Security. In addition, you have options for enabling accessibility, adding bookmarks from style sheets, converting an Excel workbook, and similar settings unique to each Microsoft program. With Microsoft Publisher and PostScript/EPS files you have identical support for choosing Adobe PDF Settings and Security options. In Figure 7.11 the options are shown for Microsoft Word.

---

**FIGURE 7.11**

Settings for Microsoft Office applications include options for enabling accessibility and converting heads and styles to bookmarks.

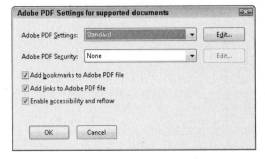

## Cross-Reference

Specific uses for enabling accessibility and adding bookmarks and links to PDFs from Microsoft Office applications are covered in Chapters 8 and 25. ■

After making choices for the options you want to use for file conversions, click the OK button in the Preferences dialog box. All the settings are set as new defaults until you change them. These settings are applied to documents you import from a file, from multiple files, and when you use the Open command in Acrobat.

## Converting multiple files to PDF

The menu command you had available in Acrobat 7 for converting multiple files to PDF was Create PDF⇨From Multiple Files. This command disappeared from the Create PDF task button in Acrobat 8, and a new task button (Combine Files) was added in Acrobat 8 that has been rebranded as Combine in Acrobat 9 and X. You can still use the Create task button and choose Merge Files into a single PDF or use the Combine task button and choose the same menu command.

In Acrobat, you can convert multiple files to PDF or combine multiple PDF documents together in either a PDF file or a PDF Portfolio. Acrobat 8 supported PDF Packages that are gone in Acrobat 9 and above in favor of the new PDF Portfolios feature. Because there are so many options available when working with the Combine task button and menu commands, I added a chapter to cover all you need to know about working with both Combine and PDF Portfolios.

### Cross-Reference

For more information on combining files into a single PDF document and creating PDF Portfolios, see Chapter 11. ∎

## Transforming Clipboard images

Suppose you have a map contained as part of a layout and you want to clip out the map and send it off to a friend for directions to an event, or perhaps you want to take a screenshot of an FTP client application to show log-on instructions, or maybe you want to clarify the use of a dialog box in Acrobat or another application. All of these examples and many more are excellent candidates for screen captures.

To capture a screenshot of the entire monitor screen in Windows, press the Shift+PrtScrn (Print Screen) or PrtSc keys. The keystrokes copy the current view of your monitor to the Clipboard. You can launch Acrobat or maximize it and select From Clipboard from the Create task button pull-down menu. The Clipboard data opens as a PDF document in the Acrobat Document pane. If you have a menu or dialog box open, the screen capture includes the foreground items in the capture like the screenshots shown throughout this book. Screens captured on Windows through these methods create 96-ppi (pixels per inch) images; captures on the Mac are 72 ppi.

If you want to capture a dialog box without the background on Windows, use Alt+PrtScrn (or PrtSc). The dialog box screenshots in this book were all taken by using these key modifiers.

### Note

Copying a screenshot to the Clipboard works with any program or at the operating system level when capturing desktop or folder views, accessories, or virtually any view you see on your computer monitor. Once data are on the Clipboard, you can open Acrobat and convert the Clipboard data to a PDF document. ∎

# Converting Clipboard images (Mac)

Converting Clipboard data on the Mac is handled exactly the same as when converting Clipboard data on Windows. However, if you want to first take a screenshot on the Mac, you use Acrobat instead of keystrokes.

On the Mac version of Acrobat you have additional commands for capturing screenshots. These commands are not necessary on Windows, where your keyboard can easily capture screenshots; but on the Mac, no keystrokes exist for capturing a screen and saving the captured data to the Clipboard. All Mac keystrokes used for capturing screenshots record the data in a file saved to the Desktop as a .png file.

To capture a screen to the Clipboard, select File ⇨ Create and choose one of the three screen capture items you see listed in the menu as shown in Figure 7.12:

- **From Screen Capture.** Selecting this option is the same as using ⌘+Shift+3. The entire monitor window is captured and converted to PDF.

- **From Window Capture.** Using this option is like pressing ⌘+Shift+4 and then pressing the spacebar. A camera icon appears as the cursor. Move the icon on top of a window and click to capture just that window.

- **From Selection Capture.** Using this option is like pressing ⌘+Shift+4, but without following with pressing the Spacebar. A crosshair appears as a new cursor. Click and drag the area to capture and release the mouse button. The selected area is converted to PDF.

When you select one of the options for capturing a screen, the screen capture is made and the capture is converted to PDF and opened in Acrobat.

---

**FIGURE 7.12**

Select File ⇨ Create and select one of the three screen captures to convert a screen, window, or selection to PDF.

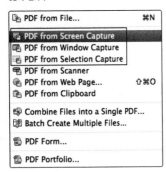

## Taking snapshots

In the Select & Zoom toolbar, select the Snapshot tool and click on a PDF page. The entire page is copied to the Clipboard. You can then create a PDF file From Clipboard Image as described in the previous section. The page you create, however, is a raster image when you convert it to PDF. You lose all text attributes when copying a page in this manner. A better solution for converting an entire page is to use the Extract Pages command.

**Cross-Reference**

For information on extracting pages, see Chapter 15. ■

The advantage of using the Snapshot tool is when taking a snapshot of a partial page in Acrobat. You can select the Snapshot tool and drag a marquee in an area you want to copy. When you release the mouse button, the selected area is copied to the Clipboard. Choose PDF from Clipboard from the Create task button to convert the selection to PDF. Again, you lose all type attributes, but you can use this method if retaining text is not an issue or if you want to crop an image. Using the Crop tool doesn't reduce the page size or file size of a PDF document. Using the Snapshot tool results in smaller file sizes when copying smaller sections of a PDF page.

Snapshots cannot be taken in password-protected files. If a file is encrypted, you need to eliminate the file encryption before using the Snapshot tool.

**Cross-Reference**

For additional information on creating snapshots and setting resolution for snapshot captures, see Chapter 14. For information on using the Crop tool, see Chapter 15. For linking to snapshots, see Chapter 21. For information on file encryption, see Chapter 24. ■

# Scanning to PDF

Click the Create task button and select PDF from Scanner. This option enables you to scan a document on your desktop scanner and convert to PDF. Acrobat offers some nice features for scanning files into Acrobat that are covered in Chapter 16. Select File ➪ Create ➪ PDF From Scanner to open the scanner dialog box.

**Cross-Reference**

There's a lot to scanning from within Acrobat and converting scanned documents to recognizable text. Look over Chapter 16, where scanning and OCR conversion are covered. ■

# Converting Web Pages to PDF

You use the File ➪ Create ➪ PDF from Web Page menu command to convert Web pages to PDF. You can also use Create PDF task button and choose PDF From Web Page to convert

Web pages hosted on Web sites or HTML files stored locally on your computer or networked servers.

Web Capture provides a complex set of preferences and tools with different options for converting Web pages, a Web site, Web links, HTML form fields, animations, or multiple sites to PDF. A captured Web site converts HTML, text files, and images to PDF, and each Web page is appended to the converted document. Conversion to PDF from Web sites can provide many opportunities for archiving information, analyzing data, creating search indexes, and many more uses where information needs to reside locally on computers.

Web pages containing animation such as Flash animation can be converted to PDF in Acrobat 6 and later. When animated pages are captured, the animation effects are viewed in the PDF file in any Acrobat viewer.

## Understanding Web site structure

To understand how to capture a Web site and convert the documents to PDF, you need a fundamental understanding of a Web page and the structure of a site. A Web page is a file created with the Hypertext Markup Language (HTML). There is nothing specific to the length of a Web page. A page may be a screen the size of $640 \times 480$ pixels or a length equivalent to several hundred letter-sized pages. Size, in terms of linear length, is usually determined by the page content and amount of space needed to display the page. PDF files, on the other hand, have fixed lengths up to $200 \times 200$ inches. You can determine the fixed size of the PDF page prior to converting the Web site from HTML to PDF. After the PDF page size is determined, any Web pages captured adhere to the fixed size. If a Web page is larger than the established PDF page, the overflow automatically creates additional PDF pages. Hence, a single converted Web page may result in several PDF pages.

Web site design typically follows a hierarchical order. The home page rests at the topmost level where direct links from this page occupy a second level. Subsequently, links from the second level refer to pages at a third level and so on.

When pages are captured with Acrobat, the user can specify the number of levels to convert. Be forewarned, however, that even two levels of a Web site can occupy many Web pages. The number of pages and the speed of your Internet connection determine the amount of time needed to capture a site.

## Understanding captured pages structure

One or more levels can be captured from a Web site. You decide the number of levels to convert in the Create PDF from Web Page dialog box. PDF pages are converted and placed in a new PDF file or appended to an existing PDF file. One nice feature with Create PDF from Web Page is that it can seek out and append only new pages that have not yet been downloaded.

After pages are converted to PDF they can be viewed in Acrobat. Any URL links on the converted Web page are preserved in the resultant PDF and can be used to append files to the

PDF or open the link destinations in your Web browser. The file types that can be converted to PDF include the following:

- **Adobe PDF format.** Although not converted to PDF because they already appear in the format, PDF pages can be downloaded with Create PDF from Web Page.

## Note

XML forms created in Adobe LiveCycle Designer are not converted (nor do they appear in the Acrobat Document pane) when using the Create ⇨ PDF From Web Page command. Designer forms are added to blank pages converted to PDF as file attachments. ∎

- **FDF.** Form Data Format files can be captured and converted to PDF. An FDF file might be form data exported from a PDF form.

- **GIF Image Format (Graphics Interchange Format).** GIF images, as well as the last image in an animated GIF, can be captured when you convert a Web site to PDF. GIFs, like JPEGs within the HTML file, can also appear on separate PDF pages.

- **HTML documents.** HTML files can be converted to PDF. The hypertext links from the original HTML file are active in the PDF document as long as the destination documents and URLs have also been converted.

- **JPEG (Joint Photographic Experts Group) image format.** Images used in the HTML documents are also captured and converted to PDF. JPEGs may be part of the converted HTML page. When captured, they can be part of a captured HTML page and can also appear individually on PDF pages.

- **Multimedia Content.** Multimedia content including Flash animation can be embedded in Web pages converted to PDF.

- **Plain text.** Any text-only documents contained on a Web site, such as an ASCII text document, can be converted to PDF. When capturing text-only files, you have the opportunity to control many text attributes and page formats.

- **PNG image format.** Portable Network Graphics (PNG) contained in Web pages can be converted to PDF just like GIF and JPEG images.

- **XDP.** Forms created with Adobe LiveCycle Designer can be saved in XDP (XML Data Package) that can be understood by an XFA plug-in.

- **XFDF.** XML-based FDF files typically exported from PDF forms can be converted to PDF.

- **Image maps.** Image maps created in HTML are converted to PDF. The links associated with the map are active in the PDF as long as the link destinations are also converted.

- **Password-secure areas.** A password-secure area of a Web site can also be converted to PDF. In order to access a secure site, however, you need the password(s).

## Determining accepted file types and links

If a Web page link to another Web page or URL exists, it is preserved in the converted PDF document. Links to pages, sites, and various actions work similarly to the way they do directly on the Web site. However, if a PDF document contains a link to another PDF document, the converted file doesn't preserve the link. When the site is converted, the captured pages reside in a single PDF document. In order to maintain PDF links that open other PDF documents, the destination documents need to be captured as individual pages or extracted and saved from the converted pages.

Links to other levels are also inactive if they have not been converted during the capture. You can append individual linked pages to the converted PDF document by clicking Web links. Selections for converting individual links can be made available in a dialog box that opens after clicking a Web link. You can then append one or more links to the converted document. You can find the specifics on how to accomplish this task in "Appending pages" a little later in this chapter.

For executed animation, such as an animation from a GIF file or other programming application, the download contains only the last image in the sequence. A mouseover effect that changes an image is preserved in the converted PDF document as long as you download both the original image and the image associated with the mouseover. Additionally, you can capture sounds contained in documents.

You can also convert form fields to PDF, and field types such as radio buttons, check boxes, list boxes, and combo boxes often convert with the data intact. You might want to convert a form that has a list of countries and use the form field in your own PDF forms. The Acrobat implementation of JavaScript varies considerably from JavaScript written for Web pages, and therefore many JavaScripts do not work in converted Web pages.

## Cross-Reference
**For more information on form field types, see Chapters 30 and 31.** ∎

For Web pages that contain non-English characters, you need to have the appropriate resources loaded in order to download and convert the files. Japanese characters, for example, require installation of the Far East language files and additional system files. Using non-English characters requires you to make additional settings choices for Language Scripts. The options are available in the HTML Conversion Settings dialog box in the Fonts and Encoding tab. For making adjustments in the HTML Conversion Settings dialog box, see the section "Choosing Conversion Settings" later in this chapter.

### Using bookmarks in converted pages

After you convert a Web site to PDF, you can edit the document in Acrobat as you would any other PDF. Links to pages become editable links — that is, you can modify their properties. When a site has been converted to PDF, all the PDF pages contain bookmarks linked to the respective pages, as shown in Figure 7.13. The first bookmark is a regular (unstructured) bookmark that contains the domain name from which the site was captured. All bookmarks appearing below the server name are structured bookmarks linked to the converted pages. With the exception of specific Web applications, you can edit these bookmarks like any other bookmarks created in Acrobat. Additionally, you can use structured bookmarks for page editing by moving and deleting the bookmarks and associated pages.

## Cross-Reference

For more information on bookmarks, see Chapter 21. ∎

**FIGURE 7.13**

A captured Web site converted to PDF displays the domain name server as a normal bookmark and several structured bookmarks.

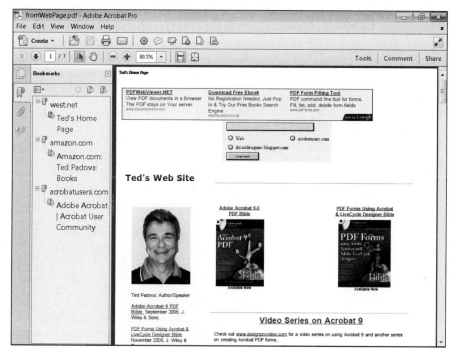

# Capturing Web pages

To begin capturing Web pages, choose File ➪ Create PDF ➪ From Web Page. The Create PDF from Web Page dialog box opens.

In the Create PDF from Web Page dialog box, various settings determine many different attributes for how a Web page is converted to PDF and how it appears in the Acrobat Document pane. The first level of controls is handled in the Create PDF from Web Page dialog box. Additional buttons in this dialog box open other dialog boxes, where you apply many more settings. If this is your first attempt at capturing a Web page, open the Create PDF from Web Page dialog box. Type a URL in the URL text box.

The default view shows you an abbreviated list of options as shown in the top of Figure 7.14. Click the Capture Multiple Levels button in the dialog box to expand the options as shown at the bottom of Figure 7.14. When the options are expanded, you can enter the number of levels in the Get only text box. Type 1 for the levels and click the Create button.

FIGURE 7.14

When you select the File ⇨ Create ⇨ PDF From Web Page command, the Create PDF from Web Page dialog box opens.

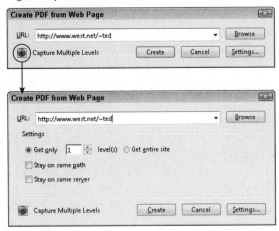

## Caution

**Be certain the Levels text box is set to 1 on your first attempt. Entering any other value may keep you waiting for some time depending on how many pages download from additional levels.** ■

Depending on the site, the number of different links from the site to other URLs, and the structure of the HTML pages, you often need to wade through the maze of dialog boxes that control settings for the PDF conversion from the HTML files. You don't need to memorize all of these settings; just use the following section as a reference when you capture Web pages.

### Adjusting settings in the Create PDF from Web Page dialog box

The controls available to you in the Create PDF from Web Page dialog box begin with the URL you type in the URL text box. This URL determines the site where the pages, which are converted, are hosted. After you enter the URL, the remaining selections you need to set include:

- **Get only *x* levels.** First, you need to click the Capture Multiple Pages button to expand the dialog box as shown in Figure 7.14. Appended pages can contain more than one level. The URL link may go to another site hosted on another server or stay on the same server. Select the levels to be downloaded by clicking the up or down arrows or entering a numeric value in the Get only text box.

## Caution

A Web site can have two levels of extraordinary size. If the Home page is on the first level and many links are contained on the Home page, all the associated links are at the second level. If you're downloading with a slow connection, the time needed to capture the site can be quite long. ∎

- **Get Entire Site.** When you select this radio button, all levels on the Web site are downloaded.

- **Stay on same path.** When this option is enabled, all documents are confined to the directory path under the selected URL.

- **Stay on same server.** Links made to other servers are not downloaded when this option is enabled.

- **Create.** When you're ready to convert Web pages from the site identified in the URL field box, click the Create button.

- **Browse.** Selecting this button enables you to capture a Web site residing on your computer or network server. Click Browse to open a navigation dialog box where you can find the directory where HTML pages are stored and capture the pages.

- **Settings.** Click this button to make choices for the conversion options. See "Choosing Conversion settings" later in this chapter.

## Tip

An alternative to using the Create from Web Page dialog box for a single Web page stored locally on your computer is to use drag and drop. Select the HTML document to convert to PDF and drag it to the top of the Acrobat window or program icon. If you have multiple HTML files to convert, you can also use the Create From Multiple Files menu command. ∎

Although it may not be entirely practical, Web designers who are more comfortable with WYSIWYG (What You See Is What You Get) HTML editors than layout applications may find that creating layout assemblies in their favorite editor is beneficial. You can't get control over image sampling, but you can achieve a layout for screen display. Create the layout in a program such as Adobe Dreamweaver. When you're finished with the pages, launch Acrobat and select Create task button ⇨ PDF from Web Page. Click the Browse button in the Create PDF from Web Page dialog box and navigate to your HTML files. Click the Create button to convert your pages to PDF. You can send these pages as an email attachment to a colleague or print them to your desktop printer. One advantage for using this method is your client or co-worker can add comments with the Comment & Markup tools to mark corrections and/or revisions when reviewing Web page designs.

## Caution

Even though you may browse to a folder on your hard drive and convert a local Web site to PDF, any external links launch your Internet connection and capture pages on another site. If you want only local pages converted, be certain to click the Stay on same server button in the Create PDF from Web Page dialog box. ∎

## Cross-Reference

You can create Web pages from tools installed by Acrobat in Microsoft Internet Explorer in Windows only. For information related to converting Web pages to PDF from within Microsoft Internet Explorer, see Chapter 25. For more information on using Comment & Markup tools, see Chapter 19. ■

### Choosing conversion settings

Clicking the Settings button in the Create PDF from Web Page dialog box opens the Web Page Conversion Settings dialog box, which has two tabs on which you supply file conversion attributes and page layout settings. The General tab deals with the file attribute settings, as shown in Figure 7.15.

**FIGURE 7.15**

The Web Page Conversion Settings dialog box offers controls for file types and how they will be converted to PDF.

Acrobat limits your choices for file type conversion to HTML and plain text. Earlier versions of Acrobat offered separate options for converting various image formats. Choose from the File Type menu either HTML or Text, and settings adjustments for these file types are further selected from another dialog box that opens when you click the Settings button.

At the bottom of the dialog box are three PDF Settings check boxes:

- **Create bookmarks.** When you enable this option, pages converted to PDF have structured bookmarks created for each page captured. The page's title is used as the bookmark name. If the page has no title, Acrobat supplies the URL as the bookmark name.

- **Place headers & footers on new page.** A header and footer are placed on all converted pages if this option is enabled. A header in the HTML file consists of the page title appearing with the <HEAD> tag. The footer retrieves the page's URL, the page name, and a date stamp for the date and time the page was downloaded.

- **Create PDF tags.** The structure of the converted PDF matches that of the original HTML file. Items such as list elements, table cells, and similar HTML tags are preserved. The PDF document contains structured bookmarks for each of the structured items. A tagged bookmark then links to a table, list, or other HTML element.

When you select HTML in the File Type menu and click the Settings button, a dialog box opens for HTML Conversion Settings, as shown in Figure 7.16.

---

**FIGURE 7.16**

---

When you select HTML in the File Description list and click the Settings button, the HTML Conversion Settings dialog box opens.

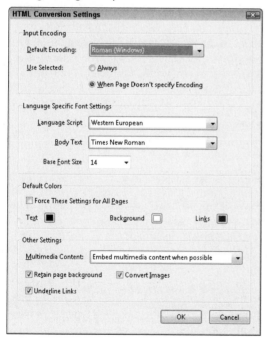

The two tabs in the HTML Conversion Settings dialog box are the General tab and the Fonts and Encoding tab. The first group of settings handles the general attributes assigned to the page layout:

- **Input Encoding.** Sets the Web page text encoding for body text, heads, and preformatted text. The default is consistent with the language you install. Other supported languages include Chinese, Japanese, Korean, and Unicode characters.

- **Language Specific Font Settings.** The items appearing under the Language Specific Font Settings section contain choices for font attributes and language choices. Choose from the menu options to select the Language, Body Text, and Base Font Size.

- **Default Colors.** Use this option to assign new default colors for Text, Background color, Links, and Alt Text. You can choose a color from a set of preset colors, or choose the option for custom colors, from a palette that opens after you click the swatch.

- **Force These Settings for All Pages.** HTML pages may or may not have assigned color values. When no color is assigned for one of these items, this setting defines the unassigned elements with the colors set in the Default Colors section. If this check box is enabled, all colors, including HTML-assigned colors, are changed to the Default Colors.

- **Multimedia.** Enables you to set options for handling multimedia clips. From the pull-down menu, you can choose from three options:

  - **Disable multimedia capture.** Movie and sound clips are ignored. Only the Web pages are converted to PDF, and no links to the media are included in the capture.

  - **Embed multimedia content when possible.** Acrobat viewers 6 and above enable you to embed multimedia clips in the PDF document. Selecting this option captures the Web page and embeds any multimedia files that meet the compatibility requirements of Acrobat. Be aware that embedded multimedia files are available only to Acrobat viewers 6.0 or later.

  - **Reference multimedia content by URL.** The captured Web page contains a link to the URL where the multimedia files are hosted.

## Cross-Reference

For more about features for handling multimedia in PDF documents, see Chapter 22. ■

- **Retain page background.** These include settings for the background colors used on the Web page, tiled image backgrounds, and table cells. When these check boxes are enabled, the original design is preserved in the PDF document.

## Tip

If you find table cells, background colors, and tiled background images distracting when you're reading Web pages either in a browser or converted to PDF, disable the Background Options check boxes before converting to PDF. The original design is changed, but the files are easily legible for both screen reading and when printed. ■

- **Convert Images.** If checked, graphics are converted. If unchecked, the graphics are not converted.

## Tip

To produce faster downloads, disable the Convert Images check box. The number of pages to be converted is significantly reduced, thereby reducing the amount of time to capture a Web site. ∎

- **Underline Links.** Displays the text used in an <A HREF . . .> tag with an underline. This option can be helpful if the text for a link is not a different color than the body copy.

After making choices in the HTML Conversion Settings dialog box, click OK and you return to the Web Page Conversion Settings dialog box shown earlier in Figure 7.15. Choose Text from the File Type menu and click the Settings button to open options for handling text conversions as shown in Figure 7.17.

**FIGURE 7.17**

Choose Text from the File Type menu and click Settings to open the Text Conversion Settings dialog box.

Options for text conversions include many similar choices you have for HTML conversions with regard to Input Encoding, Language Specific Font Settings, and font color choices. One additional option appears for Wrap Lines at Margin that controls word wrap in unformatted text.

### Choosing Page Layout conversion settings

All the settings discussed on the previous few pages were related to the General tab. In the Web Page Conversion Settings dialog box, another option is available. Page layout offers you options for describing the physical size and orientation of converted pages. Click the Page Layout tab as shown in Figure 7.18.

**FIGURE 7.18**

The Page Layout options are available from the Web Page Conversion Settings dialog box when you select the Page Layout tab.

Page layout attributes enable you to force long HTML pages into more standard page sizes for viewing or printing. If an HTML page spans several letter-sized pages, you can determine where the page breaks occur and the orientation of the converted pages. Many options are available in the Page Layout tab of the Web Page Conversion Settings dialog box:

- **Page Size.** This pull-down menu provides a variety of default page sizes. Acrobat supports page sizes from 1-inch square to 200-inches square. You can supply any value between the minimum and maximum page sizes in the Width and Height field boxes below the pull-down menu to override the fixed sizes available from the pull-down menu. To make changes in the field boxes, edit the text, click the up and down arrows in the dialog box, or click in a field box and press the up and down arrow keys on your keyboard. Press Tab and Shift+Tab to toggle between the field boxes.

- **Margins.** In the four Margins field boxes, you can set the amount of space on all four sides of the PDF page before any data appear. You make the changes for the margin sizes via the same methods described in the preceding bullet.

- **Orientation.** You choose portrait or landscape orientation from the radio button options. If a site's Web pages all conform to screen sizes such as 640 × 480, you might want to change the orientation to landscape.

- **Scale Wide Contents to fit page.** Once again, because HTML documents don't follow standard page sizes, images and text can be easily clipped when these documents are converted to a standard size. When this option is enabled, the page contents are reduced in size to fit within the page margins.

- **Switch to landscape if scaled smaller than.** The percentage value is user definable. When the page contents appear on a portrait page within the limit specified in the field box, the PDF document is automatically converted to a landscape orientation. The default is 70 percent. If the default value is used, any vertical page scaled lower than 70 percent is auto-switched to landscape as long as the orientation is selected for Portrait.

## PDF Workflow

If your workflow is dependent on capturing Web pages routinely, then you'll want to use the same conversion settings for all your Web captures. Educational facilities, government agencies, research institutes, and large corporate offices may have frequent needs for archiving research information found on the Web.

Unfortunately, Acrobat makes no provision for saving and loading Web Capture settings established in the dialog boxes discussed in the preceding pages. To develop a workflow suited to organizations or workgroups, your alternative may be setting up a single computer dedicated to the task of capturing data from the Web. The computer needs to be licensed for Acrobat, but using a single computer ensures all Web captures are performed with the same conversion settings. Users with any Acrobat viewer can retrieve the PDF files that are captured across a network or intranet. ■

### Determining download status

After you choose all settings and options in all the dialog boxes pertaining to converting Web sites to PDF, you can revisit the Create PDF from Web Page command from any one of the three methods discussed earlier. As pages are downloaded and converted to PDF, the Download Status dialog box opens displaying, appropriately, the download status. After the first page downloads, this dialog box, shown in Figure 7.19, moves to the background behind the converted Web pages.

## Caution

Web Capture places the converted PDF in memory and uses your hard drive space as an extension of RAM. The PDF is not saved to disk until you perform a Save or Save As operation. If your computer crashes or you quit without saving, the file is lost and you'll need to capture the site again. ■

**FIGURE 7.19**

The Download Status dialog box appears momentarily and then disappears as Acrobat continues to download pages and convert them to PDF.

## Appending pages

When a PDF file is open in the Document pane, you can append pages from URL links by opening a context menu on a bookmark in the Bookmarks panel and choose from a few options supporting Web page conversions as shown in Figure 7.20.

To append pages to the open PDF, choose Append Next Level in the context menu. If you choose View Web Links, a dialog box opens, reporting all the URLs visited when the conversion to PDF was made. The last option in the context menu related to converting Web pages is Open Page in Web Browser. Choosing this option, as you might suspect, opens the bookmark URL in your default Web browser.

## Locating Web addresses

Acrobat versions 7 through X are intelligent viewers when it comes to detecting URLs in text on PDF pages. You don't need a link or button to click URL text and launch your default Web browser. Acrobat versions 7 through X do that automatically for you.

In order for Acrobat viewers to recognize URLs in text, you need to be certain a Preference option is enabled in the General Preferences. Open the Preferences dialog box (Control/⌘+K) and click General in the left pane. Check Create links from URLs in the right pane as shown in Figure 7.21.

**FIGURE 7.20**

Open a context menu on a bookmark in the Bookmarks panel and you find three menu choices for working with Web page captures.

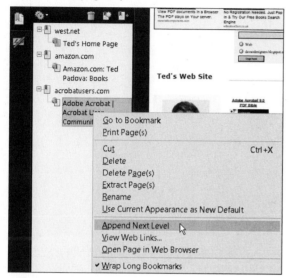

**FIGURE 7.21**

Open Preferences and check Create links from URLs from General.

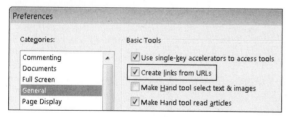

If you prepare PDF files for users of earlier versions of Acrobat viewers, then you need to create links to URLs in text if you want users to click text to launch a Web page. You can easily create links from URLs in text using a simple menu command. But don't do this if you know your entire audience uses a 7.0 viewer or above. The more links or buttons you add to a PDF, the larger your file size will be.

The text must have a URL listing beginning with `http://`, `https:`, or `www`. In addition any email address such as `designer@company.com` will be recognized as a `mailto:` link that will open your default mail client. After the Web links are converted, you can also click the link and append pages by using Web Capture. PDF authors may also create Web links for end users when distributing files to others.

To create Web links on pages containing URLs, open the Document Processing panel and click Create Links from URLs. A dialog box opens, as shown in Figure 7.22.

**FIGURE 7.22**

The Create Web Links dialog box enables you to create Web links from text for user-defined page ranges in the open PDF file.

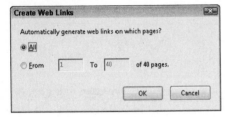

In the Create Web Links dialog box, you specify page ranges for where Acrobat should create the links. Acrobat performs this task quickly and creates all links where the proper syntax has been used to describe the URL. If you want to delete links from a PDF document, open the Document Processing panel and click Document Remove All Links. The Remove Web Links dialog box opens, and you can supply page ranges for eliminating Web links.

# Summary

In this chapter, you learned many ways to convert files to PDFs. Among the items discussed are:

- You can create PDF documents with the Adobe PDF printer. You can use the Adobe PDF printer to apply a variety of Adobe PDF Settings to the PDF conversion. Adobe PDF Settings are used by Acrobat Distiller and the Adobe PDF Printer.

- You can use Acrobat to convert a variety of different native file formats to PDF using the Create PDF From File command. Multiple files can be converted to PDF and concatenated into a single document.

- You can use Acrobat to download Web pages and convert them to PDF. Web pages residing locally on hard drives can be converted to PDF. All Web page conversions preserve page and URL links.

- You can convert data copied to the system Clipboard to PDF on both Windows and the Mac.

# 8

# Using Acrobat PDFMaker with Microsoft Programs

The last chapter covered PDF file creation from various programs and certain file types. Some of the PDF creation options you have from within Acrobat are also available directly from the authoring programs. Such is the case with the most popular Microsoft applications.

Adobe has devoted much development time to creating tools that easily convert most of the Microsoft applications to PDF along with certain other programs, such as Autodesk AutoCAD discussed in Chapter 7 and Lotus Notes. With a one-button click in almost every Microsoft program you can convert your documents to PDF.

The common tool used in these programs is Acrobat PDFMaker, created by Adobe Systems and automatically installed in every program supporting the tool when you install Acrobat.

In this chapter you learn how to use the PDFMaker tool in the most popular Microsoft programs.

## Using Acrobat with Microsoft Word

Of all the Office applications, Microsoft Word gives you the best support for PDF file creation. Microsoft Word is the only word-processing application that provides access to the structural data of the document. The structural data of the Word document such as titles, heads, tables, paragraphs, figure captions, and so on can be converted to tagged bookmarks.

Tagged bookmarks give you much more control over the PDF content. You can navigate to the element structures, and move, copy, extract, and delete pages through menu commands in the Bookmarks tab.

## Note

Depending on the Acrobat viewer you use, the PDFMaker options are different. In Acrobat Pro, you have an Embed Video tool. This tool is not available in Acrobat Standard. ■

With Word and all Microsoft Office programs you have several choices for PDF conversion. You can use the Create PDF From File command, use the Combine Task or command, drag and drop Microsoft Office files on the Acrobat Document pane, print to PostScript and convert the PostScript in Acrobat Distiller, and use a tool developed by Adobe called the Acrobat PDFMaker. This tool is installed in all Office programs and several other Microsoft programs.

## Cross-Reference

For more information on Create PDF From File, see Chapter 7. For more on using Combine Task, see Chapter 11. ■

Of all the tools available to you, using PDFMaker is your best choice. Why? Because PDFMaker provides you with more options settings to control the attributes in the converted file. If, for example, you want to set up a hierarchy order for bookmarks to appear in the converted PDF, you need to use PDFMaker. If you want to convert PowerPoint files with transitions and media effects, you need to use PDFMaker. If you want to create layered PDFs from Microsoft Visio, again, you need PDFMaker. Other PDF conversion options don't provide you with support for many of these attributes.

PDFMaker offers several tools to control PDF file creation from within Microsoft Word and all other Microsoft programs that use the PDFMaker tools. After you install Acrobat and later open Word (or other Office programs), two Acrobat icons appear on the far-left side of the toolbar and a menu command in MS Office 2003 products, and you have a separate tab in the Office 2007 Ribbon.

## Note

You have similar conversion options for using PDFMaker in Microsoft Office 2003 and Microsoft Office 2007. The user interface is obviously different between the different versions of Microsoft Office. This chapter covers using Office 2007, and all the screen shots appearing here were taken using Microsoft's newest Office release. If you're an Office 2003 user, you can find similar conversion settings using the Acrobat menu commands that are installed with PDFMaker. ■

Each of the Office 2007 and Office 2010 programs display an Acrobat tab in the Ribbon after you install Acrobat on Windows. Click the Acrobat tab and you find several tools, shown in Figure 8.1, used for handling Adobe PDF files.

FIGURE 8.1

Click the Acrobat tab in the Ribbon to display all the tools installed with PDFMaker.

# Using PDFMaker on the Mac

PDFMaker vanished from the Mac in Acrobat 9 and is not supported in Acrobat X. Earlier versions of Acrobat included the PDFMaker in the MS Office applications, but they weren't as robust as you had on Windows.

The alternative that consistently produces good PDF documents from MS Office programs is to use the File⇨Print command and print to a PDF document.

In any MS Office program choose File⇨Print. When the Print dialog box opens, choose Adobe PDF from the printer pull-down menu. Open the PDF menu and choose Save as PDF. The Save dialog box opens. Name your file and locate a target folder and click Save.

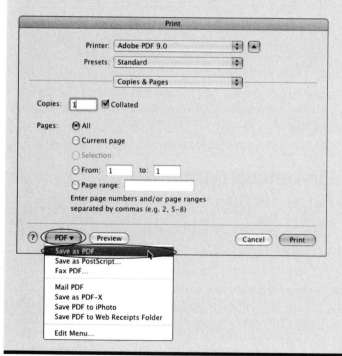

When you click the Acrobat tab in the Ribbon, you find the following tools:

- **Create PDF.** Click this button to open the Save Adobe PDF File As dialog box. Name the file and click Save to convert the Word document to a PDF.

- **Preferences.** Formerly called Conversion Settings in earlier versions of MS Office and PDFMaker, the Preferences button opens the Acrobat PDFMaker dialog box where you make choices for conversion options.

- **Create and Attach to Email.** Clicking this button performs two tasks. The Word document is converted to a PDF and the resultant PDF is attached to a new email message in your default email client.

- **Mail Merge.** A mail merge template is merged with a data file, and the template and data are converted to PDF pages.

- **Create and Send For Review.** The Word file is converted to a PDF and opens in Acrobat with the Send for Shared Review dialog box open and ready for you to make a choice for starting a shared review on Acrobat.com or an internal server.

## Cross-Reference

For more information on Shared Reviews see Chapter 20. For additional information on using Acrobat.com, see Chapter 26. ■

- **Acrobat Comments.** Click Acrobat Comments and a pull-down menu opens with commands for Importing Comments from Acrobat, Continue Integration Process, Accept All Changes in a Document, Delete All Comments in a Document, and Show Instructions — a help information dialog box.

- **Embed 3D.** Click the Embed 3D tool and the Add 3D Data dialog box opens. You can choose a 3-D file for embedding in the Word document and assign JavaScripts for setting different views and rotations.

- **Embed Video.** Click this button to embed an Adobe Flash animation or multimedia file.

# Changing conversion settings (Windows)

PDFMaker uses the PDF Library to convert Office documents to PDF. When you click the Preferences button in the Ribbon, the Acrobat PDFMaker dialog box opens. In the dialog box, five tabs offer attribute choices for how the PDF is ultimately created. The tabs are Settings, Security, Word, Bookmarks, and Video as shown in Figure 8.2.

Different programs support many different features. For example, Microsoft Visio and Autodesk AutoCAD both support layers. Programs such as Word, Excel, and PowerPoint do not support layers. Excel supports workbooks, Word supports style sheets, and PowerPoint supports media and transitions. When you open PDFMaker in any program supporting the tool, you'll find different conversion settings options. Be aware that the dialog box you see in Figure 8.2 changes when opened in other programs. In Figure 8.2, the conversion settings options are specific only to Microsoft Word.

Click Preferences in the Ribbon and the Acrobat PDFMaker dialog box opens.

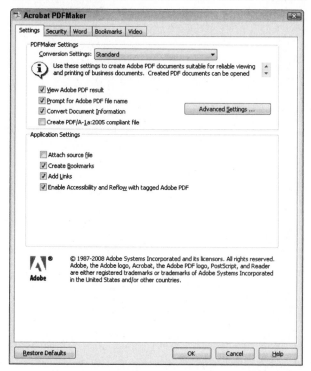

## Exploring options in the Settings panel

The Settings panel is the first of the four panels where you select options. At the top of the Settings panel is a pull-down menu for Conversion Settings. From this menu, you choose the same settings as are used by Acrobat Distiller to convert the file to a PDF. If you want to edit the settings or create a new Adobe PDF Setting, click the Advanced Settings button to open the Adobe PDF Settings dialog box shown in Figure 8.3. This enables you to make choices for attributes used to convert the document to a PDF.

Options in the Settings panel are as follows:

- **View Adobe PDF result.** When the PDF is created, the document opens in Acrobat if this check box is enabled. If it's disabled, the PDF is created and the Word file remains in view.

- **Prompt for Adobe PDF filename.** If this check box is enabled, you won't inadvertently overwrite a file with the same name. Leaving this check box enabled is a good idea.

**FIGURE 8.3**

The Adobe PDF Settings panel offers you choices for selecting the Adobe PDF Settings used to convert the file.

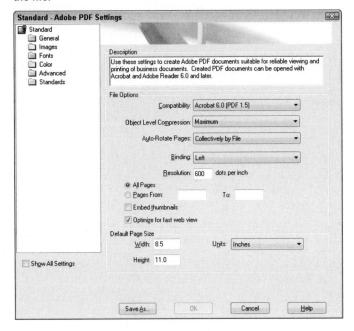

- **Convert Document Information.** This option ensures document information created in Word is added to the PDF Document Properties.

- **Create PDF/A-1a:2005 Compatible file.** Clicking this option automatically changes the Conversion Settings to the PDF/A-1a:2005(RGB) Adobe PDF Setting. The files are made compliant with PDF/A. Note that using PDF/A produces a PDF with Acrobat 5 compatibility; therefore, any features specific to PDF version 1.5 (Acrobat 6 and greater compatible) files are lost in PDF/A-compliant files.

- **Attach source file.** If you want to attach the Word file from which the PDF was created, enable this check box and the Word file is added as a file attachment.

- **Create Bookmarks.** Bookmarks are created from Word style sheets. Select this check box to convert styles and headings to Bookmarks. Make selections for what styles and headings to convert to bookmarks in the Bookmarks panel.

- **Add Links.** This option ensures that hyperlinks created in Word are converted to links in the PDF document.

- **Enable Accessibility and Reflow with tagged Adobe PDF.** This option creates document structure tags. Accessibility for the visually challenged and developmentally disabled that is contained in the Word document is preserved in the PDF. Reflowing text enables the Acrobat user to use the Reflow view. As a matter of default, leave this check box enabled. Tagged PDF documents also help you export the PDF text back out to a word processor with more data integrity than when exporting files without tags.

## Note

**If you enable accessibility and reflow, the file sizes of your PDF documents are larger compared to files exported to PDF without accessibility and tags. If you need to produce the smallest file sizes for specific purposes where you know accessibility and preserving structure are not needed, disable the check box.** ■

### Using the Security panel

Click the Security panel to open options for security settings. Security options for permissions are available only for High-Bit encryption (128-bit RC4). If you choose to add security from the Word options, the PDF document is compatible with Acrobat 5.0 viewers and greater. If you need additional security controls available in Acrobat 6, Acrobat 7, and Acrobat X compatibility options, apply the security in Acrobat.

## Cross-Reference

**For specific definitions of the security options, see Chapter 24.** ■

### Choosing options in the Word panel

Click the Word panel to choose options for Word content, as shown in Figure 8.4.

---

**FIGURE 8.4**

---

The Word panel contains items specific to some of the content in Word that can be converted in the resulting PDF document.

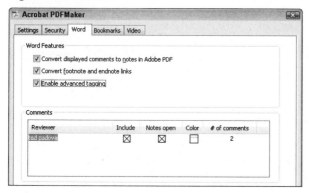

Options on the Word panel are as follows:

- **Convert displayed comments to notes in Adobe PDF.** Notes can be converted to annotation comments that will appear in a text note in the PDF file.

- **Convert footnote and endnote links.** Bookmark links are added for all footnotes and endnotes.

- **Enable advanced tagging.** The tagging features available in Word that export to PDF have been split for accessibility with the Enable Accessibility and Reflow with tagged Adobe PDF files you see in Figure 8.2. This option adds settings *over and above* document accessibility. Checking this box adds document structure for character styles such as underlines, superscript, subscript, outline, strikeouts, and so on that can be useful when exporting PDF files back to text such as exporting to Word or RTF formats. The downside for selecting this check box is that the PDF conversion will take longer and the file sizes will grow. Unless you anticipate a need for adding this kind of document structure in your converted files, leave the check box unchecked.

- **Comments.** The lower window lists all comments by author in the file. If you check the box in the Include column, the comments are converted to Acrobat comments. The Notes open column enables you to set the default for note comments with open note popup windows.

## Tip

If you have a document with comments added by several individuals and you want each person's comments appearing with different note colors, click the icon in the Color column to change color. Keep clicking the icon to continue changing color. Word scrolls through eight different colors as you keep clicking the mouse. ■

### Using the Bookmarks panel

In the Bookmarks panel, there are three items that can determine what bookmarks will be created in the PDF file:

- **Convert Word Headings to Bookmarks.** Word headings can be converted to bookmarks. In the box below the check boxes, a list of all headings and styles contained in the Word document appears. Click the box under the Bookmark column to determine what heads to convert to bookmarks.

- **Convert Word Styles to Bookmarks.** You can select user-defined styles for conversion to bookmarks. Scroll the list of elements and place a check mark for the styles you want to convert.

- **Convert Word Bookmarks.** Converts all bookmarks created in Word to PDF bookmarks.

Click the number appearing in the Levels column and a popup menu becomes visible. Click the down-pointing arrow to open the menu and select the level of nesting for the bookmarks as shown in Figure 8.5. The nesting order you determine here in the Acrobat PDFMaker settings dialog box determines the order of parent/child relationships in the Acrobat Bookmarks panel when the file is converted to PDF. (See Figure 8.6.)

**FIGURE 8.5**

The Bookmarks panel offers three choices for determining what bookmarks are created in the PDF file. Clicking a number in the Level column permits you to determine parent/child relationships for bookmarks.

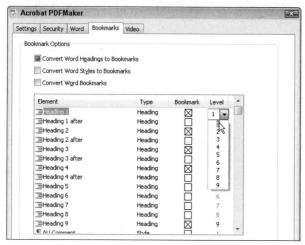

**FIGURE 8.6**

Bookmarks from subheads are nested as child bookmarks below the top-level heads according to the Level order specified in Acrobat PDFMaker.

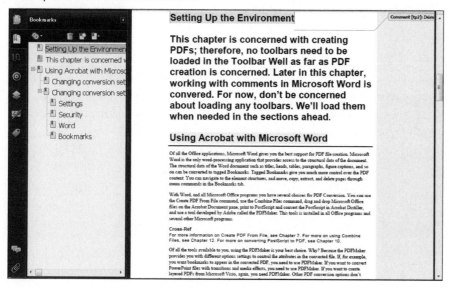

## Caution

If you select the Convert Word Styles to Bookmarks check box and you have a number of style sheets in your Word document, you end up with a huge list of bookmarks. At some point the bookmarks will appear over- whelming and difficult to manage. Unless you have a definite need for converting styles in some Word docu- ments, stick with the Convert Word Headings to Bookmarks option and convert the heads to bookmarks. ■

After you select the options in the Acrobat PDFMaker dialog box, click the Convert to PDF tool or select the menu option to convert the file. In Figure 8.6, I converted a file having three levels of heads. Notice that when the Bookmarks panel is open, you see the bookmarks nested into parent/child relationships.

## Cross-Reference

For more information on Adobe PDF bookmarks and nesting bookmarks into parent/child relationships, see Chapter 21. ■

### Exploring options in the Video panel

The Video panel in Acrobat PDFMaker offers some choices for importing video files in a Word document. Click the Video tab and the options shown in Figure 8.7 include:

- **Location.** The video can be stored in the same folder as the Word document or a folder you choose by clicking the Browse button.

- **Quality.** From the Video Quality pull-down menu choose a quality setting for the video playback. If the video file is interlaced, an option to de-interlace the file is included below the menu.

- **Encode Audio.** Choose from options in the pull-down menu for audio quality.

---

**FIGURE 8.7**

Choose from options in the Video panel for location and quality settings for imported video files.

---

# Working with comments (Windows)

Move to the right on the Ribbon and in the Review and Comment area you find Acrobat Comments. Clicking this button opens a pull-down menu as shown in Figure 8.8. The commands in the menu address merging your PDF comments back into the original Microsoft Word document. The menu items are as follows:

**FIGURE 8.8**

Click Acrobat Comments to open the pull-down menu for managing comments.

- **Import Comments from Acrobat.** This is a *round-trip* process — that is, you need to start with a Microsoft Word document, send it out to be reviewed, and then merge the received comments back into the Word file. In addition, when you create the PDF file in the first place, you must use PDFMaker. When you select the menu item, the Import Comments from Adobe Acrobat help window opens. Read the helpful tips on how to import comments and click OK to proceed. The next dialog box that opens is Import Comments from Adobe Acrobat, as shown in Figure 8.9. In the dialog box, you make choices for what files to select, what comments to import, and whether you want to filter the comments.

**FIGURE 8.9**

The Import Comments from Adobe Acrobat dialog box offers choices for file selection and the comment types to import into the Word document.

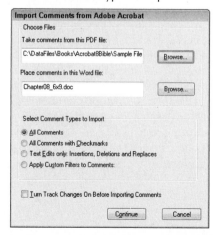

- **Continue Integration Process.** This continues the integration of PDF comments in the Word document for text edits such as inserts and deletions. If review tracking is on, you can merge tracked changes.

- **Accept All Changes in Document.** After the comment integration, select this menu command to accept the comments. Comments such as text marked for deletion are deleted; text marked with insertion adds the inserted comments; and so on.

- **Delete All Comments in Document.** All comments imported from the PDF document are deleted from the Word file.

- **Show Instructions.** The dialog box that opens when you choose the Import Comments from Acrobat command (see the first bullet in this list) also opens when you choose the Show Instructions menu command.

To make the process for importing comments from Acrobat easier (or Exporting comments from Acrobat to Word), take a look at the steps that follow, which describe a workflow for exchanging comments in Word and PDF documents.

### STEPS: Integrating Acrobat comments in Word documents (Windows only)

1.  **Convert a Word document to PDF using the PDFMaker Create PDF Tool.** Be certain to use PDFMaker to convert your Word file to PDF.

## Caution

You must be certain to check Enable Accessibility and Reflow with tagged Adobe PDF in the Settings panel in order to export/import comments between Acrobat PDF and Word files. ■

2.  **Mark up the PDF file in Acrobat using the Comment & Markup tools.** Be certain to use the Text Edits tools in the Comment & Markup toolbar to comment on the PDF file. Text Edit comments get merged directly into the Microsoft Word document stream, whereas other comments are just applied as note comments in Word.

## Cross-Reference

For more information on commenting and using the Text Edits tools, see Chapter 19. ■

3.  **Initiate an export of comments to Word.** You can export comments from Acrobat to Word or Import comments in Word from a PDF file. In Acrobat you use the Comments panel and choose Export Comments to Word command in the Comments List panel. In Word you use the Acrobat Comments ➪ Import Comments from Acrobat menu command. Either menu selection opens the Import Comments from Adobe Acrobat dialog box. If you start in Acrobat, Microsoft Word is launched and the Import Comments from Adobe Acrobat Wizard is handled from within Word. The first dialog box describes the process for integrating your PDF comments back to a Word document. Click OK after reading the help information.

4. **Choose files and comment types.** The second dialog box is the Import Comments from Adobe Acrobat Wizard shown earlier in Figure 8.9. Choose the Word file you want to use for exporting comments and click Continue.

5. **Import the comments.** Your comments are imported into the Word document in a seamless operation. After all the comments are imported you should see the Successful Import dialog box open, as shown in Figure 8.10.

**FIGURE 8.10**

If your comments are successfully imported, the Successful Import dialog box opens.

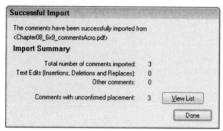

6. **Integrate Text Edits.** Open the Acrobat Comments pull-down menu in the Ribbon and choose Continue Integration Process. Another dialog box opens as shown in Figure 8.11, where you can selectively choose comments to integrate or click the Apply All Remaining button to integrate all Text Edits. After the comments are integrated, another dialog box opens and reports the results. Click Done and your integration is complete.

**FIGURE 8.11**

Click Apply to apply each comment as you review it in the New Text window, or click Apply All Remaining to import all Text Edits comments.

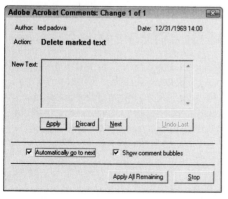

## Converting snippets to PDF

You may have a passage of text, a graphic image, a table, a footnote or some other portion of data on a page in MS Word and want just a selected area converted to a PDF document. If this is your task, just select the data you want to convert in your Word document and click the Create PDF button in the Ribbon. The Acrobat PDFMaker dialog box opens. Select Options.

The default for the Page Range is All, which of course means that all pages in the Word document are converted to PDF when you click OK. Notice the Selection radio button in Figure 8.12. When you select any data in a Word file, the Selection radio button becomes active. Click this button and your selected data are converted to PDF.

### FIGURE 8.12

Select data in a Word document and click Create PDF in the Ribbon. Select Options. Click Selection in the Acrobat PDFMaker dialog box to convert the selection to a PDF file.

## Converting Microsoft Excel Files to PDF

When converting Microsoft Excel files, as with any other program using the PDFMaker, you'll want to open the Acrobat Ribbon. As is the case with Word, the tools are installed in Excel after you install Acrobat. When you open the Acrobat Ribbon and compare the tool choices with the same Ribbon opened in Word, you see a few differences between the Ribbon tools shown for Word in Figure 8.1 and the Ribbon tools for Excel shown in Figure 8.13.

Notice the Mail Merge and Acrobat Comments tools are unique to Word and don't appear in the Excel menu. The remaining tools are the same as you find in Word; however, when converting to PDF, you have some different options to choose from for creating PDF files from Excel.

FIGURE 8.13

The Acrobat menu as shown in Microsoft Excel

Open the Acrobat PDFMaker dialog box by selecting Preferences. The Acrobat PDFMaker dialog box opens, as shown in Figure 8.14.

FIGURE 8.14

Select Preferences to open the Acrobat PDFMaker dialog box.

Compare Figure 8.14 with the Acrobat PDFMaker dialog box opened in Word in Figure 8.2. All the settings are identical in the Excel Acrobat PDFMaker dialog box as the same dialog box opened from Word, with the exception of the last three items:

- **Convert Comments.** Check this box when you want Excel comments converted to comment notes in the resultant PDF file.

- **Fit Worksheet to a single page.** Check this box to avoid tiling individual worksheet pages.

- **Fit to paper width.** Check this box to fit the spreadsheet to the width of the document page.

- **Prompt for selecting Excel Sheets.** Check this box to individually select worksheets in a workbook you want converted to PDF. If you create workbooks with multiple worksheets, be sure to keep this box checked as a default.

To understand a little more about converting Excel workbooks to PDF, follow these steps.

### STEPS: Converting an Excel Workbook to PDF

1. **Open an Excel workbook.** Try to use an Excel file having several worksheets in a workbook.

2. **Change conversion settings.** Click the Acrobat tab in the Ribbon and click the Preferences button. In the Change Acrobat PDFMaker dialog box select the check boxes for Create Bookmarks and Prompt for selecting Excel Sheets. You can additionally make other choices such as Fit Worksheet to a single page if you like. Click OK to return to the Ribbon options.

3. **Convert to PDF.** Click the Create PDF tool in the Ribbon.

4. **Select worksheets.** As soon as you make a choice to convert to PDF, a second Acrobat PDFMaker dialog box opens. Because you selected Prompt for selecting Excel Sheets in the first Acrobat PDFMaker dialog box, Acrobat prompts you to select the worksheets you want to convert to PDF.

    Click the Entire Workbook radio button if you want all sheets converted to PDF, or individually select the sheets you want to convert and click the Add button. In my example I want to convert the first 5M sheet, the second 5M sheet, and the fourth 5M sheet you see listed in Figure 8.15. After making your selection(s), click the Convert to PDF button and your worksheet(s) is converted to PDF.

5. **View the PDF.** If you elected to view the PDF after conversion by selecting the View Adobe PDF result check box in the Acrobat PDFMaker dialog box, your file opens automatically in Acrobat. If you didn't check the box, open Acrobat and click the Open tool to locate and open your converted document. Click the Bookmarks panel and you should see bookmarks added for each worksheet in the converted workbook, as shown in Figure 8.16.

**FIGURE 8.15**

Select the sheets you want to convert and click the Add button.

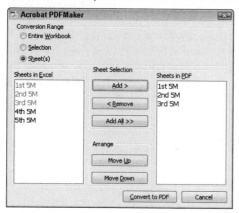

**FIGURE 8.16**

Click the Bookmarks panel and you'll find bookmarks associated with each worksheet in the converted workbook.

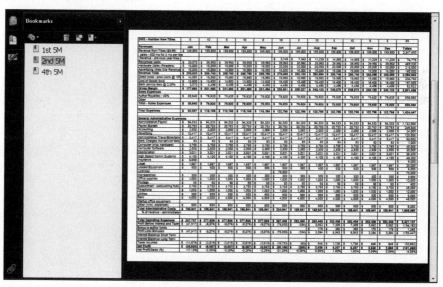

# Converting Microsoft PowerPoint Files to PDF

PowerPoint Conversion Settings offer a few more options than you find with either Word or Excel. To open the Acrobat PDFMaker dialog box, click the Acrobat tab in the Ribbon and click Preferences. When the Acrobat PDFMaker dialog box opens you see four new items in the Applications settings that don't appear in the Word or Excel Acrobat PDFMaker dialog box.

The items shown in Figure 8.17 include the following:

- **Convert Multimedia.** Imported media such as sound and video in PowerPoint files can be converted to PDF media.
- **Preserve Slide Transitions.** Slide transitions can be saved in the PDF file and viewed when you view the PDF in Full Screen mode in an Acrobat viewer.

**FIGURE 8.17**

Click Preferences in the Ribbon in PowerPoint to open the Acrobat PDFMaker dialog box.

- **Convert hidden slides to PDF pages.** Check this box if you have hidden slides in PowerPoint and you want the hidden slides to appear as pages in the resultant PDF.

- **Convert Speaker Notes.** Speaker notes are converted to PDF when you check this box.

# Changing Microsoft Publisher Files to PDF

Microsoft Publisher is Microsoft's effort at developing a more commercial and professional program designed for prepress and printing. Print shops and service bureaus shied away from Publisher in earlier versions for lack of essential tools such as adding printer's marks, color separation tools, and changing halftone frequency. However, Microsoft continued development of the product, and the latest version of Publisher includes all the features needed for prepress and commercial printing.

Unlike Word, Excel, and PowerPoint, Publisher doesn't have a separate Ribbon bar. From the top of the Ribbon, click Adobe PDF and a pull-down menu opens as shown in Figure 8.18. To open the Preferences similar to the Preferences button chosen in the other Office applications, choose Change Conversion Settings and the Acrobat PDFMaker dialog box opens as shown in Figure 8.19.

**FIGURE 8.18**

The Adobe PDF pull-down menu in Microsoft Publisher

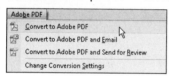

When it comes to exports to PDF, Adobe supports some of the much-needed file attributes required to print files on press. When you open the Acrobat PDFMaker from the Adobe PDF menu in Microsoft Publisher, the Acrobat PDFMaker dialog box displays some settings choices not found in any of the other Acrobat PDFMaker dialog boxes.

## Note

When you first launch Microsoft Publisher after installing Acrobat, you are prompted in a dialog box for enabling macros. Because the Acrobat PDFMaker is a macro, you need to grant permissions for using the macro or you won't see the Adobe PDF menu or the Acrobat conversion tools. ∎

As shown in Figure 8.19, you have some unique settings that apply only to Microsoft Publisher. These settings include the following:

- **Conversion Settings.** The default Adobe PDF Setting is Press Quality. Like the other Acrobat PDFMaker dialog boxes, you can change the setting by clicking the Advanced Settings button.

- **Preserve Spot Color in Adobe PDF.** If spot colors are used in the Publisher file, you need to check this box to preserve the spot colors. If you fail to do so, spot colors are converted to CMYK.

**FIGURE 8.19**

Acrobat PDFMaker preferences opened from Microsoft Publisher

- **Print Crop Marks.** As you can see by comparing this Acrobat PDFMaker dialog box with the others shown for Word, Excel, and PowerPoint, you see the first option for adding crop marks when a file is converted to PDF. This setting is very important if you have bleeds on pages in the Publisher document.

- **Allow Bleeds.** If bleeds are contained in the PowerPoint file, you must check the box to allow bleeds. When the box is checked, you have another setting to print separate bleed marks.

- **Preserve Transparency in Adobe PDF.** You can check the box to preserve transparency and let Acrobat flatten the transparency at print time.

The features added to the PowerPoint Acrobat PDFMaker are all related to commercial printing.

## Cross-Reference

For more information on commercial printing and transparency flattening, see Chapter 29. ■

# Converting Web Pages from Internet Explorer to PDF (Windows Only)

In Chapter 7, I talked about PDF conversion using the Create PDF From Web Page command. In Chapter 25 I talk about PDFs and the Web. But because this chapter is focused on using the Acrobat PDFMaker tool, I thought it best to talk about the Acrobat PDFMaker and Microsoft Internet Explorer here in Chapter 8.

If you're working in an Acrobat session and you want to convert one or more pages to PDF, it makes sense to use the Create PDF From Web Page command. You don't need to launch a Web browser and open a page you want to convert to PDF. You can do all that within Acrobat.

So why does Adobe supply yet another tool for Web page conversion to PDF? Because sometimes you browse the Internet and find a page you want to convert to PDF. Because you're already in a Web browser, it makes sense to convert a Web page from the browser versus launching Acrobat and typing a URL in the Create PDF From Web Page dialog box.

As an example, let me share with you one Web page conversion I use routinely. When I book my airline tickets online, the ticket provider displays an itinerary showing my flight number, travel times, and travel dates. Of course the provider displays a print-ready Web page that I can send off to my printer, but I'm prone to losing things, and printing paper is a surefire target for a lost item in my travel bag.

As an alternative to printing Web pages, I just do a quick conversion to PDF and copy my PDF to the laptop I carry to conferences and as a backup to a flash drive. When I'm in a hotel, I just open the PDF to check on my departure when I finish up my travels.

You may find many other uses for converting Web pages to PDF. Perhaps a map to a location, a latest recipe you saw on Emeril's show, some research information you're collecting, a new product description you want to study, or many other similar uses. Personally, I find it much easier to locate a PDF file on my computer than that last piece of paper I printed to my desktop printer.

## Changing a Web page to PDF using PDFMaker

If you use Microsoft Internet Explorer on Windows, then you have the Acrobat PDFMaker installed in Explorer. In Internet Explorer you can click the pull-down menu adjacent to the Convert tool in the Internet Explorer toolbar to open the Adobe PDF menu and view the menu options, as shown in Figure 8.20. Notice in the menu you have a command for Preferences. Click Preferences in the menu and you find conversion options similar to those you use when creating a PDF from a Web page.

**FIGURE 8.20**

Open the Convert pull-down menu to view the options for converting Web pages to PDF.

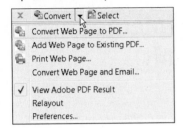

## Cross-Reference

**To learn more about conversion settings for Web page conversion to PDF, see Chapter 7. ■**

To convert a Web page to PDF, open a Web page in Internet Explorer and click the Convert tool to open a pull-down menu. Choose Convert Web Page to PDF. Acrobat begins the conversion process, and you'll see a progress bar similar to the one shown in Figure 8.21.

**FIGURE 8.21**

A progress bar reports the conversion of a Web page to PDF.

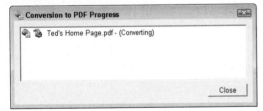

After conversion, the Web page opens in Acrobat. Notice that pages converted with Internet Explorer also include structured bookmarks like pages converted with the Create PDF From Web Page tool. If you open a context menu on a structured bookmark, you'll see the same menu options as you find with Web pages converted with the Create PDF From Web Page tool. Pages converted to PDF from Internet Explorer can also have additional pages appended to the converted file by selecting Append Next Level in a context menu, as shown in Figure 8.22.

## Cross-Reference

**For more information on structured bookmarks and options for appending Web pages, see Chapter 7. ■**

FIGURE 8.22

Creating PDFs from Acrobat PDFMaker in Internet Explorer produces structured bookmarks and menu options the same as when using the Create PDF From Web Page tool.

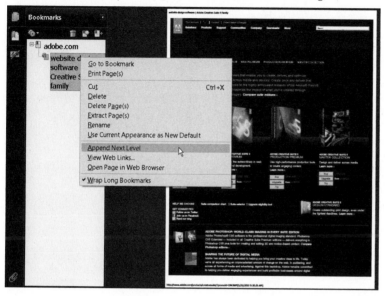

## Tip

Mac users may feel a little left out when converting Web pages to PDF from within programs such as Apple's Safari. No PDFMaker exists on the Mac for Safari or Microsoft Internet Explorer. However, the Mac user can still create PDF documents from any Web browser. Just open a Web page and select File ⇨ Print. In the Print dialog box click the PDF button to open a pull-down menu and select Save as PDF. Your Web page is converted to PDF when you save the file. You don't have an option for appending Web pages as the Windows users have when using PDFMaker, but you can always use either the Create PDF From Web Page tool or navigate to other Web pages and print them to PDF. ■

## Changing Web Page selections to PDF

At times you may want to use a portion of a Web page and convert it to PDF. You might find an airline schedule from your town to other cities and want just the information for departures from your town. You don't need a long table of flight schedules departing from other areas in the country. You may find a list of recent DVD releases and only want to select a few from a long list on a huge Web page, or you might want to capture a table without all the text preceding and following the table. These circumstances are ideal candidates for converting partial data on a Web page to a PDF document, and Acrobat supports your every desire when using Microsoft IE and Acrobat.

To convert a selection on a Web page to a PDF file, follow these steps.

### Steps: Converting Web Page Selections to PDF (Windows only)

1. **Open a Web page in Microsoft Internet Explorer.** Note that these steps pertain only to Microsoft Internet Explorer on Windows.

2. **Drag through the content you want to convert to a PDF file.** You can drag through text and images, tables, and form fields on a Web page to select the data you want to convert to PDF.

3. **Open a context menu on the selection.** Right-click the mouse button to open a context menu on the selection as shown in Figure 8.23.

**FIGURE 8.23**

Create a selection and open a context menu.

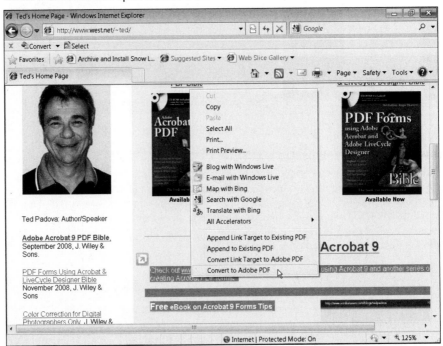

4. **Convert to PDF.** From the context menu options, choose Convert to Adobe PDF.

5. **View the resultant PDF in Acrobat.** PDFMaker converts the selection to a PDF file and opens in your Acrobat viewer.

Notice in Figure 8.23 you see a Select button adjacent to the Convert button in Internet Explorer. Click this button and you can select sections on a Web page to convert to PDF. While the Select button is active, click an area on a Web page. Move to another area and click again. When you click the Convert to PDF button or choose Convert to PDF from a context menu, all the items you selected are converted to PDF.

If you want to deselect items, click the Select button again and the PDFMaker deselects all selected items. You can then click the Select button again and start over, selecting items for conversion to PDF.

# Converting Microsoft Outlook Emails to PDF (Windows Only)

Acrobat PDFMaker is also installed with Microsoft Outlook. When you open Outlook, you'll find two tools in the toolbar installed by Acrobat.

The first tool is the Create Adobe PDF from selected messages, and the second tool is Create Adobe PDF from folders. To convert mail messages listed in the Outlook Inbox or other mailbox, select messages you want to convert to PDF. You might have a mail thread related to a specific topic where you want to archive all mail related to the given topic. Use the Shift key or Control key to select messages in the mailbox you want to archive. After selecting the messages, click the Create Adobe PDF from selected messages tool. The Save Adobe PDF File As dialog box opens as shown in Figure 8.24.

**FIGURE 8.24**

Click Create PDF from selected messages to open the Save Adobe PDF File As dialog box.

Click the Save button after identifying a target folder for the saved file, and PDFMaker converts your selected messages to PDF. The final result is a PDF Portfolio. In the PDF Portfolio you'll find each message converted to a PDF file. You can search the content of the portfolio and find results based on text searches. The PDF Portfolio provides you with many options for viewing, modifying, and managing your converted messages.

## Cross-Reference

There's so much to working with PDF Portfolios that I've dedicated a chapter exclusively to combining files and working with PDF Portfolios. See Chapter 11 for more information. ∎

The second button you find in Outlook is the Create PDF from folder tool. Click this tool and you can convert an entire mailbox of messages to PDF.

# Summary

Among the many options you have for converting MS Office files to PDF, the following was covered in this chapter:

- Microsoft Office applications such as Word, Excel, and PowerPoint export directly to PDF with the assistance of PDFMaker. Office applications retain document structure and convert structured elements to bookmarks and links in exported PDFs when Acrobat PDFMaker is used.

- Acrobat PDFMaker for Microsoft Publisher supports many features used for commercial printing.

- Microsoft Internet Explorer supports PDFs created with PDFMaker very similar to PDFs produced with Create PDF From Web Page.

- You can convert selected portions of a Web page to PDF using a context menu command.

- Microsoft Outlook files can be converted to PDF and assembled in PDF Portfolios using PDFMaker in Outlook.

# Exporting to PDF from Authoring Applications

C hapter 7 covered PDF creation from all the supported file formats contained in the Convert to PDF preferences. In Chapter 8 you learned about using the PDFMaker with Microsoft programs. Other PDF creation tools exist with programs such as QuarkXPress, CorelDraw, and Lotus Notes, and the list of programs supporting PDF creation continues to grow.

PDF exports from host applications are best with Adobe's own Creative Suite applications. Many of the Adobe CS programs were created from the ground up using core PDF technology.

This chapter deals with PDF exports from the Creative Suite programs. Some options you find with exports to PDF in Adobe Programs are supported in other applications, but none have as comprehensive a set of PDF export choices as do the Adobe programs. If you're a user of any one of the Creative Suite applications, then this chapter is for you.

**IN THIS CHAPTER**

**Working with Adobe Creative Suite**

**Using Acrobat with non-Adobe programs**

## Working with Acrobat and the Adobe Creative Suite

The Adobe Creative Suite (CS5) comes in several flavors. The Creative Suite Design Standard edition includes Adobe Illustrator CS, Adobe InDesign CS, Adobe Photoshop CS, Adobe Bride CS, Adobe Device Central CS, Adobe Acrobat Pro, and Adobe Version Cue CS. The Adobe Creative Suite Design Premium edition includes all these programs but replaces Adobe Photoshop CS with Adobe Photoshop CS Extended and adds Adobe Flash and Adobe Dreamweaver and Fireworks. Additional

Creative Suite bundles are the Web Premium, the Web Standard, the Production Premium, and the top end Adobe Master Collection that includes every program in all the other bundles. Most of the CS applications support PDF documents with direct exports and imports. For the remainder of this chapter I'll refer to the CS5 and applications simply as the Creative Suite or CS programs. As of this writing, the current version is Adobe Creative Suite 5.

# Using Acrobat and Adobe Photoshop

Adobe Photoshop CS supports creating and importing PDFs. When you create a PDF, you use the Save As command and save, and like all CS applications in the CS versions, the exports use Adobe PDF Settings to convert to PDF. When you import PDF documents that were not originally created in Photoshop, the files are rasterized. The process of rasterizing files converts all objects, such as type and vector objects, to raster images (pixels).

## Saving to PDF from Photoshop

Creating a PDF file from Photoshop is nothing more than choosing the Photoshop PDF format from the Save dialog box. Photoshop supports many different file formats for opening and saving documents. In versions prior to Photoshop 6.0, you had to flatten all layers before you could save a document as a PDF file. In versions 6.0 and later, you can preserve layers and vector art. When you save a layered file from Photoshop CS as a Photoshop PDF and open it again in Photoshop, all layers are retained; however, a layered Photoshop file saved as PDF opens in Acrobat as a single-layer document. Type and vector art work the same way. You can create type without rasterizing it and save the file as a PDF. Later, if you want to edit the file, you can reopen it back in Photoshop and edit the type. What's more, you can search the text in Acrobat when you save the file as PDF from Photoshop.

## Caution

Flattening layers in Photoshop always rasterizes vector art and type. If you want to preserve vector art and type, you need to save the layered file as a Photoshop PDF document. ■

To save a multilayered Photoshop image, Photoshop document, or flattened image, you use the Save As command. In Photoshop CS, choose File ➪ Save As. The Save As PDF dialog box opens. This dialog box is the same when saving from all other CS applications. If you're familiar with Acrobat Distiller, the Save Adobe PDF dialog box and the various panes contained within appear similar to the tabs in Acrobat Distiller. However, while the CS applications use a similar UI for consistency, they do *not* use Acrobat Distiller to create the PDF.

When saving as Photoshop PDF, the first pane in the Save Adobe PDF dialog box is the General settings, as shown in Figure 9.1. Options choices you make in the Save Adobe PDF dialog box include:

- **Adobe PDF Preset.** All the presets you create in Distiller are available from the pull-down menu. Any new presets created in Distiller are immediately made available to all CS programs.

- **Standard.** From the Standard pull-down menu you can select from the PDF/X subsets.

- **Compatibility.** Acrobat compatibility choices are available from the Compatibility pull-down menu. You find compatibility choices dating back to Acrobat 4 compatibility with all subsequent compatibility choices up to the current version when Acrobat was last upgraded. Because Acrobat's development cycle usually is ahead of the CS programs, you find the most recent Acrobat compatibility choice for Acrobat not available until you see the next upgrade of the Creative Suite that follows the most recent upgrade to Acrobat.

- **Description.** This area in the General pane is a text description of the compatibility option you choose.

- **Preserve Photoshop Editing Capabilities.** If you choose to uncheck the Preserve Photoshop Editing Capabilities and later open the PDF in Photoshop, the file is rasterized and all layers are flattened. Preserving Photoshop Editing Capabilities preserves layers and type. The type can be searched in Acrobat. If you don't need to preserve type and vector objects, remove the check mark and flatten the file. Flattened images result in smaller file sizes.

**FIGURE 9.1**

To export directly to PDF, use the Save or Save As dialog box in Photoshop. As with all other CS applications, the Save Adobe PDF dialog box opens.

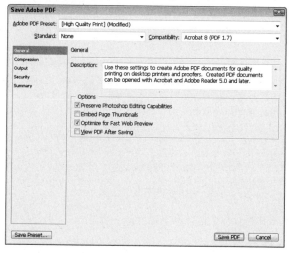

## Cross-Reference
For more on opening and rasterizing files in Photoshop, see the section "Acquiring PDF files in Photoshop" later in this chapter. ■

- **Embed Page Thumbnails.** As a general rule, be certain to leave this option off. This option was used for legacy formats and Acrobat no longer looks at embedded thumbnails. If for some reason you need to create page thumbnails, do it in Acrobat.

- **Optimize for Fast Web Preview.** Keep this option checked to optimize files. When downloading from the Web, files are downloaded much faster.

- **View PDF After Saving.** Checking this option launches your default Acrobat viewer and opens the file in Acrobat.

Click Compression in the left pane to open the compression choices. The options shown in Figure 9.2 include:

- **Compression.** In the Options area, leave Bicubic Downsampling To at the default. This option is likely to be the best choice for just about all your images. The two text boxes enable you to downsample images. For Photoshop files you're best off changing resolution before you come to the save options. Leave these two text boxes at the defaults and use the Image ⇨ Image Size command in Photoshop to make resolution changes.

  Your choices include None, JPEG, JPEG2000, and ZIP. None adds no compression to the file. JPEG is a lossy compression scheme offering various levels of compression that you choose from the Image Quality pull-down menu. JPEG2000 requires Acrobat 6 compatibility or greater. Compression is greater with JPEG2000 than with JPEG. This compression scheme works with transparent layers and alpha channels. ZIP compression is lossless. Files are not compressed as much as with JPEG, but the data integrity is optimal. ZIP compression is usually preferred for images with large amounts of a single color.

  Convert 16 Bits/Channel Image to 8 Bits/Channel. Sixteen-bit images, such as those created with 16-bit or more scanners or digital cameras supporting Camera Raw and 16-bit cannot be converted to PDF using the Create PDF ⇨ From File command. Sixteen-bit images, however, can be saved from Photoshop as Photoshop PDFs and opened in Acrobat. To preserve 16-bit images, save with Acrobat 6 compatibility or later.

- **Tile Size.** You're not likely to use Tile Size, because Acrobat supports large document sizes when printing to large format printers. Use this option to print tiled pages on desktop printers when you want to piece pages together for proofs.

Click Output in the left pane and your choices appear, as shown in Figure 9.3.

You can handle color conversion and intent profiles here in the Save Adobe PDF dialog box, but you're most likely to handle these choices in your printer driver or layout program. The bottom half of the pane is only accessible if you select one of the PDF/X options in the Standards pull-down menu.

## Cross-Reference

For more on color handling and profile conversion, see Chapter 28. For more on PDF/X, see Chapter 29. ∎

**FIGURE 9.2**

Click Compression to advance to the next pane in the Save Adobe PDF dialog box.

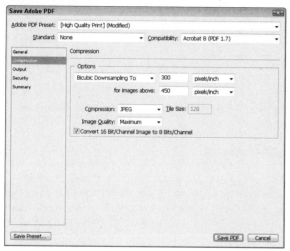

**FIGURE 9.3**

Output options offer choices for color profiling and color conversion.

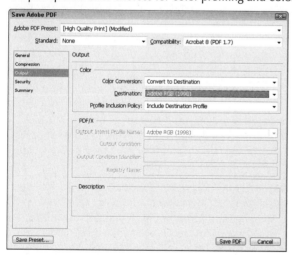

Click Security and the Security options are displayed. If you want security, click the check boxes and make choices for the security permissions you want to restrict.

The last pane displays a summary of the settings you chose to use to export to PDF. Click Save PDF and the file is saved as a Photoshop PDF file.

## Working with Photoshop color modes

Photoshop provides a number of choices for the color mode used to express your image. You can open files from different color modes, convert color modes in Photoshop, and save among different formats available for a given color mode. File formats are dependent on color modes, and some format options are not available if the image data are defined in a mode not acceptable to the format.

## Tip

See Table 9.1, later in this section, for Photoshop PDF exports supported by the Photoshop color modes and relative uses for each mode. ■

Color mode choices in Photoshop include the following:

- **Bitmap.** The image is expressed in two colors: black and white. In Photoshop terms, images in the bitmap mode are referred to as line art. In Acrobat terms, this color mode is called monochrome bitmap. Bitmap images are usually about one-eighth the size of a grayscale file. The bitmap format can be used with Acrobat's OCR functionality for converting the image data to rich text.

- **Grayscale.** This is your anchor mode in Photoshop. Grayscale is like a black-and-white photo, a halftone, or a Charlie Chaplin movie. You see grayscale images everywhere, including the pages in this book. I refer to this as an anchor mode because you can convert to any of the other modes from grayscale. RGB files cannot be converted directly to bitmaps or duotones. You first need to convert RGB to grayscale, and then to either a bitmap or duotone. From grayscale, although the color is not regained, you can also convert back to any of the other color modes. Grayscale images significantly reduce file sizes — they're approximately one-third the size of an RGB file, but larger than the bitmaps.

- **RGB.** For screen views, multimedia, and Web graphics, RGB is the most commonly used mode. It has a color gamut much larger than CMYK and is best suited for display on computer monitors. A few printing devices can take advantage of RGB, such as film recorders, large inkjet printers, and some desktop color printers. In most cases, however, this mode is not used for printing files to commercial output devices, especially when color-separating and using high-end digital prepress.

- **CMYK.** The process colors of Cyan, Magenta, Yellow, and Black are used in offset printing and most commercial output devices. The color gamut is much narrower than RGB; and when you convert an image from RGB to CMYK using Photoshop's mode conversion command, you usually see some noticeable dilution of color appearing on your monitor. When exporting files to PDF directly from Photoshop or when opening files in other applications and then distilling them, you should always make your color conversions first in Photoshop.

- **Lab.** Lab color, in theory, encompasses all the color from both the RGB and CMYK color spaces. This color mode is based on a mathematical model to describe all perceptible color within the human universe. In practicality, its color space is limited to approximately 6 million colors, about 10+ million less than RGB color. Lab color is device-independent color, which theoretically means the color is true regardless of the device on which your image is edited and printed. Lab mode is commonly preferred by high-end color editing professionals when printing color separations on PostScript Level 2 and PostScript 3 devices. Earlier versions of PDFs saved from Lab color images had problems printing four-color separations. With Acrobat, you can print Lab images to process separations.

## Cross-Reference

For more information on printing color separations, see Chapter 29. ■

- **Multichannel.** If you convert any of the other color modes to Multichannel mode, all the individual channels used to define the image color are converted to grayscale. The resulting document is a grayscale image with multiple channels. With regard to exporting to PDF, you likely won't use this mode.

- **Duotone.** The Duotone mode can actually support one of four individual color modes. Monotone is selectable from the Duotone mode, which holds a single color value in the image, like a tint. Duotone defines the image in two color values, Tritone in three, and Quadtone in four. When you export to PDF from Photoshop, all of these modes are supported.

- **Indexed Color.** Whereas the other color modes such as RGB, Lab, and CMYK define an image with a wide color gamut (up to millions of colors), the Indexed Color mode limits the total colors to a maximum of 256. Color reduction in images is ideal for Web graphics where the fewer colors significantly reduce the file sizes. You can export indexed color images directly to PDF format from Photoshop.

**TABLE 9.1**

### Photoshop Color Modes

| Color Mode | Export to PDF | Screen View | Print Composite | Print Separations |
|---|---|---|---|---|
| Bitmap | Yes | Yes | Yes | No |
| Grayscale | Yes | Yes | Yes | No |
| RGB Color | Yes | Yes | Yes* | Yes |
| CMYK Color | Yes | No | Yes | Yes |
| Lab Color | Yes | Yes | Yes | Yes |
| Multichannel | Yes | No | No | No |
| Duotone | Yes | Yes | No | Yes |
| Indexed Color | Yes | Yes | No | Yes |
| 16-bit | Yes | No | No | Yes |

* When working with high-end commercial devices, CMYK is preferred.

## Acquiring PDF files in Photoshop

PDF documents may be composed of many different elements depending on the design of the original file. If you design a page in a layout program for which you create text, import Photoshop images, and also import EPS illustrations, the different elements retain their characteristics when converted to PDF. Text, for example, remains as text, raster images such as Photoshop files remain as raster images, and EPS illustrations remain as EPS vector objects. Although the images, text, and line art may be compressed when a PDF file/document is created, all the text and line art remain as vector elements. In Photoshop, if you open an illustration or text created in any program other than Photoshop, the document elements are rasterized and lose their vector-based attributes. Photoshop rasterizes PDF documents much as it does with any EPS file.

In Photoshop, you have several methods of handling PDF imports. PDF documents opened in Photoshop are handled with the File ⇨ Open command, File ⇨ Place command, File ⇨ Import command, and through a File ⇨ Automate command. Each of the methods offers different options, so let's take the methods individually.

### Opening PDF files in Photoshop

When you choose File ⇨ Open, select a PDF file, and click Open, the Import PDF dialog box appears. If your PDF document has multiple pages you can select one, all, or any number of pages to open. Press Ctrl/⌘ and click individual page thumbnails in the Import PDF dialog box shown in Figure 9.4 to select pages in a noncontiguous order. Click the first page, press the Shift key, and click the last page to select all pages.

---

**FIGURE 9.4**

The Import PDF dialog box enables you to pick the page number in a multi-page file to place in Photoshop.

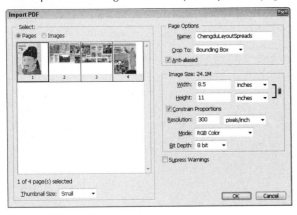

Options choices in the Import PDF dialog box include the following:

- **Crop To.** There are six choices you can make from the pull-down menu. For Photoshop files, files are imported the same size no matter which option you select. The options are more significant when using Adobe InDesign.

- **Resolution.** The default resolution regardless of the size is 72 ppi. You can choose to supply a user-defined resolution in this dialog box. If the original raster images were at a resolution different from the amount supplied in this dialog box, the images are resampled. Text and line art will be rasterized according to the amount you define in the dialog box without interpolation.

## Note

Image resampling is a method for tossing away pixels (downsampling) or manufacturing new pixels (upsampling). Either way the process is referred to as *interpolation,* where Photoshop makes some guesses as to which pixels to toss or which pixels to create. ■

- **Mode.** Choose a color mode — Grayscale, RGB, CMYK, or Lab color — from the pull-down menu.

- **Bit Depth.** Choose either 8- or 16-bit for the bit depth. If the PDF contains photos, changing an 8-bit depth file to 16-bit won't add more data to the file. Any tone adjustments using Photoshop's Levels and Curves result in the same data loss on 16-bit as you find with 8-bit images, if the original image file(s) was 8-bit.

## Tip

For much better tone separation, working with true 16-bit images results in less data loss and smoother tonal transitions. You can convert 8-bit images to 16-bit in Photoshop. Open a PDF using the 8-bit option. Once opened in Photoshop select Image ⇨ Mode ⇨ 16-bit. Next, select Image ⇨ Image Size and downsample the image 50 percent. Select 71 percent for either the Width or Height and check the Resample check box. Use Bicubic for the method, click OK, and the image resolution is downsampled 50 percent. The pixels are compressed in a tighter relationship, resulting in a true 16-bit image. The file now contains enough data to prevent data loss when making tone corrections with Levels and Curves. ■

- **Anti-aliased.** Use this option to smooth edges of text, line art, and images that are interpolated through resampling. If you disable this option, text will appear with jagged edges. Text in PDF files rasterized in Photoshop looks best when anti-aliased and the display is more consistent with the original font used when the PDF was created.

- **Suppress Warnings.** Check this box to open the files without having to respond to any warning dialog boxes that might report problems with the pages.

One problem you may encounter when rasterizing PDF documents in Photoshop is maintaining font integrity. Photoshop displays a warning dialog box when it encounters a font that is not installed on your system, which presents problems when you attempt to rasterize the font. If such a problem exists, the font can be eliminated from the document or changed after you open the file in Photoshop and edit the type layer.

When files are password-protected, users are prevented from opening a PDF file in Photoshop or any other application without a password to open the file. If you attempt to open a secure document, an alert dialog box opens, prompting you for a password.

## Cross-Reference

For information about Acrobat security, see Chapter 24. ■

## PDF Workflow

If you want to convert catalogs and lengthy documents to HTML-supported files, the PDF to PSD conversion can be useful. You can set up Actions in Photoshop to downsample images, convert color modes, and save copies of the converted files in HTML-supported formats. ■

### Placing PDF files in Photoshop

Instead of opening a PDF file through the File ⇨ Open command, you can use File ⇨ Place to add a PDF to an open Photoshop document. Placing PDFs in all versions of Photoshop prior to CS2 rasterized the placed file. In Photoshop CS, placed PDF files retain all vector attributes. When you select Place, the Place PDF dialog box opens, as shown in Figure 9.5.

FIGURE 9.5

The Place PDF dialog box lets you pick the page number in a multi-page file to place in Photoshop.

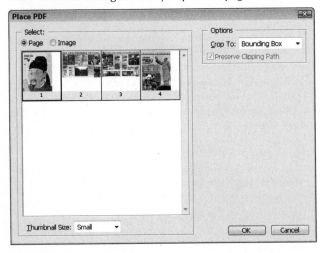

The file appears within a bounding box containing handles in each corner, as shown in Figure 9.6. Click and drag a handle to resize the placed image. You can size the image up or down in the Photoshop document window. When finished scaling, press the Enter (Windows) or Return (Mac) key. Pressing the key after sizing rasterizes the file. All vector attributes are lost, and when you save the file as Photoshop PDF you won't be able to select text.

FIGURE 9.6

Placed PDF files retain all vector attributes.

### Using comments in Photoshop

Photoshop supports the use of Comment tools. You can create a note or sound attachment in Photoshop much like you do in Acrobat. The comment is an object and won't be rasterized with any other Photoshop data. You can delete the annotation at any time by selecting the Note icon or Attach Sound icon and pressing the Backspace (Windows) or Delete (Mac) key.

You can also import comments from PDF files into Photoshop. You must use the Comment Note tool because Photoshop does not support the other comment types available in Acrobat. If a Note is contained in a PDF document and you want to import the Note into Photoshop, choose File ➪ Import ➪ Annotations. Photoshop can import an annotation only from PDF files.

## Cross-Reference

For more information about comment notes and sound attachments, see Chapter 19. ■

### Creating PDF presentations

All the features for Photoshop discussed thus far are derived from the top-level menu commands directly in Photoshop. You can also use Adobe Bridge to convert image files to PDF. Among options you find in Adobe Bridge is a command for converting image files to a PDF presentation. In the Bridge window you can select files to choose in your presentation, invoke a menu command, and Photoshop does the work to create a presentation complete with slide transitions and user-defined time intervals. If you have Photoshop you also have Adobe Bridge. Open Adobe Bridge and follow the steps below to create a presentation.

## STEPS: Saving a PDF Presentation

1. **Select image files to include in a PDF presentation.** Open Adobe Bridge and open the folder containing images you want to include in a presentation. You can add files from other folders, but your task is a little easier if you first copy all the files you want to include in the presentation to a common folder.

2. **Select Tools ⇨ Photoshop ⇨ PDF Presentation.** With the files selected in the Bridge window, open the menu command, as shown in Figure 9.7.

**FIGURE 9.7**

Choose Tools ⇨ Photoshop ⇨ PDF Presentation in the Adobe Bridge window.

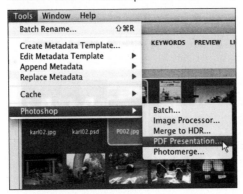

3. **Set the Presentation attributes.** The PDF Presentation dialog box opens, as shown in Figure 9.8. Click Presentation for the Output Options and make a choice for the time interval for advancing slides by editing the Advance Every text box. If you want the presentation to run in a continuous loop, check Loop after Last Page. If you want transitions, select a transition effect from the Transition pull-down menu. Note that you can also click the Browse button if you want to add more files to your presentation than those viewed in the Bridge window.

4. **Save the Presentation.** Click Save, and the Save Adobe PDF dialog box, shown in Figure 9.1 at the beginning of this chapter, opens. Adjust settings as you like in the various panes in the dialog box. You might want to use some image downsampling in the Compression pane if you build a presentation from images taken with a digital camera. If you shot Camera Raw files with a camera of 5 or more megapixels, use the Compression options for lowering image resolution.

5. **View the presentation.** Click Save, and Photoshop opens each image, samples the image, and converts to PDF. When the save is completed, open the file in Acrobat. Your presentation appears in Full Screen mode and slides change according to the interval specified in Step 3.

**FIGURE 9.8**

Click Presentation and make choices for advancing slides and transition effects.

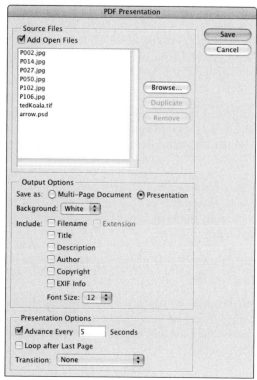

# Using Adobe Illustrator CS

Adobe Illustrator, as with other Adobe programs, is built on core PDF technology. In fact, the native Adobe Illustrator file format is PDF, and as such it is one of the best applications supporting direct export to PDF.

Illustrator has evolved to a sophisticated integration with PDF and supports the following: transparency, editing capability, layers, blending modes, text, and filters. Further integration with the program in non-PDF workflows embraces exports for Web design, where its current iteration supports one-step optimization for formats such as GIF, JPEG, PNG, SWF, and SVG.

## Saving PDFs from Adobe Illustrator CS

To export PDF files from Adobe Illustrator, you use the File ⇨ Save command. The format options available to you include the native Adobe Illustrator format (.AI), Adobe PDF (*.PDF), Illustrator EPS (*EPS), Illustrator Template (*AIT), SVG (*SVG), and SVG Compressed

(*SVGZ). In Illustrator, choose File ⇨ Save from a new document window. A Save dialog box opens that enables you to name the file, choose the destination, and select one of the formats just noted.

Additional file formats appear in the Export dialog box (File ⇨ Export). Formats supported in this dialog box include AutoCAD Drawing (*DWG), AutoCAD Interchange File (*DXF), BMP (*BMP), Enhanced Metafile (*EMF), Flash (*SWF), JPEG (*JPG), Macintosh PICT (*PCT), Photoshop (*PSD), PNG (*PNG), Targa (*TGA), Text Format (*TXT), TIFF (*TIF), and Windows Metafile (wmf).

If you choose Adobe Illustrator (.AI) as the file format and click Save, the Illustrator Options dialog box opens. In this dialog box you have an option to Create a PDF Compatible File. Check the box and click OK and your Illustrator document is saved in native format that can be opened directly in Acrobat. No other PDF conversion is necessary.

If you want to convert to PDF from a layered Illustrator document and have the layers appear in Acrobat, you need to save your Illustrator file as Adobe PDF. (*.PDF) When you select Acrobat PDF and click the Save button, the Save Adobe PDF dialog box opens with many similar settings found when saving Photoshop files.

A few differences appear in the Save Adobe PDF dialog box when you compare the options to Photoshop. These options are as follows:

- **General.** In the General tab you find two additional settings, as shown in Figure 9.9. The Create Acrobat Layers from Top-Level Layers check box is active for Acrobat 6 compatible files and later. Check the box when you want an Illustrator file exported to PDF with Adobe PDF Layers.

**FIGURE 9.9**

Two additional options appear in the Illustrator Save Adobe PDF General settings when comparing the options to those found in Photoshop.

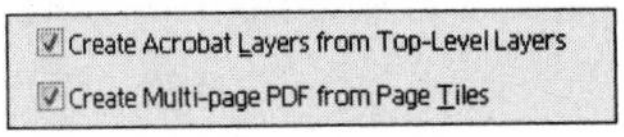

The Create Multi-page PDF from Page Tiles is used for creating multiple pages in Illustrator (see "Creating multi-page PDFs" later in this chapter).

- **Compression.** The appearance of the Compression pane is different than Photoshop, but you have all the options for downsampling files and the same compression options as found in Photoshop.
- **Marks and Bleeds.** Click Marks and Bleeds in the left pane, and the options in the right pane change to settings you can apply for setting printer's marks. Options are similar to those you find when setting marks in the Acrobat Print dialog box.

## Cross-Reference

For information on setting printer's marks in the Print dialog box, see Chapter 28. ■

- **Output.** The same color conversion and support for PDF/X compliance options are available to Illustrator as found in Photoshop. One option is added in Illustrator to mark the file if the source document uses trapping.

## Cross-Reference

For more information on trapping, see Chapter 29. ■

- **Advanced.** Illustrator has an Advanced pane where Font subsetting, overprint assignments, and transparency flattening options appear, as shown in Figure 9.10.

### FIGURE 9.10

Advanced settings offer options for font embedding, overprinting, and transparency flattening.

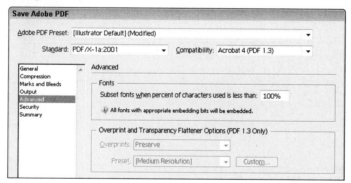

## Cross-Reference

For more on font subsetting, transparency flattening, and overprinting, see Chapter 29. ■

### Saving layered files to PDF

You can save layered Illustrator CS files to PDF with Adobe PDF Layers. Creating layered PDF documents from Illustrator is supported in Illustrator CS version 1 and above. To create PDF layers you need an authoring program capable of creating layers and capable of saving or exporting to PDF 1.5 format (Acrobat 6 compatibility) and above — Illustrator CS does both.

When saving files with layers to PDF, create the default layer view you want to appear in Acrobat. As shown in Figure 9.11, one layer in an Illustrator file is hidden and four layers are visible. The layer visibility you see in Illustrator is the same visibility you'll see in Acrobat when saving as PDF.

FIGURE 9.11

When saving to PDF with layers, create the layer view in the authoring program that you want to appear as the default view in Acrobat.

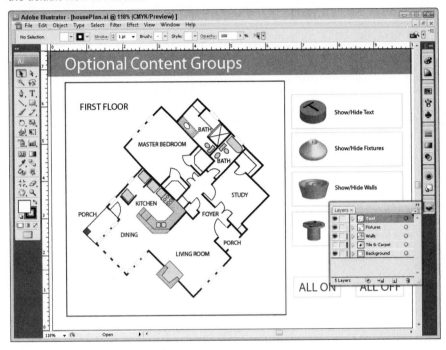

In Illustrator, choose File ⇨ Save or Save As and select PDF as the format. In the Adobe PDF Options dialog box select Acrobat 6 or greater compatibility and check the box for Create Acrobat Layers from Top-Level Layers. If the box is not checked, you won't see layers in the resultant PDF document.

When you open the PDF in Acrobat, you see the same layer view as when the file was saved from Illustrator, as shown in Figure 9.12.

## Creating multi-page PDFs

Quite often, with just about any application, users find ways to work with a program in a manner that was not intended by a developer. This is most apparent when looking at the way designers use Adobe Illustrator. Illustrator was created for artists who needed an electronic artboard to create illustrations and drawings. But when the program got to the hands of the graphic artists, it was frequently used as a page layout program. For years graphic artists pleaded with Adobe to offer support for multiple pages. No matter how many rich features were added to Adobe InDesign (which was created as a page layout program), the die-hard Illustrator users never abandoned their favorite tool. Today, great numbers of designers still first grab Illustrator to create page layouts.

**FIGURE 9.12**

The default layer view in Acrobat appears the same as the view from Illustrator when the file was saved.

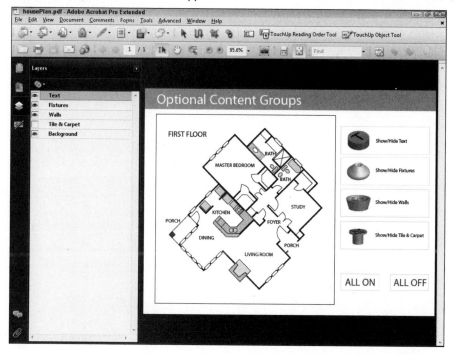

It wasn't until Illustrator CS2 was released that Adobe responded. Perhaps not completely the way designers wanted to work with multiple pages, but in part, Illustrator now supports multiple pages. The only way you can create a multi-page document in Illustrator is when exporting to Adobe PDF.

Illustrator's approach to multiple page documents is quite different from that of any other application. If creating multi-page documents in Illustrator is your interest, follow the steps below:

## STEPS: Creating Multi-Page PDFs from Adobe Illustrator

1. **Set up the page size.** For this demonstration I want to create four buttons to use in Acrobat as navigation buttons to move back and forth in a PDF document. Two buttons are needed for default appearances and two buttons will appear as rollovers, so when the cursor appears over a button, the button color or shape changes — much like you find in Web page designs. Rather than create four separate files, I want to create a single PDF document with four separate pages.

For buttons, my page size needs to be just large enough for all four buttons. When I select File ⇨ New in Illustrator, I specify my page size for 2 inches by 2 inches. These dimensions are sufficient to create four pages each at 1-inch square. The Illustrator artboard can be set up as a single page only. The page will be tiled to produce individual smaller pages when you create the PDF file. Therefore, 2 square inches is large enough to create four separate pages each at 1 square inch.

Note that you could create an artboard large enough to accommodate several letter- or tabloid-size pages if you want to use Illustrator for a traditional page layout.

2. **Create the button icons.** You can use font characters from Symbols, Wingdings, or other stylized fonts, draw shapes, or add symbols from the Symbols panel, and so on. In my example, I use some characters from the Symbol font that appear as left and right arrows. I copied the two characters and changed the color on the duplicated characters. All this is arbitrary. Feel free to use any design of your choice. The point is you need four images centered in four quadrants, as shown in Figure 9.13. Notice guidelines were drawn to help position the characters in each quadrant.

**FIGURE 9.13**

Create four shapes to be used as navigation buttons and position the shapes in the center of each quadrant on the 2-x-2-inch page.

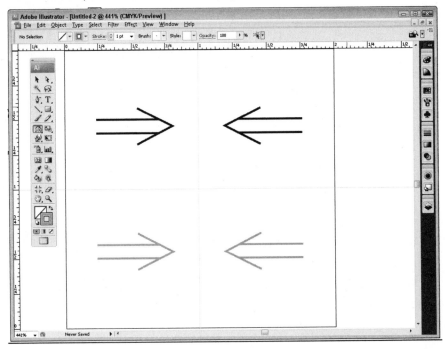

3. **Set Print Attributes.** Chose File ⇨ Print and select Adobe PDF for the Printer and Adobe PDF 9.0 for the PPD at the top of the Print dialog box. Under the Media area, choose Custom and type **1** for the Width and Height. The Print dialog box General settings should appear, as shown in Figure 9.14.

Set print attributes for Printer, PPD, and Size.

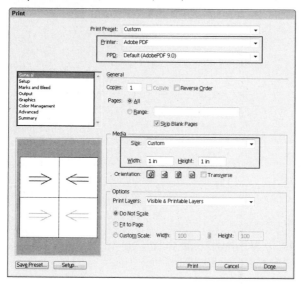

4. **Set the Tile attributes.** Click Setup in the left pane of the Print dialog box and select Tile Imageable Areas from the Tiling pull-down menu. The tiled pages should appear with dashed lines in the page thumbnail preview, as shown in Figure 9.15. If you don't see dashed lines, the file won't export as multiple pages.

5. **Click Done.** Be certain to click Done and not Cancel or Print to preserve the settings.

6. **Save as Adobe PDF.** You must use the Adobe PDF (*.PDF) file format. A Native Illustrator .ai format won't produce multiple pages. Select File ⇨ Save As and choose Adobe PDF (*.PDF) for the Type (Windows) or Format (Mac). Click Save and the Save Adobe PDF dialog box opens.

7. **Check Create Multiple-page PDF from Page Tiles in the General settings.** (See Figure 9.9 earlier in this chapter.) Click Save PDF and the file is saved.

**FIGURE 9.15**

Select Tile Imageable Areas and observe the preview to be certain the pages are defined with dashed lines.

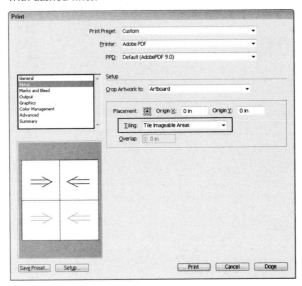

8. **Open the PDF in Acrobat.** When the file opens, click the Pages pane. You should see four separate pages, as shown in Figure 9.16.

## Tip

You can bypass the step to open the Save As dialog box by clicking Print in Step 5 and simply print to a PDF document. Clicking Done sets up the pages for exporting to PDF and permits you to continue editing if needed. ∎

A file like the one created in these steps can be used as button faces with button form fields. Rather than have four separate files, you can choose any image in a multi-page document to add as a button face in Acrobat. In the Appearance settings in Button properties the Select Icon dialog box lists all pages in a PDF document. You can scroll the elevator bar on the right side of the dialog box to view different pages, as shown in Figure 9.17.

## Cross-Reference

For more information on creating button faces, see Chapters 21 and 32. ∎

**FIGURE 9.16**

Open the file in Acrobat and click the Pages tab to view thumbnails of the pages in the document.

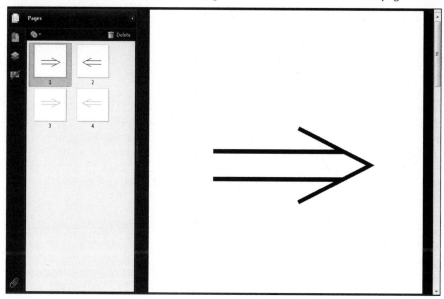

**FIGURE 9.17**

When assigning appearances in Button properties, you can choose any page in a multi-page document for a button appearance.

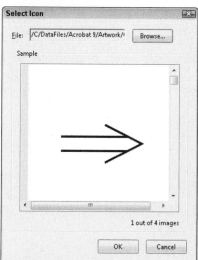

### Saving SWF files

Acrobat versions 6 and above support many different kinds of media formats including Adobe Flash SWF. Using Illustrator CS you can create vector objects as animated sequences to embellish PDFs such as forms, diagrams, electronic brochures, and similar documents where you want to add animation to amplify your messages. To understand a little more about saving SWF files from Illustrator and importing them in Acrobat, follow these steps.

### STEPS: Exporting SWF Files to Acrobat

1. **Create a sequence in Illustrator.** Either draw vector shapes in Illustrator or drag a symbol from the Symbols palette to the document page. The shape you create is on a layer. Duplicate the shape and paste it to a second layer. Continue adding new layers and shapes to complete a sequence. You can change size, rotations, or shape designs for each shape on a different layer. In my example shown in Figure 9.18, I created a shape on one layer and sized the objects up 25 percent on each new layer.

## Tip

To easily create a sequence for motion objects, drag a symbol from Illustrator's Symbols palette to the document page. Press the Control/Option key and click+drag to duplicate the shape. Press Control/⌘+D several times to repeat the duplication. Select all the objects and open the Layers palette flyout menu. Select Release to Layers (Sequence) from the palette menu commands. All your objects are distributed to separate layers. ■

FIGURE 9.18

Add a shape to separate layers.

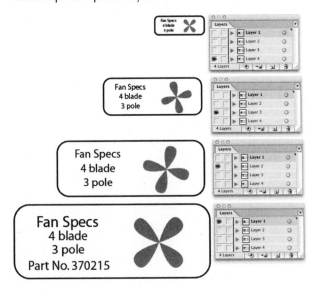

2. **Export to SWF.** Choose File ⇨ Export. In the Export dialog box, select Flash (swf) from the Format pull-down menu. Add a filename, select a target folder, and click the Export button. The SWF Options dialog box opens.

3. **Choose the Export option.** Choose All Layers to SWF Frames from the Export As pull-down menu. Click the Advanced button to display the Advanced settings.

4. **Set the SWF file format options.** In the SWF Options dialog box shown in Figure 9.19 are choices for the frame rate, exporting HTML-compatible files, and various appearance options. Be certain to check the box where you see Export Static Layers and make other choices as desired. Click OK to continue the export to SWF.

**FIGURE 9.19**

Set options in the SWF Options dialog box Advanced settings.

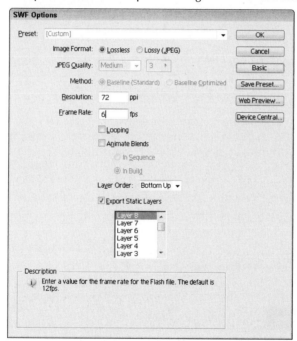

5. **Save the Illustrator file.** When you export to a file format from Illustrator, your file is not yet saved. If you want to return to the document to make additional edits, save the file. Choose File ⇨ Save and save the file as an .ai file with Create PDF Compatible File checked.

6. **Import the SWF file in Acrobat (Acrobat Pro/ Pro Extended only).** Open the Multimedia toolbar and select the Flash tool. Drag a rectangle on the document page

where you want to import the SWF file (or just double-click the get the default size of the SWF file. Click the Browse button in the Insert Flash dialog box, locate your SWF file, and import it. When you import the SWF file, the first frame in the sequence appears within the movie rectangle, as shown in Figure 9.20.

**FIGURE 9.20**

Select the Flash tool from the Multimedia toolbar and drag open a rectangle to import a Flash SWF file.

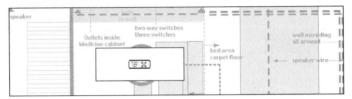

7. **Play the movie clip.** Select the Hand tool and click the movie frame. Figure 9.21 displays the last frame in a sequence. The effect is that the message box appears to explode in view as the sequence is played.

Whether you create SWF files from Illustrator or Adobe Flash, the SWF file imports in Acrobat are the same. Use the Flash tool in the Multimedia toolbar and locate an SWF file on your hard drive. Open the file and choose Acrobat 6 compatibility. You can add play buttons in Acrobat to play, stop, pause, and resume, and add JavaScripts for a variety of different play options. You can also convert Web pages containing SWF files to PDF. When Web pages are captured using Acrobat, the SWF files play as movies in the converted PDF.

## Cross-Reference

To learn more about importing SWF, movie files, and adding play buttons and Acrobat 5 and 6 compatibility, see Chapter 22. For more on capturing Web pages, see Chapter 7. ■

**FIGURE 9.21**

Select the Hand tool and click the movie box to play the sequence.

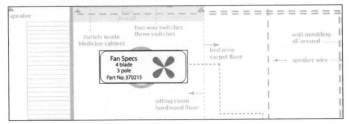

### Opening Illustrator files in Acrobat

Illustrator native files do not need conversion to PDF to be viewed in Acrobat. Acrobat supports opening native Illustrator .ai documents. When you click the Open tool, choose File ⇨ Open, or select Create PDF From File and select a native Illustrator .ai file, the file opens in Acrobat without conversion to PDF. All this is possible if the original Illustrator document was saved with an option for Create PDF Compatible File. When you save Illustrator files as native documents and click the Save button in the Save or Save As dialog box, the Illustrator Options dialog box opens, as shown in Figure 9.22. Under the Options, select the Create PDF Compatible File check box. You can then open the file in Acrobat without converting it to PDF.

**FIGURE 9.22**

Saving with PDF compatibility results in file types that can be opened in Acrobat without conversion to PDF.

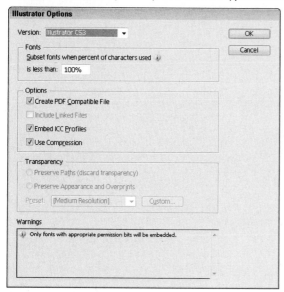

# Exploring Acrobat and Adobe InDesign

When it comes to original authoring programs to create designs for just about any use that ultimately end up as a PDF document, my personal choice is Adobe InDesign. Whether a slide presentation, an Acrobat PDF form, a form that you use a PDF template for in Adobe LiveCycle Designer, a brochure, a pamphlet, or any other kind of document outside a simple office memo, InDesign is the premier tool of choice.

With Adobe InDesign, you can create layered files, expand your design horizons to new levels, create bookmarks and hyperlinks, export movie and Flash files, and a number of different features you just don't have available in any other application. With InDesign's style sheets for cells and tables, and tools for creating forms and dynamic linking to Excel spreadsheets, this program puts a control in your hands for superb PDF creation.

To export to PDF from InDesign, choose File ⇨ Export. In the Export dialog box, select Adobe PDF from the Format pull-down menu and click Save. The Export Adobe PDF dialog box then appears, as shown in Figure 9.23. Options here provide some similar settings as you find with Adobe Illustrator and Adobe Photoshop as well as a number of additional attribute choices for handling files designed for print, Web hosting, and screen viewing. You can export Bookmarks that appear in the resultant PDF file, export interactivity with buttons and actions, export HTML and hyperlinks, and create PDF documents designed for commercial printing.

**FIGURE 9.23**

InDesign can export documents with options settings to accommodate files designed for print, Web hosting, and interactive screen viewing.

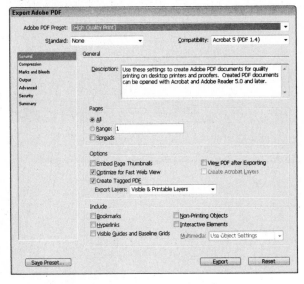

## Exporting PDFs for print

The Preset pull-down menu offers you choices for several Adobe PDF Settings that determine how your PDF is created. Among those options are selections for PDF/X files. PDF/X is a format specifically designed for printing and commercial prepress. When you export to PDF/X, you resolve colorspace problems, transparency problems, and other potential problems faced when printing documents on commercial devices.

## Exporting Adobe PDF layers

Just as when exporting layers from Illustrator, you set the default layer view in InDesign that you want to appear in Acrobat as a default view. You can add interactive buttons in InDesign and export your interactive links that are also recognized by Acrobat. In the Export Adobe PDF dialog box shown in Figure 9.23, be certain to check the boxes for Create Acrobat Layers and the Include items such as Bookmarks, Hyperlinks, and Interactive Elements. Click the Export button to export your document to PDF. In Figure 9.24, a layered InDesign CS file with interactive buttons and imported video is prepared for export to PDF.

**FIGURE 9.24**

A layout is prepared in Adobe InDesign with imported video, interactive buttons, and multiple layers.

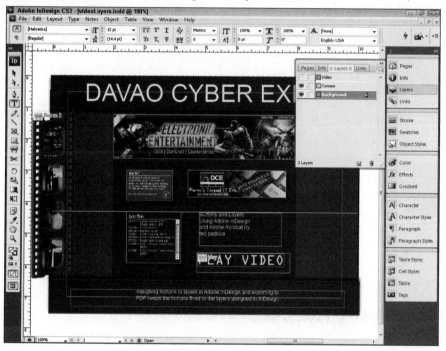

When you open the file in Acrobat, a modification of the button attributes sets a different layer visibility and plays the imported video, as shown in Figure 9.25. These kinds of design opportunities provide artists with tools to create effective presentations and electronic brochures that users who download the free Adobe Reader software can view.

## Expanding your design horizon

Something InDesign provides you that isn't available in any other program is a way to create a look where objects fall off the page when viewed in Acrobat viewers. As Brian Tamayo, a Dallas, Texas–based designer who first discovered this InDesign anomaly, says, "Think outside the page." Figure 9.26 shows you an example of an object breaking a page border.

**FIGURE 9.25**

A slight modification to the button attributes changes layer visibility and plays the imported video.

**FIGURE 9.26**

Adobe InDesign is the only program that permits you to create objects that fall off a page when viewed in InDesign.

If you want to create a PDF document with a similar design, you need to use Adobe InDesign and follow these steps.

### STEPS: Breaking Page Borders Using Adobe InDesign

1. **Open a Master Page.** Open a Master Page in an Adobe InDesign document. This technique requires you to place the object you want to use for breaking a page border in a PDF file to place the image on a Master Page.

2. **Place a graphic.** Use File ➪ Place in Adobe InDesign to import a vector object or photo and place it on a Master Page.

3. **Position the graphic.** When you place a graphic and select it, a bounding box is shown with a midpoint square. The midpoint of the graphic must be inside a page border. Move the graphic so the midpoint falls within the page border.

4. **Convert the graphic to a button.** Choose Object ➪ Interactive ➪ Convert to Button. The object must be converted to a button to be shown in the resultant PDF file.

5. **Save the file.** Complete your design and assign the Master Page to one or all pages in your InDesign document and choose File ➪ Save.

6. **Export to PDF.** Choose File ➪ Export and select Adobe PDF from the Save as type (Windows) or Format (Mac) pull-down menu. Type a name for your file and click Save.

7. **Enable Interactive Elements.** In the Export Adobe PDF dialog box shown in Figure 9.23, be certain to check the box for Interactive Elements. Click Export and view the PDF document.

## Tip

If you want an object pushed outside the page border farther than the midpoint on a selected graphic, add a 1-pixel Photoshop file to your Master Page. Click the graphic and the 1-pixel image and group them. The midpoint will change. You can move a graphic well beyond a page if so desired by spacing the graphic and 1-pixel image apart from each other. ■

# Using Acrobat with Non-Adobe Programs

A number of different application programs support PDF creation from file exports similar to the way Adobe handles exporting to PDF. Programs such as QuarkXPress, CorelDraw, and several others all have their own options for exporting native files to PDF. Many attribute choices featured in the CS programs are also available in those non-Adobe programs that export to PDF. You may need to poke around in the export dialog boxes to find various settings adjustments.

If you use a program that doesn't support direct exports to PDF, you should use the Adobe PDF print driver to create the PDF file.

## Cross-Reference

For more information on using the Adobe PDF print driver, see Chapter 7. ∎

# Summary

In this chapter, you explored converting files to PDF from a number of different imaging programs. Some of the items discussed include:

- Adobe Creative Suite is a sophisticated solution for file interoperability. All the CS applications export directly to PDF.
- Adobe Photoshop can export directly to PDF as separate files and presentations. Photoshop can open single and multiple PDF documents created by any producer and preserve text and vector art when exporting to PDF.
- Adobe Illustrator exports Flash and SWF files that can be imported in PDF documents as movie files.
- Adobe Illustrator CS and Adobe InDesign CS export to PDF with layers intact.
- Adobe InDesign CS exports links, bookmarks, and embedded media to PDF.
- Some non-Adobe programs offer export-to-PDF features similar to the CS applications. For those programs not supporting exports to PDF, you should use the Adobe PDF printer driver.

# Exporting PDF Content

To begin this section on editing PDF documents, I'll start with saving files and exporting data. As you find in this chapter, Acrobat has Save tools and commands and supports exporting your PDF data in a variety of file formats. As you learned in Part II, files are not originally authored in Acrobat, but rather, they are converted to the PDF format. If you need to perform some major editing, it's always best to try to return to the original authoring application, make your edits, and then convert to PDF. In some cases, however, you may not have an original authoring application document. In such circumstances, you may need to get the PDF data in a format that you can manipulate and edit in another program. Fortunately, Acrobat supports exporting to many different file formats that can be imported in other programs.

## Saving PDF Files

When you open a PDF document in any viewer, the Save tool in the File toolbar and the File ⇨ Save menu command are both grayed out. When you open the File menu and look at Save As, you notice the menu command is active.

After you edit a file through the use of tools or menu commands, the Save tool and Save menu command become active.

You can use the File ⇨ Save As command at any time. As you edit PDF documents, they tend to become bulky and contain unnecessary information. To optimize a file and make it the smallest file size, choose File ⇨ Save As and select the default PDF format for the file type. If you save to the same folder location with the same filename, Acrobat rewrites the file as you use Save As. You should plan on using Save As and rewriting your file after your last edits. Doing so ensures you of creating a smaller, more optimized file.

Another factor affecting optimized files is ensuring the default preferences are set to file optimization when using the Save As command. Open the Preferences dialog box (Ctrl/⌘+K) and click Documents in the left pane. In the Documents preferences pane, be certain the check box is enabled for Save As optimizes for Fast Web View. Enabling this option ensures that your files are always optimized when you use Save As.

# Exporting to PDF

By default, when you use either Save or Save As, the file type is a PDF document. Using Save offers you no other option for changing the file type; but when you select Save As, you can choose to export your PDF document in one of a number of different file formats. If you need to update a file or export data from PDF files, choose File ➪ Save As and choose a file format from the Save as type (Format on Macintosh) pull-down menu, as shown in Figure 10.1.

**FIGURE 10.1**

Choose File ➪ Save As and choose the file format to be saved from the Save as type pull-down menu.

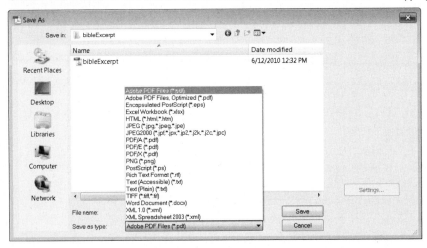

Users of Acrobat 9 may remember the File ➪ Export menu command, and that from the Export submenu you could choose a number of different export formats. In Acrobat X, the Export submenu commands have been moved to the Save As submenu as shown in Figure 10.2.

FIGURE 10.2

Choose File ➪ Save As and choose the file format to export PDF content from a number of different export formats.

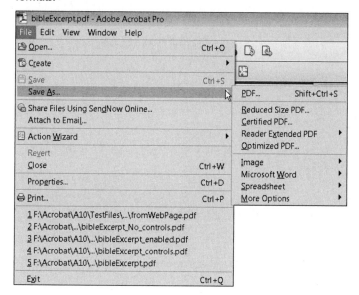

Notice in the Save As submenu that you find several choices appearing below PDF to the second separator bar (see Figure 10.2) and several choices below the second separator bar. The first five menu choices were accessed in a different menu in earlier versions of Acrobat. In Acrobat X, the new choices appearing in the Save As submenu include:

- **PDF.** Use this command to open the Save As dialog box and make choices for the file format as shown earlier in Figure 10.1.

- **Reduced Size PDF.** This option is the same as the File ➪ Reduce File Size command found in earlier versions of Acrobat. You can change the PDF version and compress the file by reducing the file size.

- **Certified PDF.** Certified documents carry a level of security and can be authenticated for reliability.

- **Reader Extended PDF.** The submenu commands provide options for enabling PDF files with special features for Adobe Reader users.

- **Optimized PDF.** In earlier versions of Acrobat, we used the Advanced ➪ PDF Optimizer menu command to open the PDF Optimizer. This command enables you to compress PDF files much more than the Smaller File option.

# Exporting Data to Different Formats

Below the second separator bar in the Save As submenu, shown in Figure 10.2, you find four commands, each with its own submenu. The menu commands are Image, Microsoft Word, Spreadsheet, and More Options. These commands enable you to export a PDF document to one of these four supported formats

## Converting to an Image exports

You can export a PDF document as any one of the following image file formats, JPEG (*.jpg, .jpeg, .jpe), JPEG2000 (.jpf, *.ipx, *.jp2, *.j2k, *.j2c, .jpc), PNG (.png), and TIFF (*.tif, *.tiff). Each entire page, including text and images, is exported as a single image file. From the Settings dialog box, you choose options for image compression and color management. The options settings for exporting image file formats are the same as the options used when importing images in Acrobat with the Create PDF From File or From Multiple Files commands discussed in Chapter 7.

## Exporting to Microsoft Word

For several generations of Acrobat, the Adobe development engineers have continually worked hard on preserving layout and appearance in documents exported to Microsoft Word and RTF formats. You'll find in Acrobat X more improvement in these areas, and to date, the best exporting features when you want to edit a file in Microsoft Word.

You can export PDF files to either a Microsoft Word format (Office 2007) or Word 97-2003 format. The conversion settings include choices for image handling and sampling as well as a feature for handling the document layout. Unlike HTML and XML files, exports to Word and

RTF embed the images in the exported text files when you choose to export images. Acrobat does not offer an option for exporting images apart from the text data.

Be aware that although you can export PDF documents directly to Microsoft Word format, the integrity of your file depends on how well you created the PDF. If the PDF was created without tags and through less desirable PDF-creation methods, the ultimate file you produce in either Word format may not be suitable for editing and converting back to PDF. Inasmuch as tags are added during conversion to PDF, the tagged structure is not retained in the resulting file.

## Cross-Reference

**For more information on programs supporting exports to PDF as structured and tagged files, see Chapters 7, 8, and 25. ■**

Notwithstanding tagging issues, the exports to Microsoft Word from Acrobat 9 and above are the best I've seen with any version of Acrobat. Clicking the Settings button in the Save As dialog box for exports to Microsoft Word or RTF opens the Save As Settings dialog box. The settings are the same for RTF as for Word-formatted file exports (shown in Figure 10.3).

**FIGURE 10.3**

Select either Microsoft Word or RTF for the file export and click the Settings button. The options in both dialog boxes are identical.

Settings for exporting to Microsoft Word or RTF formats include the following:

- **Layout Settings.** You can choose to retain the document layout by clicking the Retain Page Layout radio button, and the exported data appear in Microsoft Word almost exactly as you see the file laid out in Acrobat. Choose the Retain Flowing Text option to preserve text reflow.

- **Include Comments.** Like EPS and PostScript files discussed earlier, Comment notes can be exported to Word or with RTF files. Select the box for Include Comments and the Comment notes are exported.

- **Include Images.** You can extract image files from the PDF and embed them in the .doc or .rtf file in either of two formats. Select JPG or PNG for the image file format.

- **Run OCR if needed.** Check this option if the file contains an image that you want converted to text.

- **OCR Language.** Choose the language from the drop-down menu for the OCR recognition.

## Cross-Reference

For more information on resolutions and sampling, see Chapter 17. To learn about tagging PDF files, see Chapter 23. ∎

## Exporting to Spreadsheet formats

You can export tables to Microsoft Excel Workbooks and XML files that can be read by Microsoft Excel. In order to export a table successfully, the original file needs to have been created as a table in a program like Microsoft Word or Excel. If you try to export columns and rows that were not created as a table in an authoring program, no data are exported from the PDF file.

## Using More Options

The More Options submenu commands contain an assortment of data formats similar to the formats you have available when choosing Save As and options from the Save as type (Windows) or Format (Mac) drop-down menu.

### Exporting PDF/A, PDF/E, PDF/X (*.pdf)

Acrobat supports various standards for different uses and different markets. The PDF/A specification is used for archiving PDF documents so that files you create today can be viewed by users many years in the future. The PDF/E specification is a standard for engineers creating documents such as CAD drawings. The PDF/X specification is used by the print industry for ensuring proper output on commercial printing devices. Each of the choices you have in the Save As/Export menus offer settings respective to the standard.

### Using the Rich Text Format

Use the Rich Text Format option when you want to export text to RTF. RTF files preserve similar layout structure as when you export to MS Word formats.

## Exporting Encapsulated PostScript (*.eps) and PostScript (*.ps)

EPS files are saved as single page files. When multiple-page PDFs are saved to EPS, each page is saved as a new EPS document. PostScript files save the PDF to disk like you would print a file to disk as PostScript. PostScript files can then be redistilled in Acrobat Distiller to convert back to PDF. You can also download PostScript files to PostScript printers through a downloading utility or a hot folder, which is used for sending files directly to the printer.

Many of the options for creating either an EPS file or a PostScript file are identical. You'll notice some differences as you travel through the many options found in the Save As Settings dialog box. Select either Encapsulated PostScript (*.eps) or PostScript (*.ps) from the Files of type (Format on Mac) pull-down menu and click the Settings button. The options appear in the Save As Settings dialog box. Shown in Figure 10.4 is the EPS Save As Settings dialog box.

**FIGURE 10.4**

Select Encapsulated PostScript (*.eps) or PostScript (*.ps) from the Save as type (Format on Mac) pull-down menu. Click the Settings button to open the Save As Settings dialog box. In this figure, Save as Encapsulated PostScript (*.eps) was selected.

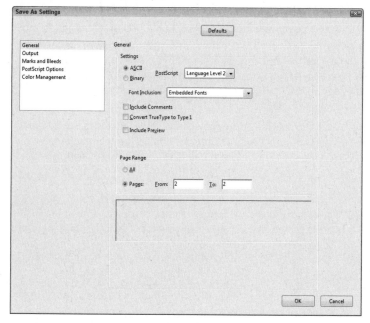

### Using General settings

On the left side of the Save As Settings dialog box are several categories for choices you make on the right side of the dialog box. The first of the categories is the General settings where you set some general attributes for the way an EPS or PostScript file is saved. These settings are as follows:

- **Defaults.** The Defaults button at the top of the dialog box returns all settings to the original defaults. You can access this button at any time as you travel through the various option categories in the list at the left side of the dialog box.

- **ASCII.** PostScript files are encoded as ASCII (American Standard Code for Information Interchange). ASCII files are larger than binary files, which is the second option for encoding selections.

## Cross-Reference
For information on color separating EPS files and Acrobat PDF, see Chapter 29. ■

- **Binary.** Binary files are much smaller than ASCII files. Use binary encoding when the PostScript language level is 2 or 3.

- **PostScript.** Select the language levels from the pull-down menu choices. For ASCII encoding use Language Level 1 from the menu. For exporting EPS files to Adobe InDesign, you can use Language Level 2. If you're using Language Level 2 or 3, select binary encoding. Use PostScript 3 only when the output devices use PostScript 3 RIPs.

- **Font Inclusion.** You have three choices for font inclusion. Choose None to not embed fonts. Choose Embedded Fonts to keep the same fonts embedded in the PDF in the exported EPS file. Choose Embedded and Referenced Fonts to keep the PDF embedded fonts and fonts referenced from fonts loaded in your system. If you're using a font that is not embedded in the PDF document but is loaded as a system font, the font is embedded in the resulting PDF.

- **Include Comments.** When the check box is enabled, any comment notes are included in the resulting EPS or PostScript document. When the PostScript document is distilled in Acrobat Distiller, the comment notes are retained in the resulting PDF document.

- **Convert TrueType to Type 1.** Check the box to convert TrueType fonts to Type 1 fonts.

- **Include Preview (EPS file exports only).** The preview is a screen view of the EPS file. If this check box is not enabled, the EPS file appears as a gray box when you place the file in another program. The data are all there, but you won't be able to see the EPS image. When this check box is enabled, a preview is embedded in the EPS file. Preview image formats are TIFF on Windows and PICT on the Macintosh.

- **Page Range.** You can export all pages by selecting the All radio button or entering the page numbers for a range of pages to be exported. EPS files are exported as individual files for each page and automatically numbered by Acrobat.

### Choosing Output options
Click the Output item in the list on the left side of the Save As Settings dialog box and the options change, as shown in Figure 10.5.

**FIGURE 10.5**

Select Output and the options change to attribute settings designed for printing and prepress.

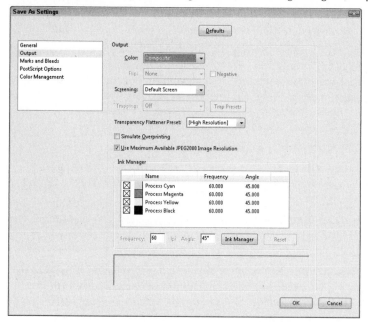

Output options enable you to control prepress output attributes, including the following:

- **Color.** The four choices for handling color in resulting EPS and PostScript file(s) are as follows:

  - **Composite.** Use this option to export the file as a composite image. If the file is a four-color image, you can still import an EPS file in a separating program and print separations. The intent for Composite is for use with composite color printing and printing separations to non-Adobe PostScript devices. For PostScript files, composites can be downloaded directly to PostScript 2 and 3 devices for In-RIP separating.

  - **Composite Gray.** If the files are grayscale, use Composite Gray.

  - **Separations.** This option creates a DCS (Desktop Color Separation) file, and each color as well as a composite is exported as separate files. If pre-separating the EPS file(s), be certain you use a program such as Adobe InDesign that supports DCS files, or you can directly download each plate to your RIP. For PostScript files, the file is separated. When you download the PostScript file, all colors print on separate plates.

## Cross-Reference

For more information about DCS files, color separations, and RIPs, see Chapter 29. ■

- **In-RIP Separations.** This option works only on Adobe PostScript 3 RIPs. A composite color image is printed to the RIP and the RIP color separates the composite file.

## Note

**Separations and In-RIP Separations are only active when you have your page setup set to a PostScript printer.** ■

- **Screening.** You make choices for screening from this pull-down menu. Unless you have some special need for embedding half-tone frequencies in the EPS file, leave the Screening set to Default Screen and handle all your frequency control at the RIP. For PostScript files, set the screening as desired before downloading the file.
- **Trapping.** You can apply trapping and choose trap presets.
- **Apply Output Preview Settings.** Select this option to simulate the output of one device on another. This option simulates the output condition defined in the Output Preview dialog box on the current output device.
- **Transparency Flattener Preset.** Choose from High Medium and Low resolutions for transparency flattening. Transparency is flattened according to your choice in the resultant EPS file.
- **Simulate Overprinting.** Overprints and knockouts can be soft-proofed on-screen for color-separated devices. The check box is grayed out unless you choose one of the separation items in the Color pull-down menu.
- **Use Maximum Available JPEG2000 Image Resolution.** For any raster images contained in the EPS file export, the file compression uses JPEG2000 at the maximum setting when this check box is enabled. If disabled, the original compression level at the time the PDF was created is used.
- **Ink Manager.** Clearing the box on the far left of each color plate eliminates the plate for separated files. Scroll the box to see any spot colors, and you can select spot colors for conversion to CMYK color.

## Cross-Reference

**For more information about separations, overprinting, transparency, trapping, and managing inks, see Chapter 29.** ■

### Selecting Marks and Bleeds options

Select the Marks and Bleeds item in the list at the left of the Save As Settings dialog box and the options for adding printer's marks appear, as shown in Figure 10.6.

The options are as follows:

- **All Marks/Marks.** You can check the box for All Marks and all the check boxes below the Style menu are checked. You can toggle on or off all check marks to create just the marks you want to appear in the resultant file.

- **Style.** You have choices for compatibility with authoring and illustration programs. Choose from different versions of InDesign, Illustrator, or QuarkXPress.

- **Line Weight.** From the pull-down menu, select line weights for the printer's marks from $^{1}/_{8}$-, $^{1}/_{4}$-, and $^{1}/_{2}$-inch choices.

Select Marks and Bleeds to add printer's marks to the EPS/PS export.

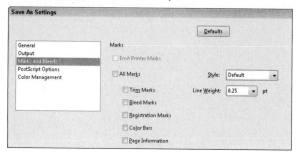

## Choosing PostScript options

Click the last item in the list for EPS/PS exports and the options shown in Figure 10.7 appear. The PostScript options offer you settings for embedded PostScript attributes in the EPS/PS file.

The PostScript options include the following:

- **Font and Resource Policy.** You determine how fonts download to a printer's RIP via three choices in the pull-down menu:

  - **Send at Start.** The entire font sets for all pages are downloaded to the printer's RIP. The file prints faster than any of the other methods, but puts a memory burden on the printing device to hold all the font matrices in memory during printing.

  - **Send by Range.** Fonts are downloaded from the first page where the fonts are used and stays in memory until the job is printed. The font downloading occurs as each font is found on a page that uses them. The job prints a little slower than when using the Send at Start option, but uses less memory initially as the job is printed.

  - **Send for Each Page.** Fonts encountered on a page are downloaded to the RIP, and then flushed as the next page is printed. The second page's fonts are then downloaded and flushed after printing, and so on. This method requires the least memory. Files print slower than when using either of the other two methods.

- **Emit CIDFontType2 as CIDFontType2 (PS Version 2015 and greater).** Use this option to preserve hinting in the original font when printing. The option is available only for Language Level 3 output.

FIGURE 10.7

Select PostScript Options to add various PostScript printing attributes to the EPS/PostScript file(s).

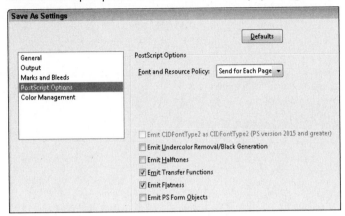

- **Emit Undercolor Removal/Black Generation.** GCR/UCR removal is necessary only if the original document contained assignments in the PostScript file converted to PDF. If you want to remove any embedded settings for handling the amount of black or compensating for black generation with different inks, check this box. If you don't know what any of this means, checking the box or not won't have an effect on your own personal documents.

- **Emit Halftones.** If a halftone frequency was embedded in the original file, you can eliminate it in the exported document. Unless you want to use embedded frequencies, leave the box checked in case you accidentally preserved a frequency in the original file for EPS files. When printing PostScript files to high-end devices, you'll want to assign frequencies at the time the PostScript file is created.

- **Emit Transfer Functions.** The same criteria as the preceding bullet apply to transfer functions. If you intend to use embedded transfer functions, leave the check box disabled. Otherwise, keep it checked as a default.

- **Emit Flatness.** Flatness settings applied in Photoshop, Illustrator, or other illustration programs are generally applied to clipping paths in images and on vector objects to ease the burden of printing complex objects. When checked, the flatness settings applied in the original authoring program are honored.

- **Emit PS Form Objects.** This option relates to PS Form XObjects. XObjects are used to create a description of multiple smaller objects repeated several times such as patterns, brushes, backgrounds, and so on. Emitting the XObjects reduces the size of the print job; however, more memory is needed to RIP the file(s).

## Using Color Management options

The Color Management option has been removed from the Output options in Acrobat 8 to a new category for Color management in Acrobat 9 and above. Click Color Management in the left pane and the right pane changes to the view you see in Figure 10.8.

---

**FIGURE 10.8**

---

Click Color Management in the left pane to display choices for managing color and choosing color profiles.

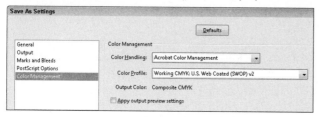

The Color Management options include:

- **Color Handling.** Make a choice from the pull-down menu for whether you want Acrobat or your printer driver to manage color or whether you want to use no color management.

- **Color Profile.** Choose a color profile from the pull-down menu.

## Caution

If you choose to let Acrobat manage color and you also choose a printer profile, you'll end up double profiling your output. The relationship between these two options is critical to understand. For a detailed explanation for how to manage color on your output, see Chapter 31. ■

- **Apply output preview settings.** Check this box to simulate an output on a specific printing device.

Click OK in the Save As Settings dialog box and click Save in the Save As dialog box. The PDF is exported in EPS or PostScript format, containing all the attributes you described for all the options listed earlier.

Because printing in Acrobat Pro takes care of all the print controls you need, exporting EPS files for printing is a task you won't need to perform unless there's some strange problem that needs to be resolved in a file that won't print. A more practical use for exporting EPS files from Acrobat is if you need to import a PDF file in another program that does not support PDF, but does support EPS. In such cases you'll find it helpful to understand all the options you have available for EPS exports.

You have many advantages in creating PostScript files from Acrobat. Files can be redistilled in Acrobat Distiller with PDF/X formats for printing and prepress, sometimes as a work-around for repurposing documents, and for downloading directly to PostScript devices — particularly for print shops using imposition software that only supports PostScript and not PDF.

## Cross-Reference

**For more information about PDF/X files, see Chapter 29.** ∎

### Exporting to HTML Web page

Earlier versions of Acrobat prior to Acrobat X provided options for exporting PDFs to HTML files, HTML files with Cascading Style Sheets, Plain Text, and XML files. Text was exported according to the encoding method you selected, and images were exported according to the format option you selected. In short you had several choices for how documents were exported to HTML/HTM. In Acrobat X you have a single choice with a single set of options choices found when you click the Settings button in the Save As dialog box. Options are limited to including images and running an OCR if needed for image files containing text.

# Summary

In this chapter you explored many methods for exporting PDF data and the file formats supported by Acrobat.

- Using the Save As command and overwriting a PDF document optimizes it and can sometimes result in much smaller file sizes.
- Acrobat can save PDFs in a variety of different formats. Many formats have an elaborate number of options settings to set attributes for the saved files.

# Part III

# Editing PDFs

Part III covers the many different editing opportunities you have available with Acrobat. In Chapter 11, you find a wealth of information dedicated to combining documents and using the Acrobat 10 PDF Portfolio features. Chapter 12 deals with text editing, followed by Chapter 13 where I cover redacting PDF files for those who need to remove sensitive information from PDFs.

In Chapter 14, I talk about editing images and objects. In Chapter 15, you find many ways for editing PDF pages in Acrobat. In Chapter 16, you find some of the new improvements for scanning paper documents that ultimately are converted to PDF and the Optical Character Recognition (OCR) features you find in Acrobat.

In Chapter 17, you'll learn how to repurpose PDF files for screen viewing and Web hosting, as well as how to automate many tasks in Acrobat using the new Actions Wizard. This section on editing PDF files concludes with Chapter 18 where I talk about adding special features for Adobe Reader users for saving PDF forms and participating in comment reviews.

# Combining, Packaging, and Attaching PDFs

I n Acrobat versions 6 and 7, we had a menu command for creating a single PDF from multiple files of different file formats. In Acrobat 8 we saw some improvements to combining files into a single PDF document, and we were introduced to PDF Packages. In Acrobat 9 PDF Portfolios were introduced. In Acrobat X we have a new interface design and some improvements to the PDF Portfolio features.

In addition to using the Combine Files options and creating PDF Portfolios, I tossed in adding file attachments to PDF documents, and I cover the various options you have when adding attachments to PDFs and PDF Portfolios.

Read on to explore Acrobat features for merging files into single PDF documents and assembling files into PDF Portfolios, and learn some of the methods Acrobat provides to you for attaching files to your documents.

# Merging Files into a Single PDF Document

The Adobe Acrobat development team has spent considerable time over the last few versions of Acrobat to improve and deliver methods for us to combine multiple files into PDF documents. Adobe claims their research has found most knowledge workers today want to communicate messages based on the delivery of different files created in different authoring programs.

You might have a spreadsheet created in Excel, a presentation created in PowerPoint, an advertisement created in Adobe InDesign, and a media file created in Adobe Flash that collectively deliver the message you want to communicate or a file you want to share for comment and review.

In Acrobat 8 we had the Combine Files menu command that was used to combine multiple files of different types into a single PDF document. The Acrobat 9 and later command for combining files was changed to Merge Files into a Single PDF. Although the nomenclature changed, the results are the same. The Merge Files into a Single PDF command is used to combine native authoring application files such as a PowerPoint file, a Word File, a PDF file, and any other file formats compatible with the Create PDF From File command and merge them into a single PDF document.

## Cross-Reference

**For more information on the file formats Acrobat supports for conversion to PDF, see Chapter 7. ■**

The Merge Files into a Single PDF command enables you to combine files of any type and neatly organize the order of your files in the Combine Files Wizard before creating the composite document.

Combining files is handled from the Create task button in the Toolbar Well or from a menu command (File ➪ Create ➪ Combine Files into a Single PDF). In Figure 11.1, you can see the pull-down menu and the menu choices you have in the Create task button. The Combine Files into Single PDF command is used to merge files from a number of different formats including PDF into a single document. The Assemble Files into a Portfolio command creates a package of documents assembled into a single PDF Portfolio file.

## Cross-Reference

**For more information on PDF Portfolios, see "Creating a PDF Portfolio" later in this chapter. ■**

### FIGURE 11.1

The Create task button provides two commands used for merging files and creating a PDF Portfolio.

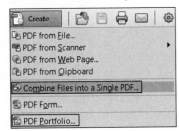

# Combining files and folders on Windows

When you want to combine files into a single PDF document you can click the Create task button and select Combine Files into a Single PDF. Likewise you can choose File ⇨ Create ⇨ Combine Files into a Single PDF. Either action opens the Combine Files dialog box. Before you use the command, there are a few restrictions you have with regard to the types of files you can combine. These restrictions include:

- **PDFs with security.** PDFs with security cannot be combined using this command.

- **Adobe LiveCycle Designer XML Forms.** Any form created in Adobe LiveCycle Designer cannot be added using this command.

- **Digital signatures.** You can use this command to add files that have digital signatures, but the signatures are removed when you combine the files.

- **Form fields.** Adding a form is no problem using the Merge Files into a Single PDF command, but if you have different files using the same field names, the fields are merged into one field. For example, if you merge a form populated with data and another identical form with the fields left blank, the data are merged together. The order of the files to be merged is important. If you have two identical forms and merge them with the blank fields file listed in the first position, both forms are merged and the second form (populated with field data) now appears with empty fields. Conversely, if the populated fields file is in the topmost position in the list along with a file with blank fields, both documents appear with the same data when you combine them. In other words, forms with identical field names inherit data from the first form in a list of files you merge.

Before I go on to explain all the features available to you when merging files into a single PDF document, launch Acrobat and follow along to see how easy it is to merge files using the revised Combine Files Wizard.

## STEPS: Using the Combine Files Command (Windows)

1. **Click the Create task button.** From the pull-down menu, select Combine Files into a Single PDF.

2. **Select files to merge.** When you select Combine Files into a Single PDF, the Combine Files Wizard opens. Click the Add Files button and a pull-down menu opens. From the menu options choose Add Files. The Add Files dialog box opens, where you can browse your hard drive and select individual files to merge into a single PDF document. Select files you want to add to the file list and click the Add Files button. You can click a file and add it to the file list and click Add Files again and locate files in different folders. If you have a folder containing all the files you want to combine, you can choose the Add Folder item from the Add Files pull-down menu. All files within a folder are then added to the list.

In Figure 11.2, I added several documents to my list: a Flash SWF file, three InDesign files, a Word file, an Excel file, and two PowerPoint files. Note that all files are in native file format.

**FIGURE 11.2**

Click the Add Files button to add files to a list.

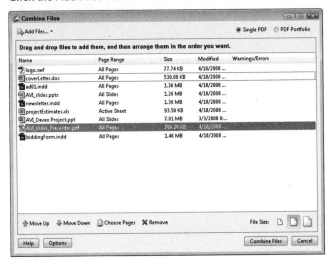

## Tip

Multiple files within the same folder can be added to your list. Click a file and Shift+click to select a group of files listed in a contiguous order. Click and press Ctrl/⌘+click to select files in a noncontiguous order. ■

3. **Arrange the files in the order you want them to appear in the merged PDF document.** Click a file in the list and use the Move Up and Move Down buttons to arrange the files in the order you want them to appear in the resultant PDF document.

4. **Choose Pages.** Click a file in the list and the Choose Pages button becomes active (see Figure 11.3). Note that if you select an Excel document, the Choose Pages button changes to Choose Sheets, and selecting a PowerPoint file changes the button name to Choose Slides. In my example, I selected an Excel Workbook (.xls file).

5. **Select Pages (or Sheets or Slides).** A preview of your document is displayed in a separate window. You can scroll pages, worksheets, slides, and so on to preview the pages. At the top of the window you can make choices for the pages you want to add to the single PDF file. Make your choices and click OK.

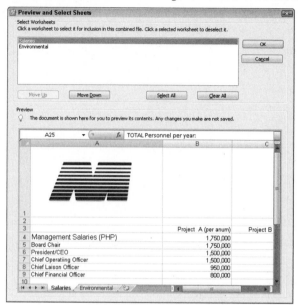

**FIGURE 11.3**

Select a file and click Choose Pages (or Sheets or Slides) to open the Preview window.

6. **Create the merged PDF document.** Click Combine Files in the Wizard window. Any files you added to your list that need conversion to PDF are converted on the fly. The original authoring program opens and files are converted to PDF. Wait for Acrobat to complete the conversion and concatenation and you'll be prompted to save your composite document.

7. **Save the composite file.** When prompted to save the file, type a filename to change the default name: Binder.1.pdf and click Save. A Save As dialog box opens. Type a name for your file, navigate to the folder you want to use for your saved file, and click Save again.

8. **Review the resultant PDF file.** The composite file opens in the Acrobat Document pane. Click the Bookmarks tab in the Navigation pane. Notice that any bookmarks in your original PDFs containing bookmarks are preserved. Additional bookmarks are added to the file linking the first page of each separate document to a bookmark. In Figure 11.4, you see my composite document with the Bookmarks pane open.

# Cross-Reference

For more information on bookmarks, see Chapter 21. ■

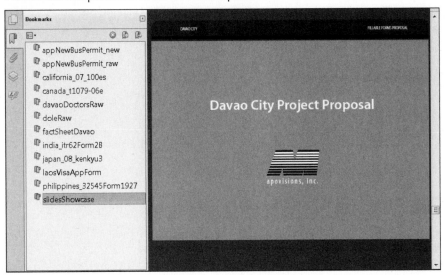

FIGURE 11.4

Preview the composite file in the Document pane.

## Combining files and folders on the Mac

As I mentioned in Chapter 8 when I covered converting Microsoft Office files to PDF, the preferred way to convert the files is to use the PDF Printer. Since the PDFMaker is not available on the Mac, you won't find native file format support for Merge Files into a Single PDF using MS Office applications.

You can use other file formats on the Mac such as Adobe InDesign .indd files, Adobe Illustrator .ai files, Adobe Flash .swf and .fla, image file formats such as gif, jpg, etc., and HTML files. Mac users can also use the Choose Pages button for MS Office files after you convert them to PDF. The nice thing about the Merge Files command is that you can also add PDF documents to the merged file.

## Using the Combine Files Wizard

In Acrobat 8, the Combine Files Wizard had two panes where you could choose attributes for your combined files or PDF Packages. In Acrobat 9 and later, the Merge Files into a Single PDF document uses a single pane in the Wizard, and the new PDF Portfolios are created in a separate interface.

As a first order of business, let's take a look at adding files to the Wizard window when you first open the Combine Files dialog box. At the top of the Wizard is a pull-down menu used to add files for combining into a single PDF document, as shown in Figure 11.5.

**FIGURE 11.5**

The Add Files pull-down menu displays four menu commands used to add files to the Wizard list of files.

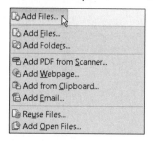

Your choices are as follows:

- **Add Files.** Use this menu command to open the Add Files dialog box. This dialog box behaves similar to an Open dialog box where you can navigate your hard drive and locate files to add to the list in the first pane.

  If you select a secure PDF or a file created in Adobe LiveCycle Designer, a warning message appears in the Combine Files dialog box as shown in Figure 11.6. As stated in the message, you cannot combine the selected file and must use the PDF Portfolio option if you want to merge the file with other documents.

**FIGURE 11.6**

A warning appears for all files that are not supported in the Combine Files Wizard.

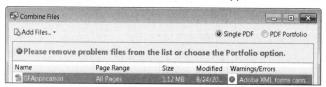

- **Add Folders.** Use this command to add a folder of files.
- **Add PDF From Scanner.** Choose this option when you want to scan a document to add to the list.
- **Add Web Page.** You can visit a URL, convert the Web page to PDF, and add it to your files to combine into a single PDF.
- **Add from Clipboard.** Any data copied to the clipboard is converted to PDF and added to the list.
- **Add Email (Windows only.** You can add emails by dragging and dropping from either Microsoft Outlook or Lotus Notes to the Combine Files list.

- **Reuse Files.** Choose this menu command and the Reuse Files dialog box shown in Figure 11.7 opens. Once you've created a PDF by combining files, you can open the Reuse Files dialog box and use one or any number of files combined together in a previous file.

  On the left side of the dialog box you see a list of files used in a previous session that were combined to create a single PDF document. On the right you see files made available for reuse. Click a file in the right pane and click Add Files to reuse it. The file is then added to the list in the Combine Files Wizard.

**FIGURE 11.7**

Reuse Files enables you to select files used in a previous Combine Files session in a new session.

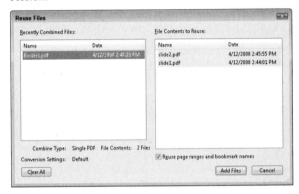

- **Add Open Files.** You can choose the Merge Files into a Single PDF command without having a file open in the Document pane. If you have a file open when you open the Wizard window, you can choose to add your open file to other files you add to the list.

## Tip

From the desktop you can select files in a folder, open a context menu, and choose Combine supported files in Acrobat. When you release the mouse button, the files are added to the Combine Files Wizard, where you can choose pages and merge the files into a single PDF document. If you want to convert the files to separate PDFs, choose the Convert to PDF command in the same context menu. ■

## Organizing files

As you move below the file list in the Wizard window, a series of buttons appear for organizing pages in the file you ultimately create, as shown in Figure 11.8.

**FIGURE 11.8**

Buttons below the file list are used to organize pages.

Your options include:

- **Move Up.** Click a file and click the Move Up button and the file is reordered in the list. If the file you select is at the top of the list, the Move Up button is grayed out and unusable.

- **Move Down.** This button behaves the opposite of the Move Up button. Clicking the button moves a selected or several selected files down. When you select a file at the bottom of the list, the button is grayed out and unusable.

- **Remove.** As you might suspect, clicking this button removes any selected file(s) from the list.

- **Choose Pages/Sheets/Slides/Layouts/Sheet Selection.** This option is available only for multiple-page documents and documents of certain file types. Most MS Office files are compatible with the Choose (*button text*) option. Click this button and the Preview Selected *button text* dialog box opens. The *button text* varies according to the file type you choose to add in the Combine Files dialog box. For MS Word files the button text is Choose Pages. With MS Excel the button text is Choose Sheets. AutoCAD files appear with Choose Layout. Microsoft Visio files appear with Sheet Selection. If you select a PowerPoint file, the button name changes to Choose Slides. Clicking any option opens a Preview dialog box like the one shown when I select Choose Slides with a PowerPoint file selected as shown in Figure 11.9.

## Tip

If you want to open the Preview and Select Pages/Slides dialog box, you can also double-click a file in the list window. ■

## Note

For simplicity, I'll refer to the item appearing in the Choose button as simply Choose or Choose Pages button when describing options for choosing pages/sheets/layouts and so on in the sections ahead. ■

### Previewing files

Files of several different file types — primarily those of the Microsoft Office flavor and PDF documents — permit you to create a PDF preview and choose pages within the document to add to your resultant file, and also offer many different editing features. However, what you do in the Preview window cannot be saved. If you want to alter content you need to return to the original authoring program and make your edits, then export back to PDF.

**FIGURE 11.9**

Click Choose Pages to open a dialog box where pages in a file can be previewed.

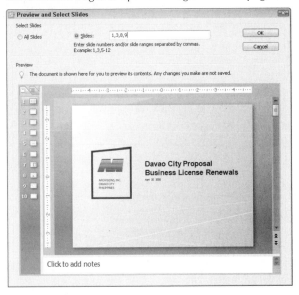

## Cross-Reference

**For more information regarding exporting to PDF, see Chapter 7. For information related to Microsoft Office and PDF creation, see Chapter 8.** ■

Once again, I can't cover all the options available to you when previewing files, but here are a few examples available with some Office applications:

- **Microsoft Word.** Click a multi-page Word document in the file list and click Choose Pages, or simply double-click the Word document and the document opens in the Preview and Select Page Range dialog box. You can select specific pages you want added to the combined file by typing values in the Pages text box at the top of the dialog box. Noncontiguous pages are separated by commas and contiguous pages are separated by dashes. For example, 1,3,7-9 denotes using pages 1, 3, and 5 through 7 for adding to the combined file.

  In long documents, it would be helpful to see a view of the document pages so you know what pages you want to include in your combined file. The Preview and Select Page Range dialog box offers you just that. In addition, you can make a number of temporary edits through commands from a context menu, as shown in Figure 11.10. For example, if you want to see a preview of your document with a larger font size, you can use the Font options to change font attributes.

**FIGURE 11.10**

Right-click (Windows) or Ctrl+click (Mac) to open a context menu where some editing commands appear.

Be aware that any edits you make won't be applied to the combined file. What you see available are commands designed to help you view files using temporary changes you can make to the document. If you need to make the changes permanent and reflected in the resultant PDF document, you must return to the original authoring program, make the changes, and save the file.

You can browse documents by tables, graphics, sections, comments, and much more. Just click the circle between the Previous and Next Page buttons represented by double arrowheads in the lower-right corner of the dialog box. A pop-up menu, shown in Figure 11.11, appears where you can choose to browse your file according to any one of 12 different options. All of the options are used for navigational purposes only. You can, for example, jump to different comments in a file, browse a file by section number, browse by table, and so on.

**FIGURE 11.11**

Click the small circle between the Previous and Next Page arrows to open a pop-up menu used for browsing different content.

- **Microsoft Excel.** Double-click an Excel Workbook file in the Wizard window or click and select Choose Sheets. The Preview and Select Sheets dialog box opens, as shown earlier in Figure 11.3. As with MS Word, you also have context menu commands. An entire workbook can be displayed, and you can scroll the pages selecting only the pages you want to appear in your combined file.

- **Microsoft PowerPoint.** You can choose a Slide Sorter view and an Outline view in PowerPoint which you open in much the same way as when opening Word and Excel files. In Figure 11.9, slides are shown in the Slide Sorter view.

  PowerPoint files can also be viewed with content changes, but like other files, the changes are only temporary while in the Preview dialog box. From a context menu you have choices for deleting slides, changing the slide design, changing layout, and changing the background.

Other similar options are available with Microsoft Visio files, Microsoft Project and Publisher files, and a number of different file formats including AutoCAD DWG and DWF files. Your clue as to whether you have an option to open files in the Preview dialog box is whether you see an active Choose button in the Combine Files Wizard. If the button is grayed out, you don't have the option to preview pages.

### Choosing conversion options

On the right side of the bottom of the Combine Files dialog box you have three icons. These icons offer options for file optimization. Click Smaller File Size, and images are downsampled to 150 ppi and compressed with a low-quality JPEG compression scheme. The file size will typically be smaller than your original file unless you used lower resolution images and low-quality JPEG compression. Click Default File Size (middle icon) to preserve the original file resolutions, and the image size attributes are the same setting identified in the Edit ⇨ Preferences ⇨ Convert to PDF Settings. Click Larger File Size to create a file with optimum results. You may not see much difference in file sizes between Default and Larger file sizes if you used high-resolution images and high-quality JPEG compression.

## Note

Using Larger File Size does not upsample images. The image resolution won't be greater than the default resolution used when an image was saved. The primary change you experience with this option is when JPEG compression is set to Maximum Quality. If you saved your images with Medium Quality, the quality setting is changed. ■

These buttons affect files that need to be converted to PDF, and PDF documents. When PDF documents are included and you make a choice for the file size, the PDF Optimizer is used to resample images.

## Caution

Creating Smaller File Sizes can result in much longer times to create a combined file. This option downsamples each image above 150 ppi and requires more time to produce the resultant PDF than the other two options. ■

At the very bottom of the Wizard window the Help, Combine Files, and Cancel buttons should be self-explanatory. Additionally, you have an Options button. Click the Options button and the Options dialog box opens, as shown in Figure 11.12.

**FIGURE 11.12**

Click the Options button at the bottom of the first pane in the Wizard to open the Options dialog box.

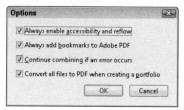

The four options you have are

- **Always enable accessibility and reflow.** This item makes your PDF conversions accessible.

## Cross-Reference

For more information on accessibility, see Chapter 23. ■

- **Always add bookmarks to Adobe PDF.** By default, the check box is enabled. If you don't want bookmarks added to the resultant file, remove the check mark.

- **Continue combining if an error occurs.** If a file cannot be combined for one reason or another, you can halt the process by removing the check mark. If the check box is enabled, Acrobat skips over corrupt files and files that cannot be added to the merged document.

- **Convert all files to PDF when creating a portfolio.** This choice relates to PDF Portfolios where you can package documents in a PDF wrapper and either convert to PDF or keep the files in their native file format. Remove the check mark if you don't want the files converted to PDF in a PDF Portfolio.

# Working with PDF Portfolios

Acrobat 8 provided a way to package PDF documents together in the form of a PDF Package. The primary thinking behind the PDF Package in Acrobat 8 was to permit you to do all the things you couldn't do when combining PDFs such as:

- **Secure files.** PDF Packages enabled you to add secure files. In order to add a secure file to a package, you need the password(s).

- **Adobe Designer XML forms.** PDF Packages enabled you to combine files that were created in Adobe Designer.

- **PDF forms.** Actually this can be both PDF forms and XML forms. When you combine forms having identical field names, the data fields remain undisturbed.

- **Preserve original document format.** When you use Merge Files into a Single PDF, any document other than PDF is converted to PDF as long as the file format is compatible with the Create PDF From File command. When creating a PDF Package, files appear with a PDF preview but they retain original file format attributes and can be exported from the package back to the original file format.

In addition to the reasons stated in the above bullet points, PDF Packages were used for aggregating data from PDF forms and exporting form data to spreadsheets.

What you had available in Acrobat 8 in terms of creating PDF Packages was a new, impressive Acrobat feature. All the advantages for having PDF Packages were implemented in Acrobat 9, but Adobe introduced a new method for packaging PDF content in the form of PDF Portfolios. In Acrobat X we find a more attractive display for PDF Portfolios and some refinement in creating layouts and assembling documents.

PDF Portfolios should be thought of more as a revelation in Acrobat functionality rather than an enhancement on packaging files. You have all the advantages you had available with PDF Packages, but PDF Portfolios are much more. In short, the focus of PDF Portfolios is on presentation, and it's presentation in a big way. The Adobe engineers have given you in Acrobat X a more improved new interface and new methods for displaying content in very exciting ways.

When you create a PDF Portfolio, you create a much different result than when merging files into one PDF document. PDF Portfolios are PDF documents and/or native application documents assembled together in a package (or collection) similar to adding file attachments to a PDF. During the assembly of a PDF Portfolio you have many different choices for how you want to display your portfolio and the documents contained therein.

PDF Portfolios opened in Acrobat 8 appear as PDF Packages. The coversheet for the PDF Package is a default coversheet created by Adobe and installed with your Acrobat installation. As you can see in Figure 11.13, a PDF Portfolio opened in Acrobat 8 informs the user that to see all features in a PDF Portfolio, the user needs to upgrade to Acrobat or Adobe Reader 9 or above.

If you open a PDF Portfolio in Acrobat 7, the file appears very similar to PDF Packages opened in Acrobat 8 viewers. In Acrobat 7 you see the coversheet and the files appear as file attachments.

## Cross-Reference

For more on file attachments see "Working with File Attachments" later in this chapter. ■

**FIGURE 11.13**

The coversheet of a PDF Portfolio opened in Acrobat 8

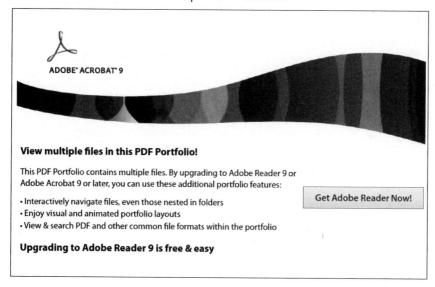

## Understanding the Create PDF Portfolio Wizard

You could jump in and create a PDF Portfolio before exploring all the options available to you. However, a little understanding of the Create PDF Portfolio Wizard is helpful before you create an Acrobat X PDF Portfolio.

You create PDF Portfolios similar to the way you assemble files in a single PDF document. There are three ways to do this: choose PDF Portfolio from the Create task button (shown earlier in Figure 11.1), use the File ⇨ Create ⇨ PDF Portfolio menu command, or click Create PDF Portfolio in the Getting Started section of the Acrobat X Welcome screen. Using any one of these three methods opens the Create PDF Portfolio Wizard shown in Figure 11.14.

You have two sets of options in the Create PDF Portfolio Wizard. First, on the left side of the window you can choose a layout. Acrobat X provides you with some default layouts that are listed in the Wizard. After choosing a layout, you can later change to another layout when editing your portfolio. The second choice you have is to add files. If you have files ready to be assembled in a portfolio, click the Add Files button on the right side of the Wizard. You can skip this step and add files later if you so desire before clicking the Finish button.

The only thing Acrobat requires of you when you first create a new PDF Portfolio is to accept the default layout or choose a layout from the list. Once you make the choice, you can change the appearance when editing the portfolio.

**FIGURE 11.14**

To launch the Create PDF Portfolio Wizard, choose Create PDF Portfolio from the Create task button, select File ⇨ Create, or click Create PDF Portfolio in the Welcome screen.

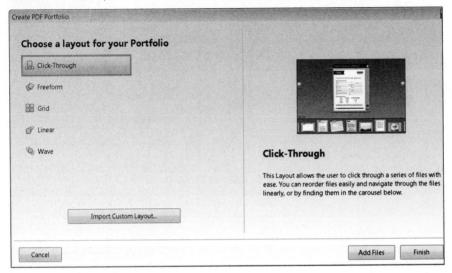

## Creating a PDF Portfolio

To understand a little more about PDF Portfolios, let's first start by following some steps to create a portfolio and then look at some of the attributes for working in the new Acrobat X PDF Portfolio interface. You start a PDF Portfolio by using one of two commands similar to the way you merge files into single PDF documents. You can choose File ⇨ Create ⇨ Assemble PDF Portfolio, or open the Create task button and select Assemble PDF Portfolio. If you are already in the Combine Files Wizard you can click the PDF Portfolio radio button. Regardless of which menu command you use, the Acrobat user interface changes to the PDF Portfolio interface where you add files, edit display appearances, specify document details, choose from among different publish options, and more.

To create a PDF Portfolio, follow these steps.

### STEPS: Creating a PDF Portfolio

1. **Click the Create task button (or open the File ⇨ Create menu) and choose Create PDF Portfolio).** After you select the menu command, the Create PDF Portfolio Wizard opens. Click Finish and the default Click-Through layout is selected for the new portfolio.

2. **Add files to the portfolio.** Click Add Files in the Add Content panel. The Add Files dialog box opens. Select files and click Open in the dialog box. Your files are shown in the portfolio, similar to what you see in Figure 11.15.

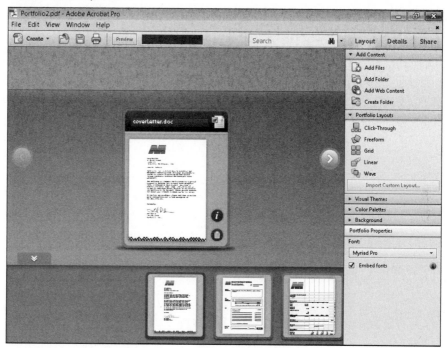

**FIGURE 11.15**

Files added to a portfolio

3. **Change the layout.** If you want to use another layout, click one of the options in the Portfolio Layouts panel. You can click each layout and see a preview as the layouts change.

4. **Change the theme.** In the Visual Themes pane you have several choices for changing a theme. Click the options and choose a theme to your liking.

5. **Edit the background.** Open the Background panel and you find a number of options for changing gradient direction and intensity, background color, and background image attributes. Play around a little and experiment with the options.

6. **Change header properties.** Click Header properties to open the Header Properties panel shown in Figure 11.16. From the Templates pull-down menu, choose Text and Image. Click Add Text and type header text in the Header Items text box. Click Add Image to import an image for the header. When the text and image are added to the portfolio, you can click and drag to position them, and scale them by dragging their corner handles.

**FIGURE 11.16**

Add a header by choosing options in the Header Properties panel.

7. **Save the portfolio.** By default, Acrobat saves your portfolio as Portfolio1, Portfolio2, Portfolio3, and so on (in a single editing session) if you don't modify the filename. To save the portfolio with a name of your choosing, select File ⇨ Save Portfolio As. In the Save As dialog box locate a target folder and type a name for your portfolio. Click the Save button and the file is saved. When you first create a portfolio, you can also choose Save Portfolio; a dialog box opens, prompting you to save and find a target folder.

8. **Preview the portfolio.** After saving the file, click the Preview button in the Quick Tools toolbar. For my example, I used the Wave layout, Tech Office Visual Theme, a background linear gradient, and text and an image for the header (see Figure 11.17).

The steps outlined here are but a fraction of the choices you have for customizing the view and adding options for PDF Portfolios. Much more is available to you, including Flash animations you can add to the Home view of your portfolios.

FIGURE 11.17

Preview the PDF Portfolio in Acrobat.

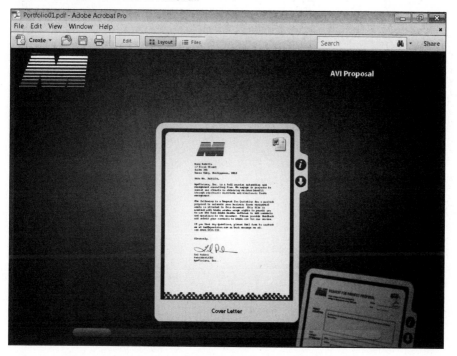

## Examining the portfolio interface

Many options are available to you in creating and setting up the display of PDF Portfolios. Some of the options you have relate to how you set up a portfolio for users to view your work, and other options relate to your editing tasks in creating the portfolios. When you choose a menu command such as File ⇨ Create ⇨ Create PDF Portfolio and click Finish in the Create PDF Portfolio Wizard without importing any files, the interface shown in Figure 11.18 opens. The various tools, panels, and menu choices you have include:

**FIGURE 11.18**

The default appearance when you begin creating a PDF Portfolio

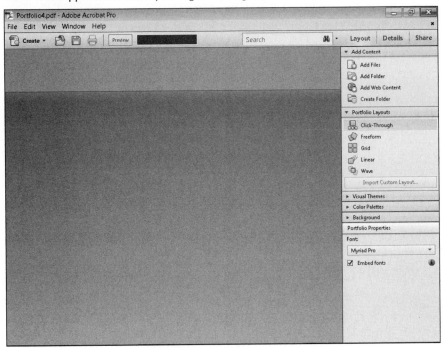

- **Menu bar.** The top-level menu bar provides an abbreviated set of menu commands for working with portfolios. If you choose some commands such as File ⇨ Open, View ⇨ Compare Documents, or open the Window menu and select another open file, you leave the PDF Portfolio currently in view.

- **Quick Tools.** A limited number of tools appear in the Quick Tools toolbar. You also find the Create task button on the left side of the Quick Tools toolbar. By default, PDF Portfolios open in Edit mode when you first assemble a portfolio. Click the Preview button to see a preview after making edits.

- **Search.** Use the text field to perform a complete text search in all files contained within a portfolio.

- **Layout buttons.** The Layout button is selected by default. When Layout is selected, the Layout panel opens. Click Details to see a detailed and sorted view of files in a portfolio. When you want to share and distribute PDF Portfolios, click the Share button to open the Share panel.

- **Panels.** Consistent with the new user interface for Acrobat X, you find a number of panels nested in the Tools panel. Here you find all the options you need for adding and removing files, changing the portfolio appearance, and choosing various file attributes.

# Discovering the PDF Portfolio panels

When creating PDF Portfolios, you see a completely different set of panels nested in the Layout panel compared to the Tools panel in normal viewer mode. The panels contain all the tools and commands you need to assemble and design your portfolio. By default, the Add Content panel is open when you create a new portfolio.

## Using the Add Content panel

The Add Content panel shown in Figure 11.19 contains items that permit you to add and manage files. The options include:

**FIGURE 11.19**

The Add Content panel opens by default when you create a new portfolio.

- **Add Files.** Click Add Files and the Add Files dialog box opens. You navigate your hard drive and select files for importing when creating a new portfolio or editing an existing portfolio. You can select multiple files in the Add Files dialog box by pressing Ctrl/⌘ and clicking files. After you select the files in the Add Files dialog box, click Open and the files are added to your portfolio.

- **Add Folder.** Click Add Folder and select a folder in the Browse for Folder dialog box that opens. When you add a folder, all the files appear in the portfolio nested inside a folder. To open a folder in a portfolio, double-click the folder just like you do when opening folders on your desktop.

- **Add Web Content.** You might think that this feature is similar to the Create PDF From Web Page feature I describe in Chapter 7. It's a logical assumption, but Acrobat handles adding Web content to portfolios quite differently from converting HTML to PDF. Click this item and a dialog box opens, prompting you to add a Web URL, a title for the link, and a description. When you click OK, a link to the Web address is added to the portfolio. When a user double-clicks the link, the Web content is shown within the portfolio. In Figure 11.20 I added a link to a YouTube video. When I view the link, I can see the video playing inside my portfolio.

## Tip

There are many different applications available for managing content, particularly content on social networks. You can use Acrobat X for content management by creating PDF Portfolios, adding Web links and files, and storing the PDFs either locally or on your Acrobat.com account. ■

**FIGURE 11.20**

Web link content is displayed inside PDF Portfolios.

- **Create Folder.** Click the last item in the Add Content panel and you add a new folder to a portfolio. To add files to a folder, double-click the folder to open it, and then click the Add Files item in the Add Content panel. Alternately, you can open a context menu and choose Add Files. If you don't open the folder, adding files places the new files outside the folder. If you have files in a portfolio that you want to place inside the folder, drag and drop the files to the folder just like adding files to folders on your desktop.

## Changing the Portfolio Layouts panel

The next panel in the Layout panel is the Portfolio Layouts panel shown in Figure 11.21. You have a few predefined layouts that are easily understood when you click one of the options. By default the Click-Through layout is selected when you open the Create PDF Portfolio Wizard. Click one of the other options in the panel to change the layout type.

The last item in the Portfolio Layouts panel is the Import Custom Layout button. Click this button and you can import layouts that either you or other users create. Creating layouts is not an easy task. If you're interested in exploring custom layouts, visit the Adobe Web site or search the Internet for tutorials.

**FIGURE 11.21**

The Portfolio Layouts panel offers options to change the layout appearance of your portfolios.

## Working with the Visual Themes panel

The Visual Themes panel shown in Figure 11.22 offers various options for theme changes, such as different-colored backgrounds and visual elements, gradient appearances, and opacity differences. You can apply any one of the different themes to a given background. To change a theme, click a theme name in the Visual Themes panel.

**FIGURE 11.22**

Visual Themes provide choices for background colors and elements, gradients, and opacity differences.

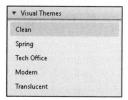

## Working with the Color Palettes panel

The Color Palettes panel shown in Figure 11.23 displays colors used in the currently selected Visual Theme. You can change colors by clicking color swatches in the panel, and you can create a new custom palette by clicking the Create from Existing button. This action opens another panel where you find a Save button to save the new custom theme.

## Changing the Background panel

The Background panel shown in Figure 11.24 provides several options for changing the background display. Options available in this panel include:

**FIGURE 11.23**

The Color Palettes panel offers options for changing theme colors and saving new custom color palettes.

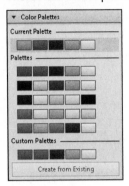

**FIGURE 11.24**

The Background panel offers options for changing the background appearance of a portfolio.

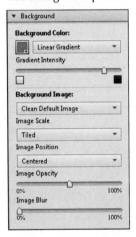

- **Background Color.** Click the swatch to the left of the drop-down menu and a color palette opens where you can change the background color.
- **Background Fill.** The drop-down menu provides choices for a solid fill, a linear gradient, and a radial gradient.
- **Gradient Intensity.** If you choose either a linear or radial gradient, you can move the slider to change the gradient intensity.

- **Background Image.** The default image option is None, meaning no image or design is used for the background. From the drop-down menu, click None to open the menu and choose from various preset image choices. Scroll to the bottom of the menu and you can import an image in the JPEG, GIF, or PNG format. Use the Image Scale and Image Position drop-down menus to size and position your imported image.

- **Image Opacity.** When you import an image, a slide appears in the Background Image panel. Move the slider left or right to change the opacity.

- **Image Blur.** To diffuse an imported image, move the slider.

### Adding a Header

The Header Properties panel shown earlier in Figure 11.16 provides options for Adding header items that appear at the top of your portfolio. You can change templates from the drop-down menu at the top of the panel, create text, add an image, and freely move the elements around after adding them by clicking and dragging.

### Choosing the Portfolio Properties panel

At the bottom of the Layout panel, you find the Portfolio Properties panel as shown in Figure 11.25. In this panel you have a choice for font selection for the header, filenames, and descriptions. To embed the fonts, check the Embed fonts check box.

**FIGURE 11.25**

The Portfolio Properties panel offers options for font selection and embedding fonts.

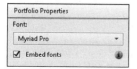

## Working with the Details panel

When you create a PDF Portfolio, the Layout panel opens by default. Adjacent to Layout, you find the Details button. Click this button and the Details panel opens as shown in Figure 11.26.

As you can see in Figure 11.26, files added to a portfolio appear in a list on the left. The order you see here is the same order you find in layout mode. You can easily change the order of the files by clicking and dragging them up or down.

To the right of each filename are columns of data. The columns that are displayed are chosen from the Columns to Display panel. Check each column you want to show in the Details display. You can adjust column sizes by dragging the separator bar that divides columns at the top of the window.

FIGURE 11.26

A PDF Portfolio displayed with the Details panel open

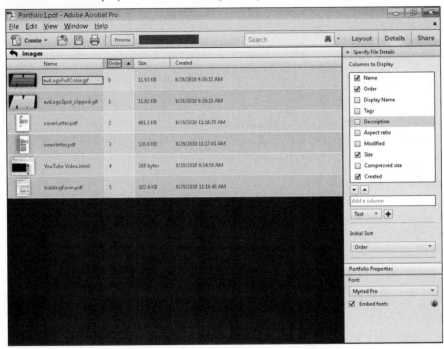

Columns are sorted according to the choice you make from the Initial Sort drop-down menu. In Figure 11.26 the columns are sorted according to the Order column where you see numerical values. To change the sort to an alpha name sort, open the Initial Sort menu and choose Display Name.

## Sharing PDF Portfolios

The third panel in the PDF Portfolio interface is the Share panel. Click the Share button to open the panel shown in Figure 11.27. In this panel you have two choices for sharing files denoted by the radio buttons at the top of the panel. Click the Use Adobe SendNow Online option to share your portfolio online on Acrobat.com, or click Attach To Email to email your portfolio. If you email a portfolio, you can fill in the To, Subject, and Comments text boxes to complete a text message.

## Cross-Reference

For more information on using Acrobat.com, see Chapter 26. ∎

**FIGURE 11.27**

Use the Share panel to deploy your PDF Portfolios to Acrobat.com or via email.

## Working with context menus in portfolios

When you add files to a portfolio, you have access to the interface controls described in the section "Examining the portfolio interface." Some of the options you have from the interface tools and menus are also available in a context menu when you right-click (Control+click on Mac) on a file. Additionally, there are a few context menu commands that you don't find in other areas in the portfolio interface.

Open a context menu on a file in a portfolio and you see the menu options as shown in Figure 11.28. A few options not yet discussed include:

Three items exist in the context menu that you don't find from the tools in the portfolio interface. The Select All and Deselect All commands enable you to select or deselect files in the portfolio. You might use Select All (also available by pressing Ctrl/⌘+A) and then choose Convert to PDF for files that were added from native file formats.

The Properties menu choice opens a File Properties dialog box. Here you can type a description as shown in Figure 11.29. The description you add to the File Properties dialog box is dynamically displayed when you view files in the Details View mode and check the Description check box in the Specify File Details panel.

**FIGURE 11.28**

Open a context menu (right-click in Windows or Ctrl+click in Mac) on a file in a portfolio.

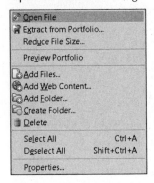

**FIGURE 11.29**

Open a context menu and choose Properties to open the File Properties dialog box.

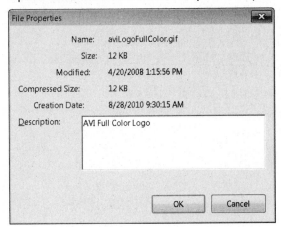

## Adding file information

Files are shown in a portfolio with two icons appearing at the lower-right side of the document. At the bottom of the page is a trash can icon. Click this icon and a dialog box opens for you to confirm deleting the file. Above the trash can icon is an *i* symbol (for Information). Click the icon and the display changes to what you see in Figure 11.30.

Use the text boxes to type corresponding information for Tags (where you can display files according to tag names when in Detail View) and a description of the file. To close the

Information window, click the X in the top-right corner and the file display returns to a thumbnail view of the first page in the file.

The Information window offers options for adding file information.

# Navigating PDF Portfolios

What I've covered up to this point is creating and editing PDF Portfolios. As a recipient of a portfolio or to help guide others in viewing your portfolio content, you'll need to become familiar with PDF Portfolio navigation and viewing.

## Previewing portfolios

Recipients who review your files see portfolios in a Preview mode. You can also view a portfolio in Preview mode after editing by clicking the Preview button in the Quick Tools toolbar.

Each of the layout views provides you with buttons or arrows to scroll documents in a portfolio. Additionally you find a bin at the bottom of the portfolio window with thumbnail images of the files contained therein, as shown in Figure 11.31. Click an arrow or thumbnail to bring the selected file to the forefront. To scroll through documents, click the arrows in the layout interface.

To create more viewing area for a document, you can collapse the document bin at the bottom of the screen. Click the down-pointing chevron to collapse the view and the document in the center of the screen expands to a larger view.

**FIGURE 11.31**

Click the arrows or a thumbnail to bring the document in view in the center of the layout screen.

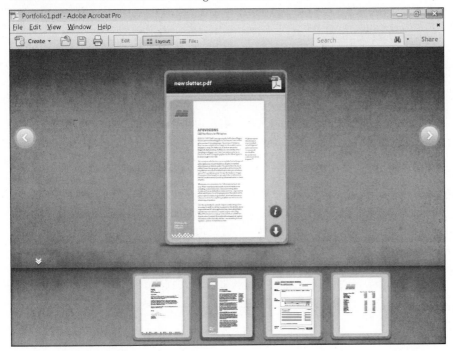

When you see a document in the layout style, only the first page of a multi-page document is in view. To navigate a document, double-click the document and it expands to a larger view similar to viewing files in Read Mode with a toolbar at the bottom of the document as shown in Figure 11.32.

## Cross-Reference
**For more information on Read Mode, see Chapter 5.** ■

To navigate pages in Read Mode, click the Up or Down arrows. To jump to a page, type the page number in the text box where you see 1 in Figure 11.32. If you want to extract the file from the portfolio and save it as a separate file, click the leftmost icon (a page with a down-pointing arrow) in the toolbar.

FIGURE 11.32

Double-click a document to view the file in Read Mode.

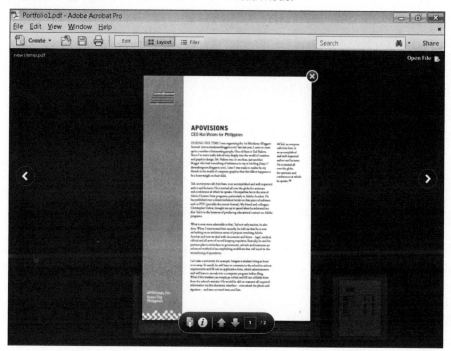

## Previewing files

Each file contained within a portfolio can be shown in a separate preview window. If you have PDF files as part of your portfolio, you can open them in Acrobat and view the files just like you view other PDF documents. If the files are native authoring application documents, the Preview displays an Open File button to use to open the file in the native application.

You open a file in Preview mode by clicking the Open File button at the top-right corner of the window (see Figure 11.32). This view is still the view within the PDF Portfolio. If you want to edit a PDF document, you can click the Open File button and open the PDF in the Normal viewer mode, where you have access to all the Acrobat tools and the menu commands.

If you want to simply browse a PDF document, you can stay in the PDF Portfolio Preview mode. You can view bookmarks, digital signatures, comments, and file attachments, and you can access other navigation panels by opening a context menu on the Navigation panel and choosing a panel you want to open.

**Cross-Reference**

For more information on using Navigation panels, see Chapter 5. ■

Open the Tools panel while in Preview mode to access Acrobat tools. From the Tools panel you have access to all Acrobat tools. If you want to add comments, open the Comments panel.

**Cross-Reference**

For more information on using the Tools panel, see Chapter 5. For more information on adding comments, see Chapter 19. ■

## Returning to default views

One thing that's critically important to know is how to return to the default view when you open a PDF Portfolio. By default you start in a Layout view. As you become familiar with navigating files in portfolios, this view will be commonplace to you, and you'll frequently want to return to the view when you branch out and explore other views such as the Preview mode or Normal viewer mode in Acrobat.

Just remember that when you click the Close button while previewing a file, the action only closes Preview mode. Your PDF Portfolio remains open. Alternately, you can open the Window menu and select the portfolio name at the bottom of the window to return to the portfolio.

## Using the Detail List view

To enter the Detail List view, click the Detail tool in the PDF Portfolio toolbar. When you enter the Detail List view, you can double-click a file icon in the far-left column to enter Preview mode. Note that you don't have context menu commands for navigation or any other operation while in the Detail List view.

# Working with File Attachments

File attachments enable you to attach any document file on your hard drive, a recorded sound, or a pasted image to an open PDF file. When you attach files, the file is embedded in the PDF document. Embedding a file provides other users with the capability to view attachments on other computers and across platforms. At first it may appear as though the attachment is a link. However, if you transport the PDF document to another computer and open the attachment, the embedded file opens in the host application.

Users on other computers need the original authoring application to view the embedded file just like files added to PDF Portfolios. You can add file attachments in Acrobat Standard and Acrobat Pro. You can also add file attachments in Adobe Reader when PDFs have been created by using Adobe LiveCycle Reader Extensions ES. If you open the Attachments panel (click the paper clip icon in the Navigation panel) in Adobe Reader, you cannot add file attachments if the file has not been enabled with Adobe LiveCycle Reader Extensions ES. An alternative for those without the LiveCycle Reader Extensions ES is to enable PDFs for Commenting in Adobe Reader using Acrobat Pro. Reader users can then add file attachments as comments.

## Cross-Reference

Enabling commenting in Adobe Reader is available only in Acrobat Pro. For more information on enabling files with Adobe Reader extensions, see Chapter 18. ■

There are two methods available to you when attaching files: you can use the Comments panel and attach a file as a comment, or use the Add Attachment menu command from the Attachments panel. When files are attached using Attach a File as a Comment, the PDF needs to be enabled with usage rights for Adobe Reader users to extract the file. Additionally, when Attach a File as a Comment is used, the file attachments show up in any comment summary you create in Acrobat. Additionally, you can add file attachments to PDF Portfolios as well as PDF documents.

## Cross-Reference

The commenting tools used for file attachments are not discussed in this chapter. However, commenting is a huge topic, and you'll find Chapter 19 devoted to all the other features all Acrobat viewers offer you for commenting. ■

When using the Attach a File menu command, any Adobe Reader user in version 7.0 and later can extract the file attachment without the file enabled with usage rights. Unlike using commenting tools, files attached using the menu command do not show up in comment summaries.

## Cross-Reference

For more information on adding usage rights to PDFs for Adobe Reader, see Chapter 18. ■

Regardless of what attachment you add to a document, the attachments appear in the Attachments panel in the Navigation pane. If you add a file attachment to a PDF in a PDF Portfolio, the portfolio attachments are shown in the Attachments panel when you open the Navigation pane.

# Using the Attachments Panel

To attach a file to a PDF document, open the Attachments panel from the navigation pane by clicking the paper clip icon. From the Options menu, choose Add Attachment as shown in Figure 11.33. Browse your hard drive, select the file you want to attach, and click Open.

To use the Attach File as a Comment tool, open the Comments panel and open the Annotations panel. Click the Attach File tool in the first row of tools. Move the cursor to a document page and click. The Add Attachment dialog box opens, in which you navigate to a file and select it for the attachment. Any file on your computer can be used as a file attachment. Select a file and click Open. The File Attachment Properties dialog box opens with the Appearance tab in view as shown in Figure 11.34.

Choose Add Attachment from the Options menu in the Attach panel.

Select a file to attach and the File Attachment Properties dialog box opens.

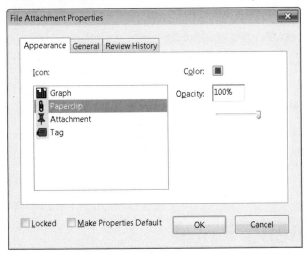

The Appearance properties for file attachments offer you choices for icon appearances to represent file attachments. Choose from one of the four icon choices shown in Figure 11.34. By default the Paperclip icon is used.

The General tab shown in Figure 11.35 has editable fields used for Author name, Subject, and a Description. By default, the Author name is supplied by your Identity preferences.

## Cross-Reference

**For information on editing Identity preferences, see Chapter 19. ■**

**FIGURE 11.35**

The General properties offer choices for author name, subject, and a description of the attached file.

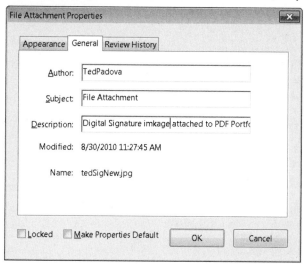

The Review History tab is used for review sessions where information related to the review history and migration history are viewed.

## Cross-Reference

**For information on review and migration history, see Chapter 20. ■**

If you position the cursor over a file attachment icon, a tooltip displays the author name, file-name, and the description information.

Attach a File as a Comment does not support an associated pop-up note. Double-clicking an attachment icon opens the file attachment.

## Note

**You must have the original authoring application to open file attachments when the attachments are other than PDF. ■**

You can use PDF documents like a security wrapper for any file you want to exchange with colleagues and co-workers. Use the Attach a File as a Comment tool and attach one or more files to a PDF document. Secure the PDF with Password Security and use the E-mail tool to send the file to members of your workgroup. You can protect the document with password security and prevent unauthorized users from opening your PDF or extracting attached files. In this regard you can use Acrobat to secure any document you create in any authoring program. Of course, you can also secure PDF Portfolios and use files within a portfolio very similar to using file attachments.

## Cross-Reference

**For more information on using password security, see Chapter 24.** ■

File attachments are embedded in PDFs, and double-clicking the Attach a File as a Comment icon provides you with access to the file. If you want to save an embedded file to disk without opening the file, open a context menu and select Save Attachment. Acrobat opens a dialog box where you can navigate your hard drive and designate a location for the file to be saved to. Neither opening a file nor saving the attachment file to disk removes the file attachment. If you want to delete a file attachment, open a context menu on the attachment icon and select Delete Attachment or select the icon and press Delete or the Del key.

# Summary

In this chapter, you explored creating PDFs from multiple files, working with PDF Portfolios, and attaching files to PDF documents.

- Separate files can be merged together in a single PDF file using the Combine Files task button.
- A PDF Portfolio is created with either several different menu commands or by using the same Combine Files Wizard.
- PDF Portfolios open in a separate user interface much different than the Normal viewer mode in Acrobat 9 and later viewers.
- PDF Portfolios can contain secure files and Adobe Designer XML forms. Creating a single PDF from multiple files does not support secure files or Designer forms.
- PDF Portfolios use a number of different user-selectable templates for the display the Home page and the Layout view.
- Headers added to a PDF Portfolio appear on all pages, including the Home page.
- Files can be sorted in the Detail List view by dragging them up or down in the window.
- Navigating PDF Portfolios can be handled in the Layout view, the Preview view, and in the Detail List view.
- PDF Portfolios can be published on Acrobat.com.
- File attachments can be added to PDFs.

- Attachments can be made as file attachment comments or using a menu command in the Attachments panel.

- If files are attached, you can extract the attachments in Adobe Reader.

- If you attach files other than PDF, you need the original application program that created the document installed on your computer in order to open the attached file.

- File attachments are viewed according to the PDF file in the Attachments panel. When viewing file attachments made on PDFs in a PDF Portfolio, only the attachments on the current file in view can be seen in the Attachments panel.

# Editing Text

I deally, you should always return to an original document when you want to make changes on PDF pages that were converted from an authoring application. With all of Acrobat's impressive features, it is not designed to be used as a page layout program. The options you have in Acrobat for text editing are limited to tweaks and minor corrections. In as much as Acrobat 9 (and Acrobat X) greatly improved text editing on PDFs, returning to your authoring program, editing the pages, and converting them back to PDF is a preferred method.

For minor edits and for purposes of editing PDF files where original documents have been lost or are unavailable, Acrobat does provide you with tools and means for text editing. As you look through this chapter, realize that the pages ahead are intended to describe methods for minor corrections and text editing when you don't have an option for returning to an original document.

## Using the Edit Document Text Tool

For minor text edits, you can use the Edit Document Text tool. This tool is found in the Content panel. Click the Tools button and then click Content to open the panel. Under Add/Edit Text, click Edit Document Text. Before you attempt to change text passages on a PDF page, you need to keep a few things in mind. Some of the considerations include:

- **Font embedding.** If you attempt to edit an embedded font, Acrobat prompts you in a dialog box to unembed the font. Text editing is only possible after a font is unembedded. Depending on the permissions granted by the font developer, some fonts can't be unembedded. If Acrobat informs you that font editing cannot occur, you need to make your changes in the original authoring document.

- **Tagged and untagged PDF documents.** Selecting text with the Edit Document Text tool was problematic with earlier versions of Acrobat. Blocks of text in untagged files were interpreted as separate passages and could not be selected in a contiguous area. Acrobat now has a more intelligent interpretation of text on a page, and tagged as well as untagged files display no difference when selecting text. In Figure 12.1, a page of text is selected with the Edit Document Text tool in an untagged document.

**FIGURE 12.1**

You can select multiple blocks of text with the Edit Document Text tool in untagged PDF files.

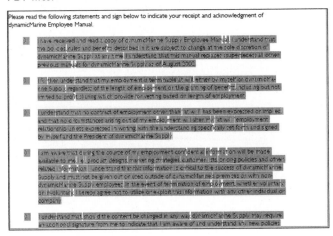

The ability to select lines of text, a paragraph, or multiple paragraphs with the Edit Document Text tool is not dependent on whether a PDF is tagged or untagged; but rather, it's dependent on the structure and content of a PDF. In some documents, you can't select more than single lines of text like the file shown in Figure 12.2.

## Cross-Reference

For more information on tagged and structured PDF documents, see Chapter 23. For information on creating tagged PDF files, see Chapter 9. ■

**FIGURE 12.2**

The Edit Document Text tool can select only single lines of text on a page in some PDF documents.

- **Property changes.** You can apply property changes for fonts, such as color, size, and other attributes, to text without unembedding the font.

Fortunately, Acrobat alerts you ahead of time if you attempt to edit a PDF document with embedded fonts and those fonts aren't installed on your computer. To edit fonts on a page, select the Edit Document Text tool, and click and drag over a body of text to be changed. Acrobat pauses momentarily as it surveys your installed fonts and the font embedded in the PDF document. Enter your changes and the selected text is replaced with the new text you typed.

You'll be able to see on-screen whether your text editing results in an acceptable appearance and the edits are properly applied. If the text scrambles and you lose total control over the document page, you need to either find the original authoring document or export text from Acrobat into a word processor or layout program to make the changes.

## Prepress

Editing text passages are fine for screen displays when the text flows in an acceptable manner. For high-end printing and prepress, you might be able to make changes and minor edits successfully without experiencing printing problems. However, for any kind of paragraph editing you are best off returning to the authoring application. You might get away with some edits in Acrobat, but eventually they will catch up with you. If you do make a spelling error change or other minor text edit, be certain to re-embed the font (see "Changing text attributes" later in this chapter). ■

In addition to selecting the Properties menu command, a context menu opened from an Edit Document Text tool selection offers menu commands for insertion of special characters. Four choices are available to you when you open a context menu and select the Insert menu command. From the submenu, you can choose:

- **Line Break.** This choice adds a line break from the cursor insertion. This command is handy when creating new text on a page or when pasting text. Text lines may extend beyond the page width when creating new text or pasting text. You can create line breaks to keep text within a specific area of the page.

- **Soft Hyphen.** This choice adds a soft hyphen for text scrolling to a new line.

- **Non-Breaking Space.** To add spaces without line breaks, choose nonbreaking space.

- **Em Dash.** To add an em dash (—) at the cursor insertion, choose em dash.

When text is selected and you insert a special character, the selected text is deleted and the new character is added. If you use special characters in some files, the results may be less than desirable. Line breaks can flow text into following paragraphs and the text can overlap, making the page unreadable. If you encounter such problems and the edits are necessary to make your files more readable, you must return the file to the authoring program, make the edits, and re-create the PDF document.

## Changing text attributes

You can make many text attribute changes without unembedding fonts. You can change colors, point sizes in lines of text, character and word spacing, and other similar text attributes, as well as make changes related to the document structure. You make all of these changes in the TouchUp Properties dialog box.

To edit text properties, select the characters, words, or paragraph(s) you want to change. Be certain the text is highlighted and open a context menu, as shown in Figure 12.3. From the menu options, select Properties.

**FIGURE 12.3**

To change text properties, select the text to be changed with the Edit Document Text tool and then select Properties from the menu options.

## Cross-Reference

Two tools enable text selection — the Edit Document Text tool and the Select tool. Always use the Edit Document Text tool context menu when opening the TouchUp Properties dialog box. The Select tool context menu does not provide access to the TouchUp Properties dialog box. For information related to using the Select tool, see "Using the Select Tool" later in this chapter. ■

After you select Properties from the context menu, the TouchUp Properties dialog box opens, as shown in Figure 12.4. The first two tabs relate to changing tags and document structure. Leave these alone for the moment and look at the third tab labeled Text. The properties contained on it relate to changing font attributes for the selected text.

**FIGURE 12.4**

Select the Text tab in the TouchUp Properties dialog box to make changes to font attributes.

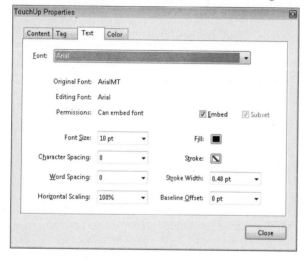

## Cross-Reference

For information on using the Content and Tag panels, see Chapter 23. ■

Items contained in the Text tab include:

- **Font.** This pull-down menu contains a list of fonts for all the fonts loaded in your system and fonts embedded in the document. Keep in mind that just because a font is listed in the pull-down menu doesn't mean you can select the font. If the font is an embedded/subsetted font and you don't have a compatible font loaded in your system, Acrobat won't let you use that font. Fonts loaded in your system can be selected to replace fonts that are both embedded and not embedded.

## Note

The font list in the pull-down menu shows a line dividing the list at the top of the menu. All fonts appearing above the line are embedded fonts in the document. All fonts below the line are loaded in your system. ■

- **Font Size.** You select a preset font size from this pull-down menu. If the desired size is not listed among the menu choices, select the font size in the field box and type a new value to change the size.

- **Character Spacing.** You can move characters in a line of text closer together or farther apart. The values shown in the pull-down menu are measured in em spaces. Choose from the menu choices or type a value in the field box. Using negative (–) values moves the characters together.

- **Word Spacing.** This option controls the space between whole words. You make choices for distance the same way you do for the preceding Character Spacing option.

- **Horizontal Scaling.** Sizing of individual characters (narrower or wider) is set according to the percentage of the original size. Values above 100 percent scale characters larger than the original font. Values below 100 percent result in smaller characters.

- **Embed.** Check the box to embed the selected font.

- **Subset.** Check the box to subset the font.

## Caution

In order to legally embed a font, you must own a copy of the font to be embedded and comply with the licensing restrictions of the font manufacturer. Be certain to review the licensing agreement that came with your fonts to verify embedding the font(s) is permitted. Some developers do not license fonts for embedding. ■

- **Fill.** The color swatch shows the default color of the selected font. Clicking the color swatch opens a pop-up menu, as shown in Figure 12.5. You select preset colors from the palette. When you click Other Color the system color palette opens. You can create custom colors from the system color palette and apply them to the text fill.

### FIGURE 12.5

Click the color swatch in the TouchUp Properties dialog box to open the pop-up menu used for making color selections.

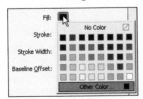

- **Stroke Width.** You change the weight (in points) of stroke outlines (if a font has a stroke) by making choices in the pull-down menu or by typing values in the field box.

## Prepress

If you intend to print your PDFs for color separations, don't make color changes in Acrobat. Acrobat only supports RGB colors with no support for CMYK or spot colors using the TouchUp Properties dialog box. If color changes to text are needed, you would be best off returning to the original authoring application and making the color changes, and then recreating the PDF file. For more information on RGB, Spot, and Process color, see Chapter 29. ∎

## Tip

If you want to create outline text, select No color from the Fill Color pop-up menu and add a stroke color and width. When stroke fills are set to No color, the fills appear transparent and show the background color. ∎

- **Baseline Offset.** You can raise or lower text above the baseline or below it. To move text up, enter positive values in the field box. To move text below the baseline, use negative values.

After making choices in the TouchUp Properties dialog box, click the Close button. The changes you make in the dialog box are reflected only on text you selected with the Edit Document Text tool.

## Adding new text to a document

You can also use the Edit Document Text tool to add a new line of text in a document. Select the Edit Document Text tool, press the Ctrl/Option key, and then click the mouse button in the area you want to add new text. The New Text Font dialog box opens as shown in Figure 12.6.

**FIGURE 12.6**

Ctrl/Option+click a document page when you have the Edit Document Text tool selected and the New Text Font dialog box opens. Select a font from the Font pull-down menu and select text alignment — Horizontal or Vertical — from the Mode pull-down menu.

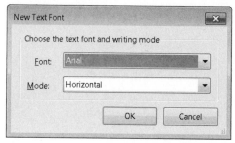

From the Font pull-down menu, you can select any font loaded in your system. You're safe when choosing a font from the Font pull-down menu in the New Text Font dialog box since all fonts appearing in the menu are only those fonts loaded in your system.

From the Mode pull-down menu, you can select between Horizontal or Vertical alignment. Click OK in the dialog box and the cursor blinks at the location where you clicked the mouse button. The words "New Text" appear in a text field box. Type the text you want to add and open the TouchUp Properties dialog box by choosing Properties from a context menu. Select the check boxes for embedding and subsetting to embed the new text font in the document.

## Tip

Acrobat does not permit any edits on text where a font has been embedded and the font is not installed on your system. To resolve the problem, you can select the text, open the TouchUp Properties dialog box, and select a system font from the Font pull-down menu. After you change a font to one available to your system, you can make text edits. Note that this workaround can only be used with fonts that don't carry licensing restrictions. ∎

# Copying text with the Edit Document Text tool

The Edit Document Text tool is probably the last tool you want to use for copying text and pasting the text into other programs. I mention it here so you know what limitations you have in Acrobat for copying text with this tool. Inasmuch as the Edit Document Text tool enables you to copy multiple lines of text, you are limited to single paragraphs or short blocks of text.

To copy text with the Edit Document Text tool, click and drag the tool through the text block(s) you want to copy. The text is selected as you drag the mouse cursor. After making a selection, open a context menu and select Copy, as shown in Figure 12.7. Alternately, you can press Ctrl/⌘+C.

**FIGURE 12.7**

Open a context menu on selected text and choose Copy.

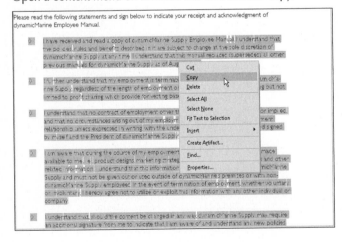

To paste text in a word processor or other application where pasting text is permitted, open the application and select the Paste command. Typically, you find Paste under the Edit menu. The text formatting of the pasted text can sometimes be better preserved if you copy text from tagged PDF documents.

# Setting Text Editing Preferences

You have some options for preference choices when using tools for text editing. Using the Edit Document Text tool doesn't require you to make any preference changes. However, when using the Select tool you have some options in the General preferences settings. To open the Preferences dialog box, press Ctrl/⌘+K. When the Preferences dialog box opens, click General in the left pane. At the top of the right pane under the Basic Tools category are options that affect selecting text, as shown in Figure 12.8.

**FIGURE 12.8**

Open the Preferences dialog box and click General in the left pane. Under the Basic Tools category are options for handling text selections.

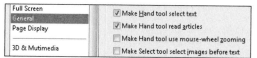

## Selecting the order of objects

The Basic Tools options shown in Figure 12.8 reflect the order that objects are selected (consider a text block as an object as you review this section). When you check the box for *Make Select tool select images before text*, images are selected first when images and text occupy the same space on a page. You use the Select tool to click in an area and the selection is made according to the preference choice made in the Selection section of the General preferences. Selecting the *Make Hand tool select text* check box and removing the *Make Select tool select images before text* reverses the order and, hence, text is selected before images when they both occupy the same space.

When I refer to occupying the same space, I'm talking about an image that may have a bounding box larger than the displayed image and text appears over the bounding box area, or when text is superimposed over an image.

## Using the Hand tool for text selections

If you're editing text on a page, you can choose to make text selections with the Hand tool instead of the Select tool or the Edit Document Text tool. The preference setting for using the

Hand tool to select text is located in the General preferences as shown in Figure 12.8. Unfortunately, there is no context menu option for switching the Hand tool between selecting text and using the Hand tool for moving the document page. You can see the menu options in Figure 12.9 when opening a context menu with the Hand tool selected.

---

**FIGURE 12.9**

A context menu opened from the Hand tool provides no option for switching the tool behavior between text selections and moving a document page around the Document pane.

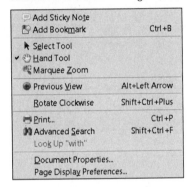

With the Hand tool, you can move a page around in the Document pane or scroll pages when viewing pages in views other than Single Page view. If you move the cursor above any text, quickly drag the page around the Document pane to move the page. If you wait a moment, the cursor changes and any dragging you do selects text. If you accidentally select text when you wanted to move the page, deselect the text by clicking outside a text block. This can be frustrating because if you don't click and drag fast enough, the Hand tool will select text when the respective preference option is selected. To disengage the text selection with the Hand tool, press the Spacebar on your keyboard. While the Spacebar is held down, the Hand tool returns to normal behavior and you can move the document page around the Document pane.

## Caution

If you enable text selection with the Hand tool and it's not working, you need to make an adjustment in the Accessibility preferences. Open the Preferences dialog box and click Accessibility in the left pane. Remove the check mark for Always display keyboard selection cursor. If this item is checked, the Hand tool preference options cannot be changed. ■

# Using the Select Tool

The Select tool is a much better choice than the Edit Document Text tool for selecting text to be copied from a PDF document and pasted in an editor, especially if you have multiple text blocks to copy. With this tool you can select multiple blocks of text and text in columns. However, you cannot make text edits with the tool like you do with the Edit Document Text tool. By default, the Select tool appears in the top-level toolbar adjacent to the Hand tool.

To select text with the Select tool, click and drag the tool through the text on a page you want to copy. If a single column appears on the page, click just before the first character to be selected and drag down to the last character. Alternately, you can press the Alt/Option key and drag through a column of text to select it. Generally using the Alt/Option key enables you to create a more precise selection when columns are positioned close together. Acrobat won't copy the text in the adjacent column as long as you stay within the boundaries of the column you are selecting. Figure 12.10 shows text selected with the Select tool where only one column in a multiple-column layout is selected.

In conjunction with the Select tool, shortcut keys and mouse clicks provide several ways to make various text selections, including the following:

- **Select a word.** Double-click a word, space, or character.
- **Select a line of text.** Triple-click anywhere on a line of text.
- **Select all text on a page.** Click four times (rapid successive clicks) to select all text on a page.
- **Select a column of text.** Click outside the text area and drag through the column or press the Alt/Option key as you drag the Select tool through a column of text.
- **Select a contiguous block of text.** Click and drag through the block of text or click the cursor at the beginning of the text to be selected, press Shift, and click at the end of the text block.
- **Deselect text.** Click outside of the text selection or press Ctrl/⌘+Shift+A.

Depending on choices you make for copying text, text pasted in other programs can retain certain formatting attributes. Your options for what you copy are derived from menu choices when you select text with the Select tool and open a context menu. When you select text, open a context menu as shown in Figure 12.11.

The options shown in the context menu provide choices for marking text with a Highlight, Cross Out, Underline, Replace, and adding a note. These items are used for commenting on PDF files. Additionally, adding a Bookmark and creating a link appear in the context menu. The remaining options in the menu are used for copying and exporting text.

## FIGURE 12.10

To select a column of text, use the Select tool and drag down the column length.

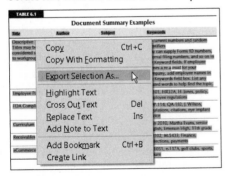

## FIGURE 12.11

Select text with the Select tool and open a context menu.

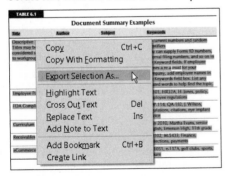

# Copying text

Most often you'll find a difference when pasting text copied from tagged and untagged documents. In Figure 12.12, text was copied from an untagged file in Acrobat and pasted into a Microsoft Word document. Much of the text and paragraph formatting was lost when the data was pasted.

Text pasted from an untagged file loses much of the text and paragraph formatting.

Copying text from tagged PDF documents typically provides much better results, as shown in Figure 12.13.

## Cross-Reference

For information related to tagging PDF documents, see Chapter 23. ■

## Copying multiple pages of text

If you view PDF files in a Single Page view, you can drag through the text on the page in view to select it. However, if you want to copy text on multiple pages, you need to change the view in a Scrolling mode. Zoom out of the document so you can see several pages in the Document pane and drag through the text you want to copy. If you need to copy more pages than those in view, drag the cursor to the bottom of the Acrobat window. The document pages scroll to place more pages in view. Keep the mouse button pressed as the pages appear in view, and release the mouse button on the last page you want to copy. In Figure 12.14, you can see a document in a Scrolling view and text selected on multiple pages.

To copy the text, select one of the Copy commands at the top of the context menu or choose Edit ⇨ Copy.

Text pasted from a tagged file retains much of the text and paragraph formatting.

This Employee Manual is an important document intended to help you become acquainted with dynamicMarine Supply. This manual will serve as a guide; it is not the final word in all cases. Individual circumstances may call for individual attention. Because the general business atmosphere of dynamicMarine Supply and economic conditions are always changing, the contents of this manual may be changed at any time at the discretion of dynamicMarine. No changes in any benefit, policy or rule will be made without due consideration of the mutual advantages, disadvantages, benefits and responsibilities such changes will have on you as an employee and on dynamicMarine.
Please read the following statements and sign below to indicate your receipt and acknowledgment of dynamicMarine Employee Manual.

- I have received and read a copy of dynamicMarine Supply Employee Manual. I understand that the policies, rules and benefits described in it are subject to change at the sole discretion of dynamicMarine Supply at any time. I understand that this manual replaces (supersedes) all other previous manuals for dynamicMarine Supply as of August 2002.
- I further understand that my employment is terminable at will, either by myself or dynamicMarine Supply, regardless of the length of employment or the granting of benefits, including but not limited to profit sharing which provide for vesting based on length of employment.
- I understand that no contract of employment other than "at will" has been expressed or implied, and that no circumstances arising out of my employment will alter my "at will" employment relationship unless expressed in writing, with the understanding specifically set forth and signed by myself and the President of dynamicMarine Supply.
- I am aware that during the course of my employment confidential information will be made available to me, i.e., product designs, marketing strategies, customer lists, pricing policies and other related information. I understand that this information is critical to the success of dynamicMarine Supply and must not be given out or used outside of dynamicMarine's premises or with non dynamicMarine Supply employees. In the event of termination of employment, whether voluntary or involuntary, I hereby agree not to utilize or exploit this information with any other individual or company.
- I understand that, should the content be changed in any way, dynamicMarine Supply may require an additional signature from me to indicate that I am aware of and understand any new policies.

## Using the Select All command

If you have a need to select all the text on a page or throughout a PDF document, you can use the Select All menu command. Depending on the tool you use and the page view mode, text selections behave differently. You must first determine whether you want to select all the text on a page or all text in the document. When selecting text on a PDF page, be certain the page layout view is set to a One Full Page layout. Click the Select tool and choose Edit ⇨ Select All or press Ctrl/⌘+A. All the text on a single page is selected. To copy the text you just selected, open a pop-up or context menu and select Copy. All the text is copied to the Clipboard and ready to paste into an editor.

If you want to select all text in a PDF document, change the page view to Scrolling Pages mode. Click the Select tool and choose Edit ⇨ Select All or press Ctrl/⌘+A.

This method only works when you use the Select tool. If you select all text using the Edit Document Text tool, the selected text is confined to a bounding box and you must first click in a bounding box area in order to use the Select All command. On any given page there can be one or more bounding boxes, and using Select All selects all text only within a single bounding box. Regardless of which page layout view you choose, the Edit Document Text tool doesn't permit text selections across multiple pages.

**FIGURE 12.14**

Click Scrolling Pages in the Page Display Toolbar and drag the Select tool through multiple pages to select the text.

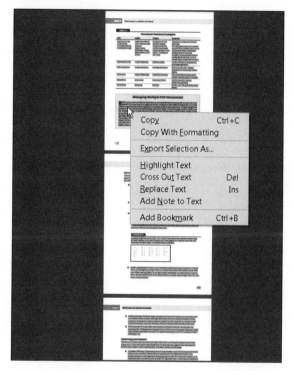

## Copying a file to the Clipboard (Windows only)

Clicking the Select tool and choosing the Select All command selects all text in a document. You can also accomplish the same task by choosing Edit ➪ Copy File to Clipboard. Open your word processor and you can paste the text into a new document.

If you don't see the menu command, you don't have OLE-compliant applications installed on your computer. Microsoft's OLE (Object Linking and Embedding) is installed by default with Office applications on Windows. If the menu command does not appear, use the Select All menu command to achieve the same results.

Copying and pasting text in word processors is best achieved by exporting PDFs using the File ➪ Save As command or by using File ➪ Export. You can export files as Microsoft Word and RTF (Rich Text Format) by selecting menu options from the task button pull-down menu. Much improved retention of formatting and page layout was added to Acrobat 9, and you'll find these methods much better than using copy/paste commands.

## Cross-Reference

For more on exporting PDF data, see Chapter 10. ■

## Tip

If you have some major text editing needed on one or two pages in a document, you can use the Extract Pages command from the Document menu to create a new PDF of just the pages you need to edit. Choose File ⇨ Save As or File ⇨ Export and save to Microsoft Word format. Edit the pages in Word and export to PDF. Open the original document and use the Document ⇨ Replace pages command to replace the pages in your file with the new PDF document. (For more on page editing, see Chapter 16.) ■

# Working with table data

You can copy and paste formatted text in columns and rows with the Select tool. If you want to paste data as tables or spreadsheets, Acrobat provides you options for copying table data and opening selected table data in a spreadsheet program.

## Copying and pasting table data

Select a table using the Select tool and choose Copy with Formatting from a context menu. Once copied to the Clipboard, the data can be pasted in a word processing or spreadsheet program. When you paste the data in Microsoft Word, it appears as a table. Pasting in Microsoft Excel pastes the data in a spreadsheet document. However, pasting in a spreadsheet application pastes the data in single cells across rows. Exporting data to individual cells requires exporting the data to a spreadsheet format.

## Opening selected data in a spreadsheet document

To export a table directly to Microsoft Excel, select columns and rows of text. From a context menu, select Export Selection. In the Export Selection dialog box you have several formats to choose from for exporting the table data. To open the data in Excel, choose Excel Workbook (*.xlsx), or Comma Separated Values (.csv) and click Save.

After saving the file, you need to launch Microsoft Excel and open the data file. The selected data appears in a new spreadsheet, as shown in Figure 12.15.

**FIGURE 12.15**

Select a table and export to a file supported by Microsoft Excel. Open the file in Excel and the data appears in individual cells.

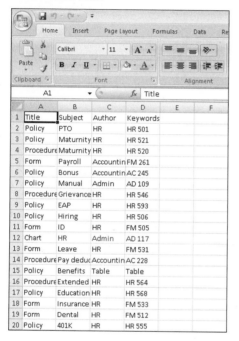

| | A | B | C | D | E | F |
|---|---|---|---|---|---|---|
| 1 | Title | Subject | Author | Keywords | | |
| 2 | Policy | PTO | HR | HR 501 | | |
| 3 | Policy | Maturnity | HR | HR 521 | | |
| 4 | Procedure | Maturnity | HR | HR 520 | | |
| 5 | Form | Payroll | Accountin | FM 261 | | |
| 6 | Policy | Bonus | Accountin | AC 245 | | |
| 7 | Policy | Manual | Admin | AD 109 | | |
| 8 | Procedure | Grievance | HR | HR 546 | | |
| 9 | Policy | EAP | HR | HR 593 | | |
| 10 | Policy | Hiring | HR | HR 506 | | |
| 11 | Form | ID | HR | FM 505 | | |
| 12 | Chart | HR | Admin | AD 117 | | |
| 13 | Form | Leave | HR | FM 531 | | |
| 14 | Procedure | Pay deduc | Accountin | AC 228 | | |
| 15 | Policy | Benefits | Table | Table | | |
| 16 | Procedure | Extended | HR | HR 564 | | |
| 17 | Policy | Education | HR | HR 568 | | |
| 18 | Form | Insurance | HR | FM 533 | | |
| 19 | Form | Dental | HR | FM 512 | | |
| 20 | Policy | 401K | HR | HR 555 | | |

# Looking Up Definitions

Whether you're editing a PDF file or browsing documents, you can find the spelling and word definition for any word in an open document. This very nice little feature in Acrobat saves you time when looking up a definition. To employ the Look Up command from a context menu, use the Hand Select tool and open a context menu. A word needs to be selected in order for the menu command to appear. After selecting a word, open a context menu and from the menu choices select Look Up "...", placing your selected word inside the quotation marks.

After you make your selection, Acrobat launches the default Web browser, which takes you to the Dictionary.com Web site. The Web page opens on the word selected in the PDF document. You can check for spelling errors, word definitions, pronunciation, and browse through a thesaurus. If you have an account for the Web site, you can click the audio button to hear an audio pronunciation through your computer speaker(s).

Currently, Acrobat only supports U.S. English as a language. Regardless of whether you have a foreign language kit installed, Acrobat launches the Dictionary.com Web site.

# Summary

In this chapter, you learned methods for editing text, copying text in PDF files, and pasting text in other editing programs.

- You use the Edit Document Text tool to make minor edits on PDF pages. You can use the tool to change font attributes, add new lines of text, and access a Properties dialog box where you can select fonts to embed and subset.

- The Edit Document Text tool is not well suited for copying and pasting text data into other programs. Text selections are limited and text formatting is lost when pasting text into other programs.

- Use the Select tool to select text on a page, across multiple pages, and all text in a document.

- When pasting text copied from a Select tool selection in a tagged file, the text data retains much integrity and can be edited with minimum character and paragraph reformatting.

- You also use the Select tool to select table data. You can copy and paste tables in other applications and save the data to a number of different file formats.

# Redacting PDFs

A marvelous feature introduced in Acrobat 8 was the Redaction tools, which are used for removing data from PDF documents. In Acrobat 9, Adobe expanded the tools to provide you with more sophisticated options for searching and redacting content in PDF files.

The Redaction tools appear in Acrobat Pro on both the Mac and Windows. You won't find Redaction features in Acrobat Standard on Windows.

In this chapter you learn about redaction, why and when it is necessary, the new Acrobat X features, and how to use all the Redaction tools.

## Understanding Redaction

Quite simply, *redaction* is the removal of visual information from a document. You might want to use redaction to remove sensitive information for security purposes, to protect rights and privacy information, to eliminate classified information, to delete names of minors in legal documents, or to delete any other information you don't want viewed by others.

Redaction is much different than blotting out or hiding text, graphics, handwriting, or any other kind of marks. If you use tools like some of the comment tools to create markups that blot out some text and graphics in a document, the items are not permanently deleted. It appears fine on-screen where you can't see items marked for deletion on a document page, but the PDF document still contains the original items. If the file is distributed, other users can access marked text and other data.

To understand why redaction tools are needed to permanently delete content from a PDF document, see the following steps.

### STEPS: Understanding the Need for Redaction

1. **Open a PDF document in Acrobat.**

2. **Open the Comments panel.**

3. **Mark out some text.** Select the Rectangle tool in the Drawing Markups panel. Draw a rectangle around some text. Alternately, you can use the Highlight tool to select text and hide it with a dark highlight color.

4. **Open the rectangle comment properties.** Right-click (Windows) or Ctrl+click (Mac) to open a context menu on the rectangle. Select Properties from the context menu.

5. **Edit the properties.** Click the Color swatch for both Color and Fill Color. From the color choices, select Black, as shown in Figure 13.1. Click the Make Properties Default check box. The next time you draw a rectangle, the rectangle will have the same style and fill color.

**FIGURE 13.1**

Set the Rectangle comment properties to black color and black fill.

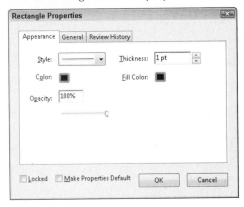

6. **Draw additional rectangles.** Using the rectangle comment tool, draw some additional rectangles to block out more text. In Figure 13.2, I have a text document with several markings where I don't want the text to be seen. On-screen this is fine, but the text is not deleted and can be extracted by other users.

7. **Copy the text.** Click the Select tool and drag through the text to select it. Choose Edit ⇨ Copy to copy the text, as shown in Figure 13.3. Note that you can also use the Search pane and search for text that you marked. You'll notice that the search results report all the hidden text.

**FIGURE 13.2**

Text on-screen is blocked out, but the text can still be extracted.

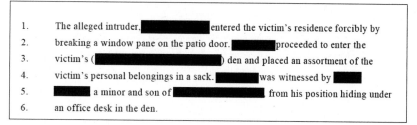

**FIGURE 13.3**

Drag through all the text with the Select tool and choose Edit ⇨ Copy.

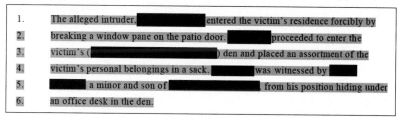

8. **Paste the text in a word processor.** In my example I open Microsoft Word and select Edit ⇨ Paste. As you can see in Figure 13.4, I was able to copy the text beneath all my comment markups.

**FIGURE 13.4**

When you paste all the text in a Word processor, the marked-out text appears in the new document window.

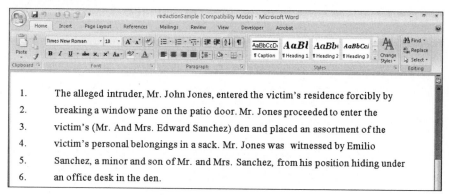

As shown in Figure 13.4, this form of redacting a document doesn't delete the marked text. You need another method to mark and eliminate data from PDFs. This is where the Redaction tools in Acrobat come into play.

# Getting a Grip on the Redaction Tools

Redaction is permanently deleting text, graphics, signatures, handwriting, and any other data you want to remove from a document. In addition to marking and deleting text and other data that you can see, a good redaction tool also provides you with a means for deleting certain metadata and hidden information in a file so all the content you decide you want to eliminate cannot be retrieved by anyone viewing your PDF files.

## Using the Redaction tools

Acrobat offers a few solutions for marking content for deletion, applying the redactions, eliminating metadata, and eliminating any hidden text. You first start a redaction session using the Redaction tools. When you open the Protection panel, the tools contained in the panel appear, as shown in Figure 13.5.

**FIGURE 13.5**

The Protection panel contains five Redaction tools.

The tools on the Redaction toolbar are as follows:

- **Mark for Redaction.** Use this tool to mark text and other data that you want to delete from a document. Marking the content does not yet delete it from the file.

- **Mark Pages to Redact.** Acrobat X introduces a new redaction feature. Use this command to mark an entire page or page range for redaction.

- **Apply Redactions.** When you are ready to permanently delete content that you marked for deletion, click the Apply Redactions tool.

- **Redaction Properties.** Use this tool to set the redaction-marking properties. You can mark content using the Mark for Redaction tool, and the markings can be adjusted for color and other attributes in the Redaction Tool Properties dialog box. Click the tool, and the Redaction Tool Properties dialog box shown in Figure 13.6 opens.

As you can see in the Redaction Tool Properties dialog box, you can select a color for your redaction marks, use text as an overlay, specify the font for the overlay text, set a number of different font attributes for the overlay text, and select from some redaction code standards. When you change the properties in this dialog box, the properties remain in effect for all redaction marks you make on a document until you again make settings adjustments in the Redaction Tool Properties dialog box.

Click the Redaction Properties tool, and the Redaction Tool Properties dialog box opens.

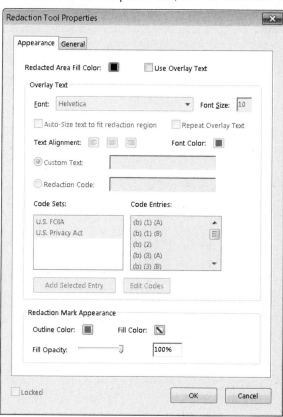

- **Find Document Text.** Click the Find Document Text tool, and the Search window opens, as shown in Figure 13.7. Type a word or phrase in the first field text box and choose a location. Your options include searching the open document or a folder location on your hard drive or network server. You can mark content for redaction in a collection of PDF documents contained in a common folder. Select the All PDF Documents in the radio button. From the pull-down menu below the radio button, select Browse for Location. The Browse For Folder dialog box opens, where you select a folder containing files you want to redact.

  Click the Search and Redact button in the Search window, and the Search window reports results of your search, as shown in Figure 13.8. As yet, no items have been marked for redaction. In the results list you see the reported results appearing next to check marks. If you want all items in the list to be redacted, click the Check All button. If you want to individually mark the results items, scroll the list, checking all boxes adjacent to the items you want to redact.

## Cross-Reference

For more information on using the Search window, see Chapter 6. ■

**FIGURE 13.7**

Click the Search and Redact button, and the Search window opens. Type a word or phrase and select either the open document or a folder of PDFs you want to mark for redaction.

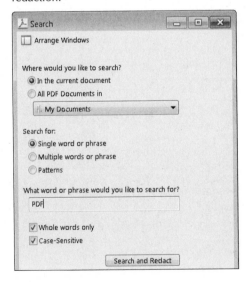

**FIGURE 13.8**

Click Check All or individually check the items you want to redact in the open PDF or from a collection of PDF files.

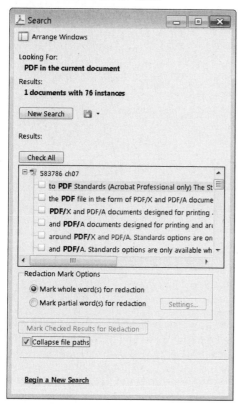

## Searching multiple words and phrases

You may want to develop a word list, import the word list into the Search and Redact window, and apply redactions from the word list. Using a word list where you can copy and paste names helps prevent spelling errors and can often make your redaction process much easier.

The Select Words button appears in the Search pane when you click the Multiple words or phrase radio button. Click the button and the Words and Phrases to Search and Redact window opens, as you see in Figure 13.9.

FIGURE 13.9

Click Select Words in the Search window to open the Words and Phrases to Search and Redact window.

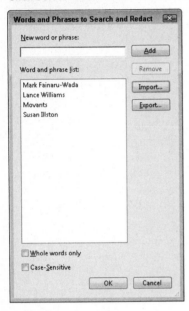

To add words to the list, type a word or words in the New word or phrase text box and click the Add button. The word(s) is moved to the Word and phrase list. You can continue adding words by typing the word name and clicking the Add button to add more words to the list.

A nice addition to the Words and Phrases to Search and Redact window is the Import button. You can import a list of words from a text file. Click the button and select the file you want to import.

As a workflow solution you can open a PDF document, copy text on a page containing several words and phrases you want to redact, and paste the copied text in a word processor or text editor. Delete the text you don't want to redact, and you're left with just those words you want to eliminate from the PDF file. Save the file as a text document and import the word list in the Search window. Using this method helps keep the spelling errors to a minimum and easily helps you form your word list.

The export button enables you to export a word list to a text file. This option can be handy when you have several documents you want to redact at different times. Perhaps during a court case you may receive documents at different intervals, but the sensitive information remains the same on all documents. As new documents come in, you can import the text file you originally exported from the Search window.

# Searching patterns

A pattern or mask is a formatted body of text — something like a social security number or phone number. Say you want to delete all social security numbers from a document, but there are many unique numbers, and without searching a pattern you would have to mark each individual number for redaction.

Acrobat takes the redundant task of marking each individual pattern such as a social security number, a zip code, an email address, a phone number, credit card numbers, and dates away by providing you with a method for searching patterns.

To search a pattern, click the Search & Remove Text tool in the Protection panel. In the Search window, click the Patterns radio button and make a choice from the pull-down menu as shown in Figure 13.10. Click the Search and Redact button, and Acrobat searches the open document or a folder of documents for the pattern and identifies it for marking for redaction in the Search window.

**FIGURE 13.10**

Click Patterns and make a choice from the drop-down menu for the type of pattern you want to search.

# Note

When you use the Multiple words or phrase option, Acrobat identifies the words that need to be marked for redaction. When you click OK in the Words and Phrases to Search and Redact window, the words are marked for redaction in the document. You then need to click the Apply Redactions tool to delete the marked words. When searching for patterns, you click the Check All button after performing a search, then click the Mark Checked Results for Redaction to mark all found instances for redaction. You then need to click the Apply Redactions tool to permanently delete the marked items. ■

# Redacting PDF Files

The tool set and options for redaction are very straightforward and intuitive. In the first section of this chapter, you looked at marking files to hide content that didn't remove the items you marked. Let's compare that first effort with a true redaction that Acrobat 8 provides for you by following some steps.

## STEPS: Redacting a PDF Document

1. **Open a file you want to eliminate some content from by using the Redaction tools.**

2. **Click the Mark for Redaction tool in the Protection panel.**

   When you first click the Mark for Redaction tool, the Using Redaction Tools help dialog box opens, as shown in Figure 13.11. This dialog box provides you with some instructions on redacting documents. If you don't want the dialog box to open in future redaction sessions, click the Don't show again check box.

When you first click the Mark for Redaction tool, the Using Redaction Tools help dialog box opens.

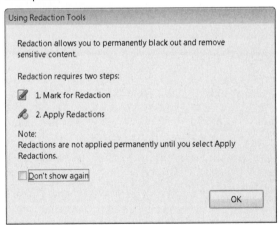

3. **Mark a graphic for redaction.** If you have a graphic in the file either as a vector object or an image file, you can remove it just like removing text. In my example I have a logotype that is a graphic object. Clicking the Mark for Redaction tool changes your cursor to a crosshair when positioned over a graphic or an I-beam cursor when positioned over text. Draw a marquee around the object, as shown in Figure 13.12, or drag the I-beam cursor through text you want to redact.

# Tip

If you want to quickly mark a graphic object for redaction, select the Mark for Redaction tool and double-click the graphic. ■

**FIGURE 13.12**

Draw a marquee around a graphic or select text to mark for redaction.

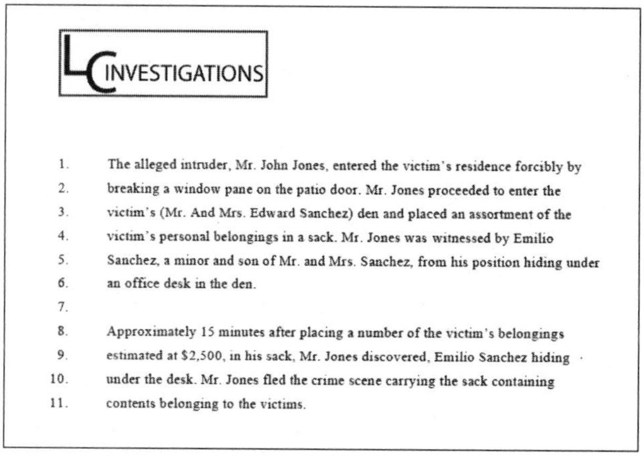

1.  The alleged intruder, Mr. John Jones, entered the victim's residence forcibly by
2.  breaking a window pane on the patio door. Mr. Jones proceeded to enter the
3.  victim's (Mr. And Mrs. Edward Sanchez) den and placed an assortment of the
4.  victim's personal belongings in a sack. Mr. Jones was witnessed by Emilio
5.  Sanchez, a minor and son of Mr. and Mrs. Sanchez, from his position hiding under
6.  an office desk in the den.
7.
8.  Approximately 15 minutes after placing a number of the victim's belongings
9.  estimated at $2,500, in his sack, Mr. Jones discovered, Emilio Sanchez hiding
10. under the desk. Mr. Jones fled the crime scene carrying the sack containing
11. contents belonging to the victims.

4.  **Mark text for redaction.** Drag the I-beam cursor through the first occurrence of text you want to redact. In my example I drag through a name I want to remove from the file.

5.  **Click the Find Document Text tool.** The Search window opens. Type any other occurrence of the text you want to redact. In my example, I type the same name as the first text marked for redaction. Click the Search and Redact button, and the first occurrence of the word to be redacted is highlighted.

6.  **Check all occurrences for redaction.** In the Search window, click the Check All button and all occurrences of the search results are now marked for redaction.

7.  **Mark the search results for redaction.** After clicking the Check All button, the Marked Checked Results button appears in the Search window. Click this button and all occurrences of the search results are now marked for redaction, as you see in Figure 13.13.

8.  **Continue marking all the content you want to eliminate in your document.** If you have other text or graphics you want to redact, follow the same steps outlined in Steps 3 to 7.

**FIGURE 13.13**

After clicking Check All or individually checking the items you want to redact in the open PDF or from a collection of PDF files, click the Mark Checked Results for Redaction button.

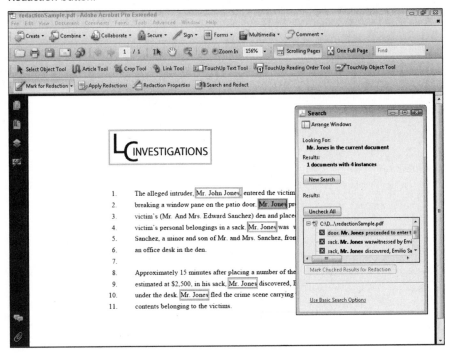

9. **Apply Redactions.** Click the Apply Redactions tool. A warning dialog box opens. Click Yes and the redactions are applied.

10. **Redact additional content.** After Acrobat redacts the items you marked, a dialog box opens, confirming your action and prompting you to examine the document for additional content. Additional content might be in the form of metadata such as Document Properties information, hidden text, and a variety of other sources you don't see when viewing a PDF file in the Document pane. Click Yes in the dialog box shown in Figure 13.14.

11. **Examine the document.** When you click Yes in the confirmation dialog box, the Examine Document panel opens. A number of different items can appear in your file that don't appear on the document pages. You might have metadata, hidden text, file attachments, hidden layers, bookmarks, and other items that use the same text you want to delete. To be certain all information is deleted from the document, the Examine Document dialog box provides a list of found items matching the items you deleted. Click the Remove button in the panel shown in Figure 13.15, and all the selected items are removed.

**FIGURE 13.14**

Click Yes to open the Examine Document dialog box.

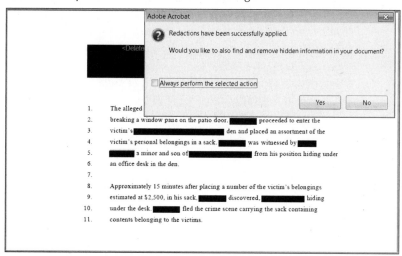

**FIGURE 13.15**

Click the Remove button in the Examine Document panel to eliminate any other occurrences of the text and graphics you want to delete.

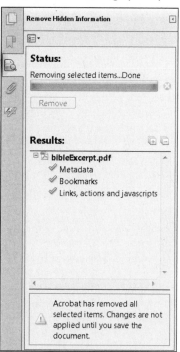

12. **Verify the redactions were made.** If you used objects with fills to redact the document, these objects are selectable and you can delete them. Click the Edit Object tool in the Content panel. Move the tool to one of your marks and click. Press the Delete (Del) key on your keyboard, and the redaction frame is deleted. You can easily see that the redaction process did indeed remove the underlying content.

    You should see that the text beneath the redaction frames has truly been deleted from your document. When you use the select tool and drag through the text, you'll notice that no selection appears where you redacted text (and/or objects) as shown in Figure 13.16. Alternately, you can verify redactions by opening the Search window and invoking a search for the words you redacted. You should see no results reported for all text that was redacted.

**FIGURE 13.16**

After removing redaction marks and selecting all the text, the redacted file shows you all the text/objects that have been successfully deleted from the file.

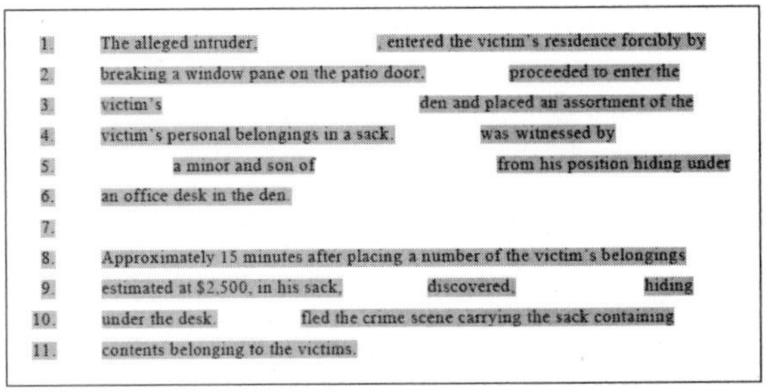

The alleged intruder, , entered the victim's residence forcibly by breaking a window pane on the patio door. proceeded to enter the victim's den and placed an assortment of the victim's personal belongings in a sack. was witnessed by a minor and son of from his position hiding under an office desk in the den.

Approximately 15 minutes after placing a number of the victim's belongings estimated at $2,500, in his sack, discovered, hiding under the desk. fled the crime scene carrying the sack containing contents belonging to the victims.

# Sanitizing a Document

You'll notice that you have another item below the redaction tools in the Protection panel labeled Sanitize Document. After applying redactions and examining a document, click this item in the Protection panel. The Sanitize Document window opens, as shown in Figure 13.17, and displays a list of items that are cleared when you click OK. The list is self-explanatory. Look over the window and you can see the data that is removed from a document when you use this command.

**FIGURE 13.17**

Click Sanitize Document in the Protection panel, and a window displays a list of items that are removed from the document when you click OK.

Adobe Acrobat

Sanitize Document removes hidden data and metadata from your document so that sensitive information is not inadvertently passed along when you publish your PDF. Sanitize Document will remove:

* Metadata
* Embedded content and attached files
* Scripts
* Hidden layers
* Embedded search indexes
* Stored form data
* Review and comment data
* Hidden data from previous document saves
* Obscured text and images
* Comments hidden within the body of the PDF file
* Unreferenced data

Press OK to begin the sanitization process by selecting a location to save your sanitized document.

☐ Do not show this message again

OK    Cancel

# Summary

This chapter was all about removing sensitive data from a document using the Redaction tools. You learned:

- Redaction involves permanently removing data from a file.

- Acrobat Pro (Windows and Mac) contains tools for redacting content, searching and redacting, applying redactions, and examining documents for content not visible on pages. Redaction options are not available in Acrobat Standard (Windows).

- Using tools other than the Redaction tools won't delete data from PDF files.

- Redaction marks can be modified for color changes, the use of text, and formatted text used to replace deleted data.

- After redacting a document, you can choose to Examine Document information for additional content that may appear as metadata or hidden text.

- You can sanitize a document at any time either without redaction or after redaction.

# Editing Images and Objects

Images and objects, such as raster images from programs like Adobe Photoshop, vector images like those created in Adobe Illustrator, and text, can be edited in external editors and dynamically updated in a PDF document. The process involves launching the external editor from within Acrobat, making changes in the external editor, and saving the file. The file is treated like a link to the PDF where the edits are updated. Acrobat itself doesn't have any image editing tools, but you can use the external editors provided through companion programs to help out when you need to make modifications to objects in a PDF file.

Like editing text, discussed in Chapter 12, image editing with Acrobat is intended to be a minor task for last-minute small changes. For major editing tasks you should return to the original authoring program. In circumstances where you do not have an original document, you may need to extend the editing a little further by updating documents or exporting them for new layouts. In this chapter, you learn how to handle images and objects for editing and exporting purposes.

## Selecting Images

Two tools in Acrobat enable you to copy images and objects. You can use the Select tool discussed in Chapter 12 to select images as well as text, and you can also use the Edit Object tool (formerly known as the TouchUp Object tool) to select images and objects. Objects can be vector-based artwork created in programs such as Adobe Illustrator and blocks of text that Acrobat interprets as objects. Only the Edit Object tool can be used to select objects; therefore, you cannot use the Select tool unless the item is an image such as a Photoshop file contained in the PDF document.

The distinction between text as text and text as an object can easily be understood in what you see selected in the Document pane. If you drag the Select tool through text, the text becomes highlighted. When you see the text highlighted, realize that the text is selected as text. When you click a text block with the Edit Object tool, you'll see a bounding box (border) around the text block but the text itself is not highlighted. When you see this view, you can be assured the text is selected as an object. In Figure 14.1, text is selected as text by dragging through it with the Select tool, and in Figure 14.2, multiple text blocks are selected as objects when dragging through text with the Edit Object tool.

**FIGURE 14.1**

Text selected with the Select tool is selected as text and highlighted.

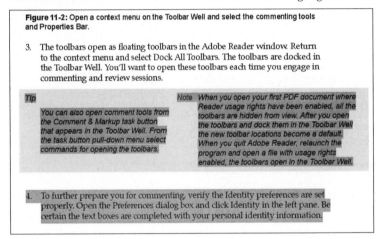

Each tool has different options and editing features associated with it. You use the Select tool, for example, when you want to select a photo image, copy it in Acrobat, and paste it in another program. Once copied to the Clipboard, you can also paste the image back into a PDF document. Additionally, you can open the Comments panel and open the Stamp drop-down menu. From the menu choice, click Paste Clipboard Image as Stamp tool. The cursor shape changes to a Stamp icon. Move the cursor to a document page and click. The image is pasted as a Stamp comment, as shown in Figure 14.3.

The Select tool permits you to save an image as a separate file. Additionally, you can edit metadata for image files using this tool.

**FIGURE 14.2**

Text selected with the Edit Object tool is selected as an object and appears with a bounding box (border).

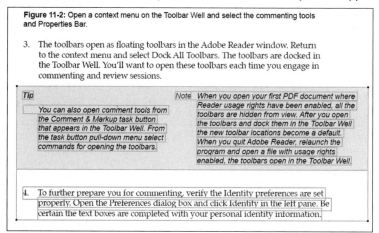

**FIGURE 14.3**

When pasting images with the Paste Image as Stamp tool, the pasted image appears as a Stamp comment.

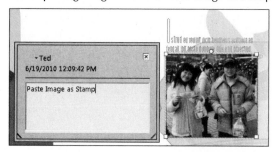

The Edit Object tool permits you to copy an image in a PDF document and paste it back to the same document or another PDF document as an image. All the paste operations remain inside Acrobat, as you cannot copy with the Edit Object tool and paste an image or object into another program. Furthermore, you cannot save an image file using the Edit Object tool as you can with the Select tool, but you can launch an external editor to edit either an image or object. When you want to edit images in Acrobat, the Edit Object tool provides you with a number of different editing options — more so than the Select tool.

## Using the Select tool

In Chapter 12, you used the Select tool to select text and tables. You can also select images with this tool. As was covered in Chapter 12, you have some preference choices for handling selections when using the Select tool. If your last visit to the General preferences was to select text before images, you need to return to the General preferences by pressing Ctrl/ ⌘+K, click General in the left pane, and select Make Select tool select images before text in the Basic Tool Options, as shown in Figure 14.4.

**FIGURE 14.4**

Open the General preferences and select the check box for Make Select tool select images before text.

Basic Tools

- ☐ Use single-key accelerators to access tools
- ☑ Create links from URLs
- ☐ Make Hand tool select text & images
- ☑ Make Hand tool read articles
- ☐ Make Hand tool use mouse-wheel zooming
- ☑ Make Select tool select images before text

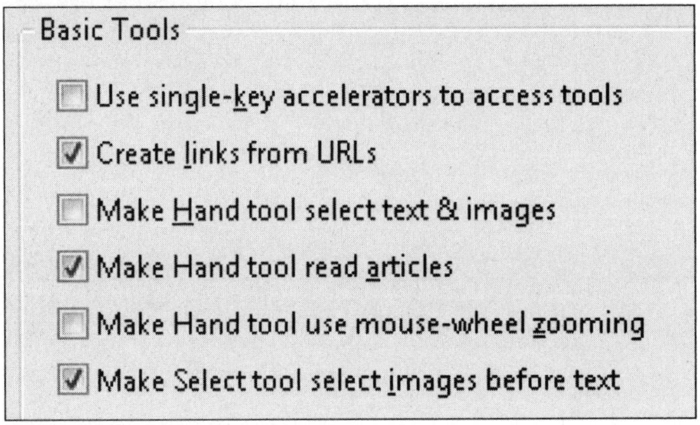

Click an image and select Copy Image from a context menu as shown in Figure 14.5.

### Adding interactivity

From the context menu, you can add a bookmark or link to the selected image. Click Bookmark from the context menu and the default view of the page is bookmarked. Click Create Link and the Create Link dialog box opens.

## Cross-Reference

For more information on creating bookmarks and links, see Chapter 21. ∎

### Pasting images

As I said earlier in this section, images copied with the Select tool are pasted back into PDF documents as Stamp comments. The appearance on-screen looks like an image pasted into a document, but it remains a comment. If you want to print images pasted from content copied with the Select tool, you need to print using the Document and Stamps option in the Print dialog box.

**FIGURE 14.5**

Open a context menu with the Select Object tool and choose Copy Image from the menu commands.

## Cross-Reference

**For more information on printing documents and stamps, see Chapter 28.** ■

Use the Select tool to paste images into other programs. Pasted images in Acrobat appear as Stamp comments, but in other programs pasting is handled as you would expect when copying and pasting between other programs. The complete image is pasted into documents such as Microsoft Office files and other application documents.

## Caution

**If you use professional layout and illustration programs designed for commercial printing, don't paste files in these applications. A preferred method is to save an image file from Acrobat and place or import the image in your design application.** ■

### Transforming pasted images

When you paste an image as a Stamp comment, you can size and rotate the image. From the four corners on a Stamp comment you see corner handles, and in the top center you see another handle. Click and drag any corner handle to size the image up or down. No modifier key is required to proportionally resize a Stamp comment. All the sizing is kept to proportions without pressing the Shift key.

To rotate a Stamp comment, place the cursor over the middle top handle. When the cursor appears over this handle, the cursor changes to a semicircle with an arrowhead, as shown in Figure 14.6. Click and drag when you see this cursor to rotate the Stamp.

**FIGURE 14.6**

Place the cursor over the top-center handle and click and drag to rotate the Stamp comment.

## Saving image files

From a context menu opened by right-clicking (Windows) or Control+clicking (Mac), you can save an image file when using the Select tool. Select Save Image As, and the Save Image As dialog box opens. From the Save as type (Windows) or Format (Mac) pull-down menu, you have options for saving in one of three file formats. Choose the default Bitmap Image Files (*.bmp), JPEG Image Files (.jpg), or TIFF Image Files (*.tif) format.

Saving as a bitmap file saves the file without compression and data loss. However, bitmap files may not retain all the data in the image. If you have images with clipping paths or drop shadows, for example, the saved image can appear significantly degraded, as shown in Figure 14.7.

**FIGURE 14.7**

Saving files with clipping paths in bitmap format can present problems with image quality. Saving the same file as a TIFF (right) preserves data integrity.

## Note

A clipping path is a mask like a cookie cutter that cuts out all the image data outside the path. Without the clipping path and drop shadow, the image in Figure 14.7 would have a white background around the image instead of transparent space. ■

JPEG files retain all data integrity; however, the downside to saving as JPEG is that the files are compressed, and you end up with data loss. Use the TIFF format when you can, and you'll save your files without data loss. As you can see in Figure 14.7, an image with a clipping path saved as a bitmap on the left is degraded compared to the correct detail shown in the TIFF export on the right.

## Tip

If you're not certain whether a BMP file will be saved, thus preserving all data integrity, you can select the image with the Select tool, copy the file to the Clipboard, and from the Create PDF Task Button pull-down menu select Create File From Clipboard Image. Acrobat creates a separate PDF document, and the image you see appears exactly as when saving as a BMP file. If the file looks good, save the PDF or return to the image and select Save Image As from a context menu. ■

### Viewing image properties

Select Image Properties from a context menu, and document metadata is reported for the image. If you shot an image with a digital camera, the data recorded by the camera is reported in the Image Information dialog box shown in Figure 14.8.

## Cross-Reference

For more information related to working with document metadata, see Chapter 6. ■

### Recognizing text using OCR

You may not see the Recognize Text Using OCR menu command when selecting images with the select tool. Images imported in a layout program won't give you the option for converting image data to recognizable text. If you have a scanned document and open the image in Acrobat, you might see this command. Use it for converting images to recognizable text.

## Cross-Reference

For more information on scanning and converting image data to recognizable text, see Chapter 16. ■

FIGURE 14.8

Select Image Properties from a context menu using the Select tool, and the Image Information dialog box opens.

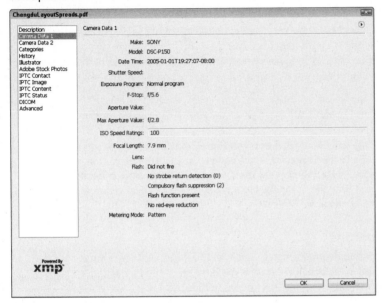

## Using the Edit Object tool

You use the Edit Object tool for selecting objects on a page. You select photo images, drawings and illustrations, and blocks of text with the tool.

### New Feature

The Edit Object tool was formerly known as the TouchUp Object tool in earlier versions of Acrobat. You access the tool by opening the Content panel and clicking Edit Object. ■

The Edit Object tool enables you to copy images and objects and paste them back into a PDF or other PDF documents you open in Acrobat. You can click an image or object or marquee several images and/or objects to select multiple items. Acrobat interprets any text you click with the Edit Object tool as an object. You can edit objects in an external editor or move the objects within a PDF document.

### Cross-Reference

For information on external editing, see the section "Editing Images and Objects Outside of Acrobat" later in this chapter. ■

You can also use the Edit Object tool to move or nudge objects. Click a single object or marquee a group of objects on a page, and then click and drag the selection to a new location. You are limited to moving objects on a single page. You can't select an object on one page and drag it to another PDF page. For moving objects to different pages you need to cut the selection, move to another page, and choose Edit ⇨ Paste. If you want to nudge objects, create a selection with the Edit Object tool and press the arrow keys on your keyboard to move the object right, left, up, or down.

## Note

**If two or more images or objects are spaced apart and each object is selectable, you can click to select an object and Shift+click to select additional images/objects. If you have objects such as vector graphics where many paths are contained within the object or you have multiple overlapping objects, marquee the objects to be certain you select all you want to copy. ■**

To copy and paste objects, including photo images, illustrations and vector objects, and text blocks, you use the Edit Object tool. To select a single object, click the object with the Edit Object tool. A keyline border shows the bounding box for the selected item. Open a context menu, and you find menu options different from those available with the Select tool, as shown in Figure 14.9.

The menu offers several commands related to handling images and objects. Select Copy to copy the image to the Clipboard, and select Cut to cut the image from the page and place it on the Clipboard. From either choice you can then paste the data on another PDF page or into another PDF document.

**FIGURE 14.9**

Select an image with the Edit Object tool and open a context menu. Select Copy from the menu choices to copy the selection.

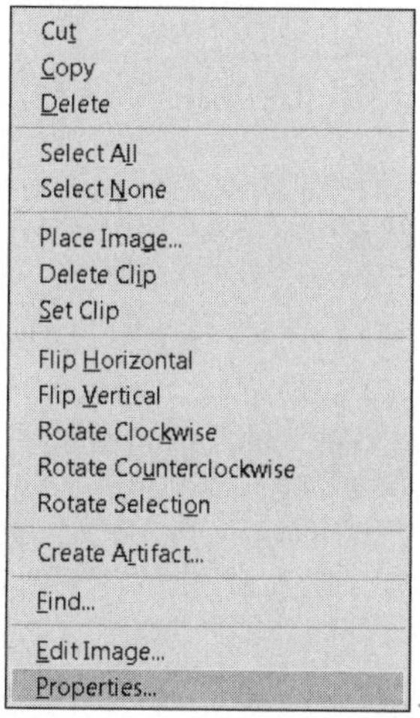

Cut
Copy
Delete

Select All
Select None

Place Image...
Delete Clip
Set Clip

Flip Horizontal
Flip Vertical
Rotate Clockwise
Rotate Counterclockwise
Rotate Selection

Create Artifact...

Find...

Edit Image...
Properties...

### Pasting images and objects

After copying with the Edit Object tool, choose Edit⇨Paste or use a context menu opened with the tool and select Paste. When pasting data, the new image or object is pasted in the foreground. If you need to keep a stacking order intact, you need to carefully plan out copying and pasting images and objects. In more complex documents, it makes sense to return to the original authoring program because you do not have commands in Acrobat to paste in front, paste in back, and paste in place. These kinds of commands are found in design programs where you can easily control the stacking order of images and objects.

If you want to replace text, images, or objects on a page with a pasted block of text, an image, or an object, select the items you want to replace after copying the item you want to paste. Choose Edit⇨Paste or use Paste from a context menu, and the pasted item replaces the selected items.

### Placing images

Placing images is like using a Place command in a layout program. When you select the command, a dialog box opens where you can select an image on your hard drive and import the image in your layout.

Acrobat supports placing images much like layout programs. Click the Edit Object tool and open a context menu on a document page. The Place Image command appears when opening a context menu on a page or when selecting an image and opening a context menu. The Open dialog box appears, where you can navigate your hard drive and locate the file you want to import in your PDF file. File formats supported using this command include Bitmap, BMP (*.bmp, *.rle, *.dlb), CompuServe GIF (*.gif), JPEG (*.jpg, *.jpeg, .jpe), JPEG2000 (.jpf, *.ipx, *.jp2, .j2k, .j2c, jpc), PCX (.pcx), PNG (.png), and TIFF (.tif, *.tiff). When one of these file formats is imported into a PDF document, Acrobat converts to PDF and imports the image.

## Cross-Reference

For more information on file formats, see Chapters 9 and 10. ∎

## Tip

If you select an image on a PDF page with the Edit Object tool and select Place Image from a context menu, the selected image is replaced with the new image you select in the Open dialog box. ∎

## Caution

Be certain to not select any objects on a page with the Edit Object tool when you use Place Image. Placing image data while an object is selected will replace the selected object. This is handy if you intentionally want to replace an object but can be troublesome if you don't want a selected object replaced. ∎

### Deleting a clip

The context menu opened with the Edit Object tool contains the Delete Clip menu command. You can delete a clipping path from an image or object that had the path applied in an image editor like Photoshop or an illustration program such as Adobe Illustrator. Deleting a path shows data outside the defined path. In Figure 14.10, you can see an image where a clipping path was created in Photoshop to hide edge artifacts on the left and after removing the clipping path on the right side of the figure where the artifacts are visible.

## FIGURE 14.10

Selecting Delete Clip from a context menu removes clipping paths assigned to objects and images.

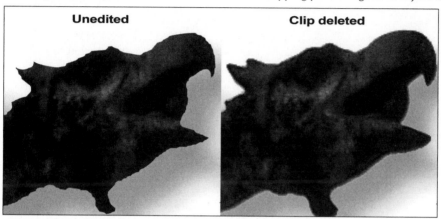

Delete Clip also performs another function. You can set a clip on an image with or without a clipping path using the Edit Object tool context menu. Once a clip has been set, use the Delete Clip command to remove the clip. To completely understand the results, see the section "Setting a clip" next.

### Setting a clip

Select the Edit Object tool, click an image on a PDF page, and from a context menu select Set Clip.

The Set Clip command enables you to clip (actually Crop) images. When using Set Clip, you'll find that three tools appear as you move the cursor around an image. The tools are shown in Figure 14.11.

## FIGURE 14.11

The Scissors, Crop, and Move tools are used when setting a clip.

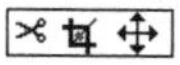

To crop an image, select the Set Clip command from a context menu opened from the Edit Object tool. The cursor immediately appears as the Scissors tool shown in Figure 14.12. This tool merely informs you that you are in Set Clip mode.

FIGURE 14.12

Select Set Clip from a context menu, and the cursor changes to a scissors icon.

Move the cursor to one of the four handles you see on the four corners of the selected image. Place the cursor directly over one of the four handles. You may need to move the cursor around a bit or zoom into the document before you see the Crop tool shown in Figure 14.13. When you see the Crop tool, drag the corner in to crop the image. You can continue using the Crop tool as long as you don't click when the cursor changes from the Crop tool to another tool.

FIGURE 14.13

Move the cursor over a corner point to see the Crop tool. Click and drag to crop the image.

When your crop appears as desired, just click the mouse button and the cursor changes from the Crop tool to the Move tool, as shown in Figure 14.14. You can click and drag the cropped image anywhere on the page.

Now, let's return to the Delete Clip command. After you have cropped an image, you can return to the full-size image before the cropping. Just open a context menu again with the Edit Object tool and select Delete Clip. The image appears as you first opened your PDF document.

Click the mouse button, and the cursor changes to the Move tool.

## Rotating images

Images can be rotated in many ways by using the context menu commands from the Edit Object tool. Open a context menu, and five separate commands appear for rotating images.

You can rotate images Horizontally and Vertically (180°), rotate Clockwise and Counterclockwise (90°), and rotate images using arbitrary rotations. The first four rotation options in the context menu should be self-evident. The more complicated rotation, Rotate Selection, requires a little explanation.

When you click an image with the Edit Object tool and choose Rotate Selection from the context menu, you won't see any change appear in the Acrobat window. Invoking the command changes modes from a scaling mode to a transformation mode. After selecting the command, move the cursor to one of the four corner handles. You need to wait for the cursor to change appearance to a line with two opposing arrowheads, as you see in Figure 14.15.

Select Rotate Selection and move the cursor to a corner handle.

Click and drag the cursor to rotate the image, and you can make an arbitrary rotation as shown in Figure 14.16. When you rotate the image as you want it, click the image, and the rotation mode is disengaged.

Click and drag to rotate the image.

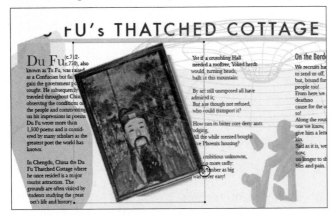

## Scaling images

You won't find a menu command for scaling images in a context menu, but scaling images is available to you.

In Acrobat, you can easily scale images. Just select the Edit Object tool and click an image. Move the cursor to a corner handle and drag the handle in or out to size an image down or up, respectively. You can constrain proportions by pressing the Shift key and dragging a corner handle.

## Creating and moving an artifact

This menu command is used when working with tagged PDF documents and accessibility. Selecting the command opens the Create Artifact dialog box. Or, if an artifact has been created, you can remove an artifact by selecting Remove Artifact.

# Cross-Reference

**For more on using the Create Artifact options, see Chapter 23.** ■

## Finding an image

A number of search options are available that pertain to images. Select Find from a context menu and the Find Element dialog box opens, as shown in Figure 14.17. A number of options appear that relate to working with accessible files. You also have options for searching annotations and OCR Suspects.

**FIGURE 14.17**

Select Find, and the Find Element dialog box opens.

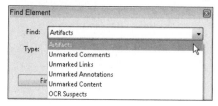

# Cross-Reference

**For more information on accessibility, see Chapter 23. For more on annotations, see Chapter 19. For more on OCR Suspects, see Chapter 16.** ■

### Showing metadata

Select this item, and the same dialog box opens when you use the Select tool to select Image Properties.

### Viewing properties

Select an image with the Edit Object tool and select Image Properties from a context menu, and you arrive at the TouchUp Properties dialog box. When the TouchUp Properties dialog box opens, click the Color tab, as shown in Figure 14.18.

**FIGURE 14.18**

Click Color in the TouchUp Properties dialog box.

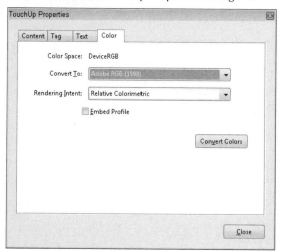

A number of tabs in the TouchUp Properties dialog box relate to accessibility and text editing, which are explained in Chapters 23 and 12, respectively. The one item in the Properties dialog box relating to image editing is contained in the Color tab.

The Color TouchUp Properties window provides you with choices for converting color profiles. The current working color space is reported at the top of the dialog box. From choices in the Convert To pull-down menu, you can choose to convert color to a working space color or an output profile. Ideally, you should stick to the working space profiles, and most often your choices will be either sRGB or Adobe RGB (1998). Output profile selections can be made in the Advanced Print Options dialog box.

## Cross-Reference

For more information on working with color workspaces and color output profiles, see Chapter 29. ■

If you want to change a color profile, make the choice for the new profile in the Convert To pull-down menu, select a Rendering Intent, and click Convert Colors. If you want the profile embedded in the image, click the Embed Profile check box before clicking Convert Colors.

## Caution

Be aware that if you embed a profile you need to make proper selections for printing files in both the Acrobat Print dialog box and switches in your printer driver. Be certain to carefully read Chapter 29 before converting color on your images. ■

As a matter of default, you'll want to keep the Rendering Intent at Relative Colorimetric. This choice is the best choice for raster image files. If you have vector images, you may want to use another rendering intent. For a comprehensive source on color management, see *Color Correction For Digital Photographers Only* (Wiley, 2006).

The item yet to be discussed in the context menu opened with the Edit Object tool is Edit Image. Selecting this command launches an external image-editing program, which is covered in the next section.

# Editing Images and Objects Outside of Acrobat

As demonstrated in the first part of this chapter, Acrobat offers you methods for copying and pasting images, moving them around the page, and exporting them to files. However, changing the physical attributes of images and shapes, other than transformations and scaling, is not something you can do in Acrobat. To modify certain appearances or attributes of raster and vector objects, you need to use an external editor. When you launch an editor from a menu command in Acrobat, you can make changes to images, text, and shapes and save your edits in the external editor. These saves are then dynamically updated in the PDF document. Acrobat treats external editing like many programs that support file links. When you edit linked files, the links are updated in the program where they are imported.

To access an external editor, you need to use the Edit Object tool. You cannot access external editors with any of the other selection tools.

## Setting TouchUp preferences

By default, Acrobat's external editors are Adobe Photoshop for image editing and Adobe Illustrator for object editing, if you have these programs installed on your computer. When you install Acrobat, the installer locates these editors on your hard drive, if they are installed, and designates them as the default editors. If you install Photoshop and/or Illustrator after Acrobat, you need to instruct Acrobat where to look for the application files to use as your image/object editors.

Choose Edit ⇨ Preferences to open the Preferences dialog box. Click the TouchUp item on the left pane of the Preferences dialog box. In the right pane are two buttons, as shown in Figure 14.19. Click Choose Image Editor to open the Choose Image Editor dialog box. The dialog box enables you to navigate your hard drive and locate Adobe Photoshop. Select the Photoshop application icon and click Open.

For page and object editing, Adobe Illustrator is the default tool, if installed. If you need to locate Illustrator, click the Choose Page/Object Editor button. Find the Illustrator application on your hard drive and select it in the Choose Page/Object Editor dialog box. Click Open, and Adobe Illustrator is enabled as your page/object editor. If you happen to use another object editor such as CorelDraw, you need to browse your hard drive and designate CorelDraw for your object editor. The same holds true for any other type of object editor.

After identifying your editors, click OK in the Preferences dialog box. The choices you made are immediately available. If Acrobat loses contact with either program, you are prompted in a dialog box that external editing cannot be done. If you see warning dialog boxes open as you attempt to use an external editor, return to the Preferences and reestablish the connection to your editors.

FIGURE 14.19

Select TouchUp in the preferences list, and the Choose buttons appear on the right side of the dialog box. Click one of the buttons to navigate your hard drive and select the respective editor.

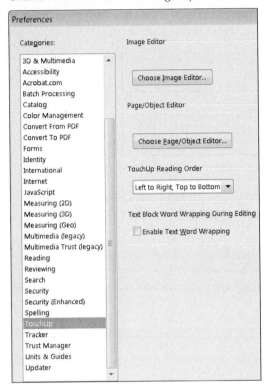

## Editing images in Adobe Photoshop

You launch Photoshop from Acrobat by selecting an image with the Edit Object tool and opening a context menu. From the menu commands, select Edit Image or press Control (Windows) or Option (Mac) and double-click. Depending on the speed of your computer and the amount of memory you have, Photoshop may take a few moments to launch. When the program opens, the image you selected is placed in a Photoshop document window.

You can change color modes and resolution, edit images for brightness and contrast, add effects, and just about anything else you can do in Photoshop to a single layer file. If you add type, add layers, or create transparency, you need to flatten all layers before saving the file. Layers added to a Photoshop file require you to use the Save As command to update the file. When you use Save As, the file is not updated in the PDF document. Flattening layers enables you to use the Save command that updates the PDF document when the file is saved. In Figure 14.20, a file in Photoshop was edited for color changes. Note that the file contains transparency and appears as a single-layer image. Because the file opened from Acrobat was a file on a single layer with transparency, all edits you make without creating additional layers enable you to still use the Save command.

You edit files in your image editor and dynamically update the PDF from which they originated.

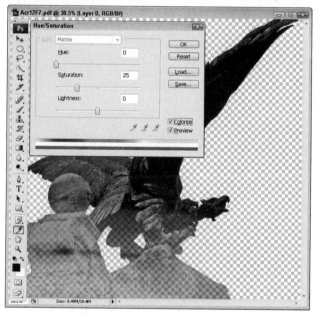

Photoshop updates the PDF document dynamically according to the edits you make with the Save command. If you add a layer to the file, you are prompted by Photoshop to Save As a new filename. Selecting Save As and writing to a new file disrupts the link. If you save in this manner, your PDF document won't update. If the file is saved without writing a new file, the updates are dynamically recorded in the PDF when you return to Acrobat.

## Editing objects in Adobe Illustrator

Objects, for the purposes of discussing external object editing, can be vector objects such as illustrations created in Illustrator, CorelDraw, or Adobe Freehand. Objects can also be text. Both vector objects and text are edited in Adobe Illustrator when you select Edit Object(s) from a context menu with the Edit Object tool.

To edit a single object, select the object with the Edit Object tool and open a context menu. The Edit Image command changes to Edit Object in the context menu. Select Edit Object and Adobe Illustrator launches. Changes you make to the object are dynamically updated when you save the file just as the file saves discussed with image editing are updated. If selecting a single object on the PDF page is difficult, you can marquee a group of objects and select Edit Objects.

If no object is selected and you open a context menu with the Edit Object tool, the menu command changes to Edit Page. To easily access the Edit Page command, you can also open a context menu outside the page boundary. When you click outside the page area, the Edit Page command appears in the context menu. Select Edit Page, and all objects are opened in Adobe Illustrator.

Be certain to not use the Save As command when editing objects. The procedures for saving files with object editing follow the same principles as described with image editing. Regardless of whether you edit a single object, multiple objects, or the entire page, the edits you make in Illustrator are updated in the PDF document only when you choose File⇨Save.

## Revising text in Adobe Illustrator

In some circumstances you may find editing text in an external editor to prove more satisfactory than editing text with the Edit Document Text tool. Editing text in Illustrator requires you to have embedded fonts loaded on your computer. Keep in mind that returning to an authoring application to apply major edits to documents is more advantageous than using the Edit Document Text tool. But, for those jobs where you don't have a document available and using the Edit Document Text tool just doesn't do the job, here's a little workaround you can try. I offer a disclaimer and tell you up front that these methods may not always work, but I've found more often than not that you can successfully edit text in Illustrator for some minor edit jobs.

One problem you can face when editing text in Illustrator is the text blocks are likely to be broken up and lose their paragraph formatting attributes. You need to select the text, cut it from the page, and paste it back, keeping the general size and position close to the original. You can then edit the text and choose File⇨Save to update the PDF document.

## Using Edit Page in Adobe Illustrator

If you want to edit an entire page in Illustrator, click the Edit Object tool on a document page without selecting an image. Open a context menu and select Edit Page. The entire page then opens in Adobe Illustrator.

### Note

If you choose Edit Objects to open text in an object editor and the PDF file was created as a tagged PDF, a dialog box opens, informing you that the tags will be removed from the document if you proceed. Click Yes in the dialog box, and the tags are removed from the document, and the selected objects open in your object editor. ■

You can also click the Edit Object tool and choose Edit⇨Select All or press Ctrl/⌘+A. All objects and their respective bounding boxes are shown as selected. Open a context menu and choose Edit Objects. All the selected objects are then opened in Adobe Illustrator.

If you edit a page or all objects on a page in Illustrator, selecting File ⇨ Save (Ctrl/⌘+S) updates the PDF document. If working on a single PDF page, you can just as easily select File ⇨ Save As in Illustrator and save to a PDF file.

If you need to completely rework a PDF document, you can also open a PDF in Adobe Illustrator. Opening a file in Illustrator is the same as selecting Edit Page. All changes you make are dynamically updated in the PDF document after saving in Illustrator.

## Cross-Reference

For more information on editing PDF pages, see Chapters 10 and 15. ∎

## Tip

If you want to edit a page in Adobe Illustrator, you can alternately open the page in Acrobat and choose Document ⇨ Extract Pages. Extract the page to edit and save as a new filename. The PDF can be opened in Adobe Illustrator, edited, and saved. When you return to Acrobat, choose Document ⇨ Replace Pages and replace the page you extracted with the page you edited in Adobe Illustrator. ∎

# Exporting Images

If you need to completely overhaul a document and want to lay it out in an authoring program, you might want to copy and paste text into a word processor, format your text, save the file, and then import the text into a program best suited for layout design, such as Adobe InDesign CS. If your PDF document contains photo images, you need to export the images and add them to your layout. Having to individually export images with the Select Image tool would be tedious for a large layout project containing many images. Fortunately, Acrobat offers you a feature for exporting all images in a PDF with a single menu command.

To export images and save them as separate files, open the Document Processing panel. Click Export All Images. The Export All Images As dialog box opens, where you can make selections for filename, destination, and the format you want to use for the exported images. In the Export All Images As dialog box, open the pull-down menu for Save as type (Windows) or Format (Mac). Four format options are available from the menu choices — JPEG, PNG, TIFF, or JPEG2000. Select one of the format options and click the Settings button to assign file attributes to the exported images.

## Cross-Reference

For more information on image file format definitions, see Chapter 10. ∎

When you select JPEG for the file type and click the Settings button, the Export All Images As JPEG Settings dialog box opens, as shown in Figure 14.21. The settings change according to the file type you select. Therefore, if you choose TIFF as a format, for example, you'll see changes for compression choices. The options for File Settings and Color Management are the same as those options discussed in Chapters 9 and 10. In addition to these settings, the

Extraction item at the bottom of the dialog box enables you to eliminate certain files when the sizes are smaller than the size you choose from the pull-down menu.

**FIGURE 14.21**

Make a choice for file format in the Export All Images As dialog box and click the Settings button. You choose options in the Export All Images As (file format) Settings dialog box for File Settings, Color Management, and Colorspace Conversion, and for eliminating image extractions falling below user-defined values.

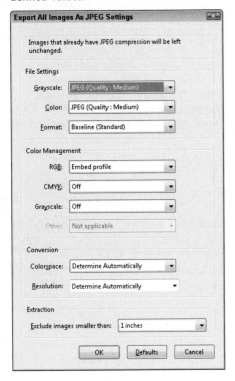

From the pull-down menu, you choose a preset option for an image's physical size. You might have icons or logos appearing on all pages constructed at .75-inch sizes. You can elect to exclude these images by selecting the 1.00 inches item in the pull-down menu. When you click OK in the Extract All Images As dialog box, all files above the size selected from the pull-down menu choice are saved as separate files in the specified format. If you want every image extracted, choose the No Limit item from the pull-down menu.

## Cross-Reference

For information on saving PDF files in other formats, see Chapter 10. ∎

# Summary

In this chapter, you learned how to edit and export images from PDF files. Among the items discussed are the following:

- You use the Select tool to select individual photo images on PDF pages. You can select only a single image with the tool. Selected images can be copied to the Clipboard.

- You can convert images copied with the Select tool to PDF with the Create PDF tool, and you can paste them into authoring programs.

- To select objects use the Edit Object tool. Objects include photo images, illustrative artwork, and text. Dragging a marquee enables you to select multiple objects. Pressing the Shift key and clicking an object toggles between adding and eliminating an object from a selection.

- You can paste objects and images copied with the Edit Object tool on PDF pages. You cannot paste them into authoring application documents.

- External editing is handled by selecting an image or an object and opening a context menu. From the menu options, select Edit Image/Object.

- If Adobe Creative Suite is installed, the default image editor is Adobe Photoshop and the default object editor is Adobe Illustrator. Select editors in the Preferences dialog box by clicking the TouchUp item in the left list and clicking the Change button on the right side of the dialog box.

- All images in a PDF can be exported as separate files with a single menu command. Choose Advanced ⇨ Document Processing ⇨ Export Images to open the Export All Images dialog box.

# Editing Pages

Chapters 12 and 14 covered editing content on PDF pages. Minor edits for text passages and images may be completed with the tools discussed in the earlier chapters. If you want to modify larger portions of a PDF document, then you'll want to know something about the tools Acrobat offers you for page editing. If you return to an authoring application and edit text, graphics, and layouts, you may want to update your PDF document according to the page edits made in other applications. Rather than re-create the entire PDF file, Acrobat enables you to selectively append, replace, delete, and extract pages in a PDF document.

When you need to add or modify content to change page designs, you have other tools such as the Add Headers and Footers dialog box and the ability to add backgrounds and watermarks. This chapter covers the page-editing tools in Acrobat and many features that can help you modify documents.

## Working with Page Thumbnails

Page Thumbnails are mini-views of PDF pages that can be displayed in various zoom sizes. To see the thumbnail view of pages in an open document, click the Page Thumbnails pane to open the pane, as shown in Figure 15.1. Thumbnail views are created on-the-fly when the pane is opened. Users of Acrobat 5 and below will remember the pane was referred to as Thumbnails. In Acrobat 6.0 viewers, the name was changed to the Pages panel, and in Acrobat X we refer to the pane as Page Thumbnails. We now refer to this pane as Page Thumbnails to differentiate it from the new Acrobat X Pages panel in the Tools panel.

FIGURE 15.1

Click the Page Thumbnails tab to open the Page Thumbnails pane, where thumbnail views of the pages are created on-the-fly.

## Navigating pages

The Page Thumbnails pane can be used to navigate pages. Clicking a thumbnail takes you to the page associated with the thumbnail. The page opens in the Document pane at the currently established zoom view. You can zoom in or out of pages in the Page Thumbnails pane by dragging the lower right handle on the rectangle appearing inside the page thumbnail. The changing zoom levels are reflected in the zoom view in the Document pane. In Figure 15.2, a rectangle shows the current page view in the Document pane. Click the handle in the lower-right corner and drag it into the center of the rectangle to zoom in on the page. Click and drag out to zoom out of the page.

The Page Thumbnails pane and the Document pane are two separate compartments in the open PDF document. Clicking in the Page Thumbnails pane activates the pane. Conversely, clicking in the Document pane activates the area where you view pages. Unfortunately, Acrobat does not highlight any part of either pane to inform you when a pane is active. So you just have to remember to click first in the area you want to be active.

If you press the Page Down key or Down Arrow key while the Document pane is active, the pages in the Document pane scroll. As each page is scrolled, the Page Thumbnails pane likewise scrolls pages, and the respective page thumbnails are highlighted. When you click in the

Page Thumbnails pane, you experience a different behavior. Pressing the Page Down key scrolls several pages down only in the Navigation pane Page Thumbnails pane. The respective pages in the Document pane are not scrolled. As you scroll through page thumbnails in the Page Thumbnails pane, the Document pane remains fixed at its current view because as you scroll in the Page Thumbnails pane, thumbnails are not actually selected. Instead, the selected thumbnail is linked to the view in the Document pane.

**FIGURE 15.2**

Thumbnails in the Page Thumbnails pane are linked to the pages in the Document pane. Click a thumbnail to navigate to the page link. Drag the red rectangle to zoom in or out of the page displayed in the Document pane.

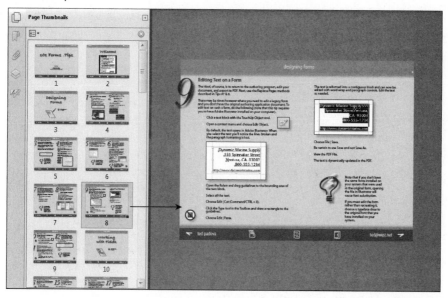

With reference to thumbnails, the term "selection" needs a little definition. When you click a page thumbnail, the number appearing below the page icon is shown selected (highlighted), and the thumbnail is further highlighted with a keyline border around the icon. Likewise, the respective page is placed in view in the Document pane. In essence, Acrobat communicates two selection messages to you. If you press the Down Arrow key on your keyboard, the page remains open in the Document pane. However, the page number highlight and keyline border move to the next page down, indicating the current thumbnail selection in the Page Thumbnails pane. In Figure 15.3, page 9 in a PDF document is selected and page 9 is open in the Document pane. When the Down Arrow key is pressed twice, page 11 becomes selected in the Page Thumbnails pane, while page 9 remains as the page viewed in the Document pane.

FIGURE 15.3

Click the cursor in the Page Thumbnails pane to activate the pane, and then press the Down Arrow key. The keyline border shows the page selection in the Page Thumbnails pane, while the highlighted page number on the previous page shows which page is in view in the Document pane.

Page 9

Page 11

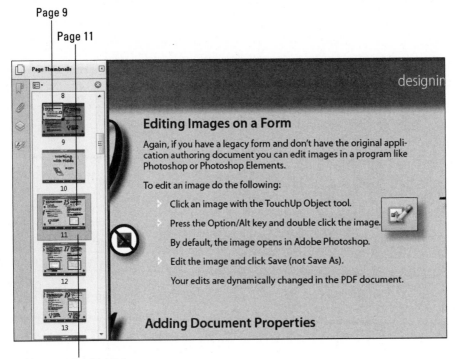

Page number highlight

# Moving Around Page Thumbnails

Quick thumbnail and page navigation is provided via a context menu. If you position the mouse cursor between the scrollbar arrows in the Page Thumbnails pane or on the far-right scrollbar in the Document pane, a context menu opens, offering you several options for navigating thumbnails/pages. Click Scroll Here to move a thumbnail/page, and the thumbnail/page at the cursor position jumps into view. For example, if you open the Page Thumbnails pane and position the cursor in the middle of a 500-page document, the thumbnail/page jumps to page 250 (or approximately the midpoint in the document).

Other nice features in the menu include Top and Bottom. If you want to jump to the beginning of the document, choose Top. If you want to jump to the end of the document, choose Bottom. The context menus operate independently so you can use the Bottom command in the Page Thumbnails pane while the Document pane displays the first page in your document. The Page Thumbnails pane jumps to the end of the document while the Document pane continues to display the first page.

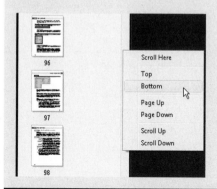

## Changing thumbnail sizes

In Acrobat 6 and later, you can reduce the size of pages to a mini-thumbnail view and enlarge the size up to a maximum thumbnail view of about 300 percent. The support for increased thumbnail views in the Page Thumbnails pane enables you to quickly find a page in a PDF document.

You reduce or enlarge page thumbnail sizes through menu commands. A context menu opened in the Page Thumbnails pane or the pane pull-down menu (known as the Options menu) includes the Enlarge Page Thumbnails and Reduce Page Thumbnails commands. Before using these commands, you should understand opening context menus.

If you click in the Page Thumbnails pane on a page thumbnail and open a context menu, the Enlarge Page Thumbnails and Reduce Page Thumbnails commands are available as options in a menu that contains many different commands for page editing. Likewise, the Options pull-down menu adjacent to the top left of the Page Thumbnails pane offers the same commands. Regardless of which menu you use, you can enlarge or reduce page thumbnail views.

To enlarge the size of the page thumbnails, click the mouse button anywhere inside the Page Thumbnails pane and open a context menu. Select Enlarge Page Thumbnails from the menu options, as shown in Figure 15.4. Return to the menu and select the same menu command to enlarge again. Repeat the steps to zoom in to the desired view.

You'll notice that Acrobat makes no provision for selecting from among a number of preset zoom sizes. You need to return to the context menu or pull-down menu to successively increase or decrease page thumbnail views. If the zoom view in the Page Thumbnails pane is larger than the pane width, click anywhere on the vertical bar on the right side of the pane and drag it to the right. The pane resizes horizontally to show more of the Page Thumbnails pane while the Document pane is reduced in size. In Figure 15.5, I enlarged the thumbnail view, using repeated steps for enlarging the thumbnails, and I widened the pane so several large thumbnails could be viewed. The tiny thumbnail on the right side of Figure 15.5 shows the selected page in the Document pane.

**FIGURE 15.4**

Open a context menu in the Page Thumbnails pane and select Enlarge Page Thumbnails. Return to the context menu and repeat the steps several times to zoom in on a page thumbnail.

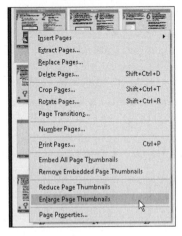

**FIGURE 15.5**

To size the Page Thumbnails pane, click the vertical bar on the right side of the pane and drag it to the right.

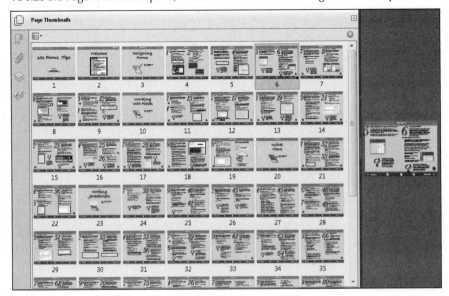

# Embedding and unembedding thumbnails

Page thumbnails are created on-the-fly each time you open the Page Thumbnails pane. In long documents, you may find your computer slowing down each time the Page Thumbnails pane is opened and the thumbnails are re-created. If this proves to be a burden, you can choose to embed thumbnails when working with the Page Thumbnails pane and avoid the delay caused by creating them.

Thumbnails add some overhead to your file. Each page thumbnail adds about 1K to the file size. Unless your files are to be viewed by users of earlier Acrobat viewers that don't support creating thumbnails on-the-fly, delete them as one of the final steps in your editing session.

To embed thumbnails, select the Embed All Page Thumbnails command from the pane Options menu or a context-sensitive menu. Thumbnails can also be created by batch-processing PDF files using a Batch Sequence or at the time of distillation when using Acrobat Distiller.

## PDF Workflow

You can delete thumbnails from PDF documents either individually in Acrobat or by using a custom action in the Custom Actions Wizard. If your work environment is such that you do a lot of editing in Acrobat and often use thumbnails, you may want to create them during distillation. When thumbnails are embedded, screen refreshes for multiple edits in long documents are faster. After you finish editing jobs and want to post PDF files on the Web or create CD-ROMs, you can batch-process the files for optimization and delete the thumbnails using the Custom Actions Wizard. Run actions to optimize multiple files and remove thumbnails. ■

## Cross-Reference

For information on creating custom actions and running batch sequences, see Chapter 17. ■

To unembed thumbnails, open a context menu on a page thumbnail and select Remove Embedded Page Thumbnails. All embedded page thumbnails are removed from the document. This step can be particularly helpful when working with Adobe Illustrator files, including the most current version of Adobe Illustrator CS and Acrobat viewers 7 or earlier. When Illustrator embeds thumbnails, a bitmap representation of the page is created as a thumbnail, and the thumbnail appearance is a poorly degraded image, as you can see on the left side of Figure 15.6. After the thumbnail is removed in Acrobat, the page thumbnail appears as you see it on the right side of Figure 15.6. Whenever you see thumbnail images with a degraded view, always check to see whether the thumbnail is embedded.

FIGURE 15.6

Adobe Illustrator exports thumbnails with a degraded bitmap view (shown left). Removing the thumbnail (shown right) improves the image quality when using Acrobat viewers 7 or earlier.

Embedded Thumbnails                    Unembedded Thumbnails

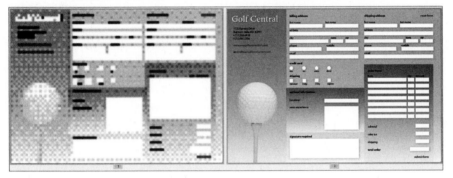

# Organizing Pages

The Page Thumbnails pane offers you a wealth of opportunity for sorting pages and reorganizing them. You can move pages around, copy and paste pages when you want to duplicate them, delete pages, print selected pages within a document, and a host of other options specific to page management.

## Reordering pages

Acrobat provides you with a marvelous slide sorter where you can shuffle pages and reorder them in a page sequence suited to your needs. Now with an opportunity to view page thumbnails in much larger views, you can easily see the content of text-only pages when no visible icons or graphics are present to distinguish differences in page content. Reorganizing pages in earlier versions of Acrobat was a little more difficult because of having to view text pages in small thumbnail views; however, now you can manage page order more easily by zooming in on pages to clearly view the content.

To rearrange pages in a PDF document, open the Page Thumbnails pane to the full width of your monitor by dragging the right side of the pane to the far right of the Document pane. Open a context menu in the Page Thumbnails pane and select Enlarge Page Thumbnails. Repeat the steps to enlarge the thumbnail views to a size that enables you to read text comfortably on the pages.

Click a page and drag the page to a spot between the pages where you want to relocate the selected page. When you move a page around the Page Thumbnails pane, a vertical bar appears where the page will be located. If the highlight bar is positioned in the area where you want to relocate a page, release the mouse button. Figure 15.7 shows page 7 selected. The page is moved to the area after page 3. Notice the vertical highlight bar appearing to the right side of page 3.

## Tip

**If you want to move pages between pages not in view in the Page Thumbnails pane, click and drag a selected page up or down in the Page Thumbnails pane, and the screen automatically scrolls to reveal hidden pages when the cursor is at the top or bottom of the pane. Keep the mouse button depressed until you find the location where you want to move a page. ■**

To select multiple pages, click a page to select it. Hold down the Control/⌘ key and click another page. If you want to select a block of contiguous pages, click the first page to be selected, hold down the Shift key, and click the last page within the group. All pages between the two selected pages are included in the selection. After you make your selection, click one of the selected pages and drag to a new location to reorder the pages.

---

**FIGURE 15.7**

To move a page in a PDF document, click a thumbnail and drag it to the area where you want to relocate the page. When you see a vertical highlight bar appear in the desired location, release the mouse button.

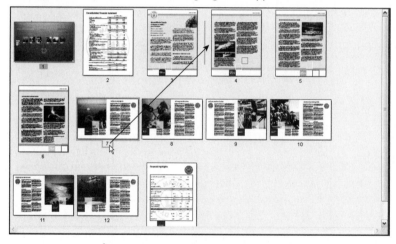

## Tip

**For a super slide sorter, open the Page Thumbnails pane and view thumbnails in a large size. Place the mouse cursor over the vertical bar to the right of the Page Thumbnails pane and drag to the right of your monitor screen. Press the F8 and F9 keys to hide the menu bar and toolbars. Resize the viewing window to fit the screen size. You'll get as much real estate on your monitor as possible. Shuffling pages is much easier in Acrobat than in almost any other program. ■**

## Copying pages

You can copy and paste pages within a PDF document or from one open PDF document to another. To copy a page with thumbnails, hold down the Ctrl/Option key as you drag a page to a new location in the same PDF file. Release the mouse button when you see the vertical highlight bar appear at the desired location. To copy a page from one PDF to another, open both PDF files and view them tiled either vertically or horizontally. The Page Thumbnails pane must be in view on both PDF documents. Click and drag the thumbnail from one file to the Page Thumbnails pane in the other document. The vertical highlight bar appears and the cursor changes, as shown in Figure 15.8. After the vertical bar is positioned at the desired location, release the mouse button, and the page drops into position.

### Cross-Reference

To learn how to tile PDF documents, see Chapter 5. ■

**FIGURE 15.8**

Dragging a thumbnail to a new location or copying between documents displays a vertical highlight bar where the page is placed.

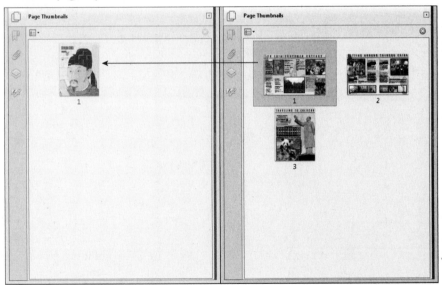

## Removing pages

The previous example behaves like a copy-and-paste sequence. You can also create a cut-and-paste action whereby the page is deleted from one PDF document and copied to another. To remove a page and place it in another PDF file, hold down the Ctrl/Option key and then click-and-drag the page to another Page Thumbnails pane in another file. The page is deleted from the original file and copied to the second file.

## Caution

**Be certain not to confuse the shortcut keys. If Control/Option is used in the page thumbnails on one document with click and drag, the page is copied. If using the same keys between two documents, the page is deleted from the file of origin and copied to the destination file. ■**

To delete a page with the Page Thumbnails pane, use a context-sensitive menu or the pane Options pull-down menu. Select a single thumbnail or Shift+click to select multiple thumbnails in a contiguous order (Ctrl/⌘+click for a noncontiguous order), and select Delete Pages from the context menu. This command opens the Delete Pages dialog box, as shown in Figure 15.9.

In the Delete Pages dialog box, by default the selected page is marked for deletion. You can make a change in the dialog box by selecting the From button and entering a contiguous page number range in the field box. The Selected radio button deletes all pages selected in the Page Thumbnails pane. You can click and select pages in a contiguous or noncontiguous group. After you select the pages you want to delete, click OK. The selected pages are deleted from the document.

**FIGURE 15.9**

When you select Delete Pages from the Pages context menu, the Delete Pages dialog box opens. Click OK to delete the selected pages.

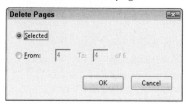

# Modifying Pages

In this context, *modifying pages* refers to the PDF page in its entirety and not individual page elements. Rather than look at changing single items on a page, such as text and graphics, this section examines some of the features for structuring pages as an extension of the commands found in the Page Thumbnails pane. Page editing discussed here relates to the insertion, extraction, and replacement of PDF pages.

## Note

**Most of the page-editing commands you have available in a context menu opened on a page thumbnail also appear in the Page Thumbnails pane. The commands for Insert Pages, Extract Pages, Replace Pages, Delete Pages, Crop Pages, and Rotate Pages appear in both menus. ■**

Before you go about creating a huge PDF document with links and buttons, understanding how Acrobat structures a page and related links is imperative. Bookmarks and other links are often created within a PDF document as user-defined navigation. Acrobat handles thumbnails and the link to the respective pages without user intervention. You have no control over the links from a thumbnail to respective pages.

## Cross-Reference

**For information on creating bookmarks and links, see Chapter 21. ■**

With regard to links and bookmarks, think of Acrobat as having a background and an overlay — the navigation items are placed on the overlay and page content is placed on the background (or layers in a PDF having Adobe PDF Layers). In regard to a single-layer PDF document, links appear as if on an overlay over the background. When viewing a PDF file, you don't see the navigation items independent of page content. This said, when you delete a page, all the links to the page are lost. Acrobat makes no provision to go to the page that follows a deleted page when links are deleted. Therefore, if you set up a bookmark to page 4 and later delete page 4, the bookmark has no place to go. Such links are commonly referred to as *dead links*.

When editing pages in Acrobat, you can choose to insert a page, delete a page, extract a page, and replace a page. If you understand the page structure, you'll know which option is right for your situation. Choices described in the Page Thumbnails pane Options menu permit access to each of the following choices by enabling you to select commands from the Document menu, or by providing a context-sensitive menu (refer to Figure 15.4) while clicking a thumbnail in the Page Thumbnails pane.

## Caution

**The menu commands for page editing are available only when you work with PDF documents that are not password protected, which prohibits page editing. If you attempt to edit pages in a secure PDF document, Acrobat prompts you for a password if the file is password protected. This behavior applies to all the options listed here. ■**

The page-editing options available either in a context menu opened on a page thumbnail or from the Page Thumbnails pane include the following:

- **Insert Pages From File.** When you select this option, the Select File to Insert dialog box opens. Select a file to insert, and click the Select button in the dialog box. The Insert Pages dialog box opens next, enabling you to choose the location for the insertion regardless of the current page viewed (see Figure 15.10). You can choose to insert a page either before or after the page in view, within a page range, or before or after the first or last page. Inserted pages do not affect any links in your document. All the pages shift left or right, depending on whether you select the Before or After option.

**FIGURE 15.10**

The Insert Pages dialog box enables you to locate the page that precedes or follows another page for the target location.

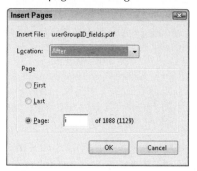

## Tip

You can also insert pages via drag-and-drop actions. Select a file from the Desktop or a folder and drag the file to the Page Thumbnails pane at the location where you want to insert a page. You can use any file type that Acrobat can convert to PDF. For example, drag a Microsoft Word or PowerPoint file to the Page Thumbnails pane and the file is converted to PDF and inserted as new pages in the existing document. ■

- **Insert Blank Page.** Use this command to insert a blank new page in a document. You can also use the command when a file is not open to create a new document with a blank page.

- **Insert Pages From Clipboard.** When you copy data using a screen shot (Windows), the Snapshot tool, or data from other applications, the data is stored on the Clipboard. In Acrobat, you can convert the Clipboard data to a PDF document using the PDF from Clipboard command in the Create task button pull-down menu or by choosing File ➪ Create PDF ➪ From Clipboard.

  Choosing the From Clipboard option opens the same dialog box shown in Figure 15.10. The Clipboard content is inserted at the location you specify in the Insert Pages dialog box.

- **Delete Pages.** When you delete a page, you delete not only its contents but also its links. If a link or bookmark is linked to a view in the deleted page, all links to the page become inoperable. When creating a presentation in Acrobat with multiple pages, you must exercise care when deleting pages to be certain links aren't broken.

  Select a single thumbnail or multiple thumbnails in the Page Thumbnails pane. Pages can be selected in a contiguous or noncontiguous selection. Open a context menu or the Options pull-down menu, or open the Page Thumbnails pane, and click Delete. The Delete Pages dialog box opens, where you can delete the selected pages by leaving the default Selected radio button active or by selecting a page range and clicking OK.

Acrobat opens a warning dialog box to confirm your choice. If you change your mind and want to keep the pages, click the Cancel button. To continue with the page deletion, click OK.

## Tip

If you begin an editing session and work on files where you insert and delete pages frequently, you may find the confirmation dialog box annoying. To eliminate the dialog box opening every time you delete a page, open the Preferences dialog box (Ctrl/⌘+K). Click General in the left pane and select the box for Do not show edit warnings in the right pane. When you return to the Document pane, all subsequent page deletions are performed without the warning dialog box opening. Be certain to exercise care when targeting pages for deletion if you are not using the edit warnings. When you want to bring back the edit warnings, open the General preferences and click Reset All Warnings. ■

- **Extract Pages.** Extracting a page is like pulling out single or multiple pages and creating a new PDF file with them. Extracting pages has no effect on bookmarks or links for the destination pages in the original document unless you delete pages when extracting them. All links are operable for pages among the extracted pages. For example, if you extract ten pages with bookmarks to each page, all the bookmarks within the extracted pages are functional in the new file. If you have a bookmark to a page not part of the extraction, the link is not operational.

  When you select the Extract Pages command, the Extract Pages dialog box opens, as shown in Figure 15.11. You supply the page range in the From/To field boxes, and check boxes exist for Delete Pages After Extracting and Extract Pages As Separate Files. You can select these two options individually or together when extracting pages.

  Pages are extracted and deleted from the original file when you select Extract Pages and you check the box for Delete Pages After Extracting. The new pages open in the foreground as a single PDF document and remain unsaved until you use the Save or Save As command.

  The other option you have in the Extract Pages dialog box is Extract Pages As Separate Files. Check this box to extract pages and save them to your hard drive instead of having them open in the Document pane. When you select the page range and click OK after checking the box to create separate files, a Browse For Folder dialog box opens, enabling you to select a target folder for the saved files. Check the box for Delete Pages After Extracting and pages are deleted from the original file after the new files are saved. Each page you select for extraction is saved as a separate file.

- **Replace Pages.** This option affects only the contents of a PDF page — the overlay is unaffected. If you have links going to or from the replaced page, all links or interactive content is preserved. When editing PDF documents where page contents need to be changed, redistilled, and inserted in the final document, always use the Replace Pages command.

  Replace Pages is particularly helpful when re-creating Acrobat PDF forms. If you create a form in an authoring program and add all the form fields in Acrobat, and then later decide you want to edit the form design, replacing the old design with a new design preserves the form fields.

FIGURE 15.11

If you want to delete the pages extracted from the original file, check the box for Delete Pages After Extracting. Checking the box for Extract Pages As Separate Files saves each page as a separate PDF to your hard drive.

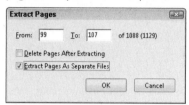

You can click a single page thumbnail or select multiple pages in a contiguous order and open a context menu. Select Replace Pages to open the Select File With New Pages dialog box. Navigate to the file containing pages that are to replace pages in the open file, and click Select.

The Replace Pages dialog box opens. In the Original area of the dialog box shown in Figure 15.12, you select the page range in the open document for the target pages to be replaced. In the Replacement section of the Replace Pages dialog box, you select the first page number of the document selected in the Select Pages to Replace dialog box. The readout to the right of the field box automatically displays the range of pages that are targeted for replacement. At the bottom of each section, notice the file-name listed for the open document and the selected document.

If you disabled the edit warnings, the pages are replaced according to the selection made in the Replace Pages dialog box. If the edit warnings are not disabled (in this case, the check box isn't selected in the General preferences dialog box), a confirmation dialog box opens. Click OK to replace the pages.

FIGURE 15.12

Specify the page range for the pages to be replaced in the first two field boxes. Enter the page number for the first page in the target file.

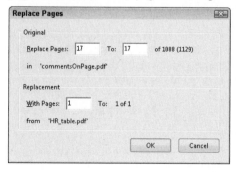

# Appending Pages to PDF Documents

If you want to create a PDF document by combining multiple files that may have been created from multiple authors and multiple authoring programs, you can choose some alternatives in Acrobat that permit you to concatenate files to form a single PDF document.

When you use the Insert Pages command, the Select File to Insert dialog box enables you to select multiple files stored in a single folder. You can select multiple files by holding down the Shift key and clicking on the target files in a listed order from within a folder, or pressing the Ctrl/⌘ key to select files in a noncontiguous order.

However, when you use the Insert Pages command, the order of the files is appended to the open PDF file, which does not follow the same file order you viewed in the list in the Select File to Insert dialog box. You have no control over rearranging the order or selecting additional files from within separate folders. Additionally, you can't add PDFs having security, forms created in Adobe Designer, or digital signatures. You can't retain form field data in multiple PDF forms having identical form data field attributes.

A much better alternative to use when appending pages is the Combine Files menu command, and in some cases the Assemble Files into a Portfolio option. Combining files permits you to establish the page order for the files you combine into one PDF document. It also enables you to choose specific pages within each PDF to add to a single PDF document. The Assemble Files into a Portfolio option permits you to assemble files into one document when you need to add PDFs having security or digital signatures, PDF forms created in Adobe LiveCycle Designer, or when aggregating forms among files having identical field names.

To review a thorough coverage on combining files using the Combine Files task button and for creating PDF Portfolios, see Chapter 11.

## Tip
You can replace pages through drag-and-drop operations when viewing two documents in tiled views and when the Page Thumbnails pane is opened for both documents. When you drag a page or a number of selected pages, hold down Ctrl+Alt (Windows) or ⌘+Option (Mac) and move the cursor in the target document on top of the page thumbnail for the first page to be replaced. Rather than place the cursor between pages where the highlight bar is shown, be certain to drop the selection on top of the page number. The target page is highlighted in black when the cursor appears directly over the page number. Release the mouse button and the pages are replaced. ■

You can approach page editing in Acrobat in many ways. Using the Page Thumbnails pane helps you access menu commands quickly. You can also access the commands just discussed with the Page Thumbnails pane collapsed by choosing the tools in the Pages pane. In addition, you can open multiple documents, view them with horizontal or vertical tiling, and drag-and-drop pages to accomplish the same results. To help in understanding how page editing with tiled views is accomplished, try following these steps for a little practice.

## STEPS: Editing Pages with Thumbnails

1. **Open two PDF documents where pages need to be arranged in a third document.** As an example for page editing, assume you have two files that need selected pages merged in a new, third file. Some of the pages need only to be copied to the new file, and some pages need to be copied and deleted from the source document.

2. **Create a new blank page.** Open the Pages pane and click Insert Blank Page.

3. **Tile the page views.** Choose Window ➪ Tile ➪ Vertically (or Ctrl/⌘+Shift+L). Click the Page Thumbnails pane in each file to open the panes. The two files you opened and the new file you created should appear similar to Figure 15.13.

4. **Replace a page.** The new document you created contains a blank page. One of the cover pages in the opened files is used as the cover in the new document. Select a page from one of the open document's Page Thumbnails pane and press Ctrl+Alt (Windows) or ⌘+Option (Mac) and drag the page to the top of the page thumbnail in the new document. When the page is targeted for replacement, the entire page is highlighted in with a keyline border, as shown in Figure 15.13.

**FIGURE 15.13**

The two opened files and the new file appear with the Page Thumbnails panels open. Drag a thumbnail image to the target file and place the cursor on top of the page number. Release the mouse button when you see a keyline border appear.

5. **Insert pages.** Select a page in one of the open documents. Press the Ctrl/⌘ key and click pages in a noncontiguous order. Release the modifier key and drag one of the selected pages below the title page in the new document. Wait until you see a highlight bar appearing below the page before releasing the mouse button.

6. **Extract pages with deletion.** Move to the second open file. In this document you copy pages to the new document while deleting them from the source document. Click a contiguous or noncontiguous group of pages to select them. Press the Ctrl/ Option key and drag the pages to the new document's Page Thumbnails pane. Pages are inserted in the new file and deleted from the source document.

7. **Close the original source documents.** Click the close button or choose File ⇨ Close to close the documents. If you want to save the file where you extracted and deleted pages, save the document and close the file.

8. **Sort the pages.** Open the Page Thumbnails pane by dragging the right side of the pane to the right side of the Acrobat window. Open a context menu and select Enlarge Page Thumbnails. Repeat the steps to enlarge pages until you have a comfortable view of the page content. Click and drag pages around the Page Thumbnails pane to reorder the pages, as shown in Figure 15.14.

**FIGURE 15.14**

Open the Page Thumbnails pane and move the pages to the desired order.

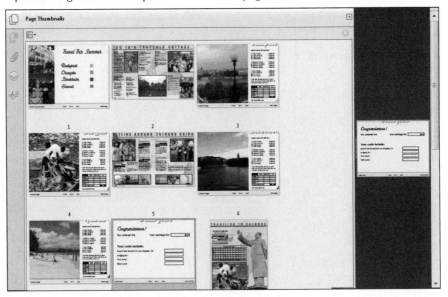

9. **Save the file.** Choose File ⇨ Save As ⇨ Save As. Supply a filename and select a destination in the Save As dialog box. Click the Save button.

Save your work periodically if you have a major editing job. When you create a new file with the Insert Blank Page command, Acrobat creates a new Untitled document, but the file is not actually saved to disk until you save the file. Save the file after a few edits; then repeat the Save command as you work on the file. When you finish the job, choose File ➪ Save As ➪ Save As and rewrite the file. Page editing can add a lot of unnecessary data to a file during an editing job. When you rewrite the file, much of the redundancy is eliminated and the file size is reduced.

## Cross-Reference

**For information on rewriting files with the Save As command, see Chapter 10.** ■

# Splitting Documents

In this chapter, I talked about pulling out pages in a PDF document that you can save as new PDF files. The Extract Pages command works fine for documents where you need to save a few pages here and there as new PDF files. But what if you have a book — a lengthy book — and you want to divide the book into individual chapters all saved as individual PDF documents? Using the Extract Pages command is going to take you a bit of time if you're working on a book with 20 or more chapters. There must be a better way.

Fortunately, Acrobat makes the task of splitting up a document and saving the split parts into individual PDF files a simple feat. You find the Split Document option in the Pages pane.

To split a document, open the Pages pane and click Split Document. The Split Document dialog box shown in Figure 15.15 offers you three options for choosing how to split a PDF document into several files.

**FIGURE 15.15**

Open the Pages pane and click Split Document to open the Split Document dialog box.

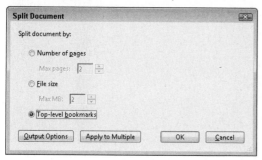

- **Number of pages.** Type a value in the text box to split a document according to the number of pages you want for the maximum page count for each file.

- **File size.** Type a value for the maximum file size for each of the split files.

- **Top-level bookmarks.** This option enables you to split a file according to the parent bookmarks in a PDF. Nested bookmarks having a child order are not recognized for splitting the document.

## Cross-Reference

**For more information on bookmarks, bookmark hierarchy, and nesting bookmarks, see Chapter 21.** ■

Regardless of the choice you make for how to split a document, be sure to visit the Output Options by clicking the Output Options button in the Split Document dialog box. The Output Options dialog box, shown in Figure 15.16, offers settings to control file naming, location, and labeling.

**FIGURE 15.16**

Click Output Options in the Split Document dialog box to open the Output Options dialog box.

Some choices you'll want to make for saving split documents include:

- **Target Folder.** Choose to use the Same folder as originals, or click the Specific Folder radio button and then the Browse button to locate a folder where you want to save the new files.

- **File name.** Three radio button options are available to you. Choose to use the bookmark names for the filenames, add a label and number before a filename such as *Part* and Acrobat automatically adds a number after the label beginning with 1, or add the label and number after the original name.

- **Use Label.** If you choose to add a label before or after the original filename, type the label in the text box here.

- **Use separator between original name and label.** Type a separator character in the text box such as an underscore if you want a separator to appear between the original file name and the label.

- **Do not overwrite existing files.** Use this option if you choose to save files to the same folder as the original files and you want to prevent overwriting the existing files.

All the options for splitting files can be applied to a single document, or you can use either the Apply to Multiple button in the Split Document dialog box or a custom action to split a folder of files.

## Cross-Reference

For more information on custom actions, see Chapter 17. ■

# Cropping Pages

In the Pages pane, you find the Crop tool. Cropping pages in Acrobat is performed with the Crop tool in the Pages pane or using a series of options in the Preflight Wizard. In Chapter 29 I talk about using the Crop tool in the Preflight Wizard. In this chapter I'll stick to using the Crop tool in the Pages toolbar.

You can select the Crop tool and draw a marquee in the document window to define the crop region and double-click the selection to open the Crop Pages dialog box shown in Figure 15.17.

When you use the Crop tool and double-click inside the crop region, the Crop Pages dialog box opens with a crop zone specified. You can edit the margins numerically where a keyline border displays the crop area dynamically as you change the margins. When you use the Crop tool, open a rectangle marquee and move the mouse cursor inside the rectangle. The cursor changes to a selection arrow, indicating that you can double-click the mouse button to open the Crop Pages dialog box. The Crop Pages dialog box enables you to refine the page cropping. You can select from the following options:

**FIGURE 15.17**

The Crop Pages dialog box displays a thumbnail image of the document page and offers options for crop margins and page ranges.

Crop area

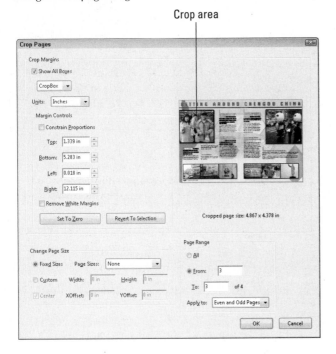

- **Crop Margins.** Four radio button options are available. When you choose one of the options, the keyline border displaying the crop region changes color according to the option selected. The four options are as follows:
  - **CropBox.** This is the default selection. It is shown with a black keyline for the cropped page when displayed or printed.
  - **ArtBox.** The Art box is shown with a red rectangle. The Art box size includes the entire bounding box for the page size.
  - **TrimBox.** The Trim box is shown with a green rectangle. Trim areas are usually determined by the printer's marks indicating the finished paper size. The paper trim is made inside the bleed box.
  - **BleedBox.** When you select the Bleed option, the keyline showing the crop area is blue. Bleeds allow colors to extend off the finished page size to account for paper trimming sizes.
- **Show All Boxes.** Displays the Crop, Trim, Bleed, and Art boxes.

- **Units.** From the pull-down menu select a unit of measure. The options include Points, Picas, Millimeters, Centimeters, and Inches.

- **Margin Controls.** Choices for margins are available for each side of the page. In the field boxes for each side, you can use the up or down arrows and watch a preview in the thumbnail at the top of the dialog box. As you press the up or down arrow, the margin line is displayed in the thumbnail. If you want to supply numeric values, enter them in the field boxes.

- **Constrain Proportions.** Check the box to keep proportions constrained. As you edit one text box in the Margin Controls, Acrobat supplies the same value in the remaining text boxes. For example, if you add 1 inch in the Top text box, Acrobat adds 1 inch to the Bottom, Left, and Right text boxes.

## Tip

To quickly adjust margins you can click in any field box and press the up and down arrow keys on your keyboard. The margins jump in increments according to the units selected from the Units pull-down menu. Press the Shift key and arrow keys and the margins jump to the next whole unit. For example, when inches are used for the units of measure, pressing Shift plus an arrow changes the amount in whole inches. ■

- **Remove White Margins.** Acrobat makes an effort to eliminate white space on the page outside any visible data. Acrobat's interpretation is confined to true white space. If a slight bit of gray appears as a border, it is not cropped.

- **Set to Zero.** This choice resets the crop margins to zero. If you change the dimensions with either of the preceding settings and want to regain the original dimensions of the crop boundary, click the Set to Zero button. From here you can redefine the margins. This button behaves much like a Reset button in other image editing programs.

- **Revert To Selection.** If you open a crop range and open the dialog box, and then change the margins or click the Set to Zero button, the crop rectangle is restored to the size it was when the dialog box was opened. That is, it's restored to the original crop area. The view displays the crop area within the current page. In other words, the thumbnail preview displays the entire page with the crop area indicated by a red rectangle.

- **Change Page Size.** You can change page sizes to standard fixed sizes by selecting options from the Page Sizes pull-down menu. You can also click the Custom radio button, and the field boxes for Height and Width become active. Change values in the field boxes to create custom page sizes. When you add printer's marks to a page or document, you can crop the page(s) larger than the page size to accommodate adding printer's marks.

## Tip

If you want to see a larger view of what's happening on your PDF document while making adjustments in the Crop Pages dialog box such as changing the page sizes, move the dialog box aside, and the background display in the Document pane dynamically updates to reflect many changes made in the Crop Pages dialog box. ■

- **Page Range.** Pages identified for cropping can be handled in the Page Range options. If All is selected, all pages in the PDF file are cropped according to the sizes you specify in the dialog box. You can target specific pages for cropping by entering values in the From and To field boxes. You select choices for Even and Odd Pages, Even Pages Only, and Odd Pages Only from the Apply to pull-down menu. The Selected option is available when you select page thumbnails in the Pages palette. If you select pages in the Page Thumbnails panel, use the Crop tool in the Pages pane and marquee a crop region on the page in view in the Document pane. Double-click the cursor inside a crop rectangle, and the Crop Pages dialog box displays the page range from the selected page thumbnails.

## Tip

When creating PDFs for slide presentations or screen views, you may occasionally have an unwanted white border around the pages. This appearance may result from creating pages in layout or illustration programs when the image data doesn't precisely match the page size. To polish up the pages and eliminate any white lines, select the Crop tool and double-click the page. In the Crop Pages dialog box, select Remove White Margins and then select All for the page range. When the pages are cropped, the excess white lines are removed. ∎

# Rotating Pages

PDF documents can contain many pages with different page sizes. You can have a business card, a letter-sized page, a tabloid page, and a huge poster all contained in the same file. Depending on the authoring program of an original document and the way a PDF is created, you may experience problems with pages appearing rotated or inverted. Acrobat offers you tools to rotate pages for viewing and printing solutions to correct such appearance problems.

You rotate pages by clicking Rotate in the Pages pane or in the Page Thumbnails pane via context or Options menus. Notice that the Rotate tool in the Pages pane appears first. Adobe added this tool as the first item in the Pages pane because through various surveys, users informed Adobe that this tool is the number one tool used in both Acrobat and Adobe Reader.

When you select Rotate Pages through any of the methods, the Rotate Pages dialog box opens. You choose the direction of rotation from a pull-down menu that enables you to rotate the page three different ways, as shown in Figure 15.18. Options in the Rotate Pages dialog box include the following:

- **Direction.** Three choices appear from the Direction pull-down menu. Select from rotating pages clockwise 90 degrees, counterclockwise 90 degrees, or 180 degrees. Selecting clockwise or counterclockwise repeatedly rotates the page in 90-degree rotations.
- **Page Range.** Select All to rotate all pages in the PDF document.

- **Selection.** If you select page thumbnails in the Page Thumbnails pane and select Rotate Pages from a context menu or by selecting Document ⇨ Rotate Pages, the Rotate Pages dialog box offers you an option for rotating selected pages.

- **Pages.** Enter the page range you want to rotate in the From and To field boxes.

- **Rotate.** The pull-down menu for Rotate offers selections for Even and Odd Pages, Even Pages Only, or Odd Pages Only. The last pull-down menu offers choices for Portrait Pages, Landscape Pages, or Pages of Any Orientation.

**FIGURE 15.18**

The Rotate Pages dialog box offers options for rotating pages in a range or by selecting even or odd pages. The Even/Odd choices can be helpful when printing to devices requiring page rotations for duplexing.

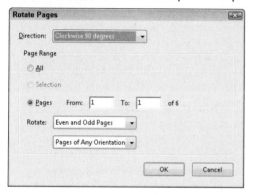

## Rotating PDF elements

When you rotate a page, all page content is rotated. If you have any layers, visible or hidden, they are rotated. Acrobat provides no means for rotating individual layers.

If you create comments on a page and later rotate the page, the comment notes rotate at the point of origin, but the note displays are not rotated. For example, if you create a comment note in the top-left corner of a page and rotate the page 90 degrees counterclockwise, the note icon on the page is rotated, eventually ending up in the lower-left corner of the page. However, the open note is viewed at the default view with the note text in its original orientation.

Form fields behave differently than notes. If you create a form field containing text, the field and contents are rotated with the page.

## Minimizing rotation problems

Among major problems with PDF page rotation involves creating PDFs from layout programs. Layout programs such as Adobe InDesign or QuarkXPress enable you to transverse pages in the Print dialog box. This control is implemented for digital prepress and printing to high-end printing devices. In addition, many PostScript Printer Description files (PPDs) used with high-end devices include transverse page options for page size selections.

## Cross-Reference

**For more information on commercial printing and PPDs, see Chapter 29. ■**

As an example, a portrait page that prints transversed is rotated 90 degrees to conserve media on roll-fed devices. If you print files to disk as PostScript and distill the files in Acrobat Distiller, don't transverse the pages. When transversed pages are opened in Acrobat, even though the auto rotate feature is enabled during distillation, Acrobat interprets the page coordinates with a 90-degree rotation. The end result is a zero point (0,0) located in the lower-right corner of the page. This interpretation can lead to problems when you're trying to define x,y coordinates for JavaScripts, replacing pages, and copying and pasting data between documents.

If you set up a landscape page in a layout program, print the file as a portrait page with the horizontal width described in field boxes for custom page sizes. Print the file to disk and distill in Acrobat Distiller. The end product is a PDF that winds up with the proper page orientation and is interpreted by Acrobat with the zero point (0,0) located in the default lower-left corner.

## Prepress

**Design and print professionals who seek to print files from PDFs can create the PDFs without transversing pages. When printing the PDFs for prepress, use the Acrobat Print dialog box to control printing, and select device PPDs from within Acrobat. If you need to repurpose documents for Web or screen presentations, you can use the same file created for prepress without having to reprint and redistill the authoring document. ■**

# Creating Headers and Footers

Headers and Footers can be used for adding page numbers, dates, and any custom data you want to add to a header and footer appearing on all or a range of pages.

When you open the Pages panel and click Header & Footer, a drop-down menu lists three options (Add, Update, and Remove). To add a new header, click Header & Footer and click Add to open the Add Header and Footer dialog box shown in Figure 15.19. You'll notice the Add Header and Footer dialog box is the same dialog box you use when adding Bates numbers (see "Using Bates numbering" later in this chapter).

The Add Header and Footer dialog box offers you the option for batch processing files. Click the Apply to Multiple button in the Add Header and Footer dialog box, and you can load files in a wizard to apply settings to multiple files.

**FIGURE 15.19**

Select Document ⇨ Add Header & Footer to open the Add Header and Footer dialog box.

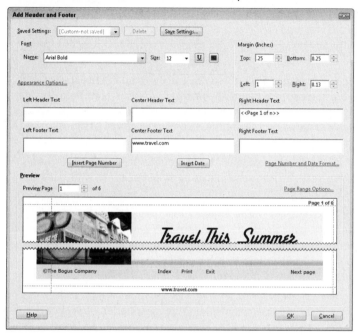

You create page headers and footers in this dialog box. Options exist for adding a date stamp, a page number, and a custom text description. In Figure 15.19, I added a page number as a header and a Web address as a footer to apply to all pages in my open document. Both headers and footers can be added in the same dialog box. Among your choices in the Add Headers and Footers dialog box are the following:

- **Saved Settings.** You can select options from the pull-down menu. By default no settings are listed in the menu. Make your settings adjustments in the dialog box and click Save Settings. Name your settings, and they are added to the Saved Settings menu. If you want to delete a saved setting, select the setting and click the Delete button.

- **Font (Name).** All the system fonts available to you from your operating system are displayed in a pull-down menu. Click the down-pointing arrow and make your font choice. You can assign a different font to each line of text in the listed items in the six boxes below the menu.

- **Font (Size).** Font sizes can be assigned individually to each line of text. If you want custom text to appear larger than a date or page number, select the item after clicking an Insert button and choose a font size from the pull-down menu. You select a font from preset point sizes. You cannot edit the field box to add a point size other than the preset sizes.

- **Margins.** The four Margins field boxes are editable. You can physically position a header or footer at any location on a page. If you add a header, the options relate to the top, left, and right field boxes. Footers relate to all but the top field box. Entering values in the lower field box has no effect on the position where the text is added when adding headers. If you use top = 5 inches, left = 3 inches, and select the left alignment radio button, the text is added 5 inches from the top and 3 inches from the left side.

  Although a header or footer extending beyond the space shown in the Preview area (denoted by dashed lines) disappears from the preview, you can move data outside the guidelines by adding values in the Margins text box and clicking OK. When you view the PDF file, the data appear at the coordinates you described in the Margins text boxes.

- **Appearance Options.** Six boxes are shown for adding data. The top row of three boxes is used for adding headers. The second row of three boxes across is used for adding footers. You can type custom text in any one of the six boxes.

- **Insert Page Number.** Click the box in the Appearance Options where you want a date to appear and type the code used for a date format. The same five date formats you have available with page numbering are also available in the Add Headers and Footers dialog box. To select a date format, you can click the Page Number and Date Format link to the right of the Insert Date button (see "Page Number and Date Format" below).

- **Insert Date.** Follow the same steps as when adding a page number. First click in the box where you want the data to appear, then choose a date format and insert it.

- **Page Number and Date Format.** The blue text is like a button. Clicking the text opens the Page Number and Date Format dialog box, as shown in Figure 15.20. From pull-down menus you select formats for Date, Page number, and a page to start adding the header and/or footer.

**FIGURE 15.20**

Click Page Number and Date format to open the Page Number and Date Format dialog box.

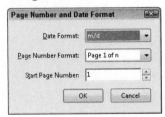

- **Page Range Options.** By default, all pages are used when you add a page header and/or footer. You can control page ranges by clicking the Page Range Options blue text. Clicking the text opens the Page Range Options dialog box shown in Figure 15.21. Select Pages from and type values in the text boxes. From the subset pull-down menu, you have All Pages, Even Pages Only, or Odd Pages Only.

**FIGURE 15.21**

Click Page Range Options to open the Page Range Options dialog box.

- **Preview.** The Preview Page text box and up/down arrows permit you to scroll through the document. Below this item are the preview boxes for headers and footers. You cannot type in either of the boxes. They are used only for previewing data added in the top six boxes.

Click OK after adding data to a header and/or footer and the data are applied to your selected page range.

## Tip

If the layout of your design elements on each page make it difficult to find a space to add a header or footer, you can use the Crop tool to add a little more space to the top, bottom, or both top and bottom of the pages. In the Crop Pages dialog box, uncheck Center and set the Y Offset to add space to the top or bottom of the pages. A 0.5 Y Offset adds one-half inch to the bottom of the page, and a –0.5 adds one-half inch to the top of the page. After cropping the pages, use the Header and Footer ⇨ Add command in the Pages panel to add a header or footer to the new space added to your pages. ■

## Updating headers and footers

If you add or delete pages, the headers and footers are not dynamic and do not change when adding or deleting pages. You need to re-edit the headers and footers to renumber pages deleted from a document or add header/footer data to pages inserted in your document. From the Header & Footer menu in the Pages panel, select Update. The Update Header and Footer dialog box opens. Options in this dialog box are identical to the Add Header and Footer dialog box.

The Update Header and Footer dialog box displays the exact same settings you used when you first added a header and/or footer. Just click OK if you want the update to be exactly the same as your original assignment of headers and footers, and the file is updated.

## Removing headers and footers

In earlier versions of Acrobat prior to version 8, the only way you could remove a background was to open the Add Header and Footer dialog box and return all settings to defaults, and then click OK. Acrobat essentially replaced your headers and footers with nothing. In Acrobat 8 through X, you have a menu command specifically used for removing headers and footers. Select Remove from the Header & Footer menu in the Pages panel. A dialog box opens, prompting you to confirm the action. Click OK and your headers and footers are removed.

# Numbering Pages

In Acrobat, page numbers appear in the Page Navigation toolbar at the top of the Acrobat window and in the Pages panel. When you open the Go To Page dialog box (View ⇨ Go To ⇨ Page or Ctrl/⌘+Alt/Option+N) and enter a value in the status bar and press Enter/Return, you may find that the destination page does not correspond with the page number you supplied in the dialog box. This is because certain documents may be numbered in sections where front matter, such as a table of contents, foreword, preface, and other such items precede the page numbering in a document. This is particularly true of books, pamphlets, essays, journals, and similar documents using numbering schemes other than integers for the front matter.

## Numbering individual PDF documents

Pages in a PDF file can be renumbered using the Page Numbering dialog box that you access with a simple menu command. Open the Pages panel and open a context menu on a page thumbnail. From the menu options, select Number Pages. The Page Numbering dialog box opens, as shown in Figure 15.22.

The Page Numbering dialog box offers options for selecting a range of pages and renumbering them in sections or throughout the entire document. The choices available to you include:

- **Pages.** This area of the dialog box asks you to specify the page range. If you want to renumber all pages with the same numbering scheme, select the All radio button. You might use this option when numbering pages with integers.

  If you enable the radio button for Selected, only the pages selected in the Pages panel are affected. By default the Selected radio button is enabled if you click a page or a page's thumbnail in the Pages panel and open the dialog box. If no page thumbnail is selected, the default radio button selection is From.

**FIGURE 15.22**

The Page Numbering dialog box offers options for numbering pages.

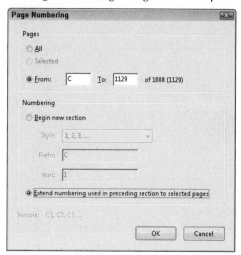

Enable the From radio button and supply a page range in the field boxes to select a page range numerically according to page position in the document. That is to say, pages 1 to X are interpreted as the first ten pages in the file regardless of the page numbering scheme used before you open the dialog box. Perhaps you want to create a separate scheme for a document's front matter. Specifying the scheme in the Numbering section of the dialog box renumbers the selection. Click OK to accept the changes. If you want to renumber another section, return to the dialog box and select a new section and new scheme. Repeat the process for all changes in page numbering according to different sections.

- **Numbering.** This portion of the dialog box offers you options for determining the page-numbering scheme you want to use. From the Style pull-down menu select a number style (refer to Figure 15.23 for your choices).

  - **Style.** If None is selected, no page number is assigned to the page. The readout in the status bar would appear similar to this: (10 of 100). The numbers within the parentheses represent the original page number order preceded by a blank space where no number (None) is specified. If you want to add a prefix, you could add alphanumeric data to the Prefix field box and supply a prefix with no number. Using the same example, the readout would appear something like this: A000 (10 of 100), where A000 is the prefix and no number follows.

    The remaining options in the Style pull-down menu are specific choices for styles of page numbers. If you have front matter where you want to use Roman numerals, you can choose between the two styles shown in Figure 15.23. Alpha characters offer you options for uppercase or lowercase letters, and integers are also available. You can combine these options with special characters by typing data in the Prefix field box.

**FIGURE 15.23**

Select number styles from the Style pull-down menu.

- **Prefix.** Type any character, number, or combination of numbers and characters in the field box for a prefix value. The prefix precedes the numbering scheme defined in the Style pull-down menu.

- **Start.** The Start item is used to indicate the number a new section starts with. Typically you use 1 to start a new section, but you can begin sections with any number you want to type in the field box. Occasionally, you may have a document where page insertions might be added later. You can number pages in a section and leave room for new additions to be made later in another editing session.

- **Extend numbering used in preceding section to selected pages.** For this option you need to select a range of page thumbnails in the Pages panel, and then open the Page Numbering dialog box. Selecting the radio button and clicking OK removes the currently assigned numbers and extends the previous section. For example, you may have Appendix A numbered A-1 through A-10. You later decide to combine Appendix B with Appendix A. Appendix B might be numbered B-1 through B-10. To extend the previous B numbered pages, you select the page thumbnails in the Pages panel, open the dialog box, and select this radio button. When you click OK, pages formerly numbered B-1 through B-10 are changed to A-11 through A-20.

## Tip

If you have multiple files you want to renumber, use a custom action to renumber a folder of PDF files. For more information on custom actions, see Chapter 17. Note that using a batch sequence for renumbering pages is limited to renumbering each document individually. You cannot consecutively number multiple files using a batch sequence for page numbering. ■

## Using Bates numbering

Bates numbering is a method to keep multiple documents in a recognizable order. The legal industry uses Bates numbering when identifying legal documents in court cases. During the discovery phase of a case in litigation, there might be an enormous number of documents submitted as evidence. A Bates numbering system is used to provide an arbitrary unique identifier for each document. The numbers are typically numeric, but they can also be alpha-numeric. There is no standardized algorithm used for a Bates numbering schema in a court case for assigning numbers to documents; however, the numbers are generally eight or more characters in length. An example of a schema that might be used to disclose documents in the legal environment is shown in Figure 15.24.

Rather than open a PDF document in Acrobat and number each file individually, the Bates numbering feature lets you batch process multiple files and add unique numbers in a numeric order to multiple files without opening them.

**FIGURE 15.24**

An example of Bates numbers that might be used in a court case

| Company | Sequence | Length <char> | Example | Multi-page divider | Example Muli-page divider | |
|---|---|---|---|---|---|---|
| Universal Gas & Electric | numeric | 10 | 2005684511 | slash / | 1001453289/5049 | |
| Small Town USA | numeric | 8 | 15678907 | slash / | 10296733/002194 | |
| ACE Construction | alphanumeric | 11 | ACE45876302 | space dash | ACE04876932 -1189 | |
| Edwards Trust | alphanumeric | 9 | ETU45632 | space asterisk | ETU94560 *1022 | |
| ATC | numeric | 8 | 08145633 | not applicable | Start Bates: 45350001 | End Bates: 45350871 |
| Ewings & Sons | numeric | 10 | 0258942356 | not applicable | Start Bates: 0250000001 | End Bates: 0250009657 |
| GC Equipment Corporation | numeric | 7 | 2034537 | dash | 5635891-56890 | |

To see how the Bates numbering feature works in Acrobat, follow these steps.

## STEPS: Adding Bates Numbers to Multiple PDFs

1. **Open the Bates Numbering dialog box.** Open the Pages panel and click Bates Numbering ⇨ Add. The Bates Numbering dialog box shown in Figure 15.25 opens.

2. **Select files to number.** Open the Add pull-down menu and choose Add Files. The Add Files dialog box opens, where you select files you want to add to the Bates Numbering dialog box. Select files from a folder or multiple folders and click the Add Files button, and the files appear in the Bates Numbering dialog box as shown in Figure 15.25.

3. **Order the documents.** Click a document and click the Up or Down buttons to organize the files in the order you want them to appear. Because the Bates numbering system uses no standardized algorithm and the numbers are arbitrary, you don't need to worry about organizing files according to dates, topics, and so on. Simply make some order arrangement that you want based on whatever criteria you elect to use.

4. **Click OK.**

**FIGURE 15.25**

Add files for Bates numbering in the Bates Numbering window.

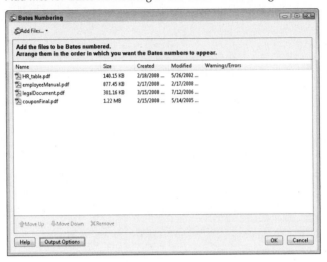

5. **Add the number schema for the select documents.** When you click OK, a slightly modified version of the Add Header and Footer dialog box opens, as shown in Figure 15.26. You can align the numbers left, center, or right by clicking in the Left, Center, or Right Header or Footer text box and then clicking the Insert Bates Number button.

   When you click Insert Bates Number, the Bates Numbering System dialog box opens. Add the total digits (including alpha characters if you use alpha characters for a number schema) in the Number of Digits text box. You have an option to type the start number, a prefix, and a suffix. Click OK, and the Bates number is shown in the field box respective to your selection. In Figure 15.26, I added a three-character prefix and six numbers for my numbering schema.

6. **Add the numbers to your selected documents.** Click OK in the Add Header and Footer dialog box and the numbers are added to all the selected PDFs. In Figure 15.27, you see one of several files where I added a Bates number. Each number in all documents is a unique number following the schema I identified in the Add Header and Footer dialog box.

**FIGURE 15.26**

Click inside the text box where you want your Bates numbers to appear and click Insert Bates Number. Add the numbering schema in the Bates Numbering System dialog box and click OK. Your Bates numbering schema then appears in the text box.

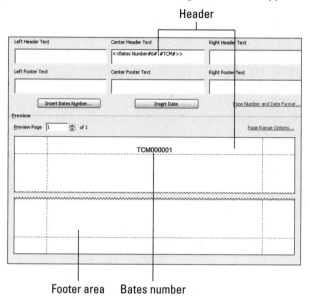

Header

Footer area    Bates number

**FIGURE 15.27**

A file where the Bates number was added as a footer

July 17, 1994

Memo:

Jim Hassleweder:

Dear Jim,

We are experiencing unusual levels of radiation in plant 17. I recommend we look into immediately diverting energy from surrounding plants and shut 17 down until we can determine the source of the problem. We are currently at unsafe levels.

Ed

TCM002467

## Removing Bates numbers

Removing Bates numbers is handled differently depending on whether a document is open in the Document pane and whether Bates numbers are actually included in the files where you want to eliminate the numbers. The various behaviors include the following:

- **No documents open in Document pane.** Choosing Header & Footer ⇨ Remove in the Pages panel opens the Header & Footer dialog box shown in Figure 15.28. You can remove Bates numbers using this dialog box.

- **Document open with no Bates number.** If you have a document open but the document contains no Bates number, an alert dialog box opens informing you that no Bates numbers are detected.

- **Document open with Bates number.** If you open a document that does contain Bates numbers, no dialog box opens. The numbers are removed by Acrobat.

**FIGURE 15.28**

When no documents are open in the Document pane, you can remove Bates numbers from multiple files using the Header & Footer dialog box.

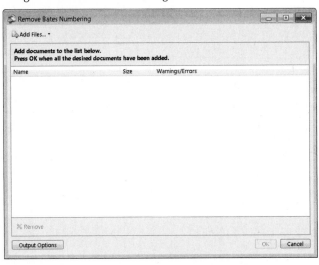

## Creating PDF Portfolios with Bates numbers

If you want to group documents according to a certain Bates numbering schema, first use the Bates Numbering dialog box and add Bates numbers to all your PDF documents. Next, use the Assemble Files into a Portfolio option in the Combine Files task button menu. Create a PDF Portfolio, and all your files are assembled in one PDF collection with Bates numbers.

## Cross-Reference

For information on how to create PDF Portfolios, see Chapter 11. ■

# Adding Watermarks and Backgrounds

You add watermarks and backgrounds in different dialog boxes, but the attributes for both items are almost identical. A few options are different in the Add Watermark dialog box, where you can add custom data in addition to importing files. You can also add a watermark in front of or behind page data. Backgrounds are only added behind page data.

## Adding backgrounds

To add a background to a PDF document, choose Background ➪ Add/Replace in the Pages panel. The Add Background dialog box opens, as shown in Figure 15.29.

---

**FIGURE 15.29**

Choose Background ➪ Add/Replace in the Pages panel to open the Add Background dialog box.

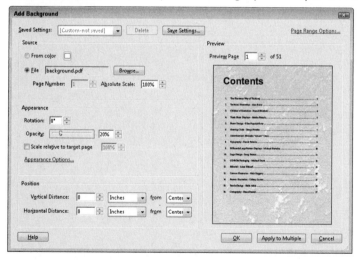

Choices you have for adding backgrounds include the following:

- **Saved Settings.** The options here are the same as when adding headers and footers. See the section "Creating headers and footers" earlier in this chapter.

- **Page Range Options.** Click the text, and the Page Range Options dialog box opens. The same dialog box with the same options is opened as when adding headers and footers. See the section "Creating headers and footers" earlier in this chapter.

- **Source.** Choose From color or File to add a background color or import a file. To change the background color, click the From color radio button, and a color palette opens, where you make a color choice to apply as a background color.

  To add a file for a background, click File and click the Browse button. The Browse dialog box opens where you select a file to import. File types supported include PDF documents, BMP, and JPEG. Note that choices for adding text along with a background are not available. Because the Add Watermark feature appears in a different dialog box, all text options are available only in the Add Watermark dialog box.

- **Appearance.** Several different options are listed in the Appearance settings. These include:

  - **Rotation.** You can rotate backgrounds in 1-degree increments by typing values in the Rotation text box or clicking the up and down arrows.

  - **Opacity.** Opacity adjustments are made by moving the slider, typing values in the text box, or clicking the up and down arrows. In Figure 15.30, objects were rotated in two separate documents. The object on the left was rotated +45 degrees. The object on the right was rotated +135 degrees with an opacity of 20 percent.

**FIGURE 15.30**

Rotations of 45 and 135 degrees. The figure on the right is adjusted for a 20 percent opacity.

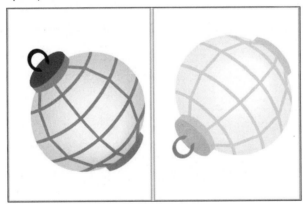

- **Scale relative to target page.** By default, the scaling is set to 100 percent. Type a value in the text box for scaling up or down to the desired value.

- **Appearance Options.** Click the Appearance Options blue text, and the Appearance Options dialog box opens, as shown in Figure 15.31. In the dialog box you can toggle on and off showing backgrounds when printing and when displayed on your monitor.

Click the Appearance Options blue text to open the Appearance Options dialog box. Check the boxes to show or hide a background when printing and when displaying on-screen.

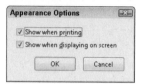

- **Position.** Set options for the position of the background by typing values in the text boxes for Vertical Distance and Horizontal Distance. From the first set of pull-down menus, select a unit of measure. The second set of pull-down menus lets you position the vertical and horizontal placement from Top, Center, and Bottom. In Figure 15.32, the position of an object with the Vertical Distance menu options is shown first, and the object position with the Horizontal Distance menu options is shown second. It also shows how the objects fall on a page when making the menu choices.
- **Preview Page.** In the preview area, you see a page preview of an imported background (or background color if you click the From color radio button). The Preview Page text box is used to type a page number, and the respective page appears in the Preview window. You can toggle through all pages and view the page previews before applying a background. Click OK in the Add Background dialog box, and the background is added to pages in the selected page range.

## Replacing backgrounds

From the Background menu, the item for adding backgrounds and replacing backgrounds opens the same dialog box. Select Background ⇨ Add/Replace in the Pages panel and follow the same steps used for adding a background. If a file contains a background, the new background you select from either a color or a file replaces the old background.

## Updating backgrounds

If you add a background to a PDF file from an image file, and then edit the image file and select Background ⇨ Update in the Pages panel, Acrobat won't update the edited background. A dynamic link is not made from Acrobat to the image file. If you want to update a background imported from an image file, you need to click again on the Browse button and identify your edited image file. Add it as you add a new background and the PDF background is updated.

**FIGURE 15.32**

Nine different positions are available from the pull-down menu choices for Vertical and Horizontal placements.

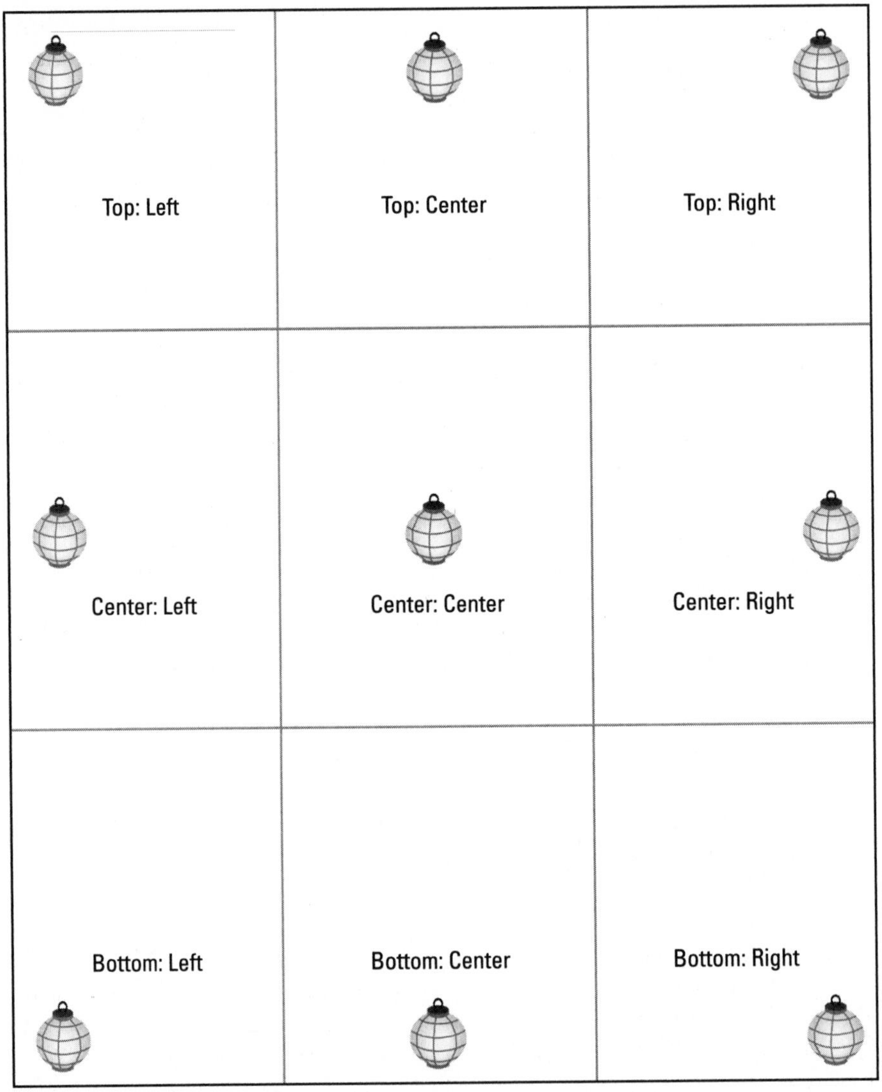

| | | |
|---|---|---|
| Top: Left | Top: Center | Top: Right |
| Center: Left | Center: Center | Center: Right |
| Bottom: Left | Bottom: Center | Bottom: Right |

## Removing backgrounds

As with the menu command for removing headers and footers, you also have a command for removing backgrounds. To remove the current background, select Background ⇨ Remove in the Pages panel and a dialog box opens. Click OK and the background is removed.

# Adding watermarks

Select Watermark ⇨ Add in the Pages panel to add a watermark to a PDF. Watermarks generally appear on top of page data, but in Acrobat 8 through X you can choose to have a watermark appear on top of or behind the page data. The Add Watermark dialog box that opens, as shown in Figure 15.33, is similar to the Add Background dialog box.

The Add Watermark dialog box contains a few different options than the Add Background dialog box. The first noticeable difference is the Source area in the Add Watermark dialog box. The first item and the default selection is Text. You have a text box where text is typed in the Add Watermark dialog box. Below the text box are some options for changing text attributes.

As yet, however, you don't have an option for creating outline text that would be helpful when creating watermarks. The only way to create outline text is to first create it in an illustration program such as Adobe Illustrator and import the text as a graphic in the Add Watermark dialog box.

In the appearance area of the Add Watermark dialog box, you find options for fixed rotations as well as arbitrary rotations. The Location options enable you to place your watermark behind or in front of the page data. The remaining choices are the same as those found in the Add Background dialog box.

**FIGURE 15.33**

Select Watermark ⇨ Add in the Pages panel to open the Add Watermark dialog box.

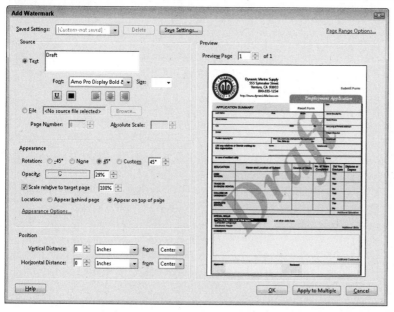

## Tip

Graphics placed behind page data only appear in transparent areas on the page. To quickly check what areas are transparent (as opposed to opaque), open the Preferences dialog box (Ctrl/⌘+K) and click Page Display in the left pane. Click the Show transparency grid check box in the right pane and click OK. All the areas appearing with transparency are shown in the Document pane. ■

To create a watermark on a PDF document, follow these steps.

### STEPS: Adding a Watermark to a PDF Document

1. **Open a file in Acrobat.** Use any PDF document that you want to appear with a watermark.

2. **Open the Add Watermark dialog box.** Click Watermark in the Pages panel and click Add. The Add Watermark dialog box opens.

3. **Type text in the Text box.** In my example, I typed Draft in the text box I'll use for watermarking draft documents.

4. **Set Font attributes.** Select a font from the Font pull-down menu, select a font size, and click the color swatch and choose a color. Note that if you select a particular hue in the color palette and you want that hue to appear lighter, you can reduce opacity with the Opacity slider. For example, to make a light gray, select the default black color and set the opacity to 20 to 30 percent.

5. **Edit appearance settings.** In my example, I wanted the text rotated, so I clicked the 45° radio button. I reduced the opacity of my black color selection to 30 percent and then I clicked the Scale relative to target page check box. This action scaled my text to fit the page size. Note that if you scale text to fit a page, any font size you select in the Source area of the dialog box works.

6. **Edit the location.** Determine whether you want your watermark on top of the page content or behind it. In my example, I wanted the watermark to appear behind my page data so I clicked the Appear behind page radio button.

7. **Preview pages.** Click the Preview Page arrows or type values in the text box to scroll through the pages to which you want to apply your watermark.

8. **Set Appearance Options.** Click the Appearance Options blue text to open the Appearance Options dialog box. Check the boxes to either show or not show the watermark when printing and screen viewing. Another check box is available to keep the watermark position and size constant on different page sizes. Check this box if you're working with files that have different page sizes and click OK.

   - **Set the Page Range.** Click the Page Range Options blue text in the top-right corner of the dialog box to open the Page Range Options dialog box. If you want all pages to appear with a watermark, you don't need to open this dialog box. If you want a page range less than all pages, type the page numbers in the from and to text boxes and click OK.

- **Save the settings.** If this is a watermark you intend to reuse with other documents, you can save the settings and use them whenever you want to apply the same watermark. Click the Save Settings button at the top of the dialog box and the Save Settings dialog box opens. Type a name for your new setting and click OK. The new setting now appears under the Saved Settings pull-down. In Figure 15.34, I added my new Draft settings to the menu.

**FIGURE 15.34**

The Settings menu after I saved my Draft custom setting

- **Click OK.** The watermark is applied to the page range you chose in the Page Range Options dialog box.

## Cross-Reference

If you don't want anyone to tamper with watermarks added to your PDF files such as changing or deleting them, you can secure your file against editing pages using Acrobat Security. For more information on how to secure PDFs, see Chapter 24. ∎

## Removing and updating watermarks

The options for removing and updating watermarks are the same as for removing and updating backgrounds. Click Watermarks and the menu commands appear for Add, Update, and Remove. If you want to modify a saved setting, choose Update. Edit your settings and click OK. Acrobat updates all pages containing watermarks. Clicking Remove in the Watermark menu opens the same dialog box as when removing backgrounds. Click OK and all watermarks are removed.

Note that if you want to remove backgrounds or watermarks from selected pages in a file while keeping backgrounds/watermarks on some pages, clicking the Remove menu item removes all watermarks/backgrounds from your document. You then need to add the watermarks/backgrounds to pages where you want them to appear.

When adding watermarks and backgrounds, you can't select pages in the Pages panel and apply watermarks/backgrounds to selected pages in the pane. You must use the Page Range dialog box to apply watermarks/backgrounds to a page range. Acrobat makes no provision for adding these items to noncontiguous pages. You have to individually apply watermarks/backgrounds to pages in a noncontiguous order.

## Tip

If you want to add a watermark or background on a form enabled with Adobe Reader usage rights, first apply the watermark or background to a PDF, and then enable the file with usage rights. If you attempt to add a watermark or background to an enabled file, you need to save a copy of the file, add the watermark or background, and then reenable the file. (For more information on enabling files with Adobe Reader extensions, see Chapter 18.) ■

# Summary

In this chapter, you explore editing pages and working with the Page Thumbnails pane.

- You can enlarge or reduce page thumbnails through successive menu commands in the Page Thumbnails pane.

- You can open the Page Thumbnails pane to full-screen size where you can sort and reorder pages.

- Page thumbnails can be used to navigate pages and zoom in on pages.

- To copy pages in a PDF document and between PDF documents, you can use page thumbnails.

- Page thumbnails are created on-the-fly when you open the Page Thumbnails pane. If you want to speed up the screen refreshes when opening the Page Thumbnails pane, you can embed thumbnails from a menu option in the Page Thumbnails pane and delete them after your editing sessions.

- Pages are inserted, deleted, extracted, and replaced through menu commands from the Page Thumbnails pane context menu or the Page Thumbnails pane.

- The Split Document command enables you to split files according to page count, file size, and top-level bookmarks.

- You crop PDF pages with the Crop tool. When you crop a page, the page view is reduced to the crop region, but all the original data in terms of page size is still contained in the file. You can return to the Crop Page dialog box and undo crops even after a file has been saved.

- You can rotate PDF pages in 90- and 180-degree rotations via menu commands in the Rotate Pages dialog box.

- Enabling a preference setting for viewing logical pages helps you navigate to pages numbered with integers.

- Opening the Page Numbering dialog box from a context menu in the Page Thumbnails pane or the Page Thumbnails pane enables you to renumber pages in a PDF file.

- To number multiple PDF documents with consecutive numbering, use the Bates Numbering dialog box. To add page numbers to a collection of PDFs without consecutive numbers, use the Batch Processing command.

- To add page numbers to a PDF document, use the Add Header and Footer dialog box.

- You can add different headers and footers to different pages in a PDF document. Each time the content for headers and footers changes, you open the Add Header and Footer dialog box, add the content, and specify the page range.

- To add a background to a document, use the Add Background dialog box. To add a watermark to a file, use the Add Watermark dialog box.

- Backgrounds and watermarks can be updated and removed.

- After you save a PDF with a watermark and/or background, the data are embedded in the PDF document. In Acrobat 8 through X, you can always return to a document and remove backgrounds and watermarks.

# Scanning and OCR Conversion

Welcome to the world of one-stop scanning and text recognition. Anyone who scanned documents in earlier versions of Acrobat will appreciate the one-step operation for scanning a text document and performing text recognition via Acrobat's Optical Character Recognition (OCR) engine and many new enhancements to Acrobat Scan. The one-stop scanning introduced in Acrobat 8 was improved in Acrobat 9 through the implementation of a new scanning technology called ClearScan, the addition of presets that support custom settings you can configure for various source materials, creating multiple files from scanned documents, adding multiple scanned documents to a PDF Portfolio, and much more with Acrobat Scan features.

When performing a scan in Acrobat, you are not limited to scanning documents for text conversions. Acrobat enables you to scan photos and images that might have some other uses. Therefore, this chapter covers all the aspects of scanning from within Acrobat using the Scan to PDF command and the Text Recognition commands.

## IN THIS CHAPTER

**Setting up a scanner**

**Scanning basics**

**Scanning paper documents**

**Working with scanning settings**

**Using WIA-compliant scanners**

**Scanning workflows**

**Correcting OCR errors**

**Exporting OCR text**

**Scanning forms**

## Configuring Scanners

Before you can scan a page in Acrobat, you need to configure your scanner and be certain it functions properly. After you complete your installation of Acrobat, it should recognize your scanner immediately. If all the scanner hardware is in place and operational and Acrobat still does not recognize your scanner, the next step is to be certain Acrobat recognizes the scanner's software. If Acrobat doesn't see your scanner, you may need to relocate software to another location on your hard drive or acquire a software update from your scanner manufacturer.

You get access to your scanner in Acrobat through one of three methods: TWAIN drivers, Acquire plug-ins, or WIA-compliant drivers.

## Using TWAIN software

TWAIN (Technology With An Important Name) software is manufacturer-supplied and should be available on the CD-ROM you receive with your scanner. In Windows, the TWAIN files are stored in the \Windows\twain_32 folder. When you install scanner software, the TWAIN driver should find the proper folder through the installer routine. On the Mac you'll find TWAIN resources in the System\Library\Image Capture\TWAIN Data Sources folder.

Many scanner manufacturers produce the equipment but use third-party developers to write the software. Adobe has certainly not tested the Scan plug-in with all scanner manufacturers and all software developers, but many of the popular brands have been thoroughly tested to work seamlessly with Acrobat. Theoretically, the TWAIN software should work in most cases. If you have problems accessing your scanner from within Acrobat, but can perform scans in other applications, then you most likely have a problem with the TWAIN driver. If this is the case, contact your scanner manufacturer and see whether it has an upgrade or whether you can get some technical support. In many cases, you can download upgrades for registered software on the Internet.

## Using Adobe Photoshop plug-in software

Acrobat supports Acquire plug-ins to use with Adobe Photoshop. More prevalent than TWAIN drivers, Photoshop plug-ins are available from just about every scanner manufacturer. If you use Adobe Photoshop or Adobe Photoshop Elements, you may need to copy your Photoshop Acquire plug-in to your Acrobat plug-ins folder. On Windows, copy the Photoshop Acquire plug-in and open the Acrobat\plug_ins\PaperCapture folder and paste your Acquire plug-in.

Mac OS X requires you to expand the Acrobat X Pro package in order to paste your Photoshop Acquire plug-in. To do so, follow these steps:

1. **Open your Applications/Adobe Acrobat X Pro folder and select (not double-click) Adobe Acrobat X Pro.**

2. **Ctrl+click to open a context menu, and select Show Package Contents.** The Contents folder appears in the Adobe Acrobat X Pro folder.

3. **Double-click the Contents folder and double-click the Plug-ins folder that comes into view.**

4. **Double-click the PaperCapture.acroplugin folder and drag your Photoshop Acquire plug-in into this folder.** (Option+click+drag to copy the plug-in to the target folder.) When you close the folders, the package is restored.

# Configuring Windows Imaging Architecture scan drivers (Windows only)

TWAIN drivers have been around for a long time and many developers are still supporting TWAIN drivers, but many newer scanners are now supporting a more recent driver technology called Windows Imaging Architecture (WIA). WIA is a Microsoft-developed technology that provides developers a relatively easy way to write support for scanners. Developers such as Acer, Compaq, Epson, Fujitsu, HP, Kodak, Microtek, Ricoh, and UMAX have all embraced WIA in many of their newer models.

The good news from Adobe is that if you have a WIA-supported scanner you can configure your scanner's scan button with Acrobat. To do so, open the Start Menu and choose Control Panels ➪ Scanners and cameras ➪ <scanner name> (on Windows 7, open the Start menu and choose Devices and Printers). The Scanners and Cameras (or Devices and Printers) window opens. Click your scanner name, click the Properties button to open the scanner properties on Windows, and then right-click the scanner name and choose Properties.

The WIA scanner properties dialog box opens as shown in Figure 16.1. Select your scanner's Scan, Copy, Photo, or other button you want to activate. When using scanners with a button to initiate a scan, choose the Scan button. Click the Start the Program radio button. Click OK; the next time you hit your Scan button on your scanner, the scan is opened in Adobe Acrobat.

---

**FIGURE 16.1**

Choose an event and click OK.

---

## Scanners and PDF

PDF is so popular that just about every developer in one market or another is supporting the Portable Document Format. Today, you find the support for PDF broadening with scanner developers. Many new scanner models support hardware buttons on the scanners for scanning to a PDF file. Additionally, you can find scanner proprietary software supporting scanning to PDF.

In some cases you can find scanners that do marvelous jobs of scanning to PDF files, but they don't support WIA architecture or TWAIN drivers — such is the case with the Fujitsu Scansnap 510 scanner. In these cases, you can use the scanner's button or the software to scan to PDF. Once the file is scanned to PDF it typically opens in Acrobat, where you can recognize text and populate forms with form fields.

# Understanding Scanning Essentials

At this point you should have your scanner and Acrobat configured properly. Before I begin discussing how to use your scanner with Acrobat, take a moment to understand some of the essential issues to deal with in performing clean, accurate scans. A few items need to be discussed: the hardware and hardware-related issues; the types of scans to be produced; and understanding your scanner capabilities. A few moments here saves you much time in producing the best scans you can expect from your equipment.

The hardware issue to consider is your scanner. The single most important issue with scanner hardware is keeping the platen clean. If you have dust and dirt on the glass, these particles show up in your scans. Keep the platen clean, and use a lint-free cloth to clean the glass. If you use a solvent, always apply the solvent to the cloth and not the scanner glass.

## Preparing a document

Just as your scans can benefit from careful attention to your scanner, exercising a little care with the source material can help produce clean scans. Bits of dust, improperly aligned pages, poor contrast, and degraded originals affect your ability to create scans that the text recognition software can read without many errors. A little preparation before scanning saves you much time in trying to clean up poorly scanned images.

## Photocopying originals

Sometimes you can improve image and text contrast by photocopying original documents. Try some experiments to test your results. Placing photocopies made from large, bulky material on the scanner bed ultimately results in better scans than when using the original material.

## Ensuring straight alignment

If you have documents with frayed edges or pages torn from a magazine, trim the edges and make them parallel to the text on the page. Precise placement of pages on the scanner bed facilitates clean scans. Even though Acrobat has a recognition capability within a 14-degree rotation, the straighter the page, the better the results. Acrobat 8 and 9 can actually rotate a scan 90 degrees and 180 degrees, and new text recognition improvements are spectacular with pages rotated 180 degrees. However, as a matter of practice, try to keep the source material rotated in the proper portrait view on the scanner platen.

## Caution

Be certain to observe copyright laws when scanning published material. If you scan text from books and magazines, you need to obtain permission from the publisher before using the material. ∎

Try to remember the axiom "garbage in, garbage out" when you approach any kind of scanning. The better the source material, the better your scanned results. Exercise a little care in the beginning, and your Acrobat scanning sessions move along much faster.

# Using Scan to PDF

As I mentioned in the beginning of this chapter, Acrobat offers you one-step scanning and OCR conversion. Before getting into all the options in dialog boxes and what they mean, let's look at scanning a document and recognizing text.

## Scanning on Windows

Scanning on Windows and the Mac follows a similar path, but there are some differences in the options you have available on one platform versus the other. For Windows users, follow the steps below to scan a document and recognize the text.

### STEPS: Scanning a Text Document (Windows)

1.  **Place a document on the scanner platen.** Be certain your scanner is configured and operational.
2.  **Choose File ⇨ Create ⇨ PDF FromScanner ⇨ Custom Scan.** Alternately, you can click the Create task button and choose PDF From Scanner ⇨ Custom Scan. The Custom Scan dialog box opens, as shown in Figure 16.2.

## Note

You have several submenu options on Windows to choose from for scanning to a PDF. If you haven't configured presets, try using the Custom Scan operation first. Later in this chapter in the section "Working with presets" you'll learn how to configure the presets. ∎

**FIGURE 16.2**

The Custom Scan dialog box opens after you select Create ⇨ PDF From Scanner ⇨ Custom Scan.

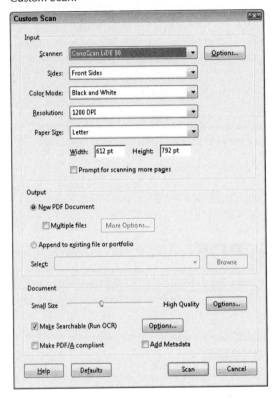

3. **Select your scanner.** The first task is to be certain your scanner appears listed on the Scanner pull-down menu in the Custom Scan dialog box. If you don't see your scanner here, then you have a configuration problem. Assuming everything is working okay, select your scanner as shown in Figure 16.2.

4. **Select the resolution.** From the Resolution pull-down menu choose a resolution setting. Higher resolutions take longer but produce much better results. At a minimum you should use 300 dpi for the scan resolution.

5. **Paper size.** Choose a paper size for the artwork. If you use A4 paper, be sure to make the choice here for A4. Also, if using US Letter paper, make the choice accordingly.

6. **Select the output.** If you have a document open in the Document pane, you can append your document with the new scan. If you want to create a separate document, click New PDF Document in the Output section of the Custom Scan dialog box.

7. **Set document quality.** For a first-time effort, leave the slider at the default.

8. **Make searchable.** Check the box for Make Searchable (Run OCR). This check box informs Acrobat to use the OCR engine to convert the scanned image to recognizable text.

9. **Click Scan.** Leave the remaining items at the defaults and click the Scan button to commence scanning. Note that the resolution settings, paper size, and clicking the Scan button apply to WIA-compliant scanners. If your scanner is not WIA compliant, you may need to use a TWAIN driver that automatically opens your scanner interface. In your scanner's software, you need to make choices for the items you don't have available in Acrobat and click the Scan button.

10. **Check the document for recognizable text.** Click the Select tool in the Toolbar Well and drag through the document. You should see the text selected as you drag, as shown in Figure 16.3.

**FIGURE 16.3**

The scanned document appears in Acrobat with selectable text.

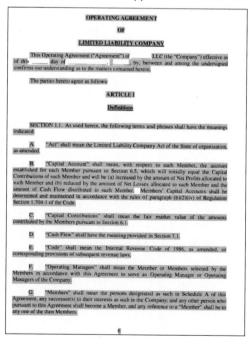

## Scanning on the Mac

Some of the new features related to setting up scanning presets are not available to Mac users. In addition, you don't have WIA support on the Mac. All your scanning occurs using a

TWAIN driver and making choices for scan attributes in your scanner's software. To create a scan in Acrobat on the Mac and recognize text, do the following.

### STEPS: Scanning a Text Document (Mac)

1. **Place a document on the scanner platen.** Be certain your scanner is configured and operational.

2. **Select Create ⇨ PDF From Scanner.** Alternately, you can click the Create task button and choose Create PDF From Scanner. The Acrobat Scan dialog box opens as shown in Figure 16.4.

**FIGURE 16.4**

Choose File ⇨ Create ⇨ PDF From Scanner to open the Acrobat Scan dialog box.

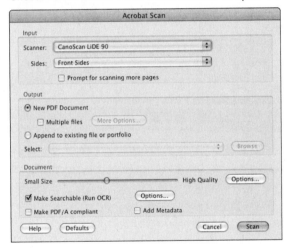

3. **Choose your scanner.** Open the Scanner pull-down menu and choose your scanner.

4. **Leave the settings at the defaults and click Scan.** The default settings are set up to create a new PDF document and make your text searchable. Leave the settings at the defaults and click Scan to open your scanner's software via the TWAIN driver.

5. **Set the scan attributes.** Make choices for resolution, color mode, and page size in your scanner's interface. In Figure 16.5 you can see a scanner interface that was opened from Acrobat using a TWAIN driver.

6. **Click Scan.** Click the Scan button to commence scanning. The converted file opens in Acrobat with recognizable text.

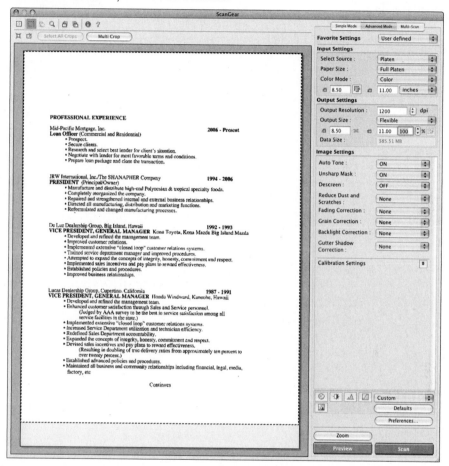

**FIGURE 16.5**

Set scan attributes in your scanner software.

# Using Acrobat Scan (Windows and Mac)

There are two different dialog boxes that open when you choose Create ⇨ PDF From Scanner. For WIA-compliant scanners on Windows only, you have a number of different options you can choose from within Acrobat. If you use a TWAIN driver that opens your scanner software to create a scan, the Acrobat Scan dialog box has much fewer options.

To differentiate the options, you have scanner settings in either the Custom Scan dialog box (like Figure 16.2) or when setting up scan presets using WIA-compliant scanners. If using a TWAIN driver, you open the Acrobat Scan dialog box (like Figure 16.4).

# Setting options in Acrobat Scan

Beginning at the top of the Acrobat Scan dialog box (refer to Figure 16.2), Input options you have available when using a TWAIN driver include:

- **Scanner.** The pull-down menu is used to select your scanner. When the scanner is online and recognized by Acrobat, you'll see the scanner plug-in software name appear in a pull-down menu. Some scanning software may not enable you to see other options such as Color Mode and Resolution in the Acrobat Scan dialog box. If these items are not available, you'll need to make the choices in the scanner plug-in. When you first select Acrobat Scan, a dialog box informs you that the Native Scanners Interface can't be hidden. In such a case, you need to make choices in your plug-in software.

- **Sides.** Choose from Single or Both sides. If your scanner is capable of scanning both sides of a paper document, the scan can be completed in one step. If your scanner doesn't support two-sided scanning, Acrobat pauses the scan and permits you to turn the paper over on the scanner platen.

- **Prompt for scanning more pages.** Check this box for multiple-pages scanning when using scanners without document feeders.

- **New PDF Document.** Click the radio button to create a scan that opens as a new PDF file. If you want to scan multiple pages and create separate new pages for each scan, check the Multiple files check box.

- **Append to existing file or portfolio.** You can append a scan to a file that is open in the Document pane where you make choices from the pull-down menu, or that you choose from your hard drive by clicking the Browse button. You can also add a scan to an existing PDF Portfolio.

## Cross-Reference

For more information on PDF Portfolios, see Chapter 11. ■

- **Optimization.** The slider is used to adjust the quality of the scanned image. This quality setting has nothing to do with text recognition. Click the Options button to open the Optimization Options dialog box as shown in Figure 16.6. The default choice is Automatic. When you click Custom Settings, you can make choices for various optimization settings. Your choices include:

  - **Compression.** For color/grayscale images, choose from Adaptive or JPEG for file compression. JPEG files result in smaller file sizes, but you experience data loss. In many cases the data loss may have no effect on appearance or Acrobat's ability to recognize text. If you do experience problems, try using Adaptive compression.

    Monochrome images are compressed with three different compression schemes depending on the choice made from the pull-down menu. JBIG2 is a JPEG compression scheme with little data loss. You can also use Adaptive like that used for color/grayscale images and CCITT Group 4, which is a common compression used by fax machines. When applying compression to images, try the defaults (Adaptive for color/grayscale and JBIG2 for monochrome) first. If your scans are presenting visual problems or Acrobat has difficulty in recognizing text, experiment with the other settings.

**FIGURE 16.6**

Click Options to open the Optimization Options dialog box.

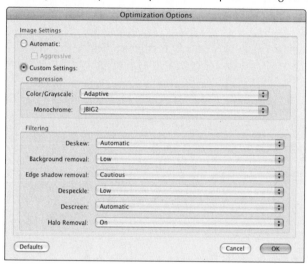

You can adjust the quality slider for the amount of compression applied to the scans. As you move the slider left, the file size is smaller but the image quality is reduced. Move the slider toward Higher if you experience problems with text recognition.

- **Deskew.** Acrobat automatically straightens crooked scans when Deskew is set to automatic. To turn off the deskewing, select Off from the pull-down menu.

- **Background removal.** Removes background data. Use this option and choose from Low, Medium, High, or Off from menu choices. When text has drop shadows or original paper copies show dust and dirt, play with the amount settings to sharpen the text.

- **Edge shadow removal.** If you want to scan in grayscale or color mode, Acrobat can eliminate levels of gray where shadows appear around type. For cleaner text scans, enable this option. Note that you need to have crisp, clean originals to see much of a difference between scanning with the option enabled versus disabled. Two settings are used for Cautious and Aggressive as well as Off. Use Aggressive for more removal.

- **Despeckle.** This item and descreen are particularly helpful when scanning documents that have been printed and are subject to moiré patterns (a condition common when scanning printed documents) or when scanning documents with dust and dirt.

- **Descreen.** Use Descreen like Despeckle mentioned previously when scanning printed documents and screened type.

- **Halo Removal.** Artifacts creating halo effects around type can be cleaned up by setting this option to On.

- **Make Searchable (Run OCR).** You can instruct Acrobat to recognize text using OCR at the time a document is scanned. If you disable this check box you can later use a menu command to run Acrobat's OCR engine. Clicking the Options button opens the Recognize Text – Settings dialog box shown in Figure 16.7. See "Setting text recognition options" later in this chapter.

- **Make PDF/A Compliant.** Check this radio button to make a PDF/A-compliant file.

## Cross-Reference

For more information on PDF/compliance, see Chapter 17. ■

- **Add Metadata.** If you check this box, the Document Properties Description dialog box opens after your scan is completed and the text recognized. You can add Title, Author, Subject, and Keywords to the Document Properties.

## Cross-Reference

For more information about editing Document Properties, see Chapter 6. ■

## Tip

The filtering options you have in Figure 16.6 are also available when choosing Optimize Scanned PDF in the Document Processing panel. Choosing this command opens the Optimize Scanned PDF dialog box. This command offers you an option to optimize scanned documents after scanning and after adding form fields when scanning forms. ■

## Setting text recognition options

If scanning for OCR, check the box for Make Searchable (Run OCR). If you want to scan images, remove the check mark from this option. For searchable text, you have more choices when you click the Options button. Clicking this button opens the Recognize Text – Settings dialog box. As shown in Figure 16.7, you have three choices for PDF Output style, which determine how the text recognition is performed:

- **Primary OCR Language.** By default, Acrobat installs 42 language dictionaries available for OCR. If you scan documents from any of the supported languages, select the appropriate language in the pull-down menu in the Recognize Text – Settings dialog box.

- **PDF Output Style.** From the pull-down menu shown in Figure 16.7, your options are as follows:

  - **ClearScan.** In earlier versions of Acrobat, this item was called Formatted Text & Graphics. When using the legacy format or the newer ClearScan technology, the bitmapped image is discarded and replaced with searchable text and graphics. If there is an instance where the OCR engine does not have confidence, the original bitmap is left in place and the best guess is placed behind, mimicking the "Searchable Image" style.

    Formatted Text and Graphics had some problems related to color images. The newer ClearScan technology does a much better job of converting scanned images to text and file sizes are much smaller.

  - **Searchable Image.** Text is also placed behind the original image, preserving the integrity of the original documents. The image scan is compressed to reduce file size. Some of the quality of the original scan is lost.

  - **Searchable Image (Exact).** This option keeps the image scan in the foreground with text placed in the background. The appearance of the scanned image does not change. Text is added on a hidden layer that gives you the capability of creating indexes and performing searches. Use this option when you don't want to change a document's appearance, but you do want to be able to search the text of that document. Something on the order of a legal document or a certificate might be an example of such a document. This option produces the largest file sizes.

## Note

See the "Searchable Images versus ClearScan" sidebar in this chapter for more details on the differences among the PDF output styles. ■

- **Downsample Images.** This option enables you to downsample images or keep them at the original scanned resolution. If None is selected, no downsampling is applied to images. The remaining options offer downsampling values at 600 dots per inch (dpi), 300 dpi, 150 dpi, and 72 dpi.

---

**FIGURE 16.7**

---

Open the PDF Output Style drop-down menu and choose from one of three options for performing the OCR.

## Searchable Images versus ClearScan

When you search OCR pages with either Searchable Image (Exact) or Searchable Image, the pages are image files with searchable text. The original file is an image file produced from your scan designed to be viewed as an original, unaltered document. This option enables you to electronically archive documents for legal purposes or when unaltered originals need to be preserved.

When you convert a document with Recognize Text Using OCR, the OCR conversion places text behind the scan. The intent is for you to be able to archive files and search them either through using the Search panel to search files on your hard disk or by searching an index where these documents have been catalogued.

The text behind PDF Image is not editable with Acrobat. However, Adobe Acrobat Capture 3.0 does have tools to edit text in a PDF Image file. If Recognize Text Using OCR misinterprets a word, you cannot make corrections to the text. The text is selectable, and you can copy the text and paste it into a word processor or text editor. If you want to examine the OCR suspects, paste the text into a word processor and review the document. Or buy a copy of Adobe Acrobat Capture 3.0 to do the edits from within the PDF file.

To copy text from a PDF Image format, select the Select tool. Click the cursor anywhere in the text and choose Edit⇨Select All (Ctrl/⌘+A). Open a context menu and select Copy File to Clipboard. Open a word processor and choose Edit⇨Paste. You may find the number of suspects to be too many to be usable. If you want to improve the OCR conversion, return to the Create PDF from Scanner dialog box and rescan the file with a higher resolution or different scanning mode.

ClearScan files (previously referred to as PDF Formatted Text & Graphics in Acrobat 6 and later) are scanned documents converted to text. When you select ClearScan in the Recognize Text dialog box, the file conversion is made to a PDF with scalable text and graphics. Recognize Text reads the bitmap configuration of words and converts them to text. This text can be edited and altered on a page. When you make text corrections, you see the changes reflected on the document page.

When capturing pages, be certain to view the options and know the difference between capturing pages as PDF Scanned Image and ClearScan documents.

After you make choices in the Recognize Text – Settings dialog box and click OK, you return to the Acrobat Scan dialog box. Click Scan and the OCR engine use the last settings you made in the Recognize Text – Settings dialog box.

# Using WIA Scan Drivers (Windows)

If you have a WIA-compliant scanner, your options for scanning from within Acrobat are much more plentiful than using the Acrobat Scan 5-button scan operation. Acrobat Scan is easy to use, but it offers fewer options than Scan to PDF on Windows.

# Working with presets

Presets are settings you can configure and retain to perform scans with a set of options that you define or that Adobe creates as a series of defaults.

Acrobat provides you with several presets used with black and white, grayscale, and color documents, and with color images. The settings for scanning each of these types of documents are preset for you. You can use them *out of the box,* or you can configure each preset for your own personal needs.

Adobe's intent is to help you simplify your scanning and OCR recognition by setting up some general options that apply for scanning a range of original document types. However, you may have some special needs. For example, you may be scanning a different paper size than the default choice for one of the scanning presets, or you may want to scan at a different resolution than the choice added to a given preset. If this is the case, you'll want to change a preset to suit your own personal scanning needs.

Take a quick look at some of the options you have available when you first start a scan. Choose Create ➪ PDF From Scanner and the submenu opens as shown in Figure 16.8. From the menu choices you have the four preset choices, a choice for Custom Scan, and a choice for Configure Presets. The Custom Scan choice is provided in case you have a scan where you want to deviate from all the presets and choose your options prior to a scan — more like a one-time use. The last item in the submenu is Configure Presets. Choose this option to configure any one of the first four presets listed in the menu.

---

**FIGURE 16.8**

Choose File ➪ Create ➪ From Scanner or click the Create task button and choose Create PDF From Scanner to open the submenu where the preset commands are listed.

To edit a preset, do the following.

## STEPS: Editing a Preset

1. **Choose File ➪ Create ➪ PDF From Scanner ➪ Configure Presets.** The Configure Presets dialog box opens as shown in Figure 16.9.

2. **Choose your scanner.** Open the Scanner pull-down menu and choose the scanner you want to use. If you have multiple scanners, all scanners configured properly appear in the menu.

3. **Choose the preset you want to edit.** From the Presets pull-down menu choose the preset you want to edit as shown in Figure 16.9.

Choose File ⇨ Create ⇨ PDF From Scanner ⇨ Configure Presets to open the Configure Presets dialog box.

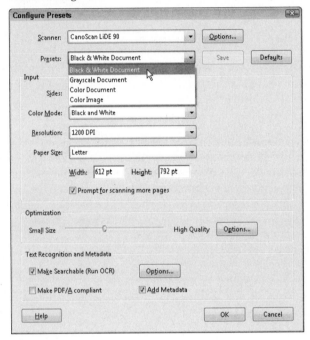

4. **Change the attributes.** From the options shown in the Configure Presets dialog box, use the menus and text boxes to make the changes you want for the preset. In my example I edited Resolution and changed my scanner's default A4 paper size to US Letter. For more detail on the options, see the section earlier in this chapter "Setting options in Acrobat Scan."

5. **Save the settings.** Click the Save button to apply your new settings to the preset. The next time you want to scan a document with the new preset, choose File ⇨ Create ⇨ From Scanner ⇨ <preset choice>.

You'll notice that when setting up the paper size you have an option choice from the Paper Size pull-down menu for Custom. Click Custom and edit the Width and Height text boxes to scan custom-size pages.

If you change a preset and you find that the settings have all been configured improperly and you want to start over, simply open the Configure Presets dialog box and choose your edited preset. Click the Defaults button to change the options back to the originally installed preset choices.

## Creating a custom scan

For an occasional scan where options don't exist in one of your presets, you may want to use the File ⇨ Create ⇨ From Scanner ⇨ Custom Scan command, or click the Create task button and choose Create PDF From Scanner ⇨ Custom Scan. Choosing either option opens the Custom Scan dialog box shown earlier in Figure 16.2.

When you perform a scan using the Custom Scan dialog box, you need to address the choices in the dialog box before clicking the Scan button. If you find yourself scanning routinely using the Custom Scan dialog box, open the Configure Presets dialog box and edit a preset.

## Setting scanner options

In both the Configure Preset and Custom Scan dialog box you find a button for Options adjacent to the Scanner pull-down menu. Click this button to open the Scanner Options dialog box (Figure 16.10) where you can make some choices for the transfer method and user interface.

**FIGURE 16.10**

Click the Options button adjacent to the Scanner pull-down menu to open the Scanner Options dialog box.

For the Transfer Method you can choose Native Mode or Memory Mode from the pull-down menu. Both modes prompt you to save your file in a Save dialog box. For faster scanning of multiple pages, choose the Memory Mode option.

For User Interface, choose between options in Acrobat or your scanner's interface. To use the options in the presets and the Custom Scan dialog box, you'll want to choose Hide Scanner's Native Interface. If the pull-down menu is grayed out, you are forced to use your scanner's interface.

The Invert Black and White Images check box is used for scanning white text on a black background. This option is a likely candidate for using the Custom Scan menu choice if you have an occasional piece of artwork designed with white text on a black background. You wouldn't want to change a preset if this type of artwork is used infrequently when scanning.

## Appending scans to files and portfolios

You can open an existing PDF document or PDF Portfolio or choose a file stored on your hard drive and append scans to the document(s). In the Custom Scan dialog box (or when configuring a preset) or when using Acrobat Scan, click the Append to existing file or portfolio radio button.

If you have a document or portfolio open in the document pane, the Select path shows the open document's directory path by default. You can change the path and select another document by clicking the Browse button.

When you scan to a PDF Portfolio, Acrobat prompts you in a dialog box to name your file. Type a name to perform the scan. The file is saved using the filename you add to the Acrobat Scan dialog box shown in Figure 16.11 and appended to a PDF Portfolio. If you scan to a file, the new scan is appended to the selected document and there is no need to type a name for the new scan.

### Cross-Reference
For more information on PDF Portfolios, see Chapter 11. ∎

**FIGURE 16.11**

When scanning to a PDF Portfolio, type a name for the new scan and click OK.

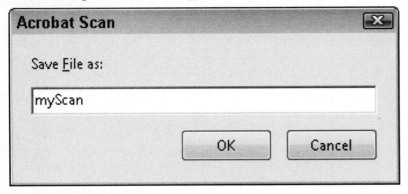

# Creating Workflow Solutions

Scanning individual pages for limited use can easily be handled by the methods described in this chapter. As you scan documents, you need to attend to feeding papers under the scanner lid and manually clicking buttons to continue scanning. If you need to convert large numbers of pages to digital content, you may want to explore other solutions. Depending on how much money you want to spend, you may want to invest in a commercial-grade scanner with a document feeder.

Some scanners support automatic document feeders. If your workflow demands scanning volumes of papers, acquiring a good scanner with an automatic document feeder is a great advantage. When you scan in Acrobat, scanned pages are successively appended to a PDF. Therefore, you can leave a stack of papers in the scanner feeder and leave it unattended. Scanning can be performed automatically overnight. When you return to your computer, the PDF file is complete with recognized text and ready for saving to your hard disk.

## Tip

If you scan using a document feeder, open the Preferences and click Documents in the left pane. In the right pane, click Automatically save document changes to temporary file every [1]. Type 1 in the text box to save your updates every minute. If the scanning operation crashes, you may be able to rescue the file up to the last minute when pages were appended to the document. ■

A more expensive solution, but not out of the question for workflows needing automated means of capturing pages, is to purchase Adobe's stand-alone product, Adobe Acrobat Capture. Combined with a scanner and document feeder, the conversion of scanned images to text is handled in a single operation. You have other solutions from third-party vendors that support industrial-strength scanning and OCR conversion with the capability of converting the final file to PDF format.

## PDF Workflow

Users in government and educational workflows seeking to scan volumes of text for document accessibility will find purchasing auto document feeding scanners and Adobe Acrobat Capture, or other software capable of batch scanning and OCR conversion, to be a much more effective means for converting publications and documents to accessible PDFs. Some hardware screen readers use proprietary software to read TIFF image files for document accessibility. Acrobat PDF is a much better solution over TIFF images and proprietary formats, because once converted to PDF, the document content is searchable and much smaller. If scanning textbooks and government papers is your task, PDF is a much better file format for document accessibility. ■

# Using Text Recognition

You may have files scanned as image files and want to convert them to recognizable text, which is similar to performing OCR tasks in earlier versions of Acrobat. You handle scanning and OCR recognition in one of two ways in Acrobat. You can scan a document and run the OCR recognition in one step, or you can scan documents, save them as PDF files, and later use Acrobat to run the OCR recognition. The latter case might use other scanning programs such as a Photoshop plug-in or a dedicated scanning tool to perform the scans.

If you don't have a scanner or you're looking for a more efficient way to scan documents and recognize text, you can use a digital camera and a copy stand. A digital camera fires off images ten to one over a flatbed scanner, and you can import the images directly into Acrobat and run the Text Recognition command. If using a digital camera be certain to shoot JPEG images and not Camera Raw. Acrobat converts JPEGs to PDF via the Create PDF From File or the Merge Files into a Single PDF commands. Camera Raw conversion is not supported.

If you have scanned image files or digital camera files and you want to convert to searchable text, perform the following steps.

### STEPS: Converting Image Files to Searchable Text

1. **Open files in Acrobat.** Use the File ➪ Create ➪ From File or the File ➪ Create ➪ Merge Files into a Single PDF menu command to convert image files to PDF.

## Cross-Reference

For more information on converting image files to PDF, see Chapter 7. ■

2. **Recognize text.** Select In the Current File under the heading Convert to Searchable Text in the Content panel to open the Recognize Text dialog box shown in Figure 16.12.

3. **Set the PDF output style.** Click the Edit button in the Recognize Text dialog box to open the Recognize Text – Settings dialog box. (This is the same dialog box shown earlier in this chapter in Figure 16.7.) From the PDF Output Style pull-down menu, select ClearScan. If you don't make this selection, you can't change misspelled words later with the changes visible on the document page(s). Click OK to return to the Recognize Text dialog box.

4. **Run the OCR engine.** Click OK to start the OCR engine converting the image file to recognizable text.

**FIGURE 16.12**

Click In Current File in the Content panel to open the Recognize Text dialog box.

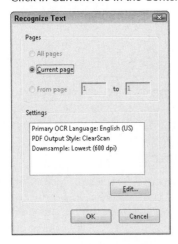

5. **Check for suspect words.** After Acrobat completes the text recognition, open the More menu under Convert To Searchable Text in the Content panel and click Find First OCR Suspect. The Find Element dialog box opens as shown in Figure 16.13. Suspect words are reported in the Suspect text box. If the word is correct as it is reported in the Suspect text box, click Accept and Find to move to the next suspect. If the word is incorrect, type the correct spelling on the document page and click Accept and Find to change the spelling and move to the next suspect. Continue moving through the document until you correct all suspects.

**FIGURE 16.13**

Click Accept and Find if the correct word is displayed in the Find Element dialog box.

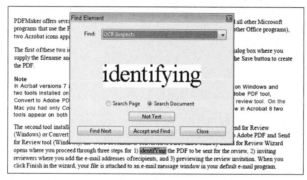

6. **Save the PDF.** Select File ⇨ Save As ⇨ PDF to optimize the file and update your corrections.

# Recognizing text in multiple files

If you set up a workflow where you perform scans on multiple scanners and save files as PDFs or an image format compatible with the Create PDF From File command, you can recognize text in multiple files.

You can also recognize text in multiple documents using a single menu command. Open the More menu in the Content panel and choose In Multiple Files. The files can be saved in any format compatible with the Create PDF From File menu command.

To recognize text in multiple files, follow these steps.

### STEPS: Performing OCR on Multiple Files

1. **Open the More menu in the Content panel and click In Multiple Files.** The Paper Capture Multiple Files dialog box opens.

2. **Add files.** Open the Add Files pull-down menu and choose from one of three menu commands. Add Files enables you to add individual files. Add Folders enables you to add a folder of scans. Add Open Files enables you to add all files open in the Document pane. You can combine choices in the Paper Capture Multiple Files dialog box. For example, you can add individual files, add a folder, and add some files open in Acrobat and list them in the Paper Capture Multiple Files dialog box shown in Figure 16.14.

**FIGURE 16.14**

Open the Add Files pull-down menu and choose files to add to a list for OCR conversion.

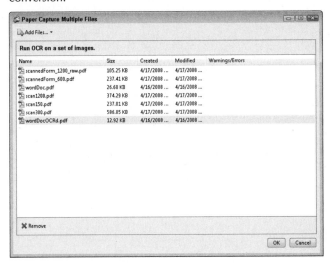

3. **Set the Output options.** Click OK in the Paper Capture Multiple Files dialog box to open the Output Options dialog box as shown in Figure 16.15. Make choices for the folder where you want to save the files, adding text to the filename, and an output format. You can also open the PDF Optimizer and choose optimization settings for the saved files.

4. **Click OK to start the OCR process and save the files.**

## Cross-Reference

For more information on optimizing files using the PDF Optimizer, see Chapter 17. ■

**FIGURE 16.15**

Make choices in the Output Options dialog box and click OK.

## Understanding suspect words

A *suspect* word is one that the OCR engine interprets differently from the closest match found in the Primary OCR Language Dictionary. The word is suspect because it doesn't have a match in the Primary OCR Language Dictionary. You might have proper names, industry terminology, abbreviations, and so on that the OCR engine marks as suspects. Simply because the word(s) is marked as a suspect doesn't necessarily require changing the word. Therefore, when you review suspects, you have two choices: Either change the word to a correct spelling or inform Acrobat to leave it as is and move to the next suspect.

After the Recognize Text dialog box closes, the converted page(s) doesn't appear any different from before you began the OCR conversion. In order to see any words that may have been misinterpreted during the conversions, you need to access a menu command and tell Acrobat you want to view the suspect words. You have two choices in the OCR Text Recognition submenu.

## Note

**In order to correct OCR suspects in Acrobat, you need to convert pages with the ClearScan output style. ■**

If you open the Recognize Text panel and click Find First Suspect, Acrobat shows the first word that it interprets as a suspect, which means the interpretation of the OCR engine did not exactly match a word in its dictionary. The suspect word is highlighted in the document pane.

If you open the Recognize Text panel and click Find All Suspects, all the suspect words are highlighted with a red border across all pages converted. At a glance you can see the number of suspects that need to be reviewed.

## Tip

**When examining suspect words you should plan on zooming in to the suspects. If you prefer to view a page in a zoomed-out view, select the Loupe tool to zoom in on suspect words. You can keep the page view smaller while zooming in on suspects with the Loupe tool. ■**

To leave a word unedited, you can choose either Find Next or Accept and Find. If the OCR engine recognized a graphic (such as a signature) as text, you can also select "Not Text" to return it to the original bitmap image. If you choose Find Next, the bitmap image of the text stays in place and the text behind the bitmap stays as is. When you click the Accept and Find button, the bitmap is thrown away and the word behind the bitmap is promoted to the text location. As you work with the text corrections, realize that you have two layers. The bitmap is the scanned image, and Recognize Text created the text below the scanned image. Therefore, as you edit the text corrections you can choose to throw away the bitmap image on top of the text layer or choose to preserve it. To make a correction, edit a suspect word and click Accept and Find. The new text you edited is promoted to the text layer while the bitmap is thrown away.

## PDF Workflow

**If you want to develop a workflow in an office environment, you may want to have several machines perform the function of scanning documents and have other computers perform OCR functions. You can scan images in software such as Adobe Photoshop and save your files in either an image format or as Photoshop PDFs. The scans can be routed to other workstations used for the OCR conversion. ■**

# Reducing suspects

When you begin a new Acrobat session and want to scan many pages with OCR Text Recognition, scanning one or two pages representative of the pages you want to convert and examining the number of suspects in your sample scan is a good idea. If the suspects outnumber the number of correct interpretations, editing the suspect words could take you more time than typing the document in a word processor. At some point the ratio of the number of suspects to correct words can make capturing pages more of a burden than a solution.

If the number of suspect words is extraordinary, you may want to scan another few pages using different settings. For example, increase the image resolution or scan in a different color mode. Change the attributes in the Acrobat Scan dialog box or adjust settings in your Acquire plug-in to produce scans more suitable for capturing pages. Run Text Recognition and examine the suspects. When a scan results in fewer suspects, you can then go about scanning the remaining pages. In Figure 16.16, I scanned a page at 200 ppi and converted the page with Recognize Text Using OCR. After viewing the number of suspects, I decided to scan the page again with a higher resolution. The results of my OCR suspects with a higher resolution (600 ppi) were significantly reduced, as you can see in Figure 16.17.

---

**FIGURE 16.16**

I scanned a page and converted it with Recognize Text Using OCR. After I chose Find All OCR Suspects, I determined that the number of suspects made this job too difficult to edit in Acrobat.

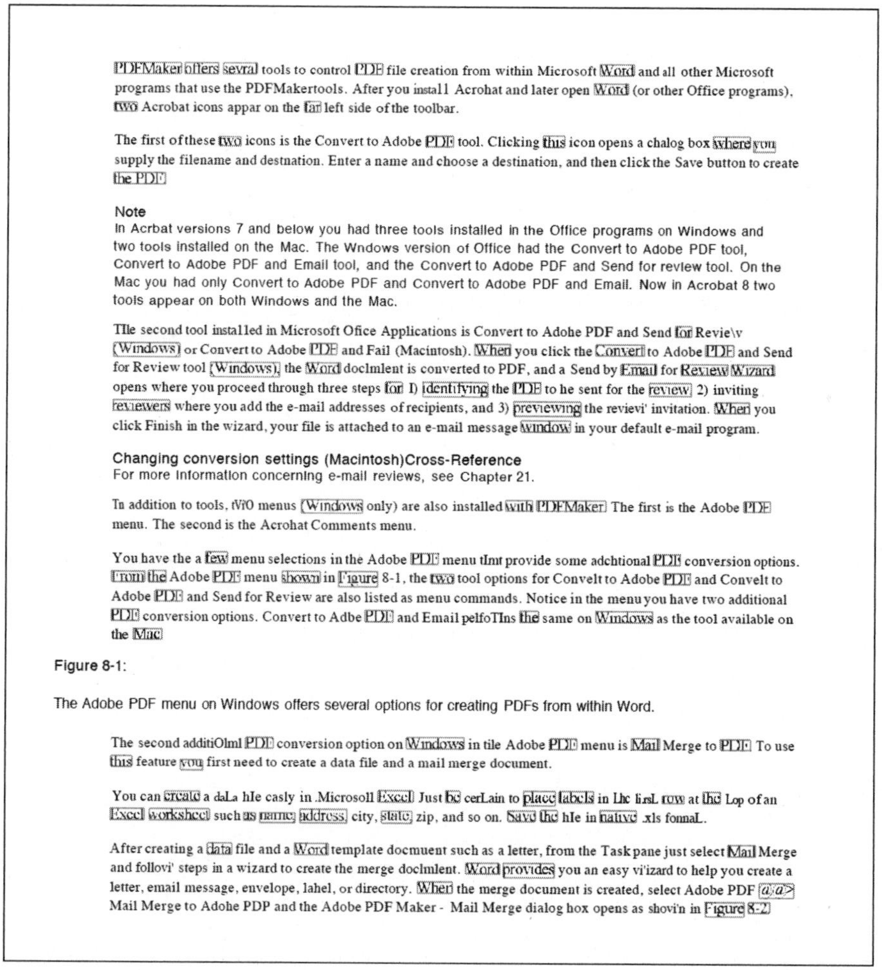

PDFMaker offers sevral tools to control PDF file creation from within Microsoft Word and all other Microsoft programs that use the PDFMakertools. After you install Acrobat and later open Word (or other Office programs), two Acrobat icons appar on the far left side of the toolbar.

The first of these two icons is the Convert to Adobe PDF tool. Clicking this icon opens a chalog box where you supply the filename and destnation. Enter a name and choose a destination, and then click the Save button to create the PDF.

Note
In Acrbat versions 7 and below you had three tools installed in the Office programs on Windows and two tools installed on the Mac. The Wndows version of Office had the Convert to Adobe PDF tool, Convert to Adobe PDF and Email tool, and the Convert to Adobe PDF and Send for review tool. On the Mac you had only Convert to Adobe PDF and Convert to Adobe PDF and Email. Now in Acrbat 8 two tools appear on both Windows and the Mac.

Tlle second tool installed in Microsoft Ofice Applications is Convert to Adobe PDF and Send for Revie\w (Windows) or Convert to Adobe PDF and Fail (Macintosh). When you click the Convert to Adobe PDF and Send for Review tool (Windows), the Word doclment is converted to PDF, and a Send by Email for Review Wizard opens where you proceed through three steps for 1) identifying the PDF to he sent for the review, 2) inviting reviewers where you add the e-mail addresses of recipients, and 3) previewing the reviewi' invitation. When you click Finish in the wizard, your file is attached to an e-mail message window in your default e-mail program.

Changing conversion settings (Macintosh)Cross-Reference
For more information concerning e-mail reviews, see Chapter 21.

Tn addition to tools, tVi0 menus (Windows only) are also installed with PDFMaker. The first is the Adobe PDF menu. The second is the Acrohat Comments menu.

You have the a few menu selections in the Adobe PDF menu tlmt provide some adchtional PDF conversion options. From the Adobe PDF menu shown in Figure 8-1, the two tool options for Convelt to Adobe PDF and Convelt to Adobe PDF and Send for Review are also listed as menu commands. Notice in the menu you have two additional PDF conversion options. Convert to Adbe PDF and Email pelfoTlns the same on Windows as the tool available on the Mac.

Figure 8-1:

The Adobe PDF menu on Windows offers several options for creating PDFs from within Word.

The second additiOlml PDF conversion option on Windows in tile Adobe PDF menu is Mail Merge to PDF. To use this feature you first need to create a data file and a mail merge document.

You can create a daLa hIe casly in .Microsoll Excel Just be cerLain to place labcls in Lhe finL row at the Lop of an Excel worksheet such as name, address, city, statc, zip, and so on. Save the hle in native .xls fonnaL.

After creating a data file and a Word template docmuent such as a letter, from the Task pane just select Mail Merge and follovi' steps in a wizard to create the merge doclmlent. Word provides you an easy vi'izard to help you create a letter, email message, envelope, lahel, or directory. When the merge document is created, select Adobe PDF a a Mail Merge to Adohe PDP and the Adobe PDF Maker - Mail Merge dialog hox opens as shovi'n in Figure 8-2.

FIGURE 16.17

I scanned the same page from Figure 16.16 at a higher resolution and converted it again. Fewer suspects were found and the job of correcting the suspects was more manageable.

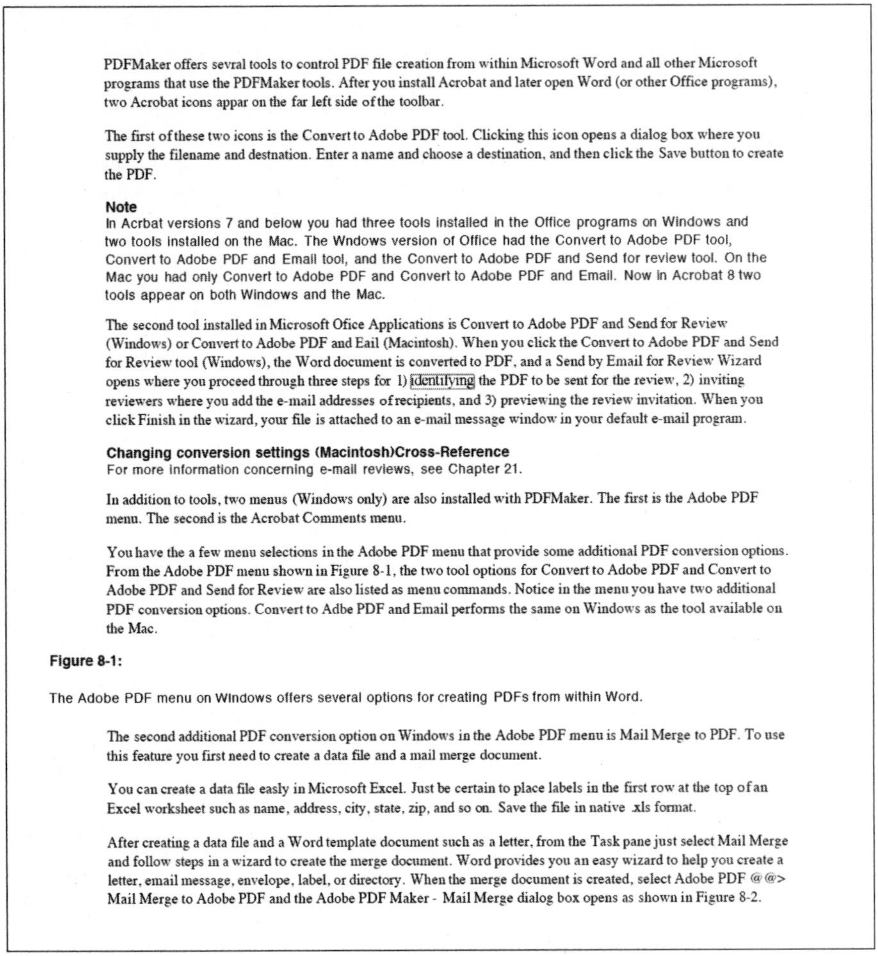

PDFMaker offers sevral tools to control PDF file creation from within Microsoft Word and all other Microsoft programs that use the PDFMaker tools. After you install Acrobat and later open Word (or other Office programs), two Acrobat icons appar on the far left side of the toolbar.

The first of these two icons is the Convert to Adobe PDF tool. Clicking this icon opens a dialog box where you supply the filename and destnation. Enter a name and choose a destination, and then click the Save button to create the PDF.

**Note**
In Acrbat versions 7 and below you had three tools installed in the Office programs on Windows and two tools installed on the Mac. The Wndows version of Office had the Convert to Adobe PDF tool, Convert to Adobe PDF and Email tool, and the Convert to Adobe PDF and Send for review tool. On the Mac you had only Convert to Adobe PDF and Convert to Adobe PDF and Email. Now in Acrobat 8 two tools appear on both Windows and the Mac.

The second tool installed in Microsoft Ofice Applications is Convert to Adobe PDF and Send for Review (Windows) or Convert to Adobe PDF and Eail (Macintosh). When you click the Convert to Adobe PDF and Send for Review tool (Windows), the Word document is converted to PDF, and a Send by Email for Review Wizard opens where you proceed through three steps for 1) identifying the PDF to be sent for the review, 2) inviting reviewers where you add the e-mail addresses of recipients, and 3) previewing the review invitation. When you click Finish in the wizard, your file is attached to an e-mail message window in your default e-mail program.

**Changing conversion settings (Macintosh)Cross-Reference**
For more information concerning e-mail reviews, see Chapter 21.

In addition to tools, two menus (Windows only) are also installed with PDFMaker. The first is the Adobe PDF menu. The second is the Acrobat Comments menu.

You have the a few menu selections in the Adobe PDF menu that provide some additional PDF conversion options. From the Adobe PDF menu shown in Figure 8-1, the two tool options for Convert to Adobe PDF and Convert to Adobe PDF and Send for Review are also listed as menu commands. Notice in the menu you have two additional PDF conversion options. Convert to Adbe PDF and Email performs the same on Windows as the tool available on the Mac.

**Figure 8-1:**

The Adobe PDF menu on Windows offers several options for creating PDFs from within Word.

The second additional PDF conversion option on Windows in the Adobe PDF menu is Mail Merge to PDF. To use this feature you first need to create a data file and a mail merge document.

You can create a data file easily in Microsoft Excel. Just be certain to place labels in the first row at the top of an Excel worksheet such as name, address, city, state, zip, and so on. Save the file in native .xls format.

After creating a data file and a Word template document such as a letter, from the Task pane just select Mail Merge and follow steps in a wizard to create the merge document. Word provides you an easy wizard to help you create a letter, email message, envelope, label, or directory. When the merge document is created, select Adobe PDF @ @> Mail Merge to Adobe PDF and the Adobe PDF Maker - Mail Merge dialog box opens as shown in Figure 8-2.

# Exporting OCR text

If you want to take your scanned text to a word processor for editing and integration with other text documents, Acrobat provides an easy way to transfer data to word processors. After scanning a document with Scan to PDF with Make Searchable (Run OCR) or after running Text Recognition Using OCR on an image file, follow these steps to export your text to Microsoft Word.

## STEPS: Exporting Recognized Text to Microsoft Word

1. **Export text.** After recognizing text, choose File ⇨ Save As ⇨ Word Document. Note that you can also choose Rich Text Format (RTF) if you want to import the text in another application.

2. **Save the file.** A Save As dialog box opens. Choose a target location and type a file-name in the Save As dialog box. Click Save to save the file in Microsoft Word format.

3. **Launch Microsoft Word.**

4. **Open the Word file.** Click the Microsoft Office button and choose Open. Locate the saved file and open it in Word. The text is shown with formatting as shown in Figure 16.18.

**FIGURE 16.18**

Exported text is shown in Microsoft Word.

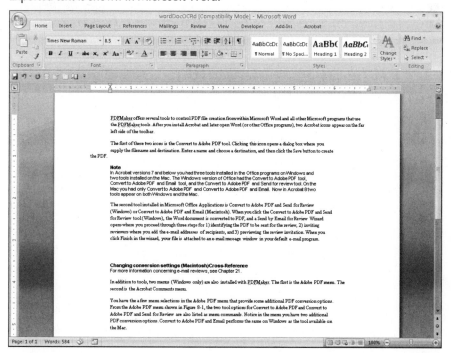

## Cross-Reference

**For more information on exporting PDF data, see Chapter 10. For more information on working with Acrobat and Microsoft Word, see Chapter 8.** ■

# Scanning Paper Forms

If you scan paper forms that you want populated with form fields in Acrobat or Adobe LiveCycle Designer and you want to use auto field detection in Acrobat, you need to start with a form that has sufficient resolution for the form fields to be recognized by Acrobat. If the resolution and image contrast aren't sufficient for Acrobat to recognize form fields, your results will vary and you may often find very few fields created by Acrobat on low-resolution scans.

## Cross-Reference

For more information on auto field detection in Acrobat, see Chapter 30. For more information on creating forms in Adobe LiveCycle Designer, see PDF Forms Using Acrobat and LiveCycle Designer Bible (Wiley Publishing). ∎

Developing a workflow for scanning forms using your scanner and Acrobat requires some practice and testing. Scanners vary considerably with quality, options, and resolution choices. The first thing you need to do is run a series of tests to determine what settings are optimum for recognizing fields automatically in Acrobat. Some considerations include:

- **Resolution.** More is generally better when it comes to scanning forms. Almost all desktop scanners support two resolutions. Optical resolution is the true resolution of your scanner. You may have a 600-ppi (pixels per inch) scanner that supports an optical resolution of 600 ppi. Your scanner also supports an interpolated resolution. For the 600-ppi scanner, the interpolated resolution is likely to be 1200 ppi. A 1200-ppi optical resolution scanner often supports an interpolated resolution of 2400 ppi, and so on.

  Interpolated resolution is best suited for line art drawings. Because most office forms are black and white, your scan resolution for forms at the highest interpolated resolution (up to 1200 ppi) of your scanner usually produces the best results when it comes to recognizing form fields. In Figure 16.19 you can see three scans I created using Acrobat Scan. The form on the left is a 150-ppi scan. In the middle is a 300-ppi scan and on the right is a 600-ppi scan. Although auto field detection isn't perfect, you can see that the 600-ppi scan produced more fields when the command was run in Acrobat.

## Note

The sample form used in these figures is a complex form having rows and columns of fields. Auto field detection provides you with a start in a complex form. You can expect to do some editing in Acrobat or Adobe LiveCycle Designer to polish up the fields and add fields where the auto recognition of form fields missed adding fields to the form. In much simpler forms, the auto field detection command does a superb job of automatically populating a form. See Chapter 30 for more on auto field detection. ∎

- **Color Mode.** Black and white art is generally scanned in a line art (bitmap) color mode. However, when it comes to OCR Text Recognition and ultimately using auto field detection, the anti-aliasing of grayscale scans most often provides you with better results.

**FIGURE 16.19**

Three scans after selecting Edit in the Forms panel and using auto field detection. On the left is a 150-ppi scan, in the middle is a 300-ppi scan, and on the right is a 600-ppi scan. The scans were performed on a scanner with an optical resolution of 600 ppi and an interpolated resolution of 1200 ppi.

- **Make Searchable (Run OCR).** When you use Scan to PDF for scanning forms on which you want to use the auto field detection, be certain to check the box for Make Searchable (Run OCR) in the Custom Scan dialog box. (See Figure 16.2 earlier in this chapter.) Using auto field detection produces no results if you attempt to run the command on a scan that hasn't been converted with the OCR engine.

## Tip

Note that ClearScan works well for documents you intend to view in Acrobat. However, forms, and especially forms with check boxes, might be best scanned using Searchable Image. If ClearScan is picking up check boxes and converting the check boxes to fonts, change the PDF output style to Searchable Image. ∎

- **Clean Up.** Ideally, you're best off using Scan to PDF and achieve optimum results using the controls in your scanner software for brightness, contrast, color mode choices, and scanning resolution. However, if your scanner software doesn't produce good results when recognizing form fields on your scans, you may be able to do a little image editing to adjust brightness and contrast. You'll need a program like Adobe Photoshop or Adobe Photoshop Elements to adjust Levels (Photoshop and Elements) and Curves (Photoshop only).

  If you do plan to do some image editing to adjust your scans' brightness and contrast, turn off Make Searchable (Run OCR) if using Acrobat Scan. After editing a scan in Photoshop or Photoshop Elements, save it as a Photoshop PDF file, open it in Acrobat, and choose In Current File in the Content panel. After running the OCR engine, you can then click Edit in the Forms panel.

Plan to do a lot of testing if you need to scan many forms and populate them with form fields in Acrobat or Adobe LiveCycle Designer. Try scanning forms with different resolutions to pinpoint the resolution setting that works best for your forms. After you find the settings that work best, go about scanning the forms you need to prepare in Acrobat.

## Tip

If the quality of your original forms is poor and you can't adjust contrast in Photoshop or Elements sufficiently to convert text with the OCR Engine and ultimately recognize fields, you can use Photoshop or Photoshop Elements to improve image brightness. Duplicate the Background layer in the Layers palette in either program. For the layer's blending mode, change the default Normal to Multiply. Add more duplicate layers using the Multiply blending mode until you see enough brightness in areas such as text, lines, boxes, and so on. Flatten the layers and make your final adjustments in the Levels dialog box. ■

# Converting a paper form to a fillable form

When scanning forms, you can use a one-button action to perform three steps in your paper form conversion to a PDF fillable form. When you click Create in the Forms panel, the Create or Edit Form Wizard provides a choice for creating a form from a paper form. When you make the choice, Acrobat Scan is used to scan the form, the scan is recognized using the OCR engine, and the form is automatically populated with form fields using Acrobat's ability to auto detect fields on a page.

## Note

The steps to convert a paper form can be completed in Acrobat Standard and Acrobat Pro. ■

To convert a paper form to a fillable form, follow these steps.

### STEPS: Scanning a Form in Acrobat

1. **Click Create in the Forms Panel.** The Create or Edit Form Wizard opens as shown in Figure 16.20.

2. **Click A paper form.** From the radio button choices, click A paper form and click Next.

**FIGURE 16.20**

Select A paper form and click Next.

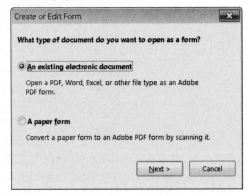

3. **Choose a preset or custom option (WIA-compliant scanners).** When you click Next in the Create or Edit Form Wizard, an Acrobat Scan dialog box opens as shown in Figure 16.21. If you have a preset already created for scanning forms, click the option (Black and White or Grayscale). If you want to adjust scan options, click Custom. In the Custom Scan dialog box make your choices for scan options.

**FIGURE 16.21**

Click a preset or click Custom.

If scanning using a TWAIN driver, your scanner software opens, where you make your scan adjustments.

4. **Click Scan.** If you choose a preset, your scan commences and you don't need this step. If setting up a custom scan or using a TWAIN driver, click the scan button in the scanner's interface to start the scan.

5. **Edit the form.** The scan finishes and the OCR engine recognizes text. The document is then moved to Form Editing Mode where Acrobat automatically detects fields and populates the form. In many cases you may need to edit a form such as the form shown in Figure 16.22. In this form, Acrobat missed a few fields and the check box fields weren't recognized. The fields are added while you stay in Form Editing Mode.

6. **Save the form.** Preview the form by clicking the Preview button and test the fields. When all fields appear on the form, choose File ⇨ Save to save the form.

## Note

When you open a scan in Form Editing Mode, Acrobat prompts you in a dialog box to use Run Form Field Recognition. Click Yes in the Add or Edit Form Fields dialog box. Acrobat searches the document for the placement of field objects on the form. ∎

## Cross-Reference

For more information on Form Editing Mode and adding fields to forms, see Chapter 30. ∎

**FIGURE 16.22**

The scan moves to Form Editing Mode where auto field detection populates the form with field objects.

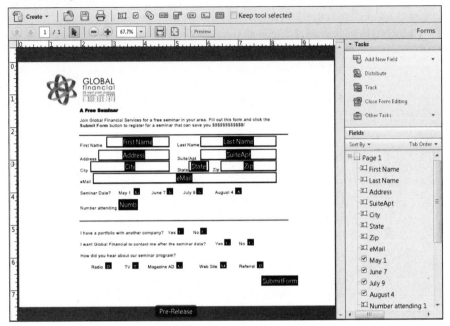

## Using a digital camera in lieu of a scanner

If you have a number of forms you want to scan from paper and convert to either Acrobat PDF forms or Adobe LiveCycle Designer XML forms, you can use a good quality digital camera in lieu of a scanner. After properly setting up a camera, you can shoot a dozen paper documents or more in the same time as it takes to scan forms — and the ratio broadens when you need to scan forms at 1200 ppi or higher.

To use a digital camera, you need to consider some of the following:

- **Camera type.** You may find some point-and-shoot cameras providing you with satisfactory results, but the best results come from a DSLR (Digital Single Lens Reflex) camera and a good quality macro lens.

- **Copy stand.** For best results, either buy or create a makeshift copy stand. Outfit the stand with daylight lights and use cross lighting to avoid shadows.

- **Save as JPEG and Raw.** When running tests with your camera, save files to your camera's media card in JPEG and Camera Raw file formats. You can test the images to see if the JPEG files produce good results when running form field recognition. If you don't get the results with JPEG as you do when using Camera Raw images, you can set up some defaults in the Camera Raw converter in either Photoshop Elements or Adobe Photoshop to automate preparing Raw files for Acrobat.

- **Set up an action in Photoshop.** If you work with Adobe Photoshop, you can create an action to automate image correction and saving files to Photoshop PDF format. You can let an action run overnight if you have a huge number of files to convert to PDF forms.

- **Set up a nested Action in Acrobat.** Two things need to be accomplished for preparing forms for editing in Acrobat or Adobe LiveCycle Designer: you need to Recognize Text Using OCR and Detect Form Fields. You can create a Custom Action as described in Chapter 17 to perform both actions.

## Note

You can use the Recognize in Multiple Files Using OCR command to batch process the OCR function. However, using this command only gets you halfway. You still need to set up a batch sequence to use Detect Form Fields to populate the scanned forms. ■

## Cross-Reference

For more information on creating batch sequences with Custom Actions, see Chapter 17. ■

If you have just a few forms, it makes no sense to go through the trouble of setting up a copy stand, shooting forms with a digital camera, editing the forms in Photoshop or Photoshop Elements, and creating a batch sequence. However, if you have 20, 50, or 100 or more forms to convert from paper to electronic forms, you'll find that using a digital camera can save you more time over scanning forms.

# Summary

In this chapter, you learned how to scan documents using Acrobat Scan and how to convert scanned images to text using Acrobat's OCR engine.

- Acrobat Scan provides choices for using presets and customizing presets with WIA-compliant scanners on Windows.

- Create PDF From Scanner on the Mac and when using noncompliant WIA scanners use TWAIN drivers or Adobe Photoshop Acquire plug-ins.

- Properly preparing the scanner and documents for scanning in Acrobat improves the quality of the scans. The scanner platen should be clean, the documents should be straight, and the contrast should be sharp.

- When scanning images in Acrobat, use the scanning software to establish resolution, image mode, and brightness controls before scanning. Test your results thoroughly to create a formula that works well for the type of documents you scan.

- Workflow automation can be greatly improved by purchasing Adobe's stand-alone product Adobe Acrobat Capture. When using Adobe Acrobat Capture with a scanner supporting a document feeder, the scanning and capturing can be performed with unattended operation.

- Acrobat Capture is a stand-alone application for optical character recognition used for converting scanned images into editable text.

- Acrobat uses a new technology called ClearScan that replaces the Formatted Text & Graphics PDF output style used with earlier versions of Acrobat.

- Text can be converted and saved as a PDF ClearScan output style, where you can edit text and change the appearance of the original scan. Text can be converted with Optical Character Recognition and saved using the Searchable Image option, which preserves the original document appearance and adds a text layer behind the image.

- Acrobat enables you to perform OCR text recognition on multiple scanned documents saved in any format compatible with the Create PDF From File command.

- OCR suspects are marked when the OCR engine does not find an exact word match in its dictionary. Text editing is performed in the Find Element dialog box.

- To import text into Microsoft Word, use the File ⇨ Save As ⇨ Word Document command in Acrobat to export to a Word file and open the exported file in Microsoft Word.

- Scanned paper forms can be populated with form fields when you enter Form Editing Mode. Acrobat automatically uses auto field detection to place field objects on a page when you enter Form Editing Mode.

- You can convert a paper form to a fillable PDF form using a single menu command in Acrobat.

- Digital cameras can be used in lieu of a scanner and can often speed up the scanning process.

# Repurposing and Creating Actions

P DF documents designed for one purpose, such as for commercial printing, might need to be repurposed for other output intent such as Web hosting or for copying to CD-ROMs. Rather than going back to the original authoring program and recreating PDFs for each purpose, you can use tools in Acrobat that enable you to downsample file sizes and strip unnecessary content. The resulting documents can then be more efficiently viewed on Web sites or exchanged via email.

You may have several files that need to be repurposed or edited in some other way using menu commands. Rather than open each file independently and apply menu commands, you can create batch sequences that apply commands to several files in one operation.

In this chapter, you learn how to repurpose PDF documents using some Acrobat tools and methods for downsizing file sizes and eliminating content unnecessary for other viewing purposes. In addition, you take a look at automating tasks by creating custom actions.

**IN THIS CHAPTER**

**Downsizing files**

**Creating Custom Actions**

## Reducing File Sizes

Reducing file sizes often occurs with downsampling images — that is to say, reducing the image resolution of all raster images or compressing images with higher compression options. In addition, you can reduce file sizes by eliminating redundant backgrounds; eliminating objects such as form fields, comments, bookmarks, and destinations; unembedding fonts; and/or compressing the document structure. You can handle file-size reductions at the time of PDF creation when you control file compression, image sampling, and font embedding for PDFs designed for a specific output purpose. However, if you create PDFs for one purpose, such as commercial printing, and later want to host the same file on a Web site, you need to either create a new PDF document specifically for the new purpose or use Acrobat tools to create smaller file sizes more suited for other output purposes. Fortunately, several means are available to you for squeezing file sizes down and optimizing PDFs for multiple purposes.

## Using the Reduce File Size command

Both Acrobat Standard and Pro offer a menu command that enables you to reduce file sizes. Open a document and choose File ➪ Save As ➪ Reduced Size PDF. The Reduce File Size dialog box opens, as shown in Figure 17.1.

**FIGURE 17.1**

Choose File ➪ Save As ➪ Smaller File to open the Reduce File Size dialog box, where you can select options for Acrobat version compatibility.

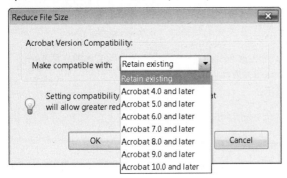

The Reduce File Size dialog box offers a drop-down menu with options for selecting Acrobat compatibility. The default is Retain existing, which means that the original PDF compatibility will not be changed when the file is reduced in size. If your PDF documents are to be viewed by Acrobat users of version 4 or later, choose Acrobat 4 and later compatibility. If all users are using Acrobat 6 through X viewers, use Acrobat 6, 7, 8, 9 or X compatibility, respectively. You might use Acrobat 4 compatibility for printing purposes because all the transparency will be flattened in Acrobat 4–compatible files.

## Caution

If you want to use many of the features available in Adobe Reader 8 through X, such as commenting and markup and form field saving, you must use Acrobat 8 compatibility or greater. If you want to use features for viewing PDF Portfolios, you need to use Acrobat 9 or above compatibility. For more information on using Adobe Reader with usage rights enabled, see Chapter 18. For information on commenting, see Chapter 19. For more information on PDF Portfolios, see Chapter 11. ■

After you make the menu selection and click OK, the Save As dialog box opens. Provide a file-name and save the file to disk. As a matter of practice it's a good idea to write a new file to disk in case the file reduction fails and you need to return to the original file to try another method of file reduction.

## Sanitizing documents

PDF files can contain artifacts and unnecessary elements that were either left behind from the original authoring program or that are not necessary for viewing content on the Web or screen viewing.

### New Feature

You can eliminate hidden information, metadata, hidden layers, scripts, and more from your files, which can greatly reduce the file size. If you don't need any of the information identified in Figure 17.2, open the Protection panel and click Sanitize Document. The dialog box shown in Figure 17.2 opens. Click OK and save the file. ∎

---

**FIGURE 17.2**

Open the Protection panel and click Sanitize Document to strip unnecessary elements and help reduce file size.

# Using PDF Optimizer (Acrobat Pro only)

Sanitizing documents and eliminating items supported in the Sanitize Document dialog box might get you only a slight file reduction. A more aggressive tool is the PDF Optimizer that can significantly reduce file sizes — especially files with high-resolution images.

With PDF Optimizer you make the choices from a number of different settings in the PDF Optimizer dialog box for what data is affected during optimization. The PDF Optimizer also offers you an option for analyzing a file so you can see what part of the PDF document occupies higher percentages of memory.

For a fast look at how to use the PDF Optimizer, use the steps that follow. Later in this chapter, I'll point out the various options you have when using the PDF Optimizer.

## STEPS: Using PDF Optimizer

1. **Open a PDF file in Acrobat.** Try to use the same file you used in the section "Sanitizing documents" earlier in this chapter.

2. **Open the PDF Optimizer.** Select File ⇨ Save As ⇨ Advanced PDF Optimization to open the dialog box shown in Figure 17.3.

**FIGURE 17.3**

Downsample files to 72 ppi for all images above 108 ppi.

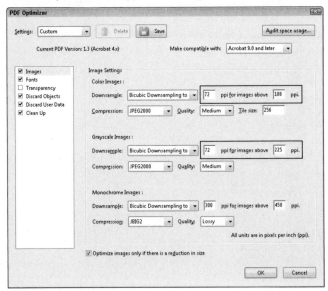

3. **Downsample images.** The PDF Optimizer has a number of different panes that offer settings for a number of different file attributes. The opening pane has options for downsampling files. Where you see Color Images and Grayscale Images you find text boxes where sampling amounts are edited. Type **72** and **108** for the sampling amounts for both sets of text boxes, as you see in Figure 17.3.

   Click the listed items on the left side of the dialog box, and you are offered a number of other choices for changing and removing data. For now, just use the defaults after changing the resolution amounts for color and grayscale images.

4. **Save the file.** Click OK and you are prompted to save your file. Type a new filename and click Save. The PDF Optimizer displays a progress bar as it optimizes the file.

5. **Examine the file size.** After the PDF Optimizer completes its task, open the Description properties. Press Ctrl/⌘+D and check the file size. You should see a substantial reduction in file size.

When you want to get the most out of reducing file sizes, you'll note that you can use both PDF Optimizer and Examine Document. Whether you first use one or the other method is unimportant. The final results are exactly the same file size.

## Tip

You can also open the PDF Optimizer when saving files. Select File ⇨ Save As and choose Adobe PDF Files, Optimized from the Save as type (Windows) or Format (Mac) pull-down menu when the Save As dialog box opens. Click the Settings button in the Save As dialog box and the PDF Optimizer window opens. You can choose a preset or make custom settings for the way you want to optimize your file. Click Save and the file is optimized and saved to disk. (For more on saving files, see Chapter 10.) ∎

### Auditing space usage

As a matter of practice, the first step you want to perform when optimizing files with the PDF Optimizer is to analyze a file so you can see what content occupies the larger amounts of memory. Analyzing a document and using the PDF Optimizer are handled in the PDF Optimizer dialog box, which opens when you choose Advanced ⇨ PDF Optimizer and is shown in Figure 17.3.

Click the button labeled Audit space usage. Depending on the size and complexity of the document, the analysis can take a little time. When the analysis completes, the dialog box shown in Figure 17.4 opens.

In the example shown in the preceding figure, notice that most of the document space is used for document overhead (68.95%) with Images occupying the second largest space at 23.62%. Document overhead might include items such as Named Destinations and links, while Images contains the space for image files. If the image resolution in this document is higher than images suited for screen viewing at 72 pixels per inch (ppi), then downsampling the images by reducing resolution would compact the file and make it significantly smaller. If you have documents designed for print and want to repurpose the documents for Web viewing, image downsampling is likely to be one of the things you'll want to adjust in the PDF Optimizer.

FIGURE 17.4

After the analysis is completed, the Audit Space Usage dialog box opens, where space usage according to different objects/elements is reported as a percentage of the total space.

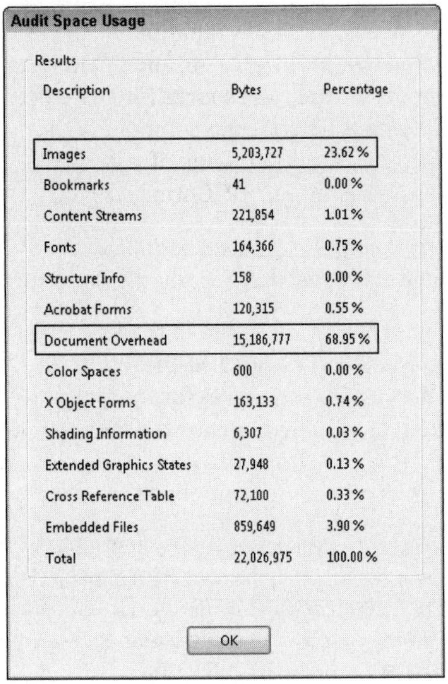

**Audit Space Usage**

Results

| Description | Bytes | Percentage |
|---|---|---|
| Images | 5,203,727 | 23.62 % |
| Bookmarks | 41 | 0.00 % |
| Content Streams | 221,854 | 1.01 % |
| Fonts | 164,366 | 0.75 % |
| Structure Info | 158 | 0.00 % |
| Acrobat Forms | 120,315 | 0.55 % |
| Document Overhead | 15,186,777 | 68.95 % |
| Color Spaces | 600 | 0.00 % |
| X Object Forms | 163,133 | 0.74 % |
| Shading Information | 6,307 | 0.03 % |
| Extended Graphics States | 27,948 | 0.13 % |
| Cross Reference Table | 72,100 | 0.33 % |
| Embedded Files | 859,649 | 3.90 % |
| Total | 22,026,975 | 100.00 % |

OK

## Optimizing files

Using the PDF Optimizer, you control a number of different attributes that contribute to a document's structure and content. By adjusting the number of different options found in the PDF Optimizer dialog box, you have the opportunity to produce documents much smaller than when using the Examine Document menu command. The options found in the PDF Optimizer include a Settings option, an option for changing PDF compatibility, and categories listed on the left side of the dialog box. Click one of the items listed in the left pane, and the right pane changes much like when using the Preferences dialog box. These categories include Images, Fonts, Transparency, Discard Objects, Discard User Data, and Clean Up.

### Set option

The Settings option appears first in the PDF Optimizer, but it's the last setting you address. When you open the PDF Optimizer, the default is Standard. Select Custom or make changes to any setting and the Save button becomes active. When you click Save, Acrobat prompts you to save your new settings as a preset. After saving, the name you define for the preset is added to the pull-down menu. When you return to the PDF Optimizer in another Acrobat session, you can select from the number of different presets and click OK to optimize files with the same settings defined for the respective preset. If you want to clear a preset from the pull-down menu, select a preset in the menu and click the Delete button.

### Make compatible with

From the Make compatible with a pull-down menu, you select Acrobat compatibility levels. You can make your optimized document compatible with Acrobat 4, 5, 6, 7, 8, and 9. The Retain existing menu command keeps the compatibility the same as the source file. When the need arises to serve users with earlier compatibility files, change the menu command to the desired compatibility level. By default, Retain Existing is selected in the menu. If you change from Acrobat 5 to Acrobat 6 or 7, some other attribute settings in the PDF Optimizer change to reflect choices supported by newer versions of Acrobat.

### Images

To reduce file size with the PDF Optimizer, use the first set of options found in the left pane; the default Images pane appears (refer to Figure 17.3). You can make choices for downsampling color, grayscale, and bitmap images by typing values in the field boxes for the sampling amounts desired. To the right of the downsampling amount, another field box is used to identify images that are downsampled. This box instructs Acrobat to look for any image above the setting defined in the field box and downsamples the file to the amount supplied in the first field box.

## Cross-Reference

The Images pane offers choices for the downsampling method. The default method is Bicubic Downsampling. Leave the choice for Bicubic Downsampling at the default selection. To learn more about the other methods and what they mean, see Chapter 9. ∎

The Compression pull-down menu offers choices for Retain existing, JPEG, JPEG2000 (an additional setting available when Acrobat 6 through 9 compatibility is selected), and Zip compression. The Retain existing setting honors the original compression used when the PDF was created.

## Cross-Reference

For more information on the JPEG and JPEG2000 file formats, see Chapter 7. ∎

For either form of JPEG compression you have additional choices for the amount of compression from the Quality pull-down menu. If you choose a JPEG compression and use Minimum for the Quality choice, your images may appear severely degraded. As a general rule, Medium quality results in satisfactory image quality for Web hosting. If you try one setting and the images look too degraded, you can return to the original file, apply a different Quality setting, and then examine the results.

Zip compression is a lossless compression scheme, which means that files are compressed without data loss. For Acrobat 4 and 5 compatibility, Zip offers a good choice when you want to maximize image quality. When using Acrobat 6 through 9 compatibility, you can select

JPEG2000 for a better compression result and select Lossless from the Quality pull-down menu, which will save all the image data.

### Fonts

Fonts will not always appear in a list in the Fonts pane when you click the word Fonts on the left side of the PDF Optimizer. Only fonts that are available for unembedding are listed on the left side of the Fonts pane. If no fonts appear in the list, you can move on to the Transparency settings. If fonts are listed in the box in the left side of the pane, select the fonts to unembed and click the Unembed button adjacent to the right chevron.

In the right box are fonts listed for unembedding. If you want to keep the font embedded, select it in the right box and click the Retain button adjacent to the left chevron. To select multiple fonts in either window, press Shift+click to select a list in a contiguous group, or press Ctrl/⌘+click to select fonts in a noncontiguous group.

## Note

By default, always choose to embed fonts in your documents unless you have some special reason for wanting to reduce the file size to a minimum and font appearances won't matter. One of the great things about PDF documents is that they retain the original design look, including font appearances, when files are exchanged among computer systems. ■

### Transparency

Transparent images and objects can be flattened in Acrobat 9 for all PDF documents created in Acrobat 5 and greater. If you select Acrobat 4 compatibility, transparency is automatically flattened because Acrobat 4 compatibility does not support transparency. When you select all other compatibility versions, you have options for flattening the transparency.

## Cross-Reference

For information on using transparency-flattening settings, see Chapter 29. ■

### Discard Objects

Discarding items such as comments, form actions, JavaScript actions, cross-references, and thumbnails affects document functionality as you might suspect. If the respective items are eliminated, any PDF interactivity created with these items is also eliminated. If you know that one or any group of these items won't have an effect on the way the repurposed document is viewed or printed, enable the check boxes for the items you want to remove.

One benefit to using the Discard Objects pane is to flatten form fields. You might have a PDF form with form fields containing data. After the form is completed, you may want to archive it on a handheld or mobile device. As of this writing, there aren't any PDF viewers that display form data. Click Discard Objects in the left pane and check the box for Flatten Form Fields, as shown in Figure 17.5. The field data on the PDF form is stamped down on the document and can be viewed on devices where PDF viewers cannot display live form data.

FIGURE 17.5

Check the box for Flatten Form Fields in the Discard Objects pane and save the file to retain data and eliminate field objects.

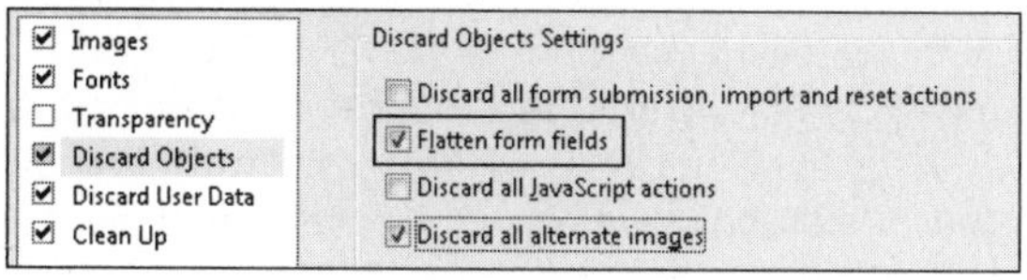

### Discard User Data

Comments, multimedia, file attachments, hidden layers, and more are listed in the Discard User Data pane. Like Discard Objects, if you choose to eliminate the items, the result can affect the way PDFs are viewed and remove some interactivity. Choose these items wisely to retain the kind of interactive features you want in the resultant file.

### Clean Up

Click Clean Up in the left pane and you find a list of items checked by default that can be used safely without affecting the functionality of your document. Select the box for Remove unreferenced named destinations if the check box is not checked. Settings such as removing invalid bookmarks, links, and destinations won't affect the document viewing, but removing the unnecessary items helps reduce file size. As a matter of practice, leave all the options in this pane checked. After you make your preferred settings in the PDF Optimizer, click the Save button if you want to save the settings as a new preset or click OK to start the optimization process.

# Using Batch Processing with Custom Actions

If you have multiple files that need to be refined for distribution on network servers, Web sites, or CD-ROM or when you want to automate many different tasks, then you'll want to create a Custom Action. Custom Actions were known as *Batch Sequences* in earlier versions of Acrobat and are a defined series of commands in a specific order that can be run on multiple files. You create the Custom Actions from a list of executable functions and determine the commands and order of the sequence.

Custom Actions help you automate tasks in Acrobat that might otherwise take considerable time, such as manually applying a common set of commands on many different files. After you develop one or more actions, you can run the sequence(s) on selected PDF files, a folder of PDF files, or multiple folders of PDF files.

Tasks such as setting opening views of PDF documents, adding document descriptions, adding page numbers, or running the PDF Optimizer can be applied to multiple files you might want to distribute on CD-ROM or on Web sites. Before distributing files, you can run an action as a final step in your production workflow to be sure all files have common attributes.

## Creating a Custom Action

If you used Batch Sequences in earlier versions of Acrobat, you'll find the new Custom Actions feature in Acrobat X to be very similar. Although the interface has changed, adding actions to form a sequence of steps is quite similar to the former Batch Sequence feature. At first glance it looks like a major overhaul for automating Acrobat tasks, but most of the choices you have in the Custom Actions Wizard are the same as those found in the Batch Sequence window.

## Using the Custom Actions Wizard

You can access Custom Actions controls in the Action Wizard panel. When you open the panel, you find a few predefined actions and two menu items used for Create New Action and Edit Actions. To create an action, click the Create New Action menu item in the Action Wizard panel and the Create New Action Wizard shown in Figure 17.6 opens. To manage actions for editing the action results or changing other attributes, click Edit Actions in the Action Wizard panel.

### FIGURE 17.6

Click Create New Action in the Action Wizard panel to open the Create New Action Wizard.

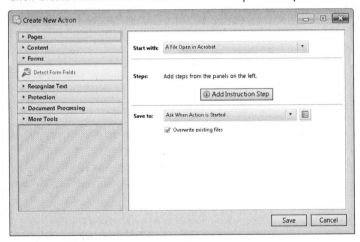

The Create New Action Wizard contains options for identifying tasks, choosing a target destination for the task results, and exporting or importing actions. More specifically, the wizard contains:

- **Items list.** In the left pane of the Create New Action Wizard, you find a list of items that are available for inclusion in a Custom Action. Click a topic to expand the heading, such as the Forms item shown in Figure 17.6. Each item listed below the relative heading is available for inclusion in a new action.

- **Start with.** The Start with drop-down menu provides options for an action performed on a target such as an open file, a file on your computer, a file in a folder, a scanned file, or combine several files into a single PDF.

- **Add Instruction Step.** Click the button to type instructions as an action is run. You can add several instruction steps between each action step.

- **Steps.** By default, the Tasks item is empty. As you add one or more items from the left pane, the respective items are displayed in a list.

- **Save to.** The Save to drop-down menu offers options for an action output such as saving to a specific folder, saving files to an original folder, not saving any changes, or prompting you for a choice when an action is run.

## Creating a Custom Action

Running actions is designed for automating common tasks. Suppose you have many pages of text that you have scanned and you want to recognize the text using OCR, add some metadata for a document description, set the open options, and secure the files with a password. All of these steps can be combined in a single action, and with the click of an action button, you can sit back and watch Acrobat complete the task.

## Cross-Reference
For more information on using OCR, see Chapter 16. For more information on adding metadata for document descriptions and setting open options, see Chapter 6. For more information on adding password security, see Chapter 24. ■

To understand how to create and use actions, follow these steps.

### STEPS: Creating a Custom Action

1. **Open the Custom Actions Wizard.** Open the Action Wizard panel and click Create New Action.

2. **Add an action.** Open the Recognize Text item in the left pane of the Create New Action Wizard and click Recognize Text (using OCR). The item is moved to the Steps list in the right pane.

3. **Choose a source.** If you want to use the same action many times, you may want to have Acrobat prompt you when the action is run to locate the folder where all the source files are contained. From the Start with drop-down menu, choose Ask When Action is Started.

4. **Choose an output destination.** Where are the files going to be saved? If you run the action several times, you'll want Acrobat to prompt you to identify a new folder. From the Save to drop-down menu, choose Ask When Action is Started.

5. **Add a second action.** Open the Content item and click Add Document Description in the left pane. The item is added on the right below the first action.

6. **Change settings.** Notice the icon as a mini menu to the right of the item name. Click the icon to open a settings dialog box for adjusting options. For the first action, you left the settings at the default. For the description, type in a title, subject, and author in the text boxes. Click OK and you return to the Custom Actions Wizard.

7. **Add a third action.** Open the Document Processing item and click Set Open Options in the pane to add the item below the Description task.

8. **Edit settings.** Click the mini menu icon to open the Set Open Options dialog box. Click Page Only under Initial View, choose single page for Page Layout, and uncheck Leave As Is under Open Action. From the Magnification drop-down menu, choose Fit Page. Click OK to accept the new changes.

9. **Add a final action.** Click Protext to open the menu and then click Encrypt.

10. **Set Options.** Click the mini menu icon and choose a security method such as Password Security and add a password to prevent changes in the document. (For more information on adding security to prevent document changes, see Chapter 24.) Click OK and you return to the Create New Action Wizard. If you added the items in the steps outlined here, your Create New Action Wizard should look like Figure 17.7.

**FIGURE 17.7**

The Custom Actions Wizard with four tasks listed.

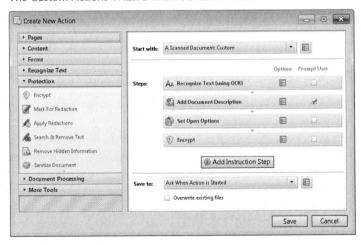

11. **Save the Action.** Click Save and Acrobat prompts you in a Name Sequence dialog box to name your action. Type a name for the action and click OK; the action is saved.

Up to this point, you have created and saved an action. In order to run the action, you need to dismiss the Custom Actions Wizard if it is open. Click Cancel and you return to the Acrobat window. Choose File ➪ Action Wizard and you see a submenu containing the existing actions and your new action. Select your action name, and the Run Sequence Confirmation dialog box opens, as shown in Figure 17.8.

**FIGURE 17.8**

The Run Sequence Confirmation dialog box lists all the commands to be performed by the action.

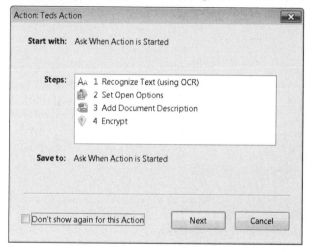

Click Next and the Actions Wizard Select Files dialog box opens. Because you chose to have Acrobat prompt you at runtime for this action, the dialog box is used for you to identify files. Click Add Files in the dialog box and click OK to run the action on the selected files.

## Managing actions

You may want to modify, rename, or delete actions. To change attributes for actions, open the Action Wizard and click Edit Actions in the Action Wizard panel. The Edit Actions dialog box opens and displays your Custom Actions. In Figure 17.9 you see the actions provided by Adobe and a custom action I created at the bottom of the list.

**FIGURE 17.9**

Click Edit Actions in the Actions Wizard panel to open the Edit Actions Wizard.

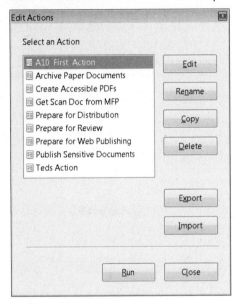

The Edit Actions dialog box offers you the following choices:

- **Edit.** Click an action name in the Select an Action list in the left window, and click Edit to change that action's steps and attributes.

- **Rename.** Click Rename to change the name for an action.

- **Delete.** Click this button to remove an action from the list and the File ⇨ PDF Actions submenu.

- **Export Action.** You may work in an enterprise office atmosphere where many co-workers are using Acrobat for similar tasks. One user can create an action and deploy it to other users. When you click Export Action, you are prompted for a folder location and the export is saved as a file that you can send to other users.

- **Import Action.** Click this button to import an action that was exported from this dialog box.

- **Run.** Click an action in the Select an Action list and click Run to run the action.

## Creating custom sequences

The term Custom Actions is a bit misleading because you are limited to choosing from a number of preset conditions provided by Acrobat. For a more authentic customized action, you can write a JavaScript to greatly expand your world of Custom Actions.

To understand more about writing a JavaScript action, follow these steps.

### STEPS: Creating a JavaScript Action

1. **Create a new action.** Open the Create New Action Wizard by clicking Create New Action in the Action Wizard panel.

2. **Add Execute JavaScript to the Tasks list.** Open the More Tools list and click Execute JavaScript.

3. **Set the Source and Output options.** Select Ask When Action is Run from the Save to drop-down menu.

4. **Add the JavaScript code to execute the action.** Click the mini menu icon in the Execute JavaScript bar and the JavaScript Editor opens. Type the following code to add a Stamp comment to a selected group of files.

## Note

Line numbers in the following code are for reference only. Do not type the numbers in the JavaScript Editor. ■

```
1. // adds a stamp to the first page //
2. var annot = this.addAnnot ({
3. page:0,
4. type: "Stamp",
5. name: "Draft",
6. rect: [400, 700, 600, 790],
7. pop-upOpen: false,
8. author: "Ted",
9. contents: "First Review",
10. });
```

## Note

The coordinates for the position of the note are set for a standard U.S. Letter size page (8.5 × 11 inches, portrait view). If you run the sequence on documents with different size pages or orientation, the results may not show the stamp on a page. ■

5. **Save the JavaScript.** Click OK in the JavaScript Editor dialog box.

6. **Save the action.** Click Save in the Custom Actions Wizard.

7. **Name the action.** When you click Save, you are prompted to name the action. Type a name and click OK; you return to the Acrobat window.

8. **Run the action.** Choose File ⇨ PDF Action ⇨ <the name of your action>. Select a folder of files and an output location.

9. **Examine the results.** Open one of the files in the output folder, and you should see a Stamp comment added to the first page in the document as shown in Figure 17.10.

FIGURE 17.10

The Stamp comment is added to the first page of all documents processed with the Add Stamp routine created in the JavaScript Editor.

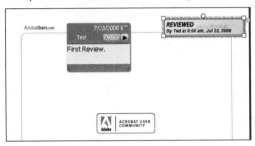

## Tip

**To find coordinates to add to the script above, drag a rectangle with the Rectangle comment tool where you want your comment annotation to appear. Open the JavaScript Debugger (Ctrl/⌘+J) and type the following code in the Debugger window:**

```
this.getAnnots()[0].rect;
```

**With the cursor placed on the line of code, press the Num Pad Enter key. The Debugger window reports the x,y coordinates at the four corners of the rectangle.** ■

## Cross-Reference

**For more information on creating stamps and using pop-up note windows, see Chapter 20.** ■

The preceding steps create a Stamp comment (from the Stamp comment you last used in Acrobat) (Line 2) at the coordinates (Line 6) — note that the page size where the stamps are added is a standard U.S. Letter 8.5 × 11 inches in portrait view. The note pop-up window is closed by default (Line 7), and the content of the note pop-up is *First Review* (Line 9). You can change the position of the note by editing the coordinates in Line 6, change the contents in Line 9, or change the stamp type in Line 4. The code can be easily modified, or you can copy and paste the code in the JavaScript Editor if you want to create other similar sequences.

## Cross-Reference

**For more information on writing JavaScripts, see Chapter 32.** ■

# Summary

In this chapter, you learned how to optimize PDF documents and create Actions for automating document processing.

- File sizes can be reduced with the Reduce File Size menu command.

- Sanitize Document offers some options for deleting content from files to help reduce file size.

- The PDF Optimizer (Acrobat Pro only) is used to reduce file sizes and eliminate unnecessary data in PDF files. PDF Optimizer can often reduce file sizes more than when using the Reduce File Size command.

- Selecting options in the Discard Objects pane in the PDF Optimizer other than the default options can interfere with the PDF functionality. Care must be exercised in selecting options to prevent potential problems.

- The Flatten form fields option in the Discard Objects pane discards field objects while retaining data for optimizing forms when the fields are no longer needed.

- What were formerly known as Batch Sequences in earlier versions of Acrobat are now called Custom Actions in Acrobat X.

- Custom Actions help you automate the processing of multiple PDF documents. From a standard set of sequence options, you can create actions for a limited number of tasks. When more custom options are needed, you can add JavaScripts for processing files with custom settings.

# Enabling Features for Adobe Reader

**E**nabling features for Adobe Reader or adding *special features* for Reader users is a means whereby certain features not appearing in the default Adobe Reader program can be added to PDF documents. This enabling function can be handled by one of two applications. You can use a server product such as the Adobe LiveCycle Reader® Extensions ES or Adobe Acrobat X Standard or Pro.

In Acrobat 7, a single enabling feature was introduced that added these special features to permit Adobe Reader users participation in email–based reviews. When a PDF document was enabled for commenting and markup, all the comment tools appeared in Adobe Reader, they were usable, and the comments could be saved using Reader.

In Acrobat 8, Adobe introduced more enabling features such as those for saving form data and adding digital signatures. These options are not part of Adobe Reader. But when opening an enabled file in Reader, you can take advantage of the special features for saving form data and adding digital signatures.

In Acrobat 9, Adobe broadened the enabling features to include the Acrobat Standard users (Windows only).

# Understanding the Restrictions for Enabling Features

As logic would have it, you're no doubt thinking there must be some restriction or limitation on enabling PDF files in Acrobat. After all, how could Adobe hope to sell one product that starts at $30,000 when a user could find the same thing purchasing a copy of Acrobat?

There are indeed limitations, and they are all spelled out in the End User License Agreement (EULA) you agree to when installing Acrobat. Just in case you are confused about language in the agreement after reading it, let me paraphrase the licensing agreement and amplify some of the conditions. In addition to what is covered in this chapter, you should carefully read the agreement and understand the limitations of use.

## Recognizing the target audience

Prior to Acrobat 8 there was no opportunity for users to enable features in PDF files that permit Adobe Reader users the ability to fill in form data, save the data, and digitally sign documents. Adobe recognized a clear distinction between users who have occasional and limited needs versus enterprises that distribute PDF forms to many thousands of people.

Small to medium businesses might have needs for people to fill out small batches of forms for travel expense claims, purchase orders, personal time-off forms, and so on. Some of the data such as data compiled from expense forms might need to be exported to an Excel spreadsheet and integrated into an accounting program.

You might also have an annual charity golf tournament with a few hundred participants, a small annual conference with fewer than 300 registrants, or a similar need to distribute forms and collect data.

These kinds of examples fit within Adobe's EULA and target audience. On the other hand, if you have a commercial Web site and you're collecting PDF forms for point of sale purchases where the numbers of potential customers may be in the thousands, then this kind of use for your PDF-enabled forms is a clear violation of the licensing agreement.

## Licensing restrictions

The language in the EULA suggests that you can enable PDF forms with forms saving for Adobe Reader users for up to 500 instances of a given document. The document usage can be one of two ways. You can distribute an unlimited number of enabled forms, but you can only aggregate up to 500 forms — something like hosting a form on your Web site where you might get less than 500 registrants for a conference. The other instance is distributing forms to 500 named individuals, and you can aggregate any number of those forms — something like expense accounts that people fill out and return monthly.

## Note

For an up-to-date description of the Acrobat EULA or any other Adobe product, visit www.adobe.com/products/eulas. On the opening Web page you'll find links to Acrobat and other Adobe products specifying the conditions of the license agreements. ■

## Enforcing the restrictions

Adobe uses no special coding or technology to ensure users are complying with the licensing agreement. Adobe believes that the enforcement for restricting users to the limitations is vested in the amount of work people need to perform. For limited use, the enabling features in Acrobat 9 and above serve a need for many PDF authors. However, the kind of use an LCRE user needs to process volumes of forms, such as parsing data and routing data to databases, is something to be found only in the server products from Adobe.

There remains a clear distinction between industrial strength use and limited use, not only in the licensing agreement but also in practicality. The enabling features do not diminish the need for the Adobe LiveCycle Reader® Extensions ES. Quite the contrary: Workgroups that begin to work more with enabling PDFs with Reader extensions are likely to experience needs for evolving to more sophisticated uses that can only be satisfied using LCRE.

# Enabling PDF Documents with Reader Extensions

In Acrobat 9 Pro and above, you can enable PDFs with special usage rights for adding comments and markups and save the comments once added in Adobe Reader. You can enable PDF forms using Standard or Pro, adding features for Adobe Reader users, and permitting them to save form data and add digital signatures.

PDF files can be enabled for Comment & Markup, Digital Signatures, Digital Signature Tool (Acrobat 8 and higher), Typewriter tool, and Forms Fill/Save. How you go about enabling files from Acrobat is handled through the File ➪ Save As submenu. You choose from one of three menu commands for adding special features to PDF documents for Adobe Reader users.

## Enabling PDFs for text additions

When you choose File ➪ Save As ➪ Reader Extended PDF File, the submenu offers three choices. This first menu choice is Enable Adding Text in Adobe Reader. If you make this choice and save the file, Adobe Reader users can use the Typewriter tool to type text on a PDF file. This is helpful when a user wants to fill out a form that doesn't have form fields.

## Cross-Reference

For more information on using the Typewriter tool and filling out PDF forms, see Chapter 30. ■

## Authorizing PDFs for commenting (Acrobat Pro)

The second submenu command offers an option for enabling a PDF for commenting in Adobe Reader. The first time you select this command an application alert dialog box opens informing you that certain editing functions normally available to Acrobat users will be restricted. If you check the Don't show again check box, as shown in Figure 18.1, the dialog box won't appear when enabling future documents.

**FIGURE 18.1**

The first time you enable a file for commenting in Adobe Reader, an application alert dialog box opens.

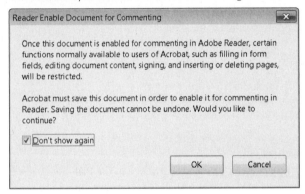

Click OK in the application alert dialog box and a Save As dialog box opens. Type a new name for your file to avoid overwriting the original and click the Save button. The PDF is now enabled with Adobe Reader usage rights for commenting and markup.

When an Adobe Reader user opens the enabled PDF document, the Comment & Markup tools are all accessible. You can add the same kind of comments as you can with either Acrobat Standard or Acrobat Pro. After adding comments, the Reader user also has access to a File ⇨ Save command. This command is not available unless a file has been enabled. Selecting File ⇨ Save permits the Reader user the opportunity to save all comments added to the PDF.

## Cross-Reference

For more information on limitations of Adobe Reader, see Chapter 4. For more information on comment and markup, see Chapter 20. ■

## Enabling PDFs for form saves

The third option provides you with a complete set of enabling features for Adobe Reader users. In Acrobat Pro and Acrobat Standard, select File ⇨ Save As ⇨ Reader Extended

PDF ⇨ Enable Additional Features in Adobe Reader, and the Enable Usage Rights in Adobe Reader dialog box opens, as shown in Figure 18.2.

**FIGURE 18.2**

Select File ⇨ Save As ⇨ Reader Extended PDF ⇨ Enable Additional Features in Adobe Reader and a dialog box opens informing you of the features that you can enable.

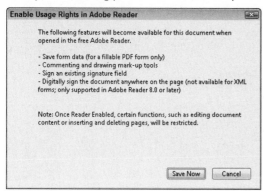

Click Save Now and all the features listed in the dialog box are enabled in the PDF file for Adobe Reader users. This option provides a complete set of enabling features, including the following:

- **Save form data (for fillable PDF forms only).** Adobe Reader users can add data to PDF forms containing form fields and save the edited file.

- **Commenting and drawing markup tools (Acrobat Pro only).** The same comment and markup tools are available to Adobe Reader users as when enabling files for Comment & Markup and Review & Comment. All comments can be saved.

- **Sign an existing signature field.** Adobe Reader users can add a digital signature to a signature field on a form and save the edits.

- **Digitally sign the document on the page (supported in Adobe Reader 8 only).** As the text implies, this feature is available only to users of Adobe Reader 8 and above. It is also not available for XML forms created with LiveCycle Designer. A Reader 8 and above user can sign a document without the appearance of a signature file and save the edits.

When you click Save Now, the file is enabled with the usage rights.

## Cross-Reference

For more information on fillable form fields, see Chapters 30 and 31. For more information on using digital signatures, see Chapter 24. ■

# Editing Enabled PDF Files

Upon occasion, you may enable a PDF document using any one of the enabling options available in Acrobat Pro and then later decide you want to edit the file. When you enable a PDF document and try to edit it in Acrobat, an application alert dialog box opens as shown in Figure 18.3.

If you try to edit an enabled file in Acrobat, an alert dialog box opens informing you that you can't edit the file.

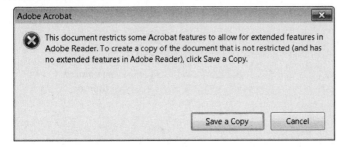

To edit an enabled file in Acrobat you first need to save a copy of the document. When you open nonenabled PDF files, the File menu lists commands for Save and Save As. When you open an enabled file in Acrobat you find the commands Save, Save As, and Save a Copy. The addition of the Save a Copy command is unique to enabled PDF files, and only this command will remove the restrictions applied when the PDF was enabled. The usage rights are removed when you save a copy, so after editing you need to re-enable the form.

Select File ➪ Save a Copy and the Save a Copy dialog box opens as you see in Figure 18.4. Click the Save a Copy button and a second Save a Copy dialog box opens, where you can name the copy and select a folder where you want to save it. Once you save a copy, your copy file is not open in the Acrobat Document pane. It's merely saved to disk. Your original file remains open and it's not editable. Close the open file, then select File ➪ Open or click the Open tool in the Toolbar Well. When the Open dialog box appears, select the copy file and open it in Acrobat. You can edit this file and enable it after you complete your editing tasks.

You'll find that most of the kinds of editing you typically perform on a PDF document aren't available with enabled documents. Items such as changing any of the Document Properties (Description, Security, Initial View, Custom, and Advanced), adding headers and footers, changing backgrounds, adding comments, editing form fields, changing JavaScripts, and so on are all unavailable to you when working on an enabled PDF document. To edit any of these items, select File ➪ Save a Copy and open the copy file.

**FIGURE 18.4**

Click the Save a Copy button to save an editable copy of the enabled PDF document.

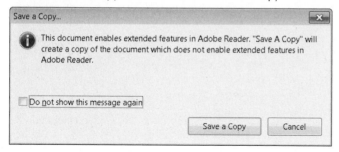

## Cross-Reference

**For more information on changing Document Properties, see Chapter 6. For more information on adding headers and footers and changing backgrounds, see Chapter 15. For more information on adding comments, see Chapter 19. For more information on editing form fields, see Chapter 31. For more information on editing JavaScripts, see Chapter 32. ■**

# Summary

In this chapter, you learned how to extend features on PDF files for Adobe Reader users for adding text, commenting, and saving form data.

- Adobe LiveCycle Reader® Extensions ES (LCRE) is a server product used for enterprise-enabling features for Adobe Reader users.

- The End User License Agreement (EULA) specifies the limitations you have for enabling PDFs with Reader extensions. When enabling forms for form saves for Reader users from within Acrobat, you are limited to 500 instances of use for unknown users. For known users, such as within a company of less than 500 employees, there is no limit to the number of uses of enabled forms.

- Acrobat Standard and Pro provide features for enabling PDF files for saving form data and digital signatures for Adobe Reader users.

# Part IV

# Using PDF Interactivity

art IV deals with PDF interactivity, whether it be collaboration with others on sharing information or adding interactive features to PDF documents. In Chapter 19, we start with comment and markup, where I cover using all the commenting features you have available in all Acrobat viewers. In Chapter 20, we move on to working in review sessions using the new Share panel.

In Chapter 21, you find the many ways to make your PDF documents more interactive through adding bookmarks, links, and buttons. In Chapter 22, I talk about adding rich media to PDFs. This part finishes up in Chapter 23 with making PDF documents accessible for people using screen readers.

# Annotating PDFs

Adobe Acrobat and Reader are the perfect tools for workgroup collaboration. With sophisticated tool sets and a number of menu options, Acrobat provides you with the ability to comment and mark up PDF documents and share your annotations with users dynamically on Web sites, through Acrobat.com, or through file exchanges on network servers or via email. For example, you can mark up documents, send your comments to a group of colleagues, ask for return comments, and track the review history. Where PDF documents may be too large to efficiently exchange files in emails, you can export comments to smaller data files or summarize them and create new PDF documents from comment summaries that can be sent to members of your workgroup. You can compare documents for changes, for comment status, and for errors and omissions, and, as with Acrobat 7 and 8 Pro, you can add usage rights in Acrobat X Pro to documents so Adobe Reader users can participate in reviews.

The review and comment tools and methods in Acrobat are extraordinary in number. Just because Acrobat provides these great tools doesn't necessarily mean you'll use all of them in your daily work activities. The best way to decide what tools work best for you and your colleagues is to review this chapter thoroughly and choose the tools you favor and then the features in review and markup that work best in your environment. In this chapter, you learn how to use all the comment tools and compare documents for reviewing purposes.

## PDF Workflow

All the tools and features discussed in this chapter are related to workflow environments. Regardless of what industry you work in, the many features related to review and comment and comparing documents can be applied to virtually all environments with two or more individuals collaborating on common projects. ∎

# Setting Commenting Preferences

Acrobat provides an elaborate set of preference options that enable you to control comment views and behavior. As you draw comments on PDF pages you may see pop-up windows, connector lines across a page, changes in page views, and a host of other strange behaviors that might confuse you. Before you begin a commenting session, you should familiarize yourself with the commenting preferences and plan to return to the preference settings several times to completely understand how you control comment behavior in Acrobat.

Open the preference settings by pressing Ctrl/⌘+K or choosing Edit ⇨ Preferences (Windows) or Acrobat ⇨ Preferences (Mac). In the left pane, select Commenting. In the right pane, you'll see a long list of preference settings, as shown in Figure 19.1. Take a moment to review these settings before you begin a commenting session.

---

**FIGURE 19.1**

Open the Commenting Preferences by pressing Ctrl/⌘+K or choosing Edit ⇨ Preferences. When the Preferences dialog box opens, select Commenting in the left pane.

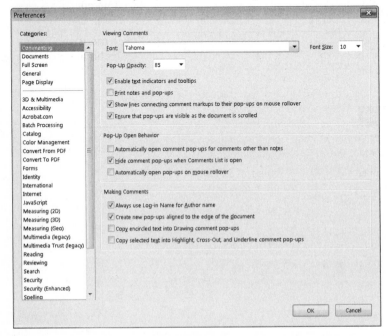

- **Font (Windows only).** The comment tools are used to mark up text and create icons, symbols, and graphic objects on pages. Most of the comment tools have associated pop-up notes where you type remarks in a note window. By default, the font used for the note text is Tahoma. To change the font, select another font from the pull-down menu. All fonts loaded in your system are available from the menu choices. The fonts you use are not embedded in the file. If you exchange PDFs containing comment notes with other users, the fonts default to another user's preference settings.

  Note that changing fonts and arbitrary font sizes is not available on the Mac. On the Mac the default Tahoma font is used and sizes are limited to Small, Medium, and Large.

- **Font Size.** Font point sizes range from 4 points to 144 points. You can type a number between these values in the field box or select one from the preset point sizes from the pull-down menu. Changing font size applies to note pop-up windows you see on your computer. If you change font size and share the file with other users, fonts appear in sizes set by individual user preferences.

- **Pop-up Opacity.** A pop-up note background color is white. At 100 percent opacity the note is opaque and hides underlying page data. You can change the opacity of pop-up notes for a transparent view so the background data can be seen when a pop-up note window is open. You adjust the level of transparency by typing a value in the field box or selecting one from the preset choices in the pull-down menu. The default is 85 percent.

- **Enable text indicators and tooltips.** Turns on or off tooltips when the Hand tool approaches a comment icon. The tooltip reports text contained in a comment note when the note is collapsed.

- **Print notes and pop-ups.** Enabling this check box prints the pop-up note contents for all pop-up note windows regardless of whether they are opened or collapsed.

- **Show lines connecting comment markups to their pop-ups on mouse rollover.** When you place the cursor over a comment markup, a line appears between the comment mark and the pop-up note, as shown in Figure 19.2.

**FIGURE 19.2**

When the preference setting is enabled, connector lines are displayed on a mouseover between the comment and the associated note window.

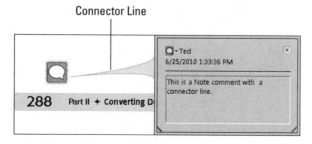

- **Ensure that pop-ups are visible as the document is scrolled.** If a comment note extends beyond one page in a continuous page view, the note is visible when scrolling pages.

- **Automatically open comment pop-ups for comments other than notes.** As you create comments with drawing tools, the Text Box tool, or Pencil tool, the pop-up note windows are collapsed by default. If you want a pop-up note window opened and ready to accept type when creating comments, check the box.

- **Hide comment pop-ups when Comments List is opened.** The Comments List is contained in the Comment panel. When you open the Comment panel, the list shows expanded comment notes with the content displayed in the pane. To hide the pop-ups in the Document pane when the Comment panel is opened, enable the check box. If you set this item as a default, you can expand comments in the Comment panel by clicking icons to see the content of the pop-ups.

- **Automatically open pop-ups on mouse rollover.** Pop-up note windows can be opened or closed. Double-clicking a collapsed pop-up note window opens the window. If you want to have a pop-up note window open automatically as the cursor is placed over a comment icon, select this check box.

- **Always use Login Name for Author name.** Another set of preferences appears when you click Identity in the left pane. The Login Name specified in the Identity preferences is used for the author name on all comments when this check box is enabled. If you are a single user on a workstation, setting the Identity preferences and enabling this check box saves you time creating comments when you want to add your name as the author name.

- **Create new pop-ups aligned to the edge of the document.** By default, the top-left corner of a pop-up note window is aligned to the top-left corner of the comment icon. If you enable this check box, no matter where you create the note icon, the pop-up notes are aligned to the right edge of the document.

- **Copy encircled text into Drawing comment pop-ups.** When proofreading a document and using the Markup tools you mark text with the Rectangle tool, Circle tool, or Cloud tool. When this preference option is checked, the text you surround with one of these tools is placed in a comment note.

- **Copy selected text into Highlight, Cross-Out, and Underline comment pop-ups.** This enables the text selected with the Highlight Text, Cross Out Text, and Underline Text tools to automatically appear in the pop-up note window.

As you can see, there are many different preference settings. How you want to view comments and the methods used for review and comment is influenced by the options you set in the Commenting preferences. Take some time to play with these settings as you use the tools discussed in this chapter.

# Looking at the Annotation & Drawing Markup Tools

Users of Acrobat Pro, Acrobat Standard (Windows), and Adobe Reader (when a file is enabled with usage rights) can access the Annotation & Drawing Markup tools.

Users of earlier versions of Acrobat will notice that all Annotation & Drawing Markup tools are added to the Comment panel. You access the Comment panel by clicking the Comment button adjacent to the Tools button. In Acrobat X all annotation tools and notes are contained in the panel on the right side of the Acrobat window.

As shown in Figure 19.3, commenting tools are organized into two groups: the Annotations group and the Drawing Markups group.

**FIGURE 19.3**

Click the Comment button to open the Comments subpanels.

# Using the Annotation Tools

The Annotation & Drawing Markup tools are intended for use by anyone reviewing and marking up documents. Much like you might use a highlighter on paper documents, the commenting tools enable you to electronically comment and mark up PDF documents. A variety of tools with different icon symbols offer you an extensive library of tools that can help you facilitate a review process.

Most comment tools have a symbol or icon that appears where the comment is created. They also have a note pop-up window where you add text to clarify a meaning associated with the mark you add to a document. These pop-up note windows have identical attributes. How you manage note pop-ups and change the properties works the same regardless of the comment mark you create, with the exception of the Callout and Text Box tools. I explain how to use the Sticky Note tool in this section. All the features described for the Sticky Note tool are the same as when handling note pop-up windows for all the comment tools that accommodate note pop-ups.

## Using the Sticky Note tool

 The Sticky Note tool is the most common commenting tool used in Acrobat and the oldest of the commenting tools, dating back to Acrobat 2. To create a comment note, click the Sticky Note tool in the Annotations panel. After you select the tool, click a document page. What you see first is the Note comment icon. Double-click the icon and an associated note window opens where you can add text for the note.

You can also create a Sticky Note by opening a context menu with the Hand tool and selecting Add Sticky Note. This action adds a note comment that appears when you double-click the note icon, and that also appears listed in the Comments List panel below the Drawing Markups panel.

### Managing notes

The color of a note pop-up and the note icon is yellow by default. At the top of the note pop-up the title bar is colored yellow and the area where you add the contents is white. The title bar contains information supplied by Acrobat that includes the subject of the note, the author, and the date and time the note is created. You can move a note pop-up independently of the note icon by clicking and dragging the title bar.

## Note Nomenclature

The tool you use to create notes is the Sticky Note tool. In earlier versions of Acrobat, this tool was called the Note tool. When referring to the tool throughout this chapter, I refer to it by its proper name in Acrobat 8 through X (Sticky Note tool). When you add comments from most of the other commenting tools, the tools have an associated note pop-up window. Throughout this chapter, I refer to this window as the pop-up note window or simply refer to it as a note or note window.

The official names for the tool panels where you select tools for comments and markups are the Annotations and Drawing Markups panels. For simplicity and ease of reading, I often refer to the tools in both panels as the commenting tools. When you see a reference to the commenting tools, realize that I'm talking about both the Annotation & Drawing Markup tools.

## Cross-Reference

The Subject of a note by default is titled Sticky Note. The default Author name is derived from either your computer logon name or your Identity, depending on how your preferences are established. For information on how to change the Subject and Author in the title bar, see "Sticky Note tool properties" later in this chapter. ■

You delete note pop-up windows and Sticky Note icons either by selecting the note icon and pressing the Delete/Backspace or Del key on your keyboard or through a context menu selection. If you use a keystroke to delete a note, you must be certain to select the icon; then press the Delete/Backspace or Del key. Selecting the title bar in a note pop-up and using the same keys won't delete the note.

To resize a note pop-up window, grab the lower-right corner of the window and drag in or out to resize smaller or larger, respectively. Note pop-ups containing more text that can be viewed in the current window size use scroll bars, so you can scroll the window much like you would when viewing pages in the Document pane. Only vertical scroll bars are shown in the pop-up windows. As you type text in the window, text wraps to the horizontal width, thereby eliminating a need for horizontal scroll bars. As you size a note pop-up window horizontally, the text rewraps to conform to the horizontal width.

You open context menus from either the note icon or the note pop-up window. When opening a context menu from the note pop-up window, you have two choices: open the context menu from the title bar or open the context menu from inside the note window on text selected in the window. Depending on where you open the context menu, the menu selections are different. Opening a context menu from the title bar or from the note icon shows identical menu options.

In Figure 19.4, I opened a context menu on a pop-up note window. The menu options are the same as if I had opened the context menu from the note icon. In Figure 19.5, I selected text inside the note window and opened the context menu. In this figure, text was selected in the note window that adds the Cut, Copy, Paste, and other text-related commands to the context menu. In both menus, you can select Delete to remove the note pop-up menu and the note icon.

## Tip

If you accidentally delete a note or several notes, you can select Edit ⇨ Undo to bring back the note and Sticky Note icon. Successively select the Undo command and you can bring back several Sticky Note icons and note windows. ■

The context menus are similar, and most commands existing in the smaller menu are the same as those found in the larger menu. If two notes are selected, additional menu commands appear in a context menu.

**FIGURE 19.4**

This context menu is opened from the note pop-up window title bar. From the menu options, select Delete to remove the note icon and the note pop-up menu.

**FIGURE 19.5**

When you open a context menu from selected text, the menu options change.

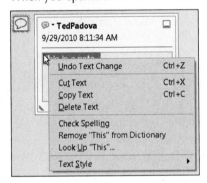

Click the Select Object tool in the Content panel and open a context menu on one of the note icons. You see different menu commands when two or more comment icons are selected as shown in Figure 19.6. The options you have in the context menu are the same as those you find when opening a context menu on two or more form fields.

## Cross-Reference

Most of the context menu commands you see when two or more comment icons are selected should be self-explanatory. For a detailed description of the menu commands, I cover the same commands when managing form fields in Chapter 30. ■

In Figure 19.5, you see a long list of menu commands. Let's take a look at these commands; the same commands found in the context menu shown in Figure 19.4 operate the same way:

- **Cut Text/Copy Text.** These items work as you might assume from using any text editor or word processor. The commands relate to typing text in the note pop-up window. You can also highlight text and use key modifiers (Ctrl/⌘+C for Copy; Ctrl/⌘+X for Cut; Ctrl/⌘+V for Paste).

**FIGURE 19.6**

Drag the Select Object tool through comment icons to select two or more. Open a context menu, and new menu commands appear for organizing comments.

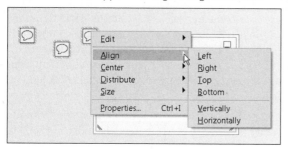

- **Delete Text.** Select text and choose Delete Text. The selected text is deleted.

- **Check Spelling.** When you select Check Spelling in the note pop-up menu, the Check Spelling dialog box opens. When the dialog box opens, click the Start button and Acrobat checks the spelling for all the text typed in the note pop-up. When Acrobat finds a misspelled word, it is highlighted and a list of suggestions that closely match the spelling is shown in the lower window. Select a word with the correct spelling and click the Change button.

- **Remove "..." from Dictionary.** This menu item is active only when you have a word selected in the note pop-up window and that note is contained in your custom dictionary. It's a nifty little feature in Acrobat. Because Acrobat automatically spell-checks text you type in the comment note pop-up window by matching your words to those found in its dictionary, words not matched are underlined in red with a wavy line similar to those used in programs such as Microsoft Word. If you want Acrobat to alert you whenever you type a specific word, remove that word from the dictionary. Then Acrobat displays the word with a red underline each time you use it.

  When would you use this feature? Assume for a moment that you want to use a generic reference to users as opposed to a masculine or feminine reference. Highlight the word *he* or *she* and open a context menu from the note pop-up window. Select Remove "*he*" from Dictionary. Each time you type the word *he*, Acrobat underlines the word because it can't find a match in the dictionary. When you review your notes, you might substitute *s/he* for the word *he*.

- **Look Up "...".** The default menu command is Look Up Definition. When a word is selected, the menu command changes to Look Up *selected word*. For example, if you select a word like *reply*, the menu command changes to Look Up "reply." Select the menu command, which launches your Web browser, opening to the Dictionary.com Web site where the word is searched and a definition is displayed on the Web page.

## Cross-Reference

For more information on looking up a definition and the Dictionary.com Web site, see Chapter 12. ■

- **Text Style.** From a submenu, select from Bold, Italic, Underline, Superscript, Subscript, or Clear Formatting. Select any one of the formatting options to apply to selected text. You can combine format changes by selecting text and a format option, and then return to the context menu and select another option, and so on.

- **Set Status.** Two submenu items are listed when you select Set Status. The Migration submenu command has three additional submenu options for migrating comments. (Comments can be migrated when you make document revisions and you want to migrate comments from an earlier PDF to a revised PDF.) The Review submenu command enables you to choose from various status settings such as None, Accepted, Cancelled, Completed, and Rejected.

- **Mark Unread.** Use this command to mark comments that haven't been read. When you select the command, a bullet mark is added in the comments list adjacent to the comment note icon.

- **Mark with Checkmark.** Whereas the Set Status items are communicated to others, a check mark you add to a comment is for your own purposes. You can mark a comment as checked to denote any comments that need attention, or that are completed and require no further annotation. Check marks are visible in the Comment panel and can be toggled on or off in the pane as well as the context menu. Check marks can be added to comments with or without your participation in a review session. You can choose to have your comments sorted by those with check marks and those comments without check marks.

- **Minimize Pop-Up Note.** Selecting this command closes the note window. Click back on the Sticky Note icon and the note window opens again. The same close action is also available by clicking the minimize icon in the top-right corner of the note pop-up window.

- **Reset Pop-Up Note Location.** If you move a note pop-up window, selecting this menu command returns the note pop-up to the default position.

- **Delete.** Deletes the comment pop-up note and the note icon.

- **Reply.** When participating in a review, you select the Reply command to reply to comments made from other users. A new window opens in which you type a reply message. From the pop-up bar you can review a thread and click the Reply button to send your comments to others via email, using Acrobat.com, to a network folder, or to a Web-hosted server.

## Cross-Reference

For more information on comment reviews, see Chapter 20. ■

- **Show Comments List.** Selecting this item opens the Comment panel. Any comments in the open document are expanded in a list view in the Comment panel. When the Comment panel is open, this option toggles to Hide Comments List.

- **Make Current Properties Default.** Any attributes you changed in the Properties dialog box (see Properties below) such as changing the Author name or Subject can be set to new defaults. After making settings choices, select this menu item and all subsequent notes you add will use the same new defaults.

- **Properties.** Opens the Properties dialog box.

## Cross-Reference

For more information on migration and reviews, see Chapter 20.

### Setting Sticky Note tool properties

Each comment created from any tool supporting a pop-up note has properties that you can change in a properties dialog box. Properties changes are generally applied to note pop-up windows and icon shapes for a particular tool. In addition, a variety of properties are specific to different tools that offer you many options for viewing and displaying comments and tracking the history of the comments made on a document.

With respect to note pop-ups and those properties assigned to the Sticky Note tool, you have choices for changing the default color, opacity, author name, and a few other options. Keep in mind that not all property changes are contained in the properties dialog box. Attributes such as font selection and point sizes are globally applied to note pop-ups in the Comment preferences.

# Setting Up the Author Name for Comment Notes

If you add comment markups where associated note pop-ups are available, you may find the comment note author name to be the same as your computer log-on name. If you open a comment note Properties dialog box and change the name, and then open a context menu on the note icon and choose Make Current Properties Default, the author name doesn't honor the new default. It can be annoying to keep opening comment properties and changing the name on each individual comment note.

There is a reason for Acrobat not adhering to your wishes, and it lies with the Commenting Preferences settings. If you want to change your author name from your computer log-on name, open the Preferences dialog box (Ctrl/⌘+K). Click Commenting in the left pane, and in the right pane where you find Making Comments, you find a setting that enables you to use the author name. By default, Always use Log-in Name for Author name is checked. This check mark overrides the defaults you try to change using the comment note properties.

Remove the check mark, and the next time you change the author name and set new defaults, all your comment author names are changed to your liking.

Making Comments

- ☑ Always use Log-in Name for Author name
- ☑ Create new pop-ups aligned to the edge of the document
- ☐ Copy encircled text into Drawing comment pop-ups
- ☐ Copy selected text into Highlight, Cross-Out, and Underline comment pop-ups

## Cross-Reference

**For information about Commenting preferences, see "Setting Commenting Preferences" at the beginning of this chapter.** ■

Additionally, you have many options available to you in the Properties Bar. If you want certain attributes to be changed for a given comment type, first look at the Properties Bar after selecting a comment tool to see if a property you want to change exists in the toolbar.

In the Sticky Note tool you find attributes for changing pop-up note color, text color, icon shapes, and a variety of font styles. It is easier to change these attributes using the Properties Bar rather than the Properties dialog box. For other properties changes, such as comment author, subject, opacity settings, and editing the review history, you need to use the Properties dialog box.

You open the properties dialog box from a context menu. Be certain to place the cursor on a pop-up note title bar or the note icon before opening a context menu. Select Properties from the menu choices and the Sticky Note Properties dialog box opens, as shown in Figure 19.7.

## Note

**When you create a comment with any of the Comment tools, the Hand tool is automatically selected upon releasing the mouse button. You can select a comment mark/icon or pop-up note with the Hand tool or the Select Object tool. Use either tool to open a context menu where the menu options enable you to select Properties. However, other menu items vary between the two context menus. For information regarding menu options from context menus opened with the Select Object tool, see the discussion on Drawing Markup tools later in this chapter.** ■

## Tip

**To keep a comment tool selected without returning to the Hand tool after creating a comment, check the box in the Properties Bar for Keep tool selected.** ■

The Sticky Note Properties dialog box contains three tabs. Select a tab and make choices for the items contained in the dialog box. For pop-up note properties, the items you can change include the following:

- **Appearance.** Options in the Appearance tab relate to the note icon appearances and the pop-up note window appearance.
  - **Icon.** From the scrollable list, select an item that changes the Note icon appearance. Selections you make in this list are dynamic and change the appearance of the icon in the Document pane as you click a name in the list. If you move the Note Properties dialog box out of the view of the note icon, you can see the appearance changes as you make selections in the list. Sixteen different icons are available to choose from, as shown in Figure 19.8. The same options are also available in the Properties Bar. Click the Icon button in the Properties Bar and a pull-down menu opens, where the same choices are listed.

**FIGURE 19.7**

Select Properties from a context menu and the Sticky Note Properties dialog box opens.

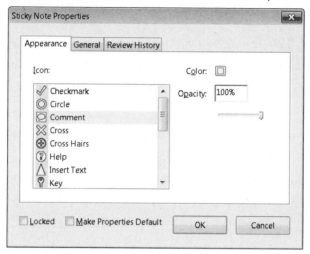

**FIGURE 19.8**

You select icon shapes from the Icon list in the Appearance tab in the Note Properties dialog box or in the Icon pull-down menu in the Properties Bar. You can choose from 16 different shapes.

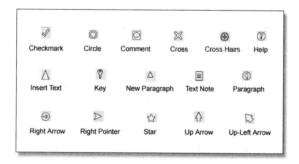

- **Color.** Click the color swatch to open the pop-up color palette shown in Figure 19.9. You select preset colors from the swatches in the palette. You may add custom colors by selecting the Other Color item in the palette, which opens the system color palette. In the system color palette, make color choices and the new custom color is applied to the note.

FIGURE 19.9

Click the color swatch to select from preset colors or select Other Color to open the system color palette, where you select custom colors.

Changing color in the Appearance properties affects both the color of the note icon and the pop-up note title bar. If you mark up and review documents in workgroups, different colors assigned to different participants can help you ascertain at a glance which participant made a given comment.

For a quick change in note colors, use the Properties Bar, where you see the same color attributes found in the Properties dialog box in the Properties Bar Color pull-down menu.

- **Opacity.** Global opacity settings are applied in the Commenting Preferences dialog box. You can override the default opacity setting in the Appearance properties for any given note pop-up window.

  Additionally, opacity adjustments can be made in the Properties Bar by choosing fixed opacity percentages from the Opacity pull-down menu. One distinction between adjusting opacity in the Properties dialog box and making adjustments in the Properties Bar is that the Properties dialog box enables you to choose different opacities at 1 percent increments. The Properties Bar is limited to fixed opacity settings in 20 percent increments.

- **Locked.** Select the Locked check box to lock a note. When notes are locked, the position of the note icon is fixed to the Document pane and cannot be moved when you leave the Note Properties dialog box. All other options in the Note Properties dialog box are grayed out, preventing you from making any further attribute changes. If you lock a note, you can move the pop-up window and resize it. The note contents, however, are locked and changes can't be made to the text in the pop-up note window. If you want to make changes to the properties or the pop-up note contents, return to the Note Properties dialog box and uncheck the Locked check box.

- **General.** Click the General tab to make changes for items appearing in the note pop-up title bar. Two editable fields are available, as shown in Figure 19.10. The changes you make in the Author and Subject fields are dynamic and are reflected in the Document pane when you edit a field and tab to the next field. You can see the changes you make here before leaving the Note Properties dialog box.

**FIGURE 19.10**

Make changes to the Author name and the pop-up note Subject in the General preferences.

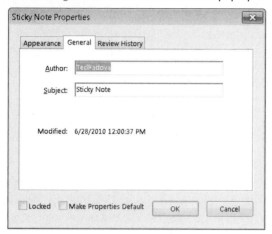

- **Author.** The Author name is supplied by default according to how you set your Commenting preferences. If you use the Identity preferences, the Author name is supplied from the information added in the Identity preferences (see "Setting Commenting Preferences" earlier in this chapter). If you don't use Identity for the Author title, the name is derived from your computer log-on name. You might see names like Owner, Administrator, or a specific name you used in setting up your operating system.

  If you want to change the Author name and override the preferences, select the General tab and edit the Author name. The name edited in the General preferences is applied to the selected note. All other notes are left undisturbed. Note that you also need to change Identity preferences if you want to make a new default for the author name. (See the sidebar "Setting up the author name for comment notes" earlier in this chapter.)

- **Subject.** By default, the Subject of a note for the Sticky Note comment is titled *Sticky Note,* which appears in the top-left corner of the pop-up note title bar. When you use other comment tools, the subject defines the tool used. For example, when using the Highlight tool, you'll see *Highlight* as the subject, using an Approved stamp comment places *Approved* in the Subject field, and so on.

  You can change the subject in the General properties by typing text in the Subject line. You can add long text descriptions for the Subject; however, the text remains on a single line in the pop-up note properties dialog box. (The total characters you can type for the Subject field are 255.) Text won't scroll to a second line. The amount of text shown for the Subject field relates to the horizontal width of the note window. As you expand the width, more text is visible in the title bar if you add a long Subject name. As you size down the width, text is clipped to accommodate the note size.

Text added to both the Author and Subject text boxes is searchable using Acrobat Search when you check the box in the Search panel for Include Comments.

## Cross-Reference

For more information on using Acrobat Search, see Chapter 6. ■

- **Modified.** This item is informational and supplied automatically by Acrobat from your system clock. The field is not editable. The readout displays the date and time the note was modified.
- **Review History.** The Review History lists all comment and status changes in a scrollable list. The list is informational and not editable.

After making changes in the Note Properties dialog box, click the OK button to apply the changes. Clicking on the close box or pressing the Esc key cancels any changes you make to note properties.

## Tip

The Properties dialog boxes for all Comment tools are not dynamic in Acrobat 9. You need to exit the Properties dialog box before making any other edits in your document or accessing any tool or menu command. ■

### Setting default properties

If you use the Make Current Properties Default menu command from a context menu opened on a comment tool or comment pop-up note, the new default is applied only in your current Acrobat session. Quit Acrobat and all the defaults are lost.

You can globally change defaults for comment and markup tools and retain the new defaults in subsequent Acrobat sessions. To set these defaults, open a context menu on any annotation or markup. A properties dialog box for the selected tool opens. Make any settings changes, click OK in the properties dialog box, and your new defaults remain in effect until you change them again or select Reset Toolbar from the same context menu.

## Tip

If you're proofreading a document and you prefer another term or word, you can find word definitions or access a thesaurus by opening a context menu with the Hand tool and selecting Add Note. Type a word in the note pop-up window and highlight the word. Open a context menu from the highlighted word and select LookUp "...". The Dictionary.com Web site opens in your Web browser with the word definition, access to a thesaurus, and an encyclopedia on the open Web page. ■

# Working with the Text Edit tools

The Text Edit tools can be used for any kind of review session; however, they were designed to be used for comments that you want to export to source documents that originated in programs such as Microsoft Word and Autodesk AutoCAD.

## Cross-Reference

For more information on exporting comments to Microsoft Word, see Chapter 8. ■

Open the Comment panel and you find the Text Edit tools displayed in the second row of the Annotations pane. The Text Edit tools include:

- **Insert Text At Cursor.** Select the menu command and move the cursor to the document page. The cursor appearance changes to an I-beam, informing you that text can be selected. Rather than selecting text, clicking the cursor at a specific location is the method most often used with this tool. The intent is to suggest to a reviewer that text needs to be inserted at the cursor position. When you click a document page, a caret is marked on the page at the insertion location and a note pop-up window opens. Type the text to be inserted in the note pop-up.

- **Replace Selected Text.** Use this tool to mark text for replacement. The line appears similar to the Cross Out Text for Deletion mark, but the caret at the end of the mark distinguishes this tool from the Cross Out Text for Deletion tool. A note pop-up window opens where you can add comments. The note contents do not include the text marked for replacement.

- **Strikethrough.** Select text and the text mark appears as a strikethrough. The symbol is used to mark text that needs to be deleted. A note pop-up window opens, where you can add comments.

- **Underline Selected Text.** Use this tool to underline the selected text. A note pop-up window opens where you can add comments.

- **Add Note to Text.** Select a word, a paragraph, or a body of text. When you release the mouse button, a note pop-up window opens in which you can add a comment. Selecting the text does not include the selected text in the pop-up note.

# Working with the Highlight tool

 Earlier versions of Acrobat contained three different highlight tools. In Acrobat X you have the Highlight tool, which behaves like a yellow marker. Drag over text and you get a yellow highlight. Double-click the annotation and you can add text in a Note window.

# Attaching files as comments

You use the Attach File as Comment tool to attach files as comments. Users of Adobe Reader can open your attached files without any special usage rights added to the files for Adobe Reader users. The Attach File as Comment tool differs somewhat from another tool you have available for adding file attachments to PDFs. For detailed information related to using the Attach File as Comment tool and using the Attachments panel for adding file attachments to PDFs, see Chapter 11.

# Recording audio comments

The Attach File as Comment tool has a drop-down menu. Open the menu and you find the Record Audio Comment tool. This tool is used to add audio to a PDF document. You need to have a microphone properly set up on your computer, and you can use audio recordings in lieu of or in addition to other comments you add to a document. For more information on using the Record Audio Comment tool and adding rich media to PDF files, see Chapter 22.

# Using the Stamp tool

The Stamp tool is part of the Commenting tools, but it differs greatly from the other tools found in the Comments panel. Rather than mark data on a PDF page and add notes to the marks, Stamps enable you to apply icons of your own choosing to express statements about a document's status or add custom icons and symbols for communicating messages. Stamps offer a wide range of flexibility for marking documents similar to analog stamps you might use for stamping approvals, drafts, confidentiality, and so on. You can use one of a number of different icons supplied by Acrobat when you install the program, or you can create your own custom icons tailored to your workflow or company needs.

## Cross-Reference

When PDFs contain usage rights for Adobe Reader, all the features related to the Stamp tool, including creating your own custom stamps, are treated in Adobe Reader the same as in Acrobat Standard and Acrobat Pro. To learn more about usage rights with Adobe Reader, see Chapters 4 and 18. ∎

Whether you use a preset stamp provided with your Acrobat installation or create a custom stamp, each stamp has an associated note pop-up window where you add comments. You select stamps from menu options in the Stamp pull-down menu where stamps are organized by categories. Add a stamp to a page by clicking the Stamp tool after selecting a stamp from a category; or you can click and drag the Stamp tool to size the icon. After creating a stamp, you access Stamp properties by opening a context menu and selecting Properties.

### Selecting stamps

Using a stamp begins with selecting from among many different stamp images found in submenus from the Stamp tool pull-down menu. Click the down-pointing arrow and the first three menu commands (following the Show Stamps Palette command) list categories for stamps installed with Acrobat. If you have at least one Custom stamp added to your stamps library, then the custom category you added appears in addition to the three default categories. Notice in Figure 19.11 that I added a custom category called My Custom Stamps that appears at the top of the Stamps pull-down menu below the Show Stamps Palette command.

Selecting one of the menu items opens a submenu where you select specific stamps from the respective category, as shown in Figure 19.11.

**FIGURE 19.11**

Select the pull-down menu from the Stamp tool and select a Stamp category. Select a subcategory and slide the mouse over to the Stamp name. Release the mouse button and the selection becomes the new default stamp.

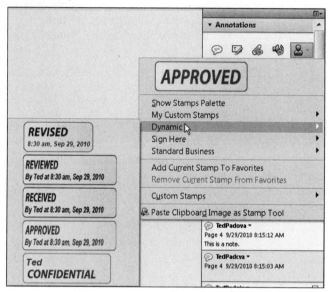

## Adding a stamp to a page

The stamp name you select in the menu becomes the new default stamp. When you click the Stamp tool or click and drag open a rectangle with the Stamp tool, the default stamp is added to the document page. Stamps are created by default with the pop-up note window collapsed unless you enable the Commenting preferences for "Automatically open comment pop-ups for comments other than notes." To open the pop-up note window, click the mouse button on the stamp image. The pop-up note opens and appears the same as other pop-up note windows for other Comment tools.

If you want to resize a stamp after creating it on a page, select the Hand tool and click the stamp icon to select it. Move the cursor to a corner handle and the cursor changes shape to a diagonal line with two opposing arrowheads, as shown in the lower-left handle in Figure 19.12. Drag the handle in or out to resize the stamp.

## Note

**Stamps are always proportionately sized when you drag any one of the corner handles. You don't need to drag handles with a modifier key to proportionately size the image.** ■

Stamps can also be rotated. Click the top-center handle and the cursor changes to a circle with an arrowhead, as shown in Figure 19.12. Drag left or right and the stamp icon rotates. You can rotate stamps in arbitrary 1-degree rotations or in constrained 45-degree rotations. To perform an arbitrary rotation, drag the center handle left or right. To constrain rotations to 45 degrees, press the Shift key and drag the center handle left or right. When you rotate a stamp, the note pop-up remains fixed in the same view as when you first open the note.

**FIGURE 19.12**

To resize a stamp, click a corner handle using the Hand tool and drag in or out to size the icon. To rotate a stamp, click and drag the top center handle left or right to rotate counterclockwise or clockwise, respectively. Pressing the Shift key constrains rotations to 45 degrees.

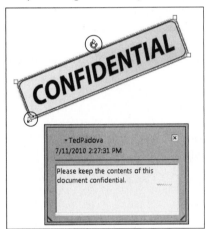

## Cross-Reference

**You can also size and rotate images and objects. For more information on scaling and rotating items in Acrobat, see Chapter 14.** ■

Acrobat offers you an assortment of stamps you can select from the category submenus in the Stamp tool pull-down menu. These stamps are created for general office uses, and you'll find many common stamp types among the sets. The three categories of stamps and their respective types and icons are shown in Figure 19.13.

You should think of these stamps as a starter set and use them for some traditional office markups when the need arises. The real power of stamps, however, lies in creating custom stamps where you can use virtually any illustration or photo image.

**FIGURE 19.13**

Choose stamps from three categories. The stamps installed with Acrobat are general office stamps used in many traditional workflows.

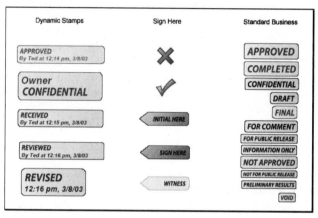

# Resizing Stamps

The stamps you find installed by Acrobat are all vector art images created in Adobe Illustrator. When you resize vector art images, the display quality remains the same no matter how large you size the stamp.

When creating custom stamps you can use a program such as Adobe Illustrator and use vector art for your stamp design. You can also create custom stamps from Photoshop files. These files, however, are raster art. If you size raster artwork above a 100 percent actual view size, you can see distortion in your stamp image.

If you plan on using photographs or other artwork created in Adobe Photoshop, be certain to anticipate the largest size you might need to size up a stamp icon. When you view a Photoshop image created at 72 ppi (pixels per inch), the largest size you can see on your monitor without distortion is a 100 percent actual size view. If you size the stamp up 200 percent or more, you'll notice image degradation, and the image is likely to display jagged edges.

If you anticipate sizing stamps up to a 400 percent view, for example, create your stamps from Photoshop images at 288 ppi. This calculation is determined by taking 72 ppi and multiplying times 4 ($72 \times 4 = 288$). Hence, when you size the stamp up to 400 percent, the actual size view is 72 ppi. As size increases, resolution decreases.

If you plan your work and anticipate the size you might use for custom stamps created from Photoshop files, you can avoid any display problems when viewing files in Acrobat. The sizing issues only have to do with physically sizing a stamp image containing raster artwork. If you use zoom tools in Acrobat, the stamps appear at the same size no matter what zoom level you view a document page.

### Changing stamp properties

You change stamp properties in the Stamp Properties dialog box. You have the same options in the Stamp Properties as those found in the Note Properties dialog box, with one exception. In the Note Properties dialog box, you make choices for the icon appearance from a list in the dialog box. Because stamps have appearances determined before you create the stamp, no options are available for changing properties for the stamp image. The color options in the Stamp Properties dialog box apply to comment notes and not the stamp images. Opacity settings, however, can be applied to the stamp image.

If you want to change the appearance of a stamp, you need to delete the stamp and create a new stamp after selecting the category and stamp name from the category submenu. You delete stamps by opening a context menu and selecting Delete, or selecting the stamp icon and pressing the Backspace/Delete or Del key.

### Creating custom stamps

You might create custom stamps with a company logo or personal identification so users in your workgroup or recipients of your files can see at a quick glance that files received are coming from you. You might use a custom stamp for approving documents in a review session, for asking others to review one of your documents, or for other business uses such as marking documents for signatures, confidentiality, time stamping, or other similar tasks.

To understand how custom stamps are created, follow these steps.

### STEPS: Creating a Custom Stamp

1. **Create the stamp icon image.** Using your favorite authoring program capable of exporting to one of the formats supported by creating a custom stamp, create an icon or image you want to use for your stamp. My tool of choice for creating custom stamps is Adobe Illustrator — but feel free to use the program you like to create your stamp image.

   File formats compatible with custom stamp creation are shown in Figure 19.14. (See the sidebar on file format compatibility later in this chapter.)

2. **Select an image to use as the new custom stamp.** Open Acrobat and select Create Custom Stamp from the Stamp tool pull-down menu. The Select Image for Custom Stamp dialog box opens. Click the Browse button in the dialog box and select your image file in the Open dialog box. Click Open and you return to the Select Image for Custom Stamp dialog box with a preview of your new stamp, as shown in Figure 19.15.

3. **Create a new stamp category.** Click OK in the Select Image for Custom Stamp dialog box and you arrive at the Create Custom Stamp dialog box. The Category text box appears with the default text: *<type here to name a new category>*. Select the text and type a new category name. (Note you can also select a category from the pull-down menu and add your new stamp to an existing category.) In my example, I typed MyStamps for a new category.

**FIGURE 19.14**

File formats compatible with creating custom stamps as available with Acrobat Pro.

**FIGURE 19.15**

Select a file and an image preview is shown in the Select Image for Custom Stamp dialog box.

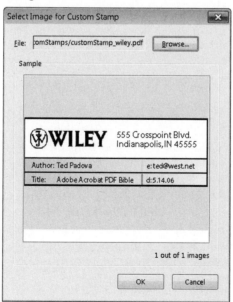

4. **Name your stamp.** Tab to the Name text box in the Create Custom Stamp dialog box and type a name for your stamp. I used the name Author Stamp for my stamp, as shown in Figure 19.16.

**FIGURE 19.16**

Type a Category and Name for your new custom stamp.

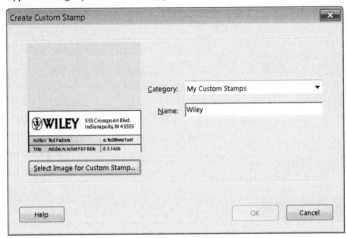

If you want to downsample a large image file, check the Down sample stamp to reduce file size check box. If you want to change your design and not use the image shown in the preview, you can click the Select Image for Custom Stamp button and locate another image.

When all the attributes are assigned for your new stamp, click OK.

5. **Use your new stamp.** Open the Stamp pull-down menu and you should see your new stamp category. Select the category name and the new stamp appears in a submenu, as shown in Figure 19.17. Click the new stamp and click in a document to apply the stamp.

## Appending stamps to a new category

After creating a custom stamp and adding a new category, the next time you open the Create Custom Stamp dialog box, you have a choice for adding a new category or appending a new stamp to your existing category. Here's how you append a stamp to an existing category.

### STEPS: Appending Stamps to an Existing Category

1. **Select Manage Stamps from the Stamp tool pull-down menu.** The Manage Custom Stamps dialog box opens, as shown in Figure 19.18.

2. **Click Create.** Click the Create button and the Select Image for Custom Stamp dialog box opens.

3. **Add a new stamp.** Follow the same steps for adding a stamp as you do when creating a new stamp. When you arrive at the Create Custom Stamp dialog box, select the category you want to add your stamp from in the Category pull-down menu. Type a name for your stamp and you arrive at the Manage Custom Stamps dialog box, as shown in Figure 19.18. In Figure 19.18, I appended a stamp to the MyStamps category.

4. **Click OK.** Your new stamp appears listed in the category submenu.

**FIGURE 19.17**

Select the stamp from the new category submenu and click in a document to add the stamp.

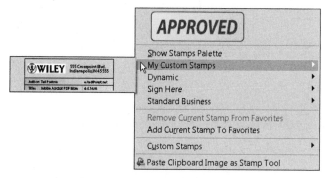

**FIGURE 19.18**

The Manage Custom Stamps dialog box shows all stamps appended to categories.

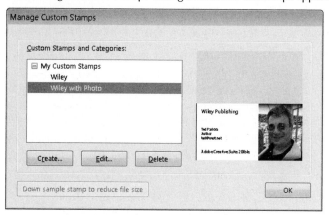

In the Manage Custom Stamps dialog box, you have several tools for managing stamps. Click the Create button to append stamps to a category or create new categories. Select a stamp and click Edit to modify an appearance, category name, or stamp name. Select a stamp and click Delete to remove a stamp from a category, or select a category and click Delete to remove an entire category. Click a stamp and click the Down sample stamp to reduce file size option if you want to downsample images. Apply edits and click OK. When you return to the Stamp tool pull-down menu, the additions/deletions are shown when you open the menu.

## Attaching files

File attachments enable you to attach any document file, recorded sound, or pasted image on your hard drive to an open PDF file. When you attach files, the file is embedded in the PDF document. Embedding a file provides other users with the capability to view attachments on other computers and across platforms. At first it may appear as though the attachment is a link. However, if you transport the PDF document to another computer and open the attachment, the embedded file opens in the host application. Users on other computers need the original authoring application to view the embedded file. You can add file attachments in Acrobat Standard and Acrobat Pro. You can also add file attachments in Adobe Reader when PDFs have been created with usage rights for Adobe Reader.

### Cross-Reference
For more information on using File Attachments and the File Attachments panel, see Chapter 11. ■

# Using the Drawing Markup Tools

As I mentioned earlier in this chapter when introducing the Annotation & Drawing Markup tools, the tools in the Comment panel can be categorized into two subsets. All the previous pages in this chapter dealt with the comment tools from the Sticky Note tool through the Attachment and Text Edit tools. Beginning with the Callout tool and moving to the right in the Drawing Markups panel, you have tools that fit into the Markup tools category.

Markup tools offer you a range of different tools that can be used with technical drawings, manuals, brochures, and design pieces, as well as routine office memos and other such documents. These tools deviate from the standard highlighter and Text Edits tools in that they tend to be used as graphic enhancements for communicating messages. If you're an engineer or technical writer, you may be inclined to use all the tools. If you're a business professional, you may pick and choose certain tools when reviewing and marking up documents. At the least, Acrobat provides a tool for just about any user in any environment when it comes to review and markup.

## Using the Text Box tool

 You use the Text Box tool for creating large blocks of text. You have more control over fonts, text attributes, and flexibility with the Text Box tool than when using a Note comment. Notice in Figure 19.19 the text in the text box and the options available in the Properties Bar at the bottom of the Toolbar Well. When you select text in the text box, you have an abundant number of font attribute choices in the Properties Bar.

**FIGURE 19.19**

Markups shown are the (1) Cloud tool, (2) Callout tool, (3) Line tool, (4) Text Box tool, and (5) Properties Bar.

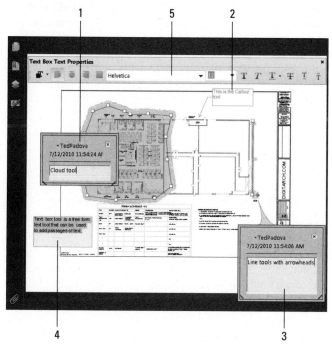

## Using the Callout tool

 The Callout tool is used to note attention to an object, block of text, image, or other element on a page where you want to focus comments about a specific item. Notice in Figure 19.19 the callout in the upper-right corner of the figure.

## Using the Cloud tool

The Cloud tool is used like the Polygon Line tool, where you click, release the mouse button, move the cursor, click, move the cursor again, and continue until you draw a polygon shape. Return to the point of origin and release the mouse button and Acrobat closes the path. The paths appear as a cloud shape. The shape can be filled and stroked. In Figure 19.19, a shape was drawn with the Cloud tool, and an opacity of 50 percent was applied so the underlying area could be viewed with transparency.

## Using the Line tools

You use the Line tools with or without arrowheads. You can add arrowheads and change line styles in the line tools properties.

In the Text Box Properties dialog box, you can change opacity for text boxes, background colors, and line styles for borders. The remaining options are similar to properties for other comment tools.

# The Default Font Attributes

During the initial days of the Acrobat 8 release, many users complained that they didn't know how to change the font color for Text Box comments from the default red text to black text. Perhaps more important to Text Box comments than any other commenting tool, you need to consistently be aware that there are two areas where you change properties for comment and markup tools.

When you open a context menu on a comment or markup tool and choose Properties, the Properties dialog box opens. You make choices as I've consistently addressed in this chapter for changing various properties. However, all properties for many tools are not included in the Properties dialog box — particularly the Text Box font attributes. To change text attributes for Text Box comments, you need to make those changes in the Properties Bar. The Text Box Text Properties open in the Properties Bar when the cursor is active inside a Text Box comment.

You can open and close the Properties Bar by pressing Ctrl/⌘+E, or by opening a context menu on the Toolbar Well and choosing Properties Bar.

Once you change text properties in the Text Box Text Properties Bar, click outside the Text Box and then click the Text Box again and open a context menu. From the menu options choose Make Current Properties Default to change the default for the text attributes. Note that while you see an I-beam cursor, opening a context menu won't provide you an option to change the defaults, which is why you need to first click outside the Text Box comment area.

# Drawing tools

The Line tools are used for creating straight lines. You might use Line tools with or without arrowheads to illustrate points of interest, point out where background elements need to be moved, point to an object, or similar kinds of notations. These tools include:

- **Arrow tool.** The Arrow tool can be used with arrowheads, although applying arrowheads is a matter of user preference. You can draw straight lines on a 360-degree axis.

- **Line tool.** The Line tool can have the same attributes assigned as the preceding Arrow tool, making them indistinguishable from each other. The intent is for the Arrow tool to provide you with a line for arrowheads, whereas the Line tool remains without arrowheads. When marking up a document and using both line tools, you don't need to keep addressing the Line Properties dialog box each time you want to toggle on or off arrowheads. It's a matter of user preference, though, as you can choose to add or eliminate arrowheads from either tool.

- **Oval tool.** Using this tool involves the same process as the Rectangle tool for constraining objects to circles. Oval shapes are drawn without adding the Shift key.

- **Rectangle tool.** Use this tool to draw rectangular or square shapes. To keep the object constrained to a square, hold down the Shift key as you click and drag.

- **Polygon tool.** Use the same sequence of clicking and moving as described earlier for the Cloud tool. When you release the mouse button back at the point of origin, the shape closes with flat edges instead of semicircles like the Cloud tool.

- **Polygon Line tool.** The Polygon Line tool also creates straight lines, but the lines are connected as you click the cursor to move in another direction. When you finish drawing a shape or lines with angles, double-click the mouse button to complete the line.

- **Pencil tool.** You use the Pencil tool to draw freeform lines. Whereas all the line tools draw straight lines, you use the Pencil tool for marking a page by drawing with a pencil, as you would with pencil and paper. The properties for pencil markings include choices for line weights, line colors, and line opacity settings.

  Pencil comments are one contiguous line. If you stop drawing by releasing the mouse button, click, and drag again, a new comment is added to the document.

- **Eraser tool.** The Eraser tool erases lines drawn with the Pencil tool. Lines drawn with other tools cannot be erased with this tool. When you draw a line with the Pencil tool and erase part of the line, the remaining portion of a Pencil comment is interpreted as a single comment. Broken lines where you may have several smaller lines remaining after erasing part of a Pencil comment are considered part of the same comment.

A note pop-up is associated with the entire group of Drawing tools. You can access tool properties by opening a context menu on a mark drawn with any tool. In the Properties dialog box for the respective tool, you can change stroke and fill colors and opacities. For strokes, you can change line weights. As with other comment tools, you also have available in the Properties dialog box General attributes options and Review History options.

### Drawing tools and context menus

One addition to an open context menu on one of the drawing tools is the Flip Line command. If you have an arrowhead on one side of a line and you want the direction to be pointing in the opposite way, open a context menu and select Flip Line.

### Setting Line tool properties

Many of the same Sticky Note properties — color assignment, opacity, author, subject, and reviewing — are available for line tools. Additional line tool properties include line weights and end caps. More options are available for end caps in the Properties dialog box than in the Properties Bar. In Figure 19.20, the line attributes are compared between settings with the Properties Bar on the left and the Properties dialog box on the right.

Line styles are the same in both the Properties Bar and the Properties dialog box, as shown in Figure 19.21.

**FIGURE 19.20**

Line settings available in the Properties Bar and the Properties dialog box

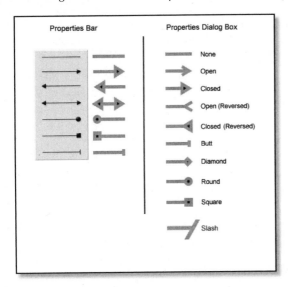

### Managing line comments

To move drawing objects, align them, or reshape them, you need to select an object with the Hand tool. If you experience difficulty selecting a line, it may be because the Make Hand tool select text check box for the Hand tool preference option is selected. If selecting drawing tool objects is awkward, open the Preferences dialog box (Ctrl/⌘+K) and select General in the left pane. Disable the check box for Make Hand tool select text.

FIGURE 19.21

Line Style properties are the same in the Properties Bar and the Properties dialog box.

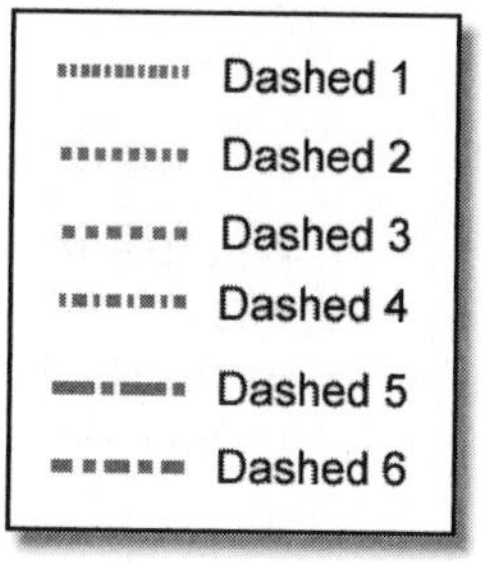

| | |
|---|---|
| ▪▪▪▪▪▪▪▪ | Dashed 1 |
| ▪▪▪▪▪▪▪ | Dashed 2 |
| ▪ ▪ ▪ ▪ ▪ | Dashed 3 |
| ▪▪▪▪▪▪ | Dashed 4 |
| ▬ ▪ ▬▪ | Dashed 5 |
| ▪ ▪ ▪ ▪ | Dashed 6 |

## Tip

**If you want to keep the Hand tool preferences set to select text with the tool and you have difficulty selecting markups, open the Comments tab and click a comment to select it.** ■

## Cross-Reference

**For more information on using the Hand tool for text selections, see Chapter 12.** ■

Click an object, and handles appear either at the line ends or at each end of line segments around polygon objects (see Figure 19.22). You can drag any handle in or out to resize or reshape objects. To move an object, click a line or a fill color and drag the shape.

**FIGURE 19.22**

To reshape objects, select the Hand tool, click a handle (square shape on a line), and drag to change the shape.

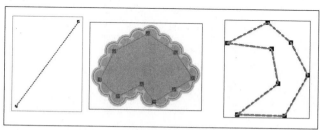

Drawing tools comments can be copied, cut, pasted, deleted, aligned, distributed, and sized. Use the Select Object tool and open a context menu while one or more objects are selected. Choose a menu command for the operation desired.

## Tip

When selecting objects with the Select Object tool, you can draw a marquee through objects to select them. You don't need to completely surround comments within a marquee to select them. ∎

# Adding Comments to Video Files

Once you convert a video file to PDF, import a multimedia file in a PDF, or add a multimedia file to a PDF Portfolio, you can add comment markups to the media. All the comment tools you use for marking up PDF documents are available to you when commenting on media clips.

Adobe has added some special features to commenting on media. When you use any one of the Annotation & Drawing Markup tools that support a note pop-up window and when using the Callout or Text Box tool, the time code for the video frame is reported in the first line of text in the note.

In Figure 19.23, I added comments to four video frames in a movie clip. Notice that the time code for each frame is reported in all the notes.

---

**FIGURE 19.23**

All the Annotation & Drawing Markup tools are supported when commenting on media clips. The first line of text in the notes reports the time code for the clip.

As with any type of comments and markup, you can view the annotations in the Comments List panel. When you click a comment shown in the Comments List panel, the video jumps to the frame where the comment was added.

# Using the Comments List Panel

The Comments List panel conveniently contains many menu commands for managing comments. By default, the Comments List panel dynamically displays the comments you add to a file. At the top of the Comments List panel, you find a Search field and three icons adjacent to down-pointing arrows. To search content in notes, type the search criteria in the text box and press Enter/Return. Search results are displayed in the Comments List panel.

Click an arrow adjacent to one of the three icons and a drop-down menu opens. The three menus include:

- **Sort Comments.** Open the menu and you can choose from Type, Page, Author, or Date for sorting comments in the Comments List panel. Additional options are available displaying comments that you have checked, check mark status, and an option to print or create a comment summary.

- **Filter Comments.** Use this menu to filter comments according to comment type and reviewer.

- **Options.** Use this menu to print comments and export comment data. Printing comments offers an option to print a comment summary and create a custom summary. In Figure 19.24, you see the Create Comment Summary dialog box that appears when you choose Create Comment Summary from the Options menu.

**FIGURE 19.24**

Layouts are dynamically displayed when you choose a summary option in the Summarize Options dialog box.

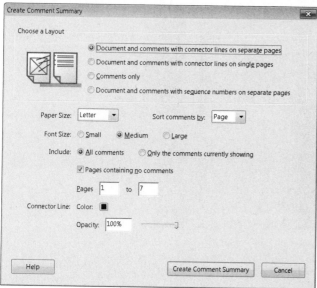

# Summary

In this chapter, you learned how to use the Annotation & Drawing Markup tools and work with the Comments panel.

- Acrobat provides an extensive set of Comment preferences. Before beginning any review session you should review the preference settings by choosing Edit ⇨ Preferences and clicking on Commenting in the left pane.

- Comment tools are found in the Annotations and Drawing Markups panels.

- Most comments created in Acrobat have associated note pop-up windows where you can type comments.

- You access comment properties by opening context menus from a note icon or pop-up note title bar.

- You can create custom stamps in Acrobat from a variety of different file formats.

- Acrobat enables you to add all the comment and markup types to video frames in movie clips and Flash video files.

- The Comments List panel displays all comments in a PDF document. Menus are available in the Comments List panel, where you can mark status changes in comments, check comment status, and filter comments.

- Comments can be filtered and sorted to isolate authors, types, dates, and other criteria. When exporting comments, only the sorted comments in view in the Comment panel are exported.

# Working with Review Sessions

Throughout this book, I address the use of PDFs on the Web, and in several chapters, I've talked about Acrobat.com. As I discussed in Chapter 7, you can download selected Web pages or entire Web sites and have all the HTML pages converted to PDF. In Chapter 11, I talked about sharing PDF Portfolios on Acrobat.com.

Coming ahead in Chapter 26, I talk about Web conferencing and sharing files. In Chapter 27, I talk about eBooks and downloading eBooks; in Chapter 31, I talk about submitting form data to Acrobat.com; and in other chapters you find similar discussions on Acrobat PDFs hosted online and using the new sharing services provided via Acrobat.com. In short, the Web plays a major role with much of your Acrobat activity.

This chapter builds on information covered in Chapter 19 where I discussed using the commenting tools, menus, and Comments List panel. In this chapter I cover commenting through Attach for Email Review and Send for Shared Review on Acrobat.com, which are, again, other uses for PDFs and the Internet.

## Creating an Attach for Email Review

The abundant number of comment tools, properties, and menu commands are nothing more than overkill if all you want to do is add some note comments on PDF pages for your own use. Acrobat is designed with much more sophistication when it comes to commenting, and the tools provided to you are intended to help you share comments in workgroups.

Comment and review among workgroups is handled in two ways. You can set up an Attach for Email Review and exchange comments with your co-workers and colleagues where PDFs and data are exchanged through email, or you can set up a Send for Shared Review where participants upload and download comments to a shared folder on a network or Web server in the review process.

Adobe's Acrobat team wanted to make it almost seamless for any user to not only start a review session but participate in review sessions. With the ability to enable documents with usage rights for Adobe Reader users, anyone with the free Adobe Reader software can participate in an email or shared review.

## Cross-Reference

For more information on adding usage rights to PDFs, see Chapters 18 and 19. ■

# Initiating an Attach for Email Review

An Attach for Email Review is a method for you, the PDF author, to share a document that needs input from other members of a workgroup (in an email exchange), such as a proposal or draft document, and ask them to make comments for feedback. As comments are submitted, you can track comments from others and make decisions about how the comments are treated. Decisions such as accepting or rejecting comments are part of this process. The comment exchanges between you and your workgroup members are handled through email. When using this kind of review, the review initiator is the only person who sees comments from all the reviewers.

When you send a file for review, the PDF contains information about you, the author/initiator, who's invited to the review, and where the original is located on your system. When a recipient receives the email inviting him or her to review your document, the attachment to the email is a PDF the recipients use to make comments. The recipients open the PDF email attachment in Acrobat or Adobe Reader and make comments. When a reviewer finishes commenting, the reviewer sends the data back to the PDF author. The data sent from the reviewers can either be a Form Data File (FDF) or both the data and the PDF document (choices are made in Reviewing preferences accessed by Ctrl/⌘+K and clicking Reviewing). If you start with a large PDF file, the comment exchanges using FDF data require much less data transfers because the comment data are typically much smaller than original PDF files.

When reviews are initiated, you *must* send the PDF file to all reviewers. You can then make a decision in the Reviewing preferences for whether the PDF or an FDF file is returned back to you. In the Preferences dialog box, click Reviewing and type a value in the Send comments as FDF for files greater than text box. The default is 5MB. Therefore, FDF data are returned for all files greater than 5MB. You can raise or lower the number by typing a new value in the text box. This setting is applied only to comments returned back to you. If you have a PDF greater than 5MB — or any file size for that matter — you must first send the PDF document to the recipients.

When comments are returned to you either in PDF or FDF form, double-click the file attachment in your email application. Double-clicking either file type appends comments from recipients to your original PDF you used when you invited recipients to participate in a review.

## Note

Before initiating a review, be certain to add your email address in the Identity preferences. If you don't add the Identity preferences, Acrobat prompts you in a dialog box and opens the Identity preferences for you. You can't proceed until you fill in the preference text boxes. Open the Preferences dialog box and select Identity. Add your personal identity information including your email address. The email address supplied in the Identity preferences is used when emailing PDFs from within Acrobat. ■

To understand how to start an email-based review, follow these steps.

### Steps: Initiating an Email-Based Review

1. **Open a document in Acrobat Pro.** Opening a document is optional because you can begin a review without a document open in the document pane. In this example, I start with a document open in Acrobat Pro. If using Acrobat Standard, you can initiate an email-based review, but you cannot enable the document with usage rights for Adobe Reader users for commenting. Enabling usage rights in Acrobat Standard is limited to enabling forms for form saves and digital signatures. If using Acrobat Pro, you have an option for enabling the document for Reader users to participate in your review.

## Cross-Reference

For more information on enabling PDF documents using Acrobat products, see Chapter 18. ■

2. **Initiate the review.** If you want to make a comment on your document you can do so, but you need to be certain to save all your updates. After saving the file, open the Comment panel by clicking the Comment button on the Toolbar Well. Click Send for Email Review in the Review panel. The first pane in the Getting Started Wizard opens, as shown in Figure 20.1. This is the first of three panes appearing in the wizard when you initiate a review.

   By default, documents active in the document pane are specified in the field box in the first pane. If you change your mind or you start a review without a document open in Acrobat, click the Browse button and browse your hard drive to locate a file.

3. **Invite reviewers.** After identifying the file to send out for review, click the Next button to open the Invite Reviewers pane, as shown in Figure 20.2. The Address Book window will contain a list of recipients for your review. Type the email addresses for the people you want to participate in the review or click Address Book to launch your email address book to select reviewers to invite.

**FIGURE 20.1**

To start a review session, open the PDF to be used for the review and choose Attach for Email Review from the Comment task button pull-down menu or the Comments menu.

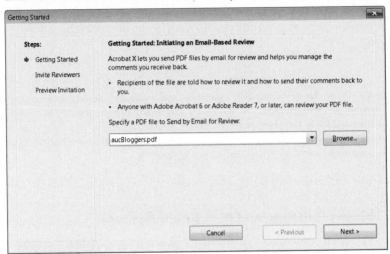

**FIGURE 20.2**

Add email addresses for the review participants.

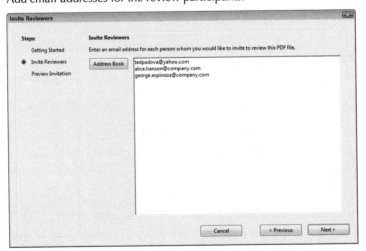

4. **Preview the invitation.** Click Next to arrive at the Preview Invitation pane, as shown in Figure 20.3. This pane displays a preview of the email message you are about to send to reviewers. You can edit the Subject or Message by typing in the respective text boxes.

**FIGURE 20.3**

Preview the message to be sent to reviewers and click Send Invitation.

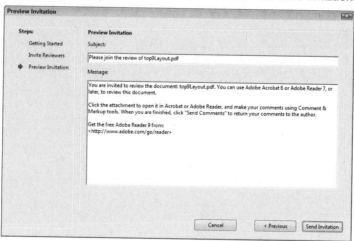

5. **Send the invitation.** Click Send Invitation in the third pane of the wizard. The Outgoing Message Notification dialog box opens as shown in Figure 20.4. This dialog box informs you that your document is attached to a new message in your default email client. You are also alerted to the fact that if you don't have your email application configured to send email automatically, you need to manually send the mail. Click OK to dismiss the dialog box.

**FIGURE 20.4**

Review the information in the Outgoing Message Notification dialog box and click OK.

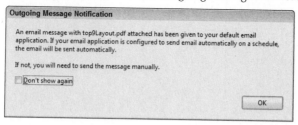

6. **Send the mail.** If your email program does not immediately send the invitation to reviewers, open your default email program and click the Send (or Send/Receive) button to commence the email initiation. In Figure 20.5, an invitation appears in Microsoft Outlook showing a recipient in the To field, the Subject of the email, and a file attachment. The message is derived from the Preview Invitation dialog box. Note

that before initiating a send, you can still edit the message. Click the Send (or Send/Receive) button to send the email and attachment to the reviewers.

**FIGURE 20.5**

If your default email program does not send the message, open the program and click the Send (or Send/Receive) button.

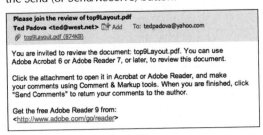

When you send your file for an email review by following the steps in the Attach for Email Review Wizard, your file is enabled automatically with Adobe Reader usage rights. There's nothing special you have to do to enable the PDF document for Adobe Reader users to participate in the review. Be certain all your Reader users are working in Adobe Reader version 7 and above and all Acrobat users are working with Acrobat 6 and above.

Any kind of review you initiate appears in the Tracker where you can monitor reviews, invite new reviewers, set deadlines. and end a review session. For more information on the Tracker, see the section "Using the Tracker" later in this chapter.

## Participating in a review

Participants in a review include you — the PDF author and review initiator — and the people you select as reviewers. In your role, you field all comments from reviewers. If you use Attach for Email Review to send comments back to users, Acrobat does permit you to reply to users' comments. A review session is designed for a single set of responses; however, if you want, you can exchange comments back and forth with the reviewers.

## Managing an Address Book for Review Sessions

When you open the Address Book from the Invite Reviewers section, shown earlier in this chapter in Figure 20.2, when using Microsoft Outlook as your default mail program, you can use names in your Address Book to invite reviewers. Just double-click the names you want to add to the email review; the names appear in the To text box at the bottom of the Address Book dialog box.

After entering email addresses in your Address Book and identifying the names you want to use for the review, click OK to add the addresses to the second pane in the Attach for Email Review Wizard.

Before you begin a review, be certain to save any edits made on the PDF. If you insert pages, delete pages, or perform a number of other edits without saving, the comments retrieved from others will appear out of place and make it difficult to understand where comments are made from the reviewers. Also, be certain to keep the original PDF in the same folder. If you decide to move the PDF to another folder, be certain to keep track of the location where the PDF resides. As you update comments, Acrobat needs to keep track of the directory path where the original PDF can be found. If Acrobat can't find the PDF, you are prompted to search for it.

## Tip

If you want to relocate a PDF file in a review to another folder while maintaining the link in Acrobat to the file, use the Tracker and send the file to a new folder. For more on the Tracker, see "Using the Tracker" later in this chapter. ■

During a review period you and your recipients use tools in Acrobat designed for use with email reviews. When starting an email review, the first time you access the Send for Email Review menu command in the Review panel, the PDF is sent to recipients. All subsequent comment exchanges between you and reviewers are handled with other tools. Be certain to not return to the Send for Email Review command if you decide to respond to user comments. Doing so sends another PDF to a recipient.

### Recipient participation

A recipient receiving your email with the PDF attachment can open the attachment directly within the email message. Double-clicking the email file attachment launches Acrobat and loads the PDF in the document pane.

## Note

Reviewers make comments with any of the comment tools discussed earlier in this chapter and in Chapter 19. After a reviewer completes a review session, the reviewer clicks the Send Comments button in the Document Message bar, as shown in Figure 20.6. ■

When the reviewer sends a response to the PDF author, the PDF author's email address is automatically supplied in the To field in the email program. The reviewer clicks Send and either a PDF or FDF is sent back to the PDF author. Again the file type is determined in the Reviewing preferences.

### Author participation

When a reviewer sends a comment to you, you double-click the email attachment and Acrobat detects that the attachment is part of an email review. A dialog box opens as shown in Figure 20.7, prompting you to merge the comments with your original file that you sent for review.

**FIGURE 20.6**

When working on a PDF in review, the Send Comments button appears in the Document Message bar.

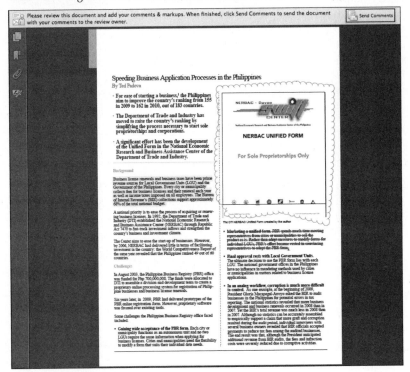

**FIGURE 20.7**

Double-click an attachment with recipient comments and you are prompted to merge the comments in your original PDF that you submitted for an email review.

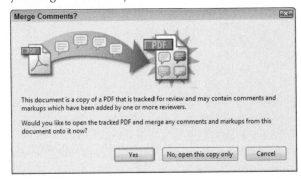

Click Yes and Acrobat opens with the Comment panel open. As comments are submitted from reviewers, you'll want to track reviews and decide to mark them for a status. If you want to reply to the recipients you can elect to send a reply to recipient comments; however, in some cases you'll want to make corrections and start a new review session. If you send a reply, each comment is treated as a separate thread in Acrobat. Instead of your having to select different tools to make responses scattered around a document page, Acrobat keeps each thread nestled together to make following a thread easier. Replies are contained in Note pop-up windows as shown in Figure 20.8. If you want to reply to a comment, open the Note drop-down menu and select Reply. Additionally you can open a context menu in the Comments List panel on a comment and choose Reply.

**FIGURE 20.8**

Comments are threads in Acrobat where you can reply in comment notes within a thread.

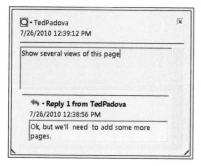

## Cross-Reference

For more on using Reply with note comments, see Chapter 19. ■

### Updating comments

You send a file to recipients for review. The reviewers then send comments back to you. Your original document needs updating to reflect the new additions added by other reviewers. When you receive an email attachment, the comment data are submitted back to you. Only a single PDF resides on your computer. If you want to merge the data sent by other reviewers with your existing PDF document, double-click the file attachment sent back to you. Acrobat updates the original PDF document with the new comments.

### Asking new reviewers to participate

You may begin a review and later decide you want to add new users to participate in the review. You can add new reviewers to a review at any time. To add a reviewer, click Track Reviews in the Review panel to open the Tracker and invite additional reviewers directly in the Tracker (see the next section in this chapter).

## Using the Tracker

The Tracker is a separate window that opens on top of the Acrobat window, where you find menu commands to help manage email-based, browser-based, and shared reviews. To open the Tracker, open the Comments panel and click Track Reviews in the Review panel. When you click Track Reviews the Tracker opens as shown in Figure 20.9.

FIGURE 20.9

The Tracker window provides information and tools for working with documents in review.

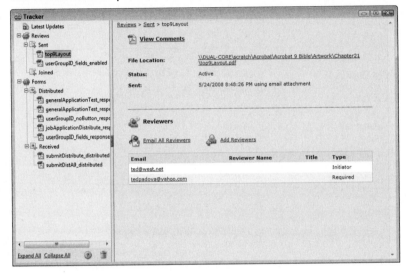

### Viewing documents in the Tracker

The left pane in the Tracker lists all documents you have in review. From the list, select a filename and open a context menu. From the menu choices select Open. The respective file opens in the document pane.

Two categories appear in the left pane in Figure 20.9. All reviews I initiated are listed in the Sent list. Expand the list to see reviews by filename. The Joined list contains all reviews sent to me by another review initiator. Additional categories can appear in the Tracker, depending on the work you perform for reviews and for distributing forms.

From a context menu opened on a document listed in the Reviews ⇨ Sent list shown in Figure 20.10, you have the following commands:

- **Open.** Opens the selected file in the document pane.
- **Stop Collecting Data.** Choose this command to stop the review process.
- **Remove Responses from Tracker.** Removes the selected file from the review.

**FIGURE 20.10**

Open a context menu on a file listed in the left pane of the Review Tracker for more options.

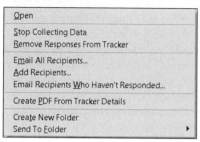

- **Email All Recipients.** Select this option to open your default email application with the To field populated with all review participants. This command is a review reminder for participants who receive an email from you to remind them to send back comments.

- **Add Recipients.** Also launches your default email application with an automated message to invite other reviewers. The selected PDF file used for initiating the original review is added as a file attachment.

- **Email Recipients Who Haven't Responded.** This is a reminder item to send an email to all those recipients who haven't send comments to you.

- **Create PDF From Tracker Details.** New in Acrobat 9, you can create a PDF file from the details for a given review session. Choose the menu item and a PDF containing details about a review opens in the document pane as a new PDF file.

- **Create New Folder.** Choose Create New Folder to open the New Folder dialog box. Type a name for the new folder and the folder appears in the Reviews ⇨ Sent list. You can add reviews and save the files together in the new folder.

- **Send To Folder.** From the submenu all the new folders you create are listed here. Rather than drag and drop files to new folders you create, open a context menu on a file and choose Send to Folder ⇨ <new folder name> to neatly organize your reviews in individual folders.

On Windows a collapsed list is marked with a plus (+) symbol. On the Mac, a collapsed list is marked with a right-pointing arrowhead. Click this symbol to expand the list. If a list is already expanded, a minus symbol (Windows) or down arrow (Mac) appears. Click this symbol to collapse the list.

## Tracking forms

The Tracker also lists all forms you have distributed. Clicking a form changes the Tracker options in the right pane. You have many new options in Acrobat 9 for tracking distributed forms. Rather than go into detail now about tracking forms, I explain more in Chapter 31.

# Working with Shared Reviews

In Acrobat 8, Adobe made an effort to make shared reviews a little easier; however, the complicated process for configuring servers remained a mystery to many Acrobat users and didn't eliminate a necessary dependence on an IT department to help configure a server for online commenting. From the beginning when browser-based reviews were introduced in Acrobat 5, Adobe has been trying to simplify review sessions for people to comment on documents in real time where all participants can see each other's comments, or comment online where people can easily exchange comments in a review session. We've seen simplicity added in each release of Acrobat, but one aspect for developing a seamless environment for online commenting was still needed.

The bottleneck in the seamless operation of the shared review process has always been working with online servers. Unless you had a properly configured server, sharing comments online was impossible in Acrobat 8 and earlier viewers. What was required was technical assistance by a company's IT department to configure a server to support online commenting. For individual users and small businesses without sophisticated IT departments, online commenting just wasn't available in Acrobat 8 and earlier viewers.

In Acrobat 9, Adobe developed the last leg of the seamless operation for online comment and review. This final element of simplicity for engaging in shared reviews is handled through the Acrobat.com services available to users in the entire Acrobat family of products. In Acrobat X, Adobe has added a little more simplicity by introducing the Share panel, where you have two very clear options for engaging in shared reviews.

When you open the Share panel, you'll immediately notice that there is no capability for Browser-Based Reviews as was available with earlier versions of Acrobat. Browser-Based Reviews have been eliminated in Acrobat X.

## Understanding shared review options

You have a few choices to make when engaging in shared reviews: you can share reviews locally on your computer or on network servers. Depending on the choice you make, the process can be very simple or quite complicated.

Among the choices you have for setting up a shared review are:

- **Acrobat.com.** You can set up review sessions on Acrobat.com without having to worry about any special configurations of a server to collect comments and integrate the comments from multiple users.

- **Network Folder.** You can configure a network folder locally on your intranet to set up a shared review among a workgroup.

- **SharePoint Workspace.** For Windows SharePoint workspaces, users need to have read and write access to engage in reviews. This option requires some help from your IT department to configure the server and set up the permissions for the participants.

For the purposes of this chapter, I'll cover only two of the options you have for conducting shared reviews: setting up network folders and using Acrobat.com.

# Using network folders

Setting up a network folder for shared reviews is intended for workgroups having internal local area networks. You begin setting up a network folder the same way as when using Acrobat.com for shared reviews. From a menu command, a wizard opens that walks you through the steps to configure a folder on a network server.

To see how easy it is to set up a network folder for shared reviews, do the following.

### STEPS: Starting a Shared Review Using a Network Folder

1. **Open the Comment task button pull-down menu and select Send For Shared Review.** The Send for Shared Review Wizard opens as shown in Figure 20.11.

Open the pull-down menu at the top of the Send for Shared Review Wizard and choose Automatically collect comments on my own internal server.

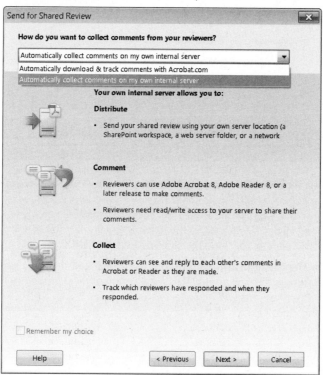

2. **Choose a location for collecting reviewer's comments.** Open the pull-down menu at the top of the Send for Shared Review Wizard and choose Automatically collect comments on my own internal server.

3. **Select a host.** Click Next in the Send for Shared Review Wizard and the second pane in the wizard opens as shown in Figure 20.12. For setting up a network folder, click the first radio button for Network folder.

**FIGURE 20.12**

Click the Network folder radio button and click the Browse button to identify a folder where the review data are collected.

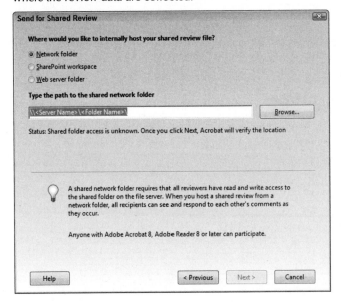

4. **Target a location to host your review.** Click the Browse button to open the Browse For Folder dialog box as shown in Figure 20.13. Choose a directory path, and if you need a new folder created, click the Make New Folder button. Name a new folder and click OK. Click OK in the Browse For Folder dialog box and you return to the second pane in the Send for Shared Review Wizard.

5. **Review the configuration summary.** Click Next and the third pane in the Send for Shared Review Wizard opens. This pane summarizes your choice for the location where the comments will be collected as shown in Figure 20.14. Review the summary and click Next.

**FIGURE 20.13**

If you want to create a new folder, click the Make New Folder button. When the directory path is established, click OK to return to the Send for Shared Review Wizard.

**FIGURE 20.14**

Review the summary and click Next to complete the network folder setup.

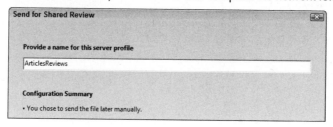

6. **Determine how you want to distribute the PDF document for review.** You basically have two choices when you arrive at the last pane in the Send for Shared Review Wizard. Choose either Adobe Acrobat or Save a local copy and manually send the file later to recipients. If you choose the second option, you have to manually send the document to reviewers. The space on the network server will collect comments from all the reviewers. When you finish the setup, the PDF document appears in the document pane with a message informing you that the file has been saved to your local hard drive and you can send the file at any time to recipients as shown in Figure 20.15.

In the Document Message bar in Figure 20.15, you find some new options for commenting. The Check for New Comments button checks the network folder for new comments that recipients add and populates your PDF document with new comments. The Publish Comments button uploads any new comments you add to the PDF file as XML data collected at the network folder.

**FIGURE 20.15**

When you finish the network folder setup, the PDF document appears in the document pane with a message informing you that you can send the file at any time to recipients.

From the pull-down menu adjacent to the Publish Comments button, you have a few choices for opening the Tracker and working offline. If you work in an area where you don't have access to your server, choose Work Offline and you can make comments while on the road. When you return to your office and connect to the network folder, your offline comments can be published.

## Setting up shared reviews on Acrobat.com

Perhaps the easiest way to initiate and participate in shared reviews is via Acrobat.com. As I've said before in this chapter, you don't have to worry about any configurations as long as you have set up your Adobe ID and can log on to Acrobat.com. This option provides you a seamless, hassle-free approach to engaging in shared reviews.

### Cross-Reference

For setting up an Adobe ID and logging on to Acrobat.com, see Chapter 26. ■

To learn how easy it is to initiate and participate in shared reviews on Acrobat.com, do the following.

## STEPS: Starting a Shared Review Using Acrobat.com

1. **Open the Review panel and click Send For Shared Review.** The Send for Shared Review Wizard opens the same as shown earlier in Figure 20.11.

2. **Choose Acrobat.com for your host.** When you open the Send for Shared Review Wizard, choose Automatically download & track comments with Acrobat.com.

3. **Log on to Acrobat.com with your Adobe ID.** Click Next to open the Send for Shared Review Adobe ID log-on pane as shown in Figure 20.16. Type your ID and password and click Sign In to log on to Acrobat.com.

**FIGURE 20.16**

Type your Adobe ID and password and click Sign In to log on to Acrobat.com.

4. **Identify recipients.** The next item you see is an email message box in the Send for Shared Review Wizard as shown in Figure 20.17. Type the names of recipients in the To text box. If you want to edit the subject and/or message you can edit the respective items in the wizard. Click Send and several things happen to your PDF document:

   - The file you send to Acrobat.com is enabled with Adobe Reader usage rights so Adobe Reader users can participate in the review.

   - The email message is sent to your list of recipients when you click the Send button.

   - The file is automatically uploaded to Acrobat.com. You don't need to bother with anything else other than identifying your recipients and clicking the send button. What could be easier?

FIGURE 20.17

Type recipient names in the To text box and click Send to initiate the review.

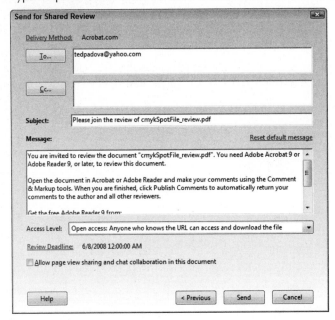

Amazingly, the list of the four preceding steps is all you have to do to initiate a shared review using Acrobat.com. Comments, publishing comments, and downloading comments is handled just like using network folders described in the section "Using Network Folders" earlier in this chapter.

Acrobat confirms your upload with a message box, as shown in Figure 20.18, when you click the Send button in the email message. As with network folder reviews, you have a Check for New Reviews button and a Publish Comments button to download recipient comments and upload your own comments.

FIGURE 20.18

The same buttons for checking for new comments and publishing comments available with network folders are identical when engaging in reviews on Acrobat.com.

When you check for comments on Acrobat.com by clicking the Check for New Comments button in the Document Message bar, new comments added in the review are reported in a message box as shown in Figure 20.19. To accept the comment, click the Click here to accept text link and the comments are downloaded and populate your PDF document on your computer.

When new comments are downloaded from Acrobat.com, a message box reports the number of comments added to your PDF file.

On Windows, you can easily monitor new comment additions on Acrobat.com in the Windows Status Bar as shown in Figure 20.20. A mouseover on the Tracker icon in the Status Bar reports any activity or no activity with shared reviews. Right-click the Tracker icon and choose Open Tracker from a context menu and the Tracker opens.

You can open the Tracker for reviews and when distributing forms from a context menu opened on the Tracker icon in the Windows Status Bar.

Additional items you have available in the Tracker when working with shared reviews include changing the deadline for a review and ending a review. In Figure 20.21 the text for these items open windows for informing recipients that a review deadline has been extended or the review has ended.

**FIGURE 20.21**

You can extend a review or end a review using the Tracker.

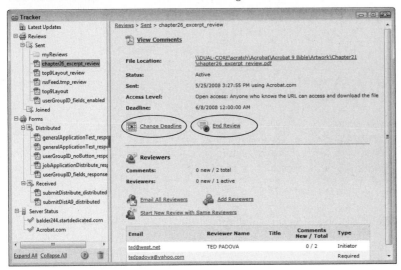

## Offering PROXY reviewers

One of the coolest things that shared reviews can offer is PROXY. Imagine an Adobe (or any company) employee wants to invite you to participate in a review. The Adobe employee uses a shared folder to start a review. However, access to the Adobe Web server is limited to only Adobe employees.

An employee decides to add you to the review, but you don't have access to the shared folder on the Adobe network. You receive the PDF via email and try to *connect* to the shared folder and, of course, you can't. Using shared reviews still makes it possible for you to add your comments to the document.

Participating in such a review provides you with new options on the status bar (see Figure 20.22) where you select Send Comments. Instead of accessing the secure network folder limited to Adobe employees, your comments are emailed to the review initiator who can then inject these comments to the review and (here's the cool part) they show up as "Reviewer name (Adobe employee) by your name," making it clear that the Adobe employee made the comment but you added it to the review cycle.

**FIGURE 20.22**

When participating as a PROXY reviewer, click Send Comments in the status bar to email your comments to the review initiator.

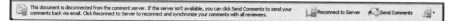

# Commenting in Real Time

An option for the hurried or impatient user is real-time commenting. Through the use of Acrobat.com and Web conferencing, you can host a meeting where you can share files. Without a commercial subscription to Acrobat Connect or Acrobat Connect Pro, your real-time commenting is limited to three people (you and two participants).

## Cross-Reference

Web conferencing and sharing files in real time is covered in Chapter 26. ■

# Summary

In this chapter, you learned how to share files for reviews via e mail and when using Acrobat.com.

- You can initiate email and shared reviews in Acrobat and participate in reviews in any Acrobat viewer. Following steps in a wizard automatically prepares a file with Adobe Reader usage rights so Adobe Reader users can participate in review sessions.

- The Tracker lists all documents initiated from Attach for Email Reviews and Send for Shared Review.

- You can host shared reviews using network folders, SharePoint servers, and Acrobat. com. When it comes to server configuration, Acrobat.com is the easiest method for sharing reviews on servers.

- When files are enabled with Adobe Reader usage rights, the Adobe Reader users can participate in ad-hoc review workflows.

# Creating Links and Actions

O ne of the truly great features Adobe Acrobat offers is the ability to create interactive documents containing hot links that invoke many different actions. Acrobat provides you with many tools and methods for making your PDFs come alive, and Acrobat helps you refine documents for user navigation and interactivity. Regardless of whether you post PDFs on Web servers, communicate via email, replicate CD-ROMs, or work with documents on local network servers, Acrobat offers tools and features that help you create dynamic documents.

In this chapter, you learn how to create links with a variety of Acrobat tools, and you learn some of the differences between several methods for linking views. With hypertext links originating from various elements such as bookmarks, page actions, links, and destinations, you have a number of action tools that provide you with an almost limitless opportunity for handling views and relationships between documents. This chapter covers creating hot links and all the different actions you can associate with links.

## Working with Bookmarks

If you use programs that support exporting to PDF with structure, you can add bookmarks automatically at the time PDF files are created. Programs such as Microsoft Word, Microsoft Excel, Microsoft PowerPoint, Microsoft Visio, Autodesk AutoCAD, Adobe PageMaker, Adobe InDesign, Adobe FrameMaker, and QuarkXPress support bookmark creation from style sheets when you use export tools in the authoring programs. Ideally, in a workflow environment where these programs are used, it is advantageous to create bookmarks from authoring applications when permitted by the program and when the bookmark action relates to page views. In other programs, or when editing PDFs with bookmarks, you may need to reassign bookmark actions, order bookmarks in a hierarchy, or create additional bookmarks.

## Cross-Reference

For more information regarding bookmark exports from authoring programs, see Chapters 8 and 9. ■

The most common bookmark action in Acrobat is navigating page views. Whereas analog bookmarks mark pages, the electronic bookmarks in a PDF document enable you to navigate to different pages and different zoom views. You can capture various page views and zoom in on images, text, tables, and so on in Acrobat as bookmark destinations. In a broader sense, you can use bookmarks to invoke actions such as opening/closing files, opening secondary files, executing menu commands, submitting forms, playing sounds and movies, executing JavaScripts, and a host of other related actions.

## Creating bookmarks

As long as you understand the sequence of steps, creating bookmarks is easy. Creating a bookmark is like capturing a snapshot. The process involves navigating to the page and view you want to capture and then creating the bookmark. Therefore, if you want to capture page 13 of a document in a Fit Page view, you navigate to page 13, click the Fit Page tool, and then create the bookmark.

You create bookmarks from several options. When the page view is in place, open the Options menu in the Bookmarks pane and select New Bookmark. You can also open a context menu on a page and select Add Bookmark from the menu options. In Figure 21.1 the Options pull-down menu in the Bookmarks pane is shown.

## Note

By default, the items Paste under Selected Bookmark and Paste after Selected Bookmark are grayed out. You need to select Cut from the menu options to make the two Paste commands active. ■

Click the Bookmarks pane to access the Options menu for bookmarks. Using a context menu, you can create a bookmark when the Navigation pane is collapsed. When you create a book- mark from a context menu while the pane is collapsed, the Navigation pane opens and the Bookmarks pane is placed in view.

If you open the Options menu in the Bookmarks pane, the menu options appear as shown in Figure 21.1. However, if you first select a bookmark and then open a context menu, the menu commands change to those shown in Figure 21.2. As shown in Figure 21.2, you have fewer menu choices in the context menu than the Options menu.

To create a bookmark, navigate to the desired page view and select New Bookmark from the Options pull-down menu in the Bookmarks pane (left).

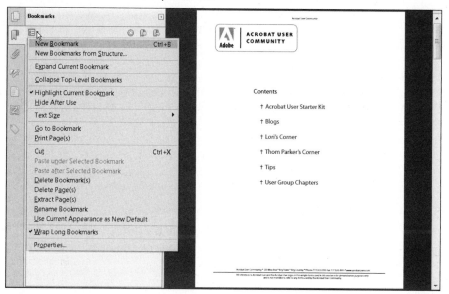

If you select a bookmark in the Bookmarks pane, the context menu is as shown here.

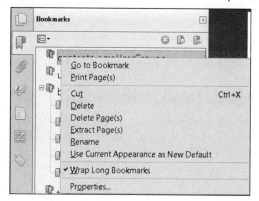

You can also use shortcut keys to create a bookmark when the Bookmarks pane is either opened or closed. Press Ctrl/⌘+B on your keyboard to create a bookmark. In all of these methods, a bookmark defaults to the name Untitled. Acrobat highlights the Untitled bookmark name after the bookmark is created. You type a name and press the Enter or Return key when you are finished typing.

On pages where text corresponds to names you want to use for bookmarks, Acrobat helps simplify the naming process. Click the Select tool and highlight the text you want to use as your bookmark name. From a context menu, select Add Bookmark. The bookmark is created and the highlighted text is used as the bookmark name. The stages of creating a bookmark in this manner are: 1) the page view is in place, 2) text is selected on the page and a context menu opened, 3) Add Bookmark is selected from the menu options (see Figure 21.3), and 4) the bookmark is created using the selected text for the bookmark name. You can also use the Options menu or modifier keys to create a bookmark while text is selected.

**FIGURE 21.3**

To automatically name a bookmark, select text with the Select tool and create the bookmark.

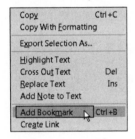

**Tip**

If you want to add a new bookmark in a list following a specific bookmark name, click the bookmark preceding the one you want to add. Leave the bookmark selected and navigate to the page and view for your new bookmark using the Navigation tools. Press Ctrl/⌘+B and the new Untitled bookmark is added below the selected bookmark in the Bookmarks pane. ■

## Managing bookmarks

Bookmarks created in a document appear in the Bookmarks pane in the order they are created, regardless of the page order. For example, if you create a bookmark on page 15, and then create another on page 12, the bookmarks are listed with page 15 before page 12 in the Bookmarks pane. At times you may want to have the Bookmarks list displayed according to page order. Additionally, bookmarks may appear more organized if they are nested in groups. If you have a category and a list of items to fit within that category, you may want to create a hierarchy that expands or collapses. Fortunately, Acrobat enables you to change the order of bookmarks without recreating them. Additionally, you can categorize the bookmarks into groups.

To reorder a bookmark, select either the page icon or bookmark name in the list and drag it up or down and left or right. A triangle with a dotted line appears when you drag a bookmark, as shown in Figure 21.4. To nest a child bookmark below a parent bookmark, drag straight up. The triangle and line show you the target area for the bookmark.

**FIGURE 21.4**

The triangle indicates where a bookmark is to be reordered.

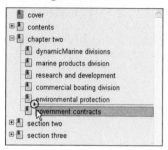

If you have a parent bookmark with several child bookmarks nested below it, you can move the parent to a new location. Drag the parent bookmark and all child bookmarks below it move with the parent. If you want to remove a child bookmark from a nest, click and drag the bookmark to the left and either down or up to the location desired.

In addition to moving bookmarks, you can cut and paste them. Select a parent or child bookmark, and from a context menu or the Bookmark pane Options menu, select Paste under Selected Bookmark or Paste after Selected Bookmark. When you choose Paste under Selected Bookmark the cut bookmark(s) is pasted as a child bookmark under the selected bookmark. Pasting after a selected bookmark pastes the cut bookmark(s) after the selected parent and all child bookmarks.

Multiple nesting is also available with bookmark organization. A bookmark can be subordinate to another bookmark that is itself nested under a parent bookmark. To subordinate a bookmark under a child bookmark, use the same method as described previously for creating the first order of children. As you drag right and up slightly, you can nest bookmarks at several levels.

You can also relocate multiple bookmarks at one time. To select several bookmarks, Shift+click each bookmark in a group. As you hold down the Shift key, you can add more bookmarks to the selection. If you click one bookmark at the top or bottom of a list and Shift+click, all bookmarks between are selected. For a noncontiguous selection, Ctrl/⌘+click. Once selected, drag the bookmarks to a new location in the list. Their order remains the same as it was before the move.

By default, new bookmarks appear at the end of a bookmark list. If you want to place a bookmark within a series of bookmarks, select the bookmark you want the new bookmark to follow. When you select New Bookmark from the Bookmarks Options menu, from a context menu, or press Ctrl/⌘+B, the new bookmark is created at the same level after the one you selected.

# Copying and Pasting Bookmarks

With all the great new features that have been continually added to Acrobat since version 6, the age-old fundamentals of bookmark copying and pasting that could have been implemented in Acrobat 1 are still not available in Acrobat X. Considering the many new wonderful features added to Acrobat 9, it's not much of a disadvantage for users to not have these features added in the newest release, but I know that many users who frequently work with long documents and continually bookmark sections of PDF documents would like to see some options for copying and pasting bookmarks.

There are some third-party developers who do offer solutions for adding more functionality to managing bookmarks. If bookmarking documents is a routine task you perform in Acrobat, you may want to search for some third-party tools to help you out. If you're an occasional bookmarker, then perhaps a workaround just might be helpful.

Assume you have several documents and in each of your PDF files you want to create a bookmark action to open files. You have the same files to open and close from within each separate document. Do you need to manually create bookmarks in each file? Not necessarily.

To begin a workaround for not having a copying and pasting bookmarks feature in Acrobat, create all the bookmark actions you want for opening files in a master file. You might have a document used as a contents page that links to other files via bookmarks. All the necessary bookmark actions designed to open secondary files would be part of this document.

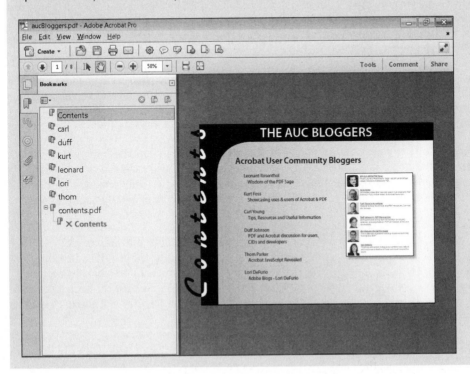

Verify all your bookmark actions work properly and save the file. Next, choose Document⇨Replace Pages and choose one of the linked files to replace all pages in your master file. If your secondary document has more pages, use the Document⇨Insert Pages command. You can always delete old pages without disturbing bookmarks assigned to open files.

After the pages are added to the master file, delete the bookmark link that opens the file you used to replace the pages. Choose File⇨Save As and save the master file under a new name. Repeat the same steps to use the same bookmarks with other files.

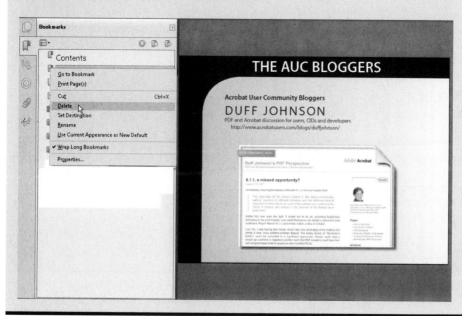

## Cross-Reference

For more information on replacing and inserting pages, see Chapter 15. ∎

# Renaming bookmarks

If you create a bookmark and want to change the bookmark name, select the bookmark to be edited from the Bookmarks pane. From the Options menu, select Rename. Acrobat highlights the name in the Bookmarks pane. Type a new name and press the Return or Enter key on your keyboard to finish editing the bookmark name. You can also click the cursor anywhere in the Document pane to finish editing the name.

You can rename bookmarks by clicking a bookmark name and then clicking the bookmark. You can also use a context menu, but be certain you first select the bookmark; then open a context menu to select the menu option for Rename. When you click a bookmark, you go to the associated bookmark view. Clicking a second time informs Acrobat you want to edit the name. To select the text, click and drag across the part of the name you want to edit or press Ctrl/⌘+A to select all text. When you type a new name, the selected text is deleted and replaced with the new text you type.

## Looking at structured bookmarks

Structured bookmarks retain document structure in files generated from tagged PDF files. You can use structured bookmarks to navigate PDF pages, reorganize the pages, and delete pages. If you create PDFs without tags, you can add structure to a document by choosing Advanced ⇨ Accessibility ⇨ Add Tags to Document. After you have a structured document and you create bookmarks, more options are available to you. For example, you can delete and extract pages via structured bookmarks.

### Cross-Reference
For more information on creating tags and working with structured documents, see Chapter 23. ■

Depending on whether you have a bookmark or a structured bookmark, context menu commands and the Options menu commands appear differently. When you open a context menu from a standard bookmark, the menu commands appear as shown in Figure 21.2. When you open a context menu from a structured bookmark, the menu commands are as they appear in Figure 21.5. Notice the items that relate to Delete Page(s) and Extract page(s) that are available when you open a context menu from a structured bookmark.

**FIGURE 21.5**

These menu commands are available when you open a structured bookmark context menu.

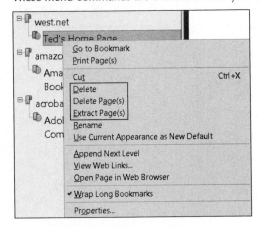

When you create a bookmark, the destination for the bookmark is a link to a page view. In the context menu for standard bookmarks, you see the menu command for Set Destination. You can navigate to a new page and select this command to change the bookmark link to a new view. With structured bookmarks, you capture the page structure (a page view, a table, a head, and so on). In the context menu, be certain to select Delete and not Delete Page(s) if you want to delete a bookmark. The Delete command deletes just the bookmark. Delete Page(s) deletes the bookmark and the page associated with the bookmark.

## Using bookmark appearances

Both bookmarks and structured bookmarks contain menu options for Use Current Appearance as New Default. This menu choice is like a bookmark style sheet where you first select the appearance of the bookmark in terms of font style and color; then you select this menu option to set the attributes as a new default. For example, change the bookmark to small text, italicized, in red; then open a context menu and select Use Current Appearance as New Default. All subsequent bookmarks you create use the same style until you change the default.

The Wrap Long Bookmarks option from either menu creates a word wrap for the bookmark name in the Bookmarks pane. By default Bookmarks are wrapped. If you want more bookmarks to appear in the vertical list, you can unwrap them. An unwrapped bookmark appears as you see in Figure 21.6. When the cursor is placed over a bookmark, a tooltip displays the entire bookmark name. When the bookmark is wrapped, it appears as you see in Figure 21.7.

**FIGURE 21.6**

When a bookmark name is longer than the pane width, a tooltip shows the complete name extended beyond the pane width.

**FIGURE 21.7**

When Wrap Long Bookmarks is selected in a Bookmarks context menu, bookmark names are wrapped to the pane width and shown in multiple lines of text. This display appears by default.

If you open the Options menu, you have more choices for how the bookmarks appear in the pane. In Figures 21.6 and 21.7, bookmarks are expanded. The minus (−) symbol (a down-pointing arrow on Mac) shows all nested child bookmarks below it. Click the symbol and the bookmark collapses to hide all child bookmarks below the parent. If you want to show all top-level bookmarks expanded, select Expand Top-Level bookmarks from the Options pull-down menu. To collapse the bookmark list, select Collapse Top-Level bookmarks from the same menu. The latter menu command is dynamic and is accessible only in the menu if you have first expanded bookmarks.

Select Hide After Use from the Options menu if you want to hide the Bookmarks pane after you select a bookmark. To change text sizes, make selections from the Options pull-down menu. Select Size and choose from one of the three submenu items for Small, Medium, or Large point sizes.

## Adding special characters to bookmark names

Acrobat doesn't offer much in terms of changing fonts and font attributes for bookmark names. However, you are not limited to the default font used for bookmarks; and, when you need some special characters or foreign language text for a bookmark name, you can garner a little help from your operating system.

On Windows, open the Character Map. This file is located by clicking the Start Menu and choosing Programs ⇨ Accessories ⇨ System Tools ⇨ Character Map (Windows XP and Vista). On Windows, open the Start menu and open All Programs. Open Accessories and open System Tools. Double-click Character Map. The Character Map program opens as shown in Figure 21.8.

From the Font drop-down menu, choose a font. Be certain to use fonts with Unicode character equivalents. Not all fonts and not all characters within a font will work. You need to look around for those fonts having a Unicode character set. For starters, try to pick some of the Adobe OpenType Pro fonts when you want to add special characters to your bookmark names.

Click a character in the scrollable window and click Select. The character is added to the Characters to copy text box. You can add several characters to the text box. When finished, click Copy and the character(s) is copied to the Clipboard. Open the Bookmarks pane and create a new bookmark, or edit a bookmark name and choose Edit ⇨ Paste. The character(s) is pasted into a bookmark name. In Figure 21.9 I created several bookmarks using nonstandard characters.

**FIGURE 21.8**

Choose Programs ⇨ Accessories ⇨ System Tools ⇨ Character Map

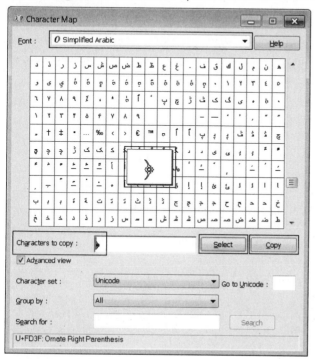

**FIGURE 21.9**

Special characters copied from the Character Map and pasted into bookmark names

On the Mac, you'll find a menu command in the Edit menu used for a similar purpose. Open the Edit menu and choose Special Characters (Mac only). The Characters window opens as shown in Figure 21.10. To insert a special character on the Mac, place the cursor inside a bookmark name and double-click a character in the Characters window. Alternately, you can also click a character and click the Insert button in the Characters window.

**FIGURE 21.10**

Choose Edit ➪ Special Characters on the Mac to open the Characters window.

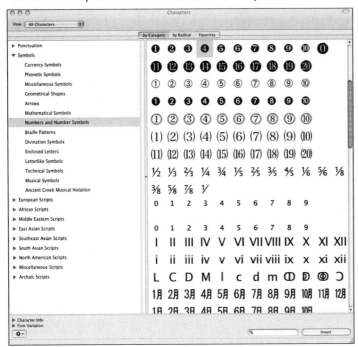

## Using bookmark properties

The Options pull-down menu offers you choices for text sizes. For other text attribute changes you need to use the Bookmark Properties dialog box. Select Properties from a context menu and the Bookmark Properties dialog box shown in Figure 21.11 opens.

**FIGURE 21.11**

The Bookmark Properties dialog box opens when you open a context menu from either a standard bookmark or a structured bookmark.

You select type styles from the Style pull-down menu. Select from Plain, Bold, Italic, or Bold_ Italic. Clicking the Color swatch opens the color pop-up window where you select preset colors or custom colors. You can capture changes from these style options when you select the Use Current Appearance as New Default menu command previously discussed.

The Actions tab enables you to change bookmark actions. By default, the bookmark action is set to open a view within the active PDF document. You can assign many other actions to bookmarks in the Actions properties.

## Cross-Reference
For assigning bookmark actions, see the section "Working with the Link Tool" later in this chapter. ■

## Using the Properties Bar

The Properties Bar also offers options for appearance settings. Using the Properties Bar is a trade-off. On the one hand, it's so much easier to make changes to bookmark appearances using the toolbar; but on the other hand, it takes up a row in the Toolbar Well. If your monitor is large enough and your viewing space adequate to comfortably see page content, then take a look at the options you have in the Properties Bar shown in Figure 21.12. To open the Properties Bar, open a context menu on the Toolbar Well and choose Properties Bar or press Ctrl/⌘+E.

---

**FIGURE 21.12**

Select a bookmark and the Properties Bar reflects options for editing bookmark appearances.

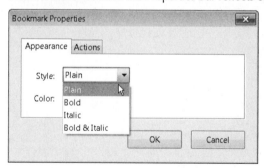

When you select a bookmark, options in the Properties Bar include the following:

- **Style.** Click Plain and a pull-down menu opens displaying font attribute choices.
- **Color.** Click the Color down arrow and the color palette opens, where you can assign a preset color or a custom color to a bookmark name.

All in all, the Properties Bar is helpful when you need to make bookmark appearance and property changes. If the Toolbar Well isn't too crowded, keep this toolbar open when you make edits for bookmarks and other types of link options.

## Setting bookmark opening views

If you create bookmarks in a document and want the document to open with the Bookmarks pane open, you can save the PDF document in a manner where the Bookmarks pane opens in the Navigation pane each time the PDF is opened.

Choose File ➪ Properties or press Ctrl/⌘+D to open the Document Properties dialog box. Click the Initial View tab. From the Navigation pane pull-down menu, select Bookmarks Panel and Page, as shown in Figure 21.13. Save the file after making the properties change. The next time you open the document, the Bookmarks pane opens.

**FIGURE 21.13**

Choose Bookmarks Panel and Page from the Navigation pane pull-down menu.

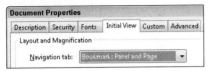

### Cross-Reference

For more information on setting Initial Views, see Chapter 5. ∎

The width of the Bookmarks pane is a user default specific to Acrobat on the end user's computer and not the file you distribute. If you open the Bookmarks pane to a wider view than the default, each time you open a PDF with the bookmarks in view, the Bookmarks pane is opened at the width you last adjusted. If you save the file with the Initial View showing Bookmarks and pages, Acrobat does not take into consideration your Bookmarks pane width. Other users who open your files see the Bookmarks pane sized to their personal pane width default sizes. This default is made from the last time you adjusted the pane size.

# Working with Articles

Acrobat offers a feature to link text blocks together for easy navigation through columns of text. User-specified ranges of text can be linked together, thereby forming an article. Articles help a user navigate through a PDF file, enabling the user to read logical sequences of paragraphs throughout a document. Working with articles is particularly helpful when you view PDF files on the World Wide Web. PDF files can be downloaded a page at a time in a Web browser. If you have a column or group of paragraphs of text that begins on page 1 and continues on page 54, an article thread can assist a reader in jumping from page 1 to page 54 without his or her having to download the remaining pages in the document.

## Viewing and navigating articles

You need to know a few basics on navigating through an article in a PDF. To determine whether articles exist, choose View ⇨ Show/Hide ⇨ Navigation Panes ⇨ Articles. A pane opens with tabs for Articles. You can dock the pane in the Navigation pane by dragging the Articles tab to the pane as shown in Figure 21.14.

**FIGURE 21.14**

Drag the Articles tab to the Navigation pane to dock the pane.

The Articles pane displays any articles existing in the PDF file in the pane list. If you select the Add Article Box tool in the Document Processing panel, the article definition boundaries are shown. In Figure 21.15, the Add Article Box tool is selected. The defined article is contained within a rectangular box with an identifier at the top of the box. In this example, 1-1 indicates that this is article number 1 and box number 1. If the article is continued on another page, the subsequent boxes read 1-2, 1-3, 1-4, and so on, indicating they are continuations of the same article thread. If you create a second article, the article begins with numbers 2-1, indicating the second article in the document and the first box of the second article.

### Viewing Article properties

The article properties are contained in a dialog box that opens immediately after you create an article or double-click an article with the Add Article Box tool. The Article Properties dialog box shown in Figure 21.16 is informational. When you view Article Properties, information supplied at the time the article was created is displayed for four data fields. The Title, Subject, Author, and Keywords fields are the same as those found in the Document Information dialog box. Inasmuch as the data for these fields are identical to that found in document information, Acrobat Search does not take advantage of the article properties information. Properties are designed to help you find information about an article before you jump to the page where the article is contained. All the fields are editable when you open the Article Properties dialog box.

**FIGURE 21.15**

Select the Add Article Box tool and the article boundaries are shown on pages.

**FIGURE 21.16**

The Article Properties dialog box displays user-supplied information for Title, Subject, Author, and Keywords fields. These fields are not searchable with Acrobat Search.

## Viewing articles

Articles are viewed at the maximum view that can be accommodated in the Acrobat window. If you have the Tools panel and the Navigation pane open, articles are displayed at maximum width between the panes. If the panes are collapsed, articles are viewed at maximum width in the Document pane. In other words, Acrobat provides you a maximum view without cutting off text, regardless of what panes you may have open.

In order to read articles you need to have a preference option enabled in the General preferences dialog box. Open Preferences (Ctrl/⌘+K) and click General in the left pane. Check Make Hand tool read articles in the right pane. If the check box is disabled, the Hand tool won't recognize articles.

Alternately, you can open the Articles pane by choosing View ⇨ ⇨ Show/Hide ⇨ Navigation Panes ⇨ Articles. The Articles pane can remain open as an individual pane, or you can drag it to the Navigation pane and dock it. The pane pull-down menu in the Articles pane offers only one option. If you select Hide After Use from the pane pull-down menu, the pane disappears when you view an article. If you want to have the pane remain open, but want more viewing area in the document, dock the Articles pane in the Navigation pane.

Double-click an article to jump to the first view in the thread. When you double-click an article in the Article pane, the article jumps in view in the document pane and the Article pane displays an arrow adjacent to the selected article in the Articles pane. In Figure 21.14 you see the arrow in view in the first article. The change in the icon appearance in the Articles pane keeps you informed of what article is currently being viewed.

Acrobat places the top-left corner where the article begins in view when you double-click an article name in the Articles pane or choose Read Article from the Articles pane Options menu. You immediately see a right-pointing arrow blink on the left side of the first line of text. Once an article is in view, select the Hand tool and position the cursor over the article (be certain the General preferences are set up to read articles with the Hand tool). The cursor changes to a Hand tool icon with an arrow pointing down. As you read articles, the cursor changes according to the direction Acrobat takes you when you're reading an article. For example, if you're viewing a column up instead of down, the cursor changes to inform you which direction you're going. The different cursor views are shown in Figure 21.17.

**FIGURE 21.17**

When you view articles, different cursors inform you ahead of time the direction you need to navigate.

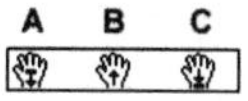

You can use several keyboard shortcuts to help you navigate with the Add Article Box tool. The cursor changes according to the following modifier keys:

- **Click.** The first click zooms to a zoom level up to 800 percent. If you read columns of text, you may find the zoom level lower, such as 200 percent. Click the cursor again to continue reading down a column. Click at the end of an article box, and the view takes you to the beginning of the next column.
- **Shift+click.** Moves backward or up a column.
- **Ctrl+click or Option+click.** Moves to the beginning of the article.
- **Return or Enter.** Moves forward down the column or to the top of the next column.
- **Shift+Return or Shift+Enter.** Moves up or to the previous column.

## Defining articles

You define articles by drawing rectangular boxes around the text you want to include as part of your article thread. While you're using the Add Article Box tool, the rectangular boxes are visible. When the tool is not active, the rectangular boxes are invisible.

Click and drag open a rectangle surrounding the column where you want to begin a new article. When you release the mouse button, the rectangular box displays on the page. At each corner and side of the article box are handles that you can grab and move to reshape the box. Notice that the lower-right corner of the article box contains a plus (+) symbol. When you finish your edits, deselect the Add Article Box tool to exit edit mode. You can return to edit mode and add more columns after reselecting the Add Article Box tool. Click the aforementioned plus symbol to let Acrobat know you want to extend the article thread (see the later section "Combining articles" for more on extended article threads).

## Tip

You can create article threads at the time the PDF file is either exported or distilled with Acrobat Distiller. Many layout applications support creating articles prior to exporting to PDF. In some cases, you may want to have a single article thread to help user navigation through your document. To practice, identify an article in one of the programs discussed in Chapter 7 and then export to PDF either through the program's export feature or by printing to PostScript and later distilling in Acrobat Distiller. ■

### Ending an article thread

When you reach the end of the article, Acrobat needs to know you want to finish creating the thread. To end an article thread, press Return, Enter, or Esc. Acrobat prompts you with a dialog box in which you supply the Title, Subject, Author, and Keywords fields for the article properties. This dialog box appears immediately after you define an article. Supplying the information at the time the dialog box opens is a good idea because then you won't need to worry about returning to the Article Properties dialog box for last-minute cleanup.

### Deleting articles

You might want to delete a portion of an article thread or an entire article. To delete either, select the Add Article Box tool and click an article box. Press the Backspace (Delete) key on your keyboard or open a context menu and select Delete from the menu options. A dialog box opens providing options for deleting the currently selected box or the entire article. To delete the entire article from within the Articles pane, select the article and click the Trashcan icon, or open a context menu and select Delete.

If you select the Box button in the Article dialog box, the deletion eliminates the article box within the article thread you selected when you pressed the Backspace (Delete) key on the keyboard. Clicking the Article button deletes all boxes in the thread across all pages in the document.

## Combining articles

At times you may want to join two articles to create a single article. To join two articles, you must first have them defined in the PDF document. Move to the last column of the first article and click the plus symbol in the last box. This click loads the Add Article Box tool. Next, move to the beginning of the article to be joined to the first article and Ctrl+click or Option+click inside the first box. While you press the shortcut keys, the cursor icon changes, as illustrated in Figure 21.18.

**FIGURE 21.18**

When you press the Ctrl or Option key while clicking the mouse button, the cursor changes to an icon, informing you that the selected articles are to be joined.

The numbering at the top of each box in the second article changes after the articles are joined. For example, if you have two articles, the first numbered 1-1, 1-2, 1-3, and the second article numbered 2-1, 2-2, the new numbering for the second article changes to 1-4 and 1-5. Article 2 takes on the attributes of article 1 and assumes the next order of the article boxes. In addition, the properties identified in the second article are lost. Because the continuation of the thread is from article 1, all attributes for article 1 supersede those of article 2. You can select multiple articles and join them all together in a single article by following the same steps.

## Tip

When combining two articles, always start with the article containing the attributes to be retained. For example, in the preceding case, to retain the attributes of article 2, select the plus symbol at the end of the last column in article 2 and click. Ctrl+click or Option+click in the first box for article 1. When the two articles are combined, the attributes of article 2 are retained. ∎

# Working with the Link Tool

Links are no mystery to any user who has browsed the Web. Buttons and text that open other Web pages and invoke various actions are something that's commonplace to any computer user. With Adobe Acrobat Standard, Pro, and Pro Extended, you have many tools to create hypertext links that ultimately appear very similar to the kinds of links you find on Web pages.

You use the Link tool to create links from a rectangle drawn with the tool to other pages, other documents, and a host of other link actions you can define in the Link Properties dialog box. The area within a link rectangle is the hot spot for invoking a link action. Links used with tools such as Bookmarks and Form Field buttons have the same attribute choices for the actions associated with the objects created with the respective tools.

When creating links with the Link tool, you encounter two dialog boxes used to establish link actions. For link actions used in opening a view, opening a secondary document, or opening a Web page, the action choices are contained in the Create Link dialog box, which opens when you click and drag open a link rectangle and release the mouse button. If you want to assign different link actions, you create a custom link and make attribute choices in the Link Properties dialog box. The Create Link dialog box requires you to make all option choices in the dialog box before you can access any commands in the Document pane. The dialog box is static, which means you need to cancel out of the dialog box or click OK to use menus, short-cut keys, or select objects on a page in the Document pane. When you work with the Link Properties dialog box you can access tools and menu commands, and select items such as buttons and other links on pages while the dialog box remains open.

## Creating links for page navigation

To help you understand how to use the Link tool, it might be helpful to walk through some steps first before you go on to read over all the attribute choices you have for links. To follow the steps that follow, you should have two documents. In one document you'll create a link to another file, and in the other document you'll create a link to a specific page in another file. To see how all this comes about, try following these steps.

### STEPS: Creating Links to Page Views

1. **Open a file in Acrobat.** For these steps you should have two documents. The first document should be a multiple-page file.

2. **Navigate to a page other than the opening page.** Use the Next Page tool or press the Page Down key on your keyboard to open a second page in the document. If you want to open another page, press Next Page or Page Down to scroll pages. Find a page other than the opening page. In my example, I start on page 2.

3. **Create a link.** Select the Link tool in the Content panel and draw a rectangle with the tool in the area you want the link to appear. You should have text or an icon on the page that makes it intuitive for a user to know a link exists: a graphic, blue text,

or some other indication that clicking in an area will invoke an action much like you might see on a Web page.

4. **Identify the link attributes.** When you click the link tool and draw a link rectangle, the Create Link dialog box opens. Click Open a file and click Next. The steps are shown in Figure 21.19.

5. **Select a file to open.** The Select File to Open dialog box appears after clicking Next in the Create Link dialog box. Navigate your hard drive and locate the file you want associated with the link. Click Select in the Select File to Open dialog box.

## Caution

**You should copy all PDFs that are linked to the same folder. If you create links to files scattered on your hard drive and then relocate the files, Acrobat will lose the link destinations. When copying files to the same folder, you can relocate your folder on your hard drive, network server, or CD-ROM without disturbing the link destinations.** ■

**FIGURE 21.19**

1) The Link tool is used to draw a link rectangle; 2) the Create Link dialog box opens after creating a link; 3) link actions are shown in the Create Link Properties window; and 4) clicking Next opens the Open dialog box, where a file to open from the link action is chosen.

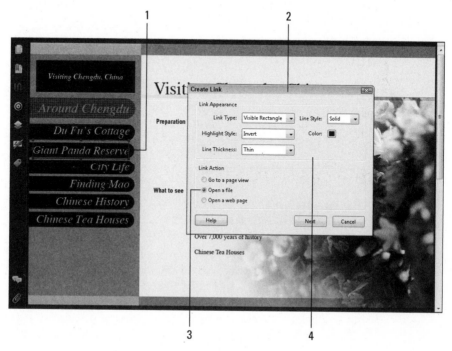

6. **Set the Open Preferences.** After identifying a file to open, the Specify Open Preference dialog box (formerly known as Window Preferences in versions prior to Acrobat 8) appears. Click Existing Window, as shown in Figure 21.20. Making this choice opens your target link while the file containing the link closes.

FIGURE 21.20

Select Existing window to open a file. The current open document closes in the Document pane as the new file opens.

7. **Save the file.** Select File ➪ Save or click the Save tool in the File toolbar to save your edits. Because this file will close when the new file opens, you need to be certain your edits are saved.

8. **Open the linked file.** Select the Hand tool and click the link. The target file should open in the Document pane.

9. **Create a second link.** Select the Link tool and draw a link rectangle. Select Go to a page view in the Create Link dialog box. Click Next to open the Create Go to View dialog box.

10. **Select the target page to open.** While the Create Go to View dialog box (shown in Figure 21.21) is open, you have complete access to all the tools and menu commands in Acrobat. Just leave the dialog box in view and click the Open tool or select File ➪ Open. Locate the file you added a link to in Step 1 and open it. Navigate to the page containing your original link by clicking the Next Page tool or the Page Down key on your keyboard. When the page is in view at the zoom level you want, click Set Link.

FIGURE 21.21

Open the target page and click Set Link.

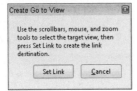

11. **Save your edits.** When you click Set Link, you are returned to the page from which the link originated (your second file in this example). Click the Save tool or select File ⇨ Save to save your edits.

12. **Test the links.** Close all documents and open the file containing the first link. Click the link and the second file opens. Click the link on that page and the first file opens, but this time the page that opens should be a page other than the first page in your document.

Note that you created two different links in these steps. The first link used the Create Link dialog box and you opened a file. When the file was opened you arrived at the default view on the first page in the file. The second link opened a page other than the opening page (in my example it was page 2). To link to specific document pages in secondary files you need to use the Go to a page view option and set the link in the Create Go to View dialog box.

The steps outlined here are but a fraction of the many different attribute choices you have for creating links and choosing actions. A host of other actions are available to you when you create custom links. Read on to find out more about creating different kinds of links.

## Linking to views

In the Create Link dialog box (opened when you draw a link rectangle with the Link tool) you make one of four radio button selections. The first three radio buttons enable you to specify link attributes in the Create Link dialog box shown back in Figure 21.19. If you select the fourth radio button and click OK, the Link Properties dialog box opens where you select different actions for the link behavior.

The first three radio button choices offer you options for selecting a page view or a file to open. Options shown in the Create Link dialog box include the following:

- **Go to a page view.** Use this option to link to a page in the open document or create a cross-document link that opens a page in another document. When you click the Next button, the Create Go to View dialog box opens as shown earlier in Figure 21.21. While the dialog box remains open, you have access to menu commands and tools. Navigate to a page in the open document or click the Open tool, open a second file, navigate to the desired page, and click Set Link.

- **Open a file.** Select this option if you want to open a PDF document or any file from another authoring program. When you click the Next button, the Select File to Open dialog box opens and allows you to select any file on your system. If you select a file other than files that can be opened in Acrobat, you (or your customer) must have the native authoring program installed in order to click the link and open the file. If you select a PDF document, you link to the Initial View in the secondary document.

## Cross-Reference

Initial View is typically the first page in a PDF document, but it can be changed to another page in the Initial View properties. For more information on setting the Initial View, see Chapter 5. ∎

- **Open a web page.** When you select this radio button, the Edit URL field is enabled. You type a URL in the Edit URL field to link to a PDF hosted on a Web site. When you add a URL, be certain to supply the complete Web address, including http://www. After you add a URL, the address becomes a new default. Each time you create a new link, the last URL added to the Edit URL field box is inherited and appears in the field box.

- **Custom Link.** Custom Link in and of itself contains no properties. You select this radio button if you want to set a different action for a link. If you select Custom Link and click OK, the Link Properties dialog box opens.

## Tip

URLs in text on PDF pages don't require links. Acrobat versions 7 and above are intelligent and they interpret URLs created in authoring programs from text with either http://www. or www. prefixes as URLs. When you place the Hand tool over URL text in a document, the Hand tool shows an icon with a Hand and a W inside the Hand indicating a live Web link. Click the link and your default Web browser opens the linked page. For earlier versions of Acrobat having URLs in text, you need to create URL links in the PDF files. Note that end users must have the option Create links from URLs enabled in the General preferences in order for Acrobat to recognize URLs from text. ■

## Cross-Reference

For more information on creating Web links, see Chapter 25. ■

## Editing a link action

If you create a link using any one of the first three radio buttons in the Create Link dialog box and later want to edit the link, you are not returned to the Create Link dialog box. The Create Link dialog box opens only after you first use the Link tool to create a link.

To change a link action, use either the Link tool or the Select Object tool. Double-click the mouse button with either tool to open the Link Properties. If you select the Hand tool and click a link, the link action is employed.

## Applying link appearance properties

The link appearance applies to the rectangle drawn when you drag the Link tool on a page in the Document pane. Default appearances are established from the last appearance settings made for the link properties. To change properties, you have two choices. You can use the Properties Bar or the Link Properties dialog box.

When using the Properties Bar, you make changes to link appearances for the items contained across the bar, as shown in Figure 21.22.

The choices in the Properties Bar include the following:

- **Color.** The Color pop-up window opens when you click the square at the far-left side of the Properties Bar. Choices for color apply to strokes only and the options are the same as you find when changing colors in Note properties.

**FIGURE 21.22**

Select a link with the Link tool or the Select Object tool to enable the options in the Properties Bar.

## Cross-Reference

**For more information on changing Note properties, see Chapter 20.** ■

- **Line Style.** You have choices from the pull-down menu for No Line, Solid, Dashed, and Underline. No lines might be used when you have a graphic image or text on a page and a link is apparent to a user. For example, if text appears blue and under-lined, you might use No Line for the line style.

- **Line Thickness.** The default shown in Figure 21.22 is 1 pt. You have choices for Thin, Medium, or Thick that translate to 1 point, 2 points, or 3 points, respectively. The line weight you choose appears in the Properties Bar. If you select No Line in the Line Style menu, 0 pt is listed in the Properties Bar.

- **Highlight Style.** Use this option to display highlights when the mouse button is pressed. When you select the Hand tool and click a link, the highlight is shown within the link rectangle while the mouse button is pressed. You can choose from No Highlight, Invert, Outline, and Inset.

- **More.** Clicking the More button opens the Link Properties dialog box just as a context menu command does.

Note that when you click the Link tool in the Advanced Editing toolbar and before you create or select a link, the Properties Bar becomes active. You can make choices for Color, Line Style, Line Thickness, and Highlight Style. But the More button is not active unless you select a link. When you click the Link tool before selecting a link and make appearance changes, the changes become a new default and will remain as a default until you change them again. If you quit Acrobat and relaunch the program, the default changes you made are still honored.

## Using link properties

To open the Link Properties dialog box, you can open a context menu and select Properties; double-click a link with the Link tool or the Select Object tool; select a link and press the Enter or Return key; or, with a link selected, click the More button in the Properties Bar. A right-click in Windows or Ctrl+click Mac opens a context menu where you can select Properties to open the Link Properties dialog box.

When the Link Properties dialog box opens, you have options nested in two tabs: the Appearance tab and the Actions tab. By default, the Appearance tab is placed in view, as shown in Figure 21.23.

FIGURE 21.23

Two tabs exist in the Link Properties dialog box where you select appearance and actions options.

The same options offered in the Properties Bar for appearance settings are available in the Appearance tab with the addition of the Link Type and a check box for Locked. Link Type is a choice you have in the Create a Link dialog box as well as here in the Link Properties. Choose from Visible Rectangle or Invisible Rectangle to make the link rectangle visible or hidden.

If you enable Locked, the link rectangle is locked to position on the document page and cannot be moved; however, when you select the Hand tool and click a locked link, the action associated with the link still executes. Locking a link also disables all option choices in the Properties Bar and the Link Properties dialog box for that link. If you need to change properties for a locked link, open the Appearance tab and disable Locked.

## Using link actions properties

Click the Actions tab to assign an action to a link. The default link action is Execute a menu item (the top item in the Actions list). Open the Select Action pull-down menu and you find a scrollable list of Action types, as shown in Figure 21.24. After you create a link with another action type, the new action becomes the default.

The Select Action pull-down menu offers a number of actions you can assign to a link. You can select an action and repeat a selection for a different action to nest action types that are executed in the order displayed in the Actions window. In Figure 21.25, three separate actions are associated with the same link. When you click the link with the Hand tool, a page opens, a Web link opens that launches your default Web browser, and a menu item is executed to quit Acrobat. From the pull-down menu, you can choose action types such as the following.

**FIGURE 21.24**

Click the Select Action pull-down menu to view all the Action types.

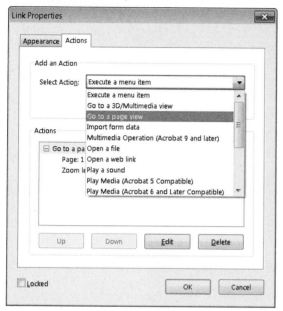

**FIGURE 21.25**

Action items can be nested in the Link Properties. The order of link execution is the same as the order listed in the Actions window.

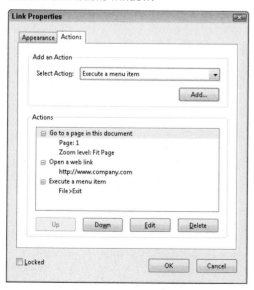

### Executing a menu item

All versions of Acrobat prior to Acrobat 8 provided options for executing almost all the menu commands you see from the top-level menus. In Acrobat 9 and above, instead of using pull-down menus in a Menu Item dialog box, the Menu Item dialog box opens, where you select from a list organized by menus with more limited commands. A number of different menu commands were eliminated from the Execute a Menu Item action beginning with Acrobat 8, including several items that relate to changing PDF content such as adding bookmarks; creating page templates; adding headers, footers, watermarks, and backgrounds; adding comments and markups; and using Forms menu commands. The Advanced menu commands have also been eliminated.

Adobe's reasoning for this is that it's answering user demand for the capability to protect files against document changes that an end user may not be aware of. For example, if you create a button that creates a bookmark or comment, adds a form field, and so on, the end user may not be aware that the button action altered the document. You are now just limited to executing a selected set of menu commands, as shown in Figure 21.26.

FIGURE 21.26

Select menu commands from the Menu Item dialog box when using the Execute a menu item action type.

### Going to a 3D/Multimedia View

If you have a PDF containing a 3-D drawing, you can create links and buttons to open different views in the drawing such as wireframe, shading, and various other views. The Add this action option opens the Select a 3D View dialog box, where you can select the views.

## Going to a page view

You add the action and the Create Go to View dialog box opens. Navigate to a page in an open document or a secondary document and click Set Link. You can also link to pages in secondary documents using the Go to a page view action in the Link Properties dialog box.

## Importing form data

When you select the Import form data option and click Add, the Select File Containing Form Data dialog box opens. Select the file containing the form data you want to import and click the Select button. Imported form data is from files saved in FDF (Form Data File) or XML format that are exported from PDF documents. When you click the Select button, the data matching identical form fields is imported. Using Import form data limits you to importing data saved only in FDF format. If you use the Forms ➪ Manage Form Data ➪ Import Data menu command, data can be imported when saved as FDF, XFDF, XML, FormFlow99 Data Files (.xfd), and TXT. Note that you must have at least one form field on the page for this to work.

## Using Multimedia Operation (Acrobat 9 and later)

Following the Import form data action you find the Multimedia Operation (Acrobat 9 and later) action. In order to use this action, you must have a multimedia file either converted to PDF or imported in a PDF document. When you add the action, the Multimedia Operations dialog box opens as shown in Figure 21.27.

**FIGURE 21.27**

Choose Multimedia Operation (Acrobat 9 and later) and click Add to open the Multimedia Operations dialog box.

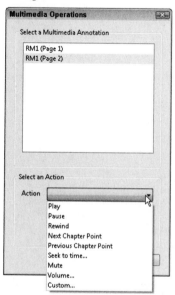

## Cross-Reference

For more information on converting multimedia files to PDF and importing media in PDF documents, see Chapter 22. ■

### Opening a file

You use Open a file to open any file on your computer. When you select the action type and click the Add button, the Open dialog box opens. Browse your hard drive and select the file you want to open. If the file is not a PDF file, you (or your customer) need to have the authoring application that created the file installed on your computer in order to execute the link action. Creating the link does not require you to have any external programs installed on your computer.

### Opening a Web link

The Open a web link option enables you to associate a link action to a Web address. Web links can be contained in PDF documents locally on your computer or within a PDF page where the PDF is hosted on a Web server. If a Web link is contained locally in a PDF document, selecting the link launches the browser configured with Acrobat and establishes a URL connection. Acrobat remains open in the background while the Web browser appears in the foreground. Always use the complete URL to identify a Web address.

When you specify a URL in the Edit URL dialog box that opens after you click the Add button in the Link Properties, you can add custom viewing in the URL address for the way you want to open a PDF document. For example, if you want to view a page other than the opening page you can add to the URL a request for opening any page number. To open a specific page, enter this text: `http://www.mycompany.com/myDoc.pdf#page=3`

In this example the file myDoc.pdf opens on page 3 in the Web browser. In addition to opening a specific page, you can add other viewing parameters such as zoom levels, page modes such as viewing layers or bookmarks, named destinations, and so on.

## Cross-Reference

For more information on setting viewing options with Web links, see Chapter 25. ■

### Playing a sound

You can create a link or button to play a sound in a PDF document. When you select the Play a sound action and click the Add button, the Select Sound File dialog box opens for you to locate a sound file on your hard drive and import the sound. Acrobat pauses a moment while the sound is converted to a format usable in Acrobat viewers. After it's imported in the PDF, the sound can be played across platforms. When the link button is selected, the sound plays. Sounds imported with the Play a sound action and those added with the Record Audio Comment tool support only Acrobat 5 media. If you use the Sound tool you can choose to import either Acrobat 5– or Acrobat 6–compatible sounds.

## Cross-Reference

For importing sounds with the Sound Attach tool, see Chapter 19. For information on using Acrobat 5– and Acrobat 6–compatible sound and media, see Chapter 22. ■

Notice the Multimedia task button pull-down menu contains a Sound Tool. You can use the Sound tool to import sounds. In addition, you can use the Record Audio Comment tool to import sound files. Playing sounds from any of these tools is identical. The Sound tool and the Record Audio Comment tool are limited to adding sounds on a page where a user needs to click or double-click a button to play the sound. The link action is more versatile as you can add sounds with nested link actions, page actions, and form fields. Sound files are supported from files saved as AIFF or WAV.

## Cross-Reference

For information on using the Sound tool, see Chapter 22, and for information on using the Attach Sound tool, see Chapter 22. ■

### Playing media (Acrobat 5 compatible) and Play media (Acrobat 6 and later compatible)

Acrobat 9 and above have an entirely new way to handle multimedia than previous versions of Acrobat. The Play Media (Acrobat 5 compatible) and Play Media (Acrobat 6 and later compatible) actions are used with legacy files where play buttons were added in Acrobat 8 and earlier. These actions are not used in Acrobat 9 when importing media using the Multimedia tools. The alternative to creating play buttons in Acrobat 9 is to use the Multimedia Operation (Acrobat 9 and later) action.

If you have legacy files with media clips and play buttons earlier than Acrobat X, you can edit the play actions by opening a link or button properties and edit the properties in the Play Media (Acrobat 6 or later compatible) dialog boxes as shown in Figure 21.28.

### Reading an article

When you select Read an article as the action type for a link, the Select Article dialog box opens when you click the Add button. If no articles are present in the PDF document, you receive a dialog box alerting you that there are no articles present and you can't use this link action. When articles are present, select the article you want to associate with the link from the listed articles in the Select Article dialog box. When you select the link in the navigation mode, Acrobat opens the page where the first box in the article appears. Additionally, the cursor changes to the Article icon that enables you to continue reading the selected article.

### Resetting a form

The Reset a form link action relates to PDF documents with form fields. When a form is filled out, you can reset the form to remove all data contained in the form fields. Acrobat provides an opportunity to clear the data from all fields or from selected fields you identify individually. A Reset a form dialog box opens, enabling you to select the fields to clear.

FIGURE 21.28

Buttons created in earlier versions of Acrobat for playing media can be edited in Acrobat 9 and above.

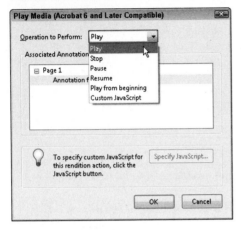

## Cross-Reference

For more information on resetting forms, see Chapter 31. ■

### Running a JavaScript

JavaScript adds great opportunity for making PDF documents interactive and dynamic. You can add JavaScripts to link button actions as well as form fields. When you select Run a JavaScript and click the Add button, the JavaScript Editor dialog box opens. You type the code in the dialog box, or copy and paste code from a text editor to the JavaScript Editor. Click OK to commit the JavaScript.

## Cross-Reference

For more information on writing JavaScripts, see Chapter 32. ■

### Setting layer visibility

For PDF documents containing layers, you first create the layer view you want in the Layers pane. Open the Layers pane and show the layers you want displayed when a user clicks the link. In Figure 21.29, four layers are hidden, as shown in the Layers pane. When you use the Set layer visibility action type, the layer view at the time you create the link is what is shown to the user when he or she clicks the link. This behavior works similarly to bookmarks in which you place in view in the Document pane your resultant view, and then create the bookmark. Layer visibility works the same. Set the visibility you want, and then set the link.

After setting your layer view for the display when the user clicks the link, create a link and click the Custom Link button. Select Set layer visibility from the Actions pull-down menu, and a dialog box opens, informing you the current layer state has been captured.

**FIGURE 21.29**

When using the Set layer visibility action type, you first show the layer view you want to display to assign it to the link action.

### Showing and hiding a field

The Show/hide a field action enables the user to allow selected form fields to be visible or hidden. Forms can be created to display and hide form fields for help menus and informational items, to protect data, and so on. You can make a hidden field visible by opening the Show/Hide Field dialog box and selecting the Hide radio button. Within this dialog box the options for both hiding and showing fields are enabled through radio buttons.

## Cross-Reference

For more information on working with Acrobat PDF forms, see Part VI. ■

### Submitting a form

Form and comment data contained in PDF documents can be transported on the World Wide Web. When a user completes a form, the data can be submitted to a URL as a Form Data File (FDF), HTML, or XML data. Additionally, the entire PDF can be submitted. The PDF author can then collect and process the data. Using form and comment data with Web servers has some requirements you need to work out with the ISP hosting your Web site. If you use forms on PDF Web pages, include a button that submits data after the user completes the form. Using the Submit a form action enables you to identify the URL where the data is submitted and determine which data type is exported from the PDF document. If comment data is to be submitted, a check box enabling comment delivery appears in the dialog box.

In Acrobat 9 and above, you can submit form data without a button. Acrobat 9 and X provide users the option for submitting form data to Acrobat.com without the need to configure Web servers and without a need for creating submit buttons. To learn more about data handling and Acrobat.com, see Chapter 31.

## Managing links

Acrobat provides many menu options for link management. You can copy/paste, align, and distribute links and more through the use of a context menu. If you need to apply these editing tasks to multiple links, select the Select Object tool and click and drag through the links you want to manage.

After selecting multiple links with either the Select Object tool or Link tool, open a context menu as shown in Figure 21.30. The context menu offers several menu categories with submenu items used for managing links.

FIGURE 21.30

Select multiple links with the Link tool or the Select Object tool and open a context menu. Select a menu category and select the command you want to use from the submenu items.

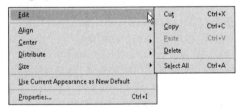

The menu items include the following:

- **Edit.** The Edit menu contains several items in a submenu for cut/copy/paste, accessible in the top-level Edit menu. You can delete a link or group of links by selecting Delete.

- **Select All.** Select All deserves some special comment. When you select a link with the Link tool or choose Edit⇨Select All, all links are selected on a page. If you click a link with the Select Object tool and choose Select All from the Edit submenu, all objects selectable with the Select Object tool are selected on the page. For example, if you have links and form fields, Select All selects all links and form fields on the target page. If you want to edit the links for deletion, alignment, copying, and so on, be certain to click the Link tool and then use Edit⇨Select All.

- **Align.** You can align multiple links Left, Right, Top, Bottom, and along the vertical and horizontal centers. Choose the respective submenu command for the alignment option of your choice.

- **Distribute.** If you have a row or column of links and you want to position them equidistant from each other, choose the Distribute command and select from either Vertically or Horizontally. Vertically distributes a column and Horizontally distributes a row of link objects.

- **Size.** As you create link rectangles, you may draw the links at different sizes. To resize links on a given page to the same size, select one of the links with the Link tool. Using a context menu, click Select All, move the Link tool to the target size link rectangle, and open a context menu. (The target link rectangle is displayed with a red keyline and red handles while the other rectangles in the selected group are highlighted blue.) Select from the submenu Height, Width, or Both. The selected link rectangles are resized to the size of the target link.

- **Properties.** Use this option to open the Link Properties dialog box. If you select more than one link rectangle, the link actions show Varies in the action list if the link actions are different among other selected links. You can apply common appearance settings to all selected links or you can edit actions if the actions are all the same among the selected links.

## Tip

If you want to change appearances for multiple links or button fields, use the Select All menu command to select all the objects, or drag through a group of objects with the Select Object tool and edit the object attributes in the Properties Bar. You can change the color of borders (and fills on button fields), line thickness, and highlight style for multiple objects. ■

# Working with Page Properties

A page action is like a link button that invokes an action when a page is opened or closed in the Document pane. You don't have to click anything because the trigger for executing the action type is handled by Acrobat when the page opens or closes. All the action types available with links are the same actions that are associated with page actions.

To create a page action, open the Page Thumbnails pane. Select a page with the Hand tool and open a context menu. From the menu options select Page Properties. The Page Properties dialog box opens with two sets of properties types available. The default page properties options are contained in the pane for Tab Order, but these settings don't have anything to do with setting a page action, so I'll skip them for the moment.

## Cross-Reference

For information related to setting tab orders, see Chapter 31. ■

It is the second tab in the Page Properties dialog box that is used for setting page actions. Click the Actions tab shown in Figure 21.31, and the options for defining actions to page behavior are displayed. Two areas are used for applying a page action to any page in a PDF document. You first select the trigger for either Page Open or Page Close and then select the action from the Select Action pull-down menu. The options in this menu are the same as you have available with link actions.

**FIGURE 21.31**

Open the Page Properties dialog box from a context menu on a page thumbnail. Click the Actions tab to open the page actions options settings.

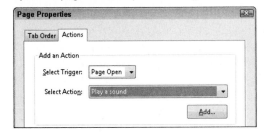

Page actions help you make your PDF documents more automated. You might select a sound to play when a page opens, as shown in Figure 21.31. You may want to set layer visibility, play a movie, or execute a menu item. Of all the options available for action types, with page actions you have the addition of an infinite number of choices when running JavaScripts. You might want to run a script that analyzes the Acrobat viewer version when a user opens a PDF document and alerts the user that Acrobat 6 is needed to properly view your document if the user opens the file in a viewer version earlier than Acrobat 6. This example and many more options are available to you when running JavaScripts from page actions.

## Cross-Reference

To see examples of JavaScripts that analyze Acrobat viewer versions and viewer types, see Chapter 32. ■

# Creating Destinations

A destination is a specific location in a document. Whereas a bookmark and a link may link to page 5 in a file, a destination links to the location where page 5 resides. If you delete page 5, bookmarks and links have no place to go and the links are often referred to as *dead links*. If you delete page 5 where a destination has been created, the destination remains at the same location — that is, following page 4 and preceding page 6. Furthermore, if you insert a page after page 4, the bookmarks and links are linked to page 6. All pages shift to make room for a new page, but the links from bookmarks and links remain fixed on a specific page. With destinations, if you insert a page after page 4, the destination takes you to the new page 5.

You can also use destinations when you want to use JavaScripts for creating pop-up menus and smart forms, and for adding other interactive features.

It all sounds pretty nifty but there's a downside to using named destinations. Adding many destinations in a PDF document adds a lot of overhead to the file size. Destinations can make a PDF bulky and slow if they are used extensively. Destinations should not be thought of as a substitute for bookmarks and links, but rather, a complement for creating interactive documents when other methods don't support the same features.

# Using destination tools

You create, organize, and display destinations within the Destinations pane. To open the panel, choose View ⇨ Show/Hide ⇨ Navigation Panes ⇨ Destinations. The Destinations pane opens in the Navigation pane.

The pane contains a few icons and a drop-down menu, as shown in Figure 21.32. In addition to the pane tools, context menus offer several menu options. You create, edit, and manage all destinations through this pane.

**FIGURE 21.32**

Open the Destinations pane by choosing View ⇨ Show/Hide ⇨ Navigation Panes ⇨ Destinations. Several icons and a list of destinations appear in the pane.

The options are as follows:

- **New.** Click the New icon or a context menu option to create new destinations. You create a destination by first navigating to the page and view, and then creating the destination, much like you create bookmarks.

- **Delete.** You can use the Trashcan icon in the pane, as well as a menu command available when opening a context menu on a selected destination to delete the destination.

- **Sort by Name.** Open the Options pull-down menu and select Sort by Name. Destinations are sorted alphabetically by name. Alternately, you can click Name or Page in the Destinations pane title bar and sort by Name or Page.

- **Sort by Page.** Open the Options pull-down menu and select Sort by Page. Destinations are sorted by page number.

- **Go to Destination.** Open a context menu on a destination and select Go to Destination. When you invoke the command, Acrobat opens the destination page.

- **Set Destination.** Also from a context menu opened in the Destinations pane, Set Destination can reassign a new target destination. First navigate to a new view, and then select Set Destination.

- **Rename.** From a context menu opened on a destination name, select Rename. The name becomes highlighted and ready for you to type text for a new name.

# Creating a pop-up menu

You can use destinations to create a pop-up menu on a page that displays menu options for navigating to other pages and other files. To create a pop-up menu that links to other pages, you create destinations and then add some JavaScript to a link or button field. When a user selects a menu item, the page destination opens in the Document pane.

Follow these steps to experience how easy it is to create an application pop-up menu.

### STEPS: Creating Application Pop-up Menus

1. **Open the Destinations pane.** Open a PDF file with multiple pages. Select View ➪ Show/Hide ➪ Navigation Panes ➪ Destinations.

2. **Create destinations.** Navigate to each page and set the view using the Zoom tools. Click New in the Destinations pane for each page view you want to capture. As you create new destinations, type a name for each destination in the Destinations pane. In my example, I created five destinations, as you can see in Figure 21.33.

---

**FIGURE 21.33**

After you add destinations, the Destinations pane displays the names you used when creating each new destination. The destinations are sorted by name in the list. To sort the list by page number, select Sort by Page from the Options pull-down menu.

3. **Create the JavaScript.** After you have finished adding new destinations, you need to do a little programming. If you haven't used the JavaScript Editor, don't panic. These steps are no more complicated than following a few simple directions.

## Cross-Reference

For a better understanding of using JavaScript and the script created here, see Chapter 32. ∎

Select the Link tool and click and drag open a link rectangle. Ideally, it's best to have some text or an icon on the page indicating that a button or link is present. If you don't use button faces and icons, you can also simply use a keyline border to show where the link appears on the page. In the Create Link dialog box, select Custom link and click OK. The Link Properties dialog box opens. Click Actions and from the Select Action pull-down menu, select Run a JavaScript.

Click Add and the JavaScript Editor opens. In the JavaScript Editor, type the following code:

```
1. var c = app.pop-upMenu
2. (["Blogs", "Thom", "Ted"]
3. ["User Groups", "Chapters"],
4. ["Forms", "Claim Forms"]);
5. this.gotoNamedDest(c);
```

See the sidebar "Analyzing the script" later in this chapter for a detailed explanation of the code. In my example, the code appears as you see in Figure 21.34.

## Note

The items category1, category 2, and so on are used to describe a category you want to appear in your pop-up menu, something like Accounting, Human Resources, Manufacturing, and so on. The items listed in the code (item1, item2, and so on) would be the destination names. You might use something like Accounting Policies, Accounting Procedures, HR Polices, HR Procedures, and so on as the destination names. ∎

**FIGURE 21.34**

JavaScript code to create an application pop-up menu

4. **Exit the JavaScript Editor and Link Properties.** Click OK in the JavaScript Editor and click OK in the Link Properties dialog box.

5. **Test the pop-up menu. Select the Hand tool and click the link.** You should see a pop-up menu similar to Figure 21.35. In this example, I included two items in the

first category to appear in a submenu. In Figure 21.35, User Groups and Forms are labels. The submenus open Chapters and Claim Form items that are the destinations.

**FIGURE 21.35**

If the pop-up menu was created properly, you should see submenu items listed when selecting a category.

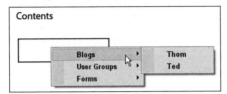

## Note

**To modify JavaScript code, select the Link tool and double-click the link. In the Link Properties dialog box select the item denoted as Run a JavaScript in the Actions list and click the Edit button. The JavaScript edit dialog box opens, where you can make changes to the code. ■**

## Cross-Reference

**For an example of a pop-up menu that opens secondary PDF documents, see Chapter 32. ■**

# Analyzing the Script

In the script, the first line of code sets a variable c for a pop-up menu. Regardless of what your destinations are named or the contents of your PDF, copy this line of code into your JavaScript Editor exactly as you see it.

Lines 2 to 4 contain the categories and submenu commands that link to the destinations you created. Here's where you need to modify your code. Where you see "category x," replace the name with a category title of your choosing. You might want to use names such as Personnel, Administration, and Finance, or you can use category names such as Designs, Illustrations, and Photos, or any other combination of names that relate to the categories you want to use. Notice that line 2 begins with an open parenthesis, (, followed by a left bracket, [. These characters are important to include in your code.

In lines 2 through 4 are three item numbers contained in quotes and separated by commas. These names need to be the same as your destination names. Type the destination names exactly, including letter case, as you created them in your Destinations pane. The order in which you add the names is unimportant. Also notice that after the last destination name and quote mark, no comma is inserted. Lines 2 and 3 end with a comma and line 4 ends with a semicolon. It is also important to type these characters just as you see them in the sample code.

Line 5, the final line of code, is the instruction to take the user to the destination selected from the menu options. Type this line exactly as you see it into your JavaScript Editor.

In this example, destinations are used to navigate pages in a PDF document via a pop-up menu. If the design of your PDF documents better suits pop-up menus, you have many options when using JavaScripts. You can also create pop-up menus with JavaScripts that open other PDF documents or specific pages in other PDF documents and that execute many different menu commands.

# Working with Buttons

In the previous section you saw how to use the Link tool to navigate pages and open files. When links are created, you need some kind of icon or text that lets a user know that a link button exists. If you add links on a page in empty white space with no border keyline, users won't know where or when to click a link button. If you want to use images or icons for button appearances, you can use another form of link tool with the Button tool that supports importing icons.

Prior to Acrobat 9, the button tool and other form field objects were limited to Acrobat Professional and Acrobat 3D. In version 9, you find the button tool and all other form tools available in Acrobat Standard (Windows) and Acrobat Pro (Windows and Mac).

## Creating a button field

Using form fields instead of links has some advantages. You can add image icons to button fields, use rollover effects, and copy and paste fields across multiple pages, and you have all the same action types accessible as those used with bookmarks, links, and page actions.

### Cross-Reference
The discussion of button fields in this chapter is limited to creating button fields with actions similar to those discussed in this chapter when creating link actions. For a more thorough discussion on using form fields in Acrobat, see Part VI. ■

Creating buttons in Acrobat 9 and above permits you to add form fields in Form Editing Mode or by using the Button tool in the Advanced Editing toolbar in Viewer mode (Acrobat 9) or the Button tool found in the Content pane (Acrobat X).

Click the Button tool in the Content pane. From the Add New Field menu in Form Editing Mode choose Button and click the tool on a document page. An abbreviated Properties window opens where you can edit the default name for the field. Click Properties and the Button Properties dialog box opens showing the General tab.

If you don't change the name when you create a button, Acrobat automatically names the field for you beginning with Button1, then Button2 for the next button you create, then Button3 and so on. When you open the Properties dialog box you can additionally change the field name in the General tab. Highlight the default name and type a new name. In this example, I want to create some navigation buttons. The name of the button I'll use is goNext, as shown in Figure 21.36.

FIGURE 21.36

Type a name for the button field in the General tab.

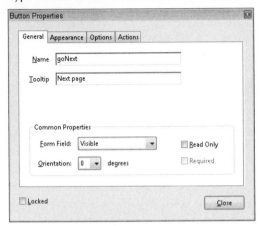

Button faces are handled in the Options tab. Click the Options tab and select Icon Only from the Layout pull-down menu. Click the Choose Icon button and the Select Icon dialog box opens. From this dialog box you need to access yet another dialog box by clicking the Browse button. The Open dialog box opens to a view where you can navigate your hard drive and select a file to import as your button face. Any file format compatible with the Create PDF from File tool is acceptable. Select a filename in the Open dialog box and click Select. Acrobat returns you to the Select Icon dialog box where you can see a preview of the imported file, as shown in Figure 21.37.

If the preview looks like the file you want to use as a button face, click OK to return to the Button Properties dialog box. Click the Actions tab where you assign the action type associated with your button. In this dialog box you make a choice for the trigger action. The default is Mouse Up, which means when the mouse button is released the action executes. Leave the Select Trigger menu option at the default and open the Select Action pull-down menu.

Select Execute a menu item from the pull-down menu. Click the Add button and the Menu Item dialog box opens. Select View ⇨ Go To ⇨ Next Page, as shown in Figure 21.38.

Now repeat the preceding steps to create a second navigation button for moving to previous pages and using a different icon to represent moving backward in the PDF file.

To move a button field, select either the Button tool or the Select Object tool. In the example here, two buttons are created to provide navigation back and forth between pages as shown in Figure 21.39. If you want to move the two buttons together, you need to use the Select Object tool. Drag the buttons to an area on the page where you can easily click the buttons to navigate pages.

**FIGURE 21.37**

The Select Icon dialog box displays a thumbnail preview of the imported file. Click OK to return to the Button Properties dialog box.

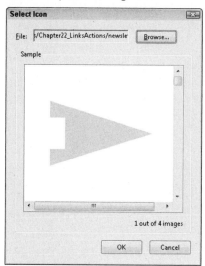

**FIGURE 21.38**

Add a menu item to navigate to the next page.

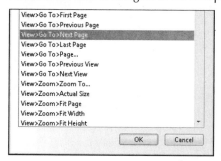

**FIGURE 21.39**

Two buttons used to navigate forward and back through document pages

## Duplicating buttons

At this point, the obvious advantage of using a button field over a link is when you want an image or icon appearance used with the button. Another advantage for using button fields over links is the ability to duplicate button fields across pages. The hard part is finished after you create the fields and add the button faces. The next step is to duplicate buttons so you don't have to copy/paste them on each page.

With the button fields in place, select the Select Object tool and click and drag through both fields. Be certain to click and drag outside the first field so as not to select it while dragging. When both fields are selected, open a context menu and select Duplicate, as shown in Figure 21.40.

**FIGURE 21.40**

Open a context menu on selected buttons and choose Duplicate.

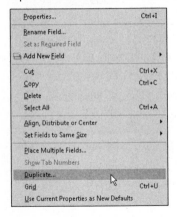

When you release the mouse button, the Duplicate field dialog box opens as shown in Figure 21.41. In the dialog box, select the page range for the duplicated fields. If you created fields on the first page, enter **2** in the first field box and enter the last page number in the second field box. Click OK and the fields with the same field properties are duplicated across the specified pages.

Click the buttons to navigate pages. Notice that each button appears in the same relative position on each page.

The important thing to remember as you work with bookmarks, links, page actions, destinations, and fields is that each is designed for different purposes. Although you can create the same results with one method or another, at times you'll favor one method over the others for a particular editing assignment. Acrobat offers many tools and features for creating dynamic interactive documents, often limited only by your imagination. The more time you invest in learning all that Acrobat affords you, the more impressive results you'll produce.

FIGURE 21.41

Enter the page range in the Duplicate Field dialog box and click OK. The fields are duplicated on the pages you specified.

## Summary

In this chapter, you learned many ways to create link actions such as bookmarks, articles, links, destination, and Page Properties.

- You can name, organize, and create bookmarks with different appearance properties. You can move, reassign, and delete standard bookmarks without affecting page content. When you delete structured bookmarks, the respective pages are deleted.

- Bookmarks support the same actions you can apply to links. Actions enable you to view pages, open documents, create Web links, and write JavaScripts and other types of commands that act as hypertext links.

- Article threads enable viewers to follow passages of text in a logical reading order.

- Links support many different actions from page navigation to running JavaScripts. Links can be copied and pasted and the link properties are retained in the pasted objects. Links cannot be duplicated across PDF pages, and links do not support content files with colors or images.

- Acrobat supports opening user-defined pages in external PDF documents via link actions.

- You select link properties in the Create Link dialog box, from a context menu command, or by double-clicking a link. All link actions are changed in the Link Properties dialog box.

- You make links from text by selecting text with the Select tool and choosing Create Link from a context menu.

- All the actions assigned to links can also be assigned to page actions. Page actions are established in the Page Properties dialog box accessed by opening a context menu on a page thumbnail and selecting Properties.

- Page actions are invoked when a page opens or a page closes.

- Destinations are similar to bookmarks. Destinations do not support actions. Destinations tend to make file sizes larger than when using bookmarks and links.

- You can use destinations, together with a JavaScript, to create pop-up menus.
- You can assign form field buttons different button faces from external files.
- Form fields are supported in Acrobat Standard (Windows) and Acrobat Pro (Windows and Mac).
- Form fields can be duplicated across multiple pages. Duplicated fields are placed on all pages in the same relative position as from where they were duplicated.

# Working with Multimedia and PDFs

Acrobat offers a wide range of possibilities with animation, motion, and sound. You can import sound files in PDFs, import movie files, import and convert Flash files to PDF, and create animation by writing JavaScript routines. With the exception of writing JavaScripts, you create animation and sound in other applications and import them in PDF documents or you can convert a media file directly to PDF.

Movie files added with the Multimedia menu choices in the Content panel are available only in Acrobat. Acrobat Standard does not have these tools and you have no way of adjusting properties for movie and sound files with Acrobat Standard. However, after you've added movie and sound files in Acrobat Pro, all Acrobat viewers, including Adobe Reader, can play the movies and sounds.

In this chapter you learn how to import multimedia files into PDF documents, set a number of import options choices, adjust media properties, and convert media files directly to PDFs.

## Working with Sound Files

You import sounds in Acrobat in one of two ways. You can use the Record Audio Comment tool and record or import a message in the form of a comment. Once recorded, the sound is embedded in Acrobat and not accessible for importing via an action. The other method of handling sound in PDF documents is to import sounds from files saved on your hard drive. By importing sounds you can invoke a sound with various action types — for example, using a page action to play a sound when the user opens or closes a page or clicks a button or link field.

## Cross-Reference

For information on using the Record Audio Comment tool and setting action types, see Chapter 19. For more information on action types, see Chapter 21. ∎

You import sound files by opening the Multimedia drop-down menu in the Content panel and clicking Sound. Be certain to understand the difference between creating an audio comment and importing a sound with the Sound tool. Using the Record Audio Comment tool enables you to record a sound or import a sound file from your hard drive. Using the Sound tool enables you to import a sound from a file saved in a format compatible for importing sounds but does not offer you an option for recording a sound. Before you can use the Sound tool, you need to either acquire or edit sounds and save them to a file format Acrobat recognizes.

## Note

The Record Audio Comment tool is available in all Acrobat viewers including Adobe Reader when PDFs have been enabled with Adobe Reader usage rights. For more information on enabling PDFs with Adobe Reader usage rights, see Chapter 18. ∎

## Creating sound files

If you are so inclined you can purchase a commercial application for editing sound and saving recordings that Acrobat can recognize. If recording sounds is an infrequent task and does not warrant the purchase of expensive commercial software, you can find sound-recording applications as shareware and in the public domain that can satisfy almost any need you have for using sounds on PDF documents.

Web sites change frequently, so you may need to do a search for public domain and shareware applications for your computer platform. As of this writing you can find sound-editing programs at www.freewarefiles.com (Windows) or www.macupdate.com (Mac). You can find applications that enable you to record sounds and save them in formats acceptable to the platform you use that can then be recognized by Acrobat. The most common of the file types Acrobat recognizes is WAV for Windows and AIFF for Mac.

## Note

You can import video and sound files that are compatible with Apple QuickTime, Flash Player, Windows Built-In Player, RealOne, and Windows Media Player. Windows media files need to be converted to QuickTime if you're importing a Windows Media file on a Mac. Windows needs a QuickTime installation in order to import QuickTime files on Windows. Sound files saved as WAV and AIFF can be imported in Acrobat running on either platform. ∎

Be certain you have a microphone properly connected to your computer according to your computer's user manual. Launch the sound-editing application you downloaded from a Web site or use a commercial application if you have one available. Most programs offer you a record button similar in appearance to a tape recorder or VCR. Click the Record button and speak into the microphone. When finished recording, click the Stop button. Depending on the application, you may be prompted in a dialog box to save the file, or you may see a window where you can further edit the sound, as shown in Figure 22.1.

To record sounds and save the sound to a file available for importing in Acrobat, use a sound-editing program.

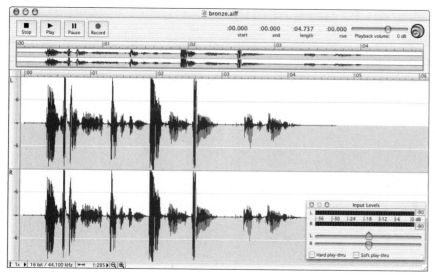

If a dialog box does not prompt you to save the recording, select Save or Save As from a menu option. Typically the commands are under the File menu, but these may vary depending on the program you use. When you save the file, be certain to save in a format acceptable to Acrobat. A WAV (Windows) or AIFF (Mac) file format can be imported in Acrobat, but be careful of any file compression applied to the file when saved. You may need to test various compression options in order to find a format that Acrobat can recognize. After choosing the format, supply a name for the file with the proper extension, as shown in Figure 22.2.

FIGURE 22.2

After editing a sound, save the file in either AIFF (Mac) or WAV (Windows) format.

## Adding sounds to page actions

A sound might be added to a Page Open or a Page Close action to provide informational instructions to complete a form, play a music score, or other similar function. In order to add a sound to a page action, you must have the sound file saved to disk as described in the preceding section. To add a sound to a page action, follow these steps.

## Note

Acrobat Standard does support importing sounds on page actions, bookmarks, and with links. Although you have no Sound tool in Acrobat Standard, you can use an action to import sounds. ■

### STEPS: Adding Sounds to Page Actions

1. **Open the Page Properties.** Be certain your sound file is available in a directory on your hard drive and click the Page Thumbnails tab in the Navigation pane. From a context menu opened on the page where you want the sound to play, select Page Properties. The Page Properties dialog box opens.

2. **Set the action trigger.** Click the Actions tab and select either Page Open or Page Close from the Select Trigger drop-down menu.

3. **Set the action type.** Open the drop-down menu for Select Action and choose Play a sound from the menu options as shown in Figure 22.3.

## Note

By default, the Play a sound menu item in the Select Action drop-down menu may not be in view. Scroll the menu down to show the command. ■

4. **Add the action to the page trigger.** Click the Add button in the Page Properties dialog box to add the sound to your PDF.

5. **Select the sound file.** The Select Sound File dialog box opens. Navigate your hard drive to find the sound to import, select it, and click the Select button. After importing the sound, click Close in the Page Properties dialog box.

**FIGURE 22.3**

Choose Play a sound from the Select Action drop-down menu.

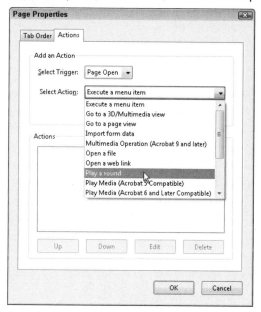

## Note

**Acrobat may pause momentarily. The sound file imported in Acrobat is converted during the import. When a sound is imported in a PDF file, the sound can then be played across platforms. Therefore, a WAV file can be played on a Mac computer and an AIFF file can be played on a Windows computer. ■**

6.   **Save the file.** Choose File ⇨ Save As and rewrite the file to disk. Close the file and reopen it to test the page action.

After you save the PDF file and reopen it, the sound is played. You can also test the sound by scrolling a page in the PDF file and returning to the page where the sound was imported. The action is dynamic and the sound plays before you save the PDF file.

## Adding sounds to form field actions

Of the mouse behavior types, you may find that Mouse Enter, On Focus, or On Blur behaviors work equally as well as using a Mouse Up or Mouse Down trigger. As an example, you might have a descriptive message display when the user places the cursor over a button field and before he or she clicks the mouse. Or you may want to invoke a sound when the user tabs out of a field as a reminder to verify data entry in a PDF form. In these situations and similar uses, the sound is played from a mouse behavior related to a data or button field. To understand how to use sound actions with data fields, follow these steps.

## STEPS: Adding Sounds to Form Fields

1. **Open a PDF document with form fields.** In Figure 22.4, I use a form with several check boxes. I want to create a sound when the user places the cursor over one of the check boxes or tabs to the field.

Four check boxes are to be configured to play a sound on a Mouse Enter trigger.

Button with sound actions

2. **Open the field properties.** Choose the Select Object tool in the Content panel and double-click the field you want to edit. If no fields exist in your document, you can add button fields in either Form Editing mode or Viewer mode. If a field exists on a form, you can use the Select Object tool in Viewer mode. The Field Type Properties dialog box opens when you double-click a field with the Select Object tool.

# Cross-Reference

For more information on creating form fields in Acrobat and using the Form Editing mode, see Chapter 30. ∎

3. **Select the mouse trigger.** In the Check Box Properties dialog box, click the Actions tab and select Mouse Enter as the Select Trigger, as shown in Figure 22.5.

4. **Add a sound action to the field.** Open the Select Action pull-down menu and select Play a sound.

5. **Select the sound file.** Click the Add button to open the Select Sound File dialog box. Select the file to import and click the Select button.

6. **Close the Check Box Properties dialog box.** Check to be certain the mouse trigger is set to Mouse Enter (or another trigger you chose to use). Click Close in the Check Box Properties dialog box.

**FIGURE 22.5**

Choose Mouse Enter from the Select Trigger pull-down menu.

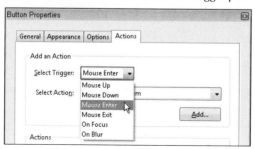

7. **Test the sound.** Select the Hand tool and place the mouse cursor over the check box where you added the sound. (Note: To play the sound by tabbing to the field, use the On Focus mouse trigger.)

When the mouse enters one of the check boxes, the respective sound plays. The sound plays completely even if the cursor leaves the field. Sounds added to forms either for page actions or field actions can be played from any Acrobat viewer.

## Tip

A sound continues to play to completion. If you want to stop the sound while editing a document, select the Select Object tool or press the R key on your keyboard to activate the Select Object tool. (Note: You need to enable Use single-key accelerators to access tools in the General Preferences to use key modifiers to select tools.) ■

## Using the Sound tool

Importing sounds with page actions, form fields, links, bookmarks, and so on limits your import options to fewer file formats and limits the attributes you can assign to the imported file. In essence, you import the file and play the sound. Not much else is available when you use the Select Action command. Another method for importing sound files in PDF documents is with the Sound tool. When you use the Sound tool to import sounds, you have a few more options for the kinds of files you can import and attributes you can assign to the imported sounds.

To import a sound with the Sound tool, select the tool from the Multimedia drop-down menu in the Content panel and double-click or drag open a rectangle on a document page. The area contained within the rectangle becomes a trigger to play the sound. When you release the mouse button, the Insert Sound dialog box opens, as shown in Figure 22.6.

## Tip

You can manage sound and movie links similarly to links and form fields where context menu options enable you to size, align, copy, paste, and distribute fields. You can access these menu commands when you select sound and movie links in a group together with links and form fields. For more information on managing links and form fields, see Chapters 21 and 30. ■

**FIGURE 22.6**

Double-click the Sound tool or click+drag a document page to open the Insert Sound dialog box.

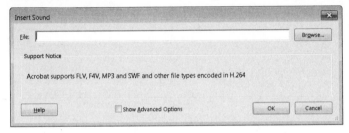

Click the Browse button and locate a file on your hard drive to import. Acrobat pauses a moment while the file is converted to a format that all Acrobat viewers recognize.

Acrobat X offers more limited support for media formats than earlier versions of the program. File formats supported by Acrobat X include SWF, FLV, F4V, MP3, and H.264 video. If you have formats other than these, then you need to convert the media to one of these formats.

In the Insert Sound dialog box, you can access additional options when you click the Show Advanced Options check box. Click the check box and the advanced options for the Insert Sound dialog box appear, as you see in Figure 22.7.

You can make choices for activation of sounds, adding a border, and adding a poster image in the advanced settings. Your choices include:

- **Enable When.** Earlier in this chapter in the section "Adding sounds to page actions" I talked about importing sounds on page actions using Page Open and Page Close triggers. If you use the Sound tool and open the advanced settings, you can trigger a sound to play on opening and closing pages. From the Enable When pull-down menu, choose the default to play a sound when the sound media box is clicked, or choose one of the other two triggers in the menu that include The page containing the content is opened or The page containing the content is closed. These last two menu choices are the same as when you use Page Action triggers to play a sound.

**FIGURE 22.7**

Click the Show Advanced Options check box to display the advanced options settings in the Insert Sound dialog box.

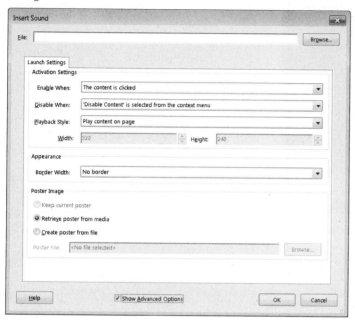

- **Disable When.** You have the same choices from this menu as you have with the Enable When menu. You can choose to stop a sound from playing when making a choice from a context menu, when a page opens, or when a page closes.

- **Playback Style.** Two choices are available from the pull-down menu. The default is to play the content on the page, in which case you won't see any visual changes on the page when the sound plays. The other choice is a floating window. A sound file does not actually appear in a floating window. A floating window is shown with a Flash file that acts like a placeholder. If you assign a poster to the sound object, the poster and sound object remain fixed on the page while a floating window like the one shown in Figure 22.8 opens.

- **Width/Height.** These text boxes are used to set the width and height of the floating window.

- **Border Width.** Choose from No border, Thin, Medium, and Thick.

**FIGURE 22.8**

A floating window assigned to a sound file

- **Transparent Background.** Assigns the background to transparency.
- **Poster Image.** Your choices are: Keep current poster, where no change in the poster occurs; Retrieve poster from file, which doesn't apply to sounds because sound files have no images in the file; and Create poster from file, where you can import any file consistent with the Create ⇨ PDF From File menu command. The Browse button opens a dialog box where you select the file you want to use for a poster.

Most of the options you have available in the Insert Sound Advanced Settings are accessible in the Properties dialog box. You can initially insert a sound using the abbreviated settings shown in Figure 22.6 and later adjust properties as needed by right-clicking with the Select Object tool on a sound import and choosing Properties.

# Importing Video Files

As with sound files, video files require that you create video clips in other authoring programs. No tools or features are contained in Acrobat for editing movies. However, after you create video clips in authoring applications, you have the wealth of import options and play opportunities similar to those used with sound files.

Video files are not limited to movie files. You can also use the various attribute choices for importing and changing properties with Adobe Flash files. Both video and Flash files can be imported and managed in Acrobat similarly.

Video editing at the high end is handled by sophisticated software such as Final Cut Pro, Adobe Premiere, Adobe After Effects, and other similar professional programs designed to offer you limitless choices for editing video and audio channels. On the low end, you have some impressive features in programs that cost very little. Adobe's marvelous consumer image editor, Adobe Photoshop Elements, is a low-cost editing program that offers you options for exporting to PDF slide shows, embedding sound files, and mixing slides and video clips. You can also use Adobe Premiere Elements 9 for Windows or Mac for video editing and media conversions.

For Mac users, Apple's own iMovie is a free application shipping with System OS X that produces QuickTime movies. iMovie supports PDF imports as well as still photos and video clips. If you happen to be a cross-platform user, a single copy of Adobe Premiere Elements 9 running on either platform is all you need to create media files that can be used cross-platform.

# Importing video (Acrobat Pro only)

In Acrobat 9, Adobe flirted with video transcoding from a video format to Adobe Flash using Acrobat Pro Extended. In Acrobat X, Pro Extended has vanished along with video transcoding to Adobe Flash. You can still use Flash files with Acrobat, but the file must be a native FLV or F4V file type.

Without all the options associated with transcoding video, importing media in Acrobat X is easy and straightforward.

For a quick look at importing a video in Acrobat, follow these steps.

### Steps: Importing a Video with Acrobat X

1. **Open a PDF document in Acrobat.**
2. **Click the Video tool in the Multimedia drop-down menu in the Content panel.**
3. **Double-click the Video tool on a document page.** When you double-click using the Video tool, the video is imported at the same size the video was originally compressed.
4. **Browse for the file location.** The Insert Video dialog box shown earlier in Figure 22.6 opens. (Note that the dialog box in Figure 22.6 is labeled Insert Sound. When you insert a video, the label changes to Insert Video.) Click the Browse button to locate the file, and leave all the other settings at the defaults.
5. **Import the video.** The Select a file dialog box opens. Select the file you want to import and click Open. Note that you may have to wait a few minutes for Acrobat to read the file.
6. **Set the attributes for importing the file.** After you click Open in the Select a file dialog box, the file path appears in the Insert Video dialog box.
7. **Click OK and the video is imported using default settings.**

For quick and easy video imports, you can follow the steps outlined here. However, Acrobat offers you a number of options for importing video files and changing properties. Becoming familiar with the options helps you take advantage of Acrobat's impressive video viewing and playback opportunities. You can make option choices during the import steps or address properties after videos have been imported.

## Using advanced settings

When you open the Insert Video dialog box you see an abbreviated set of options that are available for video imports. To expand the dialog box, click the Show Advanced Options check box to expand the dialog box to the view shown in Figure 22.9.

**FIGURE 22.9**

Click the Show Advanced Options check box to expand the Insert Video dialog box.

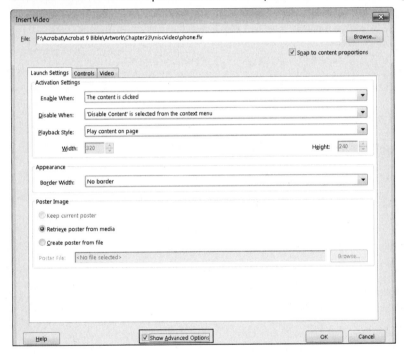

Before you import a video in Acrobat Pro, you can adjust a number of settings in the Insert Video Advanced Options dialog box. Your choices include:

- **Launch Settings.** The first of four tabs appears as the default. In the Launch settings tab you make choices for launching the video.
    - **Enable When.** Earlier in this chapter in the section "Adding sounds to page actions," I talked about triggering a sound to play based on Page Open and Page

Close actions. When using Acrobat 9 and above–compatible media, you can choose to trigger a video to play on a page open or page close action from choices in this menu.

- **Disable When.** You can stop play on the same choices you have for Enable When. If you want to stop the media from playing when you navigate to the next page, open this pull-down menu and choose The page containing the content is closed.

- **Playback Style.** Your choices are to play the content on the page or play the content in a floating window.

- **Width/Height.** You can edit the annotation frame for the size by typing values in the text boxes for floating windows only.

- **Border.** Choose from Thin, Medium, or Thick to add a border to the annotation frame.

- **Poster Image.** You make choices here for the poster image. If you click Create poster from file, click the Browse button to locate a file to use as a poster image. File formats that are supported are Adobe PDF, BMP, CompuServe GIF, JPEG, and PNG.

- **Controls.** This tab offers settings for player control displays as shown in Figure 22.10.

**FIGURE 22.10**

Click the Controls tab to show settings for playback displays.

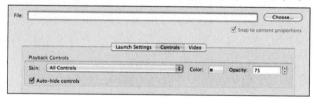

- **Skin.** The pull-down menu offers options for displaying Flash video skins that enable you to play, pause, and resume video playback. Choose the option you want from the Skin pull-down menu. For more information on skins, see the sidebar "Using skins."

- **Color.** Click the color swatch to change the skin color.

- **Opacity.** Type a value in the text box to change the opacity of the skin.

- **Auto-Hide controls.** If you check this box, the skin is hidden as the cursor moves away from the media box.

- **Video.** The Video tab enables you to add chapter points and assign actions when the video plays to a chapter point. In order to assign chapter points, the video must have been created with chapter points.

## Using Skins

Skins are Adobe Flash files that display player controls when you enable the player controls options in the Insert Video dialog box or Movie Properties. By default, Acrobat installs seven different skins you can use when playing video, with or without volume controls, muting sound, and showing captions.

You can add your own custom skins and have them appear in the Playback tab Skin pull-down menu. To add your own custom skins you'll need to use Adobe Flex and export the files as Flash movies. After you create a custom skin, you then need to add the file to the appropriate folder in Acrobat.

On Windows, open the Acrobat 10.0/Acrobat/Multimedia Skins folder and copy your custom skins to this folder.

On the Mac open the Applications/Adobe Acrobat 9 Pro folder and Control+click the Adobe Acrobat Pro icon. From the context menu options choose Show Package Contents. (Note that Multimedia Skins are not installed in the Acrobat User Data folder on the Mac). When the package contents are shown, open Contents/MacOS/Multimedia Skins. Copy your custom skins to this folder. For Mac users, the skins are available only when using H.264-compressed video or playing FLV videos.

# Importing Flash Video (Acrobat Pro Only)

The file formats you can import that are related to Adobe Flash include Flash Video (FLV) and Flash 9 and above (F4V). FLV and F4V files are native files saved from Adobe Flash. Using the Flash tool, you can import SWF Flash movie files.

If you use the Video tool, you can import both FLV and F4V files. However, the default file formats support only FLV files. If you want to use the Video tool to import an SWF file, you must change the Files of type menu choice to All Files (*.*); you'll see the SWF files accessible in the Select a file dialog box.

Another choice is to select the Flash tool from the Multimedia drop-down menu in the Content panel. When you use the Flash tool, SWF is the default format and you can import SWF files.

Double-click the Adobe Flash tool to import a Flash FLV or SWF file. The Insert Flash dialog box opens. This dialog box is similar to the Insert Video dialog box. An abbreviated list of settings is shown, similar to Figure 22.9. Clicking the Show Advanced Options check box expands the Insert Flash dialog box to display similar settings you have when importing video.

Only three tabs are shown in the Insert Flash dialog box. The tabs include:

- **Launch Settings.** The Launch Settings include identical settings you have when importing a video file.

- **Flash.** The Flash tab offers you an option to pass Flash variables (ActionScript 2.0 and 3.0 FlashVars) to a URL string.

- **Resources.** The Resources tab enables you to bind a file, multiple files, or a directory of files to video.

Like the Insert Video dialog box you make choices for the settings and select a file to import. Click the OK button to import the Flash file in a PDF document.

# Importing 3-D Content

The 3-D tool in the Multimedia drop-down menu in the Content panel is used for importing 3-D content in a PDF file. Select the tool from the Multimedia menu. Double-click the tool on a document page to open the Insert 3D dialog box.

Again, this dialog box is similar to the Insert Video dialog box. When you click the Show Advanced Options check box, the Insert 3D dialog box expands to show three tabs similar to the Insert Sound and Insert Video dialog boxes. The first tab choice is Launch Settings and offers the same choices you find in the Insert Video and Insert Flash dialog boxes. The third tab is Resources and offers the same choices you find in the Insert Flash Resources tab.

## Tip

You can also capture a view in your CAD drawing program and convert the capture to PDF. Click the Capture 3D button in the Insert 3D dialog box and open your drawing program. Navigate to the view you want to capture and make sure your screen is refreshed. Press the Print Screen key on your keyboard to open the capture automatically in Acrobat. ∎

The 3D tab is unique to the Insert 3D dialog box. The 3D tab shown in Figure 22.11 contains settings for the lighting, rendering, and animation style of the 3-D model. You have navigation choices for viewing various isometric views and choosing to open the Model Tree panel in the Acrobat viewer opening the file. You can also add a JavaScript for custom viewing and displays. Acrobat 9 had another tab for Geospatial data. This tab has been eliminated in Acrobat X.

FIGURE 22.11

The 3D tab offers unique settings for displaying 3-D imports.

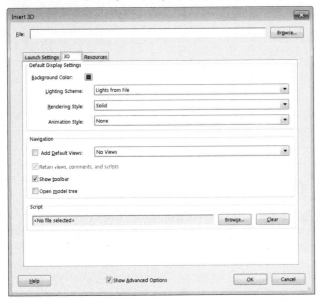

# Summary

In this chapter, you learned how to import and play video and sound in PDF documents.

- You can add sounds to page actions, links, bookmarks, and form fields, or by using the Sound tool.

- Importing sounds on actions or with the Sound tool requires you to have access to a sound file. You create and save sound files from sound-editing programs. A number of sound-editing programs are available as freeware or shareware on the Internet.

- You can edit movie files in multimedia authoring programs. Low-cost alternatives for creating movie files include Adobe Photoshop Elements, Adobe Premiere Elements, and Apple iMovie. You can save Photoshop Elements files direct to PDF. You save iMovie files in QuickTime format and import them in PDFs with the Movie tool.

- A poster is a still image that appears inside a sound or movie field. Posters for movie fields can be retrieved from a movie. Posters for sound and movie fields can be created from files including all file formats supported by the Create PDF From File menu command.

- Acrobat Pro enables you to import video from a limited number of file formats.

- The Adobe Flash tool is used to import Adobe Flash FLV, F4V, and SWF files.

- The 3D tool in Acrobat Pro enables you to convert native CAD files to PDF.

# 23

# Creating Accessibility and Tagging PDF Files

**A**dobe Acrobat is compliant with U.S. federal code regulating document accessibility for vision- and motion-challenged persons. This means that screen readers can intelligently interpret the PDFs you create; in other words, PDF files can be read aloud in a reading order as a sighted person would read a document. Through an extensive set of keyboard shortcuts available in Acrobat, almost anyone with vision or motion challenges can share your documents and read them.

In order for a document to be accessible, you must use authoring applications capable of delivering a document's structure to Acrobat. Hence, you need to know something about the internal structure of documents and what programs to use to create the structure required by Acrobat to make a document accessible. Not all the content in a document travels through the PDF creation process with information necessary to make a document completely accessible. Therefore, you need to perform some work in Acrobat to either add accessibility or to polish up a document for delivery to a screen reader in a form that makes sense to the user. In this chapter, I cover how to make documents accessible from authoring programs, as well as how to use Acrobat tools to make existing documents accessible.

## Creating Accessible Documents

The terms "document accessibility," "structure," and "tagged PDFs" may be a mystery to you. If the term "accessibility" is new, then you need to begin with an understanding of what accessible documents are before working with them. After you know more about document accessibility, you can move forward to look at how to create an accessible document, and then look at how you can edit accessible documents. Therefore, the three areas to work with are understanding accessibility, creating accessible documents from authoring programs, and finally, working with accessible documents in Acrobat.

## Understanding accessibility

Sighted people can view a document on the computer or read a printed page and easily discern the difference between titles, subtitles, columns, graphic images, graphic elements, and so on. With regard to Acrobat PDFs, you can easily see the difference between background designs, button links, bookmarks, animation, and form fields, and you typically see visual clues to know where buttons and fields exist.

With regard to screen-reading devices, which depend on software to generate audio output from an Acrobat PDF file, the software readers aren't intelligent enough to distinguish differences based on visual clues. For example, a screen reader may interpret a three-columned document as one continuous column and read the text from left to right across all three columns row by row. Obviously the output is useless to the end user working with a screen reader. Screen readers interpret headings, subheadings, and tables the same as body copy, and they offer no distinction in the structure unless the screen reader software has some clue that these items are different from the body text.

## Screen Readers

I use the term "screen reader" extensively in this chapter. When I use this term, I'm referring to tools created by third parties to read open documents aloud in Acrobat and other programs or from files in various formats saved to disk.

Screen readers range in price from $99 to over $1,000. The advantage of using third-party products with Acrobat PDF files is that they can read aloud single words as well as spell out words character by character. Through keyboard controls, users choose reading rates, audio output levels, voices, and navigation.

Screen readers are typically software programs installed on either Mac OS or Windows. More programs support Windows than Mac operating systems, but developers have been increasing their support for both platforms. The most popular screen reader used today is Freedom Scientific JAWS for Windows. Version 4.5 and later is also compatible with Flash Player 6 and later. In past years, PDF documents were not supported by many developers. Today, much more support exists for reading PDF documents with the Adobe Reader software.

For a complete list of screen readers that have been tested with Acrobat, log on to Adobe's Web site at www.adobe.com/accessibility. From Adobe's Web page you'll find URL links to vendor sites as well as general information about accessibility.

Some authoring programs provide you with an opportunity when creating the PDF file to retain the underlying structure of a document in the resulting PDF file. With a series of tags and retention of the document structure, screen readers use alternate text to make distinctions in the document much like the visual user would interpret a page. The document flow, alternate text for graphic elements, distinctions between headings, and so on can all be managed in Acrobat when the internal document structural tree is included in the PDF export. When files are not exported with the document structure, you can use Acrobat commands to add structure to PDFs. In order to make it possible for people with screen readers to navigate your PDF documents correctly, the underlying structure must be present.

PDF files fall into three categories when you are talking about a document's structure:

- **Unstructured PDF files.** Unstructured PDF documents could not be interpreted by screen readers with complete document integrity in earlier versions of Acrobat. For example, when you exported the PDF to other formats such as a Rich Text Format (RTF), the basic paragraph structure was preserved, but tables, lists, and some text formatting were lost. In Acrobat 8 and above, unstructured documents can be interpreted by screen readers with accuracy. What remains as an unstructured document when using Acrobat 8 and 9 are image files converted to PDF such as scanned documents. These files clearly are not structured.

- **Structured PDF files.** Structured PDF files can be read by screen readers, but the reliability is much less than the next category of tagged PDF documents. When you export structured PDF files to other formats, more structural content is preserved, but tables and lists can be lost. Additionally, structured documents, such as the unstructured documents discussed previously, do not support text reflows for different-sized devices.

- **Tagged PDF files.** Tagged PDFs contain both the document structure and a hierarchical structure tree where all the internal structure about the document's content is interpreted. Tagged PDFs have the highest reliability when you're repurposing files for screen reader output and saving files in other formats such as RTF, HTML, XHTML, and XML. In addition, tagged PDF files support text reflow for viewing on different-sized screens and devices and accommodate any zoom level on a monitor.

## Cross-Reference

For more information on exporting PDF content, see Chapter 9. For more on document structure, see "Understanding Structure" in this chapter. ■

## Note

Structured documents were introduced with Acrobat 4 (PDF 1.3) and tagged documents were introduced with Acrobat 5 (PDF 1.4). PDFs created prior to version 1.3 had no document structure, and PDFs created before version 1.4 could not be tagged. With later versions of Acrobat, document structure and tagging could be added to these PDFs from within Acrobat. ■

The goal for you when creating PDF documents for accessibility is to be certain you use PDF documents that are not only structured but also tagged. After you create tagged PDFs, you can work with the structure tree and modify the contents for optimum use. In terms of making Acrobat PDFs accessible, you must consider several criteria to optimize files for effective handling by screen readers:

- **Assessing accessibility.** Fortunately, Acrobat provides tools for determining whether a PDF file is an accessible document. As a first order of business you should plan on assessing a file for accessibility. If you work with legacy files or files that are created from authoring programs that don't support the export of the document structure, be certain to make the document accessible before beginning an editing session.

## Cross-Reference

For adding accessibility to PDF files from within Acrobat, see the section "Making existing PDFs accessible" later in this chapter. ∎

- **Logical reading order.** The text should follow a logical flow. You need to properly define column text in terms of the path that a screen reader follows (that is, down one column, then begin at the top of the second column, and so on). You should also mark headings and subheadings for distinction.

- **Alternative text descriptions for image and graphic elements.** Those familiar with HTML know that you can code an HTML document with alternate tags so users with text-only browsers can understand the structure of Web pages. The same principle for accessible documents applies. Alternate text needs to be inserted so the screen reader can interpret graphic elements.

- **Form field descriptions.** Form fields need to be described with text to inform a user with a screen reader that a form field is present.

- **Field tab order.** Setting the logical tab order for fields on a form is important for the visual user. With screen readers it is essential. The logical tab order for fields should be strictly followed.

- **Document security.** If documents are secured with Acrobat security, you must use 128-bit encryption compatible with Acrobat 5 and above. If you use compatibility less than Acrobat 5 or 40-bit encryption, the PDF is rendered inaccessible.

- **Links and interactivity.** Use form fields for link buttons with descriptions so the user knows that another destination or a link action is invoked if he or she selects the field.

- **Document language.** Screen readers typically deliver accessible documents in only one language. To protect your documents against inoperability with new releases, specify a document language when creating accessible PDFs. Document language specification is also important when using tools in Acrobat for checking accessibility.

## Cross-Reference

For more information on field tab order, see Chapter 31. For more information on document security, see Chapter 24. For more information on links and interactivity, see Chapter 21. ∎

# Adding accessibility in authoring applications

Not all authoring programs currently support accessibility. This phenomenon may change with new upgrades to software, so what is said today may change tomorrow. As of this writing the programs offering the best support for document accessibility include Microsoft Word version 2000 or higher, Adobe PageMaker 7.0 or higher, Adobe FrameMaker, Adobe LiveCycle Designer, and Adobe InDesign 2.0 or higher. If you use other authoring applications, you do have the option to make documents accessible with Acrobat Standard and Acrobat Pro, or Acrobat Pro Extended.

When converting Microsoft Word files to PDF, be certain to use the PDFMaker in the Word toolbar or from the Adobe PDF menu in Word. Set up the conversion settings for enabling accessibility and reflow with tagged PDF documents. This option is available in the Settings tab in the Acrobat PDFMaker dialog box. Select the "Enable Accessibility and Reflow with tagged Adobe PDF" check box.

## Cross-Reference

For more on creating PDF files with accessibility and tags from Microsoft Office applications, see Chapter 8. ■

When creating documents with text, images, charts, diagrams, and so on, using a professional layout program often works better than a word processor. Adobe InDesign CS is an ideal tool for creating layouts that you need to make accessible. When you design a document for accessibility, be precise about how you add elements on each page. The order in which you lay out documents can have an effect on the order of the exported structure. For example, adding a block of text, and then importing an image, may result in the text appearing first in the structure tree and the image following the text even if you move the elements so the image appears first on the page. The only way to observe the results of how the document structure ultimately converts to PDF is to practice and examine the tags structure tree in Acrobat versus your layouts. You can develop a workflow that minimizes the work in Acrobat to properly create the structure needed for optimum performance when read by a screen reader.

## Tip

If you arrange objects in an authoring program like Adobe InDesign and the reading order is not following the viewing order, you can cut either text or images and paste them back into the document. If, for example, an image should be first in the structure tree followed by text, but the order is reversed when you examine the tags in Acrobat, cut the text block and paste it back into the document in InDesign. Recreate the PDF and you'll find the order changed according to the order that the elements were last placed on the page. This method is not always a precise solution for reordering elements, but it can often be used to resolve problems. ■

# Making existing PDFs accessible

If you have PDF documents either from legacy files or from files converted from authoring applications that do not support exports to PDF with tags, you can use Acrobat commands to add structure to the document and make the files accessible. The first step is checking a document for accessibility. If the document contains no tags, then you can add tags in Acrobat Standard or Acrobat Pro, or Pro Extended.

### Performing a Quick Check

To determine whether a document is accessible, you can perform a Quick Check. In Acrobat Standard or Acrobat Pro, open the Accessibility panel and click Quick Check (or press Shift+Ctrl/⌘+6). In Adobe Reader, click Quick Check in the Accessibility panel (or press Shift+Ctrl/⌘+6). This method of checking the PDF is a quick analysis to determine whether tags exist in the file. When the check is completed, a dialog box opens informing you of the accessibility status. If the document is not accessible, the dialog box message states that the document is not structured and reading problems may occur.

## Note

Document accessibility can be checked in Adobe Reader. Making a document accessible, however, requires Acrobat Standard or Acrobat Pro. ∎

### Performing a Full Check (Acrobat Pro only)

Acrobat Pro offers you a more sophisticated analysis, where more file attributes are checked and a report is created either in a file or by adding comments to the open PDF document, or both. To use the Full Check option, follow these steps.

#### STEPS: Checking Accessibility in Acrobat Pro

1. **Click Full Check in the Accessibility panel.** The Accessibility Full Check dialog box opens, as shown in Figure 23.1.

2. **Check the box for Create Accessibility Report and Create comments in document.** Checking these boxes creates a report and adds comment notes in the document pertaining to the results of the analysis. All errors found during the check are reported in comment notes.

3. **Select the Checking Options for the items you want to check.** Enable the check boxes in this section for items you want to check. In this example I selected all the check boxes.

4. **When you set all the attributes, click Start Checking**. Acrobat opens a dialog box similar to Figure 23.2, reporting errors if encountered. Click OK to complete the task.

**FIGURE 23.1**

When you run a Full Check in Acrobat Pro, you can choose options for what content to check.

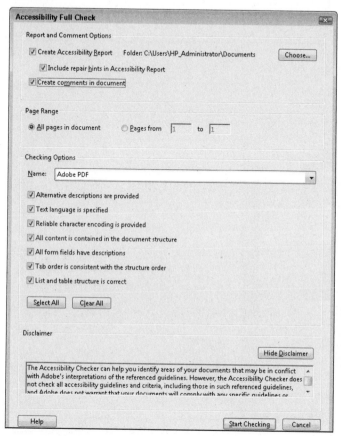

**FIGURE 23.2**

After running the Full Check, the findings are reported in a dialog box.

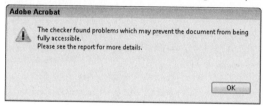

After completing the check, the Accessibility Report pane opens and displays a more detailed report as shown in Figure 23.3. If you selected Create comments in document, comment notes may appear, reporting problems in untagged documents.

The Accessibility Report panel (left side of the Acrobat window) shows you a detailed report of the full accessibility check findings.

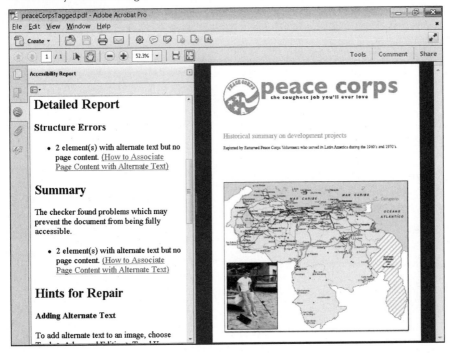

An Accessibility report is also saved to your hard drive in HTML format. If you click the Browse button in the Accessibility Full Check dialog box, you can target a location for the saved report. By default, the report is saved to your My Documents folder (Windows) or your Documents folder (Mac). Open your Web browser and select File Open. Navigate to the folder where the report is found and open the file. The report is displayed in the browser window.

The links in the HTML document link directly to the PDF file and highlight the item associated with the link. Click a link in your Web browser and the PDF file opens in the foreground with the respective item highlighted, as shown in Figure 23.4. You can correct problems by clicking links in the Web browser and correcting the problems in the PDF document.

## FIGURE 23.4

Click a link in the Web browser and the referenced item in the PDF is highlighted.

- 1 images(s) with no alternate text. (How to Add Alternate Text)
  1. No alternate text
- 1 element(s) that are not contained within the structure tree. (How to Add Tags)
  1. Inaccessible page content

### Adding accessibility

Keep in mind you are always best served by adding accessibility at the time a PDF document is created from authoring programs supporting exports to PDF with accessibility and tags. If you have files for which either returning to the authoring program is impractical or the authoring program is incapable of exporting to PDF as tagged files, click Add Tags to Document in the Accessibility panel. Or from the Tags panel in the Navigation pane, select Add Tags to Document from the Options pull-down menu. Immediately after you select the menu command from either Acrobat Standard or Acrobat Professional, a slider bar opens displaying Acrobat's progress in adding tags to the document. After completion, no confirmation dialog box opens to report the status. If problems were encountered while adding the tags, a dialog box opens, reporting the problems found.

After adding the tags, you can return to the Quick Check or Full Check menu command and check the document for accessibility.

If a file has tags and you click Add Tags to Document in the Accessibility panel, Acrobat opens a dialog box informing you that the file already has tags. Adding tags is not permitted using the menu command. If you are unhappy with the current tagging, you can remove all tags from the document, and then reapply with this method. To remove all tags, open the Tags panel in the Navigation pane. Select the topmost tag (typically labeled "Tags") and select Delete Tag from the Options drop-down menu.

## Understanding Structure

To understand more clearly the need for creating accessibility and adding tags to a document, look at Figure 23.5 as an example. This document contains several items that need attention to make the file accessible and comprehensible when read by a screen reader.

**FIGURE 23.5**

A document with images, illustrations, and text in multiple columns needs to have the structure modified for proper reading by a screen reader.

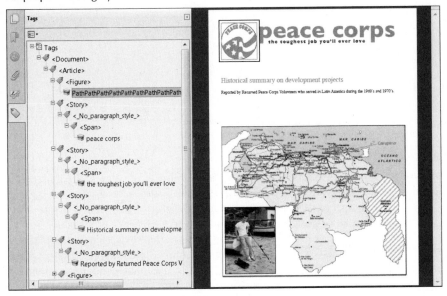

In Figure 23.5, the items of importance in terms of accessibility include the following:

- **The first element on the page is a logo.** A screen reader won't interpret the logo unless you add some alternate text to the document describing the object. Adjacent to the logo on the right side is text that a screen reader can read after you make the document accessible. If the text does not read properly, the two lines of text need to be modified for the proper interpretation by the screen reader.

- **The two lines of text are in a single column.** These lines should be read in logical order without any problems. They are shown here to illustrate the difference between the two lines and the two columns following.

- **The text is blocked in two columns.** Unless the structure is established for the screen reader to read down one column before moving to the second column, the screen reader defaults at a left-to-right reading order, reading across both columns.

- **Item four is a large map.** Alternate text for the illustration is needed for the screen reader to explain what graphic appears on the page.

- **Item five is an inset photo.** The alternate text for the map can describe the photo, or the photo can have an alternate text description. Either way, you need to create the alternate text for the screen reader to fully interpret the graphics.

When you export to PDF from authoring programs with tags, the structure of the document for the blocks of text in logical reading orders is preserved. In the example in Figure 23.5, the single and double-column text is typically not a problem when the file is read by a screen reader. Images, however, need some form of manual editing. Even the best source exporting with tags wouldn't be able to describe the visual elements in the layout. These are subjective items that need a description.

If using a program such as Microsoft Word, you can add alternate text in Word before the file is exported to PDF. In other applications you need to create the alternate text in Acrobat.

## Using the Tags panel

When you export a document from an authoring program with tags or use the Add Tags to Document menu command, a *structure tree* is created in the PDF file. The structure tree is a hierarchical order of the elements contained in the file. Elements may be in the form of heads, subheads, body text, figures, tables, annotations, and other items identified as separate individual structural elements. The hierarchy contains a nested order of the elements with parent/child relationships. A heading, for example, may have a subhead. The heading in this case is a parent element with the subheading a child element.

When a document contains tags, you view the tag elements and the structure tree in the Tags panel. Open the Tags panel and click the top item. By default, you see an icon labeled Tags with a plus (+) (Windows) or right-pointing arrow (Mac) symbol adjacent to it. Click the symbol and you open the tree at one level. Other child elements are nested below.

The Tags panel may have an extensive list of elements depending on your document length and complexity. If you want to edit an element or find it in the document, you need some help from Acrobat to find out exactly what tag in the Tags panel is related to what element on a given page. The help comes in the form of a menu command in the Tags panel. Click the down-pointing arrow adjacent to Options in the Tags panel and select Highlight Content. The content is highlighted as shown earlier in Figure 23.5.

When you return to the structure tree, the items you select are highlighted on the respective elements on pages in the Document pane. Click an element and Acrobat navigates to the page where the content is located. The object is highlighted with a keyline border, as shown in Figure 23.5.

## Adding alternate text

In the example in Figure 23.5, the logo appearing at the top of the page is an image file. When a screen reader reads the document, no specific instructions are contained in the document to interpret this image. As an option, you can create alternate text so a visually challenged person knows a graphic element exists on the page. To add alternate text in a tagged PDF document, follow these steps.

### STEPS: Adding Alternate Text to Tagged Elements

1. **Open a tagged PDF file.** Or add tags to a document. Open the Tags panel in the Navigation pane. Note: If the Tags panel is not available in the Navigation pane, choose View ➪ Show/Hide ➪ Navigation Panes ➪ Tags to open the Tags panel.

2. **Open the structure tree.** Click the Tags Root icon to the left of the text. On Windows a plus (+) symbol appears adjacent to the text. On the Mac, a right-pointing arrow appears next to the text. Clicking the icon opens the tags tree.

3. **Select Highlight Content.** If you haven't selected the menu command for highlighting content, open the Options palette in the Tags panel and select Highlight Content.

4. **Find the element for which the alternate text is to be added.** In this example, the figure below the second paragraph (<P>) was selected. When you click the Figure tag, the logo at the top-left corner of the page is highlighted. Alternately, you can also select the TouchUp Object tool, click an object on the page, and select Find Tag from Selection from the Tags palette Options pull-down menu.

5. **Open the element's properties.** Select the Edit Object tool in the Content panel. Click the element and open a context menu. Select Properties from the menu options.

6. **Add alternate text.** Click the Tags panel. Add a title for the tag by typing a title in the Title field box. The title is not necessary for, nor read by, the screen reader. Add the text you want the screen reader to read out loud in the Alternate Text field. Select the drop-down menu for Language and select a language. The edits made in this example are shown in Figure 23.6.

**FIGURE 23.6**

Fill in the fields for a title and alternate text, and select a language in the TouchUp Properties dialog box.

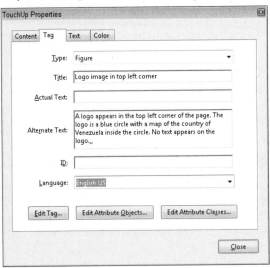

7. **Close the TouchUp Properties dialog box.**

## Using the Content tab

The Content tab contains a hierarchical list of the objects in the PDF file. Objects are listed in the order in which they appear on the page, similar to the logical structure tree in the Tags panel. Choose View ➪ Show/Hide ➪ Navigation Panes ➪ Content and you see a view similar to Figure 23.7. Click an object and move it up or down to change the order of the objects.

The Content tab can be helpful when you want to navigate to and highlight a content item listed in the tab. Click an item such as a text item or figure and the page appears in the Document pane with the respective item selected.

In addition to physically reordering objects, a number of menu commands are available from the Options pull-down menu. Among the menu commands is an option to create a New Container. Notice in Figure 23.5 that all the tags are nested within containers. You can select a tag and select New Container to add alternate text to any area in the document.

**FIGURE 23.7**

Click objects and drag up or down to reorder the objects in the Content pane.

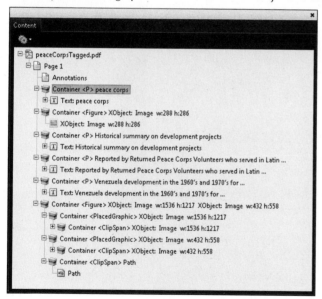

## Using the Order tab

You use the Order tab to correct reading order problems. After you create a tagged PDF document, Acrobat infers the reading order from the document structure. You may need to change the order for text and images to create a more logical flow in the document.

You use the Order tab in the navigation Pane in conjunction with the TouchUp Reading Order tool in the Accessibility panel. Select the tool and open the Order tab by choosing View ⇨ Show/Hide ⇨ Navigation Panes ⇨ Order. Acrobat lists the reading order of the elements according to page as shown in Figure 23.8. To reorder the elements or regions, click and drag a tag up or down to change the reading order. Each tagged object is numbered on a page indicating the order the tags are read. From the Touchup Reading Order dialog box you can change the attributes of tags and renumber them to change the reading order. Figure 23.8 shows the tagged elements and the reading order defined by numbers adjacent to each tagged object.

**FIGURE 23.8**

To change reading order, click and drag tags up or down in the Order tab.

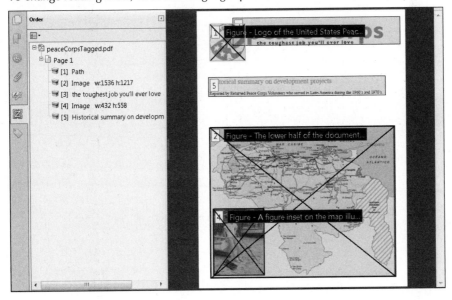

## Checking accessible tags

You can check your work easily in Acrobat by having Acrobat read the document. Choose View ⇨ Read Out Loud ⇨ Activate Read Out Loud. Return to the same menu and choose Read This Page Only. The default text-to-speech voice installed on your computer reads the text as a screen reader would interpret it. If you prepare files for screen readers, you can use Acrobat's built-in reading engine to read aloud the text in the document and the alternate tags you add to the file.

Although the Read Out Loud menu command is not intended to replace screen readers, the feature in all Acrobat viewers offers you a good means for checking files that meet accessible standards.

## Tip

You can save PDF files as accessible text. Choose File ⇨ Save As ⇨ PDF and select Text (Accessible).txt from the Save as Type (Windows) or Format (Mac) pull-down menu. The saved text is saved in the same reading order as when you read a document aloud. ∎

## Cross-Reference

For more information on Read Out Loud and controlling voices and reading speeds, see Chapter 5. ∎

In addition to using Acrobat's built-in function for reading documents aloud, you can acquire a low-cost plug-in from a third-party developer without purchasing a screen reader. PDFAloud, marketed by textHELP Systems (www.texthelp.com), is more robust than Acrobat's Read Out Loud command. With PDFAloud you can read text a word, sentence, or paragraph at a time. The plug-in also offers you synchronized colored highlighting while the text is read.

# Viewing Accessible Documents

Some accessibility requirements extend beyond text-to-speech reading. Individuals with assistive devices for visual impairments can view documents when text is zoomed and when text color significantly contrasts with background colors. You can modify the display of documents on your screen by adjusting preferences for Accessibility in the Preferences dialog box, or you can customize viewing by clicking Setup Assistant in the Accessibility panel in Acrobat and Adobe Reader, which opens the Accessibility Setup Assistant dialog box, shown in Figure 23.9.

**FIGURE 23.9**

The Accessibility Setup Assistant contains options for screen displays and reading orders.

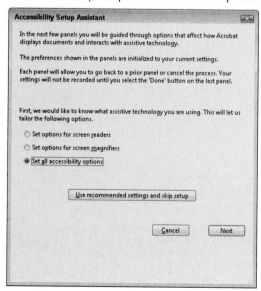

You make attribute choices in a pane and click the Next button to advance through the Accessibility Setup Assistant. You can make choices for color displays, text smoothing, zoom displays, reading orders, and page delivery by moving through the panes. When you finish, these selections will be set in the Accessibility Preferences for you.

# Summary

In this chapter, you learned how to check documents for tags and accessibility, add additional tags, and arrange reading orders.

- Screen readers can interpret accessible PDF files and create audio output for people with vision and motion challenges.

- Adobe PDFMaker for Microsoft products, version 2000 or higher, including Word, Excel, Visio, and so on; Adobe PageMaker 7 and higher; and Adobe FrameMaker, Adobe LiveCycle Designer, Adobe InDesign 2.0 and higher are capable of creating tagged and accessible PDF forms.

- You can add tags to PDF documents from a menu command within Acrobat Standard and Acrobat Pro, and Pro Extended.

- You check files for accessibility with the Quick Check command in Adobe Reader, Acrobat Standard, and Acrobat Pro and Pro Extended or with a Full Check in Acrobat Pro and Pro Extended.

- Tagged documents contain a structure tree. Elements in the tree locate respective elements in the document if you enable the Highlight Content menu command.

- You can add alternate text to elements in Acrobat by addressing the element's properties.

- You can make text and background color changes in the Accessibility Preferences dialog box or via the Accessibility Setup Assistant.

# Part V

# Publishing PDF Files

This part deals with publishing PDF files in various ways that include adding file security before deployment, hosting PDFs on the Web and hosting meetings, distributing eBooks, and printing files. In Chapter 24, you find information on securing PDF documents and adding digital signatures. Chapter 25 covers PDFs and the Web where you learn how to host PDFs on the Web, create Web links, and convert PDF content to HTML.

Chapter 26 follows with online meetings to share PDFs and PDF presentations with others via Acrobat Connect and Acrobat.com. In Chapter 27, you'll find information related to creating and viewing PDF eBooks. This part ends with printing PDF documents when hard copy is needed. In Chapter 28, you find information related to printing PDFs to desktop printers, and Chapter 29 follows with printing PDFs at commercial print shops using the Print Production tools.

# Using Authentication and Security Methods

Acrobat PDF documents can be secured using a host of different security methods and encryption tools to prevent unauthorized users from opening files and changing documents. Acrobat Security combined with digital signatures enables you to protect data and secure files for just about any purpose. There's much to learn about using Acrobat Security and digital signatures, and it's important to know what levels of security are available to you and what kinds of security you can apply in many different circumstances. This chapter covers a broad description of security and digitally signing PDF documents and the methods you use to protect files against unauthorized viewing and editing.

## Restricting the Opening and Editing of Files

Acrobat security comes in many different forms, allowing you to secure PDF files against user viewing and/or editing in many ways based on the level of security you assign to a PDF document. However, depending on what level of security you apply to a file, the document may or may not be able to be opened by users of earlier versions of Acrobat. Therefore, when you add security it is critical to know your audience and what versions of Acrobat they are using to view files.

Methods of security available in Acrobat include three types of restrictions. You can secure a file against opening and editing by using Password Security at different levels of encryption. You can also secure files using public key certificates, or if your organization is using Adobe LiveCycle Rights Management Server, you can apply security policies from there. You should think of the first method (Password Security) as security you might apply globally to PDFs when you want the public to have a password to open your PDFs or you want to restrict certain Acrobat features, such as content editing or printing. In this regard, you secure documents for what is referred to as *unknown* users. You can further delineate securing individual files into two categories. You can secure documents by applying security settings that you select via options in security windows, or you can create a security policy in which the same level of security and encryption attributes are applied to documents each time you secure files.

Think of the second method (Certificate Security) as restrictions you want to apply for a selected group of people, or what are referred to as *known* users. You might want to restrict opening documents or PDF editing to a group of co-workers, colleagues, or individuals with whom you have direct communication. This method requires the use of digital IDs and public key certificates. This form of security also uses a security policy you create from public key certificates derived from users' digital IDs.

The third method is securing files with the Adobe LiveCycle Rights Management Server. Adobe LiveCycle Rights Management as a product is not covered in this book; see the Acrobat Help Guide for more details or information. Adobe LiveCycle Rights Management Server enables you to apply server-based security policies to PDF documents. One of the great benefits of using a policy server is that you can encrypt documents for limited time use.

Keep in mind that Security Policies can be used with either Password Security or Certificate Security.

The discussion on Acrobat Security starts with the first method of applying security for a more global environment of unknown users. Later in this chapter, encryption using a security policy with public key certificates for known users is covered along with digital signatures.

## Using password security

To secure an open document, choose File ⇨ Properties. Click the Security tab in the Document Properties dialog box. Notice the Security Method pull-down menu. Four options are listed in the menu for different security methods. The default selection is No Security. Open the pull-down menu and select Password Security. The Password Security – Settings dialog box shown in Figure 24.1 opens. Depending on which compatibility option you select from the Compatibility pull-down menu, the bottom of the dialog box activates additional options or removes options. In Figure 24.1, you can see that when choosing Acrobat X compatibility, all options are available in the dialog box. If you select an earlier version, such as Acrobat 3 compatibility, some options are grayed out, such as two of the options in the Select Document Components to Encrypt section.

FIGURE 24.1

Depending on what level of compatibility you choose, the options available for Password Security change.

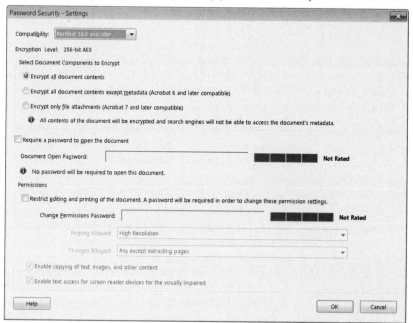

## Creating a Policy for Adding Security

If you've used earlier versions of Acrobat, accessing the Document Properties dialog box is something you are probably familiar with. It's a fast and easy way for adding document security, and it's okay when you have a single document you want to secure and never again want to secure additional documents with the same permissions and restrictions. Since Acrobat 7, Adobe Systems has made securing PDF documents much easier when you want to routinely secure PDF files using the same permissions settings. The preferred method for securing files in Acrobat 7 through X is to create a *security policy*.

To create a security policy, you use the Protection panel and open the Encrypt drop-down menu. Click Manage and a dialog box opens where you create new policies. You step through a New Security Policy Wizard where you make choices for the security method you want to use and make choices for the permissions you want to assign to a document.

Once you create the policy, you can easily apply the same policy when you want to secure additional documents without the need to select the different permissions options each time you apply security. For more detailed information on creating and using security policies, see "Using a security policy" later in this chapter.

At first glance you may not see any difference in the options for Acrobat X security compared to Acrobat 7 and later security. All the radio buttons and menu choices are the same for Acrobat 7 and later and Acrobat X. However, take a look at the Encryption Level in Figure 24.1. Acrobat 7 and 8 security used 128-bit encryption. Acrobat 9 and later provides you with 256-bit encryption.

You add Password Security via this dialog box any time you want to restrict users from opening a file and/or making changes to the content. Users must know the password you add in this dialog box in order to open a file and/or make changes. The options available to you include the following:

- **Compatibility.** The options from this pull-down menu include Acrobat 3.0, Acrobat 5.0, Acrobat 6.0, Acrobat 7.0 and later, and Acrobat X compatibility. If you select Acrobat X compatibility and save the PDF document, users need an Acrobat X viewer or greater to open the file. The same holds true when saving with Acrobat 7 and later compatibility. Users need Acrobat 7 or later to view PDFs created with Acrobat 7 and later compatibility.

- **Encryption level.** Below the Compatibility pull-down menu, Acrobat informs you what level of encryption is applied to the document based on the compatibility choice made in the pull-down menu. If you select Acrobat 3 from the Compatibility pull-down menu, the encryption level is 40-bit encryption. Acrobat 5 and Acrobat 6 compatibility are encrypted with 128-bit RC4 encryption. Acrobat 7 and 8 supports 128-bit AES. Acrobat 9.0 and X support 256-bit AES. All the higher encryption levels offer you more options for restricting printing and editing.

  - **Encrypt all document contents.** This option applies encryption to all document contents.

  - **Encrypt all document contents except metadata (Acrobat 6 and later compatible).** Use this option to apply encryption to all document contents except document metadata. As the item name implies, this level of security is compatible with Acrobat 6 and later. This is a good selection if you want to have the metadata in your secure documents available for a search engine.

  - **Encrypt only file attachments (Acrobat 7 and later compatible).** Use this option to encrypt file attachments but not the PDF document. This option is compatible only with Acrobat 7 and above. You might use this when sending an eEnvelope or a PDF Portfolio where you want to encrypt the contents only.

## Tip

Encrypting only file attachments is a nifty feature that was introduced in Acrobat 7. As an example for using this feature, you might have a document such as a memo you want to distribute to all employees. Attached to the memo you might have a financial report, draft company policy document, or some other file you want to have reviewed by management personnel only. All company personnel can see the memo, but only those who have a security password can open the file attachments. You can likewise secure files in a PDF Portfolio. The entire portfolio, or individual files within the portfolio, can be secured. ■

- **Require a password to open the document.** Select this check box if you want a user to supply a password to open the PDF document. After selecting the check box, the field box for Document Open Password becomes active and you can add a password. Before you exit the dialog box, Acrobat prompts you in another dialog box to confirm the password. Note: if you select Encrypt only file attachments (Acrobat 7 and later compatible), you must enter a password to be able to open the attachment(s).

- **Restrict editing and printing of the document. A password will be required in order to change these permission settings.** Select this check box if you want to restrict permissions from the items active in the Permissions area of the dialog box. You can use this with or without a Document Open Password. In Acrobat X, passwords are rated from Weak to Best. (See the New Feature following this list for more on the rating system.)

- **Change Permissions Password.** Fill in the field box with a password. If you also have a Document Open Password, the passwords must be different. Acrobat opens a dialog box and informs you to make different password choices if you attempt to use the same password for opening the file and setting permissions. In Acrobat X, passwords are rated from Weak to Best. (See the New Feature following this list for more on the rating system.)

- **Printing Allowed.** If you use Acrobat 3 compatibility, the options are available to either enable printing or disallow printing. The choices are None and High Resolution. Even though the choice reads High Resolution, the result simply enables users to print your file. With Acrobat 5 and above compatibility, you have a third choice for enabling printing at a lower resolution (150 dpi). If you select Low Resolution (150 dpi) from the menu options, users are restricted to printing the file at the lower resolution. This choice is typically something you might use for files intended for digital prepress and high-end printing, eBooks or eContent, or to protect your content from being printed and then rescanned.

- **Changes Allowed.** From this pull-down menu you make choices for the kinds of changes you allow users to perform on the document. Acrobat 3 compatibility offers you four choices; Acrobat 5 and above compatibility offers you five choices. These options include the following:

  - **None.** This option prevents a user from any kind of editing and content extraction.

  - **Inserting, deleting, and rotating pages.** This option is not available when using Acrobat 3 compatibility. Users are permitted to insert, delete, and rotate pages. If you create PDFs for eBooks, allowing users to rotate pages can be helpful when they view PDFs on tablets and portable devices.

  - **Page layout, filling in forms, and signing existing signature fields (Acrobat 3 only).** Select this option to enable users to extract pages, insert pages, and also perform actions on form fields.

  - **Filling in form fields and signing existing signature fields.** If you create Acrobat forms and want users to be able to fill in the form fields and digitally sign documents, enable this check box. Forms are useless to users without the ability to fill in the form fields.

- **Commenting, filling in form fields, and signing existing signature fields.** You might use this option in a review process where you want to have users comment on a design but you don't want them to make changes to your file. You can secure the document against editing, but allow commenting and form field filling in and signing. When you enable form filling in with this option or the Filling in form fields and signing existing signature fields option, users are restricted against changing your form design and cannot make edits other than filling in the fields. A good example of using this option might be having your customers fill out a form and also add comments to describe their selections.

- **Any except extracting pages.** With this option, all the permissions are available to users except extracting pages from the document and creating separate PDFs from selected pages.

- **Enable copying of text, images, and other content and access for the visually impaired.** This option is available when selecting Acrobat 3.0 and later. If you restrict permissions for any of the previous pull-down menu options, users aren't allowed to copy data. You can add permission for content copying by enabling this check box. Enable copying of text, images, and other content: The setting above was replaced with two settings in Acrobat 5.0 and higher security. This setting restricts the user from copying information from your PDF.

- **Enable text access for screen reader devices for the visually impaired.** This option is available for all versions except Acrobat 3 compatibility. As a matter of practice, checking this box is always a good idea. If you check this box, you can restrict all editing features while permitting users with screen reading devices the ability to read your files. If the check box is not enabled, screen readers and other devices designed for accessibility are not able to read the PDF document and all the options for using the View ⇨ Read Out Loud menu command are grayed out. Furthermore, users can index your files with Acrobat Pro by using Acrobat Catalog when this check box is enabled, regardless of the other items you prevent users from accessing.

## New Feature

Notice in Figure 24.1 that you find four gray boxes adjacent to the Document Open Password text box and the Change Permissions Password text box. As you type text in the password text boxes, the gray boxes change color according to the number and type of characters you type — for example, alpha characters, symbols, and numbers. The default test appears as Not Rated. As you type a password, the text changes to Weak, Medium, and Best, signifying a security rating for your password. Add more characters and change the character types, and the rating increases and dynamically displays adjacent to the password name. ■

## Cross-Reference

For more information on screen readers and accessibility, see Chapter 23. For more information on creating index files, see Chapter 6. ■

After you make choices for the password permissions, click OK, click OK again in the Document Properties dialog box, and then save your file to apply the security. If you close the document without saving, the security settings are not applied.

# Understanding Password Encryption

When you encrypt a file with password security, it's important to understand that tools exist that can decrypt files. Just about anything that can be encrypted using a password can be broken given enough time with the right tools. Software applications used for decryption run through cycles combining different characters to arrive at the right combination that accesses the encrypted file.

If you use a three-character password, the amount of time to break your password by a sophisticated decryption tool might be a matter of a few hours. As you add characters to the password, the decryption tool requires more time to explore all combinations of characters. If you add 10 to 12 characters to a password, the most sophisticated tools on the fastest computers can take decades of constant running to come up with the right combination of characters to break a password.

As a matter of practice when assigning permissions for sensitive material, always use no fewer than eight characters to secure a file. Adobe Systems has provided a sophisticated tool that enables you to protect your content if you observe a few simple rules.

In Acrobat versions prior to 9.0, only roman characters were permitted for passwords. Languages such as Middle Eastern, Hebrew, and Asian character sets were left out. When using Acrobat 9 and later, you find full Unicode support and can encrypt PDF files using a number of non-Roman character sets.

To determine the strength of the passwords you use, observe the rating scale adjacent to the password text boxes. When you see Best appear to the right of the password text boxes, you know you have a strong password that's not easy to decrypt.

## Using a security policy

Security policies are settings you save that are later used when securing documents — similar to creating style sheets in word processors or layout programs. The three different options for creating a security policy are as follows:

- **Use passwords.** This option is the same as applying a password to a document via the Document Properties Security pane. The difference between applying password security in the Password Security – Settings dialog box shown in Figure 24.1 and adding a security policy is that the latter is more efficient when you're applying the same security settings repeatedly to multiple documents. If you use the Password Security – Settings dialog box you need to set options each time you secure a document by selecting check boxes and making choices from pull-down menus. When you use a security policy, the options you choose are captured and saved as part of the policy; you just use the policy each time you want to encrypt documents with the same settings.

- **Use public key certificates.** Use this option to share files with users who have a public certificate. These certificates include ones you've added to your Trusted Identities list, or by searching online certificate directories you have access to. You can create a policy that applies different permissions to different users. Using this policy ensures that every document is encrypted with the same settings for the recipients.

- **Use Adobe LiveCycle Rights Management.** If you have access to an Adobe LiveCycle Rights Management Server, you can create a security policy that is enforced by connecting to the Adobe LiveCycle Rights Management Server. PDF documents and attachments can be secured for a selected group of users or for a period of time you determine when creating the policy. When a policy changes or expires on the server, the documents tied to the policy respect these changes as well.

To make the process of creating a security policy a little more clear, try the following steps to create a policy using password security.

### STEPS: Creating a Password Security Policy

1. **Open the Managing Security Policies Wizard.** You open the Managing Security Policy Wizard by selecting Manage Security Policies from the Secure Task Button pull-down menu. You can access the Wizard with or without a file open in the Document pane.

2. **Create a new policy.** In the Managing Security Policies Wizard, click the New button to open the New Security Policy Wizard pane, as shown in Figure 24.2. You have three options from which to choose. The default is Use passwords as shown in Figure 24.2. Leave the default settings as is and click Next. The Use the Adobe LiveCycle Rights Management Server is grayed out if you don't have access to an Adobe LiveCycle Rights Management Server or you have not subscribed to the hosted Protect PDF service from Adobe Systems.

**FIGURE 24.2**

Click New in the Managing Security Policies Wizard to open the New Security Policy dialog box.

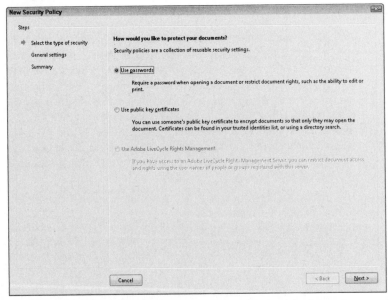

3. **Add a name and description for the new policy.** Type a policy name and description in the respective field boxes in the General Settings panel of the New Security Policy Wizard as shown in Figure 24.3. Select the box for Save passwords with the policy. The name and description you add in the second pane appear when you access the Managing Security Policies dialog box. Try to add information in the field boxes that describes the settings you use when creating the policy.

## Tip

If you want to periodically change passwords, leave the check box unchecked. Each time you use the policy, Acrobat prompts you for a new password. ∎

**FIGURE 24.3**

Name the policy and add a text description.

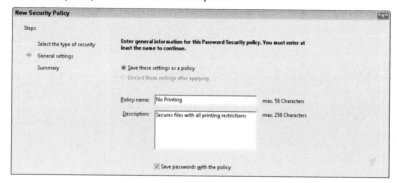

4. **Add the security settings.** Click Next. You arrive at the Document restrictions panel of the New Security Policy dialog box. This is the same dialog box you see in the Password Security–Settings dialog box shown earlier in Figure 24.1. Here you set the attributes for the security to be applied when using the policy. In my example, I selected Acrobat 7 compatibility; checked the box for "Restrict editing and printing of the document. A password will be required in order to change these permission settings"; added a password; selected None from the Print allowed pull-down menu; and checked the last check box in the dialog box.

5. **Review the policy.** Click Next. The last pane (Summary) appears with a Finish button. Click Finish to create the policy. You are returned to the Managing Security Policies dialog box where your new policy is listed in the policy list window, as shown in Figure 24.4. Notice that the name and description you added when creating the policy now appear in the Name and Description headings. Additionally you see a description of the policy details and encryption components for the policy you created. If creating multiple policies, select a policy name in the top window to change the policy details and encryption components in the lower half of the dialog box to reflect attributes for the selected policy. Click the Finish button to save the policy.

6. **Secure a document.** By default the Managing Security Policies dialog box opens as shown in Figure 24.5. Your new policy is listed in this dialog box. If you have a document open in the Document pane, you can apply the policy to the open document.

   Select the policy you created and click the Apply to Document button. Acrobat opens a dialog box informing you that you need to save your file after applying the policy to complete the security. Click OK and save the file. Your file is now secure using the permissions you identified for the policy.

**FIGURE 24.4**

Review the policy in the Summary pane.

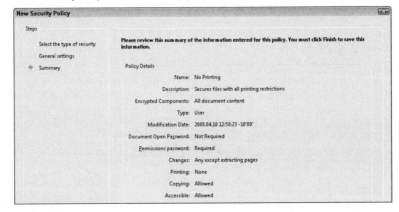

**FIGURE 24.5**

Select the policy you want to use for securing a document and click the Apply to Document button.

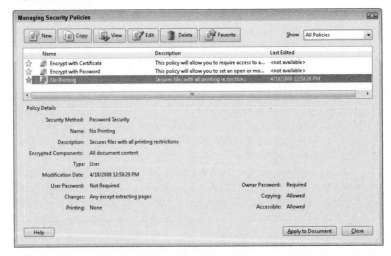

If you work with documents where you need to add different permissions depending on the document content and the users to whom you want to distribute your files, you'll want to add additional policies each designed with different permissions. As you add additional policies, you can choose what policy you want to use to secure a document.

You find your policy listed in the Managing Security Policies dialog box shown earlier in Figure 24.5. Select Manage Security Policies from the Encrypt drop-down menu in the Protection panel. Click the item and the Managing Security Policies dialog box opens. Select the policy and click Apply to Document. Click Yes when prompted in a dialog box and save the file.

## Managing security policies

You can add several policies using different permissions settings. Each time you create a new policy, it appears in the Managing Security Policies dialog box. Each time you want to secure documents with the same settings, open the Managing Security Policies dialog box and select a policy from the list. Click the Apply to Document button to secure the open document with the settings created from the selected policy.

You add or delete Favorites in the Managing Security Policies dialog box. Select Manage Security Policies to open the Managing Security Policies dialog box. In the far-left column you see a star icon adjacent to policy names. You also may not see a star icon adjacent to a policy name, as shown in Figure 24.6.

**FIGURE 24.6**

Select a policy and click the Favorite button. The policy is then listed in the Secure task button pull-down menu.

To make a policy a Favorite, select a policy where you see no star icon and click the Favorite button. If you want to remove a policy from the Favorite list, open the Managing Security Policies dialog box and select the policy you want to remove from Favorites. If it's already a Favorite, the policy appears listed with a star icon adjacent to the policy name. Click the Favorite button to remove the Favorites mark for the policy.

### Copying and editing policies

If you want to create a policy that's based on an existing policy, you can copy the policy in the Managing Security Policies dialog box and modify the policy attributes. Assume for a moment you want to add password protection to open a file and use all the same attributes of an existing policy that doesn't restrict the permissions to prompt for a password when a file is opened.

Select the policy you want to duplicate and click the Copy button. Acrobat opens the Creating a New Security Policy from an Existing Security Policy Wizard. This Wizard offers the same options as shown earlier in the New Security Policy Wizard (see Figure 24.2 earlier in this chapter) for the General Settings, Document Restrictions, and Summary. In the General Settings pane, type a new name for the new policy and type a description. Click Next and set the permissions for the policy. Click Next to open the Summary pane. Review the permissions and click Finish. Your new policy is added to the Managing Security Policies dialog box.

Select a policy and click the Edit button to get the same Wizard options as when copying files. You can modify a policy name and description and edit the permissions for an existing policy.

### Viewing and deleting policies

Select a policy and click the View button. The Viewing a Security Policy Wizard opens where you can review settings for a given policy. In this Wizard you can't make any changes to the policy. If you need to change settings, use the Edit button.

Select a policy and click the Delete button. Acrobat prompts you in a warning dialog box to confirm the action. Click Yes to delete the policy. Click No and the policy remains without changes.

# Understanding Digital IDs

A digital ID is a file that you create in Acrobat or acquire from a third-party signature provider. Your ID, also known as a *credential* or *profile* or *certificate*, is password protected and used to electronically sign or certify documents. Before you can digitally sign a document you need to create or acquire your own personal ID.

Digital IDs have two components important to understand — your personal or private digital ID and your public certificate. When you create a digital ID with Acrobat you are creating your private ID and your public certificate. The public certificate is a file you share with other users so they can encrypt files that they send to you. In order to open such encrypted files you need to supply the password used when you created your personal profile.

As a matter of understanding the security involved when using digital signatures, realize that, every time you want to sign a document you need to supply your password. Therefore, anyone having access to your computer cannot sign or certify a document on your behalf unless the user has your password. When a file is encrypted using your public certificate, the file is opened only when you have the digital ID and supply your password. Again, anyone having access to your computer cannot open a document encrypted with your public certificate unless that user has access to your password. Private digital signature IDs are used to sign and decrypt documents. Public certificates are used to encrypt documents and validate signatures.

As mentioned earlier, each digital ID has two components — the private ID and the public certificate. The private ID can be used to either digitally sign a PDF or to decrypt documents encrypted with the public certificate, and conversely, the public certificate can be used to encrypt documents or to validate digital signatures.

Digital IDs can be created in Acrobat or acquired from other parties. They can then be accessed locally from your computer or from a remote server. For a quick look at the options available when working with digital IDs and public certificates, open the More drop-down menu in the Sign and Certify panel and click Security Settings. The Security Settings dialog box opens as shown in Figure 24.7. This dialog box is used to manage and create digital IDs. You also use this dialog box to configure servers, time stamp digital IDs, and use the Adobe LiveCycle Rights Management Servers.

As shown in the dialog box, the options you have for working with digital IDs and configuring server access include the following:

- **Digital IDs.** There are three types of IDs available that include:
  - **A file.** Available on Windows and the Mac, this form of ID is similar to what you had available in earlier versions of Acrobat when using Acrobat Certificate Security. You can select Add ID (which opens the Add Digital ID dialog box to find an existing digital ID, create a new Acrobat Self-Sign, or get a third-party certificate).
  - **A roaming ID stored on a server.** This option permits you to host your ID on a Web site server. You can access your ID anywhere in the world by logging on to the server that contains your roaming ID and digitally sign documents using any one of your IDs available on the server. Roaming ID accounts are available to both Windows and Mac users.
  - **A device connected to this computer.** Use this option if you have a hardware device such as a token connected to your computer.
  - **A new digital ID I want to create now.** You use this option when you want to create your own personal ID that will be stored on your computer.

**FIGURE 24.7**

In the Security Settings dialog box you have four options for managing digital IDs and servers.

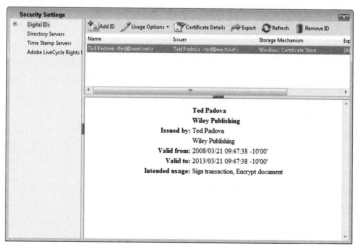

# Using Third-Party Signature Handlers

Digital signature handlers, tokens, biometrics, hardware solutions, and other similar products are available from third-party providers and offer you many different options for securing PDF documents, depending on the product and manufacturer. To find information on acquiring third-party products for signature handling, take a look at Adobe's Web site at `http://partners.adobe.com/security`. On the Adobe Security Partner Web pages you find links to digital signature and document control vendors worldwide.

If you use Acrobat for languages other than U.S. English, go to your local Web page and log on to Adobe's Web site. You might use, for example, a URL such as `www.adobe.com.fr/security` for a French language document page. This page includes a link to security partners supporting the localized products.

When you create a digital ID in Acrobat by choosing Advanced ➪ Security Settings, the Security Settings dialog box opens. Select Directory Servers and click New. The Edit Directory Server dialog box opens, where you identify a third-party server and provide log-on information and password.

- **Directory servers.** This option is used to enable you to locate specific digital ID certificates from network servers for encrypting documents using Certificate Security. Directory servers can be added by importing a configuration supplied by a System Administrator, or by entering the parameters required to configure the server.

- **Time Stamp Servers.** This option is used if you need the additional security and authentication features of a time stamp as part of your signature. As with Directory Servers, Time Stamp Servers are added by importing a configuration from a system administrator or by adding parameters required to configure the server.

- **Adobe LiveCycle Rights Management Servers.** Adobe LiveCycle Rights Management Server (`www.adobe.com/products/server/policy/main.html`) is a server-based security solution from Adobe Systems that provides dynamic control over PDF documents. Policies created with Acrobat or Adobe LiveCycle Rights Management Server are stored on the server and can be refreshed from the server. Once you've configured an Adobe Rights Management Server, all polices maintained on this server are available to you. You must log into Adobe LiveCycle Rights Management Server to use these policies. This option also requires that you access a URL provided by a System Administrator and add the server to your list of Adobe LiveCycle Rights Management Servers.

## Creating a personal digital ID

Digital IDs can be created with or without custom appearance settings. The appearance of your signature has no effect on the kind of security you add to a signature. If you want to create a custom signature appearance such as a scanned analog signature, it's usually best to first create the appearance and then create the digital ID.

## Creating a custom appearance

Appearances for your digital IDs in Acrobat viewers earlier than version 9.0 required you to use the Security preferences dialog box. In Acrobat 9 and later, you can create an appearance for a signature on-the-fly when you sign a document and need to create a signature. If you don't sign a document and start from scratch, you need to use the Security Preferences dialog box to add an appearance. What follows here assumes you are creating a new signature and not signing a form.

Open the Preferences dialog box (Ctrl/⌘+K) and click Security in the left pane. The right pane changes as shown in Figure 24.8.

**FIGURE 24.8**

Click Security in the left pane in the Preferences dialog box to change the right pane so that you can add a new appearance for a digital ID.

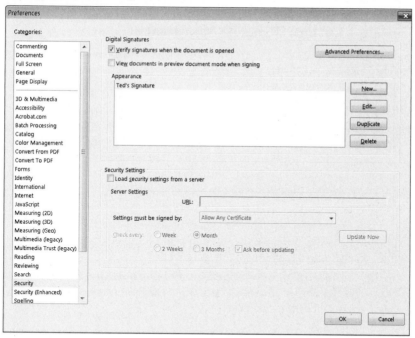

Two preferences dialog boxes are used for creating an appearance and setting some attributes for your signatures. These include:

- **Security Preferences.** You use the Security Preferences to create digital ID appearances for your personal digital IDs. If you want to add a logo, analog signature, symbol, or some text to an ID, you can do so by clicking the New button and choosing from various settings in the Configure Security Appearance dialog box.

- **Advanced Preferences.** If you have an ID configured such as the one shown in Figure 24.8, the ID(s) appears in the Appearance list in the Security Preferences dialog box. Select an ID and click Advanced Preferences to open another dialog box where a number of options exist for verifying signatures, creating them, and, on Windows, options for settings for Windows Integration. A number of different options exist in three tabs (Windows) or two tabs (Mac). For a detailed description of each item, consult the Acrobat Help document.

## Note

If you have not created a digital ID yet, you will not see anything listed in this box, but you still can create appearances that can later be used with a digital ID. ■

To understand how to create a custom appearance for a digital ID, follow these steps.

### STEPS: Creating a Custom Digital ID Appearance

1. **Open the Security preferences.** Press Ctrl/⌘+K. Click the Security item in the left pane.

2. **Click the New button in the right pane to open the Configure Signature Appearance dialog box.**

3. **Configure the appearance.** Type a title in the Title text box. This title will appear as the name for your appearance and one you'll select when configuring a digital ID. If you want to use a graphic, click the Imported graphic radio button and click File to open the Select Picture dialog box. Locate and select the graphic you want to use for the appearance. (Note that the file can be any file type supported by the Create PDF From File command.)

   Select the text items you want to display on your signature by checking boxes in the Configure Text area of the Configure Signature Appearance dialog box. In my example, I removed all check boxes, as shown in Figure 24.9.

4. **Click OK in the Configure Signature Appearance dialog box.** The signature is listed by Title in the Security preferences. Click OK in the Preference dialog box to configure your appearance for a signature.

### Creating a digital ID

The steps used to create a signature appearance are optional. You don't need to use a custom appearance when creating a digital ID. If you do create a signature appearance, you can use it when creating a new ID.

FIGURE 24.9

Type a title in the Title text box, import a graphic, and check the boxes you want to use for text appearances.

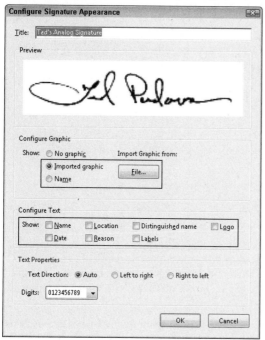

To understand how digital IDs are created, follow these steps.

## STEPS: Creating a Digital ID and Appearance

1. **Open the Security Settings dialog box.** Click Security Settings in the More drop-down menu in the Sign and Certify panel. The Security Settings Wizard, refer to Figure 24.7, opens. When the Wizard opens, click Digital IDs in the left pane.

2. **Create a Self-Signed digital ID.** Click Add ID in the Security Settings dialog box. The Add Digital ID Wizard opens, as shown in Figure 24.10. Select A new digital ID I want to create now and click Next.

3. **Select the area in which you want to store your ID.** The next pane has two options for where you can store your digital ID. Select the first radio button (New PKCS#12 digital ID file) to create a password-protected ID on either Windows or the Mac. Select the second radio button (Windows Certificate Store) if you want your ID

made available to Acrobat and Windows applications. Click Next to arrive at the new pane in the Wizard.

Click Add ID in the Security Settings dialog box to open the Add Digital ID dialog box.

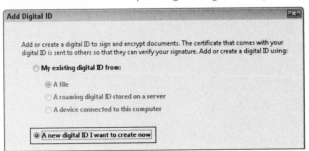

4. **Add identity information.** The next pane opens with text boxes for you to supply identity information. If you added identity information in the Identity preferences, the information is transposed to the pane shown in Figure 24.11. If you want to use special characters, non-Roman languages, or non-ASCII, check the box for Enable Unicode Support.

Choose a key algorithm from the Key Algorithm pull-down menu. In earlier versions of Acrobat the highest encryption level you had was 128-bit encryption. New in Acrobat 9 you find an option for 256-bit encryption. If you choose 256-bit encryption, you can validate signatures in Acrobat viewers earlier than version 9.0.

5. **Choose where you want to store the ID and type a password.** Click Next in the Wizard and click the Browse button to locate a folder where you want to save the ID (for New PKCS#12 digital ID files). Type a password in the Password text box and type the password again in the Confirm Password text box.

6. **Click Finish.** Click Finish in the Add Digital ID dialog box to return to the Security Settings dialog box. Your new digital ID is now ready to use.

Notice as yet, we have not selected an appearance for the digital ID. You can store multiple appearances in the Security preferences, and each time you sign a document, you can choose which appearance you want to use for your signature. You might, for example, sign documents internally in your company using one appearance, and with the same ID sign documents coming from other sources outside your company with another appearance.

**FIGURE 24.11**

Add identity information if all fields are not completed in your Identity preferences.

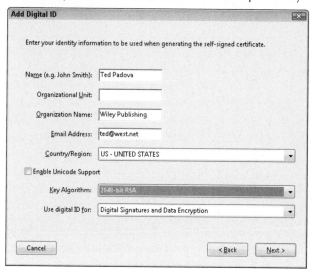

## Managing multiple IDs

If you create several IDs used for different purposes, you may have a need to remove old IDs and add new IDs. In the Security Settings you have options for assigning attributes to your IDs, adding new IDs, and removing IDs. Choose Advanced ⇨ Security Settings to open the Wizard shown earlier in this chapter in Figure 24.7.

Click an ID in the Name column to select it and click the Remove ID button to delete an ID. You also have options in the Security Settings dialog box for Exporting Certificates, selecting Usage Options, and viewing certificate details.

## Setting usage options

You can create several digital IDs and assign different usage options for each ID. After adding IDs to the Security Settings dialog box, select an ID and open the Usage Options pull-down menu. From the commands shown in Figure 24.12, you have a number of different usage options. Click one of the options shown to assign that option to the selected ID. Click another ID and assign another option. You can assign only one option to an ID. If an option is used with one ID and you apply that option to another ID, the option is removed from the first ID and assigned to your new selection. After assigning options, you'll notice the appearance of the options icons adjacent to the ID names.

FIGURE 24.12

Click an ID in the Security Settings dialog box and select a usage option.

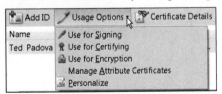

## Using signature fields

To sign a document containing a signature field, click the field with the Hand tool. The Sign Document dialog box opens, as shown in Figure 24.13. Select an ID from the Save As digital ID pull-down menu. Type your password in the Password text box and select an appearance from the Appearance pull-down menu.

When you click Sign you are prompted to save your file. Locate the folder where you want to save the file and click Save. The document is signed using the Usage Options assigned to the signature.

FIGURE 24.13

Select an ID to sign a document from the Sign As digital ID list, type the password for the ID, and choose an appearance setting.

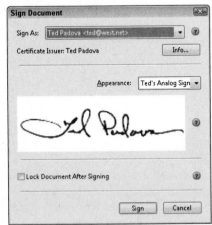

## Creating a signature field when signing a document

If no signature field appears on a document, you can sign a document by clicking Sign Document in the Sign and Certify panel. This method of signing prompts you to marquee an area on a page where you want to create a signature field on the document. Click OK in the dialog box informing you what to do and draw a rectangle. When you release the mouse button, the Sign Document dialog box opens. Follow the same steps outlined in the next section.

# Certifying a Document

You have two choices for certifying a document with a digital ID. You can choose to certify a file with or without a visible signature. In the Sign and Certify panel, click Certify with Visible Signature to have your signature shown on the document. Choose Certify without Visible Signature to add an invisible signature to the file. Using either option opens the Save as Certified Document dialog box shown in Figure 24.14.

Open the Save as Certified Document dialog box by clicking Certify with/without Digital Signature in the Sign and Certify panel.

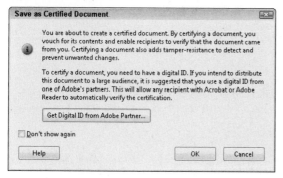

You have choices for acquiring a digital ID you have set up with an Adobe partner, or click OK to open the Sign Document dialog box where you apply a signature using the same criteria as when signing with and without signature fields.

A second option exists in the File menu. Select File ⇨ Save As Certified Document. The same dialog box opens, prompting you to select an ID from an Adobe partner or click OK to open the Sign Document dialog box.

# Using Trusted Identities and Certificate Security

Trusted identities are added to the Trusted Identities Manager dialog box. The list of trusted identities is like an address book where you can add contacts and set certificate properties. You can maintain a contact list of trusted identities from people you do business with or may do business with. Each user listed in Trusted Identities can be used to validate digital signatures and encrypt PDF documents for these users. The Trusted Identities Manager additionally permits you to set levels of trust from the users listed in your contact list.

# Understanding Encryption, Validation, and the Trusted Identities Manager

In the Manage Trusted Identities dialog box (shown in Figure 24.16), a pull-down menu provides two choices: Contacts and Certificates. Items listed in the menus do not have to match. You can have certificates in the list that are not in the Contacts list. From the Display pull-down menu you can select either Contacts or Certificates, and you can Add Contacts or Certificates respective to the menu item you select.

In order to encrypt documents you do *not* have to have a public certificate in your trusted identities. For example, a company may have a corporate-level security solution in which each employee is issued a certificate that is stored on a network server. You can search certificates on your company's LDAP (Lightweight Directory Access Protocol) server to find someone you want to encrypt for and just use their certificate without adding the certificate to your list of trusted identities.

To validate a signature, you do not have to have the public certificate in your trusted identities if you've already established a trust with a parent in the chain of trust. For example, you can create a Class 1 certificate for a security partner. So the chain might be Your Company, Inc. ⇨ Partner Class 1 ⇨ Your Name.

You can then *trust* Your Company, Inc. (the root) and therefore everybody under that chain is automatically trusted by you so you don't need any individual's certificate in your local trusted Identities for validation. However, if you want to give any user a different trust setting than the trust settings used by the parent, then you do need to add the individual's certificate to your trusted identities.

Does an individual need to send you a public certificate? The answer is no, not if the user sends you a file signed with his/her certificate. You can always get the public certificate from a file sent to you.

To acquire a public certificate from a signed document, open a context menu on the signature and select Properties. In the Signature Properties dialog box, click the Show Certificate button. The Certificate Viewer dialog box opens. Click the Export button; you are prompted to save the certificate as a file or email the certificate.

The entire range of possibilities regarding using digital IDs, signing documents, and authenticating signed or certified documents is a very complex subject. In an effort to break it down to a more simplified view, the detail in this chapter assumes you are working in an environment where you are not using a corporate-wide security solution and you're using the self-sign methods of security. If you want the highest levels of security and the most efficient means for securing documents, I encourage you to carefully review the Acrobat Help document and explore all the security information on Web pages hosted by Adobe Systems.

# Using certificate encryption

Encryption using certificates is a means for you to add security for a selected group of users. The advantage of using certificates is you can control the permissions settings individually for each user in the same PDF document. In addition, since the user needs not only a password but the digital ID file, it becomes impossible for someone else to "crack." For example, you may want to allow one user to view your document, but restrict printing. For another user you may want to disallow editing, but enable printing. For a third user you may want to allow editing and printing. All these permissions can be set for each user in the same PDF document using the Certificate Security Settings dialog box.

To encrypt a file using certificates, you need access to the public certificate. You can either search for the public certificates, which may be located on a network server, or you can collect the public certificates for each user and load them into your Trusted Identities list. Keep in mind, the Trusted Identities Manager is like an address book and merely is a convenient location where you can store contact and certificate information for users you frequently work with. During encryption you can specify permissions settings individually for each user.

# Exporting public certificates

Public certificates are used for validating signatures on documents received and encrypting files which you plan to share. For another user to validate your signature or encrypt a file unique to your profile, you need to export your public certificate and share it with other users. Your public certificate does not compromise your password settings or ability to secure your own files. Public certificates are generated from your profile, but do not send along your password to other users.

## Note

**Companies using directory servers to host public certificates do not need to export certificates. For self-sign security you also don't need to acquire a certificate from another user. A user can sign a document and you can open the signature Properties dialog box and click the Export button to gain access to the certificate. The only thing you need to be concerned about is that the first signed file you receive from a given recipient has an authentic signature from the user you know has signed the document. If you trust the file, export the certificate. You can use that certificate for all subsequent documents from the user in question. ■**

To export a public certificate you need to start with a digital ID you have already created. Select an ID in the Security Settings dialog box shown earlier in Figure 24.7. If you have more than one ID listed in the dialog box, select the ID you want to use and click the Export button. The Data Exchange File – Export Options dialog box opens, as shown in Figure 24.15.

In this dialog box you make a choice for saving your public certificate to disk or emailing the certificate directly to another user. If you select the Save the data to a file option, you can later attach it to an email message and send it to users as needed. If you select the Email the data to someone option and then click the Next button, the Compose Email dialog box opens where you add the recipient's email address. Enter an email address and click the Email button to attach the data file to a new email message. Acrobat supplies a default message in the email note for you providing instructions for the recipient, but you can edit if desired.

**FIGURE 24.15**

When exporting your certificate, you can choose to save the public certificate as a file or email the certificate to another user.

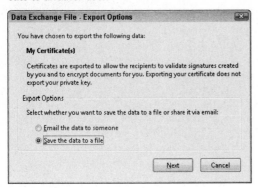

## Requesting contacts

If you want to add a contact and/or certificate to your list of trusted identities, select Advanced ➪ Manage Trusted Identities to open the Trusted Identities dialog box. Click the Request Contact button to open the Email a Request dialog box. You add your name, email address, and any contact information you want to supply in the text boxes in the Email a Request dialog box. Click the Next button to open the Compose Email dialog box. In this dialog box, you add the recipient email address. A default subject and message appear in the Compose Email dialog box informing the recipient you are requesting a copy of the individual's certificate. Click the Email button to email the request to the recipient. Note that you may need to open your default email program and click the Send or Send/Receive button to initiate a send.

# Emailing Certificates versus Exporting from Signatures

Since a user who receives a signed document from you can open the signature Properties and acquire your signature by showing the certificate and clicking an Export button, you may feel that exporting a certificate and emailing your public certificate to a user is an unnecessary step. In some cases it is unnecessary.

Where you have an advantage for exporting a certificate and emailing to others is simply adding another level of security to your workflow. If a signed document is sent to a user, the user may not be certain that the document came from you. If you sign a document, send it to a user, then email your exported certificate to the same user in a separate email, the recipient receives two mails. This workflow simply adds one more level of assurance that the certificate came from you.

When a copy of a certificate is emailed back to you, the file appears in a message window as a file attachment. Double-click the attachment to add the certificate automatically to your list of trusted identities after you approve adding the ID or click OK.

## Managing trusted identities

After you collect public certificates, you can load the certificates into your Trusted Identities list for easy management and quick access of the certificates. To load certificates, click Manage Trusted Identities in the More drop-down menu on the Sign and Certify panel. The dialog box shown in Figure 24.16 opens.

**FIGURE 24.16**

You use the Manage Trusted Identities dialog box to add identities from public certificates you collect from other users.

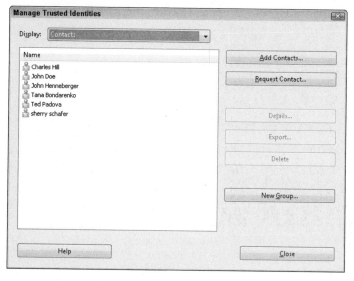

To add a recipient, click the Add Contacts button. The Choose Contacts to Import dialog box shown in Figure 24.17 opens where you can browse your hard drive or network server to locate certificates from other users. When adding identities collected by other users, click the Browse button. The Locate Certificate File dialog box opens where you navigate your hard drive and locate certificates to add to a recipient list. Click Open; the recipient's name appears in the top window of the Choose Contacts to Import dialog box. Select the name of the added contact and click the Import button to add the certificate to the identities list. You use the Search button to search through network servers configured in your Directory Servers.

Add the certificate and return to the Manage Trusted Identities dialog box and continue adding new certificates to your list of recipients.

**FIGURE 24.17**

Use the Choose Contacts to Import dialog box to add new recipient identities.

## Setting certificate security permissions

One thing to keep in mind is that when you have circumstances that require you to repeat document security for the same set of users or when encrypting documents with the same set of permissions, you'll always want to set up a security policy. In those instances where you intend to secure a document using certificates one time only, you can set permissions without creating a policy. To help simplify the process, this section refers to setting up permissions using certificates for a one-time use.

To secure a document using Certificate Security, open the Document Properties dialog box (File ➪ Properties). Click the Security tab and select Certificate Security from the Security Method pull-down menu. The Certificate Security Settings Wizard opens. The General settings panel offers you the choice to save your settings as a policy or discard the settings after applying the security. In addition you have options for what you want to encrypt, such as the document only or the document and file attachments and the type of encryption you want to apply. In Figure 24.18, you can see the options in the General settings pane. Make a choice for saving your settings as a policy or discarding the settings after applying them. If you choose to create a policy, add a name and description. At the bottom of the General pane, make a choice for the type of encryption you want to apply and click Next.

## Note

When working with PDF Portfolios, open the File menu and choose Portfolio Properties. You can use Certificate Security and apply the security settings to the entire portfolio. ■

**FIGURE 24.18**

Select Certificate Security from the Security Method pull-down menu in the Security tab from the Document Properties dialog box to open the Certificate Security Settings dialog box.

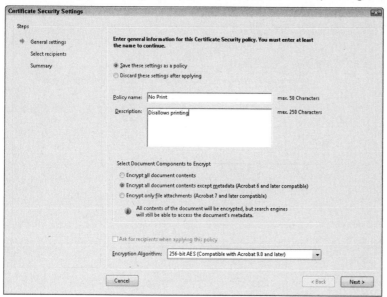

The Select Recipients pane opens, as shown in Figure 24.19. Click Browse and locate the file(s) you want to add. You can add only one file at a time. Keep clicking Browse and add all the files you want to use for this particular Certificate Security. In Figure 24.19, I added three recipients to my list.

Select a recipient in the list and click the Permissions button. The Permissions Settings dialog box opens, where you choose individual permissions for a selected recipient, as shown in Figure 24.20. Set permissions for the selected user and click OK. Select another recipient and set permissions for that user. Continue setting permissions for each user.

The great strength for using Certificate Security is that all the recipients in your list can be assigned unique permissions. For example, you can prohibit printing for one user, and allow low-resolution printing for another user and high-resolution printing for a third user. In addition, you can protect against a number of different editing options. All of these permissions settings are applied to individual recipients in the same PDF document or PDF Portfolio. Each user needs to open the file using his or her own digital ID and password.

To complete the Certificate Security, click the Next button to open the Summary panel. A summary for your policy is listed in the panel. If you want to make any changes, click the Back button. To accept the settings you made, click Finish. Save the file and all the permissions assignments to your recipients are encrypted in the document.

## FIGURE 24.19

Several certificates are added to the Select recipients pane in the Wizard.

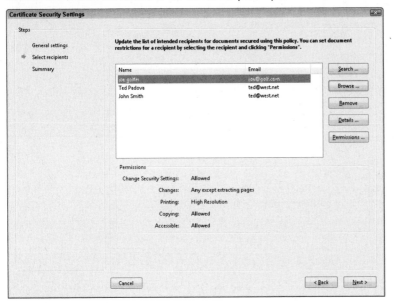

## FIGURE 24.20

Select the permissions you want to assign to the selected user and click OK.

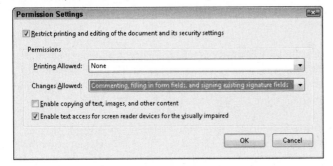

# Validating Signatures

Digital signatures would be of no value unless you could confirm that a document was signed by the individual claiming to have signed the document. For confirmation purposes you use menu commands and options to validate signatures. You have several options when validating signatures, and all depend on different circumstances, which include:

- If you have established trust with a parent, you don't need the certificate listed in your trusted identities. See the "Understanding encryption, validation, and the Trusted Identities Manager" sidebar earlier in this chapter. When you open a signed PDF from another person using a third-party security partner certificate, the signature appears as Unknown. Select Show Signature Properties from a context menu you open on the signature. In the Signature Properties dialog box, click Validate Signature. The signature appears valid without adding to your trusted identities. If you want to change the level of trust, you can add the certificate to your trusted identities and set the trust in the Manage Trusted Identities dialog box. See the "Managing trusted identities" section earlier in this chapter.

- If you open a self-signed document and the user hasn't used a third-party security partner, and you know the document has been sent to you by the PDF author, you can retrieve the certificate from the document without needing the individual to send you the certificate. You might receive files from members of your workgroup where you are confident the document you receive comes from the individual who signed it. In this case, you can open the Signature panel, select the Signature, and select Validate Signature in the Sign Options menu. Another Signature Validation dialog box opens. Click Signature Properties in this dialog box to open the Signature Properties dialog box. Open the Trust tab in the Signature Properties and click the Add to Trusted Identities button. The certificate is added to your trusted identities, where you can set the level of trust and use the certificate to validate signatures.

- If you open a document from an anonymous user or one where you question the document authenticity, you can request a certificate. You add the certificate you receive from a PDF author to your trusted identities, and you can choose to set the level of trust following the same steps outlined in the section "Managing trusted identities" earlier in this chapter.

To validate a signature, open the Security panel and choose Validate Signature from the Options menu. Choose Validate All Signatures from the same menu if you want to validate all signatures in a document where multiple signatures exist.

When you open a signed document and view signatures in the Signatures panel, an icon with a question mark may appear adjacent to the signature(s). In addition, you'll notice the text below the signature icon often states that the signature validity is unknown; or for valid signatures, the text reads: Signature is valid. You'll also find the validity of a signature reported in the Signature Message Bar as shown in Figure 24.21.

## Note

Contained in the Security Preferences (Ctrl/⌘+K and click Security in the left pane) is a check box for Verify signatures when the document is opened. If the check box is enabled, the signatures in the document are validated when the document opens. In this case, you do not need to manually access a menu command to validate a signature. Acrobat 9 and later automatically validate signatures when a document is opened. You do, however, still need to have a trusted certificate from the individual who signed the document in order to validate upon opening the file. If using an external certificate authority, you need to have an active Internet connection to your service to verify signatures. If this box is unchecked, you must manually validate your signatures. Be aware that if your document has more than ten pages, Acrobat may not validate signatures automatically upon opening the document. This behavior prevents a document from slowing down during open time. If you find documents not certifying signatures at open time, manually review the signatures in the Signatures panel and use the Validate Signature command in the Options pull-down menu. ∎

When you validate a signature, Acrobat opens a dialog box reporting the validation status. If the public certificate is loaded and the validation is true, a dialog box opens reporting the certificate is valid.

If you get UNKNOWN, this certificate is not in your trusted identities. Select the Signature Properties menu command in the Signature panel Options menu or a context menu opened on a signature in the Signatures panel. From the Summary tab select Show Certificate. From the Trust tab, select your Trust Settings and select Add to Trusted Identities. The Import Contact Settings appear when you determine which Trust Settings you want. Select OK in the Certificate Viewer window. You are returned to Signature Properties. Select Validate Signature. This signature will now be Valid. Select Close to return to the Document pane.

You can view the signature properties in the Signature Properties dialog box, which reports all the properties of the certificate including the reason for signing, the email address of the person signing the document, and the certificate fingerprint. The Signatures panel reflects a valid signature, as shown in Figure 24.21.

## FIGURE 24.21

After a signature is validated, the icon adjacent to the signature name changes to a pen and check mark, and the status is reported as valid.

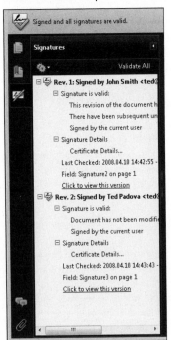

# Creating a Security Envelope

Another security option you have in Acrobat is creating a secure envelope adding any file you want to use as a file attachment. You can create eEnvelopes containing file attachments and secure the PDF and file attachment(s) against unauthorized access. Users of Acrobat or the free Adobe Reader software with access rights can open the PDFs and extract the file attachment(s).

To understand how files are attached in a Secure PDF Delivery workflow, follow these steps.

### STEPS: Creating a Secure eEnvelope

1.  **Open the Create Security Envelope dialog box.** Open the More drop-down menu in the Protection panel and click Create Security Envelope. Note that you do not need to have a document open in Acrobat to access this menu command.

2.  **Choose files to include.** The Files to Enclose panel in the Create Security Envelope Wizard opens as shown in Figure 24.22. Click the Add File to Send button to open the Files to Enclose dialog box. Navigate your hard drive, select the file you want to include, and click Open. Note that any file of any type can be added to the security envelope. In my example, I use a Microsoft Word document.

**FIGURE 24.22**

Click Add File to Send and locate the file to add to your eEnvelope.

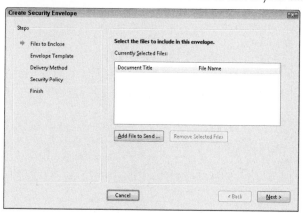

3.  **Select a template.** Click Next to open the Envelope Template panel. You can select from preinstalled templates or click the Browse button to locate a PDF file you want to use for your template. Select a preinstalled template from the list shown in Figure 24.23 and click Next.

**FIGURE 24.23**

Select a template and click Next.

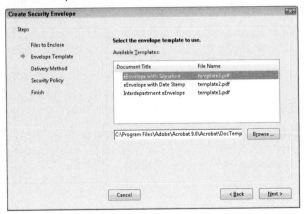

## Note

You have templates available for date stamping the envelope and signing the envelope. Choose from template2.pdf to date stamp an envelope and choose template3.pdf to open a template with a digital signature field. All templates have field boxes where you can add addressee information. ■

4. **Choose a delivery method.** The next panel that opens is the Delivery Method panel. You have two choices for delivering your eEnvelope. Choose from options for sending the envelope later or emailing it now from the two radio button options. Select Send the envelope now and click the Next button.

5. **Choose a security policy to apply.** The Security Policy pane opens, as shown in Figure 24.24. Click the Show all policies check box and select a policy in the list and click Next.

6. **Finish.** The last pane shows the directory path for the selected file. Review the summary and click Next. Click OK to attach the Security Envelope with the file attachment to a new email message, as shown in Figure 24.25. Edit the message text if you so choose and add a recipient to the To field. Click Send and your security envelope is on its way.

## FIGURE 24.24

Select a security policy and click Next.

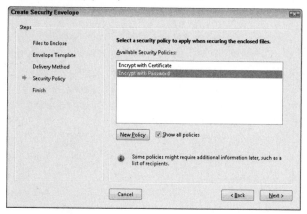

## FIGURE 24.25

Click Finish and the security envelope is attached to a new email message.

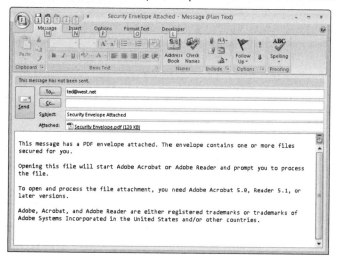

# Summary

In this chapter, you learned how to secure PDF files and apply digital signatures.

- PDF documents can be secured with built-in Acrobat Self-Signed Security and security handlers acquired from third-party developers. Files can be secured from users opening documents, editing documents, or both.

- Different levels of security can prevent users of Acrobat viewers earlier than version 6 from opening files. It is important to know your user audience and what version of Acrobat viewers they use before securing files.

- To digitally sign a document you need to create a digital ID. You create and manage digital IDs via several tools and menu commands in the Sign and Certify panel.

- You can apply appearance settings to your signatures in the form of scanned documents, icons, and symbols from files saved as PDF or other file formats compatible with the Create PDF From File command. You add signature appearances via the Security Preferences dialog box.

- You can digitally sign a document by using an existing signature field or by selecting a menu command where you are prompted to create a signature field.

- You can certify a document using your signature by selecting a menu command to certify the document.

- Trusted identities are a list of digital ID certificates from people you share information with. You can export your public certificate to a file or attach your public certificate to an email message from within Acrobat. When other users have your public certificate, they can validate your signature or encrypt documents for your use.

- You can encrypt files for a group of users by using their public certificates stored as trusted identities. A single PDF document can be secured for different users and with different permissions for each user.

- In order to validate a signature, the public certificate for that digital ID needs to be loaded into your Trusted Identities list.

- Any file of any type can be added to a secure envelope. The only way for an end user to access the file attachment is to have the password to open the attached file.

# CHAPTER 25

# Working with PDFs and the Web

Throughout this book, I address using PDFs on the Web. As I discussed in Chapter 7, you can download selected Web pages or entire Web sites and have all the HTML pages converted to PDF. In Acrobat 6 and greater you can convert media, animation, and sound to PDFs with the animated pages appearing the same in Acrobat viewers as when you see them on Web sites. In Chapter 8 I talked about using the PDFMaker with Microsoft Internet Explorer and Microsoft Outlook.

In Chapter 19, I discussed comments and, in Chapter 20, I covered online reviews. Coming ahead in Chapter 27, I talk about eBooks and downloading books as Digital Editions. In Chapter 31, I talk about submitting form data. And in other chapters, you find similar discussions on Acrobat PDFs hosted online. In short, the Web plays a major role with much of your Acrobat activity. In this chapter, I cover more about using PDFs online for viewing in Web browsers and linking to PDF views on Web sites.

## Viewing PDFs in Web Browsers

You open a PDF in a Web browser just as you open a file to view an HTML document. You specify a URL and filename to view the PDF directly in the browser or click a Web link from within a PDF document to open a URL where a PDF is hosted. For example, logging on to www. provider.com/file.pdf results in the display of the PDF page inside the browser window. This type of viewing is referred to as *inline viewing.* If you click the Read Mode button in your Web browser the PDF in appears as shown in Figure 25.1.

**FIGURE 25.1**

Inline viewing of PDFs offers you access to many Acrobat tools, which are available from the Toolbar Well, just as when viewing PDFs in Acrobat.

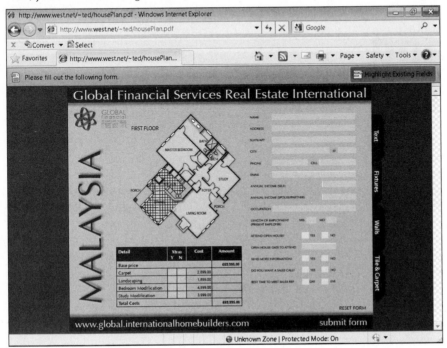

If you need access to Acrobat tools while viewing a PDF inline in a browser window, use the default view or exit Read Mode and the view changes to what you see in Figure 25.2.

You can also open PDFs on your local hard drive by selecting File ➪ Open (Windows) or File ➪ Open File (Mac). In the Open dialog box, click Browse (Windows), navigate your hard drive, and select the file you want to open. On the Mac just navigate your hard drive in the Open dialog box and select the file you want to open. Click Open and the file opens in the Web browser window. On the Mac, Safari is supported the same as you have available with Microsoft Internet Explorer.

By default, all Web-hosted PDFs are opened inside your browser. From the browser application you can save a PDF document to your hard drive by choosing File ➪ Save As.

FIGURE 25.2

Click the More Tools button in the Read Mode toolbar and you gain access to many Acrobat tools.

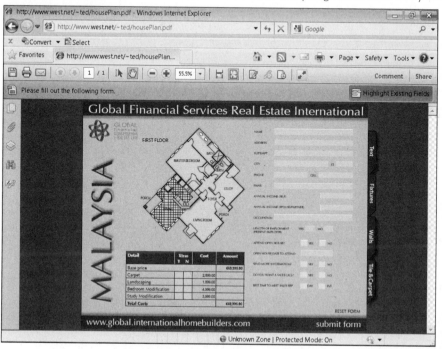

If you prefer to open Web-hosted PDFs in Acrobat, you need to adjust preferences in Acrobat. Preference options provide you with choices for viewing PDFs inside your Web browser as an inline view or viewing Web-hosted PDFs inside Acrobat the same as you would view locally hosted PDF documents. To change preferences, choose Edit ⇨ Preferences (Acrobat ⇨ Preferences on the Mac) or press Ctrl/⌘+K. In the Preferences dialog box, select Internet in the left pane. The viewing preferences appear in the right pane, as shown in Figure 25.3.

Options for handling PDFs on Web sites with Acrobat viewers include the following:

- **Display PDF in browser.** The check box is enabled by default, and PDFs viewed on Web sites are displayed as inline views in browser applications. If you disable the check box as shown in Figure 25.3, PDFs are displayed in Acrobat viewers. The default Acrobat viewer installed on your computer opens if no viewer is currently open and the target document is shown in the Acrobat viewer Document pane.

**FIGURE 25.3**

To change Web viewing preferences, open the Preferences dialog box and select Internet in the left pane.

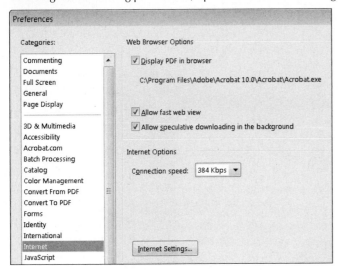

- **Allow fast web view.** This option speeds up viewing PDFs on Web servers. When this option is enabled, a single page is downloaded to your computer and shown according to how you set your preferences — in the browser window or in an Acrobat viewer window. As you scroll pages in a PDF document, each new page downloads when the page is loaded in the Document pane. If you deselect the check box, the entire PDF document is downloaded to your computer before the first page appears in the browser window or the Acrobat Document pane. You must save the PDF with Fast Web View and the server must be capable of byte-serving for fast Web view to work.

- **Allow speculative downloading in the background.** If you select the preceding Allow fast web view option, and want to continue downloading multiple-page PDF documents, check this box. As you view a page, the remaining pages continue to download until the complete PDF is downloaded from a Web site.

- **Connection Speed.** Select the speed of your Internet connection from the pull-down menu choices. This setting applies to viewing Web pages but also influences the speed selection for viewing multimedia.

- **Internet Settings.** If you click the Internet Settings button, the Internet Properties dialog box opens. In the Internet Properties dialog box you can make choices for configuring your Internet connection, choosing default applications for email, making security settings choices, setting privacy attributes, and other such system-level configurations.

# Working with Web Links

Web links to PDFs hosted on Web sites occur from within HTML documents and from within PDF files. If using an HTML editor like Adobe Dreamweaver, or writing HTML code, you create Web links the same as you link to Web pages. A PDF Web link in HTML might look like `http://www.mycompany.com/brochure.pdf` — where the link is made to the PDF instead of a document that ends with an .htm or .html extension.

Web addresses contained in the text of a PDF document can be hot links to URLs where PDFs are hosted. In earlier versions of Acrobat you needed the complete URL address including http:// for a Web link to be recognized. In Acrobat 8 and later, a URL like `www.adobe.com` is recognized as a Web link. Text in PDF documents with URL addresses can be converted to Web links via a menu command. If you distribute PDF files to users of Acrobat 6 or earlier, you need to add links to the PDF document for the users of these viewers to access Web pages from a PDF.

To create Web links from text in PDF documents, open the Document Processing panel and click Create Links from URLs. Acrobat opens the Create Web Links dialog box shown in Figure 25.4. In the dialog box you make decisions for the pages where the links are created. Select All to create Web links from all pages in the PDF. The From button enables you to supply page ranges in the two field boxes.

The Create Web Links dialog box enables you to target pages for creating Web links.

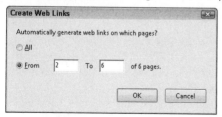

## Caution

**Be aware that you don't need to create links in PDF files distributed to Adobe Reader or Acrobat version 7 and above. However, the end user needs to have a preference option enabled in order for an Acrobat viewer to recognize text as a URL. Open the General preferences and look at the check box where you see Create links from URLs. By default the check box is checked. If this check box is not enabled, links aren't recognized from text. ∎**

Acrobat can also globally remove Web links from all pages or a specified page range. To remove Web links, open the Document Processing panel and click Remove All Links. The same options are available in the Remove Web Links dialog box as those found in the Create Web Links dialog box.

## Tip

You can create Web links only from text that has been properly identified in the text of the PDF file (either www.Company.com or http://www.company.com). If you need to add a Web link, you can easily create the text in Acrobat without having to return to the authoring program. Select the Edit Document Text tool in the Content panel. Hold down the Ctrl key (Option key on Mac) and click. The text cursor blinks where you click and is ready for you to add new type on the page. Type the URL for the Web link, deselect the text by selecting the Hand tool, and then click in the Document pane. Click Create Links from URLs in the Document Processing panel. Acrobat creates the Web link from the URL you added to the document. ■

## Adding Web links to multiple pages

You may have documents that need Web links created across multiple pages. An example might be a document that has been repurposed from an original design that was created for output to prepress and then later downsampled and hosted on a Web site. In the original design, you might have a Web link on the cover page, but for the Web-hosted document you may want to create a Web link to an order form or your home page on each page in the brochure document. Where the same URL is specified on each page and the location of the Web link is the same on every page, you can create the Web links in Acrobat after the PDF has been sampled for Web display. The following steps outline a procedure for creating Web links on multiple pages for similar designs or legacy files that don't have Web addresses added in the original authoring application document before a PDF has been created.

## Cross-Reference

For information related to repurposing documents and downsampling, see Chapter 17. ■

### STEPS: Creating Web Links on Multiple PDF Pages

1. **Add a header/footer to a multi-page PDF document.** Open the file where the Web links are to be added and click Header & Footer in the Pages panel to open the drop-down menu. Click Add to open the Add Header and Footer dialog box. In the Add Header and Footer dialog box, create a header or footer and set the type size, the alignment, the color, and the offset distance desired. In this example, I added a footer (center aligned), used Arial 8-point text, and left offsets at the defaults, as shown in Figure 25.5. (In this example, I used an incomplete URL but I started my URL address with *www.*)

2. **Click OK.**

3. **Save the file.**

4. **Open the Web link.** Move the Hand tool to a Web link and a tooltip reports the full URL address as shown in Figure 25.6. Click the link and the file opens in your Web browser.

**FIGURE 25.5**

Click one of the Header or Footer alignment boxes (Left, Center, Right) and add the URL text. Select a font, font size, and offset distance and then click the OK button.

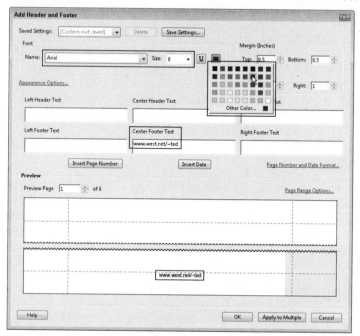

**FIGURE 25.6**

When you select the Hand tool and place the cursor over a Web link, the URL appears in a tooltip.

## Cross-Reference

For more information on creating headers and footers, see Chapter 15. ∎

## Tip

If you want Web links to appear rotated along the left or right side of your PDF document, click Rotate Pages in the Pages panel. Add a header or footer as described in the preceding steps. Click Rotate Pages and select the rotation option that turns the pages back to the original view. Save the document, and the Web links are positioned vertically on each page. ∎

# Controlling links view behavior

By default, when you click a URL link to a PDF document, whether from within your Web browser or from within Acrobat, the resulting view takes you to the same view established in your Initial View properties. Therefore, if your Initial View properties are set to Page Only, Single Page, Fit Page, and Page number 1, the PDF document opens in the Web browser according to these settings just as you would view the file in Acrobat.

The links you create to open different documents and different pages in a PDF file are often unusable when you're viewing PDFs in Web browsers. A link, for example, that opens a secondary PDF won't work in a Web browser unless you modify the link properties and link to the URL where the destination document resides. The Web browser needs URL links to open secondary files. Inasmuch as you may have all links working well for CD-ROM distribution, the links need to have some adjustments made before you can host the PDF documents with usable links on Web servers.

As an example, suppose you want to open page 2 in a PDF file on a Web server. You create a link in one document, direct the link to the URL where the PDF is hosted, and instruct the Web browser or Acrobat viewer to open page 2. To create the link, use either the Link tool or a form field button and enter the following code in an Open Web Link action:

```
http://www.west.net/~ted/pdf/manual.pdf#page=2
```

In this example, the #page=2 text following the PDF filename is the trigger to open page 2. In addition to accessing user-specified pages, you can control viewing behavior for page layouts, page views, zooms, linking to destinations, and a host of other attributes you assign to the Open Web Link action. Some examples of the code to use following the PDF document name in URL links include the following:

- **Zoom changes:** #zoom=50, #zoom=125, #zoom=200
- **Fit Page view:** #view=Fit
- **Destinations:** #nameddest=Section1
- **Open Bookmarks palette:** #pagemode=bookmarks
- **Open Pages palette:** #pagemode=thumbs
- **Collapsing palettes:** #pagemode=none
- **Combining viewing options:** #page=3&pagemode=bookmarks&zoom=125

## Tip

More information related to file links on Web hosted documents can be found on Adobe's Web site. Log on to www.adobe.com/education/pdf and type Web linking in the Search box. A number of different articles discussing Web links in PDFs are reported in the search results. In addition, you can find several articles covering Web links in PDFs on the Acrobat User Community Web site. Log on to www.acrobatusers.com and visit the blogs and articles sections. ■

The preceding are some examples for controlling view options when opening PDFs in Web browsers. For each item be aware that you need to use the complete URL address and add one of these options following the location where the PDF document is hosted. Using the page mode example, the complete open action URL might look like `http://www.mycompany.com/file.pdf#pagemode=bookmarks`.

# Opening Web links in new browser windows

If you have a PDF file viewed as an inline view in a browser window, you might want a link to a second PDF document that opens in a new browser window. Using the Open a web link action in the Button field properties always opens a Web link in the same browser window. To trigger a link action for opening a second browser window requires a JavaScript.

To set up a link to open a PDF in a second browser window, follow these steps.

### STEPS: Opening Web Links in New Browser Windows

1. **Create a button link.** Click the Button tool in the Content panel and create a button on a PDF page.

2. **Click Show All Properties in the abbreviated properties window to open the Button Properties dialog box.** Note that you can change the name of the button immediately after clicking the Button tool by typing a name in the Field Name text box.

3. **Click the Actions tab.** If you want to change appearance settings, first click Appearance and set the properties for the Button border and fill colors.

4. **Choose Run a JavaScript from the Select Action pull-down menu.**

5. **Click the Add button to open the JavaScript Editor.**

6. **Type the following code in the JavaScript Editor:**

   ```
   app.launchURL("http://www.company.com/myFile.pdf", true);
   ```

7. **Click OK in the JavaScript Editor and click Close in the Button Properties dialog box.**

The JavaScript in line 6 of the steps above opens a PDF named `myFile.pdf` hosted at company.com. The *true* flag instructs Acrobat to open the PDF in a second browser window.

## Cross-Reference

For more information on writing JavaScripts, see Chapter 32. ■

# Adding URL links to text fields

Suppose you have a form and you want a user to supply a Web address in a field. After the form is completed by a form filler, a reviewer may want to visit the URL to view the Web page. You can copy the text from the field and paste the URL in the Location bar in your Web browser. However, you can simplify the process by adding a Web link to the field so the reviewer of a form just clicks the text field to launch the default Web browser and open the associated URL.

Follow these steps to add a URL Web link to a text field.

### STEPS: Opening Web Links from Text Fields

1. **Create a text field on a form or open a form with a text field.**

2. **Click the Select Object tool in the Content panel and double-click the text field to open the Text Field Properties dialog box.**

3. **Click the Actions tab.**

4. **Choose Run a JavaScript from the Select Action pull-down menu.**

5. **Click the Add button to open the JavaScript Editor.**

6. **Type the following code in the JavaScript Editor:**

   ```
   if ( !/^\s*$/.test(event.target.value) ) app.launchURL(event.
       target.value);
   ```

7. **Click OK in the JavaScript Editor and click Close in the Text Field Properties dialog box.**

When the form filler clicks in the field, the form field is ready to accept text. After adding text, tabbing out of the field, and clicking again in the field, the JavaScript is executed and the user's default Web browser opens the URL specified in the text field.

## Cross-Reference

For more information on working with form fields, see Chapters 30 and 31. ■

# Converting PDF to HTML

In Chapter 9, I talked about exporting PDFs to a number of different file formats using the Save As command. In that chapter, you find a summary of the attributes for exporting documents from PDF including exports to HTML. In this chapter, I move forward a little and cover exporting to HTML in a little more depth.

At the onset, let me say that Adobe hasn't done much with the exports to HTML features in Acrobat. With the exception of adding an Export task button in Acrobat 8 and the File ➪ Export menu in Acrobat 9, the options you have for exporting to HTML are identical to the options you had in Acrobat 6 and 7 Standard and Professional.

Using the export to HTML features in Acrobat can get your PDF content into HTML format, but page geometry and formatting is generally lost when you try to get PDF content to HTML.

The best you can hope for is exporting text and images that permit you to use the assets in a program like Adobe Dreamweaver where you re-create the Web page using the tools and formatting capabilities of an HTML editor.

## Setting export options

You can control option settings in the Preferences dialog box (Ctrl/⌘+K) by clicking on the Convert from PDF item in the left pane. The right pane displays a list of export formats including HTML 3.2 and HTML 4.01 with CSS 1.0 (Cascading Style Sheets). Click the Edit Settings button and you see a list of options you can edit. These same options are also available to you in the Save As dialog box when you choose Save As ➪ HTML.

Open a PDF document and choose File ➪ Save As ➪ HTML (either 3.2 or 4.01 format). After selecting the Format, click the Settings button and you see the settings options as shown in Figure 25.7. Again, these options are the same as you have available in the Preferences dialog box. In addition, the Settings options are the same for both HTML formats.

**FIGURE 25.7**

The Settings adjustments in the Preferences dialog box and the Save As dialog box are identical.

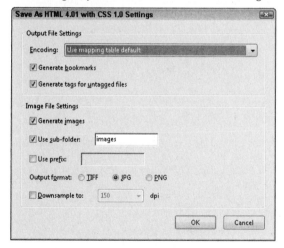

The settings options include:

- **Encoding.** A number of encoding options appear from the pull-down menu. If you have special characters in text, use either UTF-8 or UTF-16. If you use an encoding method such as UCS-4, the special characters won't be recognized.

- **Generate bookmarks.** Links to sections in the HTML document are made from the PDF bookmarks.

- **Generate tags for untagged documents.** If a document is not tagged, check this box to add tagging for accessibility.

- **Generate images.** If your PDF document has images and you want them converted to a format recognized by HTML, be certain to check this box.

- **Use sub-folder.** All images can be saved to a subfolder nested below the HTML file. Check this box to copy the images to a separate folder. The default folder name is *images*. You can edit the name and provide a name of your choosing for the folder where the images are saved.

- **Use prefix.** If you want a prefix added to your images, check the box and type a prefix name in the text box.

- **Output format.** Choose from the options for the image format you want for the exported images. Use JPG if you have photo images.

- **Downsample to.** Check this box and select an amount to downsample images. The default is 150 ppi. Change this item to 72 ppi for Web viewing.

## Converting text documents to HTML

One thing to keep in mind when you convert PDF files to HTML is that the entire PDF document is converted to a single HTML file. If you want separate HTML documents your best option is to first click Extract in the Pages panel. Enter the page numbers you want to extract for one HTML file and click OK. Convert the pages to HTML using the File ➪ Save As ➪ HTML command. Then return to the original document and extract the pages you want for your second HTML file and convert to HTML, and so on.

### Cross-Reference
For more information on extracting pages in PDFs, see Chapter 15. ■

If you have a PDF with bookmarks, you can convert to HTML with the bookmarks appearing in the HTML document and linked to the sections of the document that are bookmarked in the original PDF file. To see how to convert a text file with bookmarks, follow these steps.

### STEPS: Converting PDF Text-only Documents to HTML

1. **Open a file containing bookmarks in Acrobat.** In this example I open a file converted from Microsoft Word containing bookmarks.

2. **Open the Export to HTML dialog box.** Select File ➪ Save As ➪ HTML and choose either HTML export option.

3. **Adjust Settings.** Click the Settings button in the Save As dialog box and make setting adjustments as described in the "Setting export options" section earlier in this chapter. In this example, I check the box for Generate bookmarks. Because there are no images in my file, I don't need to address any of the options for exporting images.

4. **Click OK.** Depending on the size of your file, you may see a progress bar report the export progress or you may just see a flash on your screen. The file is exported without any confirmation dialog box.

5. **View the exported HTML in a Web browser.** Open your Web browser and select File Open. Navigate your hard drive and select the exported file and open it. If you had Bookmarks in the file, they appear as links as shown in Figure 25.8.

**FIGURE 25.8**

The exported HTML file is opened in a Web browser with links appearing for the Bookmark items that were contained in the PDF file.

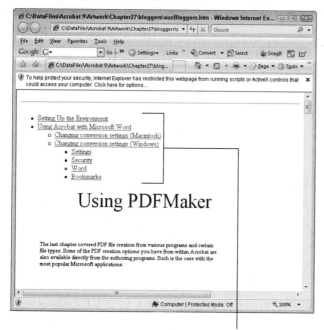

Bookmarks converted to links

# Exporting PDF files with images to HTML

The process for exporting images is much the same as exporting text files. However, the one option you'll want to edit in the Settings dialog box is the image attributes. To see how PDFs with images are converted to HTML, follow these steps.

## Steps: Converting Multi-page PDFs with Images to HTML

1. **Open a PDF file with multiple pages and images.**

2. **Select File ⇨ Save As ⇨ HTML and choose an HTML format.**

3. **Adjust Settings options.** Click Settings and select the Output format. In this example, I check the JPG radio button. Click Downsample to and select 72 from the dpi pull-down menu.

4. **Click OK.** The file may take a little time to export depending on the size of your PDF document. When the progress bar finishes, the file is ready to open in your Web browser or HTML editor.

5. **Open the file in your Web browser.** In Figure 25.9, you can see a partial view of my exported file. The original document had two letter and two tabloid pages with several images on each page. This document needs a lot of editing in an HTML editor to format text and graphics for a Web page design.

The HTML file needs a lot of work to polish up the design.

Du Fu (c.712-c.770), also known as Tu Fu, was raised as a Confucian but failed to gain the government post he sought. He subsequently traveled throughout China, observing the conditions of the people and commenting on his impressions in poems. Du Fu wrote more than 1,500 poems and is considered by many scholars as the greatest poet the world has known.
In Chengdu, China the Du Fu Thatched Cottage where he once resided is a major tourist attraction. The grounds are often visited by students studying the great poet's life and history.

English

Figure 25.10 shows the portion of the original PDF document that was exported to HTML. The best you can hope for with the PDF exports to HTML is a good starting place for editing the HTML in an HTML editor. Acrobat provides you some basic tools to get a PDF document to HTML format. From there, you can expect to do some editing in your favorite HTML editor.

One alternative you have available is to explore using a third-party plug-in designed for exporting PDFs to HTML. A number of different plug-in products are distributed by a number of developers. To find some of the latest plug-ins and obtain some demo copies you can test, visit the Adobe Plug-in finder Web site. Log on to www.adobe.com/special/acrobat/pluginfinder.html. A comprehensive list of third-party plug-ins is also listed at the PluginsWorld Web site. Log on to PluginsWorld.com to find third-party products supporting Acrobat.

FIGURE 25.10

The original PDF document that was used to export to the HTML file shown in Figure 25.9

# Summary

In this chapter, you learned how to convert Web pages to PDFs and view PDFs you download from the Web.

- PDFs can be viewed inside Web browser windows. When viewed as inline views in Web browsers, Acrobat toolbars and menu options are contained within the browser window.

- You change preferences settings for Web viewing PDFs in Windows in the Acrobat viewer Preferences dialog box.

- To make links from text in PDFs for users of Acrobat 6 and earlier, choose Advanced ⇨ Document Processing ⇨ Create Links from URLs.

- To create multiple identical Web links across several pages, use the Add Header and Footer dialog box. Type a URL as a header or footer and save the file. Close and reopen the file and the links are active in Acrobat viewers 7 and above.

- By modifying code in the Open Web Link Action properties you can control opening views and override Initial View defaults. Add the code following the URL link to adjust page views, zooms, page modes, and so on.

- You can export PDF to HTML. In most cases you need to polish up the Web page design in an HTML editor after exporting to HTML.

# Using Acrobat.com for Online Collaboration

Acrobat Connect was a new program Adobe Systems provided in version 8 and made accessible from within all Acrobat viewers as well as Adobe Bridge CS3. In Acrobat 8 you had two versions of Acrobat Connect designed to satisfy remote meeting needs for large organizations and individual users. Acrobat Connect Professional is a powerful online collaboration program, and Acrobat Connect is a personal collaboration meeting room.

In Acrobat 9, Adobe introduced a separate Acrobat.com service. Among the features available with Acrobat.com, you have another online collaboration tool called ConnectNow.

Acrobat.com is a collection of online collaboration tools that provide you free services for sharing files, sharing reviews, distributing forms, using an online word processor and collaborating in online meetings — something similar to Web conferencing.

Acrobat Connect Pro is still with us in Acrobat version X as a paid service. Through the Connect workspace you can host a meeting complete with screen sharing on your computer and a host of industrial-strength tools for conducting online meetings. ConnectNow is a free service that provides some similar features available with the Acrobat Connect Pro service, but with several fewer features, among which is the limitation of the number of people who can attend a meeting. With Connect Pro you can conduct meetings with 1,500 people. With ConnectNow you are limited to hosting meetings with three people — including yourself.

For more sophisticated online collaboration events you'll want to learn more about Acrobat Connect Pro. Log on to www.adobe.com/products/acrobatconnectpro/ to discover how this product can serve your company's online collaboration needs. In this chapter, I'll stick primarily to discussing ConnectNow as it pertains to serving individual and small group online conferencing.

# Understanding Acrobat.com

If you read Chapters 4, 20, and 31 you should have some idea of what Acrobat.com is and how to log on to find all Acrobat.com services. I briefly discussed using Acrobat.com with Adobe Reader in Chapter 4 and conducting shared reviews in Chapter 20, and discuss hosting and tracking forms coming up ahead in Chapter 31.

Acrobat.com is your central online workspace for sharing files, collecting data, engaging in review sessions, and conducting online collaboration sessions. In regard to online meetings, you have three alternatives Adobe Systems offers. These meeting room alternatives include:

- **ConnectNow (free service).** Using Acrobat.com from any Acrobat 9 or later viewer, you can conduct online meetings as a host and have a maximum of two other participants. This service is free from Adobe Systems.
- **Acrobat Connect (annual subscription fee).** In Acrobat 8, Adobe introduced Acrobat Connect. Acrobat Connect is a meeting room you use as a subscription service where you can host meetings for up to 20 people. This service is still offered by Adobe Systems.
- **Acrobat Connect Pro (annual subscription fee).** Acrobat Connect Pro is an industrial-strength application of Acrobat Connect. With Connect Pro you can host meetings of up to 1,500 people. Like Connect, this service is acquired through an annual subscription fee.

The content in this chapter is related to Acrobat.com and using the free online meeting room. If you need to host meetings with 20 or fewer people, or meetings with Acrobat Connect Pro that provides hosting meetings of up to 1,500 and a number of features such as VoIP, integrated audio, customizable layouts, multiple meeting rooms per user, and more, then log on to www.adobe.com/products/acrobatconnect/. The Adobe Acrobat Connect Web site contains information about the Connect products, free trial downloads, and online ordering and subscription services.

In addition to the meeting room service on Acrobat.com, you also have a place where you can upload files to share with other users, invite users to participate in online reviews, submit forms and have the forms uploaded to Acrobat.com for data collection and tracking, and more.

# Using ConnectNow for Online Collaboration

I'll break this chapter up into two primary areas of discussion — Web conferencing and sharing screens. To begin with, I'll cover the Acrobat.com services for Web conferencing. See the section later in this chapter "Sharing your computer screen" to learn more about sharing files on Acrobat.com.

## Getting into real-time collaboration

Before I get into using Acrobat.com for Web conferencing, I want to point out one of the outstanding features you find with the design of the Acrobat.com services. In Acrobat 8 we had Acrobat Connect to allow users to host a meeting. You might have a PowerPoint presentation that you want to step through in an online meeting to describe some aspect of your business such as the introduction of a new product, a new marketing campaign, a sales meeting, or some similar type of discussion.

Using Acrobat 8 and the PDF documents you created, using Acrobat 8 worked well for an Acrobat Connect meeting. The only pauses you experienced was a momentary delay when a new slide came into view.

In Acrobat 9 and later we have a quantum leap in the delivery of PDF files. The PDF audience palette has changed over the past several years, and people are asking for more dynamic presentations such as those you can now create with the newer version of Acrobat.com, adding Adobe Flash to PDFs as I discussed in Chapter 22, and presenting documents in the form of PDF Portfolios as I covered in Chapter 11.

If you view the media-rich PDF files in a Web conferencing application like Acrobat Connect, as was introduced with Acrobat 8, the meeting participants have to wait for video, manipulation of 3-D objects, and Adobe Flash animations. These files come across the Internet very choppy and sluggish and are painfully slow even with the fastest Internet connections.

In Acrobat 9 and later using Acrobat.com (and the new versions of ConnectNow) Adobe introduces real-time collaboration. When you choose File ➪ Collaborate ➪ Send & Collaborate Live, a recipient is invited to a real-time collaboration session. Instead of viewing your screen on a remote system and waiting for the video to play from the host machine, each participant downloads the same PDF file containing the video file. When the host triggers something like a play button, the play is sent to other users as an *event*. Instead of the video streaming to other users from the host's computer, only the events are passed to the participants. Each user then watches a video locally but the host controls the events. This is real-time collaboration and a huge development edge provided by Adobe.

## Setting up an Adobe ID

All the work you do with Acrobat.com requires you to create an Adobe ID. Each time you start a session, you need to log on with your ID (email address) and password. For the remainder of this chapter, I'll assume you've created an Adobe ID and you can log on to Acrobat.com using your log-on ID and password.

If you don't have an Adobe ID, log on to www.acrobat.com. The initial screen opens as shown in Figure 26.1.

**FIGURE 26.1**

Log on to Acrobat.com in your Web browser to open the Acrobat.com log-on page.

Type your email address and Adobe ID password and click Sign In. You arrive at the Acrobat.com workspace as shown in Figure 26.2.

If you want to bypass the log-on each time you access Acrobat.com, you can add your email address and password to your Acrobat viewer preferences.

In any Acrobat viewer, open the Preferences dialog box (Ctrl/⌘+K) and click Acrobat.com in the left pane. In the text boxes, fill in the email address you used for your Adobe ID and type your password, as shown in Figure 26.3. Check the Remember me check box. Also check Always connect when opening documents enabled for live collaboration. Setting up the Acrobat.com preferences in this manner eliminates a need to type your ID and password each time you log on to Acrobat.com.

## FIGURE 26.2

Sign on to Acrobat.com to load the Acrobat.com workspace.

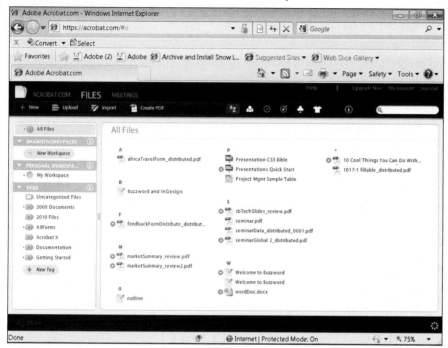

## FIGURE 26.3

Open the Preferences dialog box and add your Adobe ID information.

## Note

Setting the Acrobat.com preferences is optional. If you use your computer in a workgroup where others have access to your computer, you may want to avoid filling in the Acrobat.com preferences and use a manual logon each time you access the Acrobat.com Web site. If you are confident that no one can access your computer, go ahead and set up the preferences so you can use an automatic logon each time you visit Acrobat.com. ∎

Before you read further in this chapter, be certain to have your Adobe ID confirmed and ready to go. Make sure you can log on to Acrobat.com in your Web browser.

# Sharing your computer screen

There are some different options you have for online collaboration. You can choose to share your computer screen and control a meeting as a presenter, you can choose to share files for online comment and review, and you can choose to engage in real-time conferencing. To start with, let's take a look at sharing your computer screen in an online collaboration session.

## Starting a share session

Acrobat and Adobe Reader 9 and later make it easy to share your computer screen. Once you enter your personal meeting room you have options for controlling a meeting as a presenter, promoting other users to a presenter level, taking control over another user's computer, and allowing another user to take control over your computer. Using ConnectNow you have one of two categories to experience — that of a host and that of a participant.

To host a session, try following these steps.

### STEPS: Sharing Your Screen

1. **Log on to Acrobat.com.** Add www.acrobat.com in your Web browser Location Bar.

2. **Log on to Acrobat.com.** If you elected to not use an automatic logon by setting up your Acrobat.com preferences, log on with your Adobe ID and password. Fill in your email address and password to open your Acrobat.com workspace.

3. **Open your meeting room.** When you log on to Acrobat.com you find three items in the top-left corner of your Web browser titled Acrobat.com, Files, and Meetings. Click the Meetings button to open your meeting room.

4. **Invite people to join your meeting.** The first screen you see is the background of the ConnectNow workspace and a Get Started dialog box informing you of the URL that needs to be sent to other users for them to join your meeting room (see Figure 26.4). You can copy the URL and paste in the Location Bar in your Web browser or click the Send Email Invitation Now link. Clicking the link opens your default mail client with the URL added to a mail message. Simply fill in the To field in your mail message and send the mail to up to two recipients.

5. **Share your screen.** After sending an invitation the dialog box disappears and you find a button displayed as Share My Computer Screen. Click this button and the Start Screen Sharing dialog box opens as shown in Figure 26.5. You have a choice to share your Desktop, Windows, or Applications. Click a radio button and click Share to continue.

6. **Review the sharing information.** An Introduction to Screen Sharing window opens that provides some helpful tips on screen sharing, as shown in Figure 26.6. Look over the information and click OK to continue.

## FIGURE 26.4

The default appearance of the ConnectNow workspace

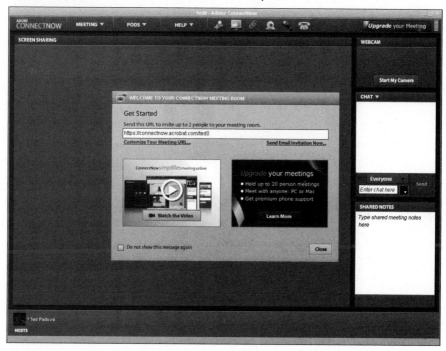

## FIGURE 26.5

Choose a sharing option and click Share.

**FIGURE 26.6**

Look over the information on screen sharing and click OK.

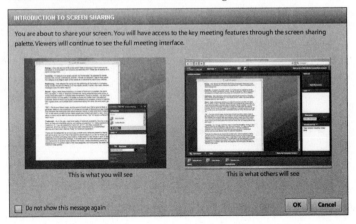

7. **Click OK.** The screen changes again where the ConnectNow Screen Sharing panel opens (see Figure 26.7) on your desktop or application window. This panel remains in the foreground no matter what application you launch and is used to control your sharing session.

8. **Invite a participant.** If you invited only one participant in Step 4, you can invite another participant in the ConnectNow Screen Sharing panel. In the Screen Sharing panel, click the Invite button shown in Figure 26.7.

   As participants log on to your meeting, you see buttons appear to Accept or Reject the person trying to attend your meeting. Click Accept as each individual you invited logs on.

9. **Start your presentation.** When the Screen Sharing panel is open, the application document behind the window remains in view for the participants. You see the screen with the ConnectNow Screen Sharing panel open as shown in Figure 26.7, but the participants see your application window only inside a screen similar to Figure 26.7.

   With the Chat panel in view, other users can text message questions to you. If you set up your session with a phone connection, other users can listen on the phone to your audio. If using an application like Yahoo! Messenger or Skype, you can have participants listen virtually anywhere in the world to your presentation.

## Examining the sharing tools

At the top of the ConnectNow workspace you find a toolbar with several menus and tools as shown in Figure 26.8. The first item you find after the ConnectNow label on the toolbar is the Meeting drop-down menu.

Open the meeting menu and you find several menu commands related to managing your meetings as shown in Figure 26.9.

**FIGURE 26.7**

After sharing your screen, the ConnectNow Screen Sharing panel opens in the foreground.

**FIGURE 26.8**

The ConnectNow toolbar

**FIGURE 26.9**

Click Meeting to open the Meeting menu.

As shown in Figure 26.9, you have a command for inviting additional participants, returning to the Screen Sharing panel, uploading files, starting your Webcam, accessing preferences, and ending your meeting and logging out.

### Loading pods

The Pods menu has several menu commands as shown in Figure 26.10, and this menu is available only to those who host a meeting.

Open the Pods menu to display the Pods menu commands.

By default, the Screen Sharing, Chat, Shared Notes, and Webcam pods are open. The Files pod displays all the files you add as attachments, and the Whiteboard opens the Tools panel discussed in the section "Participating in a sharing session." The Whiteboard is used to mark up notes on a file shared in a session by the host. The recipients have access to drawing tools when a participant shares a screen and opens the Screen Sharing panel. Clicking the Pause and Annotate button opens the same Tools panel as the host has available with the Whiteboard.

## Participating in a sharing session

If you receive an email invitation to participate in a sharing session, the only thing you need on your computer is a Web browser. Acrobat.com meeting rooms support all Web browsers on all platforms. Getting into a meeting is as simple as clicking a URL link in an email message and logging on. When you arrive at a meeting, your screen changes to the view shown in Figure 26.11. At this point a message is sent to the host who needs to accept you into the room.

## FIGURE 26.11

Join a meeting as a participant and your computer displays a screen informing you the host has been notified of your arrival.

After the host accepts you to enter the meeting room, you see the screen shared by the host as shown in Figure 26.12.

The meeting room pull-down menus shown at the top of Figure 26.12 also apply to a host sharing a computer screen. If you're a host or participant, there are some settings you'll want to make when you log on to a meeting room.

## Note

One difference you'll see between the host's computer screen at log on time and a participant is that the host has an extra button in the menu used to invite participants. The participants cannot invite others to attend a meeting hosted by another individual. ■

## FIGURE 26.12

After a host accepts you, you see the screen shared by the host.

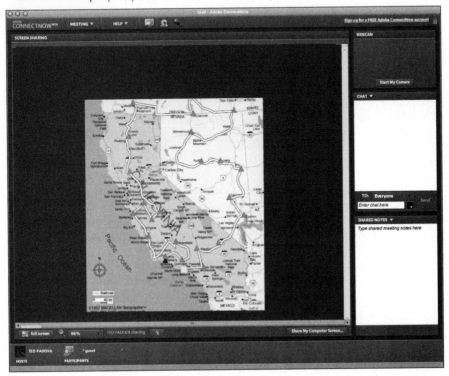

### Setting preferences

Open the Meeting pull-down menu when you log onto a meeting and choose Preferences from the menu options. The Preferences dialog box opens as shown in Figure 26.13. In this dialog box you can make some choices for handling your audio and video equipment, your chat default text size and color, and your connection speed.

### Getting help

The Help pull-down menu (accessed by clicking the Help button) provides some choices for help information. Click Troubleshooting to be taken to an Adobe Web page that provides information related to setting meetings. Click Flash Player Settings to open another Web page with information about the Adobe Flash Player.

**FIGURE 26.13**

Open the Meeting pull-down menu and make choices in the Preferences dialog box.

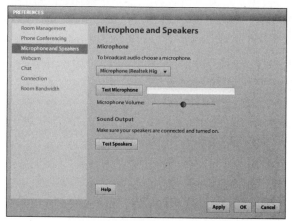

## Share My Computer Screen

Attendees can share their screens in a meeting. The host has control over what screen is shown in the meeting room; however, the host needs permission from each participant for screen sharing. Choose this menu item so your screen can be shared with others in a meeting.

## Share My Microphone

Click the Share My Microphone icon in the menu bar to open the Adobe Flash Player Settings dialog box as shown in Figure 26.14. If you want to share your microphone, click Allow and click Remember in the Adobe Flash Player Settings dialog box. While you share your microphone, other members in the meeting need to turn their microphones off to avoid an echo sound in the audio. You can minimize the echo in the audio by clicking the Advanced button in the Adobe Flash Player and making some settings choices for handling the audio.

**FIGURE 26.14**

Click the Share My Microphone button and make choices in the Adobe Flash Player Settings dialog box.

### Using the Annotation tools

When a participant shares a screen and the host gives control over the sharing to a participant, the participant's screen changes to a view similar to the host where the Screen Sharing panel opens. If a participant clicks the Annotate button in the Screen Sharing panel, the Annotations toolbar opens. When you click a number of different tools in this toolbar, a pop-up toolbar opens as shown in Figure 26.15, where you can assign attributes to the annotations you add on a document.

**FIGURE 26.15**

Click any one of a number of different tools and a pop-up toolbar opens.

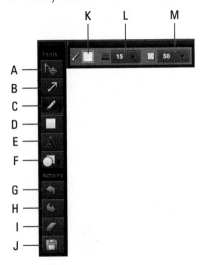

The different tools and the markup attributes you find in the Tools panel include:

- **A. Selection Arrow tool.** This tool is used to select an annotation after you draw one on a document page. When you select the object, you can use the Selection Arrow tool to reshape the annotation and rotate it.

- **B. Arrow tool.** Draw lines with arrowheads.

- **C. Highlighter Pen tool.** Highlights text.

- **D. Highlight Rectangle tool.** Used to create a rectangle to highlight text. Note text can be added to the text rectangle.

- **E. Text tool.** Add a text annotation.

- **F. Shapes tools.** Click the Shapes tools to open a pop-up toolbar as shown in Figure 26.16. You have a Line tool and several geometric shapes to choose from in the pop-up menu.

**FIGURE 26.16**

Click the Shapes tools to open the Shapes pop-up toolbar.

G. **Undo.** Undo the last action.

H. **Redo.** Redo the last action.

I. **Delete Selected Shapes tool.** Use the Selection Arrow tool to click an annotation and click this tool to delete the annotation.

J. **Save tool.** Click the Save tool and a screen capture is taken of the page and saved as a PNG file like the one shown in Figure 26.17.

**FIGURE 26.17**

Click the Save tool to take a screen capture of the annotations. A Save As dialog box opens, where you can save the file as a PNG image file.

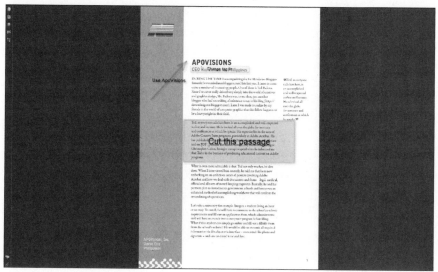

**K. Color.** Click the color swatch to open a pop-up color panel where an annotation color can be changed.

**L. Point Size.** For use with the text tool and markups that support note text, use this pull-down menu to change the text point size.

**M. Opacity.** Change the opacity of the annotation in 25 percent increments from 25 percent to 100 percent.

# Summary

In this chapter, you learned how to use the free Acrobat.com online service for conferencing and screen sharing.

- Acrobat.com is a free online service available to users of Adobe Reader X and all other Acrobat X viewers.

- Using Acrobat.com you can host Web conferences free with up to three participants (including yourself) in each session.

- Acrobat Connect and Acrobat Connect Pro are Web conferencing tools available on a subscription fee basis.

- Using ConnectNow you can share your screen with other users and promote individual users to a level where others can share their screens.

- During an Acrobat.com session you can mark up documents as a host and as a participant with real-time annotations.

# CHAPTER 2

# Working with eBooks

A few years ago, when I wrote the Adobe Acrobat 6 PDF Bible, I talked about the long-awaited arrival of eBooks and suggested the industry has been slow in delivering devices for eBook reading. Since that time there have been significant changes in developers delivering products for eBook reading and the amount of content that's been consumed by users.

Amazon.com helped spark the eBook industry with the delivery and some subsequent improvements of the Amazon Kindle Reader, where people can purchase eBooks on Amazon.com and view them on the Kindle Reader.

If Amazon created a big push for consumer adoption of eBooks, it was Apple, Inc. that created a tidal wave. In the 28 days following its introduction, Apple sold more than 1 million iPads. In less than 5 days, the Apple iBookstore sold more than 1.5 million eBooks — more eBooks sold in 5 days than Amazon sold in an entire year.

As of this writing there are additional tablet devices in development, and by the time you read this book, they should be on the market from companies like Google, Sony, HP, and a few others. Although tablet computers have been around for more than a decade, this new generation of devices offers much more for exploring content on the Web, interacting with a variety of different content, and taking a more sophisticated approach to book reading.

Regardless of the device you now use, or perhaps intend to use, there are some advantages and disadvantages to using the PDF format that you should understand. In this chapter I cover using eBooks and some of those PDF advantages and disadvantages.

# Creating eBooks

We have a new range of devices that are, among other things, designed for eBook reading. The largest market share for eBook content hosting and viewing lies with Amazon Kindle and Apple iPad. In addition, there are a number of mobile phones used today that are displaying eBooks and other content such as newspapers and magazines.

## Knowing eBook file formats

If you want to create eBooks, you need to be familiar with the types of applications that you use for the layout and design and the file formats supported on various devices. The most popular formats used for eBook creation include:

- **ePub.** The .epub format is perhaps the most widely used format for displaying eBooks. The Apple iBookstore supports ePub format for iPad (see Figure 27.1) as well as many handheld devices.

- **Mobipocket.** The .mobi format is used by Kindle readers. This is a binary format used for the rendering and display of eBooks.

- **PDF.** Adobe PDF is used for eBooks.

## Choosing the right format

If you want to create eBooks, the next thing to be aware of is an understanding of the devices that can display your work. If you choose the ePub format, your eBooks can be distributed through the Apple iBookstore, viewed on handheld devices with an ePub viewer application, and read on your computer, also with an ePub viewer application. In order to view the same eBook on the Amazon Kindle, the file needs to be converted from ePub to Mobipocket.

If you choose to create a Mobipocket eBook, the eBook can only be viewed on the Amazon Kindle or an Amazon Kindle application running on another device (see Figure 27.2). Amazon does make available a free Kindle Reader for the iPad, iPod, and iPhone.

If you decide to create an eBook as a PDF file, you need to have a PDF viewer application on the device you use to read the book. For computers, laptops, iPads, and most handheld devices, a PDF viewer is available. If you want the PDF hosted on Amazon for Kindle Readers, the PDF needs to be converted to Mobipocket format. Converting from PDF to .mobi can be done, but you may experience some conversion problems.

**FIGURE 27.1**

An ePub book viewed in the iBook Reader on an Apple iPad

## Creating content

In terms of PDF, you can use any one of the methods for PDF creation that I covered in Part II. You can export from any authoring program that supports PDF creation, and once the PDF is created, you can copy it to your device. From there you use a PDF Reader application to render and view the content.

**FIGURE 27.2**

An eBook shown in the Kindle Reader for iPad on an Apple iPad

If you want to create ePubs, you have two choices: One is to use either Microsoft Word or another word processing application such as OpenOffice.org Writer or IBM Lotus Symphony. Your other choice is to use Adobe InDesign CS5. If you use a word processor, you need to use a tool to convert the document to ePub format. One of the best tools for this conversion is a shareware program you can download from `www.stanza.com`. If you use Adobe InDesign CS5, you can export directly to the ePub format.

For creating MOBI files, you can use MS Word and submit your Word files to Amazon.com. Amazon will take care of the conversion for you.

Regardless of the application you use, you need to observe some rules that apply to eBook formats. eBooks are designed a little differently than the designs you create for print. Graphics, for example, need to be set up as inline graphics (that is, within the text and not as floating graphics). Style sheets need to be used to properly break pages. And there's much more. For a complete set of guidelines for formatting eBooks for output to a number of formats, take a look at the standards recommendations at www.smashwords.com.

## Hosting content

Here's where things get a bit sticky. If you want to create eBooks and charge money for your work, you need to submit your book to an online service that sells the books. Content providers such as Amazon Kindle and the Apple iBookstore take care of the sales, collections, and ISBN number acquisition for your book. With the hosting, the providers also add DRM (Digital Rights Management), meaning that your book is protected against unauthorized distribution.

If you decide to use PDF for the format, you're much more limited in finding a host that will sell your work and add the DRM. Adobe does provide server products that can do the job of securing content, but these products are cost-prohibitive for the consumer who wants to write a few books.

The ePub and MOBI formats are much more limiting in the visual display of content and completely lack interactivity. With PDF you can use any font; have much more freedom for the way graphics, fonts, and tables are displayed; and add interactive elements such as videos and JavaScript for button actions.

## Note

As of this writing, there are no PDF Readers for iPad, iPod, or iPhone that are capable of displaying any kind of interactivity contained in a PDF file. In addition, certain types of PDFs, such as PDF Portfolios, cannot be displayed on these devices. ■

# Acquiring Adobe Digital Editions

Since this book is about Acrobat and PDF, what follows is related to PDF only. Unfortunately, Adobe hasn't advanced well with eBook development and hosting from a non-enterprise point of view. Their efforts with Adobe Digital Editions were created back in the days of Acrobat 8, and we haven't seen updates that support the explosion of new devices.

Adobe hosts a certain amount of content on the Adobe Digital Editions Web site. You can download free eBooks, and you can purchase eBooks from Adobe that are viewed in the Adobe Digital Editions application — a free download from Adobe. Adobe Digital Editions requires the Adobe Flash Player, which makes it virtually impossible to load on the Apple iPad, iPod, or iPhone products since these devices do not support Adobe Flash.

Adobe Digital Editions is found on the Adobe Labs Web site. To install the Flash Player and activate Adobe Digital Editions, select Help ➪ Digital Editions in Acrobat or select File ➪ Digital Editions in Adobe Reader. You can also log on to www.adobe.com/products/digital editions/?source=acromenu to open the Adobe Digital Editions home page shown in Figure 27.3. The home page provides information about Adobe Digital Editions and informs you that you need to install the Adobe Flash Player application. Click the Download and Install button and the installation proceeds. You arrive at a page that confirms your installation. If the installation was not successful, you see a message informing you that your computer doesn't have the system requirements to install the Flash Player application.

**FIGURE 27.3**

Choose Help ➪ Digital Editions to arrive at the Digital Editions home page.

# Exploring the Adobe eBook Library

A number of different eBook providers are listed on Adobe's Web site. You can find eBooks in several languages distributed by a number of different providers. To view Adobe's Web page, select Help ⇨ Digital Editions (Acrobat) or File ⇨ Digital Editions (Adobe Reader). Your default Web browser opens the Adobe Digital Editions Web page. Click *Visit the Adobe Digital Editions library to browse and download eBooks and digital magazines* on the Adobe Digital Editions home page. A list of free downloads appears on the linked Web page. Click the Read button appearing adjacent to an eBook to download the file. When the file is downloaded to your computer it appears in your Adobe Digital Editions. In Figure 27.4 you can see the Adobe Digital Editions with several eBooks I downloaded to my computer.

Download eBooks from the sample library.

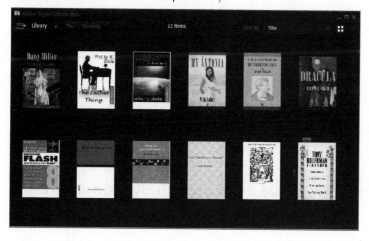

## Tip

Among the free downloads you'll find an eBook titled Inside the Publishing Revolution: The Adobe Story by Pamela Pfiffner. For an informative essay on how Adobe Systems evolved to become a major influence on how we use computers today and the relationships between the major computing developers, read this book. You'll find many interesting historical events documented and information to help you understand early strategies of the company and where Adobe is headed with the Acrobat family of products and other applications in its product line. ∎

# Reading eBooks

After installing the Adobe Digital Editions and downloading some eBooks, just click a publication you see in Figure 27.4 and your book is displayed in a reading mode within the Adobe Digital Edition interface as shown in Figure 27.5.

**FIGURE 27.5**

Click an eBook in the Adobe Digital Editions window and you can start reading the book.

For books, manuals, and large documents, you might want to look at a preference setting that can help you bookmark pages in the files you read. This type of bookmark is like an analog bookmark you might use to mark the place in a book when you pause and come back later to continue reading from the place you left off.

Open the Preferences dialog box (Ctrl/⌘+K) and click Documents in the left pane. In the right pane, check Restore last view settings when reopening documents, as shown in Figure 27.6. You can choose to open all files on the page last viewed in your Acrobat viewer. For example, if you view a PDF document and quit Acrobat after viewing page 125, and then open Acrobat in another session, the PDF opens to page 125.

## FIGURE 27.6

Check Restore last view settings when reopening documents to view the last page viewed in a document when you reopen Acrobat.

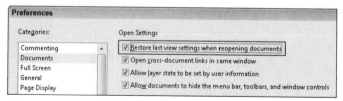

You move around the Adobe Digital Editions window by clicking tools and opening menus. From the Reading menu you can see a list of commands to change the page display and navigate pages as shown in Figure 27.7. The Library menu offers commands to display your book list as with the default thumbnail view or a list view. You also have access to the Help command that opens a FAQ (Frequently Asked Questions) Web page on Adobe's Web site where you can find some help in downloading and viewing eBooks. Another comment in the Library menu enables you to add documents to your library. Select Library ⇨ Add Item to Library and a dialog box opens where you can navigate your hard drive and select any PDF file stored locally on your hard drive and add it to your library.

## FIGURE 27.7

Open a menu at the top of the Adobe Digital Editions window to select menu commands for viewing, navigation, searching, and accessing help with eBooks.

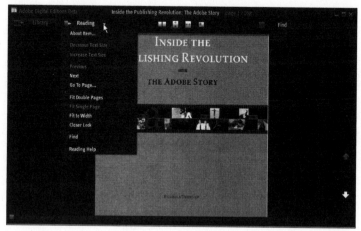

Keep in mind that the screen shots shown here are taken from the beta versions of the Adobe Digital Editions. When the product is out of beta and finally shipped, you may see different menus and menu commands.

# Summary

In this chapter, you learned methods for creating and viewing eBooks.

- The three most popular eBook formats are ePub, Mobipocket, and PDF.
- ePub and Mobipocket afford you the best options for sources hosting your work for resale.
- In order to download and view eBooks in Adobe Digital Editions, you must install the Adobe Flash Player application.
- eBooks and other PDF documents can be opened on the last viewed page when you reopen your Acrobat viewer.
- The Adobe Digital Editions library window provides tools and menu commands for viewing and navigating eBooks.

# Printing to Desktop Color Printers

O ne of the primary problems many Acrobat users experience is printing files with proper color. Notwithstanding any problems with printing fonts and getting a print out, the most problematic issues with printing PDFs that contain graphic images is accurate reproduction of color. Whether you are a creative professional or a novice to graphic design, some basic issues need to be understood when printing any kind of document containing images or other graphics to a desktop color printer.

This chapter is concerned with printing to local printers of the desktop variety from Acrobat viewers, and remarks made in this chapter are not intended for commercial printing. For professional printing and prepress, take a look at Chapter 29.

## Understanding Color Management

Quite a bit can be said about color management, and certainly more attention can be devoted to it than I have room for in this book. Quite simply, there are three basic areas you need to address in creating a color-managed workflow:

- **Monitor calibration.** There are software tools on both Windows and the Mac that can help you calibrate your monitor to eliminate color casts and color tints and set the *gamma* (neutral midtone grays) of your monitor. I won't talk about them because most are useless on LCD-type monitors, and many people are using LCDs these days. Ideally you would use a calibration device. For low-end color calibration of monitors you can purchase the Pantone Huey (`www.pantone.com/products/products.asp?idArea=2&idProduct=103`) or ColorVision Syper2express (`http://spyder.datacolor.com/product-mc-s2e.php`) calibrator for as low as $69 USA. More sophisticated calibrators such as GretagMacbeth Eye-One 2 calibrators are above $250 USA. I'll leave it up to you as to how far you want to go with calibrating your monitor, but I strongly recommend that if color output is important to you that you at least purchase one of the low-end color calibration devices.

- **Color workspace.** Whether you work in Acrobat or in an imaging program like Adobe Photoshop you need to set up your color workspace. Selections for color workspaces vary with programs. The two primary workspaces are Adobe RGB (1998) or sRGB. Choices vary according to the files you prepare and the printing equipment you use.

- **Output color profile.** Each printer and every paper you print on should have a defined color profile. Color profiles are often installed with your printer. You can also acquire or create custom color profiles to print to a specific paper on your printer.

## Note

Creating custom printer profiles requires more expensive color calibration equipment. For a source of calibration equipment, take a look at the GretagMacbeth Web site at `http://www.xrite.com/`. ∎

Don't be concerned yet about which profile to use. More important, try to understand how these three items interact with each other and what they do. First off, your monitor color profile created with a hardware device adjusts the overall brightness of your monitor. When you print a file, you want to be sure that the print outputs are not darker or lighter than the images you see on your monitor. A balance needs to be made between monitor and output so you can safely judge what a print looks like when you print to your printer.

Color workspace affects how you view color on your monitor. You want to try to get as close to seeing all the colors that can be reproduced on your printer. This happens when you choose the proper color workspace. You then select a color output profile when it comes time to print your file. Your color is converted from your workspace color to your printer's colorspace so that all the colors fit within the output space as closely as possible. Quite simply, if you see a bright red color on your computer monitor and the overall brightness matches your output, you want to be certain that same color red gets printed on your printer. This happens when the color is converted from your monitor workspace to your printer's colorspace.

Assuming you can set up your color environment to handle monitor color, workspace color, and output color, the next thing to understand is how color is managed at print time. You have some choices here. You can choose to manage color at print time through your printer, by selecting a printer profile, or by printing a converted color file that requires no color management. This is the one item that is most confusing for people to grasp — when to manage color at print time and when not to manage color. For the answer and examples, I'll cover that when we look at printing to specific printers later in this chapter.

# Selecting a Color Workspace

Your first step after calibrating your monitor in creating a color managed workflow is to choose your color workspace. In Acrobat open the Preferences dialog box by pressing Ctrl/⌘+K. In the left pane, click Color Management and the right pane changes to the view shown in Figure 28.1.

Click Color Management in the Preferences dialog box to access the Color Management options.

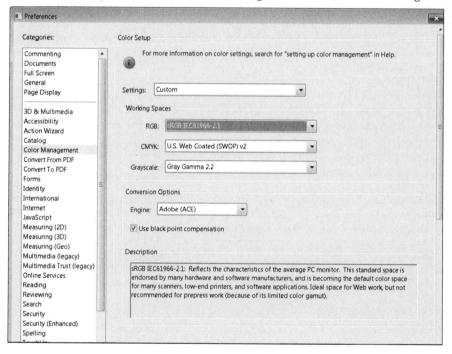

In the Working Spaces section, open the RGB pull-down menu and choose your RGB color workspace. Here you have one of two choices:

- **sRGB.** The name is much longer, as you see in Figure 28.1, but I'll use the abbreviated label and simply call this by the common term — sRGB. Traditionally, this color workspace has been used when files are prepared for screen and Web viewing. This colorspace comes as close as you can get from all the choices available to represent color consistently across all monitors. Of course, there are many variables that prevent you from matching color exactly on all monitors. We'll assume the software engineers are telling us the truth when they say that the best monitor color matching is made by selecting the sRGB colorspace.

More important, you should be aware that many desktop color printers convert color from sRGB better than other workspaces. Some online photo services and photo service providers may ask you to keep your files in sRGB. For example, if you send photos to a Costco store to print on their Noritsu photo printers, they'd ask you to keep your files in sRGB. At the desktop printer level, you'll need to either run tests or take a look at your printer's user manual to find out if your printer supports sRGB better than other color workspaces.

- **Adobe RGB (1998).** The Adobe RGB colorspace has a wider color gamut than sRGB (meaning you can see a bit more colors in this workspace). If you prepare files for press and commercial printing, you're best off using Adobe RGB. Also, some desktop color printers can take advantage of the wider color gamut, so your printer might give you more accurate color matching when converting your files from Adobe RGB to your printer's color output profile. Again though, you need to run tests or turn to the user manual to see what the manufacturer recommends.

If all your work is designed for output to desktop color printers using an RGB colorspace, you don't need to be concerned about the CMYK choices in the Color Management preferences. If you prepare files for press and commercial printing, then CMYK will be a consideration. Make a choice for the color workspace recommended by your commercial printer. If using print shops in the United States, the U.S. Web Coated (SWOP) v2 profile is likely to be your best choice. But be sure to talk to your print shop technicians first.

On Windows, set the Grayscale option to Gray Gamma 2.2, and on the Mac, set the Grayscale to Gray Gamma 1.8. Clear the check box for Output Intent overrides working spaces if your PDF files do not contain embedded Output Intent profiles.

## Cross-Reference

For more information on output intent profiles, see Chapter 29. ∎

For the Conversion options, select Adobe (ACE) for the conversion engine. On Windows, you'll have a choice for Adobe (ACE) or Microsoft ICM. On the Mac, you'll have choices for Adobe (ACE) or Apple ColorSync or Apple CMM. Use the Adobe (ACE) color engine for the best results.

Finally, check the box for Use black point compensation. Checking this option gets you closer to a rich black. Click OK in the Preferences dialog box after you make all your choices and your color settings stay intact until you change them again.

# Using Color Output Profiles

Color output profiles come in a number of different flavors. You can use color output profiles supplied by your printer manufacturer that are installed with your desktop printer, use color profiles created by paper manufacturers that are designed for use with specific printers, or create custom profiles for your printer and the papers you use.

## Note

There are several services available to you for creating custom color output profiles. If you're a creative professional, you might want to look at using a service to prepare a custom profile for your printer and the papers you use. Just go to the Internet and search for custom profiling services. Custom color profiles are offered as low as $25 US. The cost is minimal considering all the consumables you'd waste running tests to get color right on your equipment. ■

Because most users printing from Acrobat are likely to use printer profiles that were shipped with their desktop printer, I'll stick to talking about these profiles. If you're a creative professional who depends on accurate color proofing, take a look at *Color Correction For Digital Photographers Only* (Wiley Publishing, 2006) or *Color Management For Digital Photographers For Dummies* (Wiley Publishing, 2007). There's much more to color profiling than can be described here, so a little research can help you get closer to producing accurate color.

When you print your PDF files to your color desktop printer, you make a choice for using a color profile at the time you print your file. You may see a list of color profiles in the Advanced Print Setup dialog box or you may only see the name of your printer. If you see just your printer's name, color profile selection is made automatically by the print driver. Choosing a paper in your print driver options tells the printer what profile to use, hence the color profile choice is automatic.

Regardless of how the color profile is selected, a color conversion takes place from your color workspace to the colorspace of your printer. In essence, the conversion is an attempt to fit all the color you see on your monitor into the printable colorspace on your printer with as close a match as possible.

# Printing Basics in Acrobat

Before you start printing files to your printer, there are a few toggles and switches you need to verify. If you don't have some options enabled, you may have a more difficult time printing your documents. Several settings in the Print dialog box shown in Figure 28.2 are globally set for all printing on desktop printers. The essentials for setting up your printing environment and some toggles you should understand are as follows:

- **Printer selection.** From the Name pull-down menu, select the printer you want to output your file.

- **Comments and Forms.** Above the Preview area, you see the section Comments and Forms. For printing composite prints without any comments or markups, select

Document from the pull-down menu. For printing with these markups, see the section "Printing Comments, Forms, and Summaries" later in this chapter.

- **Page Scaling.** Ideally, you should print files to papers large enough to accommodate your document page size. If your document fits on a standard page size, select None for Page Scaling. If you do need to shrink a document to fit a paper smaller than the document page size, select Shrink to Printable Area or Fit to Printable Area from the Page Scaling pull-down menu. If you need to tile pages, you can make selections for tiling in the same pull-down menu.

- **Page Orientation.** On Windows, click the Properties button in the top-right corner of the Print dialog box to select either Portrait or Landscape Orientation. Note that you can also select orientation and page size by selecting File ⇨ Page Setup before you open the Print dialog box.

- **Booklet Printing.** Open the page Scaling pull-down menu and you find Booklet Printing. Select Booklet Printing to print spreads as shown in the Preview Composite in Figure 28.2. You can choose from the following three additional options for printing booklets: Print Both sides, Front side only, or Back side only. On desktop printers capable of printing two sides, you can run the print first on one side, turn the paper over, and then print the second side.

**FIGURE 28.2**

Select your printer from the Name pull-down menu. Booklet printing can be chosen from the Page Scaling pull-down menu.

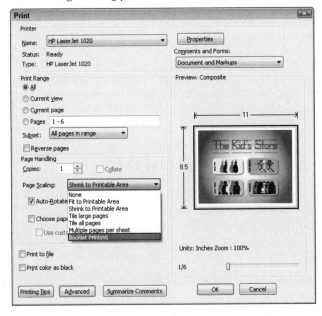

- **Tile large pages.** This option is a great benefit for those who send files to service centers for printing on large format inkjet printers. When you need a proof on your desktop printer for an oversized print, you can print multiple pages of tiled sections of the larger image. You have choices for displaying cut marks, overlap areas, and scaling.

- **Tile all pages.** Choose this option to tile all pages in a document.

- **Multiple pages per sheet.** You can reduce the number of pages printed to fit a given number of pages per sheet. You have options for customizing the number of pages per sheet and the page range per sheet.

You have some other options in the print dialog box for page range, reversing pages, using auto rotations, choosing a paper source by page size, printing to a file, and so on. All these other options are very similar to printing from other programs and should be familiar to you.

# Understanding How to Manage Color

Acrobat offers you three different options for managing color. Your choices appear when you open the Print dialog box (Ctrl/⌘+P) and click the Advanced button. In the Color Management pane open the Color Handling pull-down menu to see the options shown in Figure 28.3. The three choices include:

**FIGURE 28.3**

Open the Print dialog box, click Advanced, and click Color Management in the left pane. Open the Color Handling pull-down menu to find your options for managing color at print time.

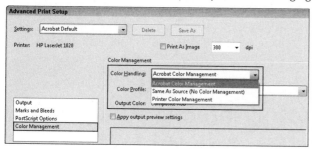

- **Acrobat Color Management.** This choice gives the control for managing color to Acrobat. If you make this choice, you need to turn off color management in your printer driver.

    If you don't turn color management off at the last stage (in the printer driver), you wind up with a double profiled print. This results in a severe color shift and color output very different than your monitor view. (See the sidebar in this chapter for more on printing with color shifts.)

## Note

See the section Printing to Desktop Printers later in this chapter to learn how to turn color management on and off in the printer driver). ∎

- **Same As Source (No Color Management).** If you convert an image in a program like Photoshop to your color output profile, the color is ready for output and no further conversion is needed. Because the color is already converted to your printer's color, you need to turn color management off throughout the print process. Most likely you won't be working with files that have embedded color output profiles in the images; therefore, you won't need to worry about printing using this option. If, perchance, you do work with images that have color converted to a printer profile, you would make this choice.

- **Printer Color Management.** When you make this choice in your Advanced Print Setup dialog box, you enable the printer to choose the color profile; however, using this option only works with PostScript printing devices. If this choice is selected, you can manage the color in the advanced print settings in your color printer driver. Typically, you'll find this option to work only when using PostScript printers. As a general rule, for non-PostScript printers, you need to use the Acrobat Color Management and choose sRGB color as your color profile.

## Cross-Reference

For more information on selecting profiles in the Advanced Print Setup dialog box, see the next section, "Printing to Desktop Printers." ∎

When printing from Acrobat you most often have one of two choices to make. Either enable your printer to determine color or enable Acrobat to determine color. If you choose to enable your printer to manage the color, you turn color management on. If you enable Acrobat to manage the color, you turn color management off. However, where you turn color on and where you turn color off varies differently between color printers. To demonstrate how color is managed, we need to look at printing Acrobat files from a few different desktop color printers.

# Printing to Desktop Printers

Print settings vary according to manufacturers, and I can't hope to cover all printers in this chapter. For a representative sample, I'll use three of the more popular color printers to show you how to print files from Acrobat. To demonstrate how color profiling is handled, I'll use Epson, HP, and Canon printers as examples. If you have a different color printer, you should be able to understand the process and apply similar choices when printing to your color printer.

When you install your printer driver, the installation utility may also install a number of color profiles. In some cases, individual profiles won't be installed — it all depends on your printer and the printer driver. If individual color profiles are not installed, then your printer driver contains profile information and makes profile choices within the driver itself. For profiles installed with your printer, you can choose profiles in Acrobat's Advanced Print Setup dialog box and control all the printing using a profile provided by your printer manufacturer.

You have a choice for how these profiles are used. You can choose to select the profile in the Print dialog box or you can choose an automatic method where the manufacturer created a no-nonsense process of automatic profile selection using your printer driver. The color profile is automatically selected when you choose the paper source.

## Printing to Epson printers

For the first example I'll use Epson printers to demonstrate how to print a PDF file from Acrobat using the printer to manage color and using Acrobat to manage color. Because the dialog boxes differ so much between platforms, I'll include printing from Windows and from the Mac in separate descriptions.

### Enabling a low-end printer to manage color on Windows

In this first example, let's take a look at how to print to an Epson low-end color printer on Windows while enabling the *printer to manage the color*. Depending on the model of your printer, you may see some slight differences in menu names, but the process will follow the same steps.

To print to an Epson printer while enabling the printer to manage the color, follow these steps.

### STEPS: Printing from Windows

1. **Open the Print dialog box.** Select File ➪ Print or press Ctrl/⌘+P to open the Print dialog box shown in Figure 28.4.

    Make all the attribute choices for printing to your printer as was described in the section "Printing Basics in Acrobat" for page orientation, page scaling, and so on.

2. **Select your printer.** Open the Name pull-down menu and select your printer as shown earlier in Figure 28.2.

**FIGURE 28.4**

Select your printer from the Name menu in the Print dialog box.

3. **Open the Advanced Print Setup dialog box.** Click Advanced in the Print dialog box.

4. **Select the color profile.** Click Color Management in the left pane of the Advanced Print Setup dialog box and open the Color Handling pull-down menu shown in Figure 28.4. From the menu options, choose Acrobat Color Management. This choice tells Acrobat to manage the color.

5. **Choose a color profile.** When using Acrobat to manage the color, you need to choose a color profile from the Color Profile pull-down menu. From the menu choices choose sRGB IEC61966-2.1. This choice is not an accurate profile for your printer and paper but it servers as a generic profile that works best for most low-end devices.

6. **Return to the Print dialog box.** Click OK in the Advanced Print Setup dialog box to return to the Print dialog box.

7. **Open the printer driver dialog box.** At this point we have made all our settings in the Acrobat workspace. Now, we need to make choices in the printer driver to decide how the color is managed. Because we do not want the printer to manage the color, we'll verify settings to ensure that indeed the printer does not manage the color.

   Click Properties in the Print dialog box to open the Printer Properties dialog box. In this example, I use an Epson Stylus C59 printer. The Epson C59 is a very low-end printer that doesn't ship with custom color profiles. Therefore, the only choice I have for managing color is to let Acrobat manage the color and choose a generic color profile such as sRGB.

8. **Choose the paper source.** This first choice determines the amount of ink to be used for your print. If printing to a glossy paper, more ink is used. If printing to a plain bond paper, less ink is used. From the Type pull-down menu, make the paper choice for the paper you use. In this example, I use Premium Glossy Photo Paper as shown in Figure 28.5.

## FIGURE 28.5

Select the paper source you use to print your files.

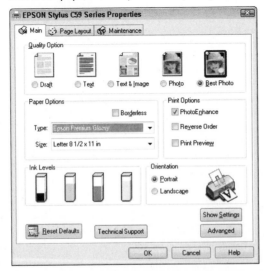

9. **Don't Color manage your output.** Now it's time to color manage your file, and this step is critical in your print production workflow. For the Epson printer without a color profile available for your paper choice, you need to click the Advanced button shown in Figure 28.6 that opens a warning dialog box. Simply click Continue to open the advanced settings dialog box as you see in Figure 28.6.

**FIGURE 28.6**

Click Advanced, and then click Continue to access the advanced settings in the Epson print driver.

A few choices need to be made in this dialog box. The most important are as follows:

- **Select a paper type.** Choose the same paper here as you did back in Step 7.

- **Turn color management off.** Because we are enabling Acrobat to determine the color, we need to be certain the Color Controls radio button is disabled. This setting tells Acrobat to manage color using the color profile we selected in Step 5.

- **Save Setting button.** If you frequently print files using the same settings, you can save your settings by clicking the Save Setting button.

10. **Print the PDF.** Click OK and OK again in the Print dialog box and your file is sent to your printer. The color is converted automatically from your source workspace of sRGB or Adobe RGB (1998) to the profile the Printer Driver automatically selects for you.

## Enabling Acrobat to determine color on the Mac

On the Mac, the Epson Printer Driver offers you different settings although the process is quite similar. Again, we are going to use the automatic method for color conversion and allow the print driver to handle the conversion.

The Acrobat Print dialog box settings and the Advanced Print Setup dialog box settings are identical on the Mac as you find in Windows. You make choices for paper orientation, page scaling, and so on in the Print dialog box and then choose Printer/ Color Management in the Advanced Print Setup dialog box just as Windows users. However, on the Mac you don't have a Properties button. All color management choices are made directly in the Acrobat Print dialog box.

To print to an Epson printer while enabling the printer to manage color on a Mac, follow these steps,

### STEPS: Printing from the Mac

1. **Select Print Settings.** Select File ⇨ Print and make the same choices as Windows users for print attributes and select Printer Color Management in the Advanced Print Setup dialog box.

2. **Select your printer.** At the top of the Acrobat Print dialog box you make a choice for your printer from the Printer pull-down menu, as shown in Figure 28.7.

---

**FIGURE 28.7**

Select your printer from the options listed in the Printer pull-down menu.

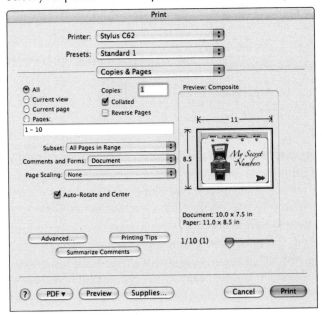

---

3. **Select the Media Type and Print Quality.** Where you see Copies & Pages, click to open a pull-down menu and select the option for Print Settings. In the Print Settings pane, you make selections for Media Type and Print Quality as shown in Figure 28.8. In this example, I use an Epson Stylus C62 printer and choose Premium Glossy Photo Paper and select Best Photo from the Print Quality pull-down menu.

**FIGURE 28.8**

Make choices for Printer, Media Type, and Print Quality in the Acrobat Print dialog box.

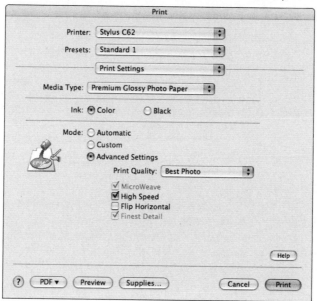

4. **Choose how to manage the color.** Now it's time to select the color management method. From the pull-down menu where you now see Print Settings, click to open the menu and select Color Management, as shown in Figure 28.9.

   Click Off (No Color Management). Making this choice tells the print driver to not manage the color.

5. **Print the file.** Click Print and the file is printed to your printer with an automatic color conversion from your workspace color to the printer color profile.

**FIGURE 28.9**

Click Print Settings to open the pull-down menu and select Color Management.

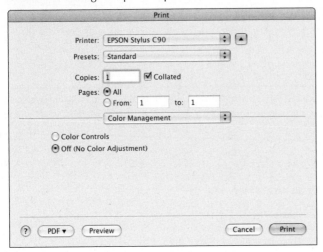

## Selecting a custom printer profile

Your second method for managing color when printing files is to select a printer profile installed with your printer driver or a custom profile you create using a color profiling system. You choose from the available list of color profiles in the Color Profile pull-down menu. Whereas the last section used a generic profile, this time we'll let Adobe Acrobat manage the color using a custom color profile. Again, the Windows options and Mac commands vary a little, so I'll discuss how to print by selecting a profile for each operating system.

### Printing using a custom printer profile on Windows

The steps are the same as those described in printing files for automatic profile selection when setting up the page and selecting a printer. When you select File ⇨ Print, you open the Acrobat Print dialog box as described in the previous section. Your steps now change when you enable Acrobat to handle the color conversion and you proceed through the Print dialog box as follows.

#### STEPS: Using Custom Color Profiles on Windows

1. **Choose Acrobat Color Management.** Open the Print dialog box and click Advanced. Click Color Management in the left pane and choose Acrobat Color Management from the Color Handling pull-down menu.

2. **Select a color profile.** Note that the Color Profile pull-down menu becomes active when you choose Acrobat Color Management. From the Color Profile pull-down menu, select the color profile designed for use with the paper you have chosen to

print your image. In this example, I use a fine art paper color profile as shown in Figure 28.10.

**FIGURE 28.10**

Choose a printer profile that matches the paper you use.

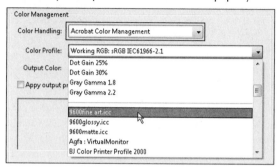

3. **Open the printer Properties.** Click Properties and the properties settings for your selected printer driver open. Check the radio button for Best Photo. From the Type pull-down menu, select the recommended paper choice. Note: If you use a custom color profile, the profile is usually shipped with guidelines for selecting proper paper.

4. **Manage the color.** Click Advanced and click Continue to arrive at the same dialog box shown earlier in Figure 28.7. The paper choice selection is automatically carried over from the previous properties dialog box (from Step 1). A different setting is in the Color Management section. This time click the ICM (Image Color Management) radio button and click Off (No Color Adjustment), as shown in Figure 28.11. Because you selected the color profile in Step 1, and you are enabling Acrobat to manage the color, you need to be sure that Color Management is OFF. If you don't turn color management off, you end up double profiling your print.

**FIGURE 28.11**

Click ICM and click Off (No Color Adjustment).

5. **Print the file.** Click OK and click Print to print the file.

### Printing using a printer profile on the Mac

All the steps to print a file enabling Acrobat to manage color are the same as Windows until you get to the printer driver. On the Mac, do the following to print a PDF document enabling Acrobat to manage color.

#### STEPS: Enabling Acrobat to Manage Color on the Mac

1. **Set the print attributes.** Follow the same steps to make choices for the print attributes and your printer. Go to the Advanced Print Options and select a printer profile for your target paper.

2. **Set the Print Settings.** Use the same settings, as shown earlier in Figure 28.8, to select the Media Type and Print Quality.

3. **Make a choice for Color Management.** Click Print Settings and select Color Management from the pull-down menu in the Print dialog box. This time, because we chose a color output profile and Acrobat is determining the color, we turn color management off. In the Color Management pane, select No Color Adjustment, as you see in Figure 28.12.

4. **Print the file.** Click Print to print the file.

**FIGURE 28.12**

Select Color Management and click No Color Adjustment.

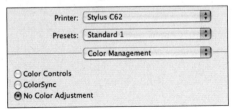

## Printing to HP inkjet printers

Regardless of the printer you use, the process for printing follows the same logic. Unfortunately each manufacturer uses different dialog boxes and different menu command names that can leave you completely confused if you try to apply steps from printing to one printer to a different printer.

The two methods for managing color (enable the printer driver to determine color by selecting Printer Color Management, or enable Acrobat to determine color by selecting a specific color profile) are applied to all printers but the dialog boxes, buttons, and menu choices appear differently.

The critical steps you need to be concerned about when printing files is the profile selection, the paper selection, and when to turn color management on or off. If you own an HP printer you probably know where to make your paper selection and your best photo selection. The more obscure setting is likely to be the color management choice. Rather than discuss each detail step for printing to an HP low-end desktop printer, let's take a look at how to manage color.

## Printing to HP printers on Windows

Again, you have two choices as follows:

- **Let your printer determine color.** For PostScript printers, you use this option. Select Printer Color Management in the Advanced Print Setup dialog box. Click Properties to open the printer driver properties. Click the Advanced tab when you arrive at the printer driver properties dialog box. Click Graphic and click Image Color Management. From the ICM Method pull-down menu, select ICM Handled by Printer, as shown in Figure 28.13.

- **Let Acrobat determine color.** Select a color profile in the Advanced Print Setup dialog box and select ICM Disabled in the Advanced tab in the HP printer driver properties.

**FIGURE 28.13**

Open Graphic and select ICM Method. Choose ICM Handled by Printer from the pull-down menu.

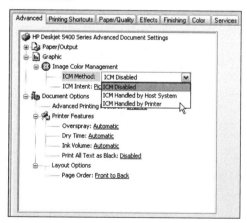

## Printing to HP printers on the Mac

HP has come a long way with printing to the Mac. The HP Next Generation Inkjet Print Products have a number of color management solutions for Mac users working with newer HP printers such as ColorSmart/sRGB shown in Figure 28.14. Rather than go into detail here, log on to: `http://h10025.www1.hp.com/ewfrf/wc/document?docname=c00284884&lc=en&cc=us&dlc=&product=3204765` where you'll find all the information you need to color manage print jobs using HP printers.

FIGURE 28.14

Select an HP paper in the Paper Type/Quality dialog box.

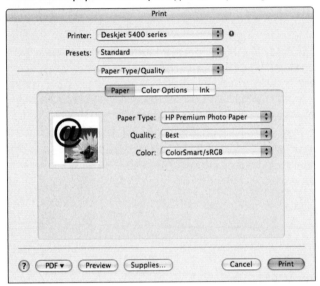

## Printing to Canon printers

Again we follow the same logic and choose to either enable or disable color management. With Canon color printers, the area in the print driver dialog box is even more hidden than you find in Epson and HP desktop printers.

### Printing to Canon printers on Windows

Using the same two options you control color management as follows:

- **Let your printer determine color.** Select Printer Color Management in the Advanced Print Setup dialog box. Click Properties in the Acrobat Print dialog box and click Manual for Color/Intensity in the Main tab, as shown in Figure 28.15.

  Click the Set button to open the Manual Color Adjustment dialog box. Check the box for Enable ICM (Windows Image Color Management), as shown in Figure 28.16.

**FIGURE 28.15**

Click the Manual radio button for Color/Intensity.

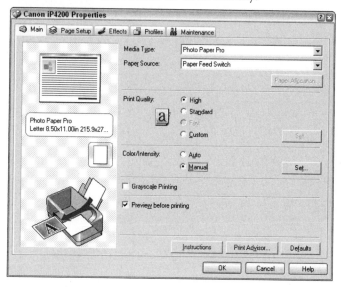

**FIGURE 28.16**

Check Enable ICM (Windows Image Color Management).

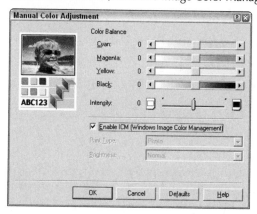

- **Let Acrobat determine color.** First select your printer profile in the Advanced Print Setup dialog box and follow the same steps as above. This time uncheck the Enable ICM (Windows Color Management) check box.

### Printing to Canon printers on the Mac

You make the same choices on the Mac as you do on Windows for how you want to manage color on a Canon printer. Enable the printer to manage the color and make a paper choice in the Quality & Media dialog box, as shown in Figure 28.17.

FIGURE 28.17

Select Quality & Media and select the paper type in the Media Type pull-down menu.

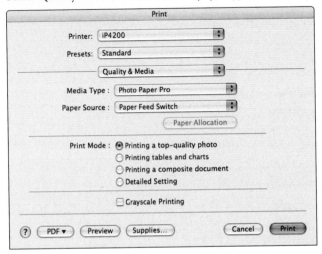

From the pull-down menu below the Presets menu, select Color Options. Here you choose BJ Standard when permitting the printer driver to determine color and None when selecting a printer profile in the Advanced Print Setup dialog box. The options are shown in Figure 28.18

# Printing Comments, Forms, and Summaries

You can print document markups as well as form field data from Acrobat viewers. The options are straightforward and easy to use. However, one limitation you should know about is that comment pop-up notes are not printed and you cannot print the content of a note.

## Tip

To see exactly what you can print when using comment notes in Acrobat, open the Print dialog box. The thumbnail preview in the Print dialog box shows you the types of comments that Acrobat will print before actually printing the file. ■

**FIGURE 28.18**

Select BJ Standard for printer color management and None when you select a printer profile.

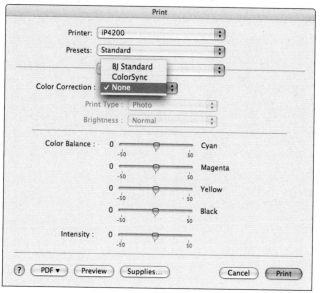

## Printing comments

To print comments, you need a file that contains some comment notes. To learn more about commenting, see Chapter 20.

To print a file with comments and markups, follow these steps.

### STEPS: Printing Document Markups

1. **Open a document containing comments and markups.** You can use the Text Edits tools, Highlight tool, and other comment tools as well as any of the Markup tools such as the Rectangle tool, Cloud tool, Callout tool, and others.

2. **Open the Print dialog box.** Select File ➪ Print.

3. **Select Document and Markups in the Comments and Forms area of the Print dialog box.** When you make the selection for Document and Markups, the page preview in the Preview Composite area of the Print dialog box shows you exactly what elements print, as you see in Figure 28.19.

**FIGURE 28.19**

Select Document and Markups from the Comments and Forms pull-down menu.

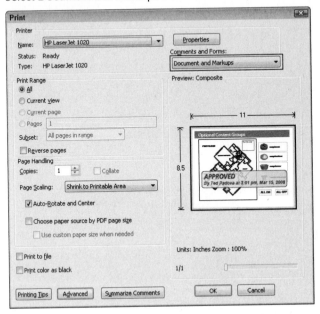

4. **Click Print.** Your print appears with the comments and markups as was shown in the Preview Composite in the Print dialog box.

You have another choice for printing comments. You can choose to print a document with just Stamp comments. From the Comments and Forms pull-down menu, select Document and Stamps. A preview also appears when you choose to print stamp comments. Just make the selection for Document and Stamps and click Print.

## Selecting and printing form field data

Another option you have is printing just form field data. You can print all form field data with just one exception. Button faces don't print. All the other fields including check boxes, radio buttons, and barcode data print.

To print just the data fields without the background content, select Form fields only in the Print dialog box in the Comments and Forms pull-down menu and print the file.

## Cross-Reference

For more information on form fields, see Chapter 31. ∎

# Creating and printing comment summaries

Yet another option you have when printing PDF documents is creating a comment summary and printing it in one step. Click the Summarize Comments button at the bottom of the Print dialog box. The Summarize Options dialog box opens, as shown in Figure 28.20, where you can make a choice for the type of comment summary you want to print. Select an option and click Print Comment Summary. The file that's printed contains just the comments in one of the four summary formats available to you.

## Cross-Reference

For more information on creating comment summaries, see Chapter 19. ∎

**FIGURE 28.20**

The Summarize Options dialog box offers choices for using one of four different templates for comment summaries.

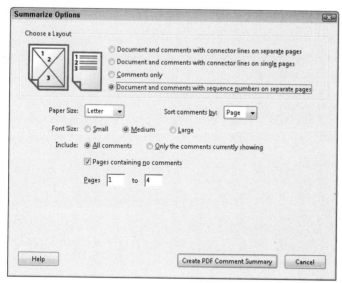

# Summary

In this chapter, you learned how to print PDF files to desktop printers and how to manage color for print output.

- A well-managed color workflow requires calibrating your monitor, using a proper workspace color, and printing using a color profile designed for your printer and paper source.

- The two most common methods for managing color with desktop color printers in Acrobat are to enable the printer to manage the color or enable Acrobat to manage the color.

- When you choose to let your printer manage color, you need to use a PostScript printer, and you turn color management on in advanced settings in your printer driver.

- When you choose to select a color profile and enable Acrobat to manage color, you turn color management off in your printer driver advanced settings.

- Comment markups can be printed with your document. You choose to print comment markups in the Acrobat Print dialog box in the Comment and Forms pull-down menu.

- You can print form field data without the background PDF design. Choose Form fields only in the Comment and Forms pull-down menu.

- You can create and print comment summaries in one step in the Print dialog box by clicking the Summarize Comments button.

# Using Commercial Printing and Prepress

At some time or another, the files you output to your desktop printer may be candidates for offset printing. The tools and commands you use for desktop printers, as I explained in Chapter 28, are sufficient for printing to all the printers you have in your office and home. However, when printing PDF documents on commercial printing devices, you must address a number of issues.

For high-end digital prepress and commercial printing, Acrobat Pro includes all the print controls that the commercial printing community desires. Combined with features for previewing color, preflighting jobs, and printing color separations, Acrobat Pro ranks as a strong competitor against any layout or other professional applications designed to serve creative professionals. In this chapter, I cover printing from Acrobat Pro using many commercial printing tools.

## Soft Proofing Color

Soft proofing color refers to viewing color on your monitor with a screen preview of the way color will be printed to hard copy. Soft proofing is a digital process whereby you use your computer monitor screen to preview things such as proper color assignments, overprints, separations, transparency, and similar issues that might cause problems on printing devices, rather than print a test proof and consume paper and ink.

With the exception of previewing overprints, all soft proofing options are contained in the Acrobat Pro programs only. Most of the options you find for soft proofing apply to high-end commercial printing; however, some features can be useful when you're printing to desktop color printers.

# Setting up your color management environment

As discussed in Chapter 28, color management is equally important when printing to commercial printing devices and prepress systems. You first begin with monitor calibration and set up your color management preferences. Whereas your workspace color choice is best using the sRGB color space for most desktop printers, the Adobe RGB (1998) color workspace is a better choice for most commercial printing equipment.

## Cross-Reference

Most of what you need for color management in Acrobat is covered in Chapter 28. ■

# Using Output Preview

Soft proofing color is handled in the Output Preview dialog box. This dialog box does not provide you options for altering the content. It is used as a viewing tool to diagnose any potential printing problems. From a Preview menu, you select one of three categories in which to preview your document — Separations, Color Warnings, or the new Acrobat 9 Object Inspector. To open the Output Preview dialog box, click Output Preview in the Print Production panel. The Output Preview dialog box opens.

## Looking at Color Warnings

Click Color Warnings in the Output Preview dialog box as shown in Figure 29.1. The Color Warnings pane opens. Several settings in the Color Warnings pane are the same as those found in the Separations pane. The unique options in this pane are the Warnings items. You use this pane to preview any problems that are shown with keylines using the colors in the Warnings areas. If you need more contrast against the background colors, click one of the Warnings color swatches to open a color palette where another color can be selected to display the Warnings keyline borders. Other areas in the Color Warnings dialog box include the Simulation Profile, Simulate Black Ink, Simulate Paper Color, Warnings, and Rich Black.

### Simulation Profile

Simulation Profile enables you to select from a list of ICC (International Color Consortium) profiles. A number of preset profiles are available from which to choose, and you can also create your own custom profiles and add them to the list. You create custom profiles with hardware/software devices that are designed specifically for calibrating monitors and creating ICC profiles. As a profile is created, it is saved as a file to your hard drive. Graphic designers can also often acquire custom profiles from print shops and service centers.

In order for Acrobat to recognize the ICC profiles you create, you must be certain that the profiles are stored in the proper directory. By default, utilities and commercial devices used for calibrating color save profiles to a directory that makes them accessible to Acrobat. If you want to remove ICC profiles so fewer profiles show up in the Proof Colors dialog box or you have problems getting a profile to the right directory, open the folder where the profiles are stored. On Windows Vista, the path is `System32\Spool\Drivers\Color`. On Mac OS X, look in `Macintosh HD:Library:ColorSync:Profiles`. When new profiles are added to the appropriate folder on your computer, you can access the profiles in Acrobat after you quit the program and relaunch it if the profile was added while Acrobat was open.

### FIGURE 29.1

Open the Output Preview dialog box and click Color Warnings.

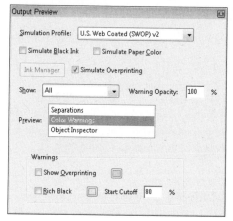

To select a profile for color proofing, open the Simulation Profile pull-down menu and choose a profile to preview. Selecting the option does not change the color in the document, and you can select different profiles from the menu selections without permanently changing color in the file.

From the pull-down menu you'll see a number of different profiles appear in a long list. Select the output device profile you want to simulate. In order to do so, you need to acquire an output profile from your printer or service bureau or use a custom profile you created and added to your Profiles folder. For printing on an offset press on coated stock in the United States, use U.S. Web Coated (SWOP) v2 if your printer doesn't have a custom profile to provide you. When you select one of the presets for soft proofing prints, the two check boxes for simulating ink and paper become accessible. (Outside the U.S. you might want to use a Japanese or European option available in the CMYK profiles from the CMYK pull-down menu.)

## Tip

To ensure your color proofing uses the same profile each time you view a file on-screen, open a document in Acrobat. Select the profile you want to use as a default from the Simulation Profile pull-down menu. Quit Acrobat and relaunch the program. The last choice you made becomes the new default. You don't need to quit the program to make the profile choice a new default, but if the program crashes during a session, you lose preferences applied in that session. Quitting after making a preference choice ensures that the preference is held in all subsequent Acrobat sessions. ■

### Simulate Black Ink

When the Simulate Black Ink check box is enabled, the preview shows you the dynamic range of the document's profile. Dynamic range is measured in values usually between 0 and 4, although some scanner developers claim dynamic ranges of 4.1, 4.2, or higher. A dynamic range of something like 3.8 yields a wide range of grays between the white point and the black point in a scanned image. If the dynamic range is high, you see details in shadows and highlights. If the dynamic range is low, highlights can get blown out and shadows lose detail. When you enable the Simulate Black Ink check box, look for the distinct tonal differences in the preview and detail in shadows and highlights.

### Simulate Paper Color

If the check box for Simulate Paper Color is enabled in the Output Preview dialog box, the preview shows you a particular shade of gray as simulated for the paper color by the profile you choose. You may find that the preview looks too gray or has too much black. This may not be the result of the profile used but rather the brightness adjustment on your monitor. If your monitor is calibrated properly and the profile accurately displays the paper color, the preview should show you an accurate representation of the document as it is printed on paper.

### Warnings

Two different warnings dynamically display potential printing problems. As you select a check box, you can move the Output Preview aside and preview the results in the document pane. When you select a box and preview the results, the display appears only when the Output Preview dialog box is open. Closing the dialog box returns you to the default view of the document page before you opened the Output Preview.

By default, the options in the Warnings section show potential problems using default colors adjacent to the warning item. You can change the warning colors by clicking the color swatch and selecting from a preset palette or selecting a custom color from your operating system color palette.

Overprints are often used to *trap* colors when files are intended for printing separations. Trapping a color creates an overlap between colors, so any movement of the paper when printed on a printing press prevents printing colors without gaps between the colors. In other cases, overprints may be assigned to colors in illustrations intentionally when a designer wants to eliminate potential trapping problems. For example, you might assign an overprint to text to avoid any trapping problems where black text is printed on top of a background color. In some instances, a designer might unintentionally assign an overprint to a color during the creative process. As a measure of checking overprints for those colors that you properly assign and to review a document for potential problems, you can use Acrobat's Show Overprinting preview to display on your monitor all the overprints created in a file. To view overprints in a PDF document, select the Show Overprinting check box in the Output Preview dialog box.

## Note

**Acrobat has an automatic overprint preview that displays CMYK files with overprint previews by default. Additionally, all files saved as PDF/X also show overprints as a default. ∎**

To understand what happens with overprints and knockouts, look at Figure 29.2. The composite image is created for printing two colors. These colors are printed on separate plates for two different inks. When the file is separated, the type is *knocked out* of the background, leaving holes in the background. Because the two colors butt up against each other, any slight movement of the paper creates a gap between where one ink color ends and the other begins. To prevent the problem, a slight bit of overprinting is added to the type. In an exaggerated view in Figure 29.2 you can see the stroke around the type character. The stroke is assigned an overprint so its color, which is the foreground color, prints on top of the background color without a knockout.

**FIGURE 29.2**

If an overprint is assigned to the type, the overprint area of the type color prints on top of the background color. If the paper moves slightly, the overprint prevents any paper color showing through gaps created by the misregistration.

### Rich black

When files are printed with rich black, all the black in the document prints with more density. This is often a common setting used when printing to inkjet printers and commercial oversized printing devices to eliminate any muddy appearance when files contain a substantial amount of black. Select the box to preview how the black will lay down on the printed output. If you see too much density in black, be certain to avoid using rich black when printing the file.

## Using Separations

One of the great features for soft proofing color in Acrobat Pro is the ability to preview a color separation where colors can be viewed individually or in combinations — for example, previewing cyan and magenta instead of previewing all colors. To preview a separation, select Separations from the Preview pull-down menu in the Output Preview dialog box. The pane changes to the view shown in Figure 29.3.

If you intend to print a file in four-color process, the Output Preview dialog box helps you identify any potential problems such as spot colors that may be contained in the file, as in the file used when I opened the Separations preview in Figure 29.3. Likewise, if a spot-color-only job contains colors not intended to be printed, they also show up.

FIGURE 29.3

The Separations window shows all colors contained in a file.

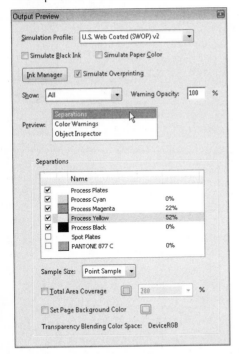

You can selectively view individual colors by disabling the check boxes adjacent to each color name, viewing selected colors only, and viewing spot colors converted to CMYK. When you click the X in a check box for a color, all images and objects containing a percentage of that color are hidden. Click again and the color is displayed.

You evaluate color values by moving the cursor around the document with the Output Preview dialog box open. Notice the percentage values on the far right side of Figure 29.3. These values represent the percent of ink at the cursor position.

## Using Object Inspector

Open the Preview pull-down menu and choose Object Inspector as shown in Figure 29.4.

The Object Inspector enables you to inspect objects in the PDF file. Objects can be text, images, and vector art. With the Object Inspector pane open in the Output Preview dialog box, move the cursor around the document. The area where you click the mouse is reported in the dialog box with feedback about the object properties.

You can review information on object properties such as color space, profile information, transparency, blending modes, image attributes such as size and resolution, and more.

**FIGURE 29.4**

The Object Inspector provides feedback on text, image, and object attributes.

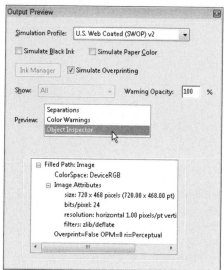

# Converting Colors

The Convert Colors tool in the Print Production panel is truly great whether you soft proof files for commercial printing or you print your PDF documents on your local desktop color printer. Click this tool and the Convert Colors dialog box opens, as shown in Figure 29.5.

**FIGURE 29.5**

Click the Convert Colors tool in the Print Production panel to open the Convert Colors dialog box.

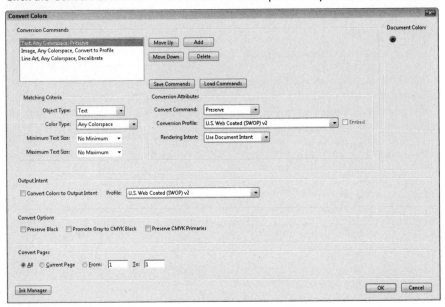

Convert Colors provides you with an impressive set of controls that enable you to selectively convert and/or preserve colors according to object type. Radical changes were made in Acrobat 9 to the convert color settings shown in Figure 29.5 as compared to earlier releases of Acrobat.

The choices you have in the Convert Colors dialog box include:

- **Conversion Commands.** Click the Add button and a new conversion item is listed in the Conversion Commands list. Select the item and you can choose the object type from the Object Type pull-down menu (see Object Type in this list) and the color type from the Color Type pull-down menu (See Color Type in this list). You can add another conversion command by clicking the Add button and define settings for a different object type. Under the Conversion attributes you can choose to preserve or convert color. The Move Up and Move Down buttons enable you to choose what commands are executed first.

- **Save/Load buttons.** You can define a series of commands and color conversion options and save the settings to a file. Click the Load button and you can load settings you create by clicking the Save button.

- **Matching Criteria.** You have choices for setting attributes according to Object Type and Color Type:

- **Object Type.** There are four choices from the pull-down menu commands. Choose Any Object to apply the conversion settings to all objects. Choose Image, Text, or Line Art to apply conversions to one of these object types. Smooth Shade is the final choice, which enables you to apply conversions to gradients. Notice in Figure 29.5 I have three different object types with different conversion settings for each type.

- **Color Type.** From the Color Type pull-down menu you choose the colorspace for the object in question. You might choose Any RGB to convert RGB color to CMYK color. The choice you make here is the existing color of the object. You make a choice for the conversion target color in another menu.

- **Minimum Text Size.** Choose from preset point sizes or type a value in the text box. (Values range from 1 to 1 million). Conversion is applied to the minimum size defined in this menu. Sizes below the minimum are ignored.

- **Maximum Text Size.** Essentially this setting is the opposite of Minimum Text Size. Define a size for the maximum point size for text.

- **Convert Command.** From the pull-down menu choose Preserve, Convert to Profile, or Decalibrate. The Preserve choice preserves the color. Convert to Profile converts the color from the Color Type setting to the selected destination Profile. Decalibrate removes profiles from the identified object in the Object Type menu.

- **Conversion Profile.** Choose a profile from this menu for the destination of the conversion.

- **Rendering Intent.** Choose from Use Document Intent, Relative Colorimetric, Absolute Colorimetric, Perceptual, or Saturation. For more information on Rendering Intents, check out the Acrobat Help file.

- **Output Intent.** Check the check box for Convert to Output Intent and choose a profile from the Profile pull-down menu for the Output Intent if you want to convert all objects to a single output intent.

- **Convert Options.** Check the boxes for handling black and CMYK primary colors in the output.

- **Convert Pages.** Choose All or a page range for the pages to be converted.

## Cross-Reference

For more information on using output profiles in the Advanced Print Setup dialog box, see Chapter 28. ∎

# Using Ink Manager

The Ink Manager dialog box enables you to change ink values and convert colors. Changes you apply to the options aren't saved with the PDF file. If you convert spot colors to CMYK, for example, and save the document, the colors are unaffected when you reopen the file. The changes applied in the Ink Manager take effect only when you print a PDF document. To open the Ink Manager, click the Ink Manager tool in the Print Production panel; the Ink Manager dialog box shown in Figure 29.6 opens.

## FIGURE 29.6

The Ink Manager enables you to change ink densities and convert color spaces.

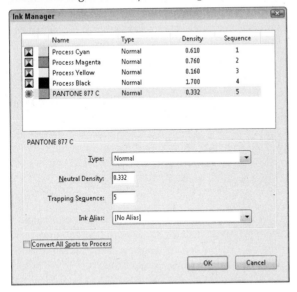

## Note

If you use the Ink Manager from inside the Color Convert dialog box, your choices can be made permanent. ■

You change density values and the trapping sequence by editing the field box. To alias spot colors, select a spot color and map the color to the same angle and density as a process color. One of the great settings in this dialog box is the check box for Converting All Spots to Process. If you have one or more colors defined as spot colors, you can convert the spot color to process color by checking the box and clicking OK. Another advantage you have with the Ink Manager is when you need to remap one spot color value to another. If you have two colors that are supposed to be printed with the same spot values (such as Pantone 185 CVC and Pantone 185 CV), you can map the color so both color names are printed on the same plate.

## Tip

You can interact with the Ink Manager directly from the Advanced Print Setup dialog box. If printing color separations from Acrobat, you can verify colors at the final stage of printing to be certain your colors are converted, remapped, or preserved by clicking the Ink Manager button in the Advanced Print Setup dialog box. ■

# Using Transparency Flattener Preview

Transparency creates problems when printing to various PostScript devices because the PostScript RIPs don't support transparency. For resolving printing problems with transparency, you need to flatten the transparency, which results in files that print success-fully on any kind of PostScript device. When transparency is flattened in a file the transparent vector objects are converted to nontransparent objects or raster images. Through this conversion, the colors meld together to form a simulated view of transparency. The amount of blending that transparent colors need depends on the amount of transparency you apply to the objects. As you move the Raster/Vector Balance slider to the left to flatten transparency, all vector objects are rasterized. When you move the slider to the right, the transparency flattener maintains as many vector objects as needed in order to successfully print the file.

You can flatten transparency in degrees, and objects in a document are affected according to the degree of transparency flattening you apply. Determining how the other objects are affected is the purpose of the transparency flattener in Acrobat.

When you use the Transparency Flattening tool in the Print Production panel, the transparency changes that you make to the PDF are preserved when you save the file. To open the Flattener Preview dialog box, click the Flattener Preview tool in the Print Production panel; the options appear as shown in Figure 29.7.

## FIGURE 29.7

When the Flattener Preview dialog box opens, click Refresh to see a preview of the document page.

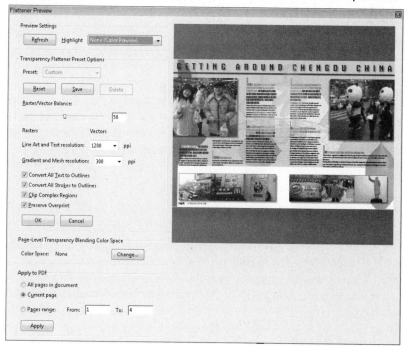

Previews are displayed only for PostScript printing devices. Be certain you have a PostScript printer selected in your Print Setup dialog box before previewing transparency. Beginning with the Highlight pull-down menu you have options for the following:

- **Refresh/Highlight.** Click Refresh when you make attribute changes to see a preview of the results. The Highlight pull-down menu offers selections for areas in the PDF file you can preview.

- **Transparency Flattener Presets.** Select a preset from the pull-down menu. Your options are Low, Medium, and High Resolution. You can reset the preset, save a preset that is added to the menu, and delete a preset after you saved one to the menu.

- **Raster/Vector Balance.** Move the slider left to add more transparency flattening. Click the Refresh button each time you make readjustment of the amount of flattening to see a preview of the results.

- **Line Art and Text Resolution.** Use the text box to edit resolution for line art.

- **Gradient and Mesh resolution.** Change values in the field box to edit the resolution you want to apply to gradients and gradient meshes.

- **Convert All Text to Outlines.** If you intend to convert text to outlines, you can see a preview for how text objects are affected in complex regions. When printing a file, you'll want to avoid globally converting text to outlines because the files are more difficult to print, and small text on output devices that print at lower resolutions may appear unsatisfactory.

- **Convert All Strokes to Outlines.** Converts all strokes to outlines. Just as is the case with text converted to outlines, the files will take longer to print if you convert strokes to outlines.

- **Clip Complex Regions.** The boundaries between vector objects and raster objects change as you move the slider. Some objects remain in vector form according to the degree of rasterization you apply. This option ensures the boundaries between the vector and raster objects fall within clipping paths, preventing artifacts appearing outside the path boundaries. As with any illustration artwork, the more clipping paths used in a file, the more difficult the printing.

- **Preserve Overprint.** Preserves all overprints assigned in the document.

- **Color Space.** Click the Change button to change the transparency blending space to a profile you can choose from the Color Space drop-down menu in the Change Page-Level Transparency Blending Space dialog box.

- **Page Range.** Apply the settings to all pages or select a page range.

- **Apply to PDF.** After making your choices from the various options, click the Apply button. You can save the PDF document and all the transparency flattening is saved with the document.

# Trapping Files

You can trap PDF files for commercial printing by applying trap presets from a selection installed as defaults or from custom trap presets you create in Acrobat. The Trap Presets dialog box provides you options for creating custom trap presets, editing a custom preset, assigning presets, and deleting custom presets. Although Acrobat provides you with trapping options, creative professionals should leave the trapping of your files to professional technicians at imaging centers. Unless you completely understand trapping, you can run into trouble by manually trapping your files. Imaging centers either use expensive custom trapping software or In-RIP trapping — both of which are much preferred over what Acrobat provides you with the trapping options.

## Tip

If you have a file that uses Overprinting but not transparency, and you want to ensure that it always prints correctly regardless of the whether the output device is overprint aware, you can flatten the overprinting via the transparency flattener. Just make sure Preserve Overprints is off. ■

## Fixing hairlines

You may need to fix hairline rules. Click the Fix Hairlines tool in the Print Production panel to open the Fix Hairlines dialog box. You can thicken up any line that falls below a specified value to a new value you supply in a field box.

To fix hairlines, click the Fix Hairlines tool in the Print Production panel. The Fix Hairlines dialog box opens, as shown in Figure 29.8. In this dialog box, you specify the amounts for hairline fixes.

**FIGURE 29.8**

Click the Fix Hairlines tool in the Print Production panel to open the Fix Hairlines dialog box.

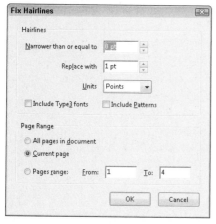

## Creating trap presets

Make adjustments as needed in the Fix Hairlines dialog box, and then click the Trap Presets tool to open the Trap Presets dialog box shown in Figure 29.9.

Click the Trap Presets tool to open the Trap Presets dialog box.

The first dialog box that opens enables you to select an existing preset or create a new one. Click the Create button to open the New Trap Preset dialog box as shown in Figure 29.10. In order to make adjustments in the dialog box you should be familiar with trapping and the acceptable amounts to apply for trap widths, miter adjustments, and attributes assigned to images and thresholds. If you know how to trap a file, you'll know what settings to apply. If you don't know anything about trapping, it's best to leave the job to your commercial printer.

Set the attributes for the trap preset in the New Trap Preset dialog box.

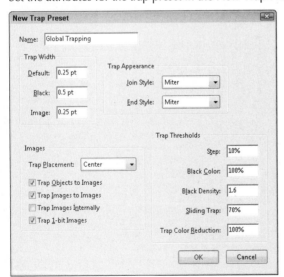

Click OK after providing a name for the new preset and making the adjustments. You are then returned to the Trap Presets dialog box where your new preset is listed in the window. Click the Assign button to apply the trap values to the document.

# Cropping Pages

Two tools appear in the Print Production panel for cropping pages in Acrobat. Ideally, you'll want to export to PDF from an authoring program with crop marks at the time you convert to PDF. Acrobat won't retain any bleeds in your document. If you don't have bleeds, these tools can help you set up the proper page size and add crop marks. A document such as a Microsoft Word file that needs to go to press is an ideal candidate for these tools because you won't find bleeds in Word files.

## Adding printer marks

When cropping pages, you'll typically add crop and other printer's marks to the cropped page so you'll know the correct trim size.

## Cropping pages

When cropping pages, the thing to remember is to first use the Add Printer Marks tool, and then use the Crop Pages tool in the Print Production panel. When you click the Crop Pages tool, the Crop Pages dialog box opens, where you set the page size, select the range of pages you want to crop, and view a preview before you exit the dialog box.

After adding crop marks, click OK; the printer marks appear on the page.

# Using PDF Optimizer

PDF Optimizer is accessed in the Save As menu (as described in Chapter 17); you can choose File ⇨ Save As ⇨ Advanced PDF Optimization. In Acrobat X, the PDF Optimizer has been removed from the Print Production tools.

A number of options appear in several panes in the PDF Optimizer for deleting nonessential data from files, changing PDF compatibility, and optimizing the file for smaller file sizes.

### Cross-Reference
For a description of PDF Optimizer as well as the available options, see Chapter 17. ∎

# Working with Job Definition Files

You use a Job Definition File (JDF) in production workflows to include information necessary for a production process and information related to the PDF creation.

You assign the information in a JDF file through a collection of dialog boxes that begins with your clicking on the JDF Job Definitions tool at the far-right side of the Print Production panel. Clicking the tool opens the JDF Job Definitions dialog box, as shown in Figure 29.11.

Click the JDF Job Definitions tool to open the JDF Job Definitions dialog box.

Click the New button to open the Create New Job Definition dialog box. You make choices for creating a new definition, using the open document's structure, or applying a definition from another file saved to your hard drive. If you create a new definition, you need to supply a name in the Name field box and click OK; the Edit JDF Job Definition dialog box opens, as shown in Figure 29.12.

In the default General tab you can define some production information and binding settings, preflight information, PDF conversion settings, and Job ID information. Click the Customer Info tab to add contact and identifying information.

The entire process for creating and using JDF files is extensive and beyond the scope of this chapter. For more information about JDF, see the Help document installed with Acrobat.

**FIGURE 29.12**

Create a new JDF Definition and the Edit JDF Definition dialog box opens.

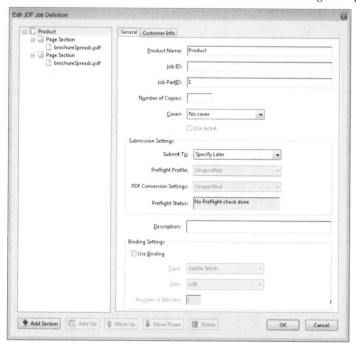

# Preflighting PDF Files

*Preflighting* is a term creative professionals and service technicians use to refer to analyzing a file for suitability for printing. A preflight assessment might examine a file for the proper color mode of images, whether images are compressed, whether fonts are either embedded or accessible to the operating system, or any number of other conditions that might interfere with successfully printing a job.

Preflight offers some impressive features such as the ability to create new Adobe PDF layers, additional presets for online publishing, and more PDF standards support.

I saved mentioning the Preflight tool in the Print Production panel for last because preflighting PDF files is a bit complicated and complex. In addition to clicking the Preflight tool, you can also press Shift+Ctrl/⌘+X. Any one of these actions opens the Preflight dialog box shown in Figure 29.13.

FIGURE 29.13

To open the Preflight dialog box, click the Preflight tool in the Print Production panel or press Shift+ Ctrl/⌘+X.

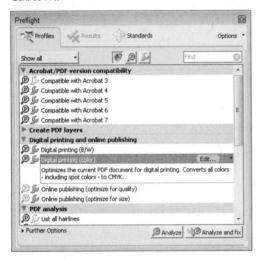

The tools used to preflight files might be stand-alone applications or features built into programs used for printing to commercial printing equipment. Prior to Acrobat 6 you needed to preflight a file before converting to PDF with a stand-alone product that analyzed the original authoring application file prior to conversion to PDF, or a third-party plug-in for Acrobat that performed preflighting on PDF files. Preflighting PDFs from within Acrobat was introduced in Acrobat 6 and has been polished and greatly improved in Acrobat 9.

As a matter of fact, there's so much to Preflight and the various options you can use, covering all features would take about half the size of this book to thoroughly explain all features. I cover some of the more important and impressive features here in this chapter. For more information on Preflighting files and complete coverage of all the options available to you, consult the complete Acrobat Help file.

## Preflighting a file

Acrobat requires you to have a file open in the document pane in order to run a preflight check unless you use a Custom Action or droplet. To preflight a document, be certain a file is open and click the Preflight tool in the Print Production panel. The Preflight dialog box shown in Figure 29.13 opens. In the scrollable and resizable window, you see a number of preinstalled profiles listed with a description for the kind of preflighting each profile performs. Use the scroll bar on the right side of the window to display additional profiles, and open and close the various disclosure triangles. If the number of items gets too many, try using the Show and search/filter options.

The Options menu contains a number of menu choices for editing profiles, importing and exporting profiles, and creating profile reports.

If a profile exists containing the conditions you want to check, select a profile and click the Analyze button. After analyzing a file, a summary report appears in the Results tab in the Preflight window as shown in Figure 29.14. Any errors in the file are reported in the summary. The summary report is listed in a hierarchy with subnotations listed under parent categories. Click the icon to the left of each category to expand the list.

FIGURE 29.14

After analyzing a file, a summary report is shown in the Results tab in the Preflight window.

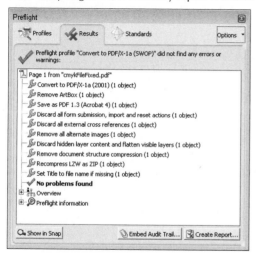

If you see errors reported after preflighting a file, you need to fix the problems either in Acrobat using Preflight's FixUps, the Print Production tools, or back in the original authoring program, and re-create the PDF file.

## Creating a new profile

If none of the preset profiles do the job of file checking for your workflow, you can create your own custom profiles. Acrobat offers you more than 400 different conditions that you can use in preflighting files. Click the Options down-pointing arrow in the Preflight window and you'll find a list of commands that relate to creating and editing profiles, as well as other commands for examining the internal structure of a PDF document as shown in Figure 29.15.

To create a new profile, choose Options ➪ Create New Preflight Profile. The Preflight: Edit Profile dialog box opens, as shown in Figure 29.16.

### FIGURE 29.15

Open the Options menu and you find all the commands you need for creating, editing, and modifying pprofiles.

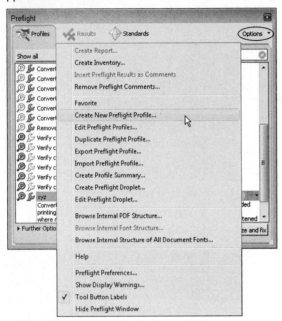

### FIGURE 29.16

Choose Options ⇨ Create New Preflight Profile to open the Preflight: Edit Profile dialog box.

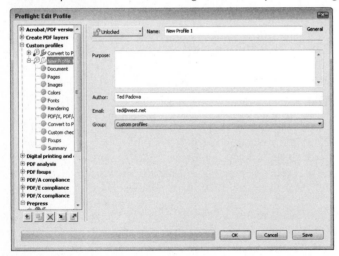

Along the left side of the dialog box you find the list of installed profiles. These profiles are listed in hierarchical order. To expand a category, click the Plus (+) symbol. To the top right of the list you find a pull-down menu. The default choice when creating a new profile is Unlocked as shown in Figure 29.16. If you attempt to edit an existing profile, the profile will be locked and you'll need to open the menu and choose Unlocked before you can make any edits.

The Name text box is where you add a name for your profile. Below the Name text box you find the Purpose text box where a description can be added to define the profile's purpose. Following the Purpose description you find an Author field, Email field, and a menu for targeting a group location for saving the file. At the bottom of the list, several tools appear for creating and managing profiles.

From left to right, the tools are as follows:

- **Create a new profile.** Click the icon to create a new profile. This tool might be used when reviewing another profile. When you open the Create New Profile menu command and arrive at the dialog box, clicking this tool does nothing. If you are on another pane and click the tool, the Preflight: Edit Profile dialog box opens as shown in Figure 29.16.

- **Duplicate the selected profile.** Click the icon to duplicate a selected profile. Once it's duplicated, you can edit the profile to change conditions.

- **Delete the selected profile.** Select a profile and click the icon to remove the profile from the list window. You cannot delete the profile if Locked is selected in the Preflight: Edit Profile pane.

- **Import.** Click the Import tool to import a profile created by a vendor or a user in your workgroup.

- **Export.** If you are responsible for creating profiles at a service center or in a company where you want to implement a set of standards, click the Export button. The profile selected when you click this button is exported to a file that you can send to other users who in turn import the profile.

To create a new custom profile, you should be at the screen shown in Figure 29.16 — that is, you should have chosen Options ⇨ Create New Profile. Type a name in the Name text box. From here, it's a matter of selecting items in the list on the left side of the dialog box and editing the changes appearing in the right pane. For example, I started a new profile by clicking Document in the left pane. I then opened the pull-down menu for the first choice and chose an icon to present a flag for the summary report. Below the icon choice (the X you see in Figure 29.17), I chose Acrobat 5 compatibility. My next choice was an icon for encryption followed by a choice for flagging the report when a PDF document is damaged. These choices are clearly shown in Figure 29.17.

FIGURE 29.17

Click an item in the left pane, and the right pane changes to reflect options you choose for the selected item.

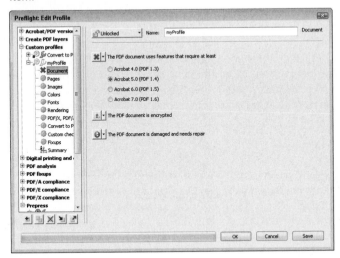

The rest of your new profile creation follows the same steps. You find the categories in the left pane, select a given category, and choose from menu items the options you want to include in the profile for preflighting the document.

After you create a new custom profile, click the Save button to save the new profile to your list of profiles.

## Generating reports and comments

After you create a profile, open a PDF document and open the Preflight dialog box. Choose the profile from the list and click the Analyze button as I described earlier in the section "Preflighting a file." A summary report then appears directly in the Preflight dialog box. This summary is an initial description of any errors found or a list of checked items and a statement confirming the file meets the conditions specified by the profile.

For a more informative document, you can create a report that lists the text summary and highlights on all pages in the document where errors are found. Click the Create Report button in the Preflight dialog box after analyzing a document to create a new PDF file as a report summary. When you open the PDF, you'll see the first page listing the summarized comments for errors found, and on each subsequent page you'll find highlights marking each area where an error was found, as shown in Figure 29.18.

FIGURE 29.18

Each page contains highlights of any errors found after preflighting a document and creating a summary report.

## Making droplets

A great feature added in Acrobat 8 was the preflight droplets. A droplet is an executable file created from the Preflight options where you can drag and drop PDF documents to preflight them. To create a droplet, follow these steps.

### STEPS: Creating a Droplet

1. **Open the Preflight dialog box.** If you don't have a PDF document open in the document pane, you can open the Preflight dialog box by choosing Advanced ➪ Preflight. You can also use the same command when a document is open.

2. **Set up the droplet.** Choose the profile you created or select an existing profile and choose Options ➪ Create Profile Droplet. The Preflight: Droplet Setup dialog box opens as shown in Figure 29.19.

   In the Preflight: Droplet Setup dialog box make choices for the location where you want the successful files saved, the files with errors saved, and the reports you want to create. You can toggle through this dialog box and get a good idea for how to identify locations and make choices for reports.

3. **Save the settings.** Click the Save button to open the Save droplet as dialog box. Locate a target folder and supply a name for your file. Click Save to save the droplet.

**FIGURE 29.19**

Make choices for saved file locations and report settings in the Preflight: Droplet Setup dialog box.

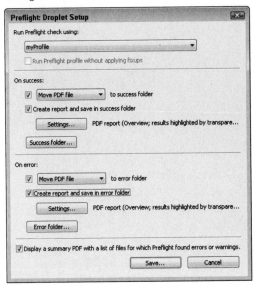

4. **Run a preflight.** Open the folder where you saved the preflight droplet and drag a PDF document or multiple PDF documents on top of the droplet icon. A Preflight dialog box opens and a progress bar shows the preflight progress.

5. **Examine the report.** After the preflight progress has completed, a preflight summary report opens as a PDF Portfolio.

## Cross-Reference

For more information on viewing files in PDF Portfolios, see Chapter 11. ∎

# Examining PDF structure

Another option you have available with the Preflight tool is examining PDF structure. You have a few choices in the Options menu in the Preflight dialog box. Open a file and open the Preflight dialog box from the Print Production panel. From the Options menu, choose Browse Internal Structure of All Document Fonts. The Preflight: Browse Internal Structure of All Document Fonts dialog box opens as shown in Figure 29.20.

**FIGURE 29.20**

Choose Options ➪ Browse Internal Structure of All Document Fonts.

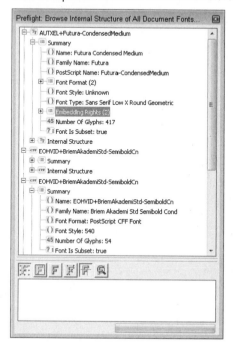

The report shows all document fonts and a detail of the font attributes. You can check this report for font embedding, subsetting, name, family, and a host of related font information.

Close the dialog box to return to the Preflight dialog box. Open the Options menu again and choose Browse Internal PDF Structure. A report is shown in the Preflight: Browse Internal PDF Structure dialog box as shown in Figure 29.21.

Here you'll find a report on the structure of the PDF in terms of page size, art, media, trim, and crop boundaries, rotations, and various content information.

## Creating an inventory

Another report you can generate using the Preflight tool is an inventory of PDF internal data and metadata. Quite simply you create the inventory report by opening a document and opening the Preflight dialog box. From the Options menu choose Create Inventory. Acrobat displays a progress bar as the report is generated. When finished, you see a report saved as a PDF file like the report shown in Figure 29.22.

**FIGURE 29.21**

Choose Options ⇨ Browse Internal Structure to display a report on the PDF structure.

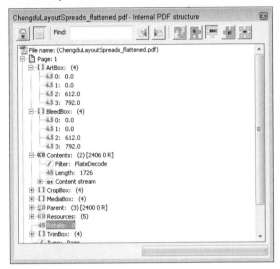

**FIGURE 29.22**

Choose Options ⇨ Create Inventory to create a PDF report of document information and metadata.

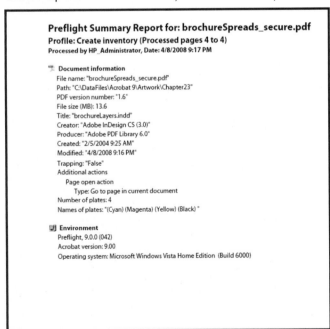

The Create Inventory command can be applied to a PDF document that has been secured with Acrobat Security. Therefore, if you don't find access to all the metadata in a file, use this feature to create a summary report.

## Cross-Reference

For more information about metadata, see Chapter 6. ■

# Checking and Fixing Up Files

Acrobat provides many options for checking files and fixing them up. You can use profiles you create for your own use and you can use profiles sent to you by service centers. But the tools you have available in Acrobat offer you an abundance of opportunity to analyze and repair files for various output sources.

In the Preflight dialog box you find settings under the Digital Printing and online publishing area. You also have PDF/X options in the Preflight dialog box to make PDF files compliant with PDF/X standards. For digital printing checks and fix-ups, look at Figure 29.23. Click this item and at the bottom of the Preflight dialog box and click the Analyze and Fix button.

---

**FIGURE 29.23**

For analyzing and fixing files to be printed on digital printing devices, make the choice in the Preflight dialog box and click Analyze and Fix.

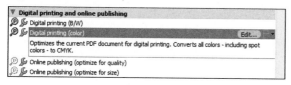

Acrobat opens another window in the Preflight dialog box that shows a progress bar as items are analyzed and it makes its best effort to fix the problems. Wait until the progress bar, shown in Figure 29.24, has finished before proceeding. As items are analyzed they are listed in the dialog box.

When Acrobat completes the analysis a report appears in the Preflight dialog box as shown in Figure 29.25. Items essential to printing the file that cannot be fixed need to be addressed back in the original authoring program. For non-essential errors and a complete fix of issues that might impair printing, Acrobat can make many files print ready.

FIGURE 29.24

Wait for the progress bar to finish.

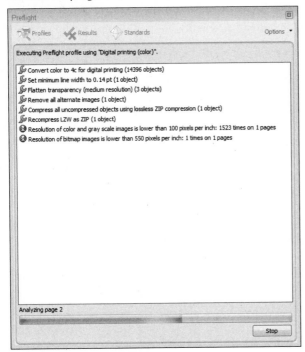

# Preparing PDFs for Commercial Printing

Acrobat Pro contains all the print controls you need for printing files to commercial devices. To access the options, choose File ⇨ Print. In the Print dialog box, click the Advanced button.

When you select Advanced in the Print dialog box in Acrobat Pro, the Advanced Print Setup dialog box shown in Figure 29.26 opens. There are four categories in the left pane. When you select a category, the right pane changes, just as the Preferences dialog box changes when you select a category.

## Note

You must have a PostScript printer selected in the Print dialog box in order to see all the options in the left pane. If the Adobe PDF Print Engine is detected, Acrobat will send the PDF directly to the printing device. ∎

## FIGURE 29.25

A report is created to show you any errors in the file.

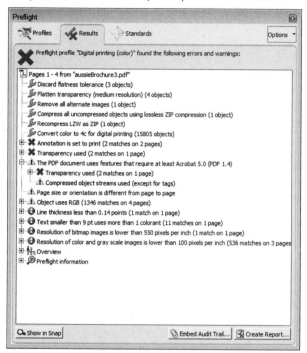

## Using Output

Output options enable you to set the color and frequency controls for the output. At the top of the dialog box a check box is available for printing the document as an image. For desktop printing when you have trouble printing the file, you can use the Print As Image option as a last resort. Print As Image rasterizes the PDF document, and type usually looks poor on the final output. Don't enable the check box for professional printing. This option is also available in the Advanced Print options for Adobe Reader and Acrobat Standard. The remaining items are used for commercial printing and include the following:

- **Color.** Select from composite or separations. Users with PostScript 3 RIPs can choose either Separations or In-Rip Separations depending on how you set up your RIP defaults. For creative professionals printing separation proofs to desktop printers, select Separations. For composite color, select Composite from the pull-down menu. For printing RC Paper or composite images to film, select Composite Gray.

## FIGURE 29.26

Click the Advanced button in the Print dialog box to open the Advanced Print Setup dialog box.

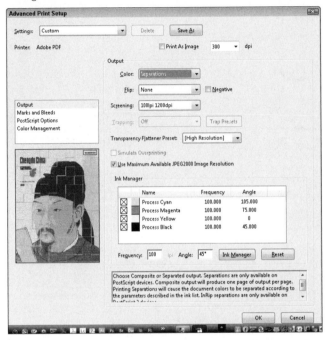

## Note

If Separations is not available, you don't have a PostScript printer capable of printing separations selected for your printer. If you don't see separations active, cancel out of the dialog box, select the Adobe PDF printer in the Print dialog box, and then click Advanced to return to the Advanced Print Settings. ■

- **Color Profile.** Select from the pull-down menu items the color profile used in your workflow.

- **Flip.** For emulsion control, select horizontal from the Flip pull-down menu to print with emulsion down. You have options for flip vertical and flip vertical & horizontal.

## Note

Adobe's print controls in Acrobat Pro are almost perfect. However, one limitation still exists in Acrobat X. There is no emulsion control for composite printing. Emulsion control is available only when printing separations. Therefore, service centers needing to print emulsion-down composites on LexJet, Mylar, transwhite, and other substrates on large-format inkjet printers need to flip files prior to PDF creation or by using the rotation tools in Acrobat. ■

- **Screening.** If you're using the Adobe PDF printer as the printer driver, the screening options won't match the device where you print your job. If you're using a device printer, the screening options for the device are derived from the PPD (PostScript Printer Description). If the frequency is not available from the pull-down menu, you select custom screens and angles from the Ink Manager (discussed later in this list).

- **Trapping.** If trapping is assigned to the document, you can turn trapping on and load a trap preset.

- **Transparency Flattener Preset.** Default and custom presets appear in the pull-down menu. Select a preset if you want to flatten transparency at print time.

- **Simulate Overprinting.** This option, also available for composite, prints only the print results in a proof, showing the results of overprints assigned in the document. This feature emulates the overprinting previews of high-end color proofers, such as what was introduced with the Imation Rainbow printer.

- **Use Maximum Available JPEG2000 Image Resolution.** When the check box is enabled, the maximum usable resolution contained in JPEG2000 images is used.

- **Frequency/Angle.** To edit the frequency and angle for each plate, type the desired values in the text boxes. Click each color and edit the Frequency and Angle text boxes.

- **Ink Manager.** Click the Ink Manager button, and the Ink Manager dialog box opens, providing options the same as those available when you click the Ink Manager tool in the Print Production panel. If spot colors are contained in the file, you can convert spot or RGB to CMYK color by selecting the Convert All Spots to Process check box. The spot color converts to CMYK when you check the box. (See "Using Ink Manager" earlier in this chapter).

## Using marks and bleeds

Select Marks and Bleeds in the left pane of the Advanced Print Setup dialog box, and the right pane changes to show options for adding printer's marks. All marks added in the Advanced Print Setup dialog box apply only to the printed file. If you want to save a file with printer's marks, use the Add Printer Marks tool in the Print Production panel.

Select All to show all printer's marks. If you want individual marks, clear All Marks and select the check boxes individually below the Marks Style pull-down menu. From the pull-down menu options, you can choose Western Style or Eastern Style. Use Eastern Style for printing files in far-eastern countries.

Marks and bleeds are also available for composite proofs as well as separations.

## Looking at PostScript options

Click PostScript Options in the Advanced Print Setup dialog box, and the right pane changes to display options for PostScript attributes as shown in Figure 29.27.

**FIGURE 29.27**

Click PostScript Options and the right pane changes to reflect options for PostScript output.

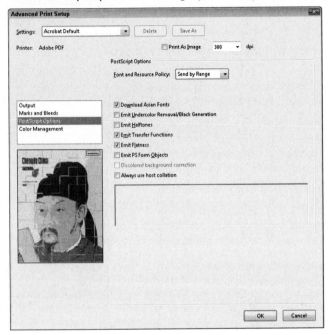

The options include the following:

- **Font and Resource Policy.** Three options are available from the pull-down menu. Select Send at Start to send all fonts to the printer as the print job starts. Select Send by Range to send fonts as they are encountered on the pages as new pages print; the fonts stay in memory until the job finishes printing. Select Send for Each page to conserve memory; the fonts are flushed after each page prints. The last selection takes more time to print but can overcome problems when you are experiencing difficulty in printing a job.

- **Print Method.** Choose from PostScript Level 2 or PostScript 3, depending on the level of PostScript used by the RIP.

- **Download Asian Fonts.** Check the box if Asian characters are in the document and not available at the RIP.

- **Convert TrueType to Type 1.** Converts TrueType to Type 1 fonts.

- **Emit CIDFontType2 as CIDFontType2 (PS version 2015 and greater).** Converts TrueType fonts to PostScript font equivalents.

- **Emit Undercolor Removal/Black Generation.** GCR/UCR removal is necessary only if the original file contained embedded settings. Clear the box to remove any embedded settings that might have been inadvertently added and saved in Photoshop. If you want to apply any embedded settings, selecting the box to Emit the settings applies them as if they were embedded in the authoring program.

- **Emit Halftones.** In the event that the PostScript file contained embedded halftones, you can preserve them here, and the frequency assigned in the Output options is used to print the file. Select the box to apply the frequency embedded in a file. You want to preserve halftones when you want an embedded halftone frequency in an image to print at a different frequency than the rest of the job.

- **Emit Transfer Functions.** Clear the box to eliminate any transfer functions that might have been embedded in Photoshop images. If you know you want images to print with embedded transfer functions you may have applied according to instructions provided from a publication house, select the box to preserve the transfer functions.

- **Emit Flatness.** If flatness was exported from files created in Adobe Photoshop with clipping paths, or if a vector art image has flatness applied, the flatness values are retained in the output.

- **Emit PS Form Objects.** PostScript XObject stores common information in a document, such as backgrounds, headers, footers, and so on. When PostScript XObjects are used, the printing is faster, but it requires more memory. To speed up the printing, select the box to emit PostScript XObjects.

- **Discolored background correction.** Corrects any problems with discoloring on backgrounds.

- **Always use host collation.** If collating is assigned in the Print dialog box, checking this box collates pages according to the settings used for the print engine.

## Using Color Management

Click Color Management in the left pane and the right pane changes to display settings for managing color. For information on options for color management and setting up color management at print time, see Chapter 28.

You can capture and save the settings you select in the Advanced Print Setup dialog box as a printing profile. Click the Save As button to open the Save Print Settings dialog box. Provide a name and click OK. You select the profiles from the pull-down menu for Settings in the top-left corner of the Advanced Print Setup dialog box.

If you create a setting and want to later delete it from the Settings pull-down menu, select the setting to delete and press the Delete button.

# Summary

In this chapter, you learned what Acrobat Pro has to offer commercial printers for outputting files on high-end printing devices.

- You can change page sizes with the Crop Pages tool. You add trim marks with the Add Printer Marks tool in the Print Production panel in Acrobat Pro.

- Both Acrobat Pro products provide several tools for soft proofing color, overprints, separation previews, and transparency flattening. Acrobat Standard and Adobe Reader do not support tools used for commercial printing.

- Traps are defined with the Trap Presets tool in Acrobat Pro.

- JDF (Job Definition Files) are defined using the JDF Job Definitions tool in Acrobat Pro.

- Preflighting files is a manner of checking a document for potential errors in printing. Acrobat Pro offers you an extended set of conditions to check files before sending them to prepress centers and print shops.

- You save PDF/X-compliant files from the Preflight dialog box. Sending PDF/X files to service centers and print shops optimizes your chances for successful output when printing to commercial printing devices.

- A set of preset profiles is installed with Acrobat Pro for preflighting jobs. You can create custom profiles by adding preset conditions in the Preflight dialog box.

- You can import and export profiles. You can acquire profiles from service centers and add them to your profile list for preflighting files.

- Acrobat provides several preflight options for examining PDF structure and content. Use the Options menu in the Preflight dialog box and choose the Browse Internal Structure and Create Inventory commands.

- Preflight droplets are executable files you create to preflight one or more PDF documents. The result is a PDF Portfolio containing a summary report of all files preflighted via a drag-and-drop function.

- The Advanced Print Setup dialog box in Acrobat Pro offers you options for color separations, printer's marks, frequency control, emulsion control, and other print attributes associated with commercial printing.

# Part VI

# Using Acrobat PDF Forms

**P**art VI is all about forms. In Chapter 30, you look at understanding PDF forms, how they are used, and using the Form Edit mode. In Chapter 31, you look at managing form data on Acrobat.com and tracking returned forms. The last chapter in this book, Chapter 32, covers using Acrobat JavaScript for adding interactive and dynamic features to PDF forms.

# Understanding Acrobat Form Tools

A dobe PDF forms can be created in Acrobat Standard (Windows) and Acrobat Pro using the form tools and many commands for creating a different kind of form. XML forms are created in Adobe Designer and Acrobat PDF forms are created in Acrobat (Standard or Pro). In some cases, an Acrobat PDF form might be preferred over an XML form. These two form types are distinctive in both the creation process and the intended use.

Before you delve into this chapter, realize that creating both Acrobat forms and Adobe LiveCycle Designer forms covers as much territory as the complete *Adobe Acrobat X PDF Bible*. As a matter of fact, I've written a book titled *PDF Forms Using Adobe Acrobat and LiveCycle Designer Bible* (Wiley Publishing 2009). That book equals the size of the *Adobe Acrobat X PDF Bible*. Therefore, all I can hope to do in this chapter is give you a brief introduction to creating PDF forms. No coverage for Adobe LiveCycle Designer appears in this book. To learn how to use LiveCycle Designer, look to the *PDF Forms Using Adobe Acrobat and LiveCycle Designer Bible*.

In this chapter, you learn how to use Form Edit Mode and create PDF forms in one of the Acrobat viewers, and find an introduction to using the different form tools. The good news is you can create PDF forms in Acrobat on either Windows or the Macintosh.

## Exploring Acrobat Forms

*Forms* in Acrobat are PDF files with data fields that appear as placeholders for user-supplied data. In Acrobat, you can use text string fields, numeric fields, check boxes, radio buttons, date fields, calculation fields, signature fields, and a variety of custom fields created with JavaScripts. The advantage of using forms in Acrobat is that doing so enables you to maintain design integrity for the appearance of a form while providing powerful control over data management. Rather than using a database manager, which may limit your ability to control fonts and graphics, Acrobat PDFs preserve all the design attributes of a document while behaving like a data manager.

## PDF Workflow

Forms are created in Acrobat or Adobe Designer. Form field data can be saved with Acrobat and also with Adobe Reader when the PDF form has been enabled with usage rights for Adobe Reader. When opening PDFs in Adobe Reader that have not been enabled with Reader Extensions, you cannot save, import, or export data. In developing PDF workflows for a company or organization, all users expected to design forms in Acrobat need to use one of the Acrobat software applications. Corporations and enterprises seeking an affordable solution for extending Adobe Reader to support forms features beyond the licensing limitations of Acrobat should look at acquiring the Adobe LiveCycle Reader Extensions ES (). For more information about LRES, log on to www.adobe.com/products/livecycle/readerextensions/. ■

## Cross-Reference

See Chapter 18 for more information on enabling PDFs for filling in and saving forms in Adobe Reader, and also for information on licensing restrictions applied to the use of enabling features in Acrobat. ■

# Recognizing the non-PDF form

The one thing to keep in mind regarding Acrobat and forms is that a form in the context of PDF is not a paper form scanned as an image and saved as PDF. Tons of these so-called forms are around offices and on the Internet. These documents may have originated as forms, but by the time you understand all of Acrobat's form creation features, you'll see that these scanned documents can hardly be called forms. Simply put, they're scanned images saved to PDF. The power of Acrobat gives you the tools to create *smart forms*. These forms can be dynamic, intuitive, and interactive, and save both you and the recipient much time in providing and gathering information.

# Developing a PDF form

PDF forms created in Acrobat usually start out as a document converted to PDF from an authoring program. Programs like Microsoft Office, Adobe InDesign, Adobe Illustrator, or one of your favorite design programs creates the layout and background for a PDF form. After the design is created in an authoring program and converted to PDF, you use tools in Acrobat to add form field objects and form field attributes.

## Cross-Reference

For information related to PDF creation from authoring programs, see the chapters in Part II. ■

## Tip

If you create a design and then add form fields in Acrobat, and then even later decide to change your design, you can edit the design back in your original authoring application. Simply save the design and open the form you created in Acrobat. Open the Pages panel, click Replace Pages, and select the modified PDF document. Replace the page, and your modified design appears without disturbing any added form fields on the original design. ■

# Filling in PDF Forms

When you receive or download a PDF form, you will encounter one of two types of forms. The so-called PDF form that was created from a scanned document or a PDF document containing no form fields is one type of form. The other type of form is the PDF document containing form fields. In all Acrobat viewers you can populate form data in either type of form.

## Using the Typewriter tool

The Typewriter tool is used to fill in a form containing no form fields. You use the Typewriter tool like a text tool is used in other authoring programs.

To use the Typewriter tool, open the Content panel and click Add or Edit Text Box. Click the page where you want to type text and an I-beam cursor appears. Type the text on a line. To adjust properties for the text you add with the Typewriter tool, click Text Box Formatting Tools in the Content panel.

The tools in the Typewriter toolbar from left to right, as shown in Figure 30.1, include the Typewriter tool, the Text Smaller tool, the Text Larger tool, Decrease Line Spacing tool, Increase Line Spacing tool, Text Color, a pull-down menu listing all your installed system fonts, and a choice for font sizes. If you want to move a text block after typing, use the Select Object tool.

**FIGURE 30.1**

Click the Typewriter tool and click a page to type text.

You have a number of options from a context menu you open using the Select Object tool on type added with the Typewriter tool. Text blocks can be aligned, centered, distributed, and sized the same as the options you find when managing field objects.

## Cross-Reference

For more information on using the context menu commands, see "Managing fields" later in this chapter. ■

## Using the Comments panel

The Typewriter tool adds annotations to your document. The text you type with the tool is not text applied to the document the same as when using other options available to you for adding text. Each line of type you add with the Typewriter tool adds the type as an annotation, and the annotations can be viewed and selected in the Comments panel. Type a few lines of text with the Typewriter tool and click Comments in the toolbar to open the Comments panel, and you see a view like the one shown in Figure 30.2.

**FIGURE 30.2**

Click Comments in the toolbar to open the Comments panel and you see a list of the entire Typewriter text added to your file.

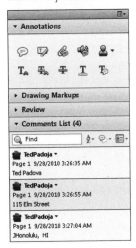

The Comments panel list of the Typewriter additions can be very handy when editing a document. If you want to delete a line of type, click the line in the Comments panel and click the Trash icon or press the Del key on your keyboard. You can also edit the type directly in the Comments panel and the changes are applied to the document page.

## Cross-Reference

For more information on annotations and using the Comments panel, see Chapter 19. ■

## Filling in forms containing form fields

As you view the form shown in Figure 30.3, notice it contains several text fields, a few combo boxes, a list box, radio buttons, check boxes, and a signature field. To fill out a text field, you need to select the Hand tool, place the cursor over the field, and click the mouse button. When you click, a blinking I-beam cursor appears, indicating that you can add text by typing on your keyboard.

**FIGURE 30.3**

A form containing many different field types: A) text fields, B) radio buttons, C) check boxes, D) combo box, E) list box, and F) signature field.

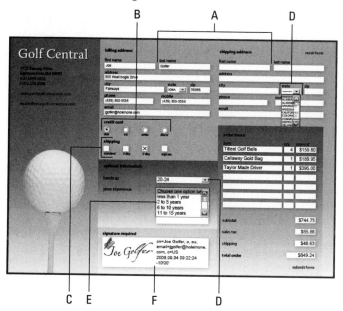

## Tip

To begin filling in a form, press the Tab key on your keyboard. When the Hand tool is selected and the cursor is not active in any field, pressing the Tab key places the cursor in the first field on the form. ∎

To navigate to the next field for more text entry, you can make one of two choices: Click in the next field or press the Tab key on your keyboard. When you press the Tab key, the cursor jumps to the next field, according to an order the PDF author specified in Acrobat when the form was designed. Be certain the Hand tool is selected and a cursor appears in a field box when you press the Tab key. If you have any other tool selected, you can tab through the fields and type data in the field boxes; however, if you click with the mouse when another tool is selected, you make edits according to the active tool.

When selecting from choices in radio button or check box fields, click in the radio button or check box. The display changes to show a small solid circle or check mark within a box or other kind of user-defined symbol from options you select for button/check box styles. When using a combo box, click the down-pointing arrow in the field and select from one of several pull-down menu choices. List boxes are scrollable fields. Scroll to the choice you want to make using the up and down arrows.

### Looking at form field navigation keystrokes

As mentioned in the preceding section, to move to the next field, you need to either click in the field or press the Tab key. Following is a list of other keystrokes that can help you move through forms to complete them:

- **Shift+Tab.** Moves to the previous field.
- **Esc.** Ends text entry.
- **Return.** Ends text entry for single line entries or adds a carriage return for multi-line fields.
- **Double-click a word in a field.** Selects the word.
- **Ctrl/⌘+A.** Selects all the text in a field.
- **Left/Right Arrow keys.** Moves the cursor one character at a time left or right.
- **Up Arrow.** Selecting options in the combo and list boxes moves up the list.
- **Down Arrow.** Selecting options in the combo and list boxes moves down the list.
- **Up/Down Arrow with combo and list boxes selected.** Moves up and down the list. When the list is collapsed, pressing the Down Arrow key opens the list.
- **Ctrl/⌘+Tab.** Accepts new entry and exits all fields. The next tab places the cursor in the first field.

## Viewing fields

You may open a form in Acrobat where the fields are not clearly visible. Creating form fields on white backgrounds for fields with no border or fill color makes a field invisible when opened in an Acrobat viewer.

If you start to fill in a form and can't see the form fields, click the Highlight Fields button on the Document message bar. All fields are highlighted with a color specified in the Forms Preferences. In Figure 30.4, the fields are white. When I click the Highlight Fields button in the top-right corner of the Document message bar, the fields are highlighted, making it easy to see where each field appears in the form.

If you don't see the Document message bar, you need to adjust a preference setting. Press Ctrl/⌘+K to open the Preferences dialog box. Click Forms in the left pane and remove the check mark where you see Always hide forms document message bar. Remove the Always hide forms document message bar check box as shown in Figure 30.5 to display the message bar in the Document pane.

## Using Auto-Complete features

While filling in a form, you can enable Acrobat to record common responses you supply in form fields. After recording responses, each time you return to similar fields, the fields are automatically filled in or a list is offered to you for selecting an option for auto-completing fields.

FIGURE 30.4

Click Highlight Fields in the Document message bar to display fields with highlights.

Document Message Bar          Highlight Fields

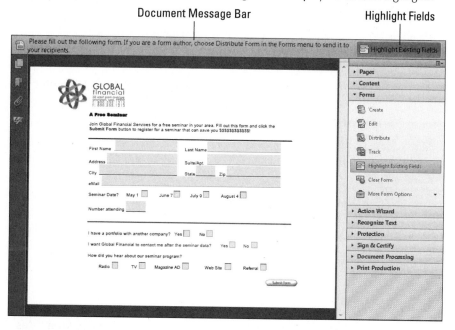

FIGURE 30.5

Remove the Always hide forms document message bar check box to display the message bar in the Document pane.

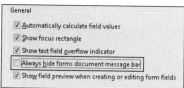

To turn the recording mechanism on, you need to address the Forms preference settings. Open the Preferences dialog box by pressing Ctrl/⌘+K and select Forms in the left pane. In the right-hand pane, open the pull-down menu under the Auto-Complete section of the Forms preferences. You can make menu choices from Off, Basic, and Advanced, as shown in Figure 30.6. Selecting Off turns the Auto-Complete feature off. Selecting Basic stores information entered in fields and uses the entries to make relevant suggestions. Select Advanced from the pull-down menu to receive suggestions from the stored list as you tab into a field. If a probability matches the list, using the Advanced option automatically fills in the field when you tab into it.

**FIGURE 30.6**

Click Forms in the Preferences dialog box and select Basic or Advanced from the Auto-Complete pull-down menu to use the auto-completion feature.

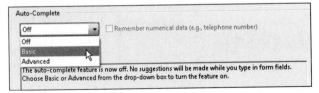

By default, numeric data are eliminated from the data stored for the suggestions. If you want to include numeric data for telephone numbers, addresses, and the like, check the Remember numerical data check box.

The list grows as you complete forms when either the Basic or Advanced choice is enabled in the pull-down menu. You can examine the list of stored entries by clicking the Edit Entry List button; the Auto-Complete Entry List dialog box opens as shown in Figure 30.7. To remove an item from the list, select it and click the Remove button. To remove all entries, click the Remove All button.

**FIGURE 30.7**

To remove entries from your suggestion list, click the Edit Entry List button in the Forms preferences. Select items in the Auto-Complete Entry List and click the Remove button.

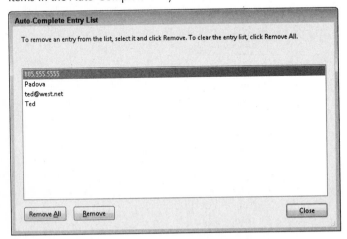

In order to record entries, you need to first make the selection for using either the Basic or Advanced Auto-Complete feature. To have suggestions for entries submitted as you type in fields, one of the two menu options needs to be enabled. When you select Off in the pull-down menu, both recording entered data and offering suggestions are turned off.

After selecting either Basic or Advanced in the Forms preferences and editing entries, fill out a form. If you recorded data after filling out one form, the next time you fill out another form you'll see suggestions, as shown in Figure 30.8. The cursor appears just below City and the suggestion (Fairways) is derived from recorded data supplied on another form.

**FIGURE 30.8**

Enter a field and a data suggestion(s) appears in a pull-down menu.

How good is the Auto-Compete feature in Acrobat? When the feature was first introduced several generations ago, it was pretty clumsy. There wasn't much sophistication in controlling what data were recorded and what data were suggested when filling in a form. After several Acrobat revisions, there remain no changes in the Auto-Fill feature. It's still quite clumsy, and you'll find sometimes it may work well for you, and in other cases you'll find turning off the Auto-Fill option less distractive when completing a form.

# Working in the Form Editing Environment

Up to this point I've covered filling in PDF forms as you might do in Adobe Reader or Adobe Acrobat. Let's shift gears now and take a look at how we create a PDF form in Acrobat — remember, the options listed here are available to you in the Acrobat commercial products including Acrobat Standard (Windows) and Acrobat Pro (Windows and Mac). If you're an Acrobat Standard user, there are no limitations you find when authoring forms in Standard. All the tools and features are identical in Acrobat Standard as they are in the Acrobat Pro products.

To enter Form Editing Mode, you begin by opening the Forms panel and clicking Start Form Wizard. This command is available to you even when you don't have a document open in the Document pane. If a document is open in the Document pane, you can also click Add or Edit Fields in the Forms panel. Choosing either command opens a PDF file in Form Editing Mode.

# Starting the Form Wizard

When you click Start Form Wizard, the Create or Edit Form Wizard opens in Acrobat. Again, you can start the Wizard with or without a file open in the Document pane. Figure 30.9 shows the Wizard as it appears on Windows (left) and the Mac (right).

The Create or Edit Form Wizard provides different options for Windows and Mac users.

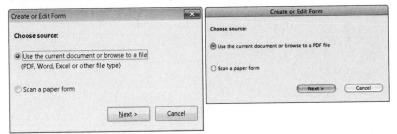

You find two options in the Wizard for creating a PDF form. Your options include:

- **An existing electronic document (Windows)/Start with a PDF document (Mac).** On Windows, you can begin with a native MS Office file, a PDF, or other file format that can be converted to PDF consistent with your viewer's support for converting documents to PDF via the File ⇨ Create ⇨ PDF From File command. Acrobat performs three functions when you choose a file format other than PDF. Your native file is first converted to PDF, and Acrobat's auto field detection operation is invoked, where Acrobat automatically recognizes fields on the form, and the form opens in Form Edit Mode.

  On the Mac, you don't have options for converting MS Office applications and several other file formats. Hence, you must begin with an existing PDF document.

- **A paper form.** Choosing this option performs several steps. Acrobat Scan is chosen where you can scan a paper document, the Recognize Text Using OCR command is invoked where the scan is converted to rich text, auto field detection is invoked, and the form opens in Form Editing Mode.

## Cross-Reference

For more information on using Acrobat Scan and the Recognize Text Using OCR command, see Chapter 16. ∎

## Cross-Reference

For more information on using Adobe LiveCycle Designer, see the PDF Forms Using Acrobat and LiveCycle Designer Bible (Wiley Publishing 2009). ∎

## Adding or editing fields

Your second choice for entering Form Editing Mode is to use the Add or Edit Fields command in the Forms panel. This option is only available when you have a PDF file open in the Document pane. You can open a PDF file without any fields, choose the Add or Edit Fields command, and Acrobat immediately assesses the document. If no form fields exist on the document, a dialog box opens asking you if you want Acrobat to detect form fields for you. If you click Yes in the dialog box, auto field detection populates the form. The form then opens in Form Editing Mode. If you click No in the dialog box, the form opens in Form Editing Mode, where you can manually edit the form by drawing field objects on the page.

## Changing modes

When you choose either the Create or the Edit command from the Forms panel, you eventually end up in the Form Editing Mode. As you can see in Figure 30.10 this mode is a completely different view as the standard Viewer mode in Acrobat in what I refer to as the Viewer mode. In this viewer interface you find several options via buttons and menus that include:

---

**FIGURE 30.10**

The Form Editing Mode displays a completely different interface than Acrobat's standard Viewer mode.

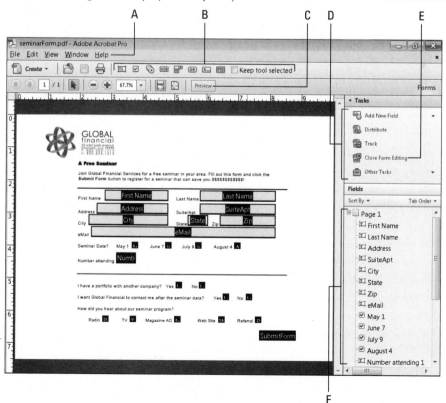

**A. Menu bar.** The same menu items are listed in the menu bar as you find in the Viewer mode. However, very few menu items can be selected when in Form Editing Mode.

**B. Form Editing Tools.** All the form tools are located in the QuickTools toolbar.

**C. Preview.** Click Preview and your form appears as a recipient will see it. In Preview you can add data to form fields, and check tab order, calculations, and other items to verify that the form field objects behave as you designed them. You still remain in Form Editing Mode when you choose this option, but the form changes from an editing view to a recipient view.

**D. Forms Tasks.** The Add New Field pull-down menu offers you all the form tools that were previously available in earlier Acrobat toolbars and also available in the QuickTools toolbar (item B above). There is no separate toolbar for form tools in Acrobat X. The only way to manually add a field is to enter the Form Editing Mode and choose a tool from this menu or expand the toolbar in the Form Editing Mode Toolbar Well.

**E. Close Form Editing.** Click this button to leave Form Editing Mode and return to Viewer mode. The only way to return to Form Editing Mode is to click Add or Edit Fields in the Forms panel.

**F. Form Fields.** The Form Editing Mode is the only place you'll find the Fields panel. You cannot access the panel in Viewer mode. To view the list of fields on a form, open the Forms panel and click Add or Edit Fields. Fields are shown listed in the Forms Fields panel.

## Editing according to mode

One thing to keep in mind is that Form Editing Mode is the place you want to use for applying fields. Most of the other kinds of editing you do with form fields can be handled in the Viewer mode. For example, if you create a text field, you first enter Form Editing Mode and create your field. Once the field is created, you can exit Form Editing Mode and make adjustments to the field properties.

Table 30.1 shows a list of the kinds of edits you can make respective to Form Editing and Viewer modes.

**TABLE 30.1**

### Form Editing According to Mode

| Editing Task | Viewer Mode | Form Editing Mode |
|---|---|---|
| Access form tools | | X |
| Copy/paste fields | X | X |
| Align/size/distribute/delete fields | X | X |

| Editing Task | Viewer Mode | Form Editing Mode |
|---|:---:|:---:|
| Place multiple fields | X | X |
| Assign actions to fields | X | X |
| Distribute form | X | X |
| Compile form data | X | |
| Show tab numbers | | X |
| Import/export form data | X | |
| Merge data into spreadsheets | X | |
| Track forms | X | X |
| Clear form data (menu command) | X | X |
| JavaScripts (Debugger, Edit All, Document, Set Document Actions) | X | X |
| Highlight fields | X | X |
| Page templates | X | |

# Creating a PDF Form

You have three means for creating an AcroForm — that is, a form created in Acrobat. You can start with a form design where fields are clearly identified with design elements such as lines and boxes, you can scan a paper form, and you can add form field objects from scratch using the form tools. For the first two options, you let Acrobat automatically add field objects through auto detecting fields that are invoked when you enter Form Editing Mode. Using the third option assumes Acrobat cannot detect any fields on a form design and you need to manually add all the field objects.

## Using auto field detection

You have a choice for how you want to open your form design. If you have an original design in a program like MS Word on Windows, you can choose to open the original Word document in Acrobat. Acrobat will convert your Word document to a PDF file, open the Form Editing Mode, and automatically detect field objects. It's all accomplished in one step, making conversion of files like MS Word, Adobe InDesign, and a host of other file formats to PDF forms a super-easy task.

Let's take a minute to see how easy it is to convert a Microsoft Office document to a PDF form by following these steps.

### STEPS: Converting a Document to a PDF Form

1. **Start the Form Wizard.** Open the Forms panel and click Create to open the Create or Edit Form Wizard shown earlier in Figure 30.9. Using this command presumes

you have a form design saved from a Microsoft Office application or other file format compatible with creating a PDF from within Acrobat (Windows).

If you're a Mac user, you need to begin with a PDF document. If you have an Office file, convert the file to PDF before using the Form Wizard.

2. **Select the file to convert.** In the Create or Edit Form Wizard click the Next button and click Browse to locate a file. Locate a file and click Next. Acrobat will convert the file, open the document in Form Editing Mode, and use auto field detection.

   Mac users can select a PDF document in the Create or Edit Form Wizard and the PDF document opens in Form Editing Mode, and auto field detection is automatically invoked.

3. **Review the Welcome to Form Editing Mode welcome dialog box.** When you enter Form Editing Mode and Acrobat automatically detects field objects, a welcome dialog box opens as shown in Figure 30.11. This dialog box offers some information about creating form field objects in Form Editing Mode. Look over the information and click OK. After you become familiar with creating forms in Acrobat, you can click the Don't show again check box to prevent the dialog box from opening in future form-editing sessions.

**FIGURE 30.11**

Look over the information in the Welcome to Form Editing dialog box and click OK.

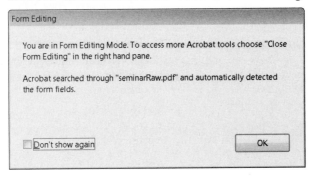

4. **Review the form.** After auto detecting fields on your form, you should always look over the form to be certain all fields were properly added. Although auto detection does a great job in adding fields to a form, it's not perfect, and you can often find a little polish is needed to finalize the form. In my example, I have a few problems on my form.

   Two extra fields were added to the form where form field objects shouldn't appear, as shown in Figure 30.12. These fields need to be deleted. The first row of boxes is check box fields that should be radio buttons designed as mutually exclusive fields. As one button is checked, the others should remain unchecked. The second row of fields is radio buttons, but they are not designed as mutually exclusive fields.

**FIGURE 30.12**

Examine the form.

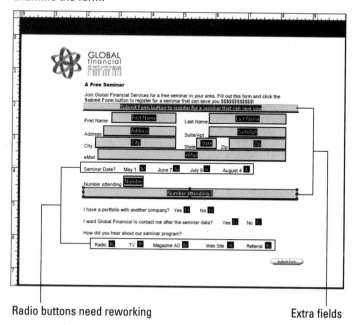

Radio buttons need reworking                    Extra fields

5. **Delete unnecessary fields.** Locate any fields that were created and not needed on your form. Click a field and press the Del or Backspace key to remove a field object. If you intend to redesign radio buttons or check boxes, delete all the buttons/check boxes in a row by dragging through the objects and pressing the Del or Backspace key.

6. **Add radio button fields.** Open the Add New Field pull-down menu and select the Radio Button tool. Move the tool to the location on the form where you want to add a radio button and click the mouse to drop the field on the page.

7. **Name the field and set the button value.** A mini properties box opens when you add a field to a page. You can type a name for the field and set a button value when adding radio buttons to a form. In Figure 30.13, I name my new radio button field seminarDate, and I set the button value to May 1.

8. **Add a new field.** Click Add another button to group and the cursor changes to a crosshair. Click or click+drag to place another button field on the page. By default, your field name remains the same. Just type another Button Value for the field. By adding buttons (or check boxes) with the same name and changing the values, you create a mutually exclusive set of radio buttons (or check boxes).

**FIGURE 30.13**

Name the field and add a button value.

9. **Preview the form.** Click Preview and add data to all your field objects. Be certain the fields are designed properly and the data you add to the form conforms properly to your form design.

10. **Save the form.** Choose File ⇨ Save As ⇨ PDF and rewrite the file. If you save periodically, rewriting the file reduces the final file size.

## Tip

While working on a form you may need to zoom in and scroll the screen to display hidden areas of your form. While in Form Editing Mode you don't have a Hand tool to scroll the window. To gain temporary access to the Hand tool, press the Spacebar and drag the screen to display hidden areas. ■

## Scanning paper forms

Converting paper forms to electronic forms is performed by first using Acrobat Scan to scan a document into a PDF file. When you open the Create or Edit Form Wizard and click the Scan a paper form radio button and then click Next, the Acrobat Scan dialog box opens as shown in Figure 30.14.

**FIGURE 30.14**

Choose the paper form option in the Create or Edit Form Wizard and the Acrobat Scan dialog box opens.

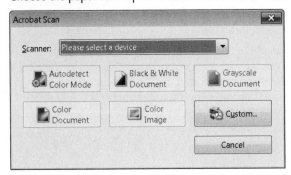

The first step in converting a paper document is to scan it using Acrobat Scan. The choices you have for scanning from within Acrobat via Acrobat Scan are all covered in Chapter 16. Look over that chapter if you want more information on scanning in Acrobat.

If you do use Acrobat Scan to convert a paper form to PDF, Acrobat automatically runs the internal OCR feature and converts the scan to rich text. From there, the file opens in Form Editing Mode and fields are automatically added via auto field detection.

You have the same issues to deal with converting a paper form to PDF as you do when converting a file to PDF in regard to the field objects. Look over the form while in Form Editing Mode and delete any unwanted fields. Be sure to double-check the form to see if all fields have been added, and check the radio buttons and check boxes for mutually exclusive fields. Like other forms you create in Acrobat, it's a good idea to check the fields in Preview mode to be certain all fields are formatted properly.

## Creating field objects manually

Forms contain different types of data fields that hold data, act as buttons that invoke actions, and call scripts to execute a series of actions. Form fields can assume different appearances as well as possess the capability to include graphic icons and images to represent hot links that invoke actions. Acrobat forms are more than a static data filing system — they can be as vivid and dynamic as your imagination.

In Acrobat, the form data fields are created by making selections from the Add New Field pull-down menu in the Forms panel in Form Editing Mode. Making a menu choice loads the cursor with a tool you use to either click the form where a field is to be placed at a default size or click and drag the cursor to create a custom size.

For an overview of the field types, look over the following list:

- **Button.** A button is usually used to invoke an action or hyperlink. A button face can be text or a graphic element created in another program that you could apply as an appearance to the button. You can also use different appearance settings in the button properties for adding stroke and fill colors. Buttons are also used to import images.

- **Check Box.** Check boxes typically appear in groups to offer the user a selection of choices. Yes and no items or a group of check boxes might be created for multiple-choice selections.

- **Combo Box.** When you view an Acrobat form, you may see a down-pointing arrow similar to the arrows appearing in panel menus. Such an arrow in a PDF form indicates the presence of a combo box. When you click the arrow, a pull-down menu opens with a list of choices. Users are limited to selecting a single choice from combo boxes. Additionally, if designed as such, users can input their own choices.

- **List Box.** A list box displays a box with scroll bars, much like windows you see in application software documents. As you scroll through a list box, you make a choice of one or more of the alternatives available by selecting items in the list.

- **Radio Button.** Radio buttons perform the same function in PDF forms as radio buttons do in dialog boxes. Usually you have two or more choices for a category. Forms are usually designed with radio buttons offering mutually exclusive choices so that when one radio button in a group is turned on, the other buttons in the group are turned off.

- **Text Field.** Text fields are boxes in which the end user types text to fill out the form. Text fields can contain alphabetical characters, numbers, or a combination of both.

- **Digital Signature.** Digital signatures can be applied to fields, PDF pages, and PDF documents. A digital signature can be used to lock out fields on a form.

- **Barcode.** The Barcode tool was not a completely new feature in Acrobat 8. Acrobat 7 supported a plug-in to create 2-D and 3-D barcodes that was shipped long after the initial release of Acrobat 7.0. With Acrobat 8.0 and above, you get the Barcode tool appearing in the Forms toolbar. This tool provides you with options for adding barcodes to a PDF form.

All these form field types and tools are available to you in Form Editing Mode from the Add New Field pull-down menu. In almost all editing sessions you'll find a need to manually add a field to a form. If using Form Field Recognition, you may add only a few form objects. If you manually create fields on a form, you'll find frequent uses for all the form tools you select from the Add New Field menu.

# Assigning Form Field Properties

Field Properties provide you with a number of options for setting field attributes for all the form field types. There are a number of common properties that all fields share such as field names, appearances, and actions choices, and there are a number of properties that are unique among the various field types.

In Acrobat X you have two different properties environments. When in Form Editing Mode you add a new field to a document, an abbreviated properties Wizard helps you identify essential properties for new fields added to a form. For all field types other than radio buttons, your properties choices are limited to typing a name for the new field. With radio buttons you have an additional choice for adding fields to a group.

When in Form Editing Mode or Viewer mode, you can open a context menu on a field and choose Properties. This choice provides you with a much more expanded version of properties choices. In the Properties dialog box, you choose options from several different panes. Depending on the field type you create, the panes in the Properties dialog box vary for different field types. Some field properties are common among several fields, while other properties are unique to each field type.

To open the Properties dialog box, click a field in Form Editing Mode or use the Select Object tool in Viewer mode and click a field. Open a context menu and choose Properties. If opening the Properties on a text field, the Text Field Properties dialog box opens, as shown in Figure 30.15.

## Tip

When creating fields in Form Editing Mode, click Show All Properties in the abbreviated properties window to open the expanded properties dialog box. ■

FIGURE 30.15

When you open the Properties dialog box on a text field, the General field properties appear as the default.

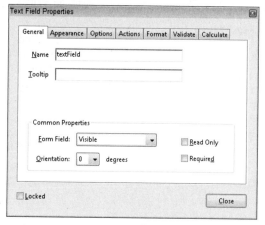

## Exploring the General properties tab

The General properties tab is the default tab where general properties are assigned. These properties are common to all field types. The properties include:

- **Name.** By default, Acrobat adds a name in the Name field. As a matter of practice you should type a descriptive name in the Name text box. Don't use names with spaces, and try to use parent/child names for fields in common groups. A parent/child name might appear as item.1, item.2, item.3, and so on; or you might have client.first, client. last, client.address, and so on.

- **Tooltip.** Type a name, and when the cursor is placed over the field in Preview mode, the text appears as a tooltip below the Hand tool cursor.

- **Form Field.** From the pull-down menu, make choices for visibility and printing. By default, the field is visible and prints when the file is printed.

- **Orientation.** A field and a field's contents can be rotated in 90-degree rotations. By default, fields are at a 0 (zero)-degree rotation. Select from 90, 180, and 270 to rotate fields in fixed rotations.

- **Read Only.** When a field is marked as Read Only, the field is not editable. The user is locked out of the field. A Read Only field might be something you use to show fixed price costs where you don't want users changing a fixed purchase price on an order form. Another example is a value that is pre-populated from a database or with fields that show results of other calculated data.

- **Required.** If a field needs to be filled in before the data is submitted, select the Required box.

- **Locked.** Locking a field prevents the field from being moved. You can still type data in the field or make a choice from options for other fields. This item is used to fix fields in position as you edit a form.

## Reviewing Appearance properties

The Appearance tab relates to form field appearances. The rectangles you draw can be assigned border colors and content fills. The text added to a field box or default text that you use for a field can be assigned different fonts, font sizes, and font colors. These options exist in the Appearance properties for all field types except barcode fields (barcode fields don't have an Appearance tab). Figure 30.16 shows the Appearance properties for a selected text field.

**FIGURE 30.16**

Click the Appearance tab for any field properties and make choices for the appearance of fields and text.

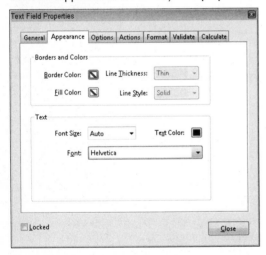

The Appearance options include the following:

- **Border Color.** The keyline created for a field is made visible with a rectangular border assigned by clicking the Border Color swatch and choosing a color.

- **Background Color.** The field box can be assigned a background color. If you want the field box displayed in a color, enable this option, click the color swatch next to it, and choose a color the same way you do for the borders. When the check box is disabled, the background appears transparent.

- **Line Thickness.** Options are the same as those available for link rectangles. Select the pull-down menu and choose from Thin, Medium, or Thick. The pull-down menu is grayed out unless you first select a Border Color.

- **Line Style.** You can choose from five style types from the pull-down menu. The Solid option shows the border as a keyline at the width specified in the Width setting. Dashed shows a dashed line; Beveled appears as a box with a beveled edge; Inset makes the field look recessed; and Underline eliminates the keyline and shows an underline for the text across the width of the field box. See Figure 30.17 for an example of these style types.

- **Font Size.** Depending on the size of the form fields you create, you may have a need to choose a different point size for the text. The default is Auto, which automatically adjusts point sizes according to the height of the field box. Choices are available for manually setting the point size for text ranges between 2 and 300 points.

**FIGURE 30.17**

Five choices for a border style are available in the Appearance tab when selecting from the Line Style pull-down menu.

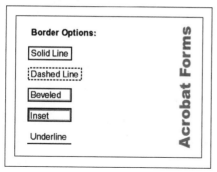

- **Text Color.** If you identify a color for text by selecting the swatch adjacent to Text Color, the field contents the end user supplies change to the selected color.

- **Font.** From the pull-down menu, select a font for the field data. All the fonts installed in your system are accessible from the pull-down menu. When designing forms for screen displays, try to use sans serif fonts for better screen views.

The Appearance settings are identical for all field types except Digital Signature fields, Radio Button fields, Check Box fields, and Barcode fields. The Radio Button and Check Box fields use fixed fonts for displaying characters in the field box. You choose what characters to use in the Options tab. When creating Radio Button and Check Box fields, you don't have a choice for Font in the Appearance properties. By default, the Adobe Pi font is used.

# Exploring the Options properties

The Options tab provides selections for specific attributes according to the type of fields you add to a page. Options are available for all fields except the Digital Signatures field. Options tab attributes for the other six field types include options for text, radio buttons, combo and list boxes, and buttons.

## Looking at text options

When you use the Text Field tool to create a field and then click the Options tab, the Properties window appears, as shown in Figure 30.18.

The Options settings in the Text Field Properties dialog box

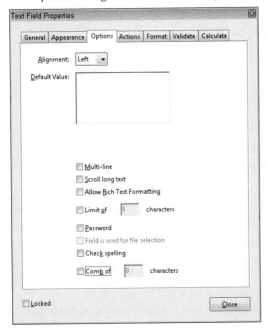

Each of the following attribute settings is optional when creating text fields:

- **Alignment.** The Alignment pull-down menu has two functions. First, any text entered in the Default field is aligned according to the option you specify from the pull-down menu choices. Alignment choices include Left, Center, and Right. Second, regardless of whether text is used in the Default field, when the end user fills out the form the cursor is positioned at the alignment selected from the pull-down menu choices. Therefore, if you select Center from the Alignment options, the text entered when filling out the form is centered within the field box.

- **Default Value.** The Default Value field can be left blank, or you can enter text that appears in the field when viewing the form. The Default item has nothing to do with the name of the field. This option is used to provide helpful information when the user fills out the form data. If no text is entered in the Default field, when you return to the form, the field appears empty. If you enter text in the Default field, the text you enter appears inside the field box and can be deleted, edited, or replaced.

- **Multi-line.** If your text field contains more than one line of text, select the Multi-line option. When you press the Return key after entering a line of text, the cursor jumps to the second line, where additional text is added to the same field. Multi-line text fields might be used, for example, as an address field to accommodate a second address line.

- **Scrolling long text.** If Multi-line is selected and text entries exceed the height of the field, you may want to add scroll bars to the field. Enable the check box to permit users to scroll lines of text. If the check box is disabled, users won't be able to scroll, but as text is added, automatic scrolling accommodates the amount of text typed in the field.

- **Allow Rich Text Formatting.** When you check this box, users can style text with bold, italic, and bold italic font styles. You may want to enable the check box if you want users to emphasize a field's contents.

- **Limit of [ ] characters.** The box for this option provides for user character limits for a given field. If you want the user to add a state value of two characters, for example, check the box and type **2** in the field box. If the user attempts to go beyond the limit, a system warning beep alerts the user that no more text can be added to the field.

- **Password.** When this option is enabled, all the text entered in the field appears as a series of asterisks when the user fills in the form. The field is not secure in the sense that you must have a given password to complete the form; it merely protects the data entry from being seen by an onlooker.

- **Field is used for file selection.** This option permits you to specify a file path as part of the field's value. The file is submitted along with the form data. Be certain to enable the Scrolling long text option described earlier in this list to enable this option.

- **Check spelling.** Spell checking is available for comments and form fields. When the check box is enabled, the field is included in a spell check. This can be helpful so the spell-checker doesn't get caught up with stopping at proper names, unique identifiers, and abbreviations that may be included in those fields.

- **Comb of [ ] characters.** When you create a text field box and enable this check box, Acrobat automatically creates a text field box with preset spacing according to the value you supply in the Characters field box. For example, if you set the value of the characters to 7, the spacing between the characters when data is added to the form spaces the characters equidistant to fit seven characters for the field size. Setting a lower value adds more space between characters, and adding higher values reduces space between characters. In Figure 30.19 you can see a comb field designed for seven characters. Be certain to disable all other check boxes. You can set the alignment of the characters by making a choice from the alignment pull-down menu, but all other check boxes need to be disabled to access the Comb of check box.

A comb field designed for seven characters

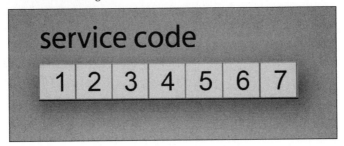

## Note
Comb fields are limited to single characters. If you need to create comb fields where two characters are contained in each subdivision, you need to create separate field boxes for each pair of characters. ■

## Tip
When you create a new form and use auto field detection, Acrobat can pick up comb fields and format them properly. Be certain to carefully design comb fields with hatch marks spaced the same height and distance in your authoring program, and you'll find Acrobat doing a good job in formatting the fields as comb fields. If hatch mark line widths, distances, or sizes vary, Acrobat won't recognize the fields as comb fields. ■

### Selecting check box and radio button options

Check boxes and radio buttons have similar Options attribute choices. When you select either field and click the Options tab, the settings common to both field types include:

- **Button/Check Box Style.** If a radio button is selected, the title is Button Style as shown in Figure 30.20. If the field is a check box, the title is listed as Check Box Style. From the pull-down menu, you select the style you want to use for the check mark inside the radio button or check box field.

- **Button/Export Value.** When creating either a check box or radio button, use the same field name for all fields in a common group where you want one radio button/ check box enabled while all the other radio buttons/check boxes are disabled. To distinguish the fields from each other, add a Button Style (radio buttons) Export Value (check boxes) that differs in each field box. You can use export values such as Yes and No or other text, or number values such as 1, 2, 3, 4, and so on.

**FIGURE 30.20**

You can choose various options for radio buttons and check boxes, including those for the style of the check marks or radio buttons.

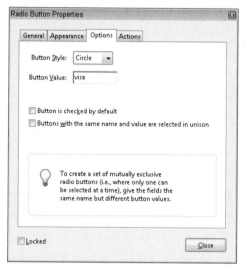

The creation of radio buttons and check boxes on Acrobat forms has been confusing to many users, and users often inappropriately create workarounds for check boxes and radio buttons to toggle them on and off. To help eliminate confusion, notice the Options properties in Figure 30.20 include a help message informing you to name fields the same name but use different export values.

- **Button/Check box is checked by default.** If you want a default value to be applied for either field type (for example, Yes), enter the export value and select the box to make the value the default. One distinction appears in the Options dialog box between radio buttons and check boxes. The second check box in the radio button properties is unique to radio buttons.

- **Buttons with the same name and value are selected in unison (applies to radio buttons only).** For data export purposes, you'll want to add a different button/ export value for each radio button and check box. If you don't need to export data to a database with unique export values for each radio button, you can add radio buttons to a page with the same export values and, by default, when a user clicks one radio button all other radio buttons are disabled. If you want all radio buttons to be selected when clicking one button in a group having the same name and export value, check this check box.

The Button/Check Box Style selection from the pull-down menu in both field types provides identical appearances. The styles are shown in Figure 30.21.

FIGURE 30.21

Six icon options are available for check boxes and radio buttons.

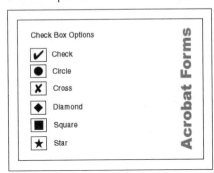

## Choosing combo box and list box options

Combo boxes enable you to create form fields with a list of selections appearing in a pull-down window. The user completing a form makes a selection from the menu items. If all items are not visible, the menu contains scroll bars made visible after selecting the down-pointing arrow to open the menu. A list box is designed as a scrollable window with an elevator bar and arrows as you see in authoring application documents, as shown in Figure 30.22.

FIGURE 30.22

View the combo box items by clicking the down arrow. After you open the menu, the scroll bars become visible. List boxes enable users to select multiple items in the scrollable window.

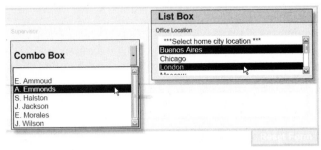

The two field types differ in several ways. First, combo boxes require less space for the form field. The combo box menu drops down from a narrow field height where the menu options are shown. List boxes require more height to make them functional to the point where at least two or three options are in view before the user attempts to scroll the window. Second, you can select only one menu option from a combo box. List boxes enable users to select multiple items. Finally, combo boxes can be designed for users to add text for a custom choice by editing any of the menu items. List boxes provide no option for users to type text in the field box, and the menu items are not editable.

The data exported with the file include the selected item from the combo boxes and all selected items for list boxes. The item choices and menu designs for the field types are created in the Options tab for the respective field type. Attributes for list boxes, shown in Figure 30.23, are also available for combo boxes.

The Options settings for list boxes have common properties also found in combo boxes.

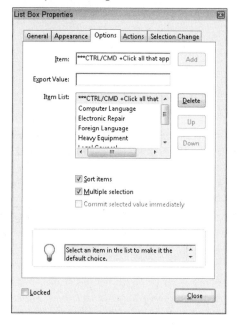

The options include:

- **Item.** You enter the name of an entry you want to appear in the scrollable list in this field.

- **Export Value.** When the data are exported, the name you enter in this field box is the exported value. If the field is left blank, the exported value is the name used in the item description typed in the Item field. If you want different export values than the name descriptions, type a value in this field box. As an example, suppose you created a consumer satisfaction survey form. In that form, the user can choose from list items such as Very Satisfied, Satisfied, and Unsatisfied, and you've specified the export values for these items to be 1, 2, and 3, respectively. When the data are analyzed, the frequency of the three items would be tabulated and defined in a legend as 1=Very Satisfied, 2=Satisfied, and 3=Unsatisfied.

- **Add.** After you enter the Item and Export Values, click the Add button to place the item in the Item List. After adding an item, you can return to the Item field and type a new item in the field box and, in turn, a new export value.

- **Item List.** As you add items, the items appear in a scrollable list window. To edit a name in the list window, delete the item, type a new name in the Item text box, and then click the Add button to add the newly edited item back in the list.

- **Delete.** If an item has been added to the list and you want to delete it, first select the item in the list. Click the Delete button to remove it from the list.

- **Up/Down.** Items are placed in the list according to the order in which they are entered. The order displayed in the list is shown in the combo box or list box when you return to the document page. If you want to reorganize items, select the item in the list and click the Up or Down button to move one level up or down, respectively. To enable the Up and Down buttons, the Sort Items option must be disabled.

- **Sort items.** When checked, the list is alphabetically sorted in ascending order. As new items are added to the list, the new fields are dynamically sorted while the option is enabled.

- **Multiple selection (List box only).** Any number of options can be selected by using modifier keys and clicking on the list items. Use Shift+click for contiguous selections and Ctrl/⌘+click for noncontiguous selections. This option applies only to list boxes.

- **Commit selected value immediately.** The choice made in the field box is saved immediately. If the check box is disabled, the choice is saved after the user exits the field by tabbing out or clicking the mouse cursor on another field or outside the field.

With the exception of the multiple selection item, the preceding options are also available for combo boxes. In addition to these options, combo boxes offer two more items that include:

- **Allow user to enter custom text.** The items listed in the Options tab are fixed in the combo box on the Acrobat form by default. If this check box is enabled, the user can create a custom value. Acrobat makes no provision for some items to be edited, and others are locked out from editing.

- **Check spelling.** Spell-checking is performed when a user types in a custom value. As text is typed, the spelling is checked.

## Selecting button options

Buttons differ from all other fields when it comes to appearance. You can create and use custom icons for button displays from PDF documents or file types compatible with Convert to PDF from File. Rather than entering data or toggling a data field, buttons typically execute an action. You might use a button to clear a form, export data, import data from a data file, or use buttons as navigation links. When you add a button to a page, the Options tab attributes change to those shown in Figure 30.24.

FIGURE 30.24

The Options tab for the Button field properties includes options for button face displays and several different mouse behaviors.

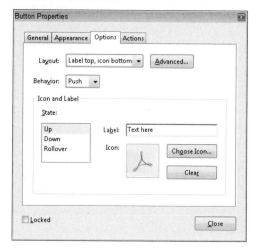

When you create a button, you make choices from the Options tab for the highlight view of the button, the behavior of the mouse cursor, and the text and icon views. The Options attributes for buttons are as follows:

- **Layout.** Several views are available for displaying a button with or without a label, which you add in the Label field described later in this list. The choices from the pull-down menu for Layout offer options for displaying a button icon with text appearing at the top, bottom, left, or right side of the icon, or over the icon. Figure 30.25 shows the different Layout options.

- **Behavior.** The Behavior options affect the appearance of the button when the button is clicked. The None option specifies no highlight when the button is clicked. Invert momentarily inverts the colors of the button when clicked. Outline displays a keyline border around the button, and Push makes the button appear to move in on Mouse Down and out on Mouse Up.

- **Icon and Label State.** Three choices are available in the list when you select Push in the Behavior pull-down menu. Up displays the highlight action when the mouse button is released. Down displays the highlight action when the mouse button is pressed. Rollover changes the icon when a second icon has been added to the rollover option. When the user moves the mouse cursor over the button without clicking, the image changes to the second icon you choose — much like a rollover effect you see on Web pages.

FIGURE 30.25

The Layout options include Label only; Icon only; Icon top, label bottom; Label top, icon bottom; Icon left, label right; Label left, icon right; and Label over icon.

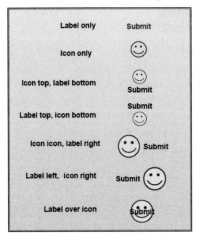

- **Label.** If you've selected a layout type that includes a label, type text in the field box for the label you want to use. Labels are shown when one of the options for the layout includes a label view with or without the icon.

- **Choose Icon.** When you use an icon for a button display, click Choose Icon to open the Select Icon dialog box. In the Select Icon dialog box, use a Browse button to open a navigation dialog box where you locate a file to select for the button face. The file can be a PDF document or a file compatible with converting to PDF from within Acrobat. The size of the file can be as small as the actual icon size or a letter-size page or larger. Acrobat automatically scales the image to fit within the form field rectangle drawn with the Button tool. When you select an icon, it is displayed as a thumbnail in the Select Icon dialog box.

## Tip

An icon library can be easily created from drawings using a font such as Zapf Dingbats or Wingdings or patterns and drawings from an illustration program. Create or place images on several pages in a layout application. Distill the file to save out as a multiple-page PDF document. When you select an icon to use for a button face, the Select Icon dialog box enables you to scroll pages in the document. You view each icon in the Sample window as a thumbnail of the currently selected page. When the desired icon is in view, click OK. The respective page is used as the icon. ■

- **Clear.** You can eliminate a selected icon by clicking the Clear button. Clear eliminates the icon without affecting any text you added in the Layout field box.

- **Advanced.** Notice the Advanced button at the top of the Options tab. Clicking the Advanced button opens the Icon Placement dialog box, where you select attributes related to scaling an icon. You can choose from icon scaling for Always, Never, Icon is

Too Big, Icon is Too Small to fit in the form field. The Scale option offers choices between Proportional and Non-proportional scaling. Click Fit to bounds to ensure the icon placement fits to the bounds of the field rectangle. Sliders provide a visual scaling reference for positioning the icon within a field rectangle.

## Choosing barcode options

Barcode fields have unique options designed to work with barcode scanners. You have options from pull-down menus and pop-up dialog boxes opened from buttons, as shown in Figure 30.26. In order to make choices for the items in the Options pane in the Barcode Field Properties dialog box, you need to know what parameters are used by your barcode scanner, fax server, or document scanner. Setting the options requires reviewing the documentation supplied by the hardware used to scan barcodes.

**FIGURE 30.26**

The Options tab for barcodes requires setting options conforming to the tools you use to scan barcodes.

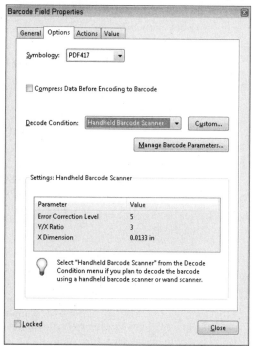

Barcodes need to calculate the data in the form in order to form the barcode. When you create barcode fields, the fields should be created with sample data on a form in order for the barcode to perform the necessary calculation to form the bar code image. You'll find at times that the barcode field isn't large enough to accommodate all data. If this occurs, you need to make the field larger or eliminate some data from the barcode.

## Cross-Reference

Managing the data is handled in the Value tab. See the section "Accessing Barcode properties" later in this chapter. ∎

# Setting Actions properties

The Actions tab enables you to set an action for any one of the eight field types; the attribute choices are identical for all fields. The same action items available for links, bookmarks, and page actions are also available to form fields. Click the Actions tab and the pane changes, as shown in Figure 30.27.

## Cross-Reference

For more information on selecting action types, see Chapter 21. ∎

From the Select Trigger pull-down menu, you make choices for different mouse behaviors that are assigned to invoke the action. From the menu options you have choices for:

- **Mouse Up.** When the user releases the mouse button, the action is invoked.
- **Mouse Down.** When the user presses the mouse button, the action is invoked.
- **Mouse Enter.** When the user moves the mouse cursor over the field, the action is invoked.
- **Mouse Exit.** When the user moves the mouse cursor away from the field, the action is invoked.
- **On Focus.** Specifies moving into the field boundaries through mouse movement or by tabbing to the field. As the cursor enters the field, the action is invoked.
- **On Blur.** Specifies moving away from the field boundaries through mouse movement or by tabbing to the field. As the cursor exits the field, the action is invoked.

Actions assigned to the cursor movements are similar to those in the context of creating links. You first select the trigger, and then select an action type from the Select Action pull-down menu. Click the Add button to add the action to the Actions list.

The action is assigned to the mouse cursor option when you click Add. The default is Mouse Up. When Mouse Up is selected, the action is invoked when the mouse button is released.

## Caution

Trigger choices other than Mouse Up may sometimes complicate filling in form fields for end users. Just about any program dealing with link buttons has adopted the Mouse Up response to invoke an action. Many users often click down, think about what they are doing, and then move the mouse away without releasing the button. This behavior enables the user to change his/her mind at the last minute. Deviating from the adopted standard might be annoying for a user. ∎

## FIGURE 30.27

Actions are available for all field types.

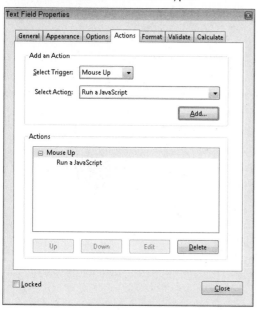

When you click the Add button, a dialog box specific to the action type you are adding opens. The actions listed in this dialog box are the same as those in the Link Properties dialog box discussed in Chapter 21. Turn back to Chapter 21 for examples of how the following action types work. A few of the more important action types used with form fields include importing form data, resetting a form, submitting a form, and showing and hiding a field.

### Importing form data

You can export the raw data from a PDF file as a Form Data File (FDF), XFDF, XML, or TXT that can later be imported into other PDF forms. To import data, you use a menu command from the list of action types (Import Form Data) or create a JavaScript. Rather than retyping the data in each form, you can import the same field data into new forms where the field names match exactly. Therefore, if a form contains field names such as First, Last, Address, City, State, and so on, all common field names from the exported data can be imported into the current form. Acrobat ignores those field names without exact matches.

## PDF Workflow

The Import Data command (in the Forms panel, select More ⇨ Manage Form Data ⇨ Import Data) enables you to develop forms for an office environment or Web server where the same data can easily be included in several documents. When designing forms, using the same field names for all common data is essential. If you import data and some fields remain blank, recheck your field names. You can edit any part of a form design or action to correct errors. ■

# Using the Acrobat Data Search

When a data file is identified for an import action, Acrobat looks to the location you specified when creating the action. Acrobat also searches other directories for the data. On the Macintosh, Acrobat looks to the Reader and Acrobat User Data directories for the data file. On Windows, Acrobat looks to the Acrobat directory, Reader directory, current directory, Windows directory, and Application Data directory. If Acrobat cannot find the data file, a dialog box opens containing a Browse button to prompt the user to locate the data file.

### Resetting a form

This action is handy for forms that need to be cleared of data and resubmitted. When the Reset a form action is invoked, data fields specified for clearing data when the field was added are cleared. When you select Reset a form and click the Add button, the Reset a Form dialog box opens. You make choices in this dialog box for what fields you want to clear. Click the Select All button and all data fields are cleared when a user clicks on the button you assign with a Reset a form action. When you use this action, it's best to associate it with Mouse Up to prevent accidental cursor movements that might clear the data and require the user to begin over again. Reset a form can also be used with a Page Action command. If you want a form to be reset every time the file is opened, the latter may be a better choice than creating a button.

## Tip

When you design a form and view the form in either Form Editing or Viewer mode, open the Forms panel and click Clear Form to reset a form. Using this command is handy if you have not yet added a Reset button to your form. ■

## Cross-Reference

For more information on using page actions, see Chapter 21. ■

### Submitting a form

Acrobat allows Form data to be emailed, submitted to Acrobat.com, or submitted to Web servers. You can design forms so users of the Adobe Reader software can submit data via email or to Web servers. When using the Submit a form action, you have access to options for the type of data format you want to submit.

## Cross-Reference

For more information on submitting form data, see Chapter 31. ■

## Looking at Format properties

The General, Appearance, and Actions tabs are available for all field types. Option attributes are available for all field types except digital signatures. The options vary significantly depending on which field type is used. For a quick glance at the tab differences according to field type, take a look at Table 30.2.

**TABLE 30.2**

## Tab Options for Field Types in the Field Properties Window

| Field Type | Appearance | Options | Actions | Format | Validate | Calculate | Selection Change | Signed | Value |
|---|---|---|---|---|---|---|---|---|---|
| Button | X | X | X | | | | | | |
| Check Box | X | X | X | | | | | | |
| Combo Box | X | X | X | X | X | X | | | |
| List Box | X | X | X | | | | X | | |
| Radio Button | X | X | X | | | | | | |
| Text | X | X | X | X | X | X | | | |
| Signature | X | | X | | | | | X | |
| Barcode | X | X | X | | | | | | X |

As shown in Table 30.2, the Format, Validate, and Calculate tab options are available only for Combo box and Text field types. To access the Format tab, select either of these field types. The Format options are the same for both field types.

When you click the Format tab, you'll find a pull-down menu for selecting a format category. To define a format, open the Select format category and choose from the menu choices the format you want to assign to the Text or Combo Box field. As each item is selected, various options pertaining to the selected category appear directly below the pull-down menu. When you select Number from the menu choices, the Number Options appear as shown in Figure 30.28.

The Select format category menu options include:

- **None.** No options are available when None is selected. Select this item if no formatting is needed for the field. An example of where None applies would be a text field where you want text data such as name, address, and so on.

- **Number.** When you select Number, the Number Options choices appear below the Select format category pull-down menu. The options for displaying numeric fields include defining the number of decimal places, indicating how the digits are separated (for example, by commas or by decimal points), and specifying any currency symbols. The Negative Number Style check boxes enable you to display negative numbers with parentheses and/or red text.

- **Percentage.** The number of decimal places you want to display for percentages is available when you select Percentage from the pull-down menu. The options are listed for number of decimal places and the separator style.

**FIGURE 30.28**

When you choose either Combo Box or Text as the field type, you can select data format options from the Format tab.

- **Date.** The date choices offer different selections for month, day, year, and time formats.

- **Time.** If you want to eliminate the date and identify only time, the Time category enables you to do so, offering choices to express time in standard and 24-hour units and a custom setting where custom formats are user-prescribed in a field box.

- **Special.** The Special category offers formatting selections for Social Security number, zip code, extended zip codes, phone numbers, and an arbitrary mask. When you select Arbitrary Mask, a field box is added where you define the mask. The acceptable values for setting up an arbitrary mask include:

  - **A.** Add *A* to the Arbitrary Mask field box, and only the alphabetical characters A–Z and a–z are acceptable for user input.

  - **X.** When you add *X* to the Arbitrary Mask field box, most printable characters from an alphanumeric character set are acceptable. ANSI values between 32–166 and 128–255 are permitted. (To learn more about what ANSI character values 32–166 and 128–255 are translated to, search the Internet for ANSI character tables. You can capture Web pages and use the tables as reference guides.)

- **O.** The letter *O* accepts all alphanumeric characters (A–Z, a–z, and 0–9).
- **9.** If you want the user to be limited to filling in numbers only, enter *9* in the Arbitrary Mask field box.
- **Custom.** Custom formatting is available by using a JavaScript. To edit the JavaScript code, click the Edit button and create a custom format script. The JavaScript Editor dialog box opens, where you type the code. As an example of using a custom JavaScript, assume that you want to add leading zeros to field numbers. You might create a JavaScript with the following code:

```
event.value = "000" + event.value;
```

The preceding code adds three leading zeros to all values supplied by the end user who completes the form field. If you want to add different characters as a suffix or prefix, enter the values you want within the quotation marks. To add a suffix, use

```
event.value = event.value + "000";
```

## Selecting Validate properties

Validate helps ensure proper information is added on the form. If a value must be within a certain minimum and maximum range, select the radio button for validating the data within the accepted values. (See Figure 30.29.) The field boxes are used to enter the minimum and maximum values. If the user attempts to enter a value outside the specified range, a warning dialog box opens, informing the user that the values entered on the form are unacceptable.

**FIGURE 30.29**

Validate is used with Combo Box and Text field types to ensure acceptable responses from user-supplied values.

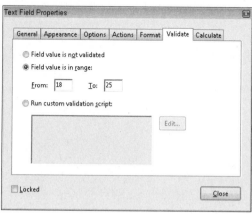

Selecting the Run custom validation script radio button and clicking the Edit button enable you to add a JavaScript. Scripts that you may want to include in this window would be those for validating comparative data fields. A password, for example, may need to be validated. If the response does not meet the condition, the user is denied access to supplying information in the field.

## Choosing Calculate properties

The Calculate tab (supported in Text and Combo fields) in the Field Properties window enables you to calculate two or more data fields. You can choose from preset calculation formulas or add a custom JavaScript for calculating fields, as shown in Figure 30.30.

The preset calculation formulas are limited to addition, multiplication, averaging, assessing the minimum in a range of fields, and assessing the maximum in a range of fields. For all other calculations you need to select the Simplified field notation or Custom calculation script radio button and click the Edit button. In the JavaScript Editor, you write JavaScripts to perform other calculations not available from the preset formulas. Simplified field notation is written in the JavaScript editor and follows syntax similar to writing formulas in spreadsheets. JavaScripts, also written in the JavaScript Editor, require you to know JavaScript as it is supported in Acrobat.

**FIGURE 30.30**

The Calculate tab offers options for calculating fields for summing data, multiplying data, and finding the average, minimum, and maximum values for selected fields. In addition, you can add custom calculations by writing JavaScripts.

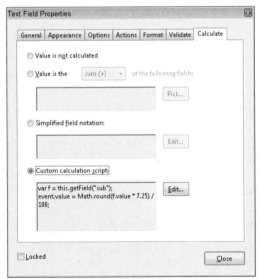

## Cross-Reference

For more information on calculating data, see Chapters 31 and 32. ■

# Employing the Selection Change properties

The Selection Change tab, shown in Figure 30.31, is available for List Box fields only. If a list box item is selected, and then a new item from the list is selected, JavaScript code can be programmed to execute an action when the change is made. As with the other dialog boxes, clicking the Edit button opens the JavaScript Editor dialog box, where you create the JavaScript code.

A variety of uses exist for the Selection Change option. You might want to create a form for consumer responses for a given product — something such as an automobile. Depending on information preceding the list box selection, some options may not be available. For example, a user specifies "four-door automobile" as one of the form choices, and then from a list, that user selects "convertible." If the manufacturer does not offer a convertible for four-door automobiles, then through use of a JavaScript in the Selection Change tab, the user is informed that this selection cannot be made based on previous information supplied in the form. The displayed warning could include information on alternative selections that the user could make.

**FIGURE 30.31**

The Selection Change tab is available only for List Box fields. When using a Selection Change option, you'll need to program JavaScript code to reflect the action when a change in selection occurs.

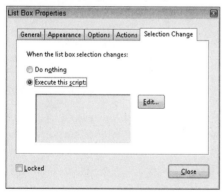

# Using the Digital Signature fields properties

The Digital Signature tool enables you to create a field used for electronically signing a document with a digital signature. The Signed tab offers options for behavior with digital signatures as follows:

- **Nothing happens when signed.** As the item description suggests, the field is signed but no action takes place upon signing.

- **Mark as read-only.** When signed, the selected fields are changed to read-only fields, locking them against further edits. You can mark all fields by selecting the radio button and choosing All fields from the pull-down menu. Choose All fields except these to isolate a few fields not marked for read-only, or select Just these fields to mark a few fields for read-only.

- **This script executes when the field is signed.** Select the radio button and click the Edit button to open the JavaScript Editor. Write a script in the JavaScript Editor that executes when the field is signed.

Digital signatures can be used to lock data fields. You can also use them to indicate approval from users or PDF authors, or you may want to display a message after a user signs a form. In Figure 30.32, a JavaScript was added to the Digital Signature Signed Properties.

The script in this example instructs a user to print the form and hand-deliver it to the accounting department. A dialog box opens after the user signs the form.

## Cross-Reference

**For setting up digital signatures and finding out more information related to signing documents, see Chapter 24. ∎**

---

**FIGURE 30.32**

For custom actions when a user signs a form, use a JavaScript.

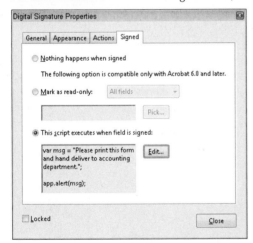

## Accessing Barcode properties

The unique property settings in the Barcode field are located in the Value tab. Options in this tab are available only with barcode fields, as shown in Figure 30.33. You have options for Encoding from a pull-down menu offering a choice between XML and Tab Delimited data.

Click the Pick button and the Field Selection dialog box opens as shown in Figure 30.34. You use this dialog box to determine what field data are added to the barcode. Uncheck those items you don't want added, such as buttons that invoke actions, temporary calculation fields, and so on. The Include field names text box offers an option to include field names along with the data in the barcode.

An additional box appears for adding a Custom calculation script. Click the radio button and click Edit to open the JavaScript Editor.

**FIGURE 30.33**

The Value tab appears only in Barcode fields.

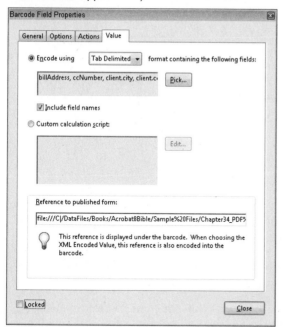

FIGURE 30.34

Click Pick and check the items you want to appear as data in the barcode.

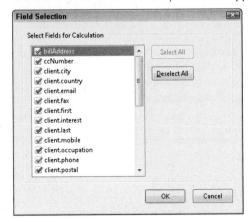

## Managing Fields

For purposes of explanation, I'll use the term *managing fields* to mean dealing with field duplication, deleting fields, and modifying field attributes. After you create a field on a PDF page, you may want to alter its size, position, or attributes. Editing form fields in Acrobat is made possible by using one of several menu commands or returning to the respective Field Properties window. This kind of editing can be performed in Form Editing Mode or Viewer mode.

### Organizing fields

To edit a form field's properties, use the Select Object tool. If you work in Form Editing Mode, the Select Object tool is the tool selection by default. Unless you choose a tool from the Add New Field menu, the only tool available to you without using a key modifier is the Select Object tool. In Viewer mode, you need to click the Select Object tool to make it the active tool. In either mode, open a context menu and choose Properties to open a field's properties. Alternately, you can also double-click a field to open the properties dialog box.

When you select multiple fields and choose Properties from the context-sensitive menu, options in the General tab, the Appearance tab, and the Actions tab are available for editing. Specific options for each different field type require that you select only common field types. For example, you can edit the appearance settings for a group of fields where the field types are different. However, to edit something like radio button field options for check mark style, you need to select only radio button fields in order to gain access to the Options tab.

## Tip

If the fields you want to select are located next to each other or you want to select many fields, use the Select Object tool and drag a marquee through the fields to be selected. When you release the mouse button, the fields inside the marquee and any fields intersected by the marquee are selected. The marquee does not need to completely surround fields for selection — just include a part of the field box within the marquee. ∎

### Renaming fields

When you create a field in Form Editing Mode, an abbreviated properties window opens where you can name a field and set field attributes as a required field — meaning the field must be filled in before the data can be submitted. If you open a context menu in either Form Editing Mode or Viewer mode, the same properties window opens offering you the same options choices as shown in Figure 30.35.

### Duplicating fields

You can duplicate a field by selecting it and holding down the Ctrl/Option key while clicking and dragging the field box. Fields can also be copied and pasted on a PDF page, between PDF pages, and between PDF documents. Select a field or multiple fields, and then choose Edit ⇨ Copy. Move to another page or open another PDF document and choose Edit ⇨ Paste. The field names and attributes are pasted together on a new page. Copying and pasting fields works well while in Form Editing or Viewer mode.

**FIGURE 30.35**

Open a context menu and choose Rename Field to open the abbreviated properties where a field name can be changed.

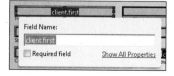

## Tip

To ensure that field names are an exact match between forms, create one form with all the fields used on other forms. Copy the fields from the original form and paste the fields in other forms requiring the same fields. By pasting the fields, you ensure all field names are identical between forms and can easily swap data between them. If you have JavaScripts at the document level, use the Document ⇨ Replace Pages command when you want to populate a form having a similar design to an original form. ∎

### Moving fields

You can relocate fields on the PDF page by using the Select Object tool and clicking and dragging the field to a new location. To constrain the angle of movement, select a field with the Select Object tool, press the Shift key, and drag the field to a new location. For precise movement, use the arrow keys to move a field box left, right, up, or down. When using the arrow keys to move a field, be certain to not use the Shift key while pressing the arrow keys because doing so resizes field boxes as opposed to moving them.

## Deleting fields

You delete fields from PDF documents in three ways. Select the field and press the Backspace key (Windows) or Delete key (Mac). You can also select the field and then choose Edit ⇨ Delete or open a context menu and choose Edit ⇨ Delete. In all cases, Acrobat removes the field without warning. If you inadvertently delete a field, you can Undo the operation by choosing Edit ⇨ Undo.

## Aligning fields

Even when you view the grids on the PDF page, aligning fields can sometimes be challenging. Acrobat simplifies field alignment by offering menu commands for aligning the field rectangles at the left, right, top, and bottom sides, as well as for specifying horizontal and vertical alignment on the PDF page. To align fields, select two or more fields and then open a context menu and select Align ⇨ Distribute Center, as shown in Figure 30.36. The alignment options for Left, Right, Top, Bottom, Horizontally, and Vertically appear in a submenu.

### FIGURE 30.36

Open a context menu using the Select Object tool on one field in a group of selected fields and choose Align from the menu.

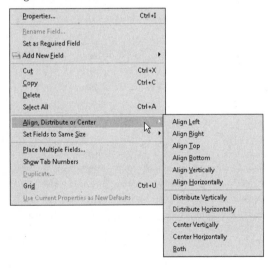

Acrobat aligns fields according to the first field selected (the anchor field appearing with a red highlight). In other words, the first field's vertical position is used to align all subsequently selected fields to the same vertical position. The same holds true for left, right, and top alignment positions. When you use the horizontal and vertical alignments, the first field selected determines the center alignment position for all subsequently selected fields. All fields are center aligned either vertically or horizontally to the anchor field.

## Tip

Fields are aligned to an anchor field when multiple fields are selected and you use the align, center, distribute, and size commands. The anchor field appears with a red border whereas the remaining selected field highlights are blue. If you want to change the anchor (the field to be used for alignment, sizing, and so on), click any other field in the selected group. Unlike other multiple object selections, you don't need to use the Shift key when selecting different fields from among a group of selected fields. All fields remain selected until you click outside the field boundaries of any selected field. ■

You can distribute fields on a PDF page by selecting multiple fields and choosing Distribute (Vertically or Horizontally) from the same submenu. Select either Horizontally or Vertically for the distribution type. The first and last fields in the group determine the beginning and ending of the field distribution. All fields within the two extremes are distributed equidistant between the first and last fields.

## Cross-Reference

For an example of how to use the Distribute commands, see "Creating multiple copies of fields" later in this chapter. ■

Center alignment is another menu command available from a context menu. When you choose Center (Vertically or Horizontally) from the same submenu shown in Figure 30.36, the selected field aligns to the horizontal or vertical center of the page. Choose Both to align a field to the center of a page. If multiple fields are selected, the alignment options take into account the relative positions of the field boxes and center the selected fields as a group while preserving their relative positions.

### Sizing fields

Field rectangles can be sized to a common physical size. Once again, the anchor field determines the size attributes for the remaining fields selected. To size fields, select multiple field boxes, and then open a context menu and choose Size Fields to Same Size and choose Width, Height, or Both from the submenu. To size field boxes individually in small increments, hold down the Ctrl/Option key and move the arrow keys. The Left and Right Arrow keys size field boxes horizontally, whereas the Up and Down arrow keys size field boxes vertically.

### Creating multiple copies of fields

To create a table array, select fields either in a single row or single column and open a context menu. From the menu options, select Place Multiple Fields. The Create Multiple Copies of Fields dialog box opens, as shown in Figure 30.37. In the Create Multiple Copies of Fields dialog box, enter a value in the field box for Copy selected fields down (for creating rows of fields) or Copy selected fields across (to create columns of fields). In Figure 30.37, I created three fields and wanted my duplicated fields to be added below the top row. Notice when you make selections in the Create Multiple Copies of Fields dialog box with the Preview check box enabled, you see a dynamic preview in the document for how the fields appear when duplicated.

## Note

**You can also create a table array by first creating a single field and then selecting options for both Copy Selected Fields down and Copy Selected Fields across. ■**

If you want to add both rows and columns, you can supply values in both field boxes for the desired number of columns and rows. The Change Width and Change Height field boxes enable you to adjust the field distance respective to each other — editing the values does not change the physical sizes of the fields. Click the Up/Down buttons for moving all fields vertically or the Left/Right buttons to move fields horizontally. When the preview box is enabled, you'll see a preview of the duplicated rows and columns before you accept the attribute choices by clicking OK.

### FIGURE 30.37

To create a table array, select a row or column of fields and open a context menu. Select Place Multiple Fields and make selections in the Create Multiple Copies of Fields dialog box for the number of rows or columns to be duplicated.

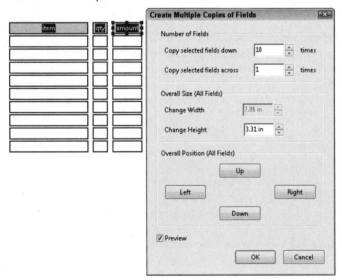

If, after you click OK, you need to polish the position of the new fields, you can move the top and bottom fields (for aligning single columns), then open a context menu and choose Align, Distribute, or Center ⇨ Vertically (or Horizontally) — depending on whether you're adjusting a row or column.

When using the Distribute command, you can distribute only single rows or columns. If you attempt to select all fields in a table and distribute several rows or columns at once, the results render an offset distribution that most likely creates an unusable alignment.

### Duplicating fields

Using the Place Multiple Fields menu command from a context menu enables you to create table arrays or individual columns or rows only on a single page. If you want to duplicate fields either on a page or through a number of pages, another menu command exists for field duplication.

You can use the Duplicate command to duplicate fields; however, in most circumstances when you want to duplicate a field, press the Ctrl/Option key and click+drag a field. The field and the properties are duplicated. If you need to change the field name, open the properties dialog box and edit the Name in the General properties.

### Setting attribute defaults

If you spend time formatting attributes for field appearances, options, and actions, you may want to assign a default attribute set for all subsequent fields created with the same form tool. After creating a field with the attributes you want, open a context menu and select Use Current Properties as New Defaults. The properties options used for the field selected, when you choose the menu command, become a new default for that field type. As you change form tools and create different fields, you can assign different defaults to different field types.

## Setting field tab orders

You have two options for setting the tab order on a form. This is one item you should address before saving your final edited form. You should be able to press the Tab key to enter the first field on a page and tab through the remaining fields in a logical order to make it easy for the end user to fill in your form. Before deploying your form, be sure to check the tab order.

The first option you have for setting Tab order is in the Pages panel. Enter Viewer mode and open the Pages panel. Open a context menu on the page where you want to set tab order. Select Properties from the menu options and the Page Properties dialog box opens, as shown in Figure 30.38. By default the Tab Order pane opens with options for setting tab order by making radio button selections.

**FIGURE 30.38**

To set tab order, open the Pages panel and open a context menu on the page where you want to edit the tab order. Select Properties from the menu choices and click Tab Order in the Page Properties dialog box.

The options for setting tab order include the following:

- **Use Row Order.** Tabs through rows from left to right. If you want to change the direction for tabbing through fields, choose File ➪ Properties. Click Advanced in the left pane and select Right Edge from the Binding pull-down menu. When you select Use Row Order and the document binding is set to Right Edge, the tab order moves from right to left.

- **Use Column Order.** Tabs through columns from left to right, or right to left if you change the binding as described in the preceding bullet.

- **Use Document Structure.** When selecting this option, you first need to use a PDF document with structure and tags. The tab order is determined by the structure tree created by the original authoring application when the file was exported to PDF.

- **Unspecified.** The default for all documents you created in earlier versions of Acrobat that you open in Acrobat 6 through 8 have the Unspecified option selected. Unless you physically change the tab order to one of the preceding options, the tab order remains true to the order set in Acrobat 5 or earlier.

The order in which you create fields and add them to a page is recorded. If you happen to create a row of fields, and then change your mind and want to add a new field in the middle of the row, Acrobat tabs to the last field in the row from the last field created. Changing the tab orders in the Page Properties won't help you fix the problem when the fields need to be reordered.

Fortunately, you do have more options for setting tab orders. The second method, and perhaps your best choice, is the Form Editing Mode for arranging fields in the proper tab order.

## Tip

You can drag and drop fields in the Fields panel to change the tab order. Click a field in the Fields panel in Form Editing Mode and drag the field up or down in the Fields panel to change the tab order. ■

If you want to see a visual order of your fields on a form, open a context menu on any field and choose Show Tab Numbers. Each field displays the tab order number in the top-left corner of the field box as shown in Figure 30.39.

**FIGURE 30.39**

Numbers on each field show you the current tab order.

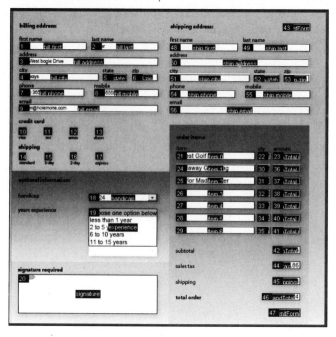

# Summary

In this chapter, you learned some of the fundamentals for creating PDF forms.

- Acrobat forms are not scanned documents converted to PDF. They are dynamic and can include interactive elements, data fields, buttons, and JavaScripts.

- Automatic form fill-in is enabled in the Preferences dialog box. Form fields can be displayed on PDF pages with a highlight color to help identify field locations.

- Data fields are created from many different field types including text, buttons, combo boxes, list boxes, signatures, check boxes, radio buttons, and barcodes.

- You set all data field attributes in the Field Properties window. Properties can be described for fields by selecting the tabs labeled Appearance, Options, Actions, Calculations, or other tabs associated with specific field types.

- Acrobat Pro and Standard have a Form Editing mode where you add field objects via a pull-down menu where the various form tools are selected.

- In Acrobat Pro and Standard, you edit forms in Form Editing Mode and fill in or check form functionality in Preview mode.

- You can edit fields with a context-sensitive menu. Acrobat has several editing commands used for aligning fields, distributing fields, and centering fields on a PDF page.

- Field duplication is handled in a context menu. You can duplicate fields on a page to create tables with the Place Multiple Fields command, or duplicate fields across multiple pages with the Duplicate command.

- The Fields panel dynamically lists all fields created in a PDF file. The panel menus and options can be of much assistance in editing field names and locating fields. The panel is in view only in Form Editing Mode.

- A form's tab order can be easily reordered by dragging fields up and down in the Fields panel.

# Working with Form Data

**A**fter you get a handle on creating form fields, as covered in Chapter 30, you'll want to know some things about managing data to help economize your efforts when working with distributed forms and performing routine calculations on data fields. When forms are completed, you have the option of printing a form, compiling form data distributed via emails or your Acrobat.com account, or sending the data off to a form server product that processes the field data. In this chapter, I cover data management from calculating field data to importing, exporting, and submitting data, and compiling data using Acrobat.com.

This chapter is targeted at users working with Adobe LiveCycle Designer as well as Acrobat. Most of what is covered in this chapter can be handled by Designer; however, if you're a Mac user or you want to do some editing in Acrobat, what follows is strictly related to working with data and form fields in Acrobat Standard or Acrobat Pro. Furthermore, the content is restricted to using Acrobat tools and commands for data management. No discussion on using server products, other than a brief explanation about additional products you can acquire, is covered in this chapter.

For Windows users, if you need to work with other data systems the best opportunity you have when working with form data is to create your form designs in Adobe LiveCycle Designer. Designer provides you with XDP, XML, and as export data format options and XDP, XML, and XFD as import format options. With Acrobat form data imports you get FDF, XFDF, XFD, TXT, and a version of XML; and export formats consisting of FDF, XFDF, XML, and TXT. Designer has much fewer import/export formats as compared to Acrobat. For more information on using

Adobe LiveCycle Designer, see *PDF Forms Using Acrobat and LiveCycle Designer Bible* (Wiley Publishing, Padova/Okamoto).

## Note

Just in case you jump to this chapter and haven't reviewed earlier chapters in this book, be aware that you have two working modes when creating/editing PDF forms. Form fields and a number of form editing tasks are handled in the Acrobat X Form Editing Mode, and other edits are performed in normal Viewer mode. When I refer to Viewer mode in this chapter, be aware that this view is the standard Acrobat editing mode you're familiar with in all viewers prior to Acrobat 9. ■

## Cross-Reference

For more information on using Form Editing Mode, see Chapter 30. ■

# Calculating Field Data

More often than not, you'll want to create forms that use some kind of calculation for data fields. Calculations might be used for summing data, calculating averages, adding complex formulas, assessing field responses, or many other conditions where results need to be placed in separate fields.

Acrobat offers you a few limited built-in functions for performing math operations. When your needs extend beyond these simple functions, you need to write JavaScripts. Some math operations, as simple as subtracting data or producing a dividend, require use of a JavaScript.

Even though I address JavaScript in some detail in the next chapter, you need to begin learning about JavaScript as it pertains to calculating data. Therefore, I'll start this chapter with some examples on using the built-in functions for calculations in Acrobat and move on, later in this section, to cover some JavaScript basics.

## Formatting for calculations

Math operations can be performed on data fields without any formatting applied to either the fields to be calculated or the result field. Although doing so is not required, as a matter of practice applying formats to all fields where calculations are made and to those fields participating in the calculation result is a good idea. As you create a PDF form, you may need to use a particular format that eventually is required either in the formula or for the text appearance in the result field. Rather than going back to the fields and changing the format, you'll save time by supplying proper formats as you create fields.

When creating text fields, open the Format tab in the Text Field Properties window and select the format you want for the field. If Number is the desired format, select Number from the pull-down menu and make choices for the number of decimal places, the display for negative numbers if it applies, and the use of a currency symbol if it applies.

## Tip

You can open the field Properties dialog box either in Form Editing Mode or Viewer mode. In Viewer mode use the Select Object tool and double-click a field object to open the Properties dialog box. ■

## Cross-Reference

For more information on using the Text Field tool, see Chapter 30. ■

Many times, once you get a field formatted, you want to replicate the attributes on subsequent fields. When you set the attributes for one field, select the field with the Select Object tool and open a context menu in either Form Editing Mode or Viewer mode. Select Use Current Properties as New Defaults. As you create additional fields, the new defaults are applied to all subsequent text fields. If you create a field that needs a different format, you can change the format for the new field without affecting the defaults.

## Tip

Although you can't create new fields while in Viewer mode using a form tool, you can duplicate a field by clicking with the Select Object tool and pressing Ctrl/Option while dragging the field. ■

## Using the preset calculation formulas

Preset math calculations include sum, product, average, minimum, and maximum. After formatting fields, select the field where you want the result to appear and click the Calculate tab in the Text Field Properties dialog box, as shown in Figure 31.1. For adding a column or row of data, select the *Value is the* radio button. The default is sum (+). Click the down-pointing arrow to open the pull-down menu to make formula choices from the list of other preset formulas.

## Note

Be certain numeric data is formatted using number format options in the Format tab of the Text Field Properties dialog box when creating form fields. ■

For summing data, leave the default as it appears and click the Pick button. The Field Selection dialog box opens, as shown in Figure 31.2. You can see the fields added to your form and grouped together. To sum a group of fields, select the check box to the left side of each field you want to add to the formula.

Click OK to leave the Field Selection dialog box and return to the Calculate properties. Click Close, and the calculation is ready. In this example, the sum of the data for the selected fields updates as the user enters data in the fields assigned to the calculation.

For performing other preset calculations, you follow the same steps. Select the formula you want to use from the pull-down menu options and select the check boxes for all fields you want to add to the calculation.

FIGURE 31.1

To add a preset calculation to a field, click the Calculate tab in the Text Field Properties dialog box. Select the calculation formula from the pull-down menu next to the "Value is the" radio button.

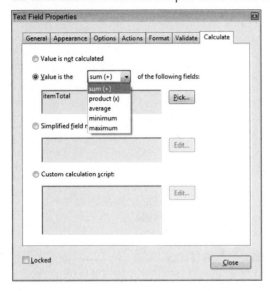

## Note

When using the Average formula, Acrobat averages all fields regardless of whether the fields used in the formula contain data. If you have three fields, but only two have values — for example, 3 and 3 — Acrobat returns a result of 2 ((3+3+0) ÷ 3=2). The preset formula doesn't take into consideration whether or not a field has data in it. To perform an average calculation where you want to average only fields containing a response, you need to write a JavaScript. ∎

### Summing data on hierarchical names

If you've read Chapter 30, you may remember that I mentioned advantages when using parent/child names for form fields. As you can see in Figure 31.2, all the fields in your form are listed in the Field Selection dialog box. If you want to sum data in large tables, clicking all the boxes in the Field Selection dialog box to select fields for columns or rows in a table can take some time. However, when you use hierarchical (or parent/child) names, the task is much easier.

In Figure 31.3, the Field Selection dialog box is open and a check mark appears next to the *itemTotal* field. Notice below this field you have a group of fields using the same parent name. The child names 0 through 6 are calculated with just the check box selection made on the parent name when summing the fields. If you write calculation scripts, your scripting is made much easier when using parent/child names.

## FIGURE 31.2

Identify the fields used for the calculation in the Field Selection dialog box by selecting the check box for each field name.

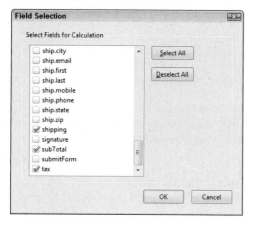

## FIGURE 31.3

If you select the Value is the Sum(+) of the following fields radio button and check a parent name in the Field Selection dialog box, all child field names are added in the calculation.

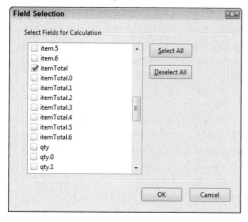

Imagine a table that contains 25 rows of data with a total field at the bottom of each column; it has 10 columns across the page. By using the parent name in the formula, you can easily create total fields at the bottom of the page by duplicating fields and editing the parent names in the Calculate properties as was described in Chapter 30.

## Using hidden fields

Complex formulas can be written in the JavaScript Editor. However, if you aren't up to speed in JavaScript programming or you want to simplify the code you write, you may want to break down a series of calculations and place results in separate fields. For example, suppose you want to calculate the result of (A – B) * C. If you don't know the code to create the calculation to first subtract two values and multiply the result by another value, you can use separate fields to hold results. In this example, you need a field to hold the result of A – B. In another calculation, you take the result field containing A – B and multiply it by C.

On the PDF form, the result of A – B is not needed for user input — it's simply a container to use as part of the larger formula. To help avoid confusion, you can hide the field. When data are contained in hidden fields, the data can still be used for calculations.

To create such a field, add a text field anywhere on a page and add the calculation in the Calculate properties. In the General properties, select Hidden from the Form Field pull-down menu. If you need to edit a hidden text field, you can do so with either the Text Field tool or the Select Object tool.

When using hidden fields, you can create calculations and access the fields in the Field Selection dialog box or use parent names in the Calculate properties as described in the preceding section.

## Cross-Reference

For more information related to hiding fields, see Chapters 21 and 30. ■

## Using simplified field notation

In addition to performing simple calculations and writing JavaScripts, the Calculate pane also offers you an option for using simplified field notation. When you select the radio button for Simplified field notation and click Edit, the JavaScript Editor dialog box opens. In the dialog box you don't write JavaScript code. The code added here is based on principles used with spreadsheet formulas.

Simplified field notation can be used in lieu of writing JavaScripts for many different math operations. As an example, suppose you want to calculate a sales tax for a subtotal field. To calculate an 8 percent sales tax with a JavaScript you would open the JavaScript Editor and type the following code:

```
1. var f = this.getField("subtotal");
2. event.value = Math.round(f.value * 8) / 100;
```

As an alternative to using JavaScript, select the Simplified field notation radio button and click the Edit button. In the JavaScript Editor, you type the following code to produce the same sales tax calculation:

```
1. subtotal * .08
```

Notice in the JavaScript code you need to identify each field used in a calculation and assign a variable to the field name. Line 1 of the preceding JavaScript code assigns the variable f to the field `subtotal`. Notice that in the Simplified Field Notation script the field name does not get assigned to a variable. You simply use all field names as they appear on the form and introduce them in your formulas.

## Caution
You cannot use hierarchical names when using simplified field notation. ∎

# Using JavaScripts

You need to write JavaScripts for all calculations that cannot be made with either the preset formulas or the simplified field notation method. If you are a novice, you'll find writing simple JavaScripts to be a relatively easy task if you understand a few basic concepts in regard to performing simple calculations, as follows:

- **Variables.** Variables consist of using characters (alphabetical and numeric) to identify a field, a result, or other variable used in the formula. You can use something as simple as a character name or a long descriptive name. Variables might be `f`, `amt`, `item0grandTotal`, `Price Amount`, and so on.

- **Identifying fields.** You need to tell Acrobat in the JavaScript code that you want to assign a variable name to a field that exists on your form. The syntax for assigning a field to a variable name might look like

  ```
  var f = this.getField("item");
  ```

  In the preceding code the field name appears in quote marks and the quote marks are contained within parentheses. The variable `f` is assigned to the field name `item` on `this` (the current open) document.

- **Algebraic formulas.** After identifying the variables, you use standard algebraic notation. Therefore, to divide one value by another (something not available to you with the preset formulas), you might enter the code shown in Figure 31.4 in the JavaScript Editor as follows:

  ```
  1. var f = this.getField("amount");
  2. var g = this.getField("itemNumber");
  3. event.value = f.value / g.value;
  ```

  The first line assigns the variable `f` to the field `amount`. The second line of code assigns the variable `g` to the field `itemNumber`. The third line of code is the formula where `f` is divided by `g`. The result is placed in the field where you add this script in the JavaScript Editor. The trigger to put the result in the field where the calculation is coded is the `event.value` item.

Without going into loops and more complex formulas, the beginning Acrobat forms author can do quite a bit by just following the preceding simple example. The code is all case sensitive, and your field names need to be identical to the name of the field on the form as you code in the JavaScript Editor.

FIGURE 31.4

Select Custom calculation script in the Calculation properties and enter the code to perform the calculation in the JavaScript Editor.

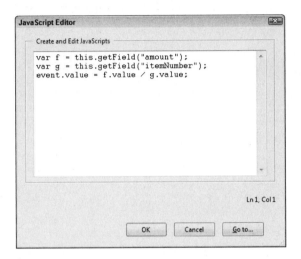

My good friend and colleague Thom Parker who hosts the JavaScript Corner on Acrobat Users (http://www.acrobatusers.com/go/javascript) fields questions almost daily from Acrobat users about JavaScript-related questions. The first question Thom asks people who contact him is, "Have you looked at the Acrobat JavaScript Scripting Reference?" This document is Thom's Bible, and even accomplished JavaScript programmers like Thom use it regularly as a reference. If you want to learn more about JavaScript, you can download the reference from www.adobe.com/devnet/acrobat/javascript.html. You can also find much help related to JavaScript on Adobe's Web site at www.adobe.com/devnet/acrobat/pdfs/js_api_reference.pdf.

# Managing Form Data

Managing form data, whether it is Acrobat PDF form data or data in the Adobe LiveCycle Designer environment, essentially falls into two categories. One category is industrial-strength data management satisfying needs of business enterprises and organizations requiring sophisticated tools beyond Acrobat for collecting and routing data. The other category is local data management you handle using Acrobat and tools within the Acrobat environment for individual and small business needs.

In regard to enterprise data management solutions, you'll find a number of server products developed by Adobe Systems to satisfy the most demanding data management needs. Adobe markets products like Adobe LiveCycle Forms (formerly Adobe LiveCycle Form Server) and several other server products designed to satisfy just about any business need for managing documents and data. All of the Adobe Server products can be found at www.adobe.com/products/server or www.adobe.com/livecycle/.

Another avenue for enterprise solutions is the Adobe Partner community. Adobe works together with a great number of third-party developers to provide an array of solutions satisfying vertical market needs. You can learn more about Adobe partners and the solutions they offer at www.adobe.com/enterprise/partners. In addition to Adobe Systems and Adobe partners, several independent developers provide more server solutions and services to help you define needs and customize your data management requirements. You can find out more about some other developers by searching the Internet.

In short, when it comes to handling data for large-scale business transactions, you need to look outside Acrobat and find a provider that can deliver the solution that fits your specific needs. One thing to keep in mind is that you don't use Acrobat to take form data for invoices and sales receipts for companies such as Sprint, Boeing, Time-Warner, and similar large enterprises and expect to write backend code to route data. You need Acrobat and some help from other products designed to work with PDF data.

As an example, take the U.S. Internal Revenue Service. The U.S. IRS certainly has more money and programming staff than one can imagine. However, the IRS has outsourced data routing since it began using online fillable PDF forms in the early 2000s — initially using the Adobe Form Server product and later using a third-party product. The IRS has never handled data routing for its huge number of forms with in-house programming staff.

In terms of local data management, and because this book is about Acrobat and what you can do with the product as it comes out of the box, you have many tools, commands, and Adobe services for managing form data. To begin understanding the handling of form data, let's start by looking at how to import and export PDF data in a local environment.

## Cross-Reference

What I can hope to do in this book is expose you to a limited view for handling data and working with PDF forms. For a more comprehensive view of creating PDF forms in Acrobat and LiveCycle Designer and managing form data, see the PDF Forms Using Acrobat and LiveCycle Designer Bible (Wiley Publishing, Padova/Okamoto). ∎

# Importing and exporting data

One of the great benefits of importing and exporting data is the ability to eliminate redundancy in re-creating common data used in different forms. Among the most common redundant data entries is your personal identifying information. Adding your name, address, phone number, and so on to forms is often a common practice. In an environment where you need to supply your personal identity information, you could keep an FDF (Form Data File) or XML file on your hard drive and load it into different PDF forms, thereby eliminating the need to re-key the data.

# Understanding PDF Form Data Formats _____

FDF is a legacy format supported by earlier versions of Acrobat from 4.0 and above. This is a proprietary Adobe format and not a data file you can use with a lot of applications or that you can open for editing. XML is a newer format introduced in Acrobat 6 and available in Acrobat 7 through X. You can open XML files in a text editor and edit the data. You can also view the data in a Web browser.

I make references to FDF/XML throughout this chapter for those who need to work with legacy files not supporting XML and for those Acrobat 6-or-greater-compatible files where XML can be used. If you have a choice when exporting or importing data in Acrobat 6–compatible files or greater, use XML as your default data file format. If you need to add JavaScript to handle the data you may want to stick with FDF as the export format.

In order to swap data between forms, you need to observe one precaution. All data fields used to import FDF/XML data must have identically matched names to the fields from which the data were exported, including case sensitivity. Therefore, the data from a field called *Name* in a PDF that exports to FDF/XML cannot be introduced in a PDF with a field called *name*. Setting up the fields is your first task, and then you can move on to data exports and imports. To clarify this concept further, I first show you how to design forms with common fields, and then export and import data.

### Creating common fields

To be certain your field names match exactly between two forms, the easiest and most efficient way to duplicate the fields is to copy fields from one form and paste them into another form. In Figure 31.5, I have a form designed as an annual tournament schedule. Some of the data from my schedule card is identical to some data on a scorecard shown in Figure 31.6.

## Tip

**You can copy/paste fields while in normal Viewer mode without having to enter Form Editing Mode. Just use the Select Object tool to select fields for copying.** ■

After copying fields from the schedule card and pasting the matching fields into the scorecard, I know I have an exact field match, and the data exported from the populated form will find the matching fields in the form shown in Figure 31.6.

## Tip

**If you need to copy all fields on the form, select the Select Object tool and press Ctrl+A (Windows) or ⌘+A (Mac) to select all fields — in either Form Editing Mode or Viewer mode. Press Ctrl+C (Windows) or ⌘+C (Mac) to copy all the selected fields to the Clipboard.** ■

**FIGURE 31.5**

A tournament schedule card populated with data

**FIGURE 31.6**

The scorecard form uses some of the exact same data as the schedule card.

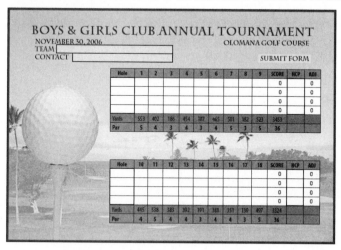

## Exporting FDF/XML data

After the forms have been created with matching fields, complete a form and fill in all the data fields. If you have some fields on one form that have been excluded on a second form, Acrobat ignores any field data where it can't find a matching field name. Therefore, you need not worry about having the same number of fields on both documents.

Exporting data from a PDF file is handled with a menu command. If you want to export the data from a form, choose Forms ⇨ Manage Form Data ⇨ Export Data. A dialog box opens where you name the file and designate a destination for the FDF/XML data.

# Exporting Form Data

The default export format when you choose Forms ⇨ Manage Form Data ⇨ Export Data is Acrobat FDF (*.fdf* extension files). In the Export Form Data As dialog box you can also choose to export data as Acrobat XFDF, XML, or Text formats. Depending on your uses for the data, be certain to check the export format shown in the Export Form Data As dialog box. The default choice is FDF. If you want to export and use XML data, choose XML Files (*.xml) from the Save as type (Windows) or Format (Mac) pull-down menu.

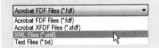

Something else to remember is that you can only export and import form data while in normal Viewer mode. You don't have access to these menu commands when in Form Editing Mode.

When you select the menu command, the Export Form Data As dialog box opens. By default, the name of your PDF file and a .fdf (or .xml) extension are supplied in the File name field box. This name is used as the FDF/XML filename. If you want to change the name, edit text in the File name field, but be certain to leave a .xml (or .fdf) extension after the filename. Click Save to save the file as an XML (or FDF) file.

The file you save as FDF/XML contains only the data from the form fields. Therefore, the file size is considerably smaller than the PDF that produced the data. The file can be stored on a local disk or network server, sent as an email attachment to another user, or uploaded to your Acrobat.com library. If another user has a PDF with the same field names, the data can be imported with one of the Acrobat products.

## Importing FDF/XML data

As with form data exports, importing FDF/XML data in PDF forms is handled with menu commands. Choose Forms ⇨ Manage Form Data ⇨ Import Data (in Viewer mode). The Select File Containing Form Data dialog box opens, where you can navigate your hard drive and find the FDF/XML file to import.

Select the FDF/XML file to be imported and click the Select button in the dialog box. When you import data from common field names, the fields are populated for all matching fields as shown in my new scorecard file after the data import in Figure 31.7. Acrobat ignores all data where no matching fields are found.

**FIGURE 31.7**

Only data with matching field names is imported. All other data is ignored.

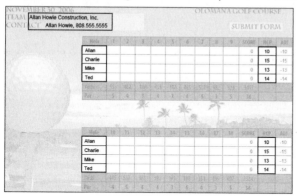

# Using Import Buttons and Page Actions

Another method you have available for importing data is to create a button or page action and use the Import form data action type. Create a button or open the Pages panel and select Page Properties from a context menu. In the Page Properties dialog box, shown in the following figure, click the Actions tab and select the Page Open trigger (this menu choice opens by default). From the Select Action pull-down menu, choose Import form data and click Add.

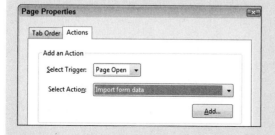

The Select File Containing Form Data dialog box opens. Select the data file you want to import and click the Select button. Save your file, and when the document opens on the target page Acrobat automatically imports data from the data file. You might use this method when you prepare forms such as a purchase order form for a vendor where you want your identifying information and the vendor information imported when preparing the order form. If you use a text file containing several vendors, click the vendor you want to use to import the respective data.

*continued*

*continued*

You'll note that you have no option for exporting data using a button or page action. In earlier versions of Acrobat you could get around the absence of an action type for exporting data by using an Execute a menu item action type. In Acrobat 8 and above, however, the Execute a menu item list is more limiting and you can't select a menu command from the list to export data using a button, bookmark, link, or page action.

Note that if you add the Import Form Data action to a button, link, bookmark, or page action, the only file format supported by the action type is FDF data. If you want to import other file formats such as TXT or XML, you need to write a JavaScript.

## Cross-Reference

**For more information on using page actions and learning more about limitations with the Execute a menu item command, see Chapter 21.** ■

## Creating spreadsheets from form data

Exporting data to spreadsheets can be handled in a few different ways. You can select from two different menu commands to export data that can be opened in a program such as Microsoft Excel, or you can aggregate form data from multiple forms into a single spreadsheet.

### Exporting data to a spreadsheet

Two different commands enable you to export PDF data and open the exported data in a spreadsheet. You can open a PDF document and click More in the Forms panel to open a drop-down menu. Click Manage Form Data ⇨ Export Data and the Export Form Data As dialog box opens. In the Export Form Data As dialog box, open the Save as type (Windows) pull-down menu or Format (Mac) pull-down menu and select Text as the file format. Click the Save button and the data can be opened in a spreadsheet program.

When you open the exported text data in MS Excel, the Text Import Wizard opens as shown in Figure 31.8. Step through the Wizard and click Finish to open the data in a new Excel spreadsheet.

Acrobat also provides a means for aggregating data from multiple forms into an Excel spreadsheet. From the More drop-down menu in the Forms panel, click Manage Form Data ⇨ Merge Data Files into Spreadsheet. This command works when you want to export data from a single file, but the real power in using the command is when you export data from multiple files. If you have a single PDF document and you use this command, the result is similar to exporting data from the Export Data command. Using the Export Data command exports to a text file, and using the Merge Data Files into Spreadsheet command exports to a CSV comma-delimited file or XML file. The text file created from the Export command is also a delimited file. As a result, you see very little difference when either file is opened in a program such as Microsoft Excel. All the data fall into rows and columns.

FIGURE 31.8

The Text Import Wizard is launched in MS Excel when you open an exported text file from Acrobat.

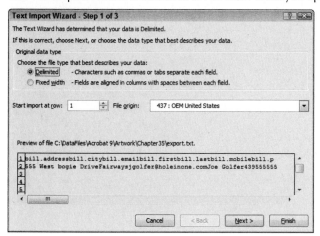

## Aggregating data from multiple files into a single spreadsheet

As I mentioned before, the real power in using the Merge Data Files into Spreadsheet command is when combining data from multiple PDFs into a spreadsheet. To see how this command works, follow these steps.

### STEPS: Combining Data from Multiple PDFs into a Spreadsheet File

1. **Collect some forms with different data fields.** To follow these steps, start with a form saved as different files having unique data. Save several forms to a common folder. In my example I used a simple form, as shown in Figure 31.9. Notice that the fields are highlighted so you can clearly see the form fields. I edited this form and changed the data for three additional forms and saved them all to the same folder.

## Note

You can add files from different folders to merge the data into a spreadsheet. ∎

2. **Open the Forms panel and click More ⇨ Manage Form Data ⇨ Merge Data Files into Spreadsheet.** Note that you don't need a document open in the document pane. If a document is open, the merge command doesn't use the open file. The Export Data From Multiple Forms dialog box opens.

3. **Add Files.** Click Add Files and select the files you want to combine together in a single spreadsheet.

   The Select File Containing Form Data dialog box opens. Select the files you want to combine together and click Select. When you return to the Export Data From Multiple Forms dialog box, the files you selected are shown in a window as you can see in Figure 31.10.

**FIGURE 31.9**

Use the same form with different data, saving each file to a common folder.

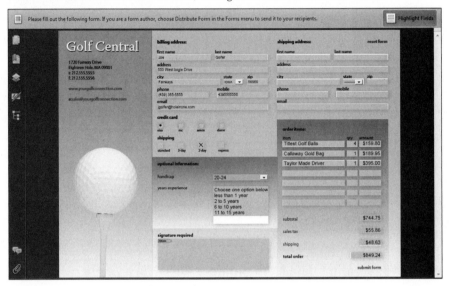

4. **Click Export.**

5. **Name and save the file.** When you click the Export button in the Export Data From Multiple Forms dialog box, the Select Folder to Save File dialog box opens. In this dialog box you locate a target folder and type a name for your file. By default the name provided in the File name text box is *report*. Edit the name and type a descriptive name for the file you save.

6. **Click Export.**

7. **View the file.** In a very short time the Export Progress dialog box opens as shown in Figure 31.11. Click the View File Now button and Microsoft Excel is launched, displaying the merged data.

## Aggregating FDF/XML data

When you create a Submit button, as I explain in the next section, "Submitting and Receiving Form Data," Adobe Reader users can't submit a PDF document back to you unless the form is enabled with Reader usage rights. If a form is not enabled, Reader users can submit the FDF/XML data back to you (without the PDF document) and you can use the Import Data command to import the FDF/XML data into a PDF form residing on your computer.

If you send files for Reader users and the data are returned to you as FDF/XML, you can aggregate the data in a spreadsheet using the same menu commands as you do when aggregating form data derived from PDF documents. Using the More ➪ Manage Form Data ➪ Merge Data Files into Spreadsheet menu command, follow the same steps as when merging PDF forms data. When you click Add Files and open the Select File Containing Form Data dialog box, notice the formats supported in the Files of type (Windows) or Format (Mac) pull-down menu. You find FDF/XML included as a format as well as PDF and XFDF.

## FIGURE 31.10

Selected files are shown in the Export Data From Multiple Forms dialog box.

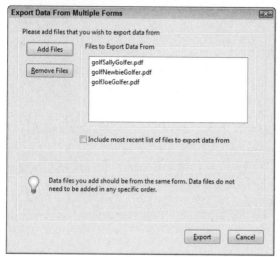

## FIGURE 31.11

Click View File Now to open the exported data in Microsoft Excel.

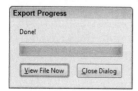

## Tip

If you use a Wizard to distribute forms, all Wizards in Acrobat automatically enable PDF forms with Adobe Reader usage rights. The only time you need to enable a PDF using the File ⇨ Save As ⇨ Reader Extended PDF File menu command is when you distribute a form manually as opposed to using a Wizard. ■

# Submitting and Receiving Form Data

We've come a long way with data exports, imports, submissions, and retrieval in Acrobat. Several generations ago, back in Acrobat 5, Adobe Reader users needed to view a PDF document inside a Web browser to submit form data. With the last few releases of Acrobat, Adobe

Reader users could click a button designed for submitting data on PDF forms inside Acrobat without having to view the PDF in a Web browser. In Acrobat 8, we were introduced to form submissions from Reader users via email attachments, where the Reader users could submit the entire PDF document with the form data back to the forms author. Inasmuch as the great developments in Acrobat 8 provided much easier forms distribution and data merging, we still had limitations with data retrieval on servers. Unless you are a programmer or have a friend in the IT department, setting up a server for data collection was out of the question.

## Cross-Reference
**For more information on viewing PDFs inside Web browsers as inline views, see Chapter 25. ■**

All this was changed in Acrobat 9. With the opportunity to manage forms on Acrobat.com many forms authors don't need to hassle with server configurations to collect and track distributed forms. You still have the option to share and collect forms via email attachments, but the great new features you find in Acrobat.com are likely to minimize the number of forms you distribute via email attachments.

## Cross-Reference
**Acrobat.com is a separate service provided by Adobe Systems. Together with Acrobat X, you can use Acrobat. com services to submit forms and collect data that can be downloaded from recipient responses from your Acrobat.com account. To learn more about using Acrobat.com, see Chapter 26. ■**

## Creating a Submit Form button

In all Acrobat viewers 8 and below that supported PDF forms, a Submit button was added to a form when you wanted the form to be sent someplace — either back to you as an email attachment or to a server where you collected forms.

In Acrobat 9 and later you have two different options for using a Submit Form button. The button can be constructed with a Submit Form action and appear on your form like it did with earlier Acrobat viewers, or a Submit Form button can appear in the Document Message Bar automatically when you distribute a form. If you have a form that you email to recipients, you can use a form containing a submit button you add to the form. If you use the Distribute command in the Forms panel, Acrobat opens a Wizard where you make choices for distributing a form, and a submit form button is automatically added in the Document Message Bar.

Distributing forms can be handled in one of several ways. You can send a form via email to recipients, in which case you'll need to perform some manual tasks to prepare your form for distribution, or you can use the Distribute Form command in either normal Viewer mode or Form Editing Mode. When distributing a form, you can elect to use Acrobat.com, your own internal server, or send forms via email attachments.

If you choose to use the Distribute Form command, Acrobat takes care of some tasks automatically for you. You don't have to create a Submit Form button, and you don't have to manually enable a PDF form with Adobe Reader usage rights. Through an easy process of walking through some Wizard steps, Acrobat takes care of these details for you.

You can also let Acrobat take care of automating tasks when you want forms emailed back to you. Again, you follow some steps via a Wizard and submit your form via an email attachment. And again, Acrobat takes care of the Submit Form button and enabling tasks.

## Cross-Reference

**For more information on enabling forms with Adobe Reader usage rights, see Chapter 18. ■**

A third option is to avoid working with a Wizard and manually send a form off to a recipient. You might have a form stored locally on your hard drive and occasionally send the form for a user to complete and send back to you. In this case, you're not interested in aggregating data from multiple users, but simply collecting some data related to some sort of specific instance.

If you decide to email a form without using a Wizard, you need to manually address two things. First, your form needs a Submit Form button with your email address specified in the Submit Form action, and the form needs to be enabled with Adobe Reader usage rights when Adobe Reader users participate as form recipients.

When you want to distribute a form using a Wizard, follow these steps:

### Steps: Distributing a Form

1. **Open a PDF form with form fields in Acrobat.** In these steps we'll set up a form for email distribution. Since we'll use a Wizard to distribute the form, we don't need a button on the form to submit the form back to you.

2. **Distribute the form.** Open the Forms panel and click Distribute in either normal Viewer mode or Form Editing Mode. The Distribute Form Wizard opens as show in Figure 31.12.

3. **Choose a collection method for acquiring the form data.** From the pull-down menu in the Wizard choose the form collection method you want to use. For this example I use Manually collect responses in my email inbox, as shown in Figure 31.12.

4. **Click Next.** The second pane in the Wizard opens as shown in Figure 31.13.

5. **Choose a method for distributing the form.** When you choose to collect data in your email inbox you have two options for distributing the form as shown in Figure 31.13. You can choose to send the form automatically to Acrobat.com (this requires you to have an MAPI compliant client email) or save a local copy and manually send the form as an email attachment later. In this example I choose Save a local copy and manually send it later.

**FIGURE 31.12**

Choose a collection method from the pull-down menu at the top of the Distribute Form Wizard.

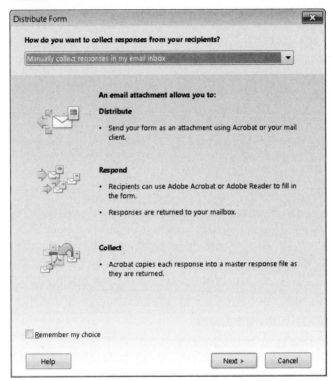

6. **Click Next.** You arrive at the last pane in the Wizard. At the bottom of the Wizard window a check box is checked by default as shown in Figure 31.14. If you keep the check box checked, email addresses of recipients are added to the Tracker to help you track the responses. If you don't want to collect the recipient email addresses uncheck the check box. Do so means the form recipient will be prompted to add your email address when the form is submitted back to you.

7. **Click Finish.** Click the Finish button in the last Wizard pane and the Tracker opens in Acrobat.

FIGURE 31.13

Choose a distribution method.

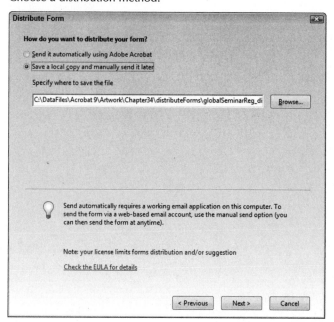

FIGURE 31.14

Click Finish after completing all the steps to distribute the form.

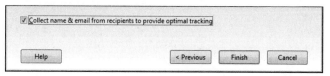

8. **Open the Original Form.** When the Tracker opens, click the blue text where you see Open Original Form, as shown in Figure 31.15.

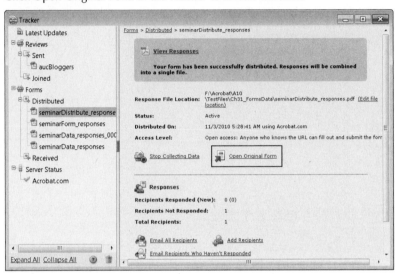

**FIGURE 31.15**

Click Open Original Form in the Tracker to review the form.

9. **Review the form.** Notice in the Document Message Bar you see the Submit Form button (see Figure 31.16) that was automatically added by Acrobat.

When the form is distributed via a Wizard, the form is automatically enabled with Adobe Reader usage rights. Enabling forms via a Wizard is available to users of Acrobat Standard as well as the Acrobat Pro and Pro Extended users.

## Cross-Reference
For more information on enabling features and using digital signatures in Adobe Reader, see Chapters 18 and 30. ■

If you chose to add a submit button to a form and not use a Wizard to distribute your form, you use a button action in the Actions tab for the Button Field Properties. From the Select Action pull-down menu you choose Submit a form and click the Add button. The Submit Form Selections dialog box opens, where you find quite a few options for choosing what data are collected when a form is returned to you via email. Let's take a look at all the options choices you have in this dialog box.

- **Enter a URL for this link.** If you have a data management system or a server product that routes data and manages a database, you can add a URL to the text box. This option requires you to have programming on your server that collects the data when it hits the URL specified in the text box. If you don't have server-side programming to manage the data, your only other option is to add an email address, as shown in Figure 31.13.

**FIGURE 31.16**

When you open the form, you find the Submit Form button in the Document Message Bar.

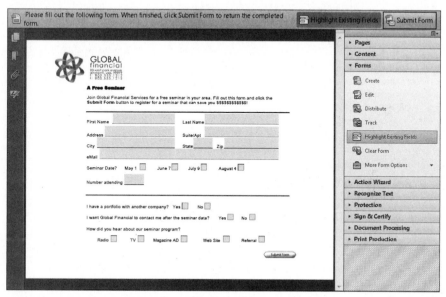

- **Export Format.** Along the left side of the dialog box you find several options for the type of export format users can send back to you.

  - **FDF Include.** The FDF data is sent to the server. The three options below the FDF Include item offer you choices for sending the Field data; Comments, which includes any comments created on a form; and Incremental changes to the PDF, which should be used when digital signatures have been used to save updates. Any one or all of the selections can be made for this data type.

  - **HTML.** The data is sent in HTML format as name/value pairs. Much as you might create a form on a Web page using HTML and JavaScript, the HTML option processes the same data type.

  - **XFDF Include.** The data are sent in XML format. Two options are available for sending the Field data or the Comments data or both. You cannot submit digital signatures via XFDF.

  - **PDF The complete document.** This option enables you to submit the PDF populated with the field data. This option is useful for Digital Signature workflows or for archiving the complete document. Additionally, if you use bar codes on forms, you'll want to have the complete PDF document sent back to you.

- **Field Selection.** On the right side of the dialog box are options for including all or selected field data in your submission. If fields are to be eliminated, select the Only these button and then click the Select fields button. The Field Selection dialog box opens, where you select which fields to use for the data export.

- **Date Options.** Dates are converted from the format specified on the form to standard date formats when the Date Options check box is enabled.

When the user clicks a Submit button, the form data from the choices you made in the dialog box are sent to the specified URL/email address. Keep in mind that if you do not have the necessary server-side programming, nothing happens to the data and it won't be found on your server. You need intervention from the host to collect and route the data.

## Tip

By default Acrobat doesn't submit the value of a button field, so if you have a form containing button fields and you want to export the buttons data as well as the text field data, select the Only these radio button in the Submit Form Selections dialog box. The Field Selection dialog box opens after you click the Select Fields button. In the Field Selection dialog box, select the check boxes for all fields you want to submit. ■

## Distributing forms via email

Deploying PDF forms in Acrobat 7 and earlier was limited to emailing PDFs and using the Submit button for users to mail data back to you. You had to deal with the data on a file-by-file basis without any tools locally on your computer to merge data or display it in a single file source. What was left out of the loop was a method for aggregating data when users returned forms to you — that is, if you don't have a server to manage data.

Acrobat 8 helped bridge the gap for data collection with the introduction of PDF Packages. In Acrobat 8 you could distribute a form and collect forms that were appended to a PDF Package where the data could be exported to a CSV file and opened in Microsoft Excel. This development in Acrobat 8 was a huge step in helping forms authors collect data from forms fillers and analyze the data.

Inasmuch as we applauded Adobe for providing us with the new features in Acrobat 8, we still had one issue that remained a problem for forms authors who didn't have sophisticated IT departments to set up servers where data could be collected. All the data collection for individual users and small businesses was dependent on email exchanges.

In Acrobat 9 and later, Adobe hasn't stepped forward in regard to data collection; rather, Adobe has leaped forward in huge bounds to help forms authors collect data. Without any need for complicated server configurations, you can now collect data on Acrobat.com, download your data for analysis, easily track forms, send reminders to users for filling out forms, and time limit your data collection.

The beauty of using a server to collect data is that you can have data collected and download the results when you have time to log on to your Acrobat.com workspace; you no longer have to depend on email collections piling up in your inbox. You can log on to Acrobat.com with a laptop while traveling, download recent responses, and keep up to date with a form collection process without having to log on to your email account.

Distributing forms in Acrobat 9 and later is handled in the Distribute Form Wizard. When you distribute a form, you have three options in the Wizard. You can collect form data on an internal server, manually collect data via email, and collect data via Acrobat.com. For data collection on your own internal server, I'll refer you to the Acrobat Help document and the Adobe Web site to browse information related to internal server configurations. For starters take a look at the Web pages found at www.adobe.com/devnet/acrobat/.

## Emailing forms using Adobe Acrobat

Distributing a form using the Distribute Form Wizard for manually collecting email responses in your mailbox is handled via a menu command. Open the Forms panel and click Distribute Form to open the Distribute Form dialog box shown earlier in Figure 31.12. From the pull-down menu at the top of the Wizard you have a choice listed as Manually collect responses in my email inbox. I covered manually distributing forms using your email inbox to collect data earlier in this chapter in the section "Creating a Submit Form button."

You have two choices for distributing a form to manually collect data in your email inbox. You can save a file and distribute it later like I explained in the section "Creating a Submit Form button" or you can use Acrobat to send the form now. When you choose Send it automatically using Adobe Acrobat (see Figure 31.13), Acrobat opens a default email message window as shown in Figure 31.17.

**FIGURE 31.17**

Acrobat opens an email message window when you choose to have Acrobat email a form.

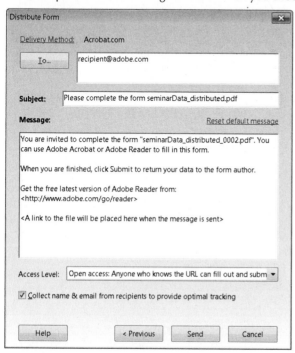

Fill in the To information and make any edits you want to make in the Subject field and the Message window. Click Send and Acrobat attaches the form to an email and sends the message and attachment.

## Analyzing data

When you collect forms from recipients. a special distributed responses PDF Portfolio document collects the data. For forms distributed via email attachments you double-click a file attachment and the form data is added to your response file. This file is created automatically when you distribute a form. In Acrobat you see a welcome page in the PDF Portfolio response file like the one shown in Figure 31.18.

**FIGURE 31.18**

As forms are collected in a PDF Portfolio response file, the Welcome Page opens when you double-click a file attachment.

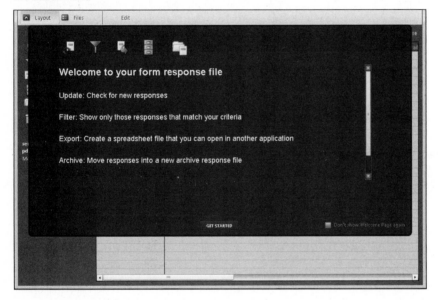

The Welcome Page has a list of items with descriptions. When you open the response file, a special set of tools is added to the left side of the Document pane. The items tasks you can perform with data collected from forms are shown in Table 31.1.

**TABLE 31.1**

## Options Available for Data Collection and Management

| Icon | Item | Description |
|------|------|-------------|
| | Update | Click Update and Acrobat checks for new updates to the response file. |
| | Filter | Choose Filter and a side panel opens where you can filter data on any field name on a form. |
| | Export | From a pull-down menu choose Sort All or Selected. If you choose Export all or Export selected, the data are exported as a CSV or XML file that can be opened in Microsoft Excel or a database. |
| | Archive | You can archive selected response data or all response data. The archive can overwrite the existing dataset file or create a new dataset file. Note: When you archive, the data is removed from your response file. |
| | Add | Click Add and you can add new responses to the response file. |

Click the Get Started button on the Welcome Page and you see the files shown in a List View in the PDF Portfolio like you see in Figure 31.19. This view is the Home view with a special layout designed for the response file. You cannot edit the layout view in the PDF Portfolio.

## Cross-Reference

For more information on PDF Portfolios and changing views, see Chapter 11. ∎

## Tip

When retrieving data that's added to your response file, you'll want to bypass the Welcome Page each time you open the file. On the Welcome Page, check Don't show Welcome Page again. The next time you open the response file you are taken directly to the view shown in Figure 31.19. ∎

You also have a List View using the response file PDF Portfolio like you do with other PDF Portfolios. The List View provides you with a little more viewing area to examine the data because the tools from the left panel in Figure 31.18 are not shown in this view, as you can see in Figure 31.20.

**FIGURE 31.19**

Responses are collected in a PDF Portfolio file with a custom layout view.

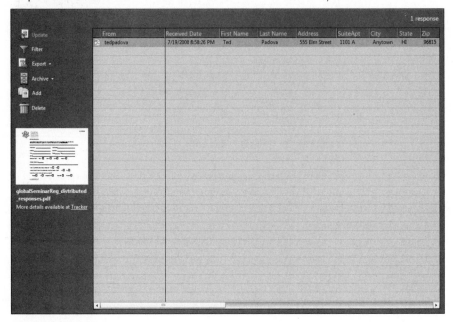

**FIGURE 31.20**

Click the List View tool to change to a List View.

In List view you also have a sort option. Click any column head and you'll find an up or down pointing arrow. Click again and the arrow changes direction. You can individually sort columns in either ascending or descending order.

While in the Home View you can sort data for any field contained on the form and reported in the response file. Click the Filter tool on the left side of the Home View and the Filter Settings open in the left panel as shown in Figure 31.21. The scrollable list contains all the field names on the form.

**FIGURE 31.21**

Click Filter to open the Filter panel.

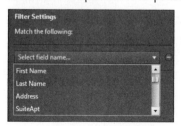

To filter data choose a field from the scrollable list. Something like State or City, if such fields exist on your form. Below the item selection you have a number of choices such as *is, contains, starts with, is blank, is not blank,* etc. Choose an item to match the date that you want. If you want to sort multiple columns, click the + Add Filter button and a new set of menus is added to the panel as shown in Figure 31.22.

**FIGURE 31.22**

Click + Add Filter and you can add multiple match items in the Filter Settings panel.

## Tip

**If you want to sort all data for a given field, use the is not blank choice in the Filter Settings. All the data in the response file is sorted for the field. ∎**

In the response file you can easily sort the data as you like. If you want to export the data to a database or spreadsheet, click Done when finished filtering the data and click the Export tool in the left panel. From the Export tool pull-down menu you can choose to export the data as all the filtered data or you can select rows in the data table and export selected data. The exported data is saved as a CSV file that can be opened in a spreadsheet program or various database programs.

If you receive a file that wasn't emailed back to you, for example a file that may be delivered on a flash drive or across a network, you can easily add files to the response file. Click the Add button and a dialog box opens, where you can choose files to add to your document.

If you want to break down the data and create separate files based on some filtering of the data, click the Archive tool in the left panel. You can choose to archive filtered data or selected data. Choose an option from the pull-down menu and the Archive Data dialog box opens as shown in Figure 31.23. From this dialog box you can choose to create a new response file or merge data with an existing response file. Either action you take removes data from the existing file while adding the data to the target file.

---

**FIGURE 31.23**

Click the Archive tool and choose an option from the Archive pull-down menu, and the Archive Data dialog box opens.

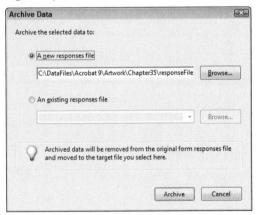

## Distributing forms via Acrobat.com

We need to roll back momentarily to the Forms ➪ Distribute Form command that opens the Distribute Form Wizard. When you open the Wizard, instead of choosing the option for distributing forms manually, choose Automatically download & organize responses with Acrobat.com.

## Note

As of this writing Acrobat.com is in public beta and may be continually changing before the service is out of beta and in final form. You may find some changes to Acrobat.com and some of the screen shots in this chapter differing from those found when Acrobat.com moves out of public beta. To stay up to date with any changes on Acrobat.com services or the appearances of the workspace, keep in touch with articles you'll find on www. acrobat.com and look for the errata page for the Acrobat X PDF Bible on the www.wiley.com web site. ■

When you choose Distribute in the Forms panel, the Distribute Form Wizard opens as shown in Figure 31.24. At first glance the Distribute Form Wizard selections for using Acrobat.com appear identical as when choosing to distribute forms via email. Upon closer look, however, you see that the descriptions for handling distribution, responses, and data collection do vary some.

**FIGURE 31.24**

The Distribute Form Wizard as it appears after choosing Automatically download & organize responses with Acrobat.com

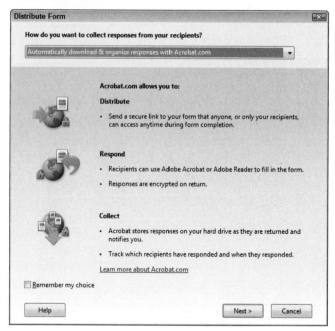

The differences between Acrobat.com and emailing forms include:

- **Distribute.** The message you send to recipients contains a secure link to your form that recipients can access. You have a choice for allowing anyone who visits your Acrobat.com library to download the form, or you can choose to restrict access to only those whom you've invited to complete the form.

- **Respond.** In addition to enabling the form the same as email distributions, responses are encrypted when returned to you.

- **Collect.** Acrobat stores responses on your hard drive as the forms are returned to you. All the forms processing actions can be monitored in the Tracker.

When you choose Automatically download & organize responses with Acrobat.com and click the Next button in the Wizard, the Distribute Form logon dialog box opens as shown in Figure 31.25. If you have an Adobe ID, use your logon information and click the Sign In button. If you don't have an Adobe ID, click the Create Adobe ID text you see in Figure 31.25.

**FIGURE 31.25**

Log on using your Adobe ID or click Create Adobe ID if you don't currently have an Adobe ID.

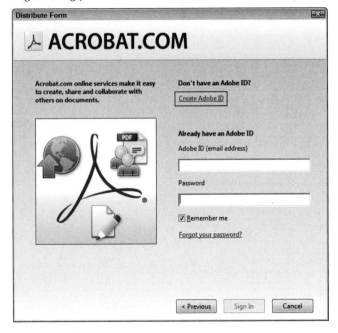

## Cross-Reference

For more information on creating an Adobe ID and setting up an account on Acrobat.com, see Chapter 26. ∎

Once you log on to Acrobat.com the next screen you see is the Distribute Form email message window. Notice the difference in Figure 31.26 and the Distribute Form email message window shown earlier in Figure 31.17. In Figure 31.26 you see an option for Access Level. Since the file is going to be a hosted file, recipients need to download the file to fill in the form. When you submit the form you have an option to choose an Access Level. You can choose to permit anyone who visits your Acrobat.com library to download the form or limit the access to only those recipients who receive an email from you.

FIGURE 31.26

Log on with your Adobe ID and the next screen you see is the Distribute Form email message window.

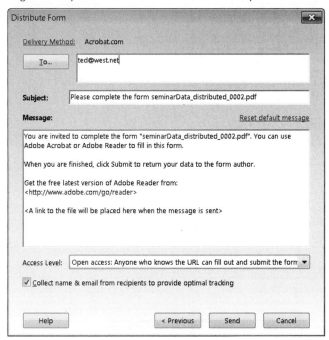

Fill in the To addresses for you form recipients, edit any changes you want made in the Subject and Message fields, choose an Access Level, and click Send. At this point Acrobat serves as your email client. The email message and attachment don't ever see your email client. Everything is handled by Acrobat, which is the reason why you had to log on in the beginning of the process. Acrobat needs a connection before the form can be sent.

## Note

If you make changes in the Message text box in the Distribute Form email message window, be certain to not disturb the URL link that appears in the message as a default. This link is needed for recipients to download your file. ∎

After Acrobat uploads the file, the Tracker opens as shown in Figure 31.27. Notice in the Tracker you see that you have similar information as shown in the Tracker in Figure 31.15. The Tracker shows you that the file was distributed to Acrobat.com, and you see an additional item for Stop Collecting Data. When you click Stop Collecting data the form is closed, so no additional data is uploaded to Acrobat.com.

FIGURE 31.27

The Tracker opens in Acrobat immediately after a form is submitted to Acrobat.com.

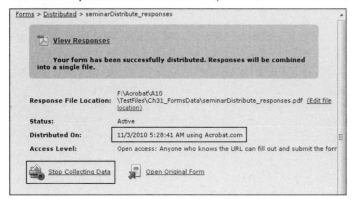

When a recipient receives an email sent by Acrobat to the recipient email address and clicks the file attachment, the recipient is taken to Acrobat.com. All recipients do not need an Acrobat.com account to access your file. The Acrobat.com window opens as shown in Figure 31.28. A recipient can download the form by clicking the Download button, fill in, and submit the form.

Recipients who arrive at your Acrobat.com workspace can click the Download button to download the form.

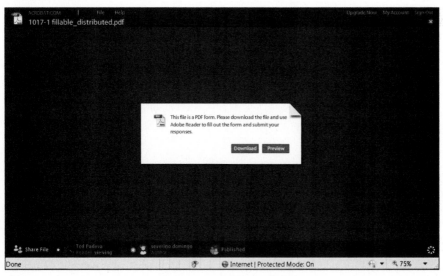

When forms are submitted to Acrobat.com, you retrieve the form via the Tracker. Open the Tracker (in the Forms Panel, click Track) and click View Responses, and the data are downloaded from Acrobat.com and added to your response file. The process for analyzing the data is the same as I covered earlier in this chapter in the section "Analyzing data."

# Using the Tracker

If you have several forms distributed and you're waiting on recipients to send back forms to you, things can quickly get a little disorganized and confusing. What you need is a management system to keep track of the forms currently being reviewed by recipients. In Acrobat your management system is available in the Tracker that you can access in either Form Editing Mode or Viewer mode by clicking Track in the Forms panel. When you choose this command, the Tracker opens as shown earlier in Figure 31.15.

In the Tracker, you see a list of forms you either distributed to be filled out or forms you were asked to fill out by another user, as shown in Figure 31.29.

**FIGURE 31.29**

The left panel in the Tracker lists all forms you have distributed and received.

In the right pane you have several options for distributed forms and forms received from other PDF authors. At the top of the right pane you handle tasks related to distributed forms, as shown earlier in Figure 31.15.

Your choices in this section of the Tracker include:

- **View Responses.** Click the blue text to open the response file where you can view and analyze the response data.

- **Edit file location.** Click the blue text to open the Choose a new response file location dialog box. The location shown in the dialog box is the folder where your dataset file is located. If you want to change the file where the data are collected, you can browse your hard drive and select a new file. You can also use this dialog box to reestablish a link to the dataset file if you happen to relocate it on your computer.

- **Stop Collecting Data.** Clicking the blue text opens a dialog box, as shown in Figure 31.30, asking you to confirm the fact that you want to terminate data collection for the form. Click Yes, and the data collection stops. Any user attempting to submit data for the form is prevented from doing so. If you want to extend the form collection period, you need to start over and redistribute the form again.

**FIGURE 31.30**

Click Yes to stop data collection on a form.

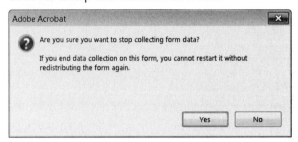

- **Open Original Form.** Click the blue text, and the original form you distributed opens in the document pane.

The bottom right side of the Tracker handles responses for a distributed form, as shown earlier in Figure 31.15.

Items you have to choose from within this section of the Tracker include:

- **Email All Recipients.** Click the blue text to send an email to all recipients of the distributed form. You might have an issue that needs some explanation and want to send a mail to all the recipients to clarify a point. When you send the mail, Acrobat acts as your mail client and sends the message (and a copy of the form again).

- **Add Recipients.** Click Add Recipients to include additional recipients to fill in the distributed form.

- **Email Recipients Who Haven't Responded.** The Tracker maintains information on recipient responses and can filter those who haven't responded. When you click the blue text, an email is sent to only those recipients who have not returned the form back to you.

# Summary

In this chapter, you learned how to distribute forms, collect form data and track forms.

- Acrobat offers a few preset calculation formulas used for calculating data. For more sophisticated calculations, you need to use Simplified Field Notation scripts and JavaScripts.

- When using hierarchical names, you can easily sum data by adding a parent name in the Calculate properties and selecting the sum (+) menu command.

- Form data can be exported from populated PDF forms in a variety of different file formats. The data can be introduced into any form having matching field names as from where the data were exported.

- To ensure that fields have the same exact names between different forms, copy fields from one document and paste the fields in all other documents.

- Button fields can be created to submit form data from any Acrobat viewer. For Adobe Reader users to submit a PDF with data back to the PDF author, the form needs to be enabled with Adobe Reader usage rights.

- Data can be exported from a PDF document directly to a spreadsheet program.

- Forms can be distributed manually via email or directly using Acrobat.com.

- Forms in progress can be managed and organized in the Tracker.

# Understanding JavaScript

With JavaScript you can create dynamic documents for not only forms, but also many other uses such as adding interactivity to files, and viewing options, animation, and similar features not available with Acrobat tools. JavaScript helps you add flare and pizzazz to your PDF files. With Acrobat Standard 9 and above (Windows), you have access to all areas where JavaScripts can be written in Standard just like the Acrobat Pro users.

As the disclaimer, I added in the introduction of this book is not about JavaScript. It would take another book the size of *Acrobat X PDF Bible* to provide complete coverage for all the JavaScript options you have in Acrobat. All I can hope to do in this chapter is provide a starting point in using JavaScript in Acrobat X and point you to sources where you can learn more. You can find much more on JavaScript in my *PDF Forms Using Adobe Acrobat and LiveCycle Designer Bible* (Wiley Publishing, 2008).

For more sophisticated uses and some sound reasoning for coding forms, look at the Acrobat JavaScript Scripting Reference and the Acrobat JavaScript Scripting Guide. Both documents are available from Adobe Systems by logging on to www.adobe.com/devnet/acrobat/.

# Getting Started with Acrobat JavaScript

Before I begin to explain some coding, let me start by making a few suggestions to the novice user who may find the programming aspects of Acrobat confusing and beyond your reach. For those who haven't coded a single line, you can easily search and find samples of code used in Acrobat forms that you can copy and paste into your designs. Search the Internet and find PDF forms that are not secure, which enables you to examine the code using search terms like PDF forms, JavaScript, Sample Forms, and do on. If, for example, you need a calculation for sales tax, search for one of the many examples of forms where a sales tax calculation is coded in a form field. You can copy and paste fields into your designs and often only need to change a variable name to make it work. Poke around and experiment and you'll find some worthwhile routines in existing PDF forms.

## Finding JavaScripts

As you peruse documents searching for JavaScripts either to paste into your own designs or to learn more about using JavaScript in Acrobat, you need to know where scripts are contained. You might copy and paste a script and find that the script doesn't execute properly. One reason is that the script relies on a function contained in another area in the document. Therefore, to gain a complete understanding of how a form works, you need to examine all the potential containers for scripts. As a matter of practice, you'll want to examine several areas in a form where JavaScripts are found.

## Tip

If you want a quick glance at JavaScripts contained in a document, click Edit All JavaScripts in the JavaScript panel. The JavaScript Editor opens and displays all JavaScripts in the document in a scrollable window. ■

JavaScripts can be contained in the following areas in a PDF document:

- **Form Fields.** Depending on the field type, you'll find JavaScripts in various tabs in the Field Properties dialog box. For text fields you can find scripts in the Format, Validate, and Calculate tabs. Other field types can have scripts contained in tabs specific to the field type.

- **Bookmarks.** JavaScripts can be contained in the Bookmarks Properties in the Actions tab.

- **Links.** Links can have JavaScripts in the Link Properties in the Actions tab.

- **Page Actions.** JavaScripts can be added to Page Open and Page Close actions.

- **Document Level JavaScripts.** JavaScript Functions can be added at the document level.

- **Document Actions.** Document Actions such as saving a file or printing a file can have JavaScripts applied when the action is invoked.

## Tip

**If you have form fields in a PDF form, you don't need to enter Form Edit Mode to add or change a JavaScript on form field objects. Use the Select Object tool and double-click or open a context menu on a field and choose Properties. The form object's Properties dialog box can be opened without entering Form Edit Mode.** ■

### Examining form field scripts

The most frequent use of JavaScript in Acrobat forms is when scripts are written for field actions. To examine JavaScripts associated with fields, select the Select Object tool and open the Field Properties. Depending on the field type, there may be several places where a script can be located. The first logical place to look is the Actions tab. Actions can contain JavaScripts for all field types. Click the Actions tab to see what actions are assigned to the field, as shown in Figure 32.1.

## Cross-Reference

**For more information on the different field types in Acrobat X, see Chapter 31.** ■

**FIGURE 32.1**

Click the Actions tab to see whether a JavaScript action has been added to the field.

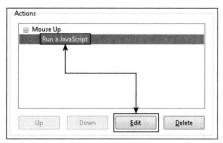

If you see JavaScript assigned to a mouse behavior, click Run a JavaScript in the Actions list and click the Edit button. Acrobat opens the JavaScript Editor and displays the code written for the script, as shown in Figure 32.2. The code in the JavaScript Editor can be copied from one field and pasted into the editor when you assign a script to another field. In addition, the field can be copied and pasted into another form. When you paste fields with JavaScript in them, the code is preserved in the pasted field.

With Text and Combo Box fields you can find JavaScripts in the Actions properties as well as the Format, Validate, and Calculate properties. If you are examining a form to understand how the field actions are executed, be certain to select each of these tabs to see whether any custom formatting or validation is used. Click the Format tab and look for Custom selected in the Select format category pull-down menu, as shown in Figure 32.3. If a JavaScript appears in either the Custom Format Script window or the Custom Keystroke Script window, click the

Edit button adjacent to where the script is written. The JavaScript Editor opens, in which you can edit the script or copy the text.

Select JavaScript in the Actions tab and click the Edit button. The JavaScript Editor dialog box opens, displaying the code.

```
JavaScript Editor

  Create and Edit JavaScripts

  this.spawnPageFromTemplate("passwords");
  this.pageNum = this.numPages-1;
  var r = [588, 454, 648, 474];
  var i = this.pageNum++
  var f =
  this.addField(String(this.pageNum),"text",i,r);
          f.textSize = 12;
          f.alignment = "right";
          f.textColor = color.black;
          f.fillColor = color.transparent;
          f.textfont = font.HelvB;
          f.borderStyle = border.s;
          f.strokeColor = color.transparent;
          f.value = util.printd("mm/dd/yy", new
  Date());

  app.execMenuItem("NewBookmark");


                                        Ln 1, Col 1

              OK        Cancel       Go to...
```

Select the Format tab and click Edit to see a script appear in the dialog box.

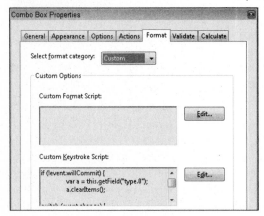

The Validate properties offer the same options. Follow the same procedures for finding JavaScripts as described earlier in this section by clicking the Validate tab and clicking Edit where you see a JavaScript in the Run custom validation script window to open the JavaScript Editor dialog box.

Field calculations are often handled in the Calculate properties. When JavaScript produces data calculations, be certain to examine the Calculate properties, as shown in Figure 32.4. However, not all field calculations are assigned to the Calculate properties, so be certain to check the Actions properties as well as Calculate in the event a calculation is performed on an action.

List Boxes offer different properties. If a List Box is used, click the Selection Change tab. A JavaScript can execute when a selection in the List Box changes. If a script appears in the dialog box, click the Edit button to open the JavaScript Edit dialog box.

Digital signatures can also be assigned custom JavaScripts. Click the Signed tab for a Digital Signature field and examine the dialog box for a custom script.

Buttons, Radio Buttons, and Check Boxes can have JavaScripts added only to the Actions properties. When opening these field types, click the Actions tab described earlier.

Barcode fields can also contain JavaScripts. The Value tab in the Barcode Properties contains an area where you can add custom JavaScripts similar to scripts you add in the Format and Validate tabs.

**FIGURE 32.4**

Click the Calculate tab to see whether a custom calculation script has been added to the field. If a script appears in the dialog box, click Edit to open the JavaScript Editor dialog box.

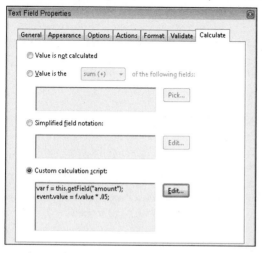

### Using Bookmarks and links

Both Bookmarks and links use the same action types as form fields. You might use a Bookmark for navigating documents rather than creating form field buttons or links on every page to open and close files. When the Bookmarks tab is open, users can click a Bookmark to open secondary files or perform other actions such as spawning pages from templates.

## Cross-Reference

**For more information on Button Field Properties, see Chapter 21.** ■

To check for JavaScripts contained in Bookmark actions, open the Bookmark Properties dialog box and click the Actions tab. JavaScripts are listed the same as when examining actions for form fields (described in the preceding section). Likewise, when you open Link Properties, you can check to see whether a JavaScript has been added as a Link action.

### Examining document-level JavaScripts

You may copy a field and paste it into another document and find an error reported when executing the JavaScript action. Although variable names are explained later, you can experience problems like this because the routine in the JavaScript might be calling a JavaScript function or global action that was contained in the original document as a document-level JavaScript. Among your tasks in dissecting a form should be an examination of any document-level JavaScripts. To find document-level JavaScript functions contained in a form, open the Tools panel and click JavaScript. From the JavaScript options, click Document JavaScripts and the JavaScript Functions dialog box opens, as shown in Figure 32.5.

In the JavaScript Functions dialog box, search for any names in the box below the Script Name box. All document-level functions are listed in this dialog box. To examine a script, select the script name and click the Edit button. The JavaScript Editor window, in which you can examine and/or copy the script, opens.

Writing functions and accessing them in JavaScript code written for field actions is much more complex. If you are new to JavaScript you may want to start with simple scripts in form fields until you learn more about how JavaScript is coded and implemented in Acrobat. As you learn more, you can develop more sophisticated routines that include functions.

### Analyzing page actions

Page actions execute when a user opens or closes a PDF page. You can assign any action type available from the Select Action types for field actions, including Run a JavaScript. When examining forms, open the Page Properties dialog box by opening a context menu in the Pages tab and selecting Properties. Click Actions when the Page Properties dialog box opens. If a JavaScript or any other page action is assigned to either the Page Open or the Page Close action, the action types are listed in the Actions window. Notice in Figure 32.6 that both a Page Open and Page Close action appear in the Actions window showing Run a JavaScript for both page actions.

## Cross-Reference

**For more information on page actions, see Chapter 21.** ■

**FIGURE 32.5**

Open the JavaScript Functions dialog box by clicking Document JavaScripts in the JavaScript panel.

**FIGURE 32.6**

When you open the Page Properties dialog box and click the Actions tab, both Page Open and Page Close actions are shown in the Actions window.

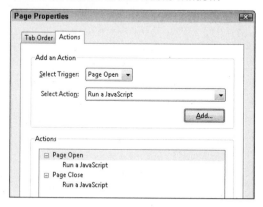

As with the other dialog boxes described earlier in this chapter, click Run a JavaScript and then click the Edit button. The JavaScript Editor window opens where you can view, edit, and/or copy the JavaScript.

### Examining document actions

Document actions execute JavaScripts for any one of five different Acrobat functions. On a document close, during a save, after a save, during a print, or after a print, a JavaScript action can be executed. To view any document actions assigned to the PDF document, open the JavaScript panel and click Set Document Actions.

## Cross-Reference

For information on creating JavaScripts on document actions, see "Using Document Actions" later in this chapter. ■

The Document Actions dialog box opens. If a JavaScript is assigned to a document action, an icon appears adjacent to the action type. You can view a script in the dialog box, as shown in Figure 32.7, or you can open the JavaScript Editor window by selecting the action name and clicking Edit.

---

**FIGURE 32.7**

Any document actions assigned to the PDF are displayed with a green circle adjacent to an action type in the Document Actions dialog box.

### Searching for page templates

Although not a JavaScript action, page templates can be called upon by JavaScript routines or additional fields can be created from template pages. Because templates can be hidden, the only way to examine JavaScripts on template pages is to first display a hidden template. As a matter of routine, you should search for page templates when examining forms.

The command for accessing page templates in Acrobat has been tossed back and forth between different menus from one version to the other. If you're coming from Acrobat 8 land, your first inclination is to search the Forms menu. However, we don't have a Forms menu in Acrobat X. You then might try to enter Forms Edit mode, and again you won't find a Page

Templates button or menu command. In Acrobat X, the Page Templates menu command has been moved to the Document Processing panel.

To display a hidden template, open the Document Processing panel and click Page Templates. If a Page Template is used in the PDF file, a template name appears in a list box in the Page Templates dialog box. If the Page Template is hidden, the square adjacent to the template name appears empty. To show the template page, click the icon adjacent to the template name. The icon changes to an eye icon inside the square. In Figure 32.8, you see four templates listed in the Page Templates dialog box. Two templates are visible and two templates are hidden.

FIGURE 32.8

Clicking the icon to the left of a template name for hidden templates makes the template visible in the PDF.

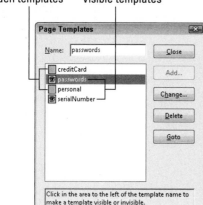

The template likely appears at the end of the document. After you make a template visible, click the GoTo button to navigate to that page. If form fields or links are on the page, you can open them and examine them for JavaScripts.

# Using the JavaScript Debugger

All of the aforementioned JavaScript locations can also be found in the JavaScript Debugger. The JavaScript Debugger dialog box enables you to examine JavaScripts from a list in the Scripts window. Press Ctrl/⌘+J or open the JavaScript panel and click JavaScript Debugger to open the dialog box shown in Figure 32.9. Select an item in the list and click the arrows to open scripts nested in a hierarchical order. When you select the script, the code is shown in the View window.

At the top of the hierarchy in the Scripts window, you'll see all the scripts associated with different actions. Click the right-pointing arrow to expand a listed item. You can expand individual items until you arrive at the action. Select the action, and the code for the item is listed in the lower View window when you select either Script or Script and Console from the pull-down menu options.

The JavaScript Debugger also helps you debug scripts you write. You can set break points that halt routines to help narrow down bugs in your code. To set a break point, click the left side of each line of code where you want a break to occur. A red circle appears after you set a break point.

**FIGURE 32.9**

Press Ctrl/⌘+J to open the JavaScript Debugger window.

## Using the JavaScript Console

The JavaScript Console is a part of the same dialog box where you find the JavaScript Debugger. In the console window you can type a line of code to test it for errors, or you can copy code from a field and paste it into the console window. To execute a segment in a routine, select the segment to be tested and press the Num Pad Enter key (or press Ctrl+Enter).

You can also execute a statement by placing the cursor at the beginning of the line to be executed. Press the Enter key on the Num Pad and the routine runs. In Figure 32.10, you see a line of code in the Console in the background. When I press the Num Pad Enter key (or Ctrl/

Ctrl+Enter) with the cursor anywhere on a line or select several lines of code, the code executes. In this example, an alert dialog box opens as you see in the foreground.

**FIGURE 32.10**

Press the Enter key on the Num Pad or press Ctrl+Enter (Windows and Mac) with the cursor anywhere on a line of code and the script is executed.

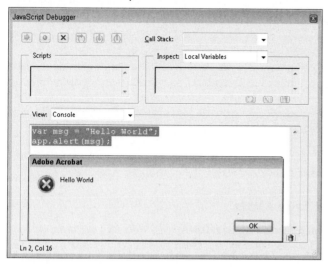

## Caution

**When testing code in the JavaScript Console, click in a line of code or select several lines of code and press the Num Pad Enter key. If you press the Enter/Return key, you'll add a paragraph return in the console window. If text is selected, the text is deleted when pressing Enter/Return.** ■

Be certain to check the Preferences dialog box when using the JavaScript Debugger and Console. Open the Preferences dialog box and click JavaScript in the left pane. On the right side of the dialog box are options for enabling the Debugger and the Console. Be certain these items are enabled before you begin editing scripts.

# Creating Viewer Options Warning Alerts

Under some circumstances, it is helpful for users to know the limitations of completing your forms before they attempt filling in data fields. If users open your forms in Adobe Reader, they cannot save the data after filling in the form unless the form is enabled with Adobe Reader usage rights. In other cases, some scripts you add to a form cannot be performed in Adobe Reader. Some examples of such scripts might be transposing data to other forms or spawning a page from a template. These actions require Acrobat. Additionally, new features introduced in Acrobat 9 and Acrobat X make some actions unusable for users with viewers earlier than Acrobat 7. Therefore, you may want to assess the viewer type and viewer version when a user opens your forms. If a version or viewer type cannot be used with the form you created, you can alert the user immediately when the file opens.

## Creating viewer type alerts

A viewer type is the Acrobat viewer used to view the PDF form. Adobe Reader, Acrobat Standard, and Acrobat Pro are the viewer types that are used in filling out PDF forms. Certain actions you add to buttons, page actions, bookmarks, and so on may not be supported by Adobe Reader. To be certain the Reader user is aware that the PDF has limitations and needs to be viewed in Acrobat Standard or Pro or Pro Extended, you can add a JavaScript with a viewer type alert. When the PDF is opened in Adobe Reader, an alert dialog box opens if the file is opened in Reader with a message informing the Reader user that the PDF can't be used in the Reader application. If the file is opened in an Acrobat product, the dialog box doesn't open.

To see how you add this type of JavaScript to a document, follow these steps.

### STEPS: Adding Viewer Type Alerts

1. **Open the JavaScript Functions dialog box.** Open a PDF and click Document JavaScripts in the JavaScript panel to open the JavaScript Functions dialog box. The location for this JavaScript is important. By adding a JavaScript at the document level, the JavaScript is run when the document opens before the first page is displayed. If the viewer type is Adobe Reader, the JavaScript displays a message. All other viewers ignore this message.

2. **Name the JavaScript function.** Type a name for the script in the Script Name text box in the JavaScript Functions dialog box. For this script I use a name such as viewerType, as shown in Figure 32.11.

**FIGURE 32.11**

Open the JavaScript Functions dialog box and type a name for your new script.

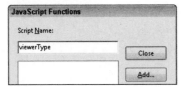

3. **Open the JavaScript Editor.** After typing a name for your script, click the Add button and the JavaScript Editor window opens.

**4. Add a JavaScript.** Enter the following code in the JavaScript Editor dialog box:

```
1. //is Reader (as opposed to Acrobat)
2. if (typeof(app.viewerType)!="undefined")
3. if(app.viewerType == "Reader")
4. {
5.   var msg = "Filling out this form requires use of Acrobat
     Standard, Acrobat Pro or Acrobat Pro Extended.";
6.   app.alert(msg);
7. }
```

## Note

The preceding line numbers are for clarification only. The line numbers are not included in the code you write in the JavaScript Editor. The code, as it is written in the JavaScript Editor, appears as shown in Figure 32.12. ∎

The // at the beginning of a line of code is a programmer's comment. The code is not executed. In line 2, the `if` statement assesses the viewer. If the viewer type in line 3 is equal (==) to Adobe Reader (`"Reader"`), then an alert dialog box opens — line 6: `app.alert(msg)`. The variable `msg` is defined in the line 5 `var msg` statement. Therefore, the variable `msg` value appears when the alert dialog box opens. If the viewer type is not `Reader`, the warning dialog box does not open.

### FIGURE 32.12

Actual code in the JavaScript Editor does not include line numbers. Numbers are used in this chapter to help describe the lines of code.

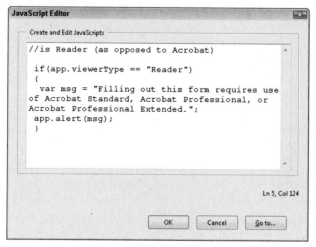

**5. Copy the script.** Press Ctrl/⌘+A to select all and press Ctrl/⌘+C to copy the text to the Clipboard. The text will remain on the Clipboard until you copy something else. We'll use this script to test it in the JavaScript Debugger later.

6. **Click OK in the JavaScript editor.** You return to the JavaScript Functions dialog box where your code is partially shown, as you can see in Figure 32.13.

FIGURE 32.13

Click OK in the JavaScript Editor and you return to the JavaScript Functions dialog box.

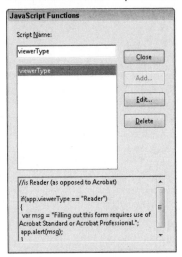

7. **Click OK in the JavaScript Functions dialog box.**
8. **Save the file.** Select File ⇨ Save or File ⇨ Save As and save the file.
9. **Open the JavaScript Debugger.** You can't test the entire script in Acrobat because the viewer type is Acrobat and not Reader, but you can take a look at the dialog box a Reader user will see before you test the script in Reader. Viewing the alert dialog box can help you find any text errors.
10. **Paste the Clipboard text in the JavaScript Debugger.** Press Ctrl/⌘+J to open the JavaScript Debugger window. Click the Trash icon to remove any text in the Console. Press Ctrl/⌘+V to paste the Clipboard text.
11. **Test the script.** Drag the cursor through the text beginning with `var msg` and continuing through `(msg):` in the second to last line. Press the Num Pad Enter key on your keyboard and the alert dialog box opens, as shown in Figure 32.14.
12. **Test the file in Adobe Reader.** To test the entire script and make sure it works properly, open the file in Adobe Reader. When the file opens, you should see the alert dialog box open.

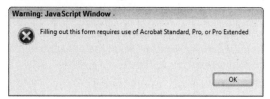

**FIGURE 32.14**

Select the text to test and press the Num Pad Enter key on your keyboard to open the application alert dialog box.

## Creating viewer version alerts

You may create JavaScripts to perform actions that are not available in earlier versions of Acrobat. The newer Acrobat 9 and above implementation of JavaScript adds more statements and reserved words than earlier versions. If it is essential for a user to complete your form in Acrobat 9 or above, you can add a page action and inform the user in an alert dialog box that Acrobat 9 or above is needed to complete the form. Follow these steps to assess the viewer version.

### STEPS: Creating a Viewer Version Alert

1. **Create a JavaScript Function.** Follow the same steps as creating a viewer type alert. Name the script viewerVersion and click the Add button in the JavaScript Functions dialog box to open the JavaScript Editor.

2. **Add a JavaScript.** Type the following code in the JavaScript Editor:

```
1. if (typeof(app.viewerVersion)!="undefined")
2. if(app.viewerVersion < 9.0)
3. {
4. var msg = "Not all features in this document work in Acrobat
   viewers lower than version 9.0. Upgrade to Adobe Acrobat 9
   Standard  Pro or Pro Extended on Windows or Adobe Acrobat 9 Pro
   on the Macintosh before proceeding.";
5. app.alert(msg);
```

In line 2, `app.viewerVersion` is used instead of the viewer type noted in the earlier example. This routine assesses the current Acrobat viewer version and displays the message in line 4 if the viewer version is earlier than Acrobat 9.0.

# Performing JavaScript Calculations

Acrobat provides only a few basic math operations. In the Calculate tab for a text or combo box field, you can choose to sum values or get a product using built-in Acrobat functions. If you want subtraction or division or any other math operations, you need to use one of the two scripting languages — Simplified Field Notation or JavaScript.

## Cross-Reference

**For more information on the built-in math functions in Acrobat, see Chapter 31. ■**

To subtract values using Simplified Field Notation, open the Calculate tab in a text or combo box field Properties dialog box and select Simplified Field Notation. Click the Edit button and type the following code:

```
1. total - discount
```

In the previous script, a field named discount is subtracted from a field named total. To calculate the same result using JavaScript, click the Custom calculation script radio button in the Calculate tab in the Properties dialog box and click Edit. In the JavaScript Editor, add the following code:

```
1. var f=this.getField("total");
2. var g = this.getField("discount");
3. event.value=f.value - g.value;
```

To divide a field named apples by a field named baskets using Simplified Field Notation, use the following script:

```
1. apples / baskets
```

To perform the same calculation using JavaScript, use the following code:

```
1. var f=this.getField("apples");
2. var g = this.getField("baskets");
3. event.value = f.value / g.value;
```

Sales tax is a common calculation required on many forms. Assuming you have one field for a subtotal and another for a grand total, open the grandTotal field and use the following code to calculate a sales tax using Simplified Field Notation.

```
1. subtotal *.0725
```

For calculating a sales tax using JavaScript, the calculation formula would be:

```
1. var f=this.getField("subTotal");
2. event.value=Math.round(f.value*7.25)/100;
```

The variable name f gets the contents of the subtotal field. The second line of code performs the calculation for variable f to compute sales tax for a tax rate of 7.25 percent. If you want to duplicate the code for one of your forms, change the tax rate accordingly.

In these examples you can quickly see that Simplified Field Notation is a much easier scripting language to work with. Many different math functions are supported with Simplified Field Notation. When you need to add other functions such as creating if/else statements or using loops, then your only choice is JavaScript.

## Using if/else statements

If/else statements are used for conditional items. For example, if one condition is true, do something; otherwise, do something else. A good use for an if/else statement might be eliminating zeros in calculation fields. By default, zeros appear in calculation fields as shown in Figure 32.15. To clear the fields of zeros, you can use an if/else statement.

**FIGURE 32.15**

A default appearance for calculation fields shows zeros according to the number format selected in the Format properties.

| Item ordered | Quantity | Unit | Total |
|---|---|---|---|
| 1. Table Alarm Clock | | $399.95 | $0.00 |
| 2. Crafted Alarm Clock | | $449.45 | $0.00 |
| 3. Modern Alarm Clock | | $699.99 | $0.00 |
| 4. Unique Wall Clock | | $484.45 | $0.00 |
| 5. Never on Time Wall Clock | | $287.99 | $0.00 |
| 6. The Grandpa Watch - 25K Gold Plated | | $799.99 | $0.00 |
| 7. The Sportsman Chronograph | | $645.45 | $0.00 |

On this form, the total fields are calculated by multiplying the quantity by the fixed unit price. If the total value is zero, we want to display the field without any value *else* we want to display the calculated value. Here's the code that eliminates the zeros when the field contents are greater than zero.

```
1. var f=this.getField("quantity");
2. var g=this.getField("unit");
3. if (f.value!=0)
4. event.value=f.value * g.value;
5. else
6. event.value="";
```

The default for the quantity field is zero and stays that way until a user adds a quantity for purchasing an item. The Unit column contains default values. Therefore, we look at the Quantity field. If the value is not zero, we want the value reported in the Total field. The else statement reports that if the quantity is zero we add nothing to the field (two quote marks with no space between the quotes).

## Calculating dates

You can add a date to a form with a simple JavaScript. To add a date to a form, create a text field. Set the attributes for the text appearance and font in the Appearance tab and click the Calculate tab. Add a JavaScript action and enter the following code:

```
1. var d = new Date();
2. console.println(util.printd("mmmm dd, yyyy", d));
```

In the preceding example, the date is reported in the format like January 27, 2009 (or whatever the current date may be). You can change date formats by editing the text within quotes. For example, change the text to read "mmm dd, yyyy", and the date is reported in the format Jul 04, 2009. Change the date to "mm/dd/yy" and the date reads 9/24/09.

The date appears in the date field when you open the PDF document. When you open a PDF document on another day, the date changes to reflect the current date. In some instances, you may want the date reported on the day a page was created and not have the date change each time the document opens in Acrobat. You can combine a script to create the date with, for example, spawning a page from a template and adding a new date field as the new page is created. (For more on spawning pages from templates, see the section "Spawning a page from a template" later in this chapter.)

In the next example we want to use a JavaScript to create a new field and add a date to the field. Here's how you do it.

### Steps: Add a New Date Field to a Page

1. **Add a button to a page.** To test the script, we'll add a button so when you click the button you can see the result. If you add a date field to a page in conjunction with another action such as spawning a page from a template, you would include the script along with the script used to spawn a page.

2. **Open the JavaScript Editor.** Use the same action as covered in previous examples to add a JavaScript action to a button.

3. **Type the script in the JavaScript Editor.** The following code creates a new field and adds a date value to the field:

```
1.   var r = [550, 765, 600, 785];
2.   var i = this.numPages-1
3.   var f = this.addField("myDate","text",i,r);
4. f.textSize = 12;
5.   f.alignment = "right";
6.   f.textColor = color.black;
7.   f.fillColor = color.transparent;
8.   f.textfont = font.HelvB;
9. f.borderStyle = border.s;
10 f.strokeColor = color.transparent;
11 f.value = util.printd("mm/dd/yy", new Date());
```

4. **Click OK in the JavaScript Editor and click Close in the Button Field Properties dialog box.**

5. **Test the script.** Click the button with the Hand tool. You should see the field added to the last page in the document.

In Step 3, the first line of code sets a variable to the coordinates (in points) for where the field rectangle will be drawn. In this example the field is drawn in the top-right corner on a standard portrait letter size page. Line 2 sets a variable to the last page in the document (remember JavaScript is zero based so the total number of pages minus 1 is the last page in the document). Line 3 is the `addField` statement adding a "text" field named *myDate* and using the page number (i) and the field coordinates (r).

Lines 4 through 10 set the attributes for the field for alignment, text color, field appearance, and so on. The last line of code creates the date field. When the field is created, it's a date stamp that won't change when the document is opened on a different date.

## Using loops

For summing columns of data, you can use the sum + preset formulas where you need results at the end of a column or row. However, at times, summing column or row data with a JavaScript is necessary. You might have a need to multiply an item by a quantity for a subtotal, and then add all the subtotals together to create a grand total. In another situation you might have a form that sums a column of numbers and calculates a sales tax after summing the fields like the example shown in Figure 32.16. In Figure 32.16 the total fields are summed and a sales tax is added to the total in the grand total field at the bottom of the far-right column. For summing data in columns, you need to create a loop that loops through all the fields used in the calculation.

**FIGURE 32.16**

A total field is calculated and a sales tax computed in the same result field.

| ITEM | QUANTITY | PRICE | TOTAL |
|---|---|---|---|
| **LIFE SAVERS** | | | |
| Life raft (small) | 2 | 799.95 | 1,599.90 |
| Life raft (medium) | 2 | 1,299.95 | 2,599.90 |
| Life raft (large) | 2 | 1,999.95 | 3,999.90 |
| Life raft (large) | 1 | 3,999.95 | 3,999.95 |
| Inflatable life raft | 1 | 1,499.00 | 1,499.00 |
| **FLARES/LAMPS** | | | |
| Flare gun | 45 | 69.99 | 3,149.55 |
| Flares (3 pak) | 63 | 19.99 | 1,259.37 |
| Flares (6 pak) | 125 | 34.99 | 4,373.75 |
| Halogen Beacon | 23 | 169.99 | 3,909.77 |
| Lantern (hi intensity) | 15 | 249.99 | 3,749.85 |
| Lantern (camp side) | 10 | 489.99 | 4,899.90 |
| Lantern (oscillating) | 20 | 889.99 | 17,799.80 |
| | | TOTAL | 37,668.90 |

For a simple loop to calculate a row of data, use the following example:

```
1. var f = this.getField("totalItem");
2. var a = f.getArray();
3. var result=0.0;
4. for (i=0; i<a.length; i++) result += a[i].value;
5. event.value = result;
```

Line 1 assigns the variable f to a parent name totalItem. The fields in a column are named totalItem.0, totalItem.1, totalItem.2, totalItem.3, and so on. Line 2 assigns the variable a to an array. Line 3 sets the variable *result* to zero. Line 4 begins the loop and the loop continues through the length of the array summing the result value. Line 5 places the end *result* value in the field.

# Using Document Actions

Document actions are actions from JavaScript routines that are implemented when a file is printed, saved, or closed. Rather than using a button to execute an action, Acrobat executes the action during one of five document conditions. A document action is executed when a file is closed, when a file is saved, after a file is saved, when a file is printed, and after a file is printed. There are many uses for executing actions on one of the document action items. You might want to delete unused fields on a form, delete all page templates, or perhaps offer a message to the user after a form has been saved or printed.

As an example, suppose forms need to be completed in an Acrobat viewer and then printed and routed by hand. You can provide instructions on what to do with the form after it finishes printing. In this case, you can set up a document action after a file has finished printing. You are assured the user sees the message because the form needs to be printed as the last step in completing the form.

Follow these steps for creating an alert dialog box with a message to instruct a user what to do with a form after it has printed.

## STEPS: Create a Document Action Showing an Alert Dialog Box

1. **Open the Document Actions dialog box.** Open a PDF file and click Set Document Actions in the JavaScript panel. The Document Actions dialog box opens.

2. **Select the Document Did Print action type.** Select one of the five items in the list box for the type of action to be used. In this example, I'll use Document Did Print as the action type.

3. **Open the JavaScript Editor.** Click Edit in the Document Actions dialog box. The JavaScript Editor dialog box opens.

4. **Code the script.** Enter the following code:

```
app.alert("Please submit the printed form to the accounting In box
    in the main office complex.",3)
```

5. **Exit the JavaScript Editor.** Click OK in the JavaScript Editor. You return to the Document Actions dialog box where your code appears when the action is selected, as shown in Figure 32.17.

## Note

**The Document Actions dialog box displays an icon adjacent to the action type and the code appears in the window below Execute this JavaScript. If you later want to delete the script, click the Edit button and highlight the text in the JavaScript Editor. Press Delete (Backspace) on the keyboard to eliminate the text.** ■

6. **Print the form.** Print the document to your desktop printer. After the PDF finishes printing, the dialog box opens.

---

**FIGURE 32.17**

Select the document action and the JavaScript code is shown in the Execute this JavaScript window.

# Working with Page Templates

One very useful tool available to you with page templates and JavaScript is the ability to create new pages from a template page. You can make templates either visible or hidden in your forms. You create new pages from template pages by spawning a page from a template. The spawned pages are duplicates of the template pages, but any fields on spawned pages are created with new field names if desired. The scripts and actions for fields added to template pages are duplicated when you spawn pages from templates. The only changes that occur are field names, so each field in your new document contains unique field names if desired.

Page templates can be spawned to create new pages or you can also use page templates to overlay data on existing pages. For example, a watermark, graphic, text, and so on, as you might add with headers and footers, can be overlaid on pages using page templates.

Creating page overlays was once a very much needed feature in earlier versions of Acrobat, but now with Acrobat's more powerful tools for creating headers and footers, the need to overlay pages using JavaScripts is more limited to conditional responses from a user who clicks a button action. For example, if the answer is yes, some content is added to a page from a template. If the answer is no, then either no page is spawned from a template or maybe a different page is spawned. However, for adding overlays to pages such as watermarks, headers, footers, page numbers, and so on, you'll find using the Add Header and Add Footer dialog boxes a better solution. For adding pages to a PDF, the *spawn* object is used (`spawnPage FromTemplate` in older versions of Acrobat).

## Cross-Reference
For more information on creating headers and footers, see Chapter 15. ∎

## Creating a page template

To create a page template, open a PDF form in which you want to convert one of the pages to a template. You may have a form where a given user response requires more information, and as a result, a new page is created in the document. You might have a file that creates a summary page after calculating data and the new page is dynamically created with a JavaScript. In another scenario, you might have a document you use for personal record keeping such as a date book, a file organizer, or some other kind of personal data management tool. In these examples, you need to frequently add new pages in a document to add more data. Creating new pages is easily handled by adding a JavaScript to spawn a page from a template. To write such a script, you first need to create a page template.

A page template is a page in a PDF file that you define as a Page Template. You can use an existing page in a document you export to PDF in an authoring program or create a separate PDF document you design for a template and later insert the page in a PDF file.

## Cross-Reference
For more information on inserting pages in PDF files, see Chapter 15. ∎

In Figure 32.18, I created a page I want to use as a template and inserted the page in a PDF file. The idea behind this page is to use a form to organize my passwords. Each time I acquire a new password for accessing Web sites or documents, I add the pertinent data in my passwords file. Since I'm always adding new passwords, I need to continually create new pages in the PDF file.

To create a Page template, follow these steps.

### Steps: Creating a Page Template

1. **Insert a page in a PDF file or use one of the existing pages in a file you want to use as a page template.**

2. **Navigate to the page you want to use for your page template.**

3. **Click Add or Edit Fields in the Forms panel.** If you are currently in Viewer mode and you want to add fields to a template page, enter Form Edit Mode. Add fields as desired using the Form tools in the Add New Field pull-down menu or open a context menu anywhere on the form and choose a field you want to add to the form.

## Cross-Reference

For more information on using Form Edit Mode and adding fields to a document, see Chapter 30. ■

4. **Return to Viewer mode.** If your template page uses form fields, add all the form fields to the template in Form Edit Mode and return to the Viewer mode by clicking the Close Form Edit button. Test all fields to make sure they work properly. In Figure 32.18, I added a number of fields to my template page.

## Note

Alternately, you can stay in Form Edit Mode and click the Preview button to test field scripts. ■

**FIGURE 32.18**

A number of fields are added to a template page.

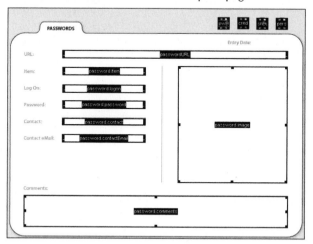

5. **Open the Page Templates dialog box.** Click Page Templates in the Document Processing panel and the Page Templates dialog box opens.

6. **Type a name for your template.** Type a name in the Name text box.

7. **Add the page as a Page Template.** Click the Add button and Acrobat prompts you in a dialog box to confirm adding the page in view in the Document pane as a page template. Click Yes and you return to the Page Templates dialog box.

   If you want your template to be hidden, click the eyeball icon in the Page Templates dialog box. The eyeball disappears, as shown in Figure 32.19, and the Page Template is hidden when you leave the Page Templates dialog box.

**FIGURE 32.19**

Add a name for the template page and click the eyeball icon to hide the template page in the document.

8. **Click Close.** When the Page Templates dialog box closes, the page is added as a page template and appears invisible in the PDF file.

## Note

You must have at least one page visible in a PDF. You cannot create a page template and hide it if the page template is the only page in the document. ∎

## Spawning a page from a template

To create new pages from your template, create a button on the page from which you want the user to spawn a new page. Either a link button or form field can be used. In the link or button properties dialog box, select Run a JavaScript as the action type.

The following code is used to spawn a page from a template.

```
1. var a = this.getTemplate("passwords");
2. a.spawn ({
3.   nPage:this.numPages,
```

```
4.    bRename:true,
5.    bOverlay:false
6. })
```

The template name I used is `passwords` as defined in the first line of code. This is the exact same name as you type in the Page Templates dialog box when you create the page template. In the second line of code, the instruction `a.spawn` spawns a page from a template. Lines 3 to 5 set the attributes for the spawned page. In line 3, the spawned page is placed after the last page in the document. You can change the value `this.numPages` to a page number and place the spawned page anywhere in the file. In line 4, any fields contained on the template page are renamed on the spawned page to provide unique field names. If the line is changed to `bRename:false`, all fields are duplicated with duplicate field names. In line 5, the code instructs Acrobat to create a new page in the document. If you change the code to `bOverlay:true`, the spawned page is superimposed over the last page in the file.

Lines 3 through 5 in the preceding script are default values. If you write the script as follows, Acrobat assumes using the defaults without specific notation for the attributes:

```
1. var a = this.getTemplate("passwords");
2. a.spawn();
```

This two-line script works fine in Acrobat 6 through X; however, there are problems executing the script properly in earlier versions of Acrobat. Be certain to use the script with six lines of code and specify all attributes of the spawned page, and you can be certain the script works in all versions of Acrobat.

You can also use an action type to instruct Acrobat to go to the newly created page. By default, spawned pages are created at the end of the PDF document. When pages are spawned, the page containing the button used to spawn a new page remains in view. To help a user navigate to the new spawned page, you can add another line of code to go to the new page. Add the following script after the last line of code used to spawn a page:

```
this.pageNum = this.numPages-1;
```

This line assesses the number of pages in the document, subtracts one from the number, and opens the last page. JavaScript is zero based; therefore, the –1 item subtracts one from the total number of pages. In JavaScript terms, page 1 is page 0.

## Tip

If you have a document with many pages and need to spawn pages periodically as the user browses the document, use a Bookmark instead of adding buttons on all the pages. A single Bookmark takes up much less memory than button fields added to every page. ∎

You can also add buttons on the template page to spawn pages from a template. In my passwords file, it would be cumbersome to always travel back to the first page to click a button that spawns a page. To make it much easier, I created a button on the template page to spawn additional pages. This way I can search through my document to see if I have an existing password already created for a given Web site. If not, no matter where I am in the document I can create a new page and add the new password.

# Creating Pop-Up Menus

Application pop-up menus can be useful for nesting action items so you can save some space on a form. You might want to have a contents page where a user navigates via menu commands to many different files stored on a CD-ROM or network server. Rather than listing all files on a page or in Bookmarks, you can categorize groups and nest them in submenus for a more economical use of space.

As an example, suppose you want to create links to other PDF documents. You have a small page and don't have enough room to display all the titles of the documents you want the user to access. By creating an application pop-up menu like the one shown in Figure 32.20, you can create categories, subcategories, and links to destinations that assist users in opening files in a relatively small section on a contents page.

## FIGURE 32.20

By adding application pop-up menus, you can create lists of destination documents in categorical groups.

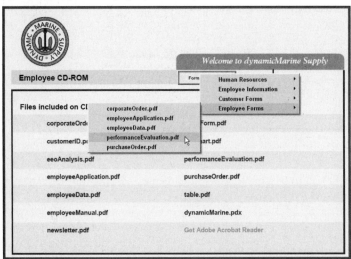

When you select the menu option, the file associated with the link opens in the Document pane. Additionally, you can create application pop-up menus to navigate pages within a document. In Figure 32.21, you can see where a pop-up menu helps out nicely. Designer and Acrobat expert Robert Connolly of pdfPictures.com creates electronic brochures that are viewed in Full Screen mode. To access the huge number of links within the documents while keeping the page design neat and attractive, Bob uses nested pop-up application menus that link to other page views, play video files, print, and navigate the document. To see some examples of the attractive eBrochures designed by Robert Connolly, log on to `www.pdf Pictures.com` where you can download some nicely assembled PDF electronic brochures and take a look at the way application pop-up menus are used in the pdfPictures files.

---

**FIGURE 32.21**

Robert Connolly of pdfPictures.com makes extensive use of application pop-up menus to preserve the attractive page designs.

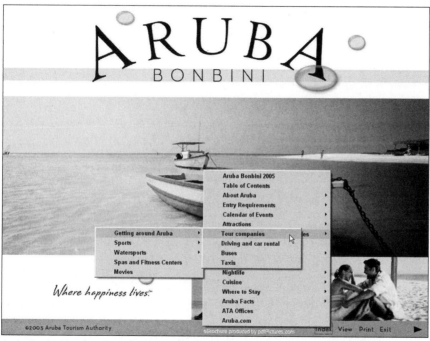

*Aruba Bonbini brochure © Aruba Tourism Authority. Reprint permission: pdfPictures.com.*

# Writing document-level JavaScripts

If you use JavaScript to open and close files, all destination files need to have a document-level JavaScript to make the open actions workable. To open each file being addressed with a JavaScript, you need to add one line of code at the document level.

For each file you want to open from a pop-up menu, open each target document and choose Document JavaScripts in the JavaScript panel. In the JavaScript Functions dialog box, type a name for the script in the field box at the top of the dialog box. Click the Add button to open the JavaScript Editor. Delete all the default text in the JavaScript Editor and type the following code:

```
this.disclosed = true;
```

Click OK in the JavaScript Editor to return to the JavaScript Functions dialog box. Click Close and save the file. Repeat the steps for all files you want to open with a JavaScript.

If you don't add the aforementioned code to the document level, the files won't open with a JavaScript. Be certain to verify that all documents contain this one line of code at the document level.

## Creating a pop-up menu

After coding functions in the destination documents, create a button field on a form used as a contents page and add the following JavaScript:

```
1. var c = app.pop-upMenu
2. (["Category 1", "1a.pdf", "1b.pdf"],
3. ["Category 2", "2a.pdf", "2b.pdf"],
4. ["Category 3", "3a.pdf", "3b.pdf"]);
5. this.slave = app.openDoc((c), this);
```

The first line of code assigns the variable c to the app.pop-upMenu method. Three categories are in lines 2 to 4. The category name is the first item in quote marks on each line. Following the category names are the filenames that open when the menu item is selected. Line 5 instructs Acrobat to open the selected file.

To create your own pop-up menus, change the category names to menu titles you want to use. Following each category, type the name of the respective document to open. Be certain to begin line 2 with an open parenthesis (and use a closed parenthesis) after the last line of code used to identify the category and filenames (line 4). Each line of code where the categories and filenames appear is contained within brackets.

The code used above works in Acrobat X, as well as earlier viewers. Updates to the JavaScript implementation in Adobe Acrobat support more refinement for coding application pop-up menus. These newer code listings can be found in the Acrobat JavaScript Reference Manual for version 8 of Acrobat. An example of a script using an application pop-up menu that opens your default Web browser and takes you to Adobe's Web site, where Web pages open for Acrobat and Adobe Reader is coded as follows:

```
1. var aParams = [
2. {cName: "Adobe Web Page", cReturn: "www.adobe.com"},
3. {cName: "-"},
4. {cName: "The Adobe Acrobat family",
5. cReturn: "http://www.adobe.com/products/acrobat/main.html"},
{cName: "Adobe Reader",
cReturn: "http://www.adobe.com/products/acrobat/readstep2.html"}
6. ];
7. // apply the function app.pop-upMenuEx to the app object, with an
   array
8. // of parameters aParams
9. var cChoice = app.pop-upMenuEx.apply( app, aParams );
```

There's much more to creating application pop-up menus and many changes to app.openDoc that was implemented in version 8 of Acrobat. Be certain to review the Acrobat JavaScript Reference Manual for code samples using these and other routines you want to implement in Acrobat.

# Working with Trusted Functions

Some Acrobat JavaScript methods have security restrictions. A number of different methods were eliminated from a non-privileged list in Acrobat 7 and continued with more restrictions in Acrobat 8 through X. Using JavaScripts for opening alert dialog boxes, opening files, and navigating pages falls into the category of non-privileged events. Adding page templates, deleting pages, inserting pages, creating new documents, adding bookmarks, and so on falls into privileged events.

One of the ideas behind adding trusted functions to enable privileged events is to protect the end user from changing a document without the user's knowledge. If you create a page action on the second page of a document that deletes pages 3 through 6, for example, the user is clearly unaware that navigating to page 2 could potentially destroy the document. To protect users from having these kinds of problems, Adobe added Trusted Functions to the Acrobat implementation of JavaScript. In order for privileges to be granted, the end user needs to copy a small JavaScript to the Acrobat JavaScript folder, thereby making the user aware that some special treatment of the PDF file is likely to occur.

## Creating new documents

When you add a Trusted Function to a document you need two scripts in two different locations. One location is in your document in any one of the areas from which you can invoke an action to run a JavaScript. The other location is a separate script saved to a text file and placed inside the Acrobat JavaScripts folder.

To make this clearer, let's first look at creating a folder-level script in the steps below, and then later we'll look at the script you add to a button inside a PDF document.

### Steps: Writing a Folder-Level Script

1. **Open a text editor.** Be certain to use a program such as WordPad or NotePad (Windows) or TextEdit (Mac). Don't use a word processing program. Some unexpected results may occur.

2. **Write the following code in your text editor.**

```
1. var trustedNewDoc = app.trustedFunction( function (nWidth,
   nHeight)
2. {
3.  app.beginPriv(); // explicitly raise privilege
```

```
   4.   app.newDoc( nWidth, nHeight );
   5.   app.endPriv();
   })
```

3. **Save the file as text only and use a.js extension.**

4. **Copy the file to your JavaScripts folder.** On Windows the directory path is C:\
   Program Files\Adobe\Acrobat 10.0\Acrobat\Javascripts.

   On the Mac, open your logon Library folder and open the Acrobat User Data: 10.0_
   x86 folder. Copy the text file to the JavaScripts folder.

The JavaScript code for this trusted function starts out with assigning the variable trusted
NewDoc to the function with width and height parameters. In line 3, you see the privileges
granted. This is like opening a locked door. The app.newDoc object creates a new document
at the nWidth and nHeight values (this is determined in the button script later in Acrobat).
The fifth line of code ends the privileges (or locks the door).

The next step is to create the script in Acrobat. In Figure 32.22, you can see where we're
headed. I have a document with several predefined page sizes. I'd like some more, so I created a template with buttons that have scripts to create new pages. Without a Trusted
Function, my buttons won't work.

**FIGURE 32.22**

A document with several predefined page sizes and buttons with JavaScripts that create blank new pages.

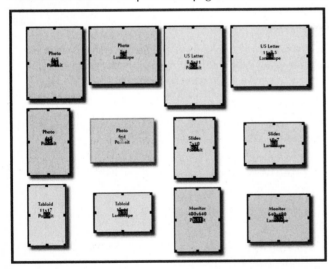

To write the button scripts in Acrobat, follow these steps.

### Steps: Using a Trusted Function in Acrobat

1.  **Create a button field.** You can use any one of the locations where JavaScripts are permitted. For this example, I'll use a button field.

2.  **Format the field.** Set the format attributes for the field name, appearance, and a button face, as described in Chapter 34.

3.  **Add a JavaScript.** Click the Actions tab and add a Run a JavaScript action. In the JavaScript Editor, type the following code:

    ```
    1. trustedNewDoc(432,288);
    ```

4.  **Click OK.**

5.  **Test the script.** Click the button with the Hand tool and a blank new document 6 x 4 inches should appear in the Document pane.

The code in the single line of text calls the Trusted Function (by function name `trusted-NewDoc`) and the values are the measurements of the new page in points. To translate the points to inches, divide by 72.

In this example, I added some preset page sizes and used buttons to create the new documents. Another alternative you have available is to create a JavaScript as a New menu item and write the code so a dialog box opens prompting you to add custom page sizes. The script is longer, but follows the same principles by writing a Trusted Function and copying it to the JavaScript folder. When adding a menu item, you don't need a script in a PDF document.

## Cross-Reference

For examples of code for creating a new menu item and scripting a routine that opens a dialog box where custom values for page sizes are added, see the JavaScript Scripting Reference at `http://partners.adobe.com/asn/acrobat/docs.jsp#javascript`. Note that the Web location may change, so be certain to search Adobe's Web site if you don't find the document at this URL. ∎

## Adding menu commands

Menu items can be added with JavaScripts written as Trusted Functions to customize your Acrobat workplace. You can add menu items for just about any kind of action and position the menu command in any one of the Acrobat menus. For an example of how to add menu items, follow the steps below.

### Steps: Adding Menu Commands with JavaScript

1.  **Launch your text editor.** Be certain to use a text editor and not a word processor.

2.  **Write the following code in the text editor:**

    ```
    1.    function totalPages(){
    2. app.alert("Total Pages: " + this.numPages);
    3.    }
    4.    function totalFields(){
    5. app.alert("Total Fields: "+ this.numFields);
    ```

```
6.    }
7.    function totalTemplates(){
8.    app.alert("Total Page Templates in this file: "+ this.
      numTemplates);
9.    }
10. app.addMenuItem ({cName: "Total Pages",
      cParent: "Tools", cExec: "totalPages()"
11. });
12. app.addMenuItem ({cName: "Number of Fields",
      cParent: "Tools", cExec: "totalFields()"
13. });
14. app.addMenuItem ({cName: "Page Templates",
      cParent: "Tools", cExec: "totalTemplates()"
15. });
```

3. **Save the text file with a.js extension.**

4. **Copy the file to your Acrobat JavaScripts folder.**

5. **Launch Acrobat.** If Acrobat was open when you added the script to the JavaScripts folder, quit the program and relaunch Acrobat.

6. **Open the Tools menu.** At the bottom of the menu you should see three additional menu commands, as shown in Figure 32.23.

FIGURE 32.23

The Tools menu shows three new menu items produced by the folder level JavaScript.

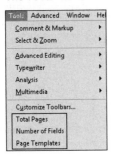

Selecting a menu item opens a dialog box reporting the total pages in the open document, the total number of fields in the open document, and the total number of templates in the open document. Particularly useful are the Total Fields and Page Templates commands. Because you don't see any indication in toolbars as to how many fields exist in the document or whether the document contains any page templates, selecting the menu commands quickly reports total fields and page templates found in the document. In Figure 32.24, selecting the Total Fields menu command opened an alert dialog box that reports the total fields in the open PDF file.

**FIGURE 32.24**

The total number of fields in a document are reported in an application alert dialog box after selecting the Total Fields menu command.

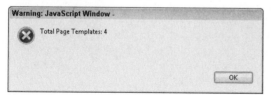

In the JavaScript to create the Tools menu items, the first eight items handle the computations for total pages, total fields, and total templates. Lines 10 through 15 contain the addMenuItem objects and attributes for the menu commands' locations (Tools menu) and displays.

# Summary

This chapter was all about JavaScript. Even if you're not a programmer, some of the simple routines you learned in this chapter can be added to your documents.

- One method for learning JavaScript is to examine forms with scripts. You can copy JavaScripts in the JavaScript Editor dialog box or copy form fields and links.

- JavaScripts are found in several places in PDF documents including fields, links, bookmarks, page actions, document-level scripts, and document actions.

- The Edit All JavaScripts command lists all JavaScripts in a document. When you're learning how a form executes JavaScripts, examining all potential areas where scripts are written is a good idea.

- Viewer types and viewer version alerts are used to inform users whether their Acrobat viewer is the correct version and type to complete a form.

- Sums of data in rows and columns are calculated with JavaScripts using loops to gather data through each pass in a loop.

- Document actions are used to execute a JavaScript when a file opens, closes, or prints.

- Pages can be spawned in a document to create new pages from a template page. When pages are spawned, all fields, links, and JavaScripts on the new spawned pages are duplicated from the template page with new field names.

- Pop-up menus can save some space on a form where lists in nested menus are scripted to open pages and/or documents.

- Trusted Functions enable you to grant temporary permissions for executing JavaScripts for privileged methods. These scripts require you to copy the scripts to the JavaScript folder in addition to the scripts you write in Acrobat.

# Final Word

Acrobat is a complex program and requires some dedicated study to master many of the features found in the application. To complement your learning after reading this book, look for online sources, Adobe support Web sites, and join the Acrobat community on www.acrobat users.com for continual updates, tips, and techniques using Acrobat and working with PDF files.

My since best wishes to you for many successful Acrobat sessions.

# Index

# Index

# Index

# Index

# Index

# Index

# Index

# Index

# Index

## M

magnification preferences, Initial View, 91–92. *See also* zooming

mail merge, 200

Make Accessible panel, 29

Make compatible with option, 451

Make Current Properties Default command, 482–483

Make PDF/A Compliant option, 422

Make Searchable... option, 422

margins

    cropping, 385–388

    in headers and footers, 392

    setting, creating PDFs from Web pages, 192

Mark for Redaction tool, 328

mark options, 262–263

Mark Pages to Redact tool, 329

Mark Unread command, 482

Mark with Checkmark command, 482

marks, preparing for commercial printing, 739

Marks and Bleeds options

    Save Adobe PDF dialog box, Illustrator, 236

    Save As Settings dialog box, 262–263

Markup tools, 498–500. *See also* Annotation & Markup tools; Drawing tools

Marquee Zoom tool, 73, 86–87

masking form fields, 781. *See also* patterns

Match All of the words option, 119

Match Any of the words option, 119

Match Exact word or phrase option, 119

math operations. *See* calculations

Maximum...returned in Results preference, 126

Measuring tool, 59

Menu bar, 11, 77, 288

menu commands, 60–61, 105. *See also specific commands*

menus

    adding to Favorites toolbar, 19

    commands, adding with JavaScript, 863–865

    context, 15–17

    down-pointing arrow, 14–15

    keyboard shortcuts, 17

    overview, 13–14

    on panels, 26

    relocated for Acrobat X, 13

    submenus, 14–15

Merge Files... command, 270

metadata, 355, 422

microphones, 577

Microsoft Office file formats, 63, 174, 178

Microsoft products. *See specific products*

Minimize Pop-Up Note command, 482

minimizing views, 98

Mobipocket format, 676

Model Tree panel, 25, 104

monitor calibration, 685–686

Move Up/Down buttons, 277

movie files, playing, 106. *See also* video files

moving

    buttons, 570

    form fields, 788

    pages to another PDF, 374–375

multichannel color mode, 229

multilayered images, 224

multimedia. *See also* sound; video

    file formats, 174

    files, playing, 105

    settings for creating PDFs from Web pages, 190

    views, going to, 105

    Web page format, converting to PDF, 183

Multimedia Operation action, 105, 557

multi-page PDFs, 238–243

multiplatform compliance, 8

## N

name wrapping, bookmarks, 537

naming. *See also* renaming

    bookmarks, 532, 538–540

    files, 135

    form fields, 763

native documents, file formats, 63. *See also* creating PDFs from, native documents; *specific document types*

navigating

    eBooks, 683

    form fields, 749–750

    PDF documents

        context menus, 72

        jumping to a page, 394

        navigation menu commands, 72–73

        page navigation commands, 72–73

        with thumbnails, 366–369

    Portfolios, 297–300

    search results, 113

navigation menu commands, 72–73

Navigation pane

    Accessibility Report panel, 102

    Articles panel, 23, 103

# Index

# Index

# Index